The First Epistle
of St. Peter

The First Epistle of St. Peter

The Greek Text with Introduction,
Notes, and Essays

Edward Gordon Selwyn

Second Edition

BAKER BOOK HOUSE
Grand Rapids, Michigan 49506

Reprinted 1981 by
Baker Book House Company
from the 1947 (second) edition
issued by Macmillan and Company (London)
ISBN: 0-8010-8199-8
First published in January 1946

First printing, June 1981
Second printing, August 1983

PHOTOLITHOPRINTED BY CUSHING - MALLOY, INC.
ANN ARBOR, MICHIGAN, UNITED STATES OF AMERICA

IN . PIAM . MEMORIAM

PATRIS . DILECTISSIMI

EDWARDI . CARI . SELWYN

TRIVM . ISTORVM . CANTABRIGIENSIVM

J. B. LIGHTFOOT . B. F. WESTCOTT

F. J. A. HORT

OLIM

AMICI . ET . DISCIPVLI

QVI . MIHI . VSQVE . A . PVERO . AMOREM

NOVI . TESTAMENTI . INSPIRAVIT

GRATO . ANIMO

HVNC . LIBRVM . DEDICO

PREFACE

THE purpose of this volume is to interpret and illuminate one of the most attractive Epistles of the New Testament. Nearly half a century has passed since Dr. Bigg's edition of it appeared in the International Critical Commentary, and there would seem therefore to be room for a full-scale commentary on the Greek Text, which, while paying special attention to the linguistic problems involved, would relate the Epistle to the currents of New Testament scholarship, both theological and critical, which have arisen in the intervening period. Circumstances of a personal character have also played their part, amongst which are a strong interest in and love for this Epistle ever since undergraduate days, a well-stocked library — partly inherited and partly acquired —, and a certain control of my time which has made concentrated work possible. Much of the book is inevitably of a kind to appeal mainly to Greek scholars, though I am bold to believe that these are somewhat more numerous, and not only among the clergy, than is often supposed. But the Epistle has a wide general interest too, for it focuses to a rare degree the interests, needs and problems of the Church of the first century, and gives classical expression to the teaching of Christianity in regard to them. They are not greatly different from those which confront thoughtful men all the world over to-day.

The work has grown in scope as it proceeded. I have deliberately excluded from my purview consideration of the rest of the " Petrine " Literature, and on this point will only say that I cannot believe the Second Epistle to reflect the same mind or spring from the same circles as the First. I have also foregone any attempt to provide an *apparatus criticus*. Much work needs to be done, especially on the patristic quotations from the Catholic Epistles, before such a task can be profitably undertaken ; and I have confined myself to the discussion of a few particular textual problems as they have arisen. In certain ways, on the other hand, I

vii

have gone beyond the limits originally planned. A growing conviction of the representative and communal character of the Epistle and detailed study of its relation to other Epistles have led me far afield ; and I hope that the results of these researches may prove to make some contribution to our understanding of the New Testament as a whole. No task, at any rate, could be more useful, if it be honestly set in hand ; for it is in the proportion and perspective which govern the faith, worship and practice of the Apostolic Church that the true lines of Christian advance will be found in our own times.

The Greek text which I have mainly used is that of Dr. Souter in his *Novum Testamentum Graece* of 1910, and my thanks are due to the Oxford University Press for permission to reprint it here. In quotations from the Bible I have usually followed the Authorized Version, and in all references to the Septuagint version of the Psalms the numeration followed is that of the English versions.

To lay down a work which has provided a continuing and sustaining interest through many chequered years is not easy, all the more as I am aware of many imperfections in it. But it is the business of scientific study, whether in the Biblical field or any other, to open doors rather than to close them ; and none has better reason than the theologian, in the measure in which he may feel that he has discharged his task, to say in the words enjoined by our Lord, " We are unprofitable servants ".

Acknowledgments are due in many directions for help in the preparation of this volume, over and above those mentioned in the text as they occur ; in particular to Dr. Lowther Clarke, the Rev. Noel Davey, his successor as Editorial Secretary of the S.P.C.K., and the Rev. Noel Brewster, Assistant Curate of All Saints, Southbourne, who have given me useful information, sometimes involving considerable research, on various matters referred to them ; to my sister, whose knowledge of German saved me much time in the elucidation of Spörri's difficult work ; to the Rev. K. E. H. Parkinson, Assistant Curate of Weeke, Winchester, for verifying the biblical references and compiling Indexes I, III, and IV ; to the Trustees and Librarians of the Thorold and

Lyttelton Library at Winchester for unfailing sympathy and help; and to the Warden and Fellows of Winchester College for the freedom of access they and their Librarian have given me to their College Library. My thanks are due also to Messrs. Mowbray for permission to incorporate in the Introduction passages from some lectures on the Epistle which they published for me in 1940 under the title of *The Epistle of Christian Courage.* I am also much indebted to my friend Dr. David Daube, Fellow of Gonville and Caius College, Cambridge, and a member of the Faculties of Divinity and Law, for the fine piece of Rabbinic scholarship which he has contributed as the Appended Note to Essay II. Above all, I owe a special debt of gratitude to my friend and neighbour Mr. E. H. Blakeney, who has laid his ripe learning and wide scholarship, and also his typographical knowledge, unreservedly at my disposal. The occurrences of his name or his initials in the book represent only a fraction of what his advice, encouragement and criticism have meant to me throughout the past seven years. Finally I wish to express my cordial thanks to Messrs. Macmillan for their willingness to accept this work for inclusion in the series of New Testament commentaries which they began to publish in this *format* with Bishop Lightfoot's *Galatians* in 1865; and also to their printers Messrs. R. & R. Clark, whose accurate reading of my manuscript and careful checking of the proofs and references have immensely lightened the labour of seeing the book through the press.

E. G. S.

WINCHESTER, *May 1st* 1945

PREFACE TO SECOND EDITION

THE present edition is essentially a reprint of the former one. The kindness of correspondents and reviewers has enabled me to make a number of verbal corrections, and I am indebted especially in this respect to the Rev. G. J. Chitty, Professor F. L. Cross and Mr. J. A. Spranger. The last-named has also sent me extensive notes on textual problems in the Epistle, of which I must defer consideration if publication of this edition is not to be delayed. For a similar reason I have not attempted to deal with one or two criticisms on matters of substance in the book, which I recognize as having weight, and shall wish at some time either to rebut or to accept.

The reception accorded to this book, in the secular press as well as in theological circles, has afforded welcome endorsement of my belief that there was still a large public which had an appetite for the serious and scholarly study of the Bible. The trend of events since the first edition was published last January has in no way served to lessen the peculiar relevance of the Epistle to our needs; and its teaching about the Church's age-long vocation, the quality of the Christian life, the patience it calls for and the undying hope which sustains it, is well calculated to inspire courage amid the confusion and distress of the present time.

E. G. S.

WINCHESTER, *June 11th*, 1946

CONTENTS

INTRODUCTION

xi

TEXT AND NOTES

ABBREVIATIONS

Ast, *Lex. Plat.* = *Lexicon Platonicum*, by D. F. Ast, 3 vols. in one. Leipzig. 1835.

Beginnings. See Jackson and Lake below.

Bengel = *Gnomon of the New Testament*, by J. A. Bengel. Engl. Tr. by A. R. Fausset. 5 vols. 1863.

Blass, *Grammar* = *Grammar of New Testament Greek*, by F. Blass. Engl. Tr. by H. St. John Thackeray. 1911.

BS = *Bible Studies*, by G. A. Deissmann. Engl. Tr. 1903.

Cabrol, *Dict. d'Arch. Chrét.* = *Dictionnaire d'Archéologie Chrétienne*, by F. Cabrol. 1907–39.

C.B.S. = Cambridge Bible for Schools and Colleges.

C.G.T. = Cambridge Greek Testament for Schools and Colleges.

1 Clem. = Clement of Rome, *Epistle to the Corinthians.*

2 Clem. = the so-called " Second Epistle of St. Clement ".

EB = *Encyclopaedia Biblica*, edited by T. K. Cheyne and J. S. Black. 4 vols. 1899–1903.

Eusebius, *H.E.* = *Eusebius' Ecclesiastical History*, acc. to the Text of Burton, with Introd. by W. Bright. 1872.

V.C. = *Vita Constantini.*

EV = English Versions (Authorized Version and Revised Version in agreement).

Exp. = *The Expositor*, London, 1875– .

Exp. T. = *The Expository Times*, Edinburgh, 1889– .

Goodwin, *MT* = *Syntax of the Moods and Tenses of the Greek Verbs*, by W. W. Goodwin.

Harnack, *Chronologie* = *Die Chronologie der Altchristlichen Literatur bis Eusebius*, by A. Harnack. 2 vols. Leipzig. 1904.

Hastings, *DAC* = *Dictionary of the Apostolic Church*, ed. by J. Hastings. 2 vols. 1915–18.

DB = *Dictionary of the Bible*, ed. by J. Hastings. 5 vols. 1898– 1904.

ERE = *Encyclopaedia of Religion and Ethics*, ed. by J. Hastings. 12 vols. 1908–21.

H^b.z.N.T. = *Handbuch zum Neuen Testament*, edited by H. Lietzmann.

I.C.C. = International Critical Commentary.

Irenaeus, *A.H.* = *Adversus Haereses.* Stieren's edition. 2 vols. 1853.

Jackson and Lake, *Beginnings* = *The Beginnings of Christianity*, Part I, by F. J. Foakes-Jackson and Kirsopp Lake. 5 vols. 1920–33.

Josephus, *Ant.* = *The Antiquities of the Jews*, by Flavius Josephus. Engl. Tr. by W. Whiston, ed. by D. S. Margoliouth.

B.J. = *The Jewish War*, by Flavius Josephus. Engl. Tr. by W. Whiston, ed. by D. S. Margoliouth.

[*N.B.* — Greek text, ed. Hudson-Havercamp. 1726.]

J.T.S. = *Journal of Theological Studies.*

Kittel, *Th.W⁰.z.N.T.* = *Theologisches Wörterbuch zum Neuen Testament*, ed. by G. Kittel [ref. usually given to author of article also].

L.A.E. = *Light from the Ancient East*, by G. A. Deissmann. Engl. Tr. by L. R. M. Strachan. 2nd ed. 1911.

Lake, *E.E.P.* = *The Earlier Epistles of St. Paul*, by Kirsopp Lake. 1911.

LS = *A Greek-English Lexicon*, by H. G. Liddell and R. Scott. 8th ed. 1897.

LXX = *The Old Testament in Greek according to the Septuagint*, ed. by H. B. Swete. 3 vols. 1887–94.

MM = *The Vocabulary of the Greek Testament*, illustrated from the Papyri and other non-literary sources. Ed. by J. H. Moulton and G. Milligan. 8 Parts. 1915–30.

Mommsen, *R.P.* = *The Provinces of the Roman Empire*, by T. Mommsen. Engl. Tr. 2 vols. 1886.

Moulton, *Grammar* = *A Grammar of New Testament Greek*, by J. H. Moulton. Vol. i. Prolegomena. 3rd ed. 1908. Vol. ii. Accidence and Word-Formation. 1929.

Oec. = Oecumenius (*c.* A.D. 600), *Commentarii in Novum Testamentum*. Pt. II. Ed. 1631.

Schürer = *The Jewish People in the Time of Jesus Christ*, by E. Schürer. Engl. Tr. of the 2nd ed. 1897.

SH = *A Critical and Exegetical Commentary on the Epistle to the Romans*, by W. Sanday and A. C. Headlam (I.C.C.).

Thl. = Theophylact, Archbishop of Bulgaria (*c.* A.D. 1080).

TS = Texts and Studies.

Weiss, *Manual* = *Manual of Introduction to the New Testament*, by B. Weiss. 2 vols. 1887–8.

WH = *The New Testament in the original Greek*. The Text revised by B. F. Westcott and F. J. A. Hort. 1896.

Wilke, *Clavis* = *Clavis Novi Testamenti*, by C. G. Wilke, edited by C. L. W. Grimm, 1868, and reissued as *Lexicon Graeco-Latinum in Libros N.T.*

Winer, *Grammar* = *Grammar of New Testament Greek*, by G. B. Winer. Engl. Tr. by W. F. Moulton. 8th Engl. ed. 1877.

Zahn, *Einleitung* = *Einleitung in das Neue Testament*, by Theodor Zahn. 2 vols. 2nd ed. 1900.

Z.N.T.W. = *Zeitschrift für die neutestamentliche Wissenschaft*. Giessen. 1900– .

SELECT BIBLIOGRAPHY

OECUMENIUS. *Commentarii in Novum Testamentum.*

CALVIN. *Commentarii in Epistolas Canonicas.* 2nd ed. 1545.

ESTIUS. *In Epistolas Commentaria.* 1679 and 1841–3.

MEYER, H. A. W. *Commentar zum Neuen Testament.* 1873–80. (Epistles of Peter and Jude, by J. E. Huther.)

LEIGHTON, Archbishop Robert. *The First Epistle General of St. Peter.* Works. Vol. i. 1846.

HORT, F. J. A. *The First Epistle of St. Peter* (i. 1–ii. 17).

BIGG, C. *The Epistles of St. Peter and St. Jude* (I.C.C.).

MAYOR, J. B. *Epistle of St. Jude and Second Epistle of St. Peter. Epistle of St. James.*

BLENKIN, G. W. *The First Epistle General of St. Peter* (C.G.T.).

PLUMPTRE, E. H. *The Epistles of St. Peter and St. Jude* (C.B.S.).

BENNETT, W. H. *The General Epistles* (Century Bible).

WAND, J. W. C. *General Epistles of St. Peter and St. Jude* (Westminster Comm.).

PERDELWITZ. R. *Die Mysterienreligion und das Problem des I. Petrusbriefes.* 1911.

SPÖRRI, T. *Der Gemeindegedanke im ersten Petrusbrief.* 1925.

WINDISCH. H. *Die Katholischen Briefe (Hᵇ.z.N.T.).* 1930.

HOLZMEISTER, U. *Commentarius in Epistolas SS. Petri et Judae.* I.

REICKE, BO. *The Disobedient Spirits and Christian Baptism.* Copenhagen. 1946.

RENAN, E. *L'Antéchrist.* 1873.

ALFORD'S Greek Testament. 1871.

CHASE, F. H. Art. in Hastings, *DB*, vol. iii, entitled " Peter, First Epistle of ".

ROBINSON, J. A. and JAMES, M. R. *The Gospel according to Peter, and the Revelation of Peter.* 1892.

HARNACK, A. *Bruchstücke des Evangeliums und der Apocalypse des Petrus.* 1893.

SWETE, H. B. *The Akhmim Fragment of the Apocryphal Gospel of St. Peter.* 1893.

MOFFATT, J. H. *An Introduction to the Literature of the New Testament.* 2nd ed. 1912. Ch. iii (A), the (First) Epistle of Peter.

SALMON, G. *Introduction to the New Testament.*

WEISS, B. *Manual of Introduction to the New Testament.*

WADE, G. W. *New Testament History.* 1922.

SWETE, H. B. *Introduction to the Old Testament in Greek.*

E. HATCH and H. A. REDPATH. *Concordance to the Septuagint.* 1897.

W. F. MOULTON and A. S. GEDEN. *Concordance to the Greek Testament.*

RAMSAY, W. M. *The Church in the Roman Empire before A.D. 170.*

ROSTOVTZEFF, M. *The Social and Economic History of the Hellenistic World.* 3 vols.

EDITIONS USED

PHILO. *Philonis Alexandri Opera quae supersunt.* Ed. L. Cohn and P. Wendland. 5 vols. 1896. [Page references also given to Mangey's edition, e.g. I. 87 M.]

CLEMENT OF ALEXANDRIA. *Clementis Alexandrini Opera.* Ed. Klotz. 4 vols. 1832. [Page references to Potter's edition, e.g. 708 P.]

MELITO. *The Homily on the Passion by Melito, Bishop of Sardis,* edited by Campbell Bonner (*Studies and Documents*, xii). 1940. [References given to page and line of the Beatty-Michigan MS., followed by the page of *Studies and Documents*, xii.]

JUSTIN MARTYR. *Justini Philosophi et Martyris Opera.* Ed. Otto. 4 vols. 1879.

INTRODUCTION

I

CHARACTER AND CONTENTS OF THE EPISTLE

THE First Epistle of St. Peter is an encyclical letter The Epistle an encyclical letter addressed to Christians dwelling in five provinces of Asia Minor. In this regard it resembles St. Paul's letter to the Ephesians, and certain other New Testament epistles ; and like Ephesians, it is without those elements of personal reminiscence and of direct handling of specific local issues which distinguish St. Paul's letters to particular churches. The author had not, it would seem, himself evangelized those i. 12 whom he addresses, though many of them may have seen or heard him, and all knew about him : he writes rather as one who had been in the background of the growth of the Church which they had experienced. The purpose of the letter is to exhort and encourage them in a time of trial ; and this he does by unfolding to them the ways of God as revealed in the Gospel, by recalling to them the example of Christ, and by expounding the principles of conduct, negative as well as positive, which were inherent in their calling and their baptism.

The keynote of the Epistle has been variously described Its synthetic character: as Hope,[1] or Pilgrimage, or Courage. But in fact, though each of these represents an important strand in the Epistle, none of them does justice to it as a whole. For despite its brevity—only 105 verses in all—it is a microcosm of Christian faith and duty, the model of a pastoral charge, composed of divers materials and of many themes. Its synthetic character is evident in the use freely made of liturgical and teaching forms current in the Church of the day, and in the close and compact interweaving of its theology and ethics ; the first bespeaking a temper of rare sympathy and understanding, the second a mind endowed with solid gifts of intellect and

[1] E.g. by Creighton, *The Mind of St. Peter.* Cf., on a more limited scale, J. W. Owen, *The Letter of the Larger Hope.*

thought. To these matters we shall return in detail later. Meanwhile it is to be observed how these qualities of heart and mind enabled the author — or the authors, if we include Silvanus — to represent and to combine features of Christianity, and indeed of religion generally, which are commonly recognized to be fundamental though they are often found in isolation.

combining the priestly elements of religion, i. 13–ii. 10   Nowhere in the New Testament, for example, are the priestly and the prophetic elements in Christianity so closely fused as in 1 Peter. The institutional, sacerdotal, sacrificial element runs as a persistent *motif* through the second half of the first chapter and the first part of the second. Deriving from the Law of Holiness in Leviticus, as interpreted by our Lord in His teaching and His sacrificial death, it passes through the implications of Christian baptism and worship to its climax in the conception of the Church as the true *sacerdotium*, fulfilling all that the Jewish priesthood had adumbrated in the past, and in its spiritual offerings of worship and well-doing representing mankind on the Godward side. The author's sense of the priest's vocation is seen likewise in

iii. 14, 15   the courtesy which he enjoins on Christians in their dealings with those who are ignorant of Christianity or hostile to it [1] : opposition is a challenge to a deepening of their consecration. Not less significant is the author's description of himself as " fellow-presbyter " with the presbyters in Asia, shewing that he felt himself to be a member of their order notwithstanding

with the prophetic, i. 10-12   his Apostolate. Yet, with all these priestly features, the Epistle has a strong prophetic vein also. Prophets had foretold and were still proclaiming the universality of the Gospel, and its cost and its reward ; the prophetic writings, and especially Deutero-Isaiah, govern the author's thought and inspire his language in matters both of doctrine and of ethics ; the moral issues and obligations that attach to faith, as summed up in the comprehensive term ἀγαθοποιΐα, are ever to the fore ; no

Is. xlv. 1   less than Isaiah does he claim that even the heathen civil power is subject to God's laws and counsels. His quotations from the Psalms and Proverbs, moreover, are those of one who represents a tradition on which the spirit of Hebrew

---

[1] Cf. Maritain, *Redeeming the Time*, ch. v., especially p. 110, for a beautiful exposition of this Christian duty.

prophecy has exercised a profound influence. Moreover, these two elements, the priestly and the prophetic, are mortised so closely together as to form a compact unity, and to point to a similar unity in the mind of the author who handled them. There is no turning from one to the other, as though they were independent. The fusion is complete.

Those who attach special importance to the mystical *and with the mystical* element may feel that on this side 1 Peter is deficient ; and it is true that the mysticism which pervades St. Paul's conception of the relation of the Church and its members to Christ, and St. John's teaching about the unity between the Father and the Son and its reflexion in the unity which binds believers to Christ and to one another through the Spirit, is absent from this Epistle. But that is not to say that it is without a mystical element. The presence of characteristic terms of the mystical way of life, such as joy and light and glory, is evidence to the contrary. The author could not *i. 6-8* write as he does of the joy and exultation and blessedness of *iv. 14* faith — of faith, too, in the midst of trial and suffering — unless he had himself experienced it. His emphasis on Christ's sufferings, moreover, is significant ; for Christ's passion is that part of His atoning death which all Christians can share, *i. 11, iv. 13* and must expect to share, in their own treading of the road of Christian life. Again, it is with the mystic's enthusiasm that he writes of the " marvellous light " into which Christians *ii. 9* have been called ; and of the glory which rests upon them *i. 8, iv. 13,* now and will be more fully theirs hereafter. The whole *14, v. 4, 10* Epistle, indeed, is warm with the glow of personal religion, as of one whose thought and teaching are grounded in the continuing sense of the Presence of God. The great themes which the author handles — the Cross and Resurrection of Christ, the *imitatio Christi*, the nature and ground of humility, the meaning of conversion and baptism — are never mere subjects of discourse, but always handled as integral parts of a living, personal faith.

Finally, these three elements of religion — the priestly, the *Its note of* prophetic and the mystical — are combined with a fourth ; *authority* with a mood of serene authority running through the Epistle which is not the less effective because it is unobtrusive. The author writes as an " apostle of Jesus Christ ". What that

betokens in the way of eyewitness and historical testimony
will be discussed later.   Here let it suffice to refer to the rich
doctrinal exposition which forms the exordium of the Epistle
and recurs elsewhere to form the basis of each passage of
iii. 13-17   exhortation ; the quiet and cheerful confidence with which
he alludes to the duty of Christians in times of trouble and
hostility ; the firm, yet humble and persuasive, spirit of his
iv. 7-11,   injunctions to those who hold office in the Church ; the
v. 1-6   entire absence of controversy throughout the work as a
whole.   Whatever view be taken of its authorship, Erasmus
was not wrong when he described it as *Epistolam profecto
dignam apostolorum principe, plenam autoritatis ac maiesta-
tis apostolicae, verbis parcam, sententiis differtam.*[1]

Analysis
of the
Epistle   Analysis of the contents of the Epistle is not easy, owing
to the compactness of its structure ; but the following may be
of some assistance to the reader.

I. *Opening salutation, embracing a Trinitarian formula*
(i. 1, 2).

II. *First Doctrinal Section* (i. 3-12).

(1) i. 3-5.   Praise to God for the resurrection of Christ,
and for the new life and new horizons opened thereby to
Christians.

(2) i. 6-9.   The rejoicing of believers in times of trial,
prompted by their love for Christ and by the perspective
given by the Christian faith.

(3) i. 10-12.   The testimony of prophecy to the universality of the Gospel which is now being realized in the expansion
of the Church.

III. *First Hortatory Section* (i. 13–ii. 3).

(1) i. 13-16.   The holiness of the Christian calling.

(2) i. 17-21.   Its ground in the transcendent events of
Christ's death and exaltation.

(3) i. 22-5.   Christian holiness the fruit of God's Word
and grace, and itself bearing fruit in charity.

[1] *Erasmi Novum Testamentum* (argumentum in 1 Petr.) : date 1521.

(4) ii. 1-3. Call to renounce evil and to persevere in the life of grace.

IV. *Second Doctrinal Section* (ii. 4-10).

(1) ii. 4, 5. The Church as God's true temple, sacerdotal in character and sacrificial in function.

(2) ii. 6-8. The Church's relation to Christ, and the choice involved in this for all men, illustrated by quotations from a primitive hymn.

(3) ii. 9, 10. Fuller statement of the nature of the Church, as fulfilling the promises, and endowed with the privileges, once given to Israel.

V. *Second Hortatory Section* (ii. 11–iii. 12).

[This passage embodies parts of a social code which appears in many other Epistles of N.T.]

(1) ii. 11, 12. Short general exhortation to integrity of life, with a view to disarming suspicion and winning unbelievers to Christianity.

(2) ii. 13-17. Nature and functions of the civil power, and the duty of Christians towards it.

(3) ii. 18-25. The duty of meekness inculcated upon Christian slaves, and its basis in the example of Christ, who is now the Shepherd and Bishop of their souls. The *imitatio Christi*.

(4) iii. 1-6. The duty of Christian wives, exemplified in dutifulness to their husbands and in modesty of outward apparel symbolizing a gentle and quiet spirit, based upon the example of Sarah.

(5) iii. 7. The duty of husbands to care for their wives.

(6) iii. 8-12. Summary of ethical qualities required of Christians, illustrated from the thirty-fourth Psalm.

VI. *Third Doctrinal Section* (iii. 13–iv. 19).

(1) iii. 13-22. The blessedness and fruitfulness of Christian patience based upon the redemptive work of Christ, whose death and resurrection were of cosmic range and significance, signalizing the overthrow of the powers of evil, delivering the baptized (typified in the deliverance of Noah),

and issuing in Christ's sovereignty over the whole spiritual order.

(2) iv. 1-6. The obligation of Christians to renounce their former pagan ways, in virtue of Christ's passion and of the certainty that they will be vindicated and their persecutors punished in the approaching Judgment.

(3) iv. 7-11. The imminence of the Judgment a call to sobriety, charity, and common service in the life of the Church, that God may be glorified through Christ.

(4) iv. 12-19. Suffering for Christ's sake rewarded by the blessedness of the Spirit's presence now and the reward of bliss hereafter. In the certainty that good and evil will alike be judged, Christians who suffer for their faith are exhorted to commit themselves into God's hands in well-doing.

VII. *Third Hortatory Section* (v. 1-11)

(1) v. 1-4. The Church's ministers charged to exercise their pastoral office willingly, and without thought of money or of power.

(2) v. 5-11. Humility incumbent upon all : so too sobriety and watchfulness, in face of the devouring zeal of the Devil. God who has called them will not fail them.

VIII. *Concluding greetings* (v. 12-14).

II

AUTHORSHIP OF THE EPISTLE

I. GENERAL CONSIDERATIONS

DISCUSSION of the authorship of the Epistle will involve us in a number of problems of literary criticism covering a wide field. The word authorship is used rather than authenticity, because the latter term is somewhat too narrow for a situation in which the employment of a secretary, whose terms of reference were often wide, was a normal feature of literary work, and in which also there lay behind the written product a coherent tradition of ideas and language on which the author or authors drew. If authenticity be held to mean a document's title to have been written as it stands, and without help of intermediary, by the reputed author, few scholars would be found to defend it in the case of I Peter ; the Apostle's language would betray him here as it did in the high-priest's palace.[1] Our task is the more complicated one of discovering, if we can, *in what sense* we may regard the Epistle as authentic. That will involve an investigation of the different strands that went to its composition, and particularly the handiwork of Silvanus whom we know to have been associated with it ; a study of the manifest interdependence of this letter with others in the N.T., with a view to discovering the substrata of tradition underlying it ; and finally an attempt to assess what may have been the Apostle's own part in the final product. If our conclusions must often be provisional and even conjectural, the tabulation of the evidence and the hypotheses it suggests may be of value to other scholars in the same field.

[1] I do not know on what ground Moulton would argue " that Peter's Greek may well have been better than his Aramaic " (*Grammar*, ii. p. 26). Dalman, it is true, says (*Sacred Sites and Ways*, p. 165) that " anyone brought up in Bethsaida would not only have understood Greek, but would have been polished with inter- course with foreigners and have had some Greek culture ". This may have been true of those who lived in Herod Philip's new capital (and perhaps the disciple Philip was such a one), but hardly of the fisher-folk who belonged to the older Bethsaida, " Fishery Home ", where the Jordan debouched into the Lake.

The evidence we look for in researches of this kind will consist in large measure of parallels, both of thought and of language, between different documents ; and we must remember that combinations of ideas and collocations of words are of greater weight than parallels between single ideas or single words.[1] But there are certain cautions which need to be observed. The vocabulary of N.T. is not a very wide one ; and the number of words which are available for the expression of a particular idea is not unlimited. Verbal parallels, therefore, often have no other reason than the fact that the word in question was the obvious and natural word to use in the circumstances. Nor are the ideas themselves infinitely numerous ; for they form part of, or derive from, a definite Gospel or κήρυγμα which was the *raison d'être* of the Christian Church and its faith. Moreover, the N.T. Epistles have as their background a common tradition out of which they spring and which they are written to transmit ; so that in many cases, where parallels exist, we are dealing not with independent writings but with an underlying tradition which is percolating through the mind and pen of the writer, often without his being aware of it. An illustration of the point, all the more instructive because it comes from a quite different field, may be found in two letters published in *The Times* in July 1938, the first from the late Professor Temperley, the second from the then Prime Minister :

Need of caution illustrated by a modern instance

(1)

SIR, — I have already pointed out in your columns that to comprehend the present state of the world the study of Castlereagh and his European phase of policy should be succeeded by a study of Canning and his policy of publicity and understanding of the nationalities problem. The utterance of the Prime Minister in your columns to-day shows a conscious (or unconscious) echo of Canning's very words.

THE PRIME MINISTER, JULY 26	CANNING
Let not him nor anyone, either in this country or elsewhere, for one moment imagine that, though we seek peace, we are willing to	Let it not be said that we cultivate peace, either because we fear or are unprepared for war. . . . Every month of peace that has since passed has but made us more cap-

[1] Cf. R. W. Chambers, *Man's Unconquerable Mind*, ch. vii.

sacrifice even for peace British honour and British vital interests. (Ministerial cheers.) We are making rapid progress with our great rearmament programme. Day by day the armed strength of this country becomes more formidable.

able of such exertion. The resources created by peace are means of war. . . . But God forbid that that occasion should arise ! — Plymouth, October 28, 1823.

If this extract and comparison are not convincing, I think this next will be :

THE PRIME MINISTER

But, while that tremendous power we are accumulating remains there as a guarantee that we can defend ourselves if we are attacked, we are not unmindful of the fact that, although it is good to have a giant's strength, it is tyrannous to use it like a giant. Our aims are not the less peaceful, but no one can imagine that we have reason to fear any foe.

CANNING

There exists a power to be wielded by Great Britain, more tremendous than was perhaps ever yet brought into action in the history of mankind. (Cheers.) But though it may be " excellent to have a giant's strength it may be tyrannous to use it like a giant ". The knowledge that we possess this strength is our security, and our business is not to seek opportunities of displaying it. — Commons, December 12, 1826.

Yours, &c.,

July 27   HAROLD TEMPERLEY

(2)

SIR, — The remarkable parallel to which Professor Harold Temperley draws attention in his letter published in *The Times* to-day, must lead many to suppose that in what I said on Tuesday in the House of Commons I had Canning's speeches in mind.

It may therefore be of interest if I say that I had never read either of the passages quoted by Professor Temperley, and, as my words were entirely my own and not taken from any brief, they indicate simply the continuity of English thought in somewhat similar circumstances, even after an interval of more than a hundred years.

Yours, &c.,

NEVILLE CHAMBERLAIN

10 Downing Street, Whitehall, July 28

2. SILVANUS

The question of the authorship of the Epistle is closely bound up with the personality and work of Silvanus, through whom St. Peter says that he writes (v 12). There is no reason

The Epistle drafted by Silvanus

for disputing the identity of this Silvanus with the Silvanus who is named in 1 Thess. i. 1 and 2 Thess. i. 1 as joint author with St. Paul and Timothy of these two Epistles,[1] nor the identity of Silvanus with the Silas who is mentioned in Acts. More difficult is the task of determining the measure of Silvanus' share in the composition of the Epistle. Some scholars, indeed (e.g. Huther in Meyer's *Commentary*, Chase in Hastings, *DB*), would not allow that he had any such share, maintaining that St. Peter is simply denoting Silvanus as the bearer of the Epistle. But this relegation of Silvanus to the office of postman is improbable, if only because the employment of an amanuensis was the normal custom in the first century A.D., and St. Peter writes ἔγραψα, not ἔπεμψα or ἐπέστειλα. The duties of an amanuensis varied from those of a scribe, often a shorthand scribe, who took down the author's words by dictation, to those of a trusted secretary who could be given wide scope in interpreting his master's mind (cf. v. 12, τοῦ πιστοῦ ἀδελφοῦ, ὡς λογίζομαι). In such cases, the usage was " precisely the same as that which still prevails in Eastern life, when the great man . . . calls over to his secretary the terms of his proposed communication, perhaps revises it rapidly, adds a few words of his own, and seals the document with his private seal ".[2] In the present case, the responsibilities of Silvanus were probably considerable ; for, even if J. A. Robinson's remark that St. Peter could not have spoken, still less written, Greek be an overstatement, we may be sure that he could not have written the good literary Greek, rich in vocabulary and often highly polished in grammar, which marks this letter. The Semitic Greek of St. Mark's Gospel is far more in keeping with the mind of one who began life as a Galilean fisherman. Nor

who was well qualified for the task

need we suppose that St. Peter was indebted to Silvanus for the style only of his letter. Silvanus was a man of marked personality and recognized position in the Church, and it is

[1] Lightfoot's judgment (*Notes on Epistles of St. Paul*, on 1 Thess. i. 1) is as follows : " The Silvanus mentioned as the bearer of St. Peter's first Epistle (1 Pet. v. 12) is probably the same person, but the name is too common to allow of the identity being pressed ". I think that the internal evidence set out below goes some way to remove the hesitation, not least the description of Silvanus as " the faithful brother ". Schmiedel in his art. " Silas, Silvanus " in *EB*, vol. iv. discusses the issue most cogently.

[2] R. Harris in *Exp.* vol. viii. p. 402

not likely that one who had been the joint author with St. Paul of two Epistles should have been relegated by St. Peter to a merely literary office. We may be confident that he would have had his own contribution to make to the substance no less than to the language of the letter, or in other words, that he drafted, or helped to draft, it ; and the receptive mind of the Apostle would have welcomed his help.[1] It will be worth while, therefore, to devote some space to the study of Silvanus, with a view to recognizing his individual peculiarities ; and the task will be doubly profitable if we are able to trace these peculiarities not only in 1 Peter but also in other N.T. writings with which he was directly associated.

Silas first appears before us at the Council at Jerusalem described in Acts xv. He and Judas Barsabbas are there described as " leading men among the brethren ", and are specially selected both to draft the circular letter to the Christians of Antioch, Syria, and Cilicia which embodied the Council's policy, and also to accompany Paul and Barnabas in conveying it to Antioch. It is evident that both were men by his of recognized standing in the Church at Jerusalem, such as position would hardly have been conceded to any but members of the Church, in the original circle of Christians there. Silas' name appears in the lists of the " Seventy " (Lk. x.) compiled by Ps.-Dorotheus, where he is called bishop of Corinth [2] ; and though these lists are valueless as evidence, the tradition receives some support from the fact that St. Paul in 1 Thess. ii. 6 speaks of Silas and himself as " apostles of Christ " — a phrase which suggests an actual commission from the Lord.[3] He may well have been one of those " eyewitnesses and ministers of the word " on whom St. Luke drew for his Gospel (Lk. i. 2) ; and the

---

[1] Cf. Burkitt, *Christian Beginnings*, pp. 131 ff. I think, therefore, that Dr. Wade's statement on this subject in his succinct but carefully balanced study of the authenticity of the Epistle (*New Testament History*, p. 312) errs on the side of caution.

[2] Cf. Milligan on 1 Thess. i. 1. For tradition as to the " Seventy " cf. Plummer on Lk. x. 1 in I.C.C. He adds, " It is not improbable that the N.T. prophets were in some cases disciples who had belonged to this body ".

[3] Cf. Bicknell, *The First and Second Epistles to the Thessalonians* (West. Comm.), p. 30. Dr. Bicknell says that the designation " indisputably includes both St. Paul and Silvanus ". Here, as often in 1 Thess., we need not assume that Timothy is also included ; for, although he was a joint author of the Epistle, the rôle which he actually played during the visit to Thessalonica described in Acts xvii. seems to have been a subordinate one.

affinities observable between 1 Peter and St. Peter's speeches in Acts (cf. below, § 7), as well as other parts of the narrative in Acts i.–xv., are perhaps to be traced to information which he supplied ; all the more as Luke and Silas were for some time fellow-travellers.

The task committed to Silas and Judas was not only that of drafting and conveying the Apostolic missive : they were also to interpret it verbally. St. Paul and Barnabas, we may suppose, were too deeply committed to the liberal policy to be the sole bearers of the letter, if its conciliatory purpose were to be achieved ; and it was decided, therefore, to reinforce them with two men of tried faith and life from the mother Church, who had not been involved in the controversy. Both men were thoroughly identified with the Council's policy, to which they would be able to give their independent testimony (ἀπαγγέλλοντας τὰ αὐτά). Both, moreover, were prophets, and therefore well able to express themselves (διὰ λόγου, Acts xv. 27, διὰ λόγου πολλοῦ, ib. 32), and to do so in a way that brought encouragement and strength to the divided community at Antioch. It is significant that both the Greek words here used, παρακαλεῖν and στηρίζειν, occur in the Thessalonian Epistles and in 1 Peter with relatively greater frequency than in the rest of St. Paul's letters to churches [1]; and that the use of the two words in combination is only found in Acts xv. 32, 1 Thess. iii. 2, 2 Thess. ii. 17, and (in close proximity, though not in combination) 1 Pet. v. 11, 12.

and his earlier collaboration with St. Paul

Silas evidently made a marked impression on St. Paul ; for, after the sharp dispute with Barnabas as to taking John Mark, St. Paul chose Silas to accompany him on the Second Missionary Journey, Timothy joining the party at Lystra. Twice during their travels, they were diverted from their projected route by " the Holy Spirit ". The suggestion is not unreasonable that this guidance came through Silas, in

---

[1] I reckon that the ratio of words in 1 and 2 Thessalonians to those in the rest of St. Paul's Epistles to churches is approximately 1 to 11 ; that of words in 1 Peter approximately 1 to 14. The occurrences of παρακαλεῖν and στηρίζειν may be shown in tabular form :

	1 and 2 Thess.	1 Peter	St. Paul's other letters to churches
παρακαλεῖν	10	3	32
στηρίζειν	4	1	2

N.B. More than half the Pauline instances are found in 2 Corinthians.

whom as a prophet such inspiration was to be expected [1]; and the reason may well have been that St. Peter was already at work on different and less controversial lines in the northern parts of the province of Asia and in Bithynia (see below, p. 45). So the party came to Troas, whence they passed to Philippi and to Thessalonica, being accompanied as far as Philippi — for so the pronoun " we " in Acts xvi. 11-18 implies — by St. Luke.   St. Luke's narratives of the events at each place add something to the portraiture of Silas.   At Philippi it is made clear that he, no less than St. Paul, was a Roman citizen ;   and it was as such that he used the alternative name Silvanus.   At Thessalonica it seems that St. Paul did most of the public preaching ;   but Silvanus (as we will now call him) was at least equally to the fore in gathering in the converts,[2] especially among the leading society women who found his charm and polish more attractive perhaps than the ruggedness of St. Paul.   The incidents at Philippi and Thessalonica mark an important moment in the history of the Church ;   for now for the first time Christianity was accused of breaking the civil law, and the persecution of it passed from being a matter of mob-violence to being the subject of police procedure.

It will be convenient to defer for the moment consideration of the preaching of St. Paul and his friends at Thessalonica, and to follow the movements of Silvanus so far as the evidence allows.   The movements of St. Paul are set out in clear sequence in Acts :   Jewish antagonism not only drove him from Thessalonica, but pursued him also to Beroea, where promising work both among Jews and Gentiles had to be interrupted.   From Beroea the Apostle went to Athens, and thence to Corinth.   The movements of Silvanus are more doubtful ;   but it is probable that he and Timothy joined St. Paul at Athens after a short interval, and were sent by him from there on missions to Philippi and Thessalonica respect-

---

[1] Cf. Redlich, *St. Paul and his Companions*, pp. 83, 65.   Canon Redlich suggests that the choice of Timothy was also due to Silas' prophetic gift ; cf. 1 Tim. i. 18.

[2] Note the isolation of St. Paul in Acts xvii. 2, 3, carried to the extent of actual quotation of his words ($\delta\nu$ $\dot{\epsilon}\gamma\dot{\omega}$ $\kappa\alpha\tau\alpha\gamma\gamma\dot{\epsilon}\lambda\lambda\omega$ $\dot{\upsilon}\mu\hat{\iota}\nu$) ; and the ensuing statement that the converts " attached themselves to Paul and Silas ".   For $\pi\rho\sigma\epsilon\kappa\lambda\eta\rho\dot{\omega}\theta\eta\sigma\alpha\nu$ should we read $\pi\rho\sigma\epsilon\kappa\sigma\lambda\lambda\dot{\eta}\theta\eta\sigma\alpha\nu$?

ively.[1] Timothy may well have been chosen to go to Thessalonica, since he had attracted less attention on the recent visit there than Silvanus; and many causes, including the desirability of cultivating still further Silvanus' acquaintance with St. Luke, may have led to his journeying to Philippi. Both men rejoined St. Paul, after their return from Macedonia, at Corinth; and it was from Corinth that the Epistles to the Thessalonians were written. In 2 Cor. i. 19 St. Paul gives us a glimpse of them both collaborating with him in the preaching of the Gospel; and it is clear that their work was marked by a very positive and earnest quality. Thereafter Silvanus passes out of sight, until he meets us again in 1 Peter v. 12, as St. Peter's associate, secretary, and envoy in Rome. The conjecture that he went from Corinth to northern Asia Minor,[2] and there laboured, perhaps in conjunction with St. Peter, is attractive; but it cannot be more than conjecture. It would have been a good partnership; for St. Peter was specially qualified, both by his gifts and by his limitations, for work amongst the Jews, while Silvanus' Roman citizenship and knowledge of Greek would commend him to the Gentiles.

Silvanus and the Thessalonian Epistles
We turn back now to the visit to Thessalonica, and to the light thrown upon it, and especially on Silvanus' part in it, by 1 and 2 Thessalonians. Acts speaks of St. Paul preaching in the synagogue during three weeks; but, as Lightfoot points out,[3] it is evident that the stay was of much longer duration than that: the three weeks of evangelistic work among the Jews led on to a period of work among the Gentiles, which in fact was the more successful. Whether Harnack's theory,[4] that 1 Thessalonians was addressed to a Gentile Christian community and 2 Thessalonians to a Jewish Christian community in the city is correct or not, the Thessalonian church was certainly a mixed one containing both elements, with the Gentile probably preponderating. And the letters are addressed to

---

[1] The sequence of events, as set out in Acts and 1 and 2 Thessalonians, is well discussed by Lake, *The Earlier Epistles of St. Paul*, pp. 73 ff.

[2] If so, the fame of his successful labours probably preceded him: cf. the allusion to "every place" in 1

Thess. i. 8.

[3] *Biblical Essays*, p. 259. The whole essay is a fine piece of Introduction to Thessalonians.

[4] Supported by Lake, *op. cit.* For a criticism of this view see Bicknell, *op. cit.*

them in the joint names of " Paul and Silvanus and Timothy ". The subscription in St. Paul's own hand (2 Thess. iii. 17) is usually taken as an indication that the actual writer was one of his companions. But that is not the only internal evidence bearing on the problem of authorship. There is "I" and also the fact that " I " and " we " are used by the authors in "we" different parts of the Epistles. Milligan discusses this passages point carefully (*op. cit.* Note C, pp. 131, 132), and his con-in these clusion may be quoted : Epistles

In view of the fact that in several of his Epistles (1 Cor., Gal., Phil., Philemon) St. Paul, after starting with an address from several persons, employs the 1st sing. throughout in the body of the letters, the continued use of the 1st pers. plur. throughout the Thessalonian Epistles is surely significant, and may be taken as indicating a closer and more continuous joint-authorship than was always the case at other times. And as we are further supported in this conclusion by all that we know regarding the special circum-stances under which the two Epistles were written, we shall do well to give its full weight to this normal use of the plural in them, and to think of it as including St. Paul's two companions along with himself wherever on other grounds this is possible.

The position actually calls for even further analysis than the above passage implies ; for, while the plural is " normal ", the singular occurs under conditions which arrest the atten-tion.[1] We can, in fact, speak of " I " passages, namely 1 Thess. ii. 18a, iii. 5, v. 27 ; 2 Thess. ii. 5-12, iii. 17. Two of these (1 Thess. v. 27 and 2 Thess. iii. 17) involve St. Paul's special position of authority and leadership among the three ; and the same may be said of 1 Thess. iii. 5.[2] But in the measure in which the 1st pers. sing. is natural and indeed inevitable in these cases, it becomes also note-worthy in the remaining two.

(*a*) In 1 Thess. ii. 18 St. Paul breaks into the singular, in a very passionate passage, to say that he had more than

---

[1] Lightfoot in his note on 1 Thess. ii. 4 (*Notes on Epistles of St. Paul*) observes this, and concludes " that a case for an epistolary plural in St. Paul's Epistles has not been made out ". So too on Rom. i. 5.

[2] Canon Deane (*St. Paul and his Letters*, pp. 90 f.) cites this passage, following so quickly on the plural in iii. 1 f., as an illustration of St. Paul's " indiscriminate use of the singular and plural pronouns ". But the sing. in iii. 5 is natural enough, if the plan for despatching Timothy to Thes-salonica was in a special measure his own.

once essayed to return (presumably from Athens) to Thessalonica, but was "frustrated by Satan". The desire was shared apparently by the others, but it was felt with a peculiar intensity and agitation by St. Paul.[1] The letter was actually written by a man of calmer temperament, we may surmise, than the Apostle.

(b) 2 Thess. ii. 3-12 is the well-known eschatological passage about the culmination of evil in the Man of Sin which is to precede the advent of the Lord. " Do you not know that while I was yet with you I told you of these things ? " St. Paul says ; and it is noteworthy that here too, as in 1 Thess. ii. 18 (and nowhere else in these two Epistles), there is an allusion to " Satan ". The sudden change from " we " to " I " and the change back to " we " in verse 13, together with the vehemence of the passage, suggests that we have here an authentic reminiscence of teaching on which St. Paul himself had laid peculiar emphasis at Thessalonica ; and the fact that it is inserted in the 1st pers. sing. suggests that it was not teaching which the others had given. Perhaps, indeed, they did not think it as appropriate as St. Paul did.

point to
Silvanus
as the
draftsman
here too

If we can thus isolate certain passages which are to be attributed to St. Paul personally, while the letters as a whole were written by one of his companions, have we any evidence as to whether this actual author was Silvanus or Timothy ? Light is thrown upon this question by the comparative study of several epistles, and this will occupy us in a moment. Meanwhile there are one or two pointers in Acts and in 1 and 2 Thessalonians themselves which suggest the answer. The first is the fact that Timothy, who was much the youngest of the party, occupied a subordinate position[2] : indeed it is only by inference (e.g. Acts xvii. 14), so far as Acts is concerned, that we know that Timothy was at Philippi or at Thessalonica at all. In 1 Thess. ii. 2, moreover, the authors allude to sufferings and indignities at Philippi, which had in fact been the fate of Paul and Silvanus only, and did not affect Timothy

---

[1] Are not the words διότι . . . Σατανᾶς (verse 18) just such as St. Paul might have written as a marginal note to the text of the letter ? For the tendency of the annotations to pass into the text itself cf. Milligan, op. cit. p. 126. With the omission of this verse, the sequence of thought in verses 17, 19 is easier.

[2] Cf. Burkitt, Christian Beginnings, " Timothy did what he was told to do, and no more ".

personally. In that case, at any rate, " we " means Paul and Silvanus. The facts raise some presumption that Silvanus played a large part in the authorship of the Epistles in question.

3. SOURCES UNDERLYING THE EPISTLE

The affinities of thought and phrase between 1 and 2 Thessalonians and 1 Peter are numerous and noteworthy, and are such as we might expect if Silvanus were a joint author in both cases ; and the evidence is set out in full in Essay II below. Here we must be content to summarize the conclusions there reached. The result of the enquiry is to indicate the existence of four main types of material current in the Church in the middle of the first century which were familiar to St. Peter and his faithful collaborator in the composition of 1 Peter, and which we are entitled to describe as " sources ". With one of these, and perhaps with more than one, we may surmise that Silvanus was personally connected ; all of them probably emerged from the prophetic circles to which he belonged by his own gifts and sympathies ; and, if the Apostle was mainly responsible for the selective use that was made of them in 1 Peter, it was Silvanus' mind that gave the final composition its literary unity and style. The four main types of material are as follows :

Four types of source underlie the Epistle

i. *Liturgical.*

The discovery of hymns and other liturgical materials, such as primitive credal forms, behind the N.T. writings has been a feature of N.T. scholarship during the present century. The point is sometimes over-pressed ; but in this Epistle we believe that the hypothesis that the περιοχή alluded to in 1 Pet. ii. 6-10 is part of a hymn solves so many problems as to be almost certain.[1] Ps. xxxiv., which is echoed in 1 Pet. ii. 2 as well as quoted in iii. 10-12, may also have been very early used as a hymn for catechumens, besides contributing to a primitive pattern of catechetical teaching. 1 Pet. iii. 18-22, though we do not share Windisch's view that it was itself in liturgical use, rests in all

[1] See Add. Notes E, F, pp. 268-81.

probability on the credal hymn quoted in 1 Tim. iii. 16.
It is worth remembering in this connexion the glimpse
which Acts xvi. gives us of St. Paul and Silvanus in prison at
Philippi, praying and singing hymns to God ; and we may
surmise that the latter was the readier hymnodist of the two.

ii. *A Persecution Fragment.*

Many of the parallels between 1 and 2 Thessalonians and
1 Peter, not to mention a number of passages in the Synoptic
Gospels and in other Epistles, are most easily explained by
the supposition that the opposition increasingly provoked
by the progress of Christianity led to the compilation of a
homiletic and hortatory document for use by evangelists and
teachers in their work of strengthening the faith of the infant
Christian communities.

iii. *Catechetical*

The existence of catechetical patterns or Forms underlying
the Epistles seems to me to have been rendered overwhelmingly probable by the work of Dr. Carrington [1] ; and modern
missionary methods make it likely that these were numerous,
being freely divided or put together to meet local needs. The
question as to whether they were oral or written is somewhat
unreal, since the probability is that enough copies became
available in manuscript for the Church's missionaries (and
some at least of the local presbyters) to possess one each,
while the rank and file of converts were content with an oral
knowledge of the tradition. We have touched only briefly
in Essay II on the strictly doctrinal Forms concerned with the
Gospel itself, though indications are given there (pp. 401 f.)
of the ample evidence that such Forms existed. But in this
Epistle St. Peter claims to have been himself an eyewitness

---

[1] *The Primitive Christian Catechism*, Cambridge, 1940. Cf. also A. M.
Hunter, *Paul and his Predecessors*;
also Dibelius' cordial appreciation of
Alfred Seeberg's *Der Katechismus der
Ur-Christenheit*, in *From Tradition to
Gospel*, pp. 27, 239 n. By " catechism ", " catechetical " we mean
Forms or patterns, both oral and
written, used in the instruction of catechumens and of those already baptized.
The question-and-answer forms which
the words suggest to us are not necessarily implied, though they are not
excluded. On the other hand, these
Forms no doubt adhered to some
kind of schematic arrangement and
formal expression, which made them
easy to memorize. The explanation of
the Parable of the Tares in Matt. xiii.
36-43 is, I think, an example of such
a Form.

of the facts of the Gospel, and he had been also the earliest exponent of their significance ; matters to which we shall turn in due course. The sources we are dealing with here are of a somewhat different kind, directed to the practical life and worship of the converts to Christianity. The sources of this character to which we believe the evidence points are :

(a) A very early baptismal Form, compiled under the influence of the Apostolic Decree of Acts xv., based on the idea of the Church as a neo-Levitical community, and containing teaching on abstinence from sensual sins, on Love as the fulfilment of Holiness, on Worship, and on the conduct expected of catechumens.[1]

(b) A Fragment on Catechumen Virtues, based largely on Prov. iii. and Ps. xxxiv., and containing teaching on Church order.

(c) A later version of the early baptismal Form which it incorporated, adding to it teaching on positive renunciation and its opposite, on Worship, the fragment on Catechumen Virtues, and a Christian social code. The preparation of this catechetical pattern may be assigned to a date round A.D. 55.

These sources represent what we may call points of crystallization in the common tradition of the Apostolic Church ; and though the definition of their contour must often remain subject to doubt, enough can be made out to compel great caution in speaking of the dependence of 1 Peter on other Epistles and *vice versa*. That St. Peter had read Romans and Ephesians is not antecedently improbable, and the author of James, if it is not in its present form by St. James himself, may have been acquainted with 1 Peter. But there is nothing in the evidence to require such suppositions. On the contrary, what the evidence points to is a high degree of interdependence of the various Epistles on a common stock of teaching and of hymnody current in the Church which is their background. When to this are added the solid core of the Apostles' own witness to the historical facts of the Gospel ; the common problems of ecclesiastical policy, both in the Church's inner life and in its relation to

The use of common sources ; accounts best for parallels between various Epistles

---

[1] The evidence on which these and the following statements rest is too detailed for insertion here, and will be found in Essay II below.

the outside world, which had to be faced and solved ; the pervasive influence of the chief leaders, notably St. Paul; and the fact that Silvanus was closely concerned in the composition of 1 and 2 Thessalonians, of 1 Peter, and perhaps also of Hebrews :— when these facts are considered, they provide all the explanation we need for the many parallels which the Epistles present.

But they do more than this : they supply a wholly sufficient answer to the statements frequently made about 1 Peter, that it is nothing more nor less than a *rechauffé* of Paulinism. These statements cover a wide range, from the "extraordinary degree of dependence on the Epistles of Paul" alleged by J. H. Ropes [1] to the "diluted Paulinism" which results in Lietzmann's view from 1 Peter having "lost the final and, religiously, the deepest motives of the genuine Paul".[2] Such statements are in any case astonishing, when we reflect that the Epistle is without allusion to what are commonly regarded as the characteristic ideas of St. Paul. Justification, for example, with all the historical and forensic arguments attached to it, is not mentioned; nor is there any trace of the Pauline contrast between faith and works, the Gospel and the Law. Both grace and sin have a different connotation in 1 Peter from that found in St. Paul's letters. The Petrine conception of the Atonement, indeed, is not only quite different from the Pauline, but seems to owe nothing to it, and springs from quite other roots in theology and experience. The doctrine of the union of the believer with Christ, which Lightfoot regarded as the central doctrine of St. Paul's theology, appears only in the phrase ἐν Χριστῷ, which is fundamentally pre-Pauline,[3] and in the idea of the participation of Christians in Christ's sufferings, where St. Peter's treatment proceeds on practical and homiletic rather than mystical and theological lines. Further, the idea of the Church in 1 Peter is conceived on neo-Levitical lines, and shews no traces of the Pauline idea of the " Body " and of Christ as its " Head ". Again, the idea of the *imitatio Christi*, which for St. Peter is the link between

and also renders the hypothesis of " Paulinism " in 1 Peter wholly unnecessary

---

[1] *The Apostolic Age*, p. 213.
[2] *The Beginnings of the Christian Church*, p. 284.
[3] Cf. E. G. Selwyn, *The Approach to Christianity*, ch. iv.

soteriology and ethics, has only very faint parallels in St. Paul ; and in his ethic humility is virtually on a par with charity, with truthfulness not far behind. In view of these facts it must be recognized that the case for Paulinism in 1 Peter, such as it is, rests on other grounds than those of a resemblance in governing ideas, except of course for those that are common to the early Christian tradition as a whole : it must rest on affinities of a less general and more particular kind. Such affinities do exist ; but it is precisely these which a synoptic study of the Epistles shews to be most simply explained by the use of common sources by their authors. Nor is the case for dependence of 1 Peter on the Pauline Epistles any better in regard to method of composition ; for, as B. Weiss observes, " the way in which the didactic and hortatory elements, instead of being separated, are closely interwoven throughout, is characteristically distinct from all the Paulines ".[1]

At the same time, when we speak of " sources " under-lying the Epistles, we need to remember that the use made of them differs from that with which we are familiar else-where in the New Testament. St. Mark and Q were known to the First and Third Evangelists as written documents and were largely incorporated as such in their respective Gospels ; and the same is true of the Travel-document, whether it be his own or another's, which St. Luke drew upon in writing Acts. In these cases the final authors and editors had direct access to their sources, and their work was directly dependent on them. They could, and did, copy them. The liturgical and catechetical sources were used in a different way. Both types of source were easily memorized and were composed with that end in view. Hymns had rhythm, and were attached to chant or tune, which is one of the most tenacious forms of association ; and they were thus easily quoted from memory, the exactness of the quotation varying at the writer's pleasure. Catechetical material was, no doubt, equally various, ranging from

Difference between sources of the Gospels and those of the Epistles

---

[1] *Manual of Introduction to N.T.* ii. p. 143 n. So Spörri describes the doctrine of the Church in 1 Peter as " so trefflicher, selbständig und origi-nal . . . vertreten . . . dass von einer epigonenhaften Nachfolge des Paulus nicht gesprochen werden kann " (*Der Gemeindegedanke im 1 P.* p. 372).

outlines or headings which were more or less invariable, after they had once received authoritative approval, to Forms which circulated widely in the Church ; but ample scope was left to individual evangelists or groups of teachers for filling the patterns in according to their sense of what they or their catechumens needed. This last point, indeed, needs to be underlined. The evangelists used their sources primarily to ensure their own accuracy in transmitting the tradition, and for their own literary purposes as authors of permanent " Gospels " : they had posterity in mind. The writers of the Epistles, on the other hand, were writing for particular communities at particular junctures in their history, and they used their sources primarily because they were already familiar to their readers. The psychological approach differs in the two cases.

1 Peter reflects the corporate tradition of the primitive Church, but is not therefore " impersonal "

We may accept, then, as true Dr. Vincent Taylor's statement [1] that 1 Peter reflects very closely the mind of the primitive Christian community. It betrays a synthetic type of mind, sensitive to the work already done by others in building up the local churches and in founding new ones, and less intent on enlarging the range of Christian ideas, with the one outstanding exception of the *imitatio Christi*, than on weaving into a new and deeper unity those which were already familiar in the Church. That is not to say, with Dibelius,[2] that " the writing lacks personal quality ". It is a question of the point of view.[3] Some cannot think of personality except in terms of striking individual characteristics. But the suppression of individual traits in the interests of a community and its mind — that is to say, humility and a

[1] *The Atonement in N.T. Teaching*, p. 48, and cf. pp. 38 f., 45. Cf. Spörri's contrast between the picture of the Church found in 1 Clement, Ignatius, and Hermas, and even in St. Paul and St. John, and that of 1 Peter, and his conclusion that " such a document [as 1 Peter] belongs to genuine primitive Christianity ", a view also held by Monnier, " C'est la piété même du premier âge qui se révèle dans ses traits essentiels " (Spörri, *op. cit.* pp. 376-8).

[2] *A Fresh Approach to the N.T. and early Christian Literature*, p. 188.

[3] Cf. T. S. Eliot's essay, " Tradition and the Individual Talent ", in *Points of View*, especially p. 29 : " The mind of the mature poet differs from that of the immature one not precisely in any valuation of ' personality ', not being necessarily more interesting, or having ' more to say ', but rather by being a more finely perfected medium in which special, or very varied, feelings are at liberty to enter into new combinations ". Such criticism is peculiarly applicable to N.T. books like 1 Peter and Revelation, which are of high poetical quality.

sensitive receptiveness of temper — is a Christian quality of
paramount importance for the Church's life. This Epistle
shews that its author had that quality ; and the Gospels too
are at least patient of the view that St. Peter had it and that
his failures were due to the individual elements in him not
being as yet fully trained to his vocation. " When thou art
converted ", our Lord said to him, " strengthen thy brethren " ; and this Epistle is a very strengthening document.
Quite apart from the element of Apostolic testimony in it,
which pervades the whole letter, and to which we shall turn
directly, there is a depth of faith and feeling in it, a simplicity of thought, a serenity of outlook, a clarity of moral
teaching, and a felicity of phrase, which leave an indelible
impression on the mind. It is not for nothing that it is one
of the most quoted books of the Bible.

iv. *Verba Christi.*

Repeated allusions are made in the Notes and in Essay II
to *verba Christi* which, even if not actually quoted as probably in iii. 9, lie below the surface of the Epistle, and usually
not far below it. Dibelius [1] has made the words of Jesus the
subject of an illuminating discussion ; and, after pointing
out how well they lent themselves to inclusion, without marks
of quotation, in any series of exhortations used by teachers
for the instruction of converts, he gives reasons for believing
that they were collected at an early date explicitly as words of The
the Lord, and therefore inspired. He cites particularly 1 Cor. Sayings
of Christ
vii. 10, ix. 14, and with no less significance the negative were col-
statement in 1 Cor. vii. 25, which implies a collection that early
lected
was definite as regards both its authority and its limits.[2]
It is for that reason that I have referred to these words by
the title *verba Christi*, the Latin denoting a certain ecclesiastical status. These collections were at first probably
numerous, being given to missionaries according to their
needs, some orally and others in writing. Further, they were
almost certainly in Greek — if any Aramaic tradition of
Christ's sayings were formed, it was short-lived and has left
no definite traces [3] — and the most probable place of their

---

[1] *From Tradition to Gospel*, ch. ix. and ch. i. pp. 20 ff.
[2] Cf. also 1 Clem. xiii. 2, xlvi. 8, Polyc. ii. 3.   [3] Dibelius, *op. cit.* pp. 32 f.

compilation was Antioch, the metropolis of the missionary movement.

The *verba Christi* belonged to the hortatory type of tradition which the Jews called *halakhah* ("walking", i.e. behaviour), as distinct from the *haggadic* tradition which was concerned with narrative. Of the latter St. Mark's Gospel is an example, of the former Q, the two being combined in the First and Third Gospels. Q was a collection of Christ's sayings compiled for hortatory purposes,[1] and these would have operated at a very early date to create a demand for as complete a collection of His words as possible. Partial collections may well have been in use before that date; others may have been excerpted from the full collection after it; but the authoritative collection itself which is represented for us by Q — though of course Q may have contained many sayings that are not recorded in St. Matthew or St. Luke — need be dated no later than the middle of the first century. It is on this collection, we may surmise, that St. Peter and Silvanus were drawing in our Epistle. Further, if this were so, we have an explanation of the fact that on the whole the *verba Christi* lying behind 1 Peter seem to be predominantly Matthaean; for it is precisely in that Gospel that we find the hortatory material in Q aggregated most markedly into "blocs" of sermon or discourse, written in the first instance not to be read so much as heard.

and are represented in the Gospel source known as Q

The frequency of allusion to the *verba Christi* is illustrated in the Subject Index at the end.

4. THE JEWISH SCRIPTURES

Use of O.T. in 1 Peter

It needs no saying that for all the Christian writers of the first two centuries the Jewish Scriptures were a primary source of information as to the meaning of Christ and Christianity; for in Him they were fulfilled. The author of 1 Peter is deeply steeped in them, as he shews both by direct quotation[2] and by frequent indirect allusions; and he knows them in the LXX form. Some of his slight deviations from

---

[1] This is so, even if, as Burkitt thought, Q contained a Passion narrative.

[2] For a list of these cf. F. H. Chase, art. "Peter, First Epistle", in Hastings, *DB*, iii. p. 781 b.

LXX may be due to quotations from memory; but in certain cases, notably ii. 6, iii. 10 ff., they are more probably due to the liturgical or catechetical sources in which the O.T. passages were in current use. These sources drew, moreover, on the Apocrypha as well as the O.T. proper; and echoes of its vocabulary, notably that of Wisdom, Ecclesiasticus, and the four books of the Maccabees, are clearly heard in our Epistle. The author was probably acquainted also with some of the works of Jewish apocalyptic, especially the Book of Enoch and the Testaments of the Twelve Patriarchs, though they may have been known to him indirectly rather than directly.

5. INFLUENCE OF GREEK LITERATURE

F. H. Chase, in the article already alluded to, gives a list of words and expressions in the Epistle which "may be briefly described as 'classical'"; and this may be supplemented by reference to Index II below. It has seemed worth while to set out in such form the passages in Greek literature which have been quoted in the Notes, since they are representative of a far larger number of illustrations which might have been given, and have an important bearing on the authorship of the Epistle. Dibelius' somewhat contemptuous description of the Epistles as "a sociological result", and his repudiation of the relevance of classical literature to their understanding,[1] is nowhere more open to criticism than in regard to 1 Peter. Its style is not only natural and unforced, indicating that it belongs to one who not only wrote, but also thought, in Greek; but it exhibits a felicity of phrase, a suppleness of expression, and a wealth of vocabulary which betoken a mind nourished in the best Greek spirit and tradition. Dr. Chase aptly speaks of the "exact correspondence between its spirit and its form"; and we may go further and say that it is the kind of correspondence which we find in the Greek tragedians and in Plato rather than that of writers such as Plutarch or Lucian. His mind is as much that of a poet as of a theologian, and of one who held, as Browning did, that "to help, strengthen, and comfort

The excellent Greek style of the Epistle

[1] *Op. cit.* pp. 6, 7.

humanity " was the poet's aim and office,[1] and that the
revelation of God in Christ was the supreme means for making
this ministry effective. Note, for example, the writer's
Aeschylean use of compounds in such words as ἀνεκλάλητος
and ἀρχιποίμην and in their aggregation in the ἄφθαρτον
καὶ ἀμίαντον καὶ ἀμάραντον of i. 4 ; his massing of
phrases as in ii. 4-10 ; the Euripidean tenderness of the
words in i. 8 in which he speaks of his readers' love for
Christ ; his verbal cadences like διὰ λόγου ζῶντος θεοῦ
καὶ μένοντος in i. 23, or ὑμῶν τὴν ἀγαθὴν ἐν Χριστῷ
ἀναστροφήν in iii. 16 ; his memorable metaphors and
similes, such as the picture of Christ as " the shepherd and
bishop of your souls " and of the Devil as " going about like
a roaring lion seeking whom he may devour "; his chaste
simplicity of phrase, as in τοῦτο χάρις παρὰ θεῷ (ii. 20) or
τῷ ἀφθάρτῳ τοῦ πραέως καὶ ἡσυχίου πνεύματος, ὅ ἐστιν
ἐνώπιον τοῦ θεοῦ πολυτελές (iii. 4). And throughout it all
there is a steady strain of the typical Greek " moderation ",
as though μηδὲν ἄγαν were one of the maxims of his upbringing : εἰ δέον ἐστί, he says of the ever-present menace
of persecution, and again, εἰ θέλοι τὸ θέλημα θεοῦ :
even in the moving words in which he speaks of Christ's
passion itself (ii. 21-5), or of his own relation to it (v. 1),
there is an element of *meiosis*, of Socratic " irony ", which is
unquestionably of Greek rather than of Hebraic *provenance*.[2]

and its
bearing
on the
problems
of author-
ship
In view of these facts, and of similar instances which
might be added to them, I cannot doubt that the Greek
models in the background — and perhaps not always in the
background only — of the author's mind are highly relevant
to the understanding of the Epistle It is not without
significance that Liddell and Scott's *Greek Lexicon* throws
far more light on this Epistle than Moulton and Milligan's
Vocabulary of the Greek Testament : its affinities, that is to
say, are far less with the vernacular of the papyri and the

---

[1] Cf. F. R. G. Duckworth, *Browning, Background and Conflict*, p. 205.
[2] Bigg claims that the non-occurrence of ἄν in 1 Peter "is sufficient to
shew that the writer was not a Greek".
But Greek writers of the period differ
widely in their usage. Thus, Mr.

Brewster tells me that in ninety
chapters of the first Book of the
Antiquities of Dionysius of Halicar-
nassus he found only thirteen cases of
ἄν, whereas it is of frequent occurence
in Dion Chrysostom. Cf. Robertson,
N.T. Gk. Gr.[3] pp. 938, 1410.

ostraka than with literary Greek. Unquestionably, such a verdict confirms the view, already seen to be probable, that it was Silvanus, not St. Peter, who drafted the Epistle ; but it is not without bearing also on St. Peter's own mind. It is clear from the way he alludes to Silvanus that there was complete sympathy between the two men ; and we may well surmise that the strain of poetry in Silvanus was not without its counterpart in the Apostle himself. The magic of Greek style is equally distributed throughout the Epistle, and distinguishes those parts which may be assigned to St. Peter's own testimony and definite direction no less than those in which he left to his amanuensis a wider discretion. What we know of St. Peter from the Gospels accords well with a strain of poetry in his temperament ; the fisherman's life on the Lake of Gennesaret with its long vigils under the stars and its opportunities for fostering the gift of wonder, the swift intuitions which so often took him ahead of his fellow-disciples, and the steady disciplining of these under the Master's eye and word before intuition could pass through penitence into faith — all these things are consonant with such a view. They would not give him the style of 1 Peter, but they would give him the qualities of mind which would have made him see in the cultured Silvanus a kindred soul after his own heart

6. THE APOSTOLIC TESTIMONY

The view that Silvanus drafted the Epistle and in doing so used material of various kinds which was already familiar to his readers and listeners accords well with the internal evidence of the letter itself and with what we know of Silvanus from other sources ; but it still leaves much to be said as to the question of authorship — a question forced on us both by the explicit words of the salutation and by the interpretation of the Epistle itself. The question still remains, In what sense (if any) was St. Peter the author ? The clue to the answer lies in the salutation : the author wrote as " an apostle of Jesus Christ ". That was his authority for writing : he wrote as an Apostle, and it was Apostolic authority that was needed by the churches whom he

The author's authority that of an Apostle and eye-witness,

addressed and in the time of trial in which he addressed them.
The very rarity of the 1st pers. sing. in the Epistle —
three times in all — makes it more distinctive when it occurs.
Thus, in ii. 11, and again in v. 1, the author separates himself
from his readers in order to give force — Apostolic force —
to his charge ; in the latter place, indeed, the assertion of
separateness follows hard on the heels of the assertion of a
common pastoral function, and the separateness is in respect
of an historical experience which only two others of the Twelve
had shared. Again in v. 12 he insists that it is he who writes
" through Silvanus ", thus renewing the Apostolic claim of
the salutation. Equally significant are the occasions on which
he uses " us " instead of " you " (i. 3, ii. 24, iii. 18, iv. 17) :
the first three passages are concerned with the historical facts
which formed the central core of the Apostolic Gospel,
namely the Passion story and its aftermath,[1] while in the
fourth the reference in ἡμῶν is to " the household of
God " of which the Twelve were the pillars. This is not the
" strictly apostolic ' we ' " of the Johannine Epistles ; but the
context shews in each case that behind the " us " of 1 Peter
lies " the authoritative witness of the original disciples "
which " governs the whole edifice of the Christian community ".[2] The author identifies himself completely with his
readers in these passages ; but he does so on the basis of the
faith they shared with him in the historically-conditioned
redemption of which he — unlike them — had been an eyewitness and an Apostle. This impression of eyewitness runs
borne out through the Epistle, and gives it a distinctive character ; and
by many it will be worth while to set down those passages which assert
passages it or imply it, or which take on more vivid meaning if read
in the in the light of it.[3] We will take them in the order of their
Epistle occurrence :

    i. 3. — The exhilaration of the "living hope" to which
Christians had been " begotten again " by Christ's resurrec-

[1] Cf. Dibelius, *From Tradition to
Gospel*, pp. 22 f.
[2] E. C. Hoskyns, *The Fourth Gospel*,
i. p. 99.
[3] Some would see in the λίθον ζῶντα
and λίθοι ζῶντες of ii. 4 an allusion to
the *Tu es Petrus* of Matt. xvi. 18.
That the metaphor of the Church as

a building, which is common both to
St. Peter and to St. Paul, has links
with this and other *verba Christi* I do
not doubt ; but I have serious hesita-
tions about connecting the λίθος of
ii. 4 with the Πέτρος and πέτρα of the
Matthaean saying.

tion vibrates through this passage with redoubled energy,
if the words are St. Peter's own ; for he was one of those who
had experienced the creative act of the risen Lord when He
" breathed on " His disciples as God had " breathed on "
Adam at the first (Jn. xx. 22), and he had felt with unique
poignancy the change from misery and despair to hope and
new life effected by the Resurrection.

i. 7, 9. — The allusion to " the genuine part of your faith "
would come aptly from one who had been sifted as wheat
(Lk. xxii. 31) ; just as none knew better than St. Peter the
difference between the beginning of faith, as he had confessed
it at Caesarea Philippi (Mk. viii. 29), and its " end " in
salvation.

i. 8. — The words οὐκ ἰδόντες imply, and are meant to
imply, that others did see, notably the Twelve ; and the more
general μὴ ὁρῶντες πιστεύοντες δέ recalls the *verbum Christi*
of Jn. xx. 29, ὅτι ἑώρακάς με, πεπίστευκας· μακάριοι οἱ μὴ
ἰδόντες, καὶ πιστεύσαντες. The themes of sight and faith are
prominent in the First Epistle of St. John, where they are
handled in a much fuller and more developed way ; but it
may be said of 1 Pet. i. 8 no less than of the Johannine
writings that " those who have not seen and yet have believed
are what they are because there once were men who believed
because they actually did see ".[1]

i. 10-12. — If the allusion here is to the prophets of the
Old Dispensation, the author may be recalling the substance
of the risen Lord's teaching on the way to Emmaus, as the
two disciples recounted it to the Twelve on their return (Lk.
xxiv. 25-7) : note especially the similarity between οὐχὶ ταῦτα
ἔδει παθεῖν τὸν Χριστὸν καὶ εἰσελθεῖν εἰς τὴν δόξαν αὐτοῦ; in
Lk. xxiv. 26 and the allusions to Christ's sufferings and glory
in 1 Pet. i. 11, iii. 18-22, iv. 13, v. 1. Similarly, the words in
i. 12, οὐχ ἑαυτοῖς ὑμῖν δὲ διηκόνουν, represent exactly the view
of the O.T. prophets' function which St. James expressed at
the Council of Jerusalem, by way of endorsing the universalist
lesson of St. Peter's vision at Joppa (Acts xv. 14-18). May
the allusion to the angels, too, in i. 12 have been prompted
by the thought of those reported to have been seen at the
empty tomb of Jesus (Jn. xx. 12 ; cf. Lk. xxiv. 4 f.) ?

[1] Hoskyns, *op. cit.* p. 97.

ii. 20-5.— This great passage recalls many incidents
which St. Peter had witnessed himself. Thus, he had seen
Christ buffeted (with κολαφιζόμενοι cf. Mk. xiv. 65, Matt.
xxvi. 67); had heard His commands to take up the cross
and follow Him (ἐπακολουθήσητε; cf. Mk. viii. 34); had
watched " His footsteps " on the way to Jerusalem (Mk.
x. 32) and to His trial and crucifixion; had observed His
patience under suffering and His silence amidst those who
reviled Him and His self-surrender to God the righteous
Judge when all human justice had been scorned; had felt
how much his own unfaith and cowardice had added to
the burden of sins which that bowed Figure carried up to
Calvary's tree; remembered how even during His Passion
Jesus had spoken of Himself as the Shepherd and of His
disciples as the sheep (Mk. xiv. 27; cf. vi. 34). Here, and
here only, in matters concerned with the Passion, does
I Peter follow St. Mark, the " Petrine " Gospel, more
closely than any of the other Evangelists. The idea of
Christ as the Suffering Servant of Is. liii. (ii. 23) and of His
voluntary death as a λύτρον (cf. λυτροῦσθαι, i. 18) are specifically Marcan traits[1]; and so too is the strongly vicarious
teaching as to His atoning death (1 Pet. i. 20, ii. 21, 24,
iii. 18, Mk. x. 45, xiv. 24) which pervades this Epistle. This
identity of attitude towards the Passion and its meaning between St. Mark and 1 Peter is significant for all who believe
the ancient tradition about that Gospel.

iii. 15.— The injunction to " meekness and fear " in
answering questioners was in sharp contrast with the Apostle's
own truculent and cowardly replies at the Lord's trial (Mk.
xiv. 71) and with his boastful words before it (Mk. xiv. 29),
but was wholly in keeping with the Lord's own meekness
before Caiaphas (Mk. xiv. 62) and before Pilate (Mk. xv. 2,
Jn. xviii. 33–xix. 11). We may well believe that memory
both of his own and of his Master's behaviour prompted St.
Peter's mind here.

v. 1.— St. Peter speaks of himself here as " witness of the
sufferings of Christ, who has experienced too a share in the
glory that is to be revealed ". Reasons have been given in
the Notes for believing that the second clause referred, and

Cf. V. Taylor, *The Atonement in New Testament Teaching*, pp. 35 ff.

would have been accepted as referring, to the Transfiguration
and to St. Peter's part in it.   If the arguments in favour of
this view are approved (and they seem to me overwhelming),
we have here a direct claim on the author's part to have been
an eyewitness.   And yet it is stated with characteristic self-
effacement ;   not to magnify his own authority, but to give
to his exhortation to his fellow-presbyters in time of stress
just that added note of certainty as to the outcome which,
because it came from his own direct experience of Christ's
sufferings and glory, could speak best to their condition.

v. 2.— The command to tend ($\pi o \iota \mu \acute{a} \nu a \tau \epsilon$) the flock of
God in their midst would come with special force from one
who had received Christ's last charge to do this very thing
(Jn. xxi. 15-17), and had often heard the Good Shepherd
speak in terms of loving solicitude of His sheep ; cf. Mk. vi.
34, Matt. x. 6, Lk. xii. 32, Jn. x. 1-18.

Though no one of these passages (with the possible
exception of v. 1) is sufficient in itself to prove that St. Peter
was the ultimate author of the Epistle, their cumulative
evidence is very strong.   The author's reference to himself in
v. 1 as " a witness of Christ's sufferings " indicates him as
having been an eyewitness of the Passion, and yet indicates it
with such an absence of self-consciousness, and so complete a
subordination of the claim to the governing purpose of the
context, that only a mind unduly suspicious could count it
false.   A similar claim is implied, though not stated, in i. 8.
Who, then, was this disciple ?   If our exegesis of v. 1b is
correct, we are tied up to a choice of three, and in effect this
would mean St. Peter.   Moreover, the other passages are not
only consonant with Petrine authorship, but take on fresh
meaning and reality on that assumption, tallying closely
with what we know of his experiences in the Gospel story,
with what both St. Mark's Gospel, with its candour about
St. Peter's failings and its reticence about his special position,
and also Acts in different ways reveal of the humility of his
character after his conversion, and with what the same two
sources tell us of his conception of the Atonement and of his
ideas about the Church.   Furthermore, all these pieces of
Petrine testimony occur in, and are indispensable parts of,
passages which are of fundamental importance to the Epistle

Bearing of this on the Petrine authorship

and constitute its spinal cord—namely, those doctrinal
sections concerned with Christ's life and death and resurrection and glory and the certainty of impending Judgment,
which give unity and background to the whole. When all
due weight has been given to the work of Silvanus in the
composition of the Epistle—work which affected its matter
as well as its style, and which bears the mark of his personality
— it still remains true that the governing mind and character
in 1 Peter are those of the Apostle himself. So far from being
" a sociological result ",[1] the Epistle bears deeply imprinted
upon it the marks of joint authorship at the hands of two
men whose names and lives we know, whose respective status
and functions in the Church were clearly demarcated, and
whose collaboration was none the less close and fruitful
because one of them was addressing his readers and hearers
with the uniqueness of Apostolic authority. 1 Peter does
undoubtedly reflect the tradition and teaching of the primitive
Church with a sympathy and sensitiveness unequalled in any
other Epistle. Yet for all that it is not anonymous, but rightly
bears the name of St. Peter. Quiller Couch's warning,[2]

---

[1] Dibelius, *op. cit.* p. 7, referring to
the style of the Epistles generally.

[2] Quoted by R. W. Chambers in
Man's Unconquerable Mind, p. 85.
The integrity of the Epistle has been
often challenged, but need not detain
us here. The extreme " critical " view
is represented by Völter's *Der erste
Petrusbrief* (1906), where it is urged
that the Epistle " wears a mask " of
Paulinism, but that all the Pauline
passages, and especially all allusions to
Christ, are really later interpolations :
" the real hero " of 1 Peter is the
Church, as is shewn by ii. 1-10.
Apart from that, nothing but a few
parts of i. 3-25 is genuine. A more
sober type of criticism detects a
division after the doxology in iv. 11,
either on literary or on historical
grounds. The former are discussed in
the note on iv. 11 ; Perdelwitz' view
(*op. cit.* p. 14) that the resumption in
iv. 12 is " dull and cumbersome "
represents a purely personal judgment
which few would support. The latter,
which are advanced by von Soden,
Usteri, and Gunkel among others,
are considered below in connexion
with the historical background of the
Epistle and particularly the persecutions alluded to in it. Special versions
of the partition theory are that of
Kühl, who regarded i. 1-iv. 11 as
governed by the relation of the Church
to the heathen world, and iv. 12 to the
end by the hostility of unbelieving
Jews—a contrast which is read into
the Epistle rather than gleaned from it
— and that of Perdelwitz, who maintained that i. 1-iv. 11 was a document based on the ideas and practices
of the Mystery Religions. His arguments are examined in detail in Add.
Note L, pp. 305-11. The genuineness
of iii. 18-iv. 1 has been suspected by
Völter, Soltau, and Holtzmann, mainly
owing to the exegetical difficulties of
these verses. The real objection to all
these theories of partition lies in the
unity of teaching and of style which
pervades the whole Epistle, a unity
which patient study of it without *parti
pris* tends only to impress more deeply
on the mind.

"Tendencies did not write *The Canterbury Tales*: Geoffrey Chaucer wrote them", is as applicable to the New Testament as to English literature.

7. I PETER AND ST. PETER'S SPEECHES IN ACTS

The internal evidence for St. Peter's authorship of the Epistle is borne out and amplified when we compare it with the speeches attributed to the Apostle in Acts. The question to what extent the speeches in Acts represent what was actually said on each occasion has been frequently debated; but there seems little to be added to what Dr. Henry J. Cadbury has written on the subject.[1] The Thucydidean principle of inserting in the historical narrative speeches that were "suited to the passions and relevant to the situations" was in vogue throughout antiquity, and gave an author much latitude.[2] At the same time we cannot rule out the possibility that some of the speeches in Acts are dependent on written sources or oral information; and the rough Semitic style and the primitive doctrine which mark parts of St. Peter's speeches (notably that in Acts x. 34-43)[3] suggest that this is so in their case. Moreover, even if this inference were incorrect, the speeches would still be relevant to our problem, for St. Luke must have had some reasons for attributing to St. Peter the ideas and the phrases which he puts into his mouth.

[marginal note: Parallels in thought and phrase between I Peter and St. Peter's speeches in Acts]

The evidence is, in fact, instructive in both respects, as the following brief summary indicates. The speeches may be reckoned as six in all:

(i) Acts ii. 14-40. *To the Crowd at Pentecost.*—The significance of Pentecost was that it was the outpouring of the Spirit of prophecy on the Church, which had been foretold by Joel as one of the portents of the End (cf. 1 Pet. i. 10-12). Christ's death was by God's determinate counsel and foreknowledge (cf. 1 Pet. i. 20, προεγνωσμένου μὲν πρὸ κατα-

---

[1] *The Making of Luke-Acts*, ch. xiv. (1927).
[2] Thuc. i. 22, Dion. Halic. *de Thucyd.* 36; and cf. Jebb's art., "The Speeches of Thucydides", in *Hellenica.*
[3] Cf. Dodd, *The Apostolic Preaching and its Developments*, Lecture I, especially the quotation from Torrey on p. 54.

βολῆς κόσμου ; and κατὰ πρόγνωσιν θεοῦ in i. 2), and His resurrection was the liberation from Hades foretold by David in Ps. xvi. The statement that Christ was not left in Hades, neither did His flesh see corruption (Acts ii. 31, taking up ii. 27) should be compared with 1 Pet. iii. 18, θανατωθεὶς μὲν σαρκὶ ζωοποιηθεὶς δὲ πνεύματι, where (as in iv. 6) the contrast between σάρξ and πνεῦμα is emphasized. In Acts, based here on Ps. xvi., the empty tomb is implied; but in the Epistle there is no overt allusion to it. In Acts ii. 32-6 Christ's resurrection and exaltation in glory are tied very closely together as in 1 Pet. i. 21, iii. 22 : it looks as though St. Peter regarded the Ascension as Christ's fare-well appearance to the Twelve rather than as an event which marked a change in Christ's own condition or mode of being. The call to " repent and be baptized " in verses 38, 39 contains teaching on the operative power, the purpose and the promise contained in baptism which has clear echoes in the Epistle. The operative power is " the name of Christ ", which also heals the sick (iii. 6, 16, iv. 7, 10, 30), brings salvation to all men (iv. 12), and wins forgiveness of sins (x. 43). The prominence of Christ's Name in the primitive preaching as the *causa causans* of salvation at once attracted the hostile attention of the Jews, so that from the very first such persecution as Christians suffered was " for the Name " (cf. Acts iv. 17, 18, v. 28, 40 f., ix. 16); and its use as well as that of the word Χριστιανός (cf. Acts xi. 26, xxvi. 28) in 1 Pet. iv. 14, 16 is perfectly natural and in no way implies a late date for the Epistle. The purpose of baptism, moreover, stated in Acts ii. 38 (cf. x. 43) as ἄφεσις ἁμαρτιῶν, is identical with that of 1 Pet. iii. 21 ; and the command to " save yourselves from this crooked generation " represents a conception of baptism to which the story of Noah would quickly attach itself as an illustration or paradigm.[1] Finally, the univer-sality of the grace promised in baptism in Acts ii. 39 has its analogy in the assumption that runs through 1 Peter ; cf. especially i. 10-12, ii. 9, 10.

(ii) Acts iii. 11-26. *In Solomon's Porch.*—The descrip-tion of Jesus as God's " Servant " (τὸν παῖδα αὐτοῦ in Acts iii. 13, 26, τὸν ἅγιον παῖδά σου in Acts iv. 27 (30)) is almost

---

[1] Cf. Dibelius, *op. cit.* p. xv.

certainly derived from the Servant-passages of Deutero-
Isaiah, a favourite book with the author of 1 Peter ; and the
context of the Passion and Resurrection in which it occurs
points to Is. liii. as expecially in mind. That conception of
the Atonement also underlies 1 Peter and probably St. Mark,
so that we have a singular doctrinal similarity in a matter of
the highest moment between all three documents. Other
parallels with 1 Peter occur in the allusion to ἄγνοια (verse
17 ; cf. 1 Pet. i. 14), to the Second Coming (verse 20, 1 Pet.
i. 7, 13, iv. 13), to the rejection of unbelievers (verse 23,
1 Pet. ii. 8) and the forgiveness of those who repent (verse
26, x. 43, 1 Pet. ii. 7, 10), and to the inevitability according to prophecy of the sufferings of Christ (verse 18, 1 Pet.
i. 20 (11)).

(iii) Acts iv. 9-12. *Before the Sanhedrin.* — These verses
record St. Peter as applying to Christ the words about the
"stone" in Ps. cxviii. 22, which Jesus had applied to Himself:
cf. Matt. xxi. 42, and 1 Pet. ii. 7, with Add. Note E below.

(iv) Acts v. 29-32. *Before the Sanhedrin.* — Here, as in
x. 39, the Cross is called τὸ ξύλον ; and so by St. Paul in
Acts xiii. 29. The word would have recalled Deut. xxi. 23,
κεκαταραμένος ὑπὸ θεοῦ πᾶς κρεμάμενος ἐπὶ ξύλου (quoted
by St. Paul in Gal. iii. 13). In Acts v. 32 St. Peter speaks of
the disciples as μάρτυρες τῶν ῥημάτων τούτων, where ῥήματα
bears its Hebraic sense of " things " or "actions" — a phrase
which suggests that the words are authentic.

(v) Acts x. 9-16, 34-43. *The Story of Cornelius.* — Among
verbal points we must note προσωπολήπτης in verse 34 and
ἀπροσωπολήπτως in 1 Pet. i. 17, and the very close identity
of teaching between the two verses ; while in verse 42 Christ is
spoken of as κριτὴς ζώντων καὶ νεκρῶν, which affords a
parallel with 1 Pet. iv. 5.

(vi) Acts xv. 7-11. *Council of Jerusalem.* — This passage
is of decisive importance for the development of St. Peter's
mind and character, expressing the beliefs resulting from his
intellectual conversion [1] through the vision at Joppa and the
baptism of Cornelius which followed it. The concreteness
and simplicity of verses 8, 9 are of special note. Points of

---

[1] On this type of conversion cf. Thouless, *An Introduction to the Psychology
of Religion*, ch. xiii.

contact with 1 Peter are the emphasis on God's choice
(ἐξελέξατο) in verse 7 (cf. ἐκλεκτοῖς in 1 Pet. i. 1, ἐκλεκτόν in
ii. 9), and the cleansing power of faith in verse 9, τῇ πίστει
καθαρίσας τὰς καρδίας αὐτῶν and 1 Pet. i. 22, τὰς ψυχὰς ὑμῶν
ἡγνικότες ἐν τῇ ὑπακοῇ τῆς ἀληθείας . . . ἐκ καθαρᾶς καρδίας
κτλ. — passages and phrases redolent of the neo-Levitical idea
of the Church already noted (*supra*, p. 19). The Apostle's
words are felt to be decisive and produce silence ; after which
St. James has little to do but to endorse St. Peter's testimony
and apply its moral. His words in verse 14 are like those in
1 Pet. ii. 4-10 which we have seen reason to assign to an early
Christian hymn.

Few would suggest that the parallels of thought and
phrase between the speeches and 1 Peter are based upon St.
Luke's reading of the Epistle ; for in both documents they
clearly belong to their contexts, and the doctrinal elements
in the speeches, notably the idea of Jesus as παῖς θεοῦ, are
obviously original and not deductions from the Epistle. On
the other hand, they are what might be expected if both
alike are utterances of the same mind, given on different
occasions. The connexion, that is to say, is not literary but
historical : the common ground lies in the mind of St. Peter
who gave, and was known to have given, teaching along
these lines and to a great extent in these terms.

8. EXTERNAL ATTESTATION

Second-
century
testimony
to the
Epistle

It is not necessary to set forth the evidence on this subject
at length, for the facts are fully discussed in many other
places [1] ; and there is little to be added to them. The *locus
classicus* for the discussion is in Eusebius, *H.E.* iii. 3, a passage
which shows clearly the extent to which the spirit of biblical
criticism — notwithstanding much that has been written to
the contrary — was a reality in the early Church. The author
distinguishes between those books of N.T. which were
" disputed " and those which were " canonical and acknow-

[1] We may mention especially the
commentaries of Bigg and Blenkin ;
Chase's art. in Hastings, *DB*, vol.
iii. ; Souter's *The Text and Canon of*
the *N.T.* ; and Lightfoot's essay on
" The Silence of Eusebius " in *Essays
on Supernatural Religion.* Cone's
discussion in *EB* is very slight.

ledged Scriptures ", and among the latter he recognizes only the First Epistle of St. Peter, among the books bearing the Apostle's name,[1] as " genuine and acknowledged among the elders of former days ". For the rest, we may sum up the matter as follows :

1. The First Epistle is first quoted from, or its language echoed, though without acknowledgment, in 1 Clement — unless we take the view that it was used by the authors of Ephesians or James. Thereafter we find similar quotations or echoes in Barnabas, Hermas, Epistle to Diognetus, Justin Martyr, and Theophilus of Antioch.

2. The existence of the Epistle as a document, though without explicit attribution to St. Peter, is first attested by Polycarp, who quotes from it or echoes it frequently.[2]

3. The earliest undoubted attribution of the Epistle to St. Peter is by Irenaeus, who quotes it as such in *A.H.* IV. ix. 2, xvi. 5, V. vii. 2.[3]

4. The Epistle is not mentioned in the Muratorian Fragment ; but this is probably due to the mutilated state of the text. It may be noted that the *Muratorianum* is not much earlier than Clement of Alexandria, who commented on 1 Peter in his *Adumbrationes* (*Hypotyposes*), and quotes from every chapter of it.

5. Little relevant evidence has come to light since Bigg's thorough discussion of the *Testimonia Veterum* in his edition of the Epistle (1901). There is no quotation from 1 Peter, for example, in the recently edited *Apostolic Tradition* of Hippolytus [4] ; the newly discovered *Homily on the Passion* of Melito throws no light on the question ; nor is the Epistle quoted in Irenaeus' *Demonstration of the Apostolic Preaching* first edited in 1907, and published in an English edition by Dr. J. A. Robinson in 1920.

---

[1] The others being 2 Peter, " which tradition had not stamped in the same way as canonical, but which nevertheless, appearing useful to many, had been studied with the other Scriptures " ; and, in a yet lesser category, the Acts, Gospel, Preaching, and Apocalypse of Peter.

[2] Cf. Lightfoot, *Essays on Supernatural Religion*, p. 50 (1889); Souter,

op. cit. p. 153, citing *The New Testament in the Apostolic Fathers* (Oxford, 1905).

[3] Chase (*DB,* iii. pp. 780 f.), however, gives grounds for believing that Papias referred to our Epistle explicitly as the Epistle of St. Peter.

[4] Burton Scott Easton, *The Apostolic Tradition of Hippolytus* ; G. H. Dix, *The Apostolic Tradition.*

The above summary is sufficient to indicate that the attestation of 1 Peter is widespread, early, and clear ; and it derives additional weight from the dubiety which from the earliest times attended the authenticity of 2 Peter and the rest of the Petrine literature.

III

OCCASION AND DATE OF THE EPISTLE

I. GENERAL CONSIDERATIONS

APART from the allusion to St. Mark and Silvanus as being with St. Peter in Rome at the time when the Epistle was written, we have only the internal evidence to guide us as to its occasion and date. This, however, is considerable ; and, if we cannot accept Renan's claim [1] that it is easy to distinguish between books written before the Fall of Jerusalem in A.D. 70 and those written after it, neither can we dismiss the matter so lightly as Goodspeed,[2] who regards this Epistle as a response to Hebrews and assigns it to the end of Domitian's reign. Special importance attaches here to the affinity between 1 Peter and Ephesians.[3] It is not a question of detailed parallels, such as are discussed below in Essay II, but of certain broad underlying assumptions and factors in the situation which are common to both. We get the impression from both Epistles of a flood-tide which has been running strongly in the Church and accounts for much in the temper and atmosphere of each. It is true that the authors stand in somewhat different proximity to the flowing tide, and touch it at different points in its course. There is a note of personal achievement and victory, of a great struggle won, in Ephesians which is absent from 1 Peter; and in Peter the tide has been arrested by events which have supervened between the writing of the two letters. But, whether in a wide reach or through a rocky spate, it is the same river that flows. Behind both Epistles flows the tide of the Church's unity and expansion. The great issue of Jew and Gentile has been settled. There is no reason to suppose that for St. Peter it had been, as for St. Paul, a life-

Comparison of 1 Peter with Ephesians,

---

[1] *L'Antéchrist*, p. xii. None the less, Renan's literary intuition is worth a good deal.

[2] *New Solutions of N.T. Problems*, p. 115.

[3] For a fresh and vigorous defence of the genuineness of Ephesians cf. A. C. Deane, *St. Paul and his Letters*, pp. 195 ff.

and-death controversy : indeed there is no trace of that or of any other controversy in his Epistle ; everything suggests that the lesson of his conversion through the vision at Joppa, and its practical application and ratification by the Council at Jerusalem, had settled for him the issue between Jewish and Gentile Christianity. But he rejoices no less than St. Paul in the upshot ; in the redemption, the call, the new inheritance, the salvation, in the Church which represents and embodies these, and even in its sufferings and trials. Nor is his mood of rejoicing daunted by the new experiences. The trials and sufferings of the Christian life fit in to the great scheme. The triumphant theme of praise and bene-diction with which this Epistle, like Ephesians, opens is strong enough to sweep past and over them, and to conclude, no less than that other letter, on the note of the glorious expansion of the Church. A like buoyant faith pervades his second passage on persecution (iii. 13-22), concluding with the overthrow of the powers of evil through Christ's passion and resurrection, the robust spiritual power given through baptism, and Christ's exaltation in glory.[1] Even the third passage (iv. 12-19), though the situation envi-saged is graver, is dominated by the emphasis on rejoicing at its beginning and the deep serenity which marks its close.

and with
1 and 2
Thes-
salonians,   This atmosphere or mood of solid achievement which links 1 Peter with Ephesians is felt more strongly if we compare it with another letter, or letters, with which it has much in common, namely 1 and 2 Thessalonians. In detail its resemblances to the Thessalonian Epistles are much closer and more numerous ; but in its general climate of feeling and thought — even though the Thessalonian Church has experienced persecution — it is far closer to Ephesians. In particular, we may note how the eschatology of 1 Peter, though clearly marked and indeed a vital part of the author's faith and outlook, stands in the same kind of proportion to his teaching as a whole as is the case in Ephesians. What has happened is that in the decade which has elapsed between Thessalonians and Ephesians " realized eschatology " nas

---

[1] Renan is surely wide of the mark when he speaks of 1 Peter as marked by " une tristesse douce, une confiance résignée " (*op. cit.* p. 115).

come to mean more than it did ; and what has brought this
about is the amazing fact of the Church's unity, with all that
it brought of expansion and of strength.   St. Peter's doctrine
of the Church, though not in conflict with St. Paul's in
Ephesians, differs from it in many ways ; but the two Epistles
are alike in presenting each a coherent conception of the
Church, based on fact and experience, and there is nothing
comparable to this in 1 and 2 Thessalonians.   It is this which, *and its*
in my judgment, forbids us to date 1 Peter earlier than A.D. 60. *bearing on the*
The doctrine and ethics of the Epistle are primitive enough ; *Epistle's date*
but it betrays a depth of corporate experience of God's grace
which points to a time when the acute controversies of the
period of the Apostolic decree had died down and the flowing
tide of expanding Christianity could be fully felt.

    This conclusion derives added confirmation from the *Meaning*
repeated " now " ($\nu\hat{\upsilon}\nu$, i. 12, ii. 10, ii. 25, iii. 21 ; $\check{\alpha}\rho\tau\iota$, i. 6, *of " now " in*
8) which makes itself heard throughout the Epistle.   Some *1 Peter*
scholars, notably Perdelwitz,[1] have narrowed down the allusions
here to the time of the readers' conversion and even regarded
it as evidence that the Epistle was written as a baptismal
homily.   But this is to strain matters too far.   In i. 6, for
example, $\check{\alpha}\rho\tau\iota$ refers to their present trials, and in i. 8 to the
contrast between the Christians of that day and the disciples
who saw Jesus in the flesh.   Even $\dot{\alpha}\rho\tau\iota\gamma\acute{\epsilon}\nu\nu\eta\tau\alpha$ in ii. 2 need
not imply that their conversion was recent ; for its use is
determined by the metaphor in $\dot{\omega}\varsigma$ $\beta\rho\acute{\epsilon}\phi\eta$ and that in turn
by the metaphorical $\gamma\acute{\alpha}\lambda\alpha$, $\alpha\dot{\upsilon}\xi\eta\theta\hat{\eta}\tau\epsilon$, $\gamma\epsilon\acute{\upsilon}\sigma\alpha\sigma\theta\epsilon$ which follow.
The occurrences of $\nu\hat{\upsilon}\nu$, on the other hand, have a significance
for the Epistle as a whole ; but it is a broad " now ", not a
narrow one.   In i. 12 $\nu\hat{\upsilon}\nu$ marks the arrival of the time ($\kappa\alpha\iota$-
$\rho\acute{o}\varsigma$) of the universal Gospel, which prophets had foretold and
studied and evangelists had proclaimed ; in iii. 21 it marks
the present fulfilment in Christian baptism of the salvation typified in Noah ; in ii. 10, 25 it means quite generally
" now that you are Christians ".   Windisch[2] is surely right
in speaking of these passages, especially i. 12, as pointing

---

[1] *Die Mysterienreligion und das Problem des I. Petrusbriefes,* p. 18.
[2] *Die Katholischen Briefe* (1930), p. 51. Cf. also Dibelius, *A Fresh Approach to the N.T. and early Christian Literature,* p. 186, " In regard to content, 1 Peter belongs in the neighbourhood of Ephesians ".

to a great mass-movement (*Missionsfeldzug*) lying behind the readers' life, as it does in Colossians and Ephesians ; though we need not follow him in the deductions he draws from this. What we may say with some confidence is that the uses of νῦν and ἄρτι in the Epistle point to a situation marked by a flood-tide of Christian expansion lately challenged and momentarily arrested by the menace or experience of persecution.

2. THE PERSONS ADDRESSED

Were the readers of Jewish or Gentile origin ?

There has been a marked division of opinion from early times as to whether the Christians addressed in this Epistle had been Jews or Gentiles before their conversion to Christianity. In the patristic age Origen, Eusebius, and the Greek Fathers generally maintained that they had been Jews, while Augustine, Jerome, and other Latin writers held the opposite view. This divergence has continued almost to our own day, the Greek view on the whole prevailing under the weighty impetus given to it by Erasmus, Calvin, Bengel, and Grotius on the threshold of the modern age. Its doughtiest champion in more recent days has been Bernhard Weiss,[1] and the facts and arguments which he adduces deserve careful attention. Chief of them is what may be termed the Jewish character of the Epistle as seen in the O.T. quotations and allusions, which would hardly be familiar to Christians of Gentile origin, and in the conception of the Church which is markedly Levitical and suitable only to those who had been nurtured in Judaism. The reference to the readers, moreover, as " strangers of the Dispersion " marks them as belonging to that part of Jewry which lay outside Palestine. Many, no doubt, had lapsed from the practice of their religion, and this accounts for the characterizations of their past life which we find in i. 18 and iv. 3-5 ; for Jewry in Asia Minor is not less likely than Jewry in Palestine in our Lord's day to have had a large fringe of people who had

---

[1] Cf. *Manual of Introduction to N.T.* ii. pp. 137 ff.; *Biblical Theology of N.T.* i. pp. 163 ff., 204 ff. Cf. also Kühl in the Weiss-Meyer commentaries; and R. H. Malden, *Problems of N.T. To-day*, p. 86 n.

put themselves, or been put, outside the pale of practising Judaism[1]; and St. Peter, who had been called to be "a fisher of men", may well have felt that his mission was chiefly to these lost sheep of the house of Israel.

This interpretation of the facts, however, encounters serious difficulties at certain points, and, though sufficient to put the extreme "Gentile" view out of court, is too narrow for its part. While, for example, the "vain conversation" (ματαία ἀναστροφή) of the readers' life before conversion admits of the view that they had been lapsed Jews, the description of it as "handed down by tradition from your fathers" (πατροπαράδοτος) could hardly have been used of any but Gentiles. Again, though many Jews may have fallen into the vices named in iv. 3-5, they are typically Gentile excesses, and certainly no Gentile could have been "surprised" if Jews abstained from taking part in them. Further, the careful attention given in ii. 18 ff. to the duties of slaves, even though based on common sources, indicates that there were many slaves among St. Peter's readers; and it is most improbable that these were Jews. The reference to the Dispersion, again, in i. 1 is far from decisive : St. Peter does not say that his readers were members of the Dispersion, but temporary residents, "domiciled" in its midst. The truth is that facts which go to prove the Epistle to have been *written* from a Jewish background do not thereby prove that the same background can be postulated of those who were to receive it. That our author's background was Jewish is indisputable ; so was that of the majority of the leaders of the Christian mission in the first age of the Church ; it was the cradle of the Church's worship and teaching; and it received formal endorsement as an integral element in Christianity in the decree of the Council at Jerusalem. Moreover, this Jewish element, with its Levitical conception of the Church as the new Israel and its preoccupation with the O.T. scriptures, came to the readers of 1 Peter not immediately. It came to them, that is to say, not as it would have come to a Jew well versed in the scriptures, but mediated through the hymns and catechetical Forms which they had learnt from their evangelists and teachers. It is significant,

Marginal note: Either view, if exclusively held, encounters serious difficulties,

---

[1] Cf. Hort, *The Romans and the Ephesians*, p. 127.

in this respect, that the books most quoted in this Epistle are the Psalms and the Proverbs, which had long been used for purposes of instruction, and also that the passage which more than any contains St. Peter's doctrine of the Church was probably part of a primitive Christian hymn.[1]

and the facts are best ac-counted for by the view that the churches addressed were " mixed "The correct interpretation of the facts would seem to lie, as so often, in refusing the dilemma, and in the view that the communities addressed in 1 Peter were " mixed " and consisted both of Jewish and Gentile Christians. The position would then be much the same as that of the Thessalonian, Roman, and Ephesian Churches ; even if earlier, as perhaps at Thessalonica,[2] Jewish and Gentile Christians had worshipped separately, the tendency to overleap these distinctions would have become increasingly strong. It is doubtful, indeed, whether there were many Churches in the first century outside Palestine, at any rate in the larger centres of population, of which the members were wholly Jewish or wholly Gentile, though in most of them Jews were probably in the majority ; and we know that in parts of Asia Minor there had been a syncretism of Jewish and pagan cults, which in some cases may have provided the spiritual background of those who afterwards became Christians.[3]

It must be remembered also that Jewish synagogues in the provinces had their " god-fearers " as well as their proselytes, and that these groups of devout but uncircumcised adherents probably played an important part in the expansion of the Church. The view that 1 Peter was addressed to Christians thus mixed in origin appears to meet all the factors in the case ; the abounding grace and salvation of which the Apostle speaks have already flowed over any Judaeo-Gentile controversies that may have existed ; and there is something in the Epistle for each and for all, whatever their spiritual past had been.[4]

---

[1] Cf. Add. Notes E, F, pp. 268-81.
[2] Cf. Harnack's theory that 1 Thess. was addressed to Gentile, and 2 Thess. to Jewish, Christians.
[3] Cf. Cumont, *Oriental Religions*, pp. 63 ff. ; Lietzmann, *The Beginnings of the Christian Church*, i. pp. 208 ff. But a note of caution is sounded by

Legge, *Forerunners and Rivals of Christianity*, ii. pp. 28 f.
[4] Even Weiss (*Biblical Theology*, i. p. 209) admits that there may have been " individual Gentiles " who had become believers and attached themselves to the Jewish Christians ; but that is not to go far enough.

There is the further question as to who had evangelized Part only of Asia Minor these Christians of Asia Minor. Or, to be more precise, who had founded the churches in those parts of Asia Minor embraced in the Address of the Epistle which St. Peter particularizes in his opening words ? The distinction has been often ignored, but it is important. For it is not clear that the whole of Asia Minor north of the Taurus mountains is intended. Ramsay, for example, who held that view,[1] has also been more than anyone responsible for the view that the Galatia visited by St. Paul was not the whole Roman province but its southern parts only ; and St. Peter was equally justified in using the term of its northern parts only, if he were so minded. Asia, again, fell into two or even three clearly marked areas — Phrygian Asia which was native but thoroughly Hellenized, the commercial urban area of the Lycus and Mæander valleys, and the main political region based on Pergamum and the river Caicus. St. Peter may well have directed his letter to the third of these only or to the first and third, and yet still have used no preciser language than he did. Further, we know that St. Paul was guided,[2] at a crucial point on his second missionary journey, to avoid preaching in " Asia " and in Bithynia ; and the last-named he never visited, while his work in Asia two years later was apparently confined to the Mæander area. No reason for this guidance of the Spirit is given in Acts ; but Rom. xv. 19, 20 tallies well with the view that it was because the Christian mission was already going forward in Bithynia and parts of Asia prosperously and peaceably, and it was undesirable that St. Paul should " build upon another man's foundations ".[3] No great boldness would be involved in the surmise that this work was under the direction of St. Peter himself, or of St. Peter and St. John.

There is nothing, therefore, in the address of 1 Peter to Road communications require us to suppose that it was intended to reach churches that were mainly Pauline. There were parts of Galatia and of Asia, and important parts too, which St. Paul had, so far as we know, not visited ; nor does he ever seem to have set

---

[1] *The Church in the Roman Empire*, p. 110.
[2] Acts xvi. 6, 7.
[3] Cf. also Latourette, *A History of* the Expansion of Christianity, i. p. 82 ; Bacon, *The Gospel and the Hellenists*, pp. 60, 61.

foot in Pontus, Cappadocia, or Bithynia. On the other hand, these were districts to which Christianity had spread at a very early date. Three of them — and indeed four, if we may reckon the Phrygia of Acts ii. 10 as meaning Galatic rather than Asian Phrygia — were represented among the pilgrims[1] who were present at Pentecost and heard St. Peter interpret that excited scene in his first sermon ; and they would have been the earliest to bring tidings of the new religion to their homes. An excellent road ran from the Cilician Gates northwards through Cappadocia and Galatia to Amisus on the Euxine, probably the first city on that coast to receive the Gospel[2] ; and at Mazaca (Caesarea) it crossed another fine route which the enterprise of Ephesian traders had utilized so effectively as to direct the commerce of Cappadocia from Sinope to their own Levantine sea-board.[3] Syrian Antioch occupied a key position in relation to both routes ; and we can be sure that the Christian Church there would lose little time in following up with a more thorough evangelization the trail of the Gospel first blazed by the returning pilgrims. In the cities, and especially the coastal cities of these provinces, Jewish settlements abounded, and it was through the synagogues, no doubt, that Christianity first made headway. But the problem of admitting Gentiles to Christian status could not have lagged far behind ; and the first evangelists must have been quickly followed by prophets and teachers bringing the news that the Gospel was universal and the terms on which the barriers between Jews and Gentiles were now down. Such is the situation which underlies i. 12. Whether St. Peter himself visited those communities in the northern half of Asia Minor we cannot say ; but his own vocation to "the circumcision" (Gal. ii. 9), their need

---

[1] Schürer, on the other hand, claims that the word κατοικοῦντες in Acts ii. 5 must connote *settled* residence (II. ii. p. 291, n. 231).

[2] Cf. Ramsay, *op. cit.* pp. 10, 225. But his reasons for believing that this would not have been before A.D. 65 are far from convincing.

[3] Cf. Toynbee, *A Study of History*, iv. 21. The distance from Mazaca to Ephesus was twice as great as to Sinope. An interesting division of Asia Minor is given by Appian, *Hist. Rom.* Prooem. 2, who distinguishes between those who "look to" (ἀφορῶντες) the "Egyptian sea", i.e. Pamphylians, Lycians, and Caria as far as Ionia, and those who look to the Euxine, Propontis, and Hellespont, i.e. Galatians, Bithynians, Mysians, and Phrygians. And cf. Rostovtzeff, *Social and Economic History of the Hellenistic World*, i. pp. 551 f.

of Apostolic guidance, and the existence of the First Epistle, make it not unlikely.[1]

3. THE SITUATION OF THOSE ADDRESSED

The people of Asia Minor in the first century of our era were highly heterogeneous. Successive migrations or invasions had introduced into the original Anatolian or Thracian stock the blood and the culture of other peoples, Phrygian, Celtic, Persian,[2] Greek, and Jewish. The oldest civilization and the most homogeneous was that of Cappadocia, whose commerce and culture have left literary remains of the third millennium B.C.[3] Its language was still in use in Strabo's time[4]: it was only slightly Hellenized and its cities were few.[5] To the west lay the Galatians, who represented a fusion of three Celtic tribes, migrants from the Pyrrhic wars, and stout allies of Rome in its struggle with Mithridates. It retained its monarchy up to 25 B.C., and its Gallic cantonal administration in imperial times ; and its law was paternal rather than Hellenic.[6] Ancyra was the capital, and here and at a few other cities Greek would have been in use, as

Characteristics of Asia Minor and its inhabitants in first century A.D.: ethnography ;

[1] Hort's suggestion in the Appendix to his unfinished edition of 1 Peter as to why the provinces mentioned in i. 1 are placed in that order has been widely accepted (cf. i. 1 n.) ; and we may surmise that the bearer of the letter, after touching at Sinope, landed at Amisus. From that point, however, or at least from Therma, there was a wide choice of means of communication with the interior, and it is likely that the letter was copied there for distribution by a number of bearers. One good road would have taken it southwards and south-eastwards through Amasia, Zela, and Sebastopolis to Sebasteia (with a possible detour from Amasia to Neo-Caesarea and Comana, rejoining the route at Zela), all of them places in Galatian Pontus or in the *regnum Polemonis* which was absorbed into it in A.D. 63. From Sebasteia a good road led south-westwards to Caesarea, the capital of Cappadocia, on the great east-west trade-route mentioned above. When the great road entered the province of

Asia, it was possible either to turn north from Kinnaborion to Kotiaeon, and thence westwards to Pergamum, or to reach Pergamum through Apameia, one of Asia's most populous and thriving cities, and Sardis. Another bearer may have gone south-westwards from Therma or Amasia to Tavium in Galatia and thence to the Galatian capital, Ancyra ; from which the Pilgrim's way, used by Jews on their pilgrimage from the Bosphorus to Jerusalem, led directly into Bithynia. The communications are well set out in Ramsay's map in *The Church in the Roman Empire*.

[2] Nock, *Conversion*, p. 42 ; Rostovtzeff, i. p. 552.

[3] Manson, *A Companion to the Bible*, p. 185 (art. by J. W. Jack).

[4] *Ib.* p. 168 (art. by W. M. Calder). Strabo himself came from Pontic Cappadocia.

[5] W. T. Arnold, *Studies of Roman Imperialism*, p. 229.

[6] Mommsen, *R.P.* (1886), i. pp. 338 f.

the *lingua franca* of trade ; but, generally speaking, the
Celtic language, like Welsh to-day, died hard. Throughout
the first century and later the cities of the plateau in Asia
Minor " remained islands of Hellenism in an Anatolian
sea ".[1] It was far otherwise, however, with the two other
regions named in the address of our Epistle. Pontus, which
formed a single province with Bithynia and yet kept its
geographical and cultural distinctiveness, was largely Hellenized.[2] Pompey had given it a cantonal administration, most
cantons forming the hinterland of some city on the coast :
Sinope was the capital of a chain of towns which stretched
for 70 miles of sea-board. Bithynia, like Asia, was rich
in populous cities, vying with one another to secure the
coveted title of " first city " or of " metropolis ", and nurtur-
ing celebrated men of letters such as Dion Chrysostom of
Prusa (A.D. 80–100), Memnon of Heraclea (A.D. 130), Arrian
(A.D. 150), and Dion Cassius (A.D. 200). Hellenism here
had been of long standing, many of its cities indeed being as
Greek as Greece itself : the tough Thracian stock of the natives
proved a good soil for it to thrive in. Greek was the normal
language, in fact, of culture, trade and social intercourse.[3]
In Asia alone the Greek cities were reckoned at five hundred,
and many of them were centres of great economic activity
economic   and wealth. The pastures of the interior, especially Galatia,
activities ; produced wool which came to be woven into cloth in Laodicea
or to be shipped across the Mediterranean from the Ionian
ports and across the Euxine from those of Bithynia. Pergamum, moreover, which had long-standing political and
commercial relationships with Egypt, developed a dye
industry, invented and gave its name to parchment, em-
broidered curtains and brocades, and was famous for its
nurture of live stock and its scientific study of agriculture.[4]
Ephesus was celebrated for its goldsmiths, like Florence and
Rome in the fifteenth and sixteenth centuries ; and flourish-
ing medical schools in this province sent their practitioners
to attend even the emperor himself. Nowhere, says Mommsen, was general culture more widely diffused or more

---

[1] Manson, *op. cit.* p. 166.   [2] Arnold, *op. cit.* p. 231.
[3] Manson, *op. cit.* p. 167; cf. Arnold, *op. cit.* p. 239.
[4] Rostovtzeff, *op. cit.* i. pp. 562 f.

influential.[1]   Capital, which in the interior was largely in the
hands of a few priest-princes controlling large areas of land,[2]
was in the maritime provinces widely distributed, and mainly
belonged to those whose enterprise and industry had created
it.   Appian writes proudly of the economic prosperity which
the " long and settled peace " of the Roman Empire had
brought to Asia Minor.[3]

If the economic condition of Asia Minor in the first distribu-
century A.D. was in general one of prosperity, the distribution wealth;
of wealth was far from equal.   In the interior the barons and
the priest-princes occupied a feudal position which paid little
heed to the lot of the bondsmen (λαοί) and slaves who
provided their manual labour.   Equally wide was the gulf
fixed between the wealthy Greek merchants of the cities and
the artisans and craftsmen, many of them slaves, whom they
employed : Rostovtzeff, indeed, speaks of social and economic
antagonism between the *bourgeoisie* and labour in the
Hellenistic world as acute.[4]   It is significant that the N.T.
Epistles shew no interest in this problem *as such* : we hear
of it only where it impinges directly on the work of the
Christian mission, as in the case of the Ephesian idol-makers
(Acts xix.), or the snobbery and callousness which it engenders
(Jas. ii. 1-9, v. 1-6) or the runaway slave (Philemon) or the
humble station of the Corinthian Christians (1 Cor. i. 26).   It
is difficult to make any general statement about the economic
condition of those whom St. Peter is addressing in this Epistle.
The fact that he has much to say to slaves, but nothing to their
masters, suggests perhaps that many of his readers were of
servile station.   On the other hand, the revelries he alludes to
in iv. 2-4 were certainly not indulged in for nothing, and in
these the readers had taken part before their conversion.   We
may reasonably surmise, therefore, that the communities in
view in this Epistle were as mixed in economic position as in
their religious background.

For the Asiatics were as mixed in religion as in race.   The religion
strangest congeries of divinities and of cults claimed their
worship, changing their names very often from one region to

---

[1] Mommsen, *op. cit.* i. pp. 360 ff.   i. p. 182 ; Manson, *op. cit.* p. 182.
[2] Foakes   Jackson   and   Kirsopp   [3] *Hist. Rom.* Prooem. 7.
Lake, *The Beginnings of Christianity*,   [4] *Op. cit.* ii. p. 1107.

another but not their character, and ranging from the primitive Ma, the Cappadocian moon-goddess, or the Phrygian Cybele or Artemis or her male counterpart, Jupiter or Dionysus Sabazius, to forms of monotheism, associated with Attis or simply with " the Highest ", which were in sympathetic contact with the Jewish synagogues. How far this syncretism of Jewish and pagan cults proceeded it is hard to say ; but it went far enough at least to attract the attention of Tacitus.[1] For the most part the native rites were of an orgiastic and often a licentious nature. The excitement of them can be felt in the *Bacchae* of Euripides and in the throbbing rhythm of Catullus' poem on Attis [2] ; and the excesses which so often accompanied their nocturnal ceremonies and processions are the subject of an express warning in 1 Pet. iv. This, however, is only one side of the picture : there was another side represented by the diets, native religious associations with social and administrative functions deriving from a remote past. Augustus encouraged the diets and gave them a recognized place as organs of opinion and local policy in the Asiatic provinces ; and in return they introduced the worship of the Roman emperor into their ceremonies. Thus, the diets of Asia and Bithynia erected temples to Augustus, whose high-priests, called Asiarchs or Bithyniarchs, exercised civil as well as religious functions. Already in his reign all the chief places on the judicial circuit had their Caesareum and their emperor-festival ; neglect of the established worship was punishable by civil law ; and Mommsen says that Asia Minor was the part of the Empire where the consequences of this in persecution were most felt.[3] It was probably these high-priests who were chiefly active in bringing Christians to justice on this score.

Privileged position of the Jews
Amid this welter of native cults, deeply embedded in the

[1] *Hist.* v. 5, an account of Judaism derived from popular prejudice, but not the less significant for that. *Inter se nihil illicitum*, he says. The monstrous accusations brought against the Christians in Pliny's time may have sprung from the evil reputation of the " Sabbathists ", as these votaries of Jehovah-Sabazius were called. Cf. Lietzmann, *The Beginnings of the Christian Church*, i. pp. 208 ff., and Cumont, *Oriental Religions*, p. 65.

[2] Cf. the interesting note on Cat. lxiii. in Macnaghten and Ramsay's *Poems of Catullus*. The town and temple of Comana in Cappadocia were noted centres of dissipated life ; cf. Rostovtzeff, i. pp. 576 f.

[3] *Op. cit.* i. pp. 345 ff.

life of the country and fostered by imperial favour, one religion stood out as of a different character. In belief, in ideals of conduct, in forms of worship, and for the most part in race, Judaism was a thing apart. Its position throughout the Empire was without exception one of privilege. In the case of Asia it rested upon four public enactments by Julius Caesar, which guaranteed to the Jews freedom of association and worship, power to acquire sites for synagogues, and the right to levy contributions and to dispose of them as they would.[1] They had also jurisdiction over their own members, exercised through their own courts[2]; and though these privileges often made them most unpopular, and sometimes led to outbursts of anti-Semitism, they were never in fact formally withdrawn.[3] The effect of this was that Judaism was treated as a *religio licita* without having to go through the formalities and submit to the conditions (including worship of the emperor) which were imposed upon the *collegia licita* of other religions. These privileges, moreover, applied to all Jews, whether or not they were Roman citizens. Bestowal of the Roman franchise in Asia Minor seems in any case to have been rare, and to have been made to individuals only[4]; but, apart from the Ionian cities and the cities, such as Apameia, founded by Seleucus I, the Jews of Asia Minor probably did not enjoy even full municipal citizenship. Politically, they were regarded as private associations of settlers (πάροικοι), having domiciliary rather than civil rights; and it is probable that they fared better so. When St. Peter addresses his readers as "domiciled among the dispersion" he is according to them the same position in relation to the Jews as the majority of Jews themselves had in relation to their comprovincials in Asia Minor.

Over this mixed population of native races, Greeks, and Jews the imperial power of Rome exercised a firm, yet tolerant and beneficent sway.[5] Of the four provinces which

The provincial administration

---

[1] Schürer, II. ii. pp. 258 ff.
[2] Cf. Acts ix. 2, xviii. 12-16.
[3] Schürer quotes Eus. *H.E.* VI. xii. 1 for cases in later times where Christians even became converts to Judaism to secure their own safety.
[4] Arnold, *op. cit.* p. 233. Even if, as

Schürer says (*op. cit.* p. 277), there were many thousands of Jews in Asia Minor who were Roman citizens, this would not be a very large proportion of the whole Jewish population.
[5] Cf. Inge, *Society in Rome under the Caesars*, pp. 87 ff.

St. Peter names, Bithynia-Pontus and Asia fell to the Senate's jurisdiction and were administered by proconsuls, while Galatia (to which the *regnum Polemonis* was added in A.D. 63) and Cappadocia were imperial provinces governed by *legati*. The latter had an eastern frontier which called for military protection ; and Galatia, though the Romans found its people trustworthy and congenial, was bordered by regions where the people were primitive and not easily governed.[1] The Romans used indirect rule, where possible, availing themselves of the services of local princes such as Deiotarus, the native diets and their presidents, the Greek municipal authorities, and the Jewish officers and courts. One thing alone they required — unconditional loyalty and obedience to Rome in all major matters of policy. It was to ensure this that they required, under the *Lex Julia* of A.D. 7, that religious activities (except in the case of the Jews) should be organized on the basis of corporations known as *collegia licita*, and that throughout Asia Minor each province should have its κοινόν or *concilium* to provide for the worship of Rome and of the reigning Caesar.[2] The Jews were exempt from this worship ; and, so long as the Christians could be regarded as a branch of Judaism, they would have enjoyed the benefits of this exemption likewise. But once that relationship ceased to be presumed, their legal position was highly precarious. And Rome's toleration during the principate extended only very reluctantly to proposals for the recognition of new societies.[3]

4. THE PERSECUTIONS ALLUDED TO IN I PETER

The persecutions mentioned in the Epistle were spasmodic, unofficial, and social rather than legal in character

It is against this background which we have thus briefly outlined that we must consider the persecutions which threatened the readers of our Epistle. They have a direct bearing on the questions both of its date and its integrity : Ramsay, for example, held that the nature of the persecution referred to in iv. 14 points inevitably to the Flavian period,

[1] For a statement of the principles on which Augustus and his successors divided the provinces cf. Strabo, *Geogr*. c. 840. 25 (Meineke).
[2] H. T. F. Duckworth, in *The Be-* ginnings of Christianity, Part I, vol. i. pp. 201 f.
[3] *A Companion to Latin Studies*, § 560.

and many German scholars maintain that the πύρωσις of iv. 12 indicates persecution so much more actual and serious than those of i. 6 ff. or iii. 13 ff. that iv. 12–v. 11 must represent, or belong to, a different document from i. 1–iv. 11. The question is also of importance because some of the deepest teaching of the Epistle is bound up with the trials through which its readers were passing. Can we grasp more clearly what these trials were ?

The passages where they are specifically referred to are three :

(*a*) 1 Pet. 1. 6.—The Christians are suffering trials (πειρασμοί) of various kinds (ποικίλοι). The choice of terms is significant. The specific term διωγμός does not occur in 1 Peter, nor does θλῖψις which is often associated with it in N.T. πειρασμός, though it is commonly the result of some evil intent, is a general term, and the plural is therefore very appropriately joined here with ποικίλοι. On our Lord's lips at the Last Supper πειρασμοί clearly means spiritual and mental trials as well as threats to His person. They are difficulties and sorrows (cf. λυπηθέντες in i. 6) caused by opposition, and they are means by which God tests (δοκιμάζει) the mettle of men's faith. False teaching within the Church is not excluded except by the fact that there is no hint of it otherwise in the Epistle. On the other hand every kind of opposition and slander is covered by it, whether coming from Jewish leaders, or from the leaders of Gentile religions such as the Asiarchs or Bithyniarchs, or from Roman authorities, or from society at large. But the qualifying words εἰ δέον ἐστί make it plain that these trials were of a local and haphazard kind, and were not experienced by all.

(*b*) 1 Pet. iii. 13-17.—We learn from this passage that some might be called to suffer " for righteousness' sake " (verse 14); but the phrase εἰ καὶ πάσχοιτε, and the words εἰ θέλοι τὸ θέλημα τοῦ θεοῦ in verse 17, point to a contingency which was regarded as remote, or at least rare. Good works and a devout and holy life, coupled with a gentle and respectful spirit in defending the Christian faith and a readiness to meet all honest enquiry about it, were the best way to disarm prejudice and calumny and win opponents over.

(*c*) 1 Pet. iv. 12-19.—The allusions here are more definite;

and the change of tone has led some scholars to the view that these verses, together with ch. v., must be ascribed to a different hand and have become accidentally attached to what has gone before. But the change must not be exaggerated. A state of πύρωσις exists, calculated to cause alarm (verse 12); but this word itself involves a metaphor which is most easily explained by reference to the "testing by fire" already mentioned in i. 7. What is significant, that is to say, is not the use of the word πύρωσις, but the fact that it is already taking place among them. The difficulty turns on the degree in which we regard the trials referred to in the earlier passages as contingent rather than actual. Some scholars, for example, have been led to the view that, in the course of the preparation of the letter, tidings of an aggravation of the position in Asia Minor reached St. Peter, and that he wrote iv. 12-19 specially in order to deal with it ; and the surmise is not unreasonable. Yet once we realize that actual persecution was spasmodic rather than general, and fortuitous rather than inevitable, we may decide that St. Peter's language is natural enough. The general ordeal (πύρωσις) lay in the complete lack of security which exposed Christians at any moment, and in any part of the empire (v. 9), to slander, defamation of character, boycott, mob-violence, and even perhaps in some cases death [1] : they were, or at any time or place might be,

[1] The martyrdom of Antipas at Pergamum (Rev. ii. 13) is of unknown date, and we cannot build anything definite upon it. It has been argued that the mention of murder in 1 Pet. iv. 15, for which the punishment was death, implies that the Christians here addressed were liable to the death penalty for their faith ; but the call in verse 19 to a life of stedfast well-doing, despite suffering, is a serious objection to that view. Verse 15 need mean no more than a clear disavowal on the Apostle's part, all the more desirable if the letter were to be seen by Roman officials and censors, of any leniency towards crimes which Roman law or policy was ascustomed to punish. Others again, notably Sir William Ramsay (*The Church in the Roman Empire*, pp. 280 ff. ; cf. also Jülicher, *Introduction to N.T.* pp. 204-15), have regarded the allusion to suffering " for the Name " (verses 14, 16) as proof of a Flavian date for the Epistle, on the ground that such persecution was not in vogue at an earlier date. But this is to give an official interpretation to language, in iv. 12-19 as also in iii. 15 and in v. 8, 9, which can be quite naturally explained otherwise. The early chapters of Acts make it clear that it was precisely " for the Name " that the Christians were persecuted by the Jews from the earliest times (Acts iv. 7, 17, v. 28, 40, 41, ix. 14, 16 ; cf. Matt. v. 10, 11) ; and the Lord Himself had foretold as much. Those who preached and taught and healed and baptized men " in Christ's name " were bound to suffer for His Name, if animosity were aroused. When Gentiles, incited by the Jews or under the impulse of their own suspicions or jealousies, took up the persecutors' rôle, it would likewise

hated of all men for Christ's sake ; society was inhospitable
and the world unjust. It was in such surroundings, full of
menace both to their faith and to their fortunes, that Christians had to play the man.

To sum up. The trials besetting the readers of 1 Peter Sum-
were spasmodic and particular rather than organized on a mary
universal scale, a matter of incidents rather than of policy,
at once ubiquitous and incalculable. The passage iv. 12-19
may indicate that in some definite way the situation had been
exacerbated while the Epistle was being written ; though this
is far from certain.[1] What the evidence points to is not
judicial procedure against a legally constituted offence, but
rather police administration which could be tightened or
relaxed at any time, as the authorities thought fit.[2] The
position is one to which we have been witnessing close
parallels during recent years in several countries, notably in
Germany. Pastor Niemöller, for example, was acquitted of
the charges brought against him, or, at least, found to have
been sufficiently punished for the few trivial offences that
were proved. But, on being released from the court, he was
immediately arrested by the Gestapo, the vast police-agency
which was the real instrument of Nazi policy. Similarly
what the Christians in the first century had to fear was not
the Roman law-court but the Roman police and the ebb and
flow of public feeling which might precipitate its action. Its
business was to keep order and to suppress suspicious movements before they became formidable. In general, the
situation was fluid. No doubt, when the emperor gave the
lead in persecution, as Nero did in A.D. 64 and as Caligula
had done among the Jews in Palestine over twenty years
previously, the activities of the police in the provinces no less
than in the capital became more vigorous, and the sufferings
of the Christians correspondingly more frequent and more
severe. At the turn of the half-century, we know that persecution broke out at Thessalonica at the instance of the Jews ;

be for His Name that Christians
would suffer. And if the matter
reached the Roman courts, and the
Christians were punished, their punishment would prove little more than that
public feeling against them had been
worked up to a pitch where the intervention of the Roman police had
become advisable.

[1] Cf. Zahn, *Einleitung*, ii. p. 34,
quoted in Hastings, *DB*, iii. p. 785 a.

[2] Cf. E. G. Hardy, *Studies in Roman History*, pp. 62, 63.

we have glimpses of it in the Epistle to the Romans, in the Epistle of St. James, and in the Epistle to the Hebrews ; and it is to Christians in Asia Minor, living in the shadow of it, that St. Peter addresses his letter.

5. THE DATE OF THE EPISTLE

Had we only St. Peter's allusions to persecution to guide us, it would be difficult to assign a date to the Epistle ; for, as Mommsen says, the persecution of the Christians in the first century was " a standing matter ",[1] and there may have been several periods in the experience of the Church in Asia Minor between A.D. 50 and 100 when the language of 1 Peter on this subject would have been appropriate. We have, however, other evidence in the Epistle which points to narrower limits. We shall see directly, for example, that both the doctrine and the ecclesiastical organization attested by the Epistle are of a quite simple and undeveloped kind, such as we might expect very early after the Christian mission had found its feet and taken from Antioch to the road. On the other hand, the feeling which the Epistle gives us of a flood-tide still flowing in the Church despite opposition from the surrounding world points to a date not much earlier than A.D. 60 ; and time must be given also for the circulation of the various liturgical and catechetical Forms which can be traced below the surface of the letter.[2] There are, moreover, certain passages in the Epistle which enable us, I think, to speak with still greater precision.

(a) St. Peter's description of his readers in i. 1 as " strangers " or " sojourners " ($\pi\alpha\rho\epsilon\pi\iota\delta\eta\mu\omega$) among the Dispersion in the five provinces he names — a description repeated and amplified in ii. 11 ($\pi\alpha\rho\omega\kappa\omega\nu\varsigma$ $\kappa\alpha\iota$ $\pi\alpha\rho\epsilon\pi\iota\delta\eta\mu\omega\nu\varsigma$) — is of great significance. Each word in this phrase in

[1] *The Provinces of the Roman Empire*, ii. p. 199 n. (ed. 1886) ; cf. also W. L. Knox, *St. Paul and the Church in Jerusalem*, p. 198.
[2] Yet this time need not be long. Scholars have been too much inclined to measure the speed at which the literature of missionary propaganda can be produced by that of their own later lucubrations on it. The speed is actually not a literary speed, but that of an army in action; and its true analogy is with the training and operational orders of a General Staff. Even quite elaborate technical manuals are compiled in time of war with great speed.

the address [1] tells a story: the recipients of his letter are
" elect ", i.e. Christians [2]; they are " sojourners ", i.e. uprooted from their old securities and forming an enclave
within their surroundings ; and the society within which
they are domiciled is, in the first instance, the Dispersion, a
word which, even if not yet possessed of the full technical
sense of later times, yet indicates the prominence of the Jewish
content of Christianity in the author's mind. Some commentators (e.g. Moffatt) give to the term παρεπίδημοι an
immediate theological significance, expressive of the idea that
Christians by virtue of belonging to God's spiritual kingdom
have ceased to belong in any true sense to any earthly society.
But this is surely a somewhat advanced and unfamiliar theological idea to insert into the opening words of a letter, and it
would be out of keeping with the writer's method revealed in
the rest of the Epistle ; for he is one of those concrete and
practical teachers who regularly leads his readers from the
known to the unknown and jumps no intervening stages. A
historical reference, therefore, is much more probable in the
term. And such a reference is not difficult to find. παρεπίδημοι
and πάροικοι connote people who do not properly belong to the
society in which they reside. Like many " evacuees " of our
own war years, they are in some sense déracinés, cut off from
home and from the social and civic securities that go with
home. Was there any occasion soon after A.D. 60 when the
use of such a phrase as ἐκλεκτοὶ παρεπίδημοι διασπορᾶς would
have struck its readers as obviously timely and appropriate ?

One such event, for which we have the clear and simple
testimony of the Jewish historian, Josephus, was the death of
St. James, the Lord's brother, in A.D. 62.[3] St. James had
been the leader of the Jewish-thinking element in Christianity
and was reckoned from the earliest times to be one of the
" pillars " of the Church.

The im-
pact of the
martyr-
dom of
St. James
the Lord's
brother
on the
Church's
position

[1] On Harnack's view that i. 1 f. and
v. 12 ff. are a much later addition to
the Epistle see Chase, *op. cit.* p. 786.
[2] The term rests on many *verba
Christi*, e.g. Mk. xiii. 20, 22, Matt. xx.
16, xxii. 14, Lk. xviii. 7, and cf.
Rom. viii. 33, Col. iii. 12, 1 Pet. ii. 9.
B. Weiss, *op. cit.* ii. pp. 137, 138, has
an excellent discussion of this point.

[3] Cf. Mayor, *The Epistle of St.
James*, 3rd ed. pp. lvii-lix, quoting
Lightfoot's discussion in his essay " St.
Paul and the Three " (*Galatians*, pp.
366 f.). A somewhat more favourable
view of Hegesippus' account of St.
James is taken by Burkitt, *Christian
Beginnings*, pp. 57-65.

I think it would be difficult to exaggerate the influence of his martyrdom on the minds of the Christians of that day ; for it meant a decisive repudiation of Christianity by Judaism. Ramsay thinks that the decisive event which shewed Christianity to be independent of Judaism was the destruction of Jerusalem [1] ; but the martyrdom at the hands of the Jewish leaders of the " apostle " who more than any other man had stood for the link with Judaism would have carried an equally clear lesson. Hitherto Christians of Jewish origin had been able to regard themselves as a kind of Jewish sect, and this attitude was shared by many non-Christian Jews ; and St. Paul's life and letters shew that the officials of the Roman Empire were prepared to take the same view and generally to extend to the Christians the privileges which the Empire had long given to the Jews. The martyrdom of St. James was instigated by a descendant of that Annas the high-priest who was the arch-conspirator in securing our Lord's condemnation ; and the work of the second Annas must have seemed to seal for ever the severance of the two religions.

still further strength-ened by that of St. Paul

The martyrdom of St. James would have sufficed in itself to justify the terms in which St. Peter addresses his readers and to make them self-explanatory. But it is possible that that event did not stand alone : indeed it must in any case have had most awkward repercussions on the way in which the Roman Empire now came to regard Christianity. The Acts of the Apostles, after shewing how fair, and sometimes even how cordial, was the attitude of the imperial officials towards the new religion, ends by leaving St. Paul a prisoner in Rome. Of the sequel to that imprisonment we have no certain knowledge. The traditional view, which was endorsed by Lightfoot,[2] is that St. Paul was released from this imprison-

[1] *Op. cit.* p. 255. But cf. also Dugmore, *The Influence of the Synagogue upon the Divine Office*, pp. 2 ff., for the view that the Revolt of Barchochba in A.D. 135 was the moment of final severance, already portended by the insertion in the *Shemoneh 'Esreh* of the anathema against heretics about forty years earlier.

[2] Cf. *Apostolic Fathers*, I. i. p. 75 n. 2. One of the crucial points in the evidence is Clement of Rome's statement that St. Paul went ἐπὶ τὸ τέρμα τῆς δύσεως (1 Clem. v.), which suggests a visit to Spain. Yet in Ps.-Sol. xvii. 14 ἕως ἐπὶ δυσμῶν means Rome, to which Pompey banished Aristo-bulus and his family.

ment and travelled to Spain and also to the Levant before
being again arrested and beheaded during or shortly after
the Neronian persecution. Others, whose arguments also
deserve respect, believe that St. Paul was executed at the end
of his imprisonment in the year 62 or 63.[1] If so, it may well
be that the martyrdom of St. James was partly responsible
for this result ; for the Emperor Nero was at that time
deeply under the influence of his infamous mistress Poppaea,
and Poppaea had strong leanings towards Judaism. What
more natural than that Poppaea's Jewish friends should tell
her that Christianity had been repudiated in the most open
way possible by the highest authorities in Judaism, and that
therefore the religion which St. Paul professed was not entitled
to Jewish privileges and could only be regarded as what the
Lex Julia had described as an " unlawful cult " ? However
that may be, and whether or not St. Paul was executed
between 61 and 63, a situation had arisen by the summer of
the year 64 when it was possible for Nero without any
difficulty to accuse the Christians in Rome of " hatred of the
human race ". For the state of public feeling in Rome
towards Christians in that year we have the concordant
testimony of two Roman historians, Suetonius and Tacitus,
the former speaking of Christianity as *superstitio nova ac
malefica* (*Nero*, 16), the latter as *exitiabilis superstitio* (*Ann.*
xv. 44) ; and though some details are doubtful about the
fearful persecution of the Christians over which Nero presided in the early August of that year, no doubt exists
that by that time Christianity had lost its civic security
vis-à-vis the State. The trumped-up charge of incendiarism
was an appeal not to evidence but to public prejudice
and animosity, and any ambiguity about the legal position of Christianity would have sufficed to make the charge
successful.

(*b*) The serenity of St. Peter's teaching about the duty **Reasons**
of Christians towards the civil power (ii. 13-17) does not **for dating**
I Peter
look as though it were written at any early date after the **before**
Neronian persecution of August A.D. 64, especially if it be **August,**
A.D. 64
the case that the emperor's outburst was followed by re-

---

[1] Wade, *N.T. History*, pp. 300,   62 (*Early Church History*, pp. 25 f.,
348 f., prefers A.D. 61 ; Vernon Bartlet   *The Acts* (Century Bible), p. 31).

pressive laws enacted specifically against the Christians.[1] The imperial power could still be looked to, when 1 Peter was written, as established, and as functioning, " for the punishment of evil-doers and the praise of them that do well " (ii. 14) ; and the persecutions alluded to are primarily, if not wholly, social and religious rather than legal, from the Gentiles certainly (iv. 4) and probably also from the Jews. The use of the cryptic " Babylon " for Rome in v. 13 suggests perhaps that in the capital the danger of some extreme and wholesale outburst of mob-violence loomed very near ; but that is a different thing from saying that it had actually occurred.

(c) If the death of St. James in the year A.D. 62 gives us a *terminus a quo* and the Neronian persecution in the summer of A.D. 64 a *terminus ad quem*, we arrive at a period of a year or eighteen months which is in no way discordant with anything that we know of the movements

St. Peter in Rome

of St. Peter, St. Mark, or Silvanus.   Of Silvanus' movements we have no later information in N.T. (apart from 1 Pet. v. 12) than that he was with St. Paul at Corinth (Acts xviii. 5, 2 Cor. i. 19) ; though the confidence which St. Peter had come to repose in him implies that he and Silvanus knew each other well.   He may have joined St. Peter when St. Paul went to Ephesus on his homeward journey.[2]   Of St. Mark we know that he was in Rome during St. Paul's captivity (Col. iv. 10 ; Philemon 24), and he was then expected to go to Asia Minor, whence somewhat later [3] St. Paul asks Timothy to bring him back with him to Rome (2 Tim. iv. 11).   From this point onwards tradition associates St. Mark closely with St. Peter ; and Papias says that he became St. Peter's " interpreter ", and as such composed his Gospel from what he remembered of the Apostle's teaching.

---

[1] Cf. Sulpicius Severus (*Chron.* ii. 29), *Hoc initio in Christianos saeviri coeptum ; post etiam datis legibus vetabatur, palamque edictis propositis Christianum esse non licebat.*   And he attributes the execution of St. Peter and St. Paul to this cause.   No other evidence of this legislation is available, but apart from the reference to edicts

and laws Ramsay (*op. cit.* p. 255 n.) thinks that Sulpicius may be using the *Histories* of Tacitus here.

[2] Cf. Knox, *op. cit.* pp. 289, 296.

[3] Swete (*St. Mark*, p. xix) thinks that St. Mark's expected visit to Asia Minor was exchanged for a visit to Egypt, which took place before 2 Timothy was written.

It is attractive to think of these two, Mark and Silvanus, writing in Rome with St. Peter as " ministers of the word " (ὑπηρέται τοῦ λόγου, Lk. i. 2), the one memorizing, and perhaps making notes on, what the Apostle taught of the historical incidents of our Lord's life, and the other concerning himself with St. Peter's testimony to his Master's teaching and its application to the needs and problems of the Christians in Asia Minor.[1]

Of St. Peter's movements from the Council of Jerusalem onwards we know singularly little. Some scholars[2] believe that he was for some time at Corinth soon after St. Paul visited that city : the existence of a Cephas-party there is a most improbable *result* of any ministry of his, but might well have called for his active intervention in order to secure its disappearance. I have already suggested that St. Peter's presence and work in Bithynia and in the Pergamene part of the province of Asia may have been the reason why St. Paul was guided to avoid evangelizing these regions on his second missionary journey. And I surmise that both there and in Corinth St. Peter's task was that of " strengthening the brethren " by general oversight and occasional visits rather than of founding new churches himself. When he went to Rome we do not know. The tradition recorded by Eusebius that St. Peter was martyred in A.D. 67 after a ministry of twenty-five years in Rome is on many grounds improbable.[3] On the other hand, the association of St. Peter with the Church of Rome for some time, at least, before his death is too well attested in tradition to allow of our doubting it.[4] I find it difficult to think that he was in Rome when St. Paul wrote Colossians or 2 Timothy, seeing that his name is not mentioned in the greetings. Some think that it was St. Paul's death which brought St. Peter to Rome, and that may well be so. But the martyrdom of St. James was likewise a critical event which would have demanded close consultation between the two great Apostles. In that event, one of St.

---

[1] Cf. R. O. P. Taylor's instructive article entitled " The Ministry of Mark " in *The Expository Times*, liv. No. 5 (Feb. 1943), pp. 136 ff.

[2] E.g. Lake, *E.E.P.* pp. 112 ff.

[3] *Ib.* p. 378.

[4] For criticisms of Merrill's view that St. Peter never went to Rome see Streeter, *The Four Gospels*, p. 489, Armitage Robinson, *Theology*, vol. x. No. 55 (Jan. 1925), pp. 48 ff., McNeile, *Introduction to N.T.* p. 36.

Paul's last acts may have been to suggest to St. Peter that he should write to the churches of northern Asia Minor an encyclical similar to that which St. Paul himself had not long since addressed to the churches of the Lycus and Mæander valleys, with such changes as the changed circumstances required. Silvanus, perhaps, was also called into counsel: it would be fitting at least that the drafter of the letter should be one who had enjoyed the trust and the friendship of them both.

**Con-
clusion**   The considerations adduced above point, then, to a date in the year 63 or the first half of 64 for the Epistle. If it were written and despatched in the autumn of A.D. 63, it could have reached the communities addressed in time to be read at the Easter festival of the following year. The point is relevant for more than one reason. We have already noted the view of some scholars that the Epistle, or at least the greater part of it, was written as a baptismal homily.[1] There is a stronger case, however, for finding the cultal point of reference in the whole celebration of the Pascha or Feast of Redemption, of which baptism was a part. Thus, we have, not only various actual and possible allusions to baptism, but also emphasis on Christ as the Lamb (i. 19), His passion ($\pi\alpha\theta\acute{\omega}\nu$, $\pi\alpha\theta\acute{\eta}\mu\alpha\tau\alpha$ frequently, which prepares the way for $\pi\acute{\alpha}\theta\sigma\varsigma$, i.e. " the Passion " in later literature), His resurrection (i. 3, 21, iii. 18-22), His second advent (i. 7, 13, iv. 13, v. 11), Vigil and Prayer and Fasting[2] (i. 13, iv. 17, v. 8), and perhaps the Eucharist (ii. 3-5).[3] This complex of *cultus* and doctrine is a very striking feature of the Epistle, and contains all the elements that were fused into the Paschal observance in Asia Minor in the second century.[4] They may well have coexisted at a much earlier date. What at least we can regard as highly probable is that baptism was associated very early with the Paschal celebrations, and that it served the very practical purpose of being the

---

[1] i. 1–iv. 11, Perdelwitz, followed by Streeter; i. 3–v. 11, Bornemann, cited by McNeile, *op. cit.* p. 209 n. Bornemann makes much of the use of Ps. xxxiv. in the Epistle.

[2] But $\nu\acute{\eta}\phi\epsilon\iota\nu$ means abstinence from wine, not food; cf. Lightfoot, on Ignatius, *Polyc.* ii.

[3] Cf. Add. Note H, pp. 294-8.

[4] Cf. Brightman, *J.T.S.* vol. xxv. pp. 254-74.

occasion when the largest number of Christians would gather together. Moreover, an Epistle like 1 Peter called for such an occasion, if it were to reach the largest number of people; and it would clearly have been supremely appropriate to it.

IV

THEOLOGY AND ETHICS OF THE EPISTLE

I. INTRODUCTORY

IN the Preface or " Hypothesis " which Oecumenius pre-
fixed to his commentary on 1 Peter, we read : " This Epistle
is written by Peter to Jews of the Dispersion who had become
Christians, and it is a teaching Epistle ; for after they had
come to the faith from Judaism, his endeavour was to
strengthen them still further ". In the words " a teaching
Epistle " the ancient commentator [1] has hit on the right
phrase, and in the clause which follows he rightly defines the
Epistle's aim. And the teaching which it gives must be
understood in the widest sense, as embracing not only what
is commonly called doctrine but also ethics or principles and
canons of conduct governing the practical life of Christians in
the Church and in the world. Indeed, in its close association
of ethics with theology, this Epistle is one of the seed-plots of
the *theologia perennis* of Christian ethical thought, immune
alike from the mysticism which tends towards the absorption
of the human soul in the divine and from the moralism which
finds its classical expression in the works of Kant. The
Christian moral life depends on man's freedom and responsibility ; but this freedom and responsibility are exercised
within a cosmic order which has God for its source, its sphere,
and its end. Thus, from the side of theology, we find faith
issuing in holiness, and holiness expressing itself in brotherly
love ; the " fear " or reverence proper to belief in God is reflected in the respect and courtesy which must govern men's
relations to one another: man's attitude of obedience and
humility before Him bespeaks a similar temper in social and
domestic life. From the side of ethics, we note how regularly
St. Peter bases his moral injunctions upon general principles,
often of a definitely theological kind : his " because " [2] is a

ii. 16

i. 13-23

v. 5

---

[1] For his probable date, about
A.D. 600, cf. C. H. Turner's art.
"Patristic Commentaries" in Hastings,

DB, ext. vol. pp. 485-8, 523 f.
[2] Cf. i. 16, 18, ii. 15, 21, iii. 9, 18,
iv. 1, 8, 14, 17, v. 5, 7.

characteristic of his thought, tracing the motives of action or of endurance to the divine Will, or to the example of Christ (especially His passion, death, and resurrection), or to the eschatological End of human destiny. This close interweaving of the two strands makes it difficult to expound the teaching of the Epistle in regard to either without some overlapping. But, as many have observed, there is overlapping in the Epistle itself ; and we may be most true to its message if we do not try to disentangle too much.

2. THE CHRISTIAN LIFE (i. 2-5)

(*a*) *Its Nature* (*i. 2*).

The address of the Epistle leads at once into a verse containing three prepositional clauses, which define severally the governing principle, the sphere, and the practical aim and character of the Christian calling.[1] There is a question whether these clauses depend on, and amplify, the word ἐκλεκτοῖς only in the preceding verse, or refer to that verse as a whole ; but the wider reference is to be preferred, for the author is no less chosen and called than his readers. Both he in his Apostolate and they in their calling as Christians and pilgrims owed their position to the " foreknowledge " of God the Father. Accidents of history — his meeting with Jesus by the Lake of Gennesaret, their severance from Judaism and from the social and legal privileges which Judaism conferred — might seem to have played their part. But the true explanation of the history and of its issue lay in that which was beyond history, namely, the counsels of the divine Providence. We are thus introduced at the outset to the conception of the divine initiative which is to recur as a constant theme throughout the Epistle. It is God's design and purpose for the universe and God's action which have called the Church into being through Christ's death and resurrection, and have given to the trials to which it was subject the character of a purifying judgment, and supply the strength and courage which it needs for its task. That is the background of the Church's life. It was all the more necessary to emphasize it

God is the source of the Christian life,

---

[1] The bearing of this verse and of other passages in I Peter on the doctrine of the Trinity are discussed below in Add. Note A, pp. 247-50.

in that the communities addressed had long traditions behind them, both Jewish and pagan, of which they were fully conscious (cf. i. 18, iv. 4) ; and what the Apostle seeks to do here is to turn their attention away from their historical antecedents to the true Cause of their new life in the Christian Church, which was the Will of God.   It is the call to shift the emphasis from history to " meta-history " (to use a phrase from Eastern theology), from tradition to the Word and Deed of God, from nature to grace.   They are what they are, not because they were what they were, but because all that has made them what they are was subject to God's transcendent purpose only now accomplished.

and the Holy Spirit its sphere, And the sphere of their life is the activity of the Spirit, which hallows them, sets them apart, makes them holy.   The instrumental use of ἐν as almost equivalent to διά is well attested in the New Testament ; but it is not necessary to find this usage here.   A better sense, and one more consonant with a later passage in this chapter (verses 13-21, especially verses 15, 16), seems to be given by the simple rendering " in " or " in the sphere of ".   Uprooted from their old loyalties and associations, these Asiatic Christians had need of new ones ; and these have been given them in the new spiritual atmosphere and environment which the Holy Spirit provides, and which is the condition of their growth.   They are an *enclave* within the world, because they are within the sphere of hallowing influences to which the world is a stranger.   No doubt for themselves as individuals the operation of these influences had a beginning in time at their baptism, as it had for the Church as a whole at Pentecost.   But no emphasis is laid on that here ; and the thought is rather of a continuous process in which the Spirit of God interacts with their spirits and conforms them ever more closely to His likeness.

and its practical end is obedience And thirdly St. Peter sets before his readers the practical purpose of the divine initiative in calling them.   We need the word " practical ", because thus early in the Epistle St. Peter strikes the note which is to sound in it throughout.   There is nothing in this verse of the ultimate vision of what the Church is to be, as we see it in the Epistle to the Ephesians, or in the Epistle to the Hebrews (ch. xii.), or in the Revelation of St. John the Divine. Nor is there at this point any allusion to the ethical " end " or *summum bonum*, whether conceived theologically (as in 1 Tim. i. 5) or in its ultimate fruition by the individual soul. Our author is aware of these wider horizons and will refer to them (i. 3-5, v. 4) ; but his outlook here is the more limited and more urgently practical one of the quality of the Church's life here and now in its earthly pilgrimage. It is to be marked by " obedience and sprinkling of the blood of Jesus Christ ". The phrase is not easy, until we realize that it summarizes, and transfers to Christianity, the ideas of obedience and of reconciliation through a sacrifice contained in Ex. xxiv., and that the " sprinkling of the blood of Jesus Christ " is a synonym for God's continuing forgiveness and grace covenanted in Christ's death.[1] With this interpretation, it sets before us the Christian ethical life as consisting in the interplay of man's endeavour after goodness with the forgiving grace of God. The word " obedience " is characteristic of Jewish ethical thought, and especially of one of its seed-plots, the Book of Deuteronomy, where obedience to God's will as revealed in His Law is regarded as the foundation of all goodness. For St. Peter the obedience is due not to the Old Law but to the New, as given by Christ in the Sermon on the Mount and elsewhere, and summarized in the " new commandment " of love to God and neighbour. But it is obedience still ; and his treatment of specific duties later in this Epistle shews how deeply the thought was impressed upon his mind.

Yet this obedience can never be fully rendered. What the author has in mind here is not that deliberate sin amounting to apostasy about which such stern words are found in the Epistle to the Hebrews (vi. 4-8, x. 26-31) and the First Epistle of St John (v. 16, 17), but rather the continuing frailty of which the saints of all ages have been conscious. " If we say that we have no sin, we deceive ourselves, and the truth is not in us " (1 Jn. i. 8) : and it is for this that God's continuing forgiveness through Christ is needed. It is the truth which forms the theme of one of the greatest of Shake-

and reconciliation to God through Christ's sacrifice

[1] The point is well brought out by Spörri, *Der Gemeindegedanke im ersten Petrusbrief*, p. 235.

speare's plays, *Measure for Measure* ; and it stands in all the clearer relief in the character of Isabel by contrast with the stern authoritarianism of Angelo.

> Why, all the souls that were, were forfeit once ;
> And He that might the vantage best have took
> Found out the remedy.

So Isabel speaks, and proclaims the true ground of Christian humility. " So many stars has not the Heaven, so many grains of sand the sea, not so many sparks the fire, not so many motes the sunlight, as the sins which He forgives." [1]

The Apostle's allusion here to the Covenant made on Sinai affords an important clue to the thought, so prominent in this Epistle, of Christianity as recapitulating, though on another and a higher plane, the history of the Chosen People. In that story the Covenant sacrifice marks a decisive moment in the making of Israel ; it is to be followed, after the wanderings in the wilderness, by their entrance into the land of Canaan which God gives them as their inheritance or possession ; and it is on that soil that the varied drama of Israel's life is unfolded in the Old Testament. St. Peter follows a similar order in his first two chapters The mention of the new Covenant here prepares the way for the teaching about the new inheritance in i. 3-25, and that again for the doctrine of the new Israel in ii. 1-10.

(b) Its transcendent Horizons (i. 3-5).

Horizons of the Church's life ;

The salutation over, St. Peter opens his Epistle in a passage of sustained eloquence, in which adoration, teaching, and exhortation are closely interwoven. It has not the torrential quality which marks the corresponding exordium to St. Paul's Ephesians, for the movement of thought and style is controlled by the objective facts of the Gospel from which it starts and of the present persecution which conditions it. But within that framework (which must be extended to include Christ's imminent revelation in triumph no less than His life and death and resurrection which are already part of history) a pattern is worked which for richness of meaning,

---

[1] Calderon, *The Mighty Magician*, quoted by R. W. Chambers, *Man's Unconquerable Mind*. Professor Chambers' chapter on *Measure for Measure* in this book is a memorable piece of literary criticism.

harmony of design, and depth and variety of colour, has few
parallels in literature.   The effect is like that of some masterpiece of tapestry or a page from one of the great illuminated
books of the tenth century.   It arrests the attention as a
whole, and absorbs it with every detail.

The framework of fact is made of Christ's resurrection, of their
the trials which the Church is suffering, and of the eschato- framework of
logical End conceived of as an Event in which the salvation evangelic
of men and the appearing of Christ coincide.   The effect of fact
these facts is to set the Christian life in a larger room, and to
endow it with relationships and aims which were closed to
human life before ; though the possibility of them had been
portended in prophecy.   Moreover, the apprehension of these
relationships and the realization of these aims required and
brought into play new spiritual activities in man — Hope,
which laid hold of the heavenly inheritance ; Love for Christ
the Redeemer, who, though unseen, was the source of joy ;
and Faith, which through every trial of circumstance, clung
fast to the truth of triumph through suffering which had.been
first exemplified in the Messiah Himself.   The whole passage
falls into three main sentences ; and in each of these sentences
all three of these themes — the fact-framework, the new relationships and aims, and the spiritual functions they call
forth — find a place.

In the glowing words of the first sentence St. Peter gathers Special
up all that the resurrection of Christ has come to mean for significance of
him and for the Christian Church, through the manifestation Christ's
of God's power and mercy on the one hand and the widening resurrection
of men's horizons and the exaltation of their hopes on the
other.   Moreover, in blessing God for this crowning mercy,
he not only implies that there were other and earlier ones,
but also uses a form of words hallowed by centuries of Jewish
worship.   For the solemn Blessing of God was a regular part
of the daily Jewish liturgy and of the due celebration of its
festivals.   No fewer than eighteen Benedictions were used in
these services.   And two themes especially recurred in them
as grounds for blessing and glorifying God.   One was the
manifestation of God's power and wisdom and goodness seen
in the creation of the world and in the bounty and beauty of
the natural order.   The other was the signal act of mercy by

which He redeemed the Chosen People out of their bondage
in the land of Egypt. Both these thoughts are taken up into
the new and Christian form of blessing which the Apostle
gives us. Instead of God's work in the creation of the world,
the thought is of His work in the " new creation " or rebirth of
Man inaugurated by the resurrection of Christ. And instead
of His deliverance of the Children of Israel from Egypt,
which was a national and political event, the thought here is
of a more universal and far-reaching deliverance, namely, the
redemption of all believers, to whatever race they belonged,
from sin and death. This was to give to redemption a
spiritual range and meaning which in Judaism it had never
attained. And it is interesting to observe that the two grounds
of Benediction — God's work in creation, and His work in
redemption thus reinterpreted — were before long to find
regular mention in the great Eucharistic *Anaphorae* of the
Christian Church.

and of
the new
hope now
opened
up

 And the immediate result of this new creation is described
by St. Peter as a " living hope ". The words imply that the
readers had known other hopes that were dead, though their
embers may still have been flickering in some hearts. We
can well conjecture what they were. There was the hope
entertained by the Jewish Christians that the leaders of
Judaism would see their tragic mistake in rejecting Christ
and would make the Holy City once again the home of a
restored theocracy ; but their hope was shattered by the
martyrdom of James, the brother of the Lord, " bishop " of
the Church in Jerusalem, at the hands of the Jewish hierarchy.
Again, there had been the hopes of those, mainly Gentile
Christians, who had believed in the friendliness of the Roman
Empire to Christianity, until events had shewn that there,
too, no reliance could be placed. And again there must have
been many who remembered the promise of the *quinquennium
Neronis*, when the young prince was guided by Seneca and
Burrus, and now found themselves disillusioned by the
cruelty and licentiousness which followed their demise. And
with those hopes lay buried all other ideas of a political
theocracy, an earthly Paradise, as the goal of human life,
which men had then conceived or might conceive in the
future. For the Apostle goes on to give body to the Church's

" living hope " in language which rules out all such projec-
tions of human optimism.

The Christian hope is of another order ; it is of an inheritance, to be possessed and used and passed on to others like
that first inheritance in Canaan which God had promised to
Moses and made a reality in Joshua's time, and yet different
from that in that it is " another country, that is a heavenly ",
which no invading armies can ravage, no sins or idolatries can
stain, no lapse of time can bring to disillusion or decay.   The
temper of mind indicated, looking at once upward and forward, is the very opposite of the disillusioned pessimism, all
too widespread in the ancient world, which finds expression
in Swinburne's words :

> From too much love of living,
>   From hope and fear set free,
> We thank with brief thanksgiving
>   Whatever gods may be
> That no life lives for ever ;
> That dead men rise up never ;
> That even the weariest river
>   Winds somewhere safe to sea.

With the idea that this world cannot supply man with abiding satisfactions our author agrees ; but it prompts him
to affirm not hope's abandonment but its redirection ; not
doubt of divine Providence, but a clearer faith, resting on a
historical revelation ; not the brevity and futility of life, but
the possibility of its entrance into a higher and richer mode
of being.

The use of the term κληρονομία would have awakened deep
chords of religious patriotism in all who cherished the
memories of Israel's past.   In classical literature and in the
vernacular of the first century it connoted no more than
property that changed hands after a death, and had no religious associations.   But for anyone nourished on the Jewish
Scriptures, it meant the Land which God had given to Israel
to be at once their own possession and the home of His worship.   The Apostle touches into life the sentiment which hung
about the term, and transfers it to a sphere of life — also their
own and also God-given — which has now been opened up for
Christians.   As yet, it stands in the same relation to their

*Christian-
ity thus
admits
men to a
new in-
heritance*

minds as the Promised Land once stood to the minds of the Patriarchs and to the Israelites in the desert ; that is to say, it was an object of hope. But it differed from the older object of hope in being, in the strict sense of the word, metaphysical ; that is, beyond the visible order and the contaminations of time.[1] It exists already, " reserved in heaven " ; and its enjoyment is assured to those on earth who are " guarded through faith " : but its content of health and eternal life will not be manifested until the End of all things is at hand. The imminence of that End is proved by the present sufferings of the Church, and therefore the eschatology already throws a sharp reflex light back upon the Church of the present. But St. Peter does not speak of the Church's life, as plainly as St. Paul and St. John do, as already an anticipation of the eternal order ; his eschatology is more primitive.

3. THE DOCTRINAL FRAMEWORK OF THE EPISTLE

World-view of the primitive Church

One of the main tasks of modern New Testament scholarship has been the attempt to elucidate the setting or pattern of doctrine in which the minds of its writers moved ; and since this pattern provided the context of much of St. Peter's thought, its principal features must be outlined. As between those who, like Loisy,[2] maintain that nothing but the eschatological element in the Gospel is to be reckoned as primitive, and the modern disciples of Wrede, on the other hand, who regard the eschatology as an early accretion upon a Gospel which was originally without it, the majority of scholars have been content to follow less extreme roads and to reach a synthesis of what is true in both views. And the outcome has been a conception of the original Gospel message, which is governed indeed by eschatology, but by an eschatology that is itself in large part already realized in the life, death, and resurrection of Jesus the Messiah.[3] There is discoverable,

---

[1] Thus, Lancelot Andrewes (*Sermons*, vol. ii. : Of the Resurrection, No. 1) speaks of " the estate of the children of the resurrection, to be the sons of God, equal to the Angels, subject to no part of death's dominion, but living in security, joy, and bliss for ever ".

[2] Cf. *Les Origines du Nouveau Testament*, ch. ii. and ch. viii.

[3] Cf. Streeter, *The Four Gospels* ; Hoskyns, *The Riddle of the New Testament*, and *The Fourth Gospel* (*passim*) ; Dodd, *The Apostolic Preaching and its Developments*.

that is to say, a world-view or pattern of thought which is common, though in many stages of development and with many differences of emphasis, to all the writers of the New Testament ; and it formed the seed-plot out of which grew the doctrinal discussions and dogmatic formulations of later Christianity.

The pattern is to be seen in its simplest form in the speeches attributed to St. Peter in the first ten chapters of the Acts of the Apostles.[1]　The primitive character of these speeches, despite the later date of the composition of Acts, is indicated by a number of features, especially by their undeveloped Christology, by their freedom from any marks of Pauline influence, and by the number of Aramaisms in certain passages : verses 35-8 of Acts x., indeed, are impossible Greek, but are clear and grammatical when translated into Aramaic.[2] We may summarize the theology of these speeches as follows :

Comparison of the Petrine speeches in Acts with I Peter as to doctrine

1. The age of fulfilment has dawned, i.e. the Messianic age has begun.　This is God's last word, just as the creation was His first word.　The event inaugurates a new·order ; the call of the elect to join the Messianic community brings new life (Acts ii. 14-36, 38, 39, iii. 12-26, iv. 8-12 (v. 17-40), x. 34-43.　Cf. I Pet. i. 10, 11, iv. 7, i. 3).

2. This has taken place through the life and death and resurrection of Jesus, which have fulfilled the prophetic element in the Jewish scriptures, and are thus shewn to have come to pass by God's " determinate counsel and foreknowledge " (Acts ii. 20-31, citing Pss. cxxxii. 11 and xvi. 8-11 ; iii. 22, citing Deut. xviii. 15-19 ; ii. 23, iii. 13, 14 (cf. Ps. xvi. 10) ; iii. 15, iv. 10, x. 43.　Cf. I Pet. i. 20, 21, iii. 18, 21, 22).

3. Jesus has been exalted, by virtue of the resurrection, to God's right hand, as Messianic head of the new Israel (Acts ii. 22-36, citing Ps. cx. 1 ; iii. 13 (cf. I Pet. i. 21) ; iv. 11, citing Ps. cxviii. 22, also quoted in I Pet. ii. 7 ; v. 30, 31 (cf. I Pet. ii. 24) ; x. 39-42).

4. The Holy Spirit in the Church is the sign of Christ's

---

[1] The problems of literary criticism raised by the affinities between these speeches and I Peter are discussed above, pp. 33-6.

[2] Dodd, *op. cit.* p. 54, quoting Torrey.　The summary here given is based on Dr. Dodd's, *op. cit.* pp. 38-45.

present power and glory, and the proof that the eschatological
hope of Israel is in course of realization (Acts ii. 33, 17-21,
citing Joel ii. 28-32 ; v. 32).

5. The Messianic events will shortly reach their consummation in the return of Christ in glory, and the judgment of
living and dead (Acts iii. 19-23, x. 42. Cf. 1 Pet. i. 5, 7, 13,
iv. 5, 13, 17, 18, v. 1, 4, 6, 10).

6. These facts and forecasts are made the basis of an
appeal for repentance, an offer of forgiveness and the gift of
the Holy Spirit, and a promise of eternal life to those who
enter the Apostolic community (Acts ii. 38, 39 (cf. Joel ii.
28 ff., Is. lvii. 19) ; iii. 19, 25, 26, citing Gen. xii. 3 ; iv. 12,
v. 31, x. 43. Cf. 1 Pet. i. 13 ff., ii. 1-3, iv. 1-5).

This pattern represents a complex of faith, fact, and hope.
The faith is the fundamental monotheistic faith of the Hebrew
scriptures and of Judaism, and the series of eschatological
events now realized are His work and carry with them a
new revelation of His nature. The facts are those which are
attested by men who have been witnesses of Christ's life,
death, and resurrection, and by others whom they have con-
vinced. These events are what have brought the new pattern
of thought into existence ; for though much of it had existed
for long past as an expectation, it only now exists as a fact
of historical experience. Christ's death, resurrection, and
second advent [1] are held together by links of peculiar strength
and cohesion, owing to the fact that the Subject of them all
is known.[2] Together they represent the central core of the
Christian creed. At the same time, the historical fulfilment
is not yet complete ; the Messianic age or age of the Spirit
has come, but not yet in full ; and faith needs, therefore, to
be supplemented by hope. He who has ascended into the
heavens to God's right hand must return, and that speedily,
to consummate His work of judgment and redemption.
Further, it is clear that any one of the main features of the

[1] The form of *Anamnesis* in the
Scottish Liturgy is thus in principle
primitive. For the view that the
cohesion of these three events is represented in the Marcan narrative of the
Transfiguration see G. H. Boobyer,
J.T.S. vol. xli. pp. 118-40.

[2] Cf. Dodd, *op. cit.* p. 68. " The

more we try to penetrate in imagination to the state of mind of the first
Christians in the earliest days, the
more we are driven to think of resurrection, exaltation and the second advent
as being, in their belief, inseparable
parts of a single divine event."

pattern may receive the main emphasis at any time. In St. Paul's Epistles, for instance, we can see the emphasis shift over from the future to the present as the expansion of the Church proceeds. In 2 Peter and Jude, as in the Apocalypse, the emphasis lies mainly on the future. In the Fourth Gospel, on the other hand, eternal life is present here and now : in other words, almost the whole interest is in that part of the eschatological pattern which has already been realized in history. One of the interesting features of 1 Peter is the closeness with which the theological pattern governing the Epistle corresponds to that of Acts i.-x. There is the same emphasis on the priority of the divine counsel, and on God's initiative in the call of the Church and His impartiality in judgment ; the same conception of Jesus as the " suffering servant " portrayed in Is. liii., a conception not found in St. Paul ; the same idea of the Church as the Messianic community. The work of the Holy Spirit is less prominent in 1 Peter than in Acts or in the Pauline letters, though 1 Pet. i. 2, 12 and iv. 14 shew that it forms part of the Apostle's presuppositions ; and, conversely, allusions to the second advent are relatively more frequent in 1 Peter than in Acts, although no more weight is put upon them. Further, there are references to details of Christ's earthly life, especially His sufferings and the way He bore them, which are unlike anything in St. Paul, but have a parallel as a supplement to the primitive pattern in St. Peter's speech recorded in Acts x. 36-41. Only in one particular, Christ's " preaching " to " the spirits in prison " (1 Pet. iii. 19, 20, iv. 6), does St. Peter introduce a doctrinal element not found in his speeches in Acts ; and there is nothing in this which may not be regarded as early. It is not too much to say that, in its presentation of the Gospel as a whole and in the balance and proportion of its parts, the teaching of this Epistle is thoroughly primitive.

4. THE LIVING GOD

(a) *God and Man.*

Nothing reveals more clearly the Hebraic character of this Epistle than the way in which it makes God and His dealings with men its central theme. Throughout the letter

The Epistle theocentric

there is to be noted a close fusion of two elements which are familiar to us in the Old Testament : (1) the doctrine of God's transcendence, His majesty and power, His holiness, His creativity, His initiative in history, His providence, judgment, and mercy, as these are taught in the prophets and in the historical books ; and (2) the doctrine of God's intimate concern with human life, its sins, its trials, and its duties, as this is set forth in the devotional literature of the Psalms. The result is that the Epistle is markedly theocentric — a fact which, as Spörri points out,[1] is not obscured but rather reaffirmed by the christocentric orientation which St. Peter gives to his idea of the Church.   From God — in relation to God — unto God : these phrases sum up the author's philosophy of history and his theology of salvation.

Only one allusion to God as Creator of the world occurs in this Epistle (iv. 19), but it is pregnant with teaching.   It starts from the most stubborn of all the difficulties which faith in the divine creation of the world has to encounter, the fact of unmerited suffering endured in, or inflicted for, carrying out God's will.   Unlike the Book of Job, it leaves on one side any attempt at speculative solution, but inculcates instead a practical attitude and activity of will.   Since God is faithful and has not created them for nothing, such sufferers are to commit their souls to His keeping, and to express this in doing good.   The challenge to men's love of God is to be met by an intenser love of neighbour, and its reward is glory and immortality at the last.   Other aspects of the divine priority in being, and the divine initiative in action, are also strongly emphasized in the Epistle.   In a world of change and decay God and His word are " living and abiding " ; Christ was " foreknown " by Him and designated as men's Redeemer " before the foundation of the world " ; the election of Christians out of the paganism in which they had lived was " according to the Father's foreknowledge " ; and it was God who had called them to their new life.   It is perhaps an overstatement to say that the Jewish conception of predestination is nowhere more prominent than in 1 Peter [2] ; but the author teaches very plainly that all Christians owe their position, and

Bearing of this upon the worth of human personality

---

[1] *Op. cit.* p. 236.
[2] E.g. Dewick, *Primitive Christian Eschatology*, p 254.

the Church its existence, not to any immanent logic of history, but to the mind and will of God ; just as, conversely, the doom of the unbelieving rests on His immutable decree (ii. 8). " It is the God-relationship that makes a man a man ", said Kierkegaard ; and St. Peter, especially in his teaching about conversion and baptism, traces the relationship up and back to its transcendent source in the prevenient activity of God. The point is of vital importance to-day when attempts are so often made to interpret human personality in terms of economics or of politics only, and without reference to man's spiritual origin.   Time may well shew, if it has not already shewn, that Christianity and Christianity alone can preserve and guarantee the true status of man.[1]

From the historical point of view, the most significant event in the rebirth or renaissance of mankind which constitutes redemption was the resurrection of Christ.[2]   For the Resurrection demonstrated that God's work of mercy in sending the Redeemer to be a sacrifice for sin was also a work of power and of judgment ; in raising Jesus from the dead, God had vindicated goodness, and men could therefore set their faith and hope in Him.   And these attributes of God are to be seen likewise in the life of the Church.   His mercy is manifested in the renovation of human personality, which made of conversion and baptism a veritable second birth, and turned a number of hitherto separate and heterogeneous individuals, bound by no ties or loyalties to one another, into a people who knew themselves to be God's people, called out of darkness into light.   It is seen too in the repeated forgiveness, spoken of as " the sprinkling of the blood of Jesus Christ ", which even the best men need.   God's power is what keeps believers' spiritual life secure, until the faith they walk by is changed to sight and final salvation is attained. His judgment is laid bare in the separation of believers from unbelievers brought about by the Incarnation ; so that He who was the cornerstone of the new temple of God was also at the same time, to unbelievers, " a stone of stumbling and

(margin note: Importance of the Resurrection in this connexion)

---

[1] Cf. V. A. Demant, *The Religious Prospect*, especially ch. ii.

[2] V. Taylor is surely mistaken when he speaks of " the small extent to which the resurrection is related to the atoning work of Christ ". *The Atonement in N.T. Teaching*, p. 46.

a rock of offence ", by which their destined rejection was sealed. St. Peter does not go as far as St John in identifying the judgment with the cross ; but he has already prepared the way for the later development.

(b) Providence and Suffering.

Suffering plays so large a part in the experience of the communities addressed in this Epistle, and appears to present so strong a challenge to the idea of the divine Providence, that the Apostle's teaching on the subject merits separate treatment. His general doctrine is given in a single passage (v.

The problem of suffering 6, 7): " Humble yourselves therefore under the mighty hand of God, that he may exalt you in due time : casting all your care upon him ; for he careth for you ". These verses affirm God's constant and effectual care of His people (as in iv. 19), which bespeaks from man the response of humility and faith ; and they correspond with striking exactness to the teaching of Christ in the Sermon on the Mount (cf. especially Matt. vi. 25-34). The persecutions to which his readers were subject gave to St. Peter's teaching about suffering a special significance, but that teaching is none the less of general application, and the context of v. 6, 7 is not in fact limited to persecution. We may note also that in 2 Thess. i. 4 ff.— a passage which has close affinities with 1 Peter and may have been drafted by Silvanus — afflictions (θλίψεις) are distinguished from persecutions (διωγμοί), though both are subject to the same laws of Christian faith, endurance, and hope. To expect of the Apostle a philosophy of suffering would be to mistake the character of his mind. But on one point he speaks clearly : the suffering of individuals is according to

Suffering according to God's will God's will. The modern view that suffering is contrary to God's will finds no countenance in this Epistle. Into the cause of it the author does not go, any more than did our Lord in His recorded teaching ; but, like our Lord, he insists that it is not to be regarded as something outside the divine purpose (cf. Matt. x. 29, 30). " If it has to be so " (i. 6), " if the will of God should be so " (iii. 17)—these words mean that God allows and takes note of suffering : it betokens in Him no impotence, but has its place in the working of His " mighty hand ". It is a school of humility, faith, and hope.

And it is this practical and spiritual adjustment to suffering which is the Apostle's main concern. The spirit in which Christians meet it may be a great advertisement to the world of what Christianity is, and may even win others to the faith. In many ways the Apostle's teaching can be paralleled in Stoicism — in its subordination of the individual, for instance, to the order of the universe, in its recognition of a divine Providence, and in its inculcation of meekness and brotherly love.[1] But in one way the Christian writer goes beyond the highest of Greek or Roman moralists. None of them went so far as to affirm the paradox of *joy in suffering*, which is so marked a feature of this Epistle.[2] The ground of this rejoicing is threefold, in that suffering purges and steels and attests the character, unites the sufferer with Christ who suffered for us, and is the prelude to a glorious recompense which will follow at the last.[3] What Christianity gives to those who suffer in Christ's name is a sense of perspective in which they can feel and see the contrast between the shortness of time and the lightness of their affliction here, and the infinite eternity and overwhelming glory beyond.

Rejoicing in suffering

" The God of all grace ", says St. Peter, " who called you unto his eternal glory in Christ, will, after you have suffered awhile, stablish, strengthen, settle you " (v. 10). It is not clear whether this stablishing and settling refer to the time of the end of all things or to the moment when the period of adversity passes ; but in either case St. Peter is bidding his readers look at their troubles in the light of their glorious destiny — to chart their lives, that is to say, on a large map. God is the God of all grace, whether He exalts or lays low : " the Lord himself giveth all good things, and he humbleth whom he will, as he will " (Tobit iv. 19). Life's normal, work-a-day trials have not the clear distinctive meaning that persecutions have as " signs " of the approaching Day of

---

[1] The Stoics had, of course, their precursors in ancient Greece, especially Sophocles. Cf. J. Adam, *The Religious Teachers of Greece*, pp. 172-5.

[2] Yet Sophocles came near it (*Philoctetes*, 1421 f.), when he makes Heracles say to the hero :

Yea, and know well, this debt is thine to pay,
Through suffering to make glorious thy life.

And Clem. Alex. *Strom.* IV. 586 [P] cites Aeschylus, *Fragm.* 315 for

τῷ πονοῦντι δ' ἐκ θεῶν
ὀφείλεται τέκνωμα τοῦ πόνου κλέος.

[3] Cf. note on i. 6.

Deliverance ; nor are they part of Christ's predictions of it But they are on the same road — not landmarks on it, indeed, but mounds and pock-holes making the going uneven and difficult ; and it is the road that leads to the same glory at the end.   St. Peter does not suggest, as he does of the persecutions, that they are matter for elation and joy ; he is too good a psychologist for that : but they have a place none the less, even if a subordinate one, in his perspective.   It is to those who suffer reproach and persecution in Christ's name that he accords the privilege of having " the spirit of glory and of God " resting upon them (iv. 14) ; but we cannot think that he would have denied this dignity and glory to any sufferer who sought to bear his trials with Christian faith and hope.

A further practical conclusion which St. Peter draws from this perspective in which he places the experiences of trial is that Christians should not be alarmed or overwhelmed with surprise [1] at their sufferings.   Crisis is a term which has no place in the Apostle's philosophy, except as applied to the critical decision between faith and unbelief ; compared with that crisis, all others shrink into insignificance.   The fact that the sufferings of Christians are part of a divine plan and indeed point forward to the joyful fulfilment of God's redemptive purpose transfigures them into the raw material of faith's victory.   St. Peter is keeping very close here to the teaching of his Master ; for this note of watchful and quiet endurance based upon the large perspective of God's purpose runs through the whole of that discourse on the last things which He gave to His disciples on the eve of the Passion.   As we read St. Mark xiii., or its parallels in St. Matthew and St. Luke, our attention is mainly caught by the succession of striking events — the outcrop of false Messiahs and false prophets, wars and rumours of wars, arrests and persecutions, and, finally, the signs of the dissolution of the natural order — which presage the end of all things and the coming of the Son of Man.   But we should do well to pay equal heed to the strain of ethical teaching which serves as a ground-bass to the eschatological themes.   " Let no man deceive you . . . be not troubled . . . take heed to yourselves . . . be not anxious beforehand what ye shall speak . . . he that en-

Persecutions and the trials of the Christian life should not cause surprise

---

[1] iv. 12, μὴ ξενίζεσθε.   Cf. note on iv. 4, and Essay II, p. 451.

dureth to the end, the same shall be saved . . take ye heed :
behold I have told you all things beforehand . . . watch and
pray " — through all these runs the claim that the suddenness
and irrationality of events shall find their match in the quietness and confidence of the Christian believers.   There is
nothing here of the half-cynical disillusionment and fatalism
of the Book of Ecclesiastes : it is not because all is vanity that
Christians are serene in trial, but because all is seen in the
light of God's purpose in Christ.

It is on this foundation of doctrine firmly laid — the
doctrine of the eternal glory laid up for us in heaven, and
already opened up to us in prospect by Christ's resurrection
— that St. Peter builds up his ethical teaching.   If the trials
of the Christian life come to be regarded not as obstacles but
as opportunities, it is possible for men to go about their
ordinary duties without self-pity and without fear.   *Lex
credendi, lex vivendi* is a motto that would make a good
summary of the Petrine teaching.

5. THE CHURCH

The word " church " does not occur in this Epistle.   The Absence
Pauline metaphor of the " body " as applied to the Church of the word
is nowhere found, nor is any mention made of its parts or " church "
" members " ; though a diversity of ministries is implied in from this Epistle
several passages.[1]   Further, while admission to the Church is
from every point of view a step of vital consequence, nothing
is said of exclusion from it of those once admitted (as in St.
Paul's Epistles) nor of apostasy from it (as in the Johannine
letters).   The Church is brought before us as a race, a people,
a temple, a flock ; and the element of order involved in these
is not without emphasis in each case.   But organization as
distinct from order figures very slightly in the total picture.
It is as though for St. Peter the Church had no outside edges,
no external boundaries : it is a flock, not a fold.

And yet, though the word " church " is absent, the thing

---

[1] Thus, the activity of " prophets " is probably alluded to in iv. 11, and (as I believe) i. 10 ; the work of " evangelists " of one sort or another is implied in i. 11 and 25 ; " deacons " may be alluded to in iv. 11 ; and " presbyters " are named and their functions discussed in v. 1-3.

betokens no lack of concreteness in the author's conception of it

Extra ecclesiam nulla salus

The Church rests upon the divine initiative

itself permeates the Epistle. It is the meeting-place of the Epistle's theology and ethics. "From God — in relation to God — unto God ": that is one of the trumpet-notes of the letter, and the Church is the subject of it. The supreme *differentia* of the Church is its faith and holiness. At the same time this faith and holiness are embodied and visible, constituting a challenge to the world around them and exposing Christians to persecution. They live in the flesh, and they suffer in the flesh (iv. 1, 2). The line of demarcation between the Church and the world is not inward and invisible alone ; it is also outward and concrete, marked by the tears and sometimes the blood of the persecuted. Moreover, the fortitude and meekness of Christians in their sufferings are so potent a means of winning others to the faith that the question may fairly be asked whether conversion should be regarded as taking place in the first instance to the Church or to Christ. Perhaps it would be true to say that, whereas in the case of the Jew it was Christ who was accepted or rejected, in the case of the Gentile (who knew nothing of the Messianic promises) it was the Church. In either case the upshot was the same. Conversion to Christ led to baptism, which was the door of admission to the Church; conversion to the Church was sealed in the same sacrament, and led to faith in Christ, and through Him in God. And the step was a crucial one, involving divine Judgment. Strictly speaking, it was not the convert who accepted or rejected Christ or the Church, but God who accepted or rejected the convert. To refuse to take the step when the opportunity is offered is to continue under the condemnation in which the whole unbelieving world is lying ; to take it is to enter the sphere of salvation. That is why, as Spörri points out,[1] we must say of St. Peter that he teaches the doctrine expressed later in the phrase, *extra ecclesiam nulla salus*.

We have already observed above that the Church owes its whole being to the initiative of God's mercy in Christ. It is both new and not new : not new, in the sense that it continues and inherits the call and the privileges of the Church of the Old Testament, but new in the sense that Israel has been rejected owing to its unbelief and that the new, universal

[1] *Op. cit.* p. 22.

Church of the Messiah has taken its place. Christians are
a twice-born people, their second or spiritual birth being the
result of God's word or creative activity, issuing from Him,
voiced by the preachers of the Gospel, and giving entrance to
a world of new values and horizons opened up by Christ's
resurrection. It is thus true that the Church's ultimate basis,
according to 1 Peter, is " the causeless, sovereign, free,
eternally unchangeable Will of Love of the Father, of the God
of grace and compassion who, in Christ, is the all-powerful
creator and lord of the Church, ever worthy to be worshipped "
(cf. i. 3, iv. 11, v. 11) [1] ; and his work is the reconciled Church.
And it is reconciled because cleansed. The rebirth and the
cleansing, i.e. forgiving of past sin, are one act. In the great
passage, i. 13-25, the two strands of thought represented by
the creative activity of God and the redemption through the
blood of Christ are inextricably interwoven ; and the faith
and holiness of the Church derive from both. And the sacrament of baptism is no mere act of bodily cleansing, but the
moral surrender of the whole man to God revealed in Christ
(iii 21, 22).

The mutually inclusive relationship which subsists between in Christ,
Christ and the Church is expressed in the phrase " in Christ ",
which occurs three times in 1 Peter ; but the phrase is not in
any way developed or made the basis of an argument, as it is
by St. Paul and St. John. It would appear that the thought
of Christ as the *sphere* of the Christian life is common ground
between the Apostle and his readers : no doctrine of mystical
union seems to underlie it or to flow from it. The close-knit
unity of the Church and its dependence upon Christ are
brought out with special force in the image of the Church as
God's true Temple, fulfilling the highest prophetic ideals of
the Temple of Israel. In this context, Christ is spoken of as who is the
like " a living stone ", i.e. a stone which is in fact a Person ; cornerstone of
and Christians are described as being likewise " personal the
" spiritual
stones " who come to Him and are aligned to Him as to a house ",
cornerstone. With Christ, therefore, the whole edifice is of
one piece, and He determines its design. And this description is combined with another. Christians are not only the
stones of which the house is built, deriving their unity from

[1] Spörri, *op. cit.* p. 237. Cf. also p. 369.

which is
both
priestly
and
sacrificial

their relationship to the whole design : they are also the body
of priests who serve in this temple and offer the spiritual
sacrifices which are its primary purpose. These sacrifices
are not further defined ; but the fact that they are described
as " acceptable to God through Jesus Christ " implies, in
view of the teaching of this Epistle elsewhere [1] as to what is
acceptable to God, that they comprise the whole Christian
life of faith and prayer, of brotherly love, and of meekness in
suffering for Christ's sake. In this passage, moreover, St.
Peter is gathering up a number of allusions to the Levitical
ordinances and the Law of Holiness [2] in the previous chapter ;
and the resultant picture of the Church is of a divinely
established institution, at once priestly and sacrificial. The
conception has far-reaching implications which are discussed
fully elsewhere.[3]

Christ the
Shepherd
of souls

ii. 25
v. 4

In yet another image St. Peter sets Christ before his
readers as the Shepherd of their souls. The thought goes
back to our Lord's own teaching, and is developed at some
length in St. John's Gospel. In this Epistle it marks the
climax of the author's exposition of the Atonement and is also
the basis of the pastoral charge committed to the Church's
ministry ; and St. Peter introduces it as though it were
already familiar to his readers. No symbols of Christ were
more popular in the earlier Christian centuries than the fish
and the shepherd ; and one may wonder whether both of
them may not be traced back to the pastoral ministry exercised by St. Peter in the first century at Rome.

The
Church's
response
in humil-
ity, which
is charac-
teristic of
its life,

in
obedience,

The distinguishing note of the Church's response to its
divine creation and appointment is expressed in a number of
terms expressive of humility ; and indeed the theme of subordination which permeates its whole social teaching, even
when this is derived from earlier sources, is based upon the
fundamental subordination of the believer to God and to His
will. Christians are " children of obedience " (i. 14). This
obedience is " obedience to the truth " (i. 22), implying a life
governed by the objective principles and standards of the
Gospel in contrast to the impulses and rationalizations (to use
a convenient modern term) by which their conduct had been

---

[1] E.g. ii. 19, iii. 4, 12, 16, iv. 2, 14, v. 5. Cf. Add. Note H, pp. 294-8.
[2] Cf. Essay II, pp. 369-74.   [3] Add. Note H.

guided in their former apostate or Gentile condition. To make progress in obedience, moreover, is one of the major purposes of their vocation (i. 2). It is instructive to note how for St. Peter faith and works go together, both being embraced in the holiness or consecration to God which was an essential mark of the Church. As Spörri observes, faith is the subjective side of the Church's being in Christ, which, on the objective side, is the creative fabric of the grace of God [1] ; and the Apostle could not think of this faith except as issuing in conduct. St. Peter would have welcomed Seneca's words, " So live with men as if God saw you ; so speak with God as if men heard you ". No echo of any controversy as to the relative precedence of faith and works is heard in St. Peter's pages, as we hear it in the pages of St. Paul or St. James. We cannot argue from this that St. Peter was unaware of the controversy, though the fact is consonant with that view. But what we can say is that in this Epistle we have the utterance of a mind for which the controversy was somewhat unreal. He did not set himself to effect a synthesis between the rival views, a task which would probably have left some mark on what he wrote. Instead, he bore fresh witness to the middle road which he had always followed and which went back to the Master Himself.

A further example of the subordinationist ethic of this *and in* Epistle is the emphasis laid upon " the spirit of God's holy *reverence* fear ". As Dr. Bigg observes, " the predominant feeling towards God is one of intense awe ".[2] What St. Peter teaches is that Christians are to be distinguished by a spirit of reverence in every walk of life, serious in their estimate of themselves as bearers of a heavenly calling ; courteous and considerate to their neighbours whether Christians or not, who are likewise the children of the one Creator ; ready to use every relationship of life as an opportunity for glorifying God ; and mindful of " that great and solemn account which they must one day give at the judgment-seat of Christ ".[3] May we note, perhaps, in St. Peter's teaching here echoes of what he himself learnt as a fisherman on the Lake of Gennesaret ? Long converse with nature in the starry night, and the

---

[1] *Op. cit.* p. 239.　　　　[2] I.C.C. p. 235 (Introd. to 2 Peter).
[3] The Bidding Prayer.

co-operation with his brother fishermen recorded in the Gospel story, must have prepared St. Peter's character for the touch of Christ's master-hand, and its response would have been just such a spirit of reverence as we find set before us here.

But there is no disparagement of natural goodness, And yet, though submission to God makes up a large part of the believer's relationship to God as conceived in this Epistle, it is not the whole of it. He stands also before God, in His presence, in harmony with Him. He is always God's servant ; but God's service is perfect freedom, and the Apostle is fully alive to the equation. With all his insistence on the priority of the divine activity in the relationship between God and man which constitutes religion, his theology is conspicuously free from any of those tendencies towards decrying nature in the interests of grace and towards extruding from the Christian revelation of God every attribute of His except transcendence, which we associate with the name of St. Augustine or of Karl Barth. We cannot imagine our author speaking of natural virtues as *splendida vitia*. There was good in the pagan world, both in its thought and in its institutions. Though St. Peter grounds the subordinationist framework of his ethics in the obedience to the will of God which was common both to Judaism and to Christianity, that framework itself is as characteristic of some of St. Paul's teaching as it is of St. Peter's, and owed something in both cases to non-Christian sources. St. Peter works out what he has to say about the ordinary round of social duty in regard to a number of specific human relationships, dealing in turn with those of citizens and the civil authorities, of slaves and masters, of wives and husbands, and of pastors and people. The range of relationships covered is not quite as large as in similar contexts in the Epistles of St. Paul ; but in both cases there can be no doubt that the Apostles are drawing upon " household codes "[1] of conduct which were well known among the Jews, and probably in the better and more thoughtful homes of the Roman Empire. Such codes were in use both in Jewish and in Stoic circles ; and the verbal similarities between St. Peter and St. Paul, when dealing with these subjects, are traceable to the fact that one or more

[1] Cf. below, Essay II, pp. 419-22.

of these codes was adapted for catechetical purposes in the
Christian churches, and so afforded a good ground-plan for
ethical teaching. So far, therefore, from despising the best
moral teaching given by Jew or pagan in their age, both
Apostles endorse it, while at the same time giving it deeper
foundations and more far-reaching ends.

The same thing holds good when we turn from contem- *nor of*
porary thought to contemporary institutions, such as the *natural institu-*
household, marriage, and the State. The attitude which St. *tions such*
Peter inculcates towards these institutions is governed by the *as the State*
detachment inevitable for those who have the other-worldly
vocation of strangers and pilgrims, and he accepts them as
part of the environment in which Christians have to shew
their mettle. But in the case of the State he goes further,
and gives it a positive claim on men's moral allegiance. This
is the more remarkable when we remember that the King or
Emperor whom he bids his readers honour was none other
than Nero,[1] and that many of the provincial governors were
both corrupt and cruel. True, the prophet who wrote Deutero-
Isaiah had spoken of the Persian king Cyrus as God's
" anointed "[2]; but it was one thing to see the divine plan and
purpose manifested in a ruler who came as the emancipator
of Israel, another to see it in a form of settled rule which often
involved the Church in cruel persecution. The explanation *The*
lies in the fact that the Apostle is not thinking of the Emperor *functions of the*
as an individual, but as performing a certain indispensable *State*
function in human society.[3] He and his subordinate officials
in the provinces are the fountain-heads of law and order, set
for the punishment of evil-doers, and " the praise of them that
do well ". There is a fine illustration of the principle in the
Play of *More* :

> MORE. Let me set up before your thoughts, good friends,
> One supposition, which if you will mark,
> You shall perceive how horrible a shape

---

[1] The case is not materially altered
if the Epistle be assigned to the later
years of Claudius' reign or to the time
of Domitian; for from the time of Tiberius onwards the Roman Principate
was a dictatorship, and the characters
of the dictators unaccountable.

[2] Is. xlv. 1.

[3] Cf. Arnold Toynbee, *Christianity
and Civilisation* (Burge Memorial
Lecture), p. 32: " So long as original
sin remains an element in human
nature, Caesar will always have much
to do ".

<blockquote>
Your innovation bears ; first 'tis a sin
Which oft th' apostle did forewarn us of,
Urging obedience to authority.
And 'twere no error if I told you all
You were in arms 'gainst God.
</blockquote>

ALL.   Marry, God forgive that.

MORE. Nay, certainly you are.

<blockquote>
For to the king God hath his office lent
Of dread, of justice, power and command ;
Hath bid him rule, and will'd you to obey.

.   .   .   .   .

What do you then
Rising 'gainst him that God Himself installs
But rise 'gainst God ?   What do you to your souls
In doing this, O desperate as you are ? [1]
</blockquote>

It is for such reasons that the author of our Epistle interprets " honour all men " by the injunctions to " love the
brotherhood ", " fear God ", and " honour the king ".   Far
more is involved than the principle that natural duties no less
than supernatural have their place in the ethics of the Kingdom.   The relationship of Christians to civil society not only
comes first in the series of relationships whose obligations
the author sets forth, but it follows hard upon a closely-knit
doctrinal passage (ii. 1-10) which deals with the character and
purpose of the Church and its relation to Christ.   Nothing
could more clearly shew the Apostle's conviction that " in the
purpose of God society is to bear on its face the impress of the
divine order ".[2]   The Christian has to live in the flesh as well
as in the Spirit, in an earthly environment as well as a heavenly,
on week-days as well as Sundays ;   and, so far from being
entitled to regard religion as a form of escapism, he is called
upon to seek, so far as he may, by his patience in suffering and
his activity in doing good, to mould society into closer conformity with the will of God.   An interesting illustration of
the principle may be found in the place given to the Emperor
Trajan in the imaginative poetry of the Middle Ages ;   as
when Dante places him in Purgatory as an example of

[1] Quoted by R. W. Chambers,
Man's Unconquerable Mind, pp. 228 f.
Professor Chambers gives a number
of reasons for attributing this play to
Shakespeare. I am the more glad to
quote from this chapter of his book, as
it is a fine piece of literary criticism.
Cf. also *Troilus and Cressida*, I. iii.
84-138.

[2] G. W. O. Addleshaw, *Dogma
and Youth Work*, p. 14.

humility,[1] or Langland makes him say :

> Ali the Clergy under Christ · might not catch me from Hell,
> But only Love and Loyalty · and my lawful judgments.[2]

Of a piece with this recognition of the validity in God's eyes of these civic and social loyalties, and of their relevance to the Christian life, is the author's insistence upon the duty of " doing good ".[3] ἀγαθοποιεῖν is, indeed, one of the key-words of the Epistle, occurring more frequently, in one form or another, than in the whole of the rest of the New Testament put together.　The other occurrences of the word, moreover, are with one exception all on the lips of our Lord Himself ; and it is in the same sense — that of active kindness and discharge of social duty — that the Epistle uses it.　Both in the Gospels and in the Epistle it is assumed that hearers and readers know what goodness is, or at least can recognize it when they see it.　There is no suggestion that it has no meaning or value apart from revelation, though revelation extends its scope.　Thus, when St. Peter bids the Christian wife put on " the ornament of a meek and quiet spirit, which is in the sight of God of great price ", he illustrates his point from a familiar figure of ancient Hebrew story ; and classical literature reminds us that it could have been matched also in many a Gentile home.　Closely allied with this attachment to ἀγαθοποιεῖν is the author's use of the word χάρις.　As Dr. Bigg points out,[4] χάρις has in this Epistle, as in the Gospels and often in the Acts, a Greek rather than a Hebrew or a Pauline sense : in 1 Pet. ii. 19, 20, indeed, χάρις is used in close connexion with ἀγαθοποιεῖν, exactly as in Lk. vi. 32-5 and in exactly the same sense.　In describing the meek endurance of suffering as " a grace in the eyes of God ", St. Peter is speaking quite simply and untheologically as a Greek might speak : he thinks of good conduct without any embarrassment as thankworthy, a glory, a favour or gracious thing in God's eyes.　Not that he thought of such goodness

The duty of well-doing

---

[1] *Purgatorio*, x. 73-93.
[2] *Piers Plowman*, xi. 139, 140.
[3] Cf. Toynbee, *op. cit.* p. 40 : " The antithesis between trying to save one's own soul by seeking and following God and trying to do one's duty to one's

neighbour is false.　The two activities are indissoluble."
[4] On 1 Peter ii. 19. A most instructive note. He goes so far as to say that " χάρις is hardly an evangelical word at all ".

as something apart from God : the heathen officials were
divinely commissioned ; and the Christian believer had the
Lord's example behind him and the hope of everlasting glory
in front of him.   But he would have been well content with
the definition of St. James : " Every good gift and every
perfect gift is from above, and cometh down from the Father
of lights, with whom is no variableness, neither shadow of
turning " (Jas. i. 17).   And again he would have found little
fault with what the author of *Piers Plowman* [1] puts into the
mouth of Imaginative :

> " Ywis, Sir ", I said,
> " To see much and suffer more · certes ", said I, " is Do-well ".

6. THE IMITATION OF CHRIST AND THE ATONEMENT

Nowhere is the connexion between theology and ethics in
this Epistle more evident than in its treatment of the Atonement.   The doctrine is quite central in St. Peter's thought,
and runs like a thread through his argument and exhortation [2] ; but the most comprehensive passage, and that which
best reveals his mind, arises out of his injunction to slaves in
ii. 18 ff.   The principle of subordination to which we have
already alluded as governing the Apostle's ethical teaching
is here touched to the finest issues.   It is noticeable that,
when dealing with those specific human relationships which
figure also in St. Paul's Epistles, and where both authors
were drawing upon household codes that were current in their
time, St. Peter dwells especially on those duties which belong
to the humbler side of each relationship.   He has much to
say on the citizen's duty to obey the civil power, but little of
the converse : he dwells much on the duty of wives to be
subject to their husbands, but has only a verse on the corresponding duty of husbands towards their wives — though it is
a verse which shews plainly that he regards the difference
between them as a difference of function and in no way of
spiritual status : he deals in detail with the duty of slaves

*Subordi-
nationist
character
of St.
Peter's
ethical
teaching*

[1] Bk. XI. 3 (quoted by R. W.
Chambers, *op. cit.* p. 138).
[2] Note especially i. 18-21, introduced
by εἰδότες ὅτι; ii. 21-5, introduced by
ὅτι; iii. 18–iv. 1, introduced by ὅτι.

The last-named passage is the subject
of separate discussion in Essay I
below, pp. 313 ff. In all these the Resurrection is an integral part of the
doctrine.

towards their masters, but omits all allusion to the reciprocal
duty of masters towards their slaves.   It seems as though St.
Peter found in the lives of those whose functions were, in one
way or another, subordinate,[1] the best expression of, and the
best opportunities for expressing, the Christian way of life.
The reason for this may be partly the humble station in life
occupied by a large proportion of the Christian communities
addressed, partly the circumstances of social ostracism in
which they found themselves, and in part also, we may surmise, the fact that St. Peter himself was a forgiven, and therefore a humbled, man.   We may assume also that our Lord's
own words, " He that will be greatest among you, let him be as
your servant ", and even more His claim to have come among
them as " one that serveth ", had sunk deep into the Apostle's
mind.   But in the last resort the meekness which he enjoins,
upon Christians generally towards their adversaries and most
signally upon slaves towards their masters, rests upon deeper
grounds than these.   The ultimate ground for it is that in
suffering meekly they will be imitating the example of Christ. 'Emphasis
    If one were asked what trait of all others in the character on the
of our Lord is dear to St. Peter, the answer is plain : it is His meekness
meekness.   And he writes about it as one who had himself of Christ
witnessed it.   St. Paul also, in a celebrated passage in his
letter to the Philippians, speaks of Christ's humiliation, and
bids his readers have in them the same mind as was in their
Master.   But the moment which St. Paul chooses as supremely
exemplifying Christ's meekness lies in the pre-temporal order,
when He laid aside His divine glory to become incarnate ;
and though he follows this act of humiliation right up to its
ultimate issue in the Cross, St. Paul has nothing corresponding to those intimate touches of detail with which St. Peter
describes Him, " who, when he was reviled, reviled not again ;
when he suffered, he threatened not ".   Nor is anything
similar to be found in any other Epistle.
    Further, St. Peter's delineation of the meekness of Christ
provides his characteristic approach to what he has to say leading to
about our Lord's passion, death, and resurrection.   In this the

---

[1] Readers of Richardson and Field-
ing will remember how often the
Christian tradition is found in the
servants' hall when absent from higher
quarters in the house. Cf. also the
fine passage from Burke on " the un-
bought grace of life " quoted by Charles
Morgan, *Reflections in a Mirror*, p. 88.

doctrine
of the
Atone-
ment
Epistle the doctrine of the Atonement grows out of Christ's meekness and patience in suffering. Other factors are brought in, and of these we shall have something to say in a moment. What is to be noted here is the way in which, in this Epistle, Christ's humility, and especially His humble bearing before His accusers, is of a piece with His sacrificial death, and indeed part and parcel of it. This is not to say that St. Peter teaches what is called " an exemplarist view " of the Atonement, such as was taught by some of the Greek fathers, and, notably, by Abelard in the Middle Ages.[1] Our author does lay emphasis on Christ's passion as an example, and appeal to His love for us as seen in the cross as a motive for our effort to follow His example. But this teaching is combined with other teaching which forbids us to say that St. Peter stands on the exemplarist side.

The
*imitatio
Christi*
St. Peter speaks of Christ as having " suffered for you, leaving you an example that ye should follow His steps ". The Greek word here translated " example " admits of two meanings. It was used sometimes of an outline design or sketch of some work of art, as it might be a painting or an embroidery, which the master drew and left for his pupils to fill in. Or again the word might be used of a pattern, such as the handwriting in a copy-book, which was meant to be copied faithfully, detail by detail, by others. Readers of Dr. Kirk's book, *The Vision of God*, may observe how these two interpretations can be held to support one or other of two great schools of Moral Theology which have left their mark on Christian history. For our immediate purpose the difference between them is of no great consequence : if the balance of scholarship inclines perhaps towards the second alternative, no rigorist conclusion should be drawn. The point which St. Peter is making is the broad one that in our Lord's patience and meekness before His accusers, and in His meek acceptance for our sakes of a felon's death, He gives us an example which we are to follow.

Import-
ance of
Is. liii.
I spoke just now of other factors which St. Peter combines with this ; and it is time now to bring these into the picture. We may begin with the use which the Apostle makes of the

---

[1] For a powerful modern exposition of this view see Dr. Rashdall's Bampton Lectures, *The Idea of Atonement in Christian Theology*.

prophecy of the Suffering Servant in Is. lii. 13–liii. The application of this great passage to our Lord's death and resurrection has long been one of the most vexed questions of New Testament theology. Professor Burkitt pointed out that the Christian use of the prophecy appears to be confined in the New Testament to those writers who used the Septuagint ; and he argued from this fact that it thus belongs to " a very early stage of Greek-speaking Christianity, but it is not quite primitive or Apostolic ".[1] Since then, opinion has varied ; but Professor Vincent Taylor's recent book *Jesus and His Sacrifice* has again tilted the scale in favour of the view that the identification of the Suffering Servant with our Lord goes back to our Lord's own authentic words. What we are told in Acts viii. of the use made of the passage by Philip the Evangelist, when instructing the Ethiopian eunuch, points in the same direction ; and we may well believe that the prophetic circle at Caesarea, of which Philip was the centre, and which we meet at a later date in the narrative of Acts, was peculiarly concerned in drawing out further implications of the prophecy and its fulfilment. Caesarea was a regular port of call and transit for those passing by sea between Palestine and other parts of the Roman Empire, and it is possible that St. Peter himself owed something to Philip for his understanding of this passage. And equally notable is the contrast between St. Paul and St. Peter in this regard ; for St. Paul's teaching about the Atonement seems uninfluenced by the prophet's picture of the Suffering Servant. Indeed, this fact alone should give us pause when we are asked to regard 1 Peter as steeped in " Paulinism ". Rather, it seems clear that St. Peter's doctrine of the Atonement is primitive in two ways : first, in that it makes so much of those details of Christ's passion which seem to rest on the testimony of an eyewitness ; secondly, in that it makes use of a prophecy in a way which we have good reason to believe to be not only primitive, but also to go back to the lips of our Lord Himself.

Three strands of allusion to the ordinances and teaching of the Old Testament are brought together in St. Peter's doctrine of Christ's death. In the first Passover sacrifice (Ex. xii.), and in its annual commemorations, the victim was

O.T. contributions to St. Peter's doctrine threefold:

[1] *Christian Beginnings*, pp. 35 ff.

a lamb which must be " without blemish " ; and St. Peter

sees in this a type of the spotless life of Christ, and a call to Christians to be holy likewise. Moreover, that sacrifice was intimately bound up with the deliverance of Israel from Egypt, and was thus an apt prefiguring of the sacrifice of Christ, by whose blood the Christian communities had been

delivered from their former " vain manner of life ". In Is. liii., where a lamb is used by way of simile, its spotlessness is not physical and ritual but moral : the scene is taken not from the altar of sacrifice, but from the farm, where lambs are slaughtered and shorn ; and the points emphasized are the lamb's helplessness and silence. It is thus a fitting illustration of the innocence and the meekness of the Suffering Servant, who is the prophet's theme, and whose sufferings and death, in the prophet's view, are the consequences of sin — though not of his own sin, but of the people's. And thus the people exclaim : " . . he was wounded for our transgressions, he was bruised for our iniquities : the chastisement of

our peace was upon him ; and with his stripes we are healed " Such was the prophetic image which St. Peter found ready to hand, and adapted to his purpose.

There is yet a third element which he brings into his picture — that of the scapegoat (Lev. xvi. 20 ff.). The author of Is. liii. may himself have drawn upon the ordinance described in Leviticus, if it was extant in his time. The ritual belongs to the Day of Atonement, and in it the high-priest transfers to the goat " all the iniquities of the children of Israel, and all their transgressions in all their sins " ; and the goat is driven away into the desert, carrying them, so that they may be heard of no more. Many commentators on 1 Peter, including Archbishop Leighton in the seventeenth century and the most recent of German editors, Hans Windisch (1930), have seen an allusion to this ordinance in the words " who his own self carried up our sins in his own body to the tree " (R.V. margin). Such an allusion would be consonant with the fact that the removal of sin rather than guilt is in the Apostle's mind, and that the issue of the Atonement on which he lays all the emphasis is the actual change and conversion of believers from former ways of sin to a better and higher kind of life, the life of righteousness. The sins of the Christians whom St. Peter addresses have been taken away, through their transfer to Him who was willing to be the " sin-bearer " [1] ; and this willingness of Christ to be the " sin-bearer " is the supreme and most moving feature of His passion and death.

Three strands are thus woven into the cord of St. Peter's thought about the Atonement — the lamb of the Passover which is " without blemish and without spot ", the Suffering Servant of Is. lii. 13–liii., and the scapegoat of the Levitical law. But none of them, not even the Isaianic prophecy, seems to bear the main weight of his teaching. They illustrate it, that is to say, rather than constitute it ; they are wound round it rather than round one another. The core of the matter lies in the observed historical fact of Christ's patience and meekness when suffering unjustly, Himself innocent. In that crucial verse which says of Christ that " when he was reviled ", He " reviled not again : when he suffered, he threatened not, but committed himself (or his cause) to him that judgeth righteously ", there is no quotation from the Law or the Prophets : the words are the Apostle's own, and have, moreover, all the simplicity of direct testimony. Shall we be wrong if we surmise that St. Peter is describing here something that he himself saw, and is reproducing for us the indelible impression which the lonely figure of his Master, standing in meek silence before His accusers and His judges, had made upon the disciple's mind ? Such glimpses as St. Peter had of our Lord either before Caiaphas or before Pilate were, no doubt, intermittent ; but St. Luke's narrative (xxii. 61) indicates that they did occur. And always the same contrast was to be seen, between the injustice, cruelty, violent words of the Jews, and the meekness, patience, silence of Him whom most he loved.

The element of eye-witness

And, indeed, we may perhaps go further still. The Greek words of the phrase " who his own self bare our sins in his own body on the tree " are translated in no less than three different ways in our English versions. The chief difficulties attach to the word " bare " and to the words " on the tree ".

---

[1] For an interesting illustration of the instinct underlying the idea of the scapegoat in modern folk-lore see the passage about the " sin-eater " in Mary Webb's *Precious Bane*, p. 36.

The word translated " bare " is the word used in the LXX of
Is. liii. 12, " he bare the sins of many ", and that would seem
to have suggested it here.   But " on the tree " is certainly a
mistranslation ; the Greek can only mean " to " or " on to "
the tree.[1]   The combination of words here is used often in the
Pentateuch of the priest bearing or carrying the sacrificial
victim to the altar ; and this image has led some scholars to
find a ritual reference here, and to infer that St. Peter is
thinking of the cross as the altar of Christ's sacrifice.   But
the idea encounters several difficulties.   In the sacrifices of
the Law, the priest carried the victim, not the people's sins,
to the altar ; moreover, this carrying was done after the
victim's death, not before it ; and yet once more " the tree "
(or, more accurately, " the wood ") does not naturally suggest
an altar, but rather the gibbet on which a felon was hanged
or crucified.   These facts suggest that those who seek to find
a reference to the ritual of sacrifice are on a wrong scent.
But, once again, how simple and direct the words appear, if
regarded as the expression of what the Apostle saw !   Somewhere, we may be sure, among those who saw Jesus tread the
road to Calvary, stood the man whom He had called to be the
first of His disciples, and who, even though he had so basely
denied Him, yet loved his Master still.   Yes, he had seen
Him carrying his own sins up the hill called Golgotha to the
cross of shame on which He was crucified with a criminal on
either side.   We may well believe that the moment marked
the climax of St. Peter's contrition as of his Master's self-
abasement.   What more natural than that it should find
expression in this context and in these very words ?[2]

The picture set before us, then, by St. Peter is of his
Master, whose life was without blemish and wholly given to
doing good, standing mute and meek before his adversaries,
in posture of complete surrender to God, and then bearing in
His own Person on the road to Calvary the burden of the

[1] Cf. Winer, *Grammar*, p. 508, "it
is only in appearance that ἐπί is joined
with verbs of rest".

[2] The argument must not be in-
verted, as though the wording of
1 Pet. ii. 23, 24 could be used as a
sufficient proof of the Petrine authorship. The claim is that if St. Peter
were the author, these verses are
congruous with that assumption, and
yield their simplest meaning in the
light of it. At the same time, if the
Petrine authorship is probable on
other grounds, a number of passages
must be held to have confirmatory
weight. Cf. pp. 27-33, above.

whole world's sins. As Archbishop Leighton, who devotes
over twenty pages to verses 23 and 24 and whose whole commentary on them is a masterpiece of rich and flowing exegesis,
wrote, " The sins of all, in all ages before and after, who were
to be saved, all their guiltiness met together on His back upon
the Cross ". But the burden was not borne in vain. Like
St. Paul, St. Peter never omits the Resurrection from his
thought upon the Atonement. Christ's work of patience and
self-abnegation was vindicated, first in the fact that He Himself rose from the dead, leaving only men's sins as the spoil
of death, and secondly in the new life to which His example
moved believers and His death and resurrection admitted
them.

Finally, the question may be asked whether, and if so how *The*
far and in what sense, the duty of following the pattern or *imitatio*
example which Christ gives us may be held to include His *Christi*
atoning death as well as His meekness and humility in suffering. Some students of the Epistle have argued that the
swift transition which is made more than once from Christ's
patience to His death is due to the fact that a similar transition
from persecution to martyrdom was ever present to the minds
of St. Peter's readers : and there may be some truth in that
view. It is not, however, certain that martyrdom was involved in the persecutions referred to in this Epistle ; and
that explanation is not needed to account for the close connexion which St. Peter makes between Christ's meekness and
His atoning death. Rather, the connexion is an inner one,
relating more to the Lord's life and character than to the
experiences of His believers in Asia Minor.

That which ties the meekness and the death so close to- The
gether is the identity of motive and of principle underlying principle
them ; and these we may assuredly copy. The motive on dying life
which St. Peter dwells is that of winning people for God — a
motive that might well come to the mind of one who had
been charged to be a " fisher of men ". Thus, wives are
bidden to shew meekness to their husbands, even if unbelievers, that so they may be won for Christ.[1] Mockers at
Christianity are to be met in a spirit of meekness and respect,
that the good life of the Christians may be able, without any

[1] iii. 1.

such impediment as a spirit of rudeness or controversy would arouse, to reach right home to their consciences.[1] For it was with just such a motive that Christ Himself died on our behalf, namely, to bring us to God. And He set no limits to that task. Rather, He embraced in it the powers of the spirit-world, evil no less than good, and reached back in time before the first recorded redemption and its ensuing covenant — that of Noah, which prefigured Christian baptism ; and God extended it, through Christ's resurrection, to include the whole realm of created spirits. With such an example of redemptive suffering before them — so grounded in the historical life of Christ, so universal in its range, and so triumphant in its issue — Christians should arm themselves with the same motive. For experience shews that that way lies redemption for them too, in the sense of freedom from sin and a God-controlled life for the future.[2]

Illustrations of this principle

This common principle underlying both the meekness and the death of Christ we may call the principle of " the dying life ". It is the principle which our Lord expressed in the command :

from our Lord's teaching ;

Whosoever will come after me, let him deny himself, and take up his cross, and follow me. For whosoever will save his life shall lose it ; but whosoever shall lose his life for my sake and the gospel's, the same shall save it (Mk. viii. 34 f.).

What is enjoined is something larger and other than asceticism, though some kind of ascetic habits will be necessary as a means to it : it is nothing less than the annulment of self-will. St. Peter is expressing this when he writes

from this Epistle;

(v. 5) : " But all of you bind upon yourselves humility in your relations one with another : for God resisteth the proud, but giveth grace unto the humble ". This humility is the root out of which meekness grows ; Christ claimed it for Himself [3] in virtue of the creatureliness which He shared with all men through His Incarnation, and it belongs to Christians by reason further of their acknowledgment of sin. And it is the

[1] iii. 15.

[2] iii. 15–iv. 6. I have given what seems to me in broad outline the Apostle's meaning in this much discussed passage. Bengel, as so often, is most helpful. For a more detailed treatment see the notes on the passage and Essay I below.

[3] Matt. xi. 29. Cf. Trench, *Synonyms of the New Testament*, § xlii., on the Greek words for humility and meekness.

indispensable condition of living in grace, just as pride interposes an unsurmountable barrier between God and man. The thought is one which Russian literature and theology during the last century have made peculiarly their own.[1] Yet Russian theology, on this matter at least, is rather Pauline than Petrine, and turns for authority for its teaching about Christ's self-humiliation more to the " kenotic " doctrine of Phil. ii. than to the historical testimony of St. Peter. On the *from ascetic* whole we shall find more to illustrate what is distinctive of St. *and moral* Peter's thought in the West than in the East. I am not *theology;* thinking especially of the much-loved work of Thomas à Kempis which bears the title *Of the Imitation of Christ* : there are, indeed, in that book some places where the author goes beyond what is to be found in the New Testament. A better illustration for our purpose is the less well-known, but not less fruitful, *Theologia Germanica*, and the contemporary works of the fourteenth-century mystical writers, Tauler, Suso, and Ruysbroek. " Behold then ", writes Ruysbroek, " the interior virtues of Christ ; humility, charity, and suffering in patience. These three virtues Jesus, our Bridegroom, practised throughout His life, and He died in them." " Nothing burneth in hell but self-will ", says the *Theologia Germanica* ; and again, " Since the life of Christ is every way most bitter to nature and the Self and the Me (for in the true life of Christ, the Self and the Me and nature must be forsaken and lost and die altogether), therefore in each of us, nature hath a horror of it ". " Leave nothing of myself in me ", is Crashaw's prayer in his poem on St. Theresa. The same teaching was the favourite theme of Jacob Boehme, and passed from him into William Law. " And now, sir ", says Law, " you see also the absolute necessity of the gospel doctrine of the cross ; viz. of *dying to self*, as the one only way to life in God. This cross, or dying to self, is the *one morality* that does man any good." [2] And the English novelist who has best described the depths of human misery, Charles Dickens, has painted an immortal embodiment of this in the character of Little Dorrit, who, while still a child, " took

[1] Cf. *The Humiliated Christ in Modern Russian Thought*, by N. Gorodetsky (1938).

[2] *The Spirit of Love* (1815 ed.), p. 54.

the place of the eldest ot the three, in all things but precedence;
was the head of the fallen family ; and bore, in her own heart,
its anxieties and shames ".   There is a fine unfolding of the
same lesson in the poems of William Blake, of which two
examples must suffice.   One has to do with the personal life,
and adheres very closely to the teaching of St. Peter :

Jesus said, Wouldest thou love one who never died
For thee, or ever die for one who had not died for thee ?
And if God dieth not for Man and giveth not Himself
Eternally for Man, Man could not exist, for man is Love,
As God is Love ; every kindness to another is a little Death
In the Divine Image ; nor can man exist but by Brotherhood.[1]

And the same truth is proclaimed on a wider scale, and
with an intenser passion, in Blake's *Milton* :

And Milton said : " I go to Eternal Death ! The Nations still
Follow after the detestable Gods of Priam, in pomp
Of warlike Selfhood, contradicting and blaspheming.
When will the Resurrection come to deliver the sleeping body
From corruptibility ? O when, Lord Jesus ! wilt Thou come ?
Tarry no longer, for my soul lies at the gate of death.
I will arise and look forth for the morning of the grave ;
I will go down to the sepulchre to see if morning breaks ;
I will go down to self-annihilation and Eternal Death ;
Lest the Last Judgement come and find me unannihilate,
And I be seiz'd and giv'n into the hands of my own Selfhood.
The Lamb of God is seen thro' mists and shadows, hov'ring
Over the sepulchres, in clouds of Jehovah and winds of Elohim,
A disk of blood, distant; and Heav'ns and Earths roll dark be-
     tween."

There is a certain fierce extravagance of statement here
which belongs rather to poetry than to theology.   But none
can deny the searching light which the passage throws upon
the recent life of nations over a large part of the earth's
surface.   In substance, moreover, it is justified by reference
to our Lord's words at the Last Supper :

And there was also a strife among them, which of them should
be accounted the greatest.

And he said unto them, The kings of the Gentiles exercise lord-
ship over them ; and they that exercise authority upon them are
called benefactors.

[1] *Jerusalem*, Bk. IV, ll. 23-8.

But ye shall not be so : but he that is greatest among you, let him be as the younger; and he that is chief, as he that doth serve.

For whether is greater, he that sitteth at meat, or he that serveth ? Is not he that sitteth at meat ? but I am among you as he that serveth (Lk. xxii. 24-7).

St. Peter heard these words, and has left us a charge to follow them.

7. SOCIOLOGY, ETHICS, AND RELIGION

Reference has already been made to the social code or codes of which St. Peter, like St. Paul, availed himself in the hortatory parts of his work [1] ; and it is now time to look at these codes from another point of view — namely, the socio- logical. Formally, these codes contain what sociologists speak of as norms or concrete patterns of behaviour, in- tended to govern conduct in certain definite social circles and relationships.[2]　This is as true of the Gentile and the Judaistic codes as of that which became current in early Christianity ; and though the differences which distinguish the Jewish from the Gentile, and the Christian from both, are important, the common features which they share, their common form and type, are no less deserving of study.　Thus, it is to be observed that they represent a discipline rather than an ethic : even in the case of the Hellenistic codes, the context is provided by the limited outlines of the gymnasium and the *polis*.　Accord- ingly, the injunctions given are highly concrete rules of specific conduct in particular relationships of life ; and they are appropriately given in the form of maxims rather than of principles.　In the case of the Jewish codes, as represented by Tobit or *Pirqe Aboth*, the context is provided by the Jewish community ; the behaviour inculcated is such as is appropri- ate to a Jew, though the fact that the community is a religious one, owing allegiance to a divine revelation, inevitably gives the code a wider scope.　The Christian code, which appears in this Epistle, is, when considered formally, narrower than

Socio- logical aspects of the social code in I Peter ;

---

[1] The evidence is fully set out in Essay II below, pp. 419-39, and the results of that discussion are here assumed.

[2] Cf. Karl Mannheim, *Diagnosis of our Time*, especially pp. 110 ff., *Man and Society*, Pt. V, ch. iv.

this : that is to say, it is confined to three clearly marked sets of relationships, civic, domestic, and ecclesiastical.

its limita-
tions and
their sig-
nificance :
This limitation of context is of great significance, both negatively and positively.   Negatively, it indicates a marked disinclination on the part of the Apostolic writers (for they are all alike in this respect) to interpret their mission as a call to express direct moral judgments on all or any issues that arise in human affairs.   The broad principles they enunciate are applicable to every sphere of life ; but the application is to be made, not directly by Church authority, but by Christians conversant from the inside with the aims and methods and

1 Cor. vi. 2
conditions of various social groups.[1]   " The saints shall judge the world " ; but this promise is subject to the principle

Lk. xii. 14
enunciated by Christ who said, " Who made me a judge or a divider among you ? "   The industrial, economic, educational, and other functional groups comprising men and women in specific and secondary relations are entitled to claim, and must work out for themselves, canons of behaviour proper to their several spheres and purposes.   This limitation in the scope of the social code of the New Testament has its positive counterpart, on the other hand, in the nature and character of the relationships in regard to which it gives specific injunctions.   They are fundamental and, among Christians, universal.   The first of these, the Christian's duty towards the State, we have already discussed at some length.   The second concerns the home, including the labour employed in it in so far as this is a matter of personal relationship.   The third derives from the position of Christians as members of a worshipping community.   No man can avoid being a citizen or belonging to a domestic circle of some kind ; and though in modern times secularism has accustomed many to live without any religious attachment, history does not suggest that this state of affairs will endure, and for practising Christians it is *eo nomine* impossible.   State, Home, and Church represent three types of grouping which no Christian can avoid.

That being so, the question must be asked how far the norms of behaviour laid down in the code are still necessary and desirable in modern social conditions.

[1] Cf. A. D. Lindsay, *Christianity and Economics*, pp. 28 ff., quoting Eucken and von Hügel.

The colossal growth of the power and claims of States in (i) in civic modern times appears to present a serious challenge to the relation-ships; doctrine of obedience taught by St. Peter and St. Paul, unless that doctrine is in some way qualified. " Render unto Caesar the things that are Caesar's " ; but what if Caesar claims authority in many domains which are not his ?   That, in fact, is what has increasingly occurred in our generation.   Compulsion, which is characteristic of the State's action, has been extended from one field of human life to another, rising sometimes to unbridled violence.   The New Testament teaching of obedience and non-resistance is, however, qualified in two ways.   In the first place, it is balanced by the principle expressed in the Apostles' answer before the Sanhedrin, " We Acts v. 29 ought to obey God rather than men " ; and a succession of martyrs from early times have testified to this principle with their lives.   There may come a moment, that is to say, when the State is so manifestly going beyond its province as to cease to deserve the loyalty of Christians, since it has ceased to fulfil its own proper functions.   No Christian may lightly judge when such a moment has come ; but he is " the servant 1 Pet. ii. of God " and " the Lord's free-man ", and cannot divest 16, 1 Cor. vii himself of his responsibility.   Secondly, the Petrine and the 22 Pauline conceptions of civic duty do, in fact, imply a liberal philosophy of the State as the true one.   The verse in which 1 Pet. ii. St. Peter concludes his passage on this subject is inconsistent 17 with any view which fails to distinguish between the State and society [1] ; and the fact that it is immediately followed by injunctions governing other social relationships tells the same tale.   The Roman principate was a dictatorship, but it left room for many liberties, especially in the provinces ; the idea of the omni-competent State was not a factor to be reckoned with in the first century, but it would have found in Christianity a resolute antagonist from the outset, if it had been.

The subjection of servants to their masters, which succeeds (ii) in the the treatment of civic duty in 1 Peter, and provides the basis relation-ship be- for some of the author's deepest ethical and theological teach- tween ing, stands on a different footing.   The use of the word οἰκέται servants and in ii. 18 shews that what the author has in mind is the institution masters; of domestic slavery, or of such industrial slavery as was found

[1] Cf. A. D. Lindsay, *The Churches and Democracy*, pp. 44 ff.

upon the premises of an employer's estate.[1] The relationship,
that is to say, is domestic and personal ; and the concern of
the code and its expositor is with the best adjustment a
Christian can make in a home where the master is harsh.   An
ethic which is purely an adjustment-ethic is fraught with
serious dangers ; an adjustment may be successful, but its
success may imperil other and higher values.[2] This charge
cannot, however, fairly be levelled against the social code as
we find it in the New Testament.   True, there are economic
and political aspects of the institution of slavery, which are
rightly held to be of great ethical import, and on which the
Apostolic writers are completely silent ; and to that extent the
limitations of their social code are undeniable.   They take
for granted what modern society unreservedly condemns.   If
that were all, we should have to agree that the code was an
example of an adjustment-ethic whose very success was its
chief drawback.   But it is not all.   For, first, whatever be
the ethical character of the institution as such, it was a sphere
of concrete personal relationships, and it is these with which
the code is primarily concerned.   It is not simply that the
time was not ripe for challenging the institution as yet (though
that is a legitimate view), nor even that the deepening and
spiritualizing of these very relationships was a pre-condition
of that time ever arriving [3]: for the future developments of the
structure of society were not within the purview of early
Christian writers.   Rather it was that these relationships
provided the sociological framework within which Christians,
both masters and servants, had to live ; and the way in which
they solved that problem affected their adjustment not only to
one another, but to God.   In other words, the social code was
blind to certain values by which men of to-day set much
store : but it was very much alive to others of which the
modern world is apt to think little.   Meekness on the part of
those who serve is a form of adjustment-ethic ; but St. Peter
turns it here into the means of pleasing God, and of being the
expression *par excellence* of what it means to follow Christ.

A further question arises here as to how far the Apostolic
teaching in regard to the reciprocal behaviour of masters and

---

[1] Cf. G. M. Trevelyan, *English Social History*, p. 321.
[2] Cf. Mannheim, *Diagnosis of our Time*, pp. 132 ff.   [3] Cf. *ibid.* p. 34.

men within the domestic circle is applicable to those immense
and highly-organized groups which characterize modern in-
dustrialism.   It is evident at once that the code does not
suffice here ;   there are many aspects of the concrete net of
relationships which make up an industry, whether large or
small, where those who are within the network must work out
its relative ethics.   But to say that the code does not suffice is
not to say that it does not apply.   The law of subordination,
for instance, on which the whole code rests, is a law of
discipline ;   and without discipline no organized group can
survive, least of all when its aims are concrete and definite
as in the case of a business, a school, or an army.   Again,
personal relationships, though less direct and constant in
industry than in the home, are equally unavoidable ;   and they
may be sweet or bitter.   Where the master or foreman reckons
himself bound to justice and kindness and the man to good
work, there a co-operative loyalty prevails, and a factory
becomes something of a family.   " Honour all men ", says ii. 17
St. Peter : all men, that is to say, are to be treated as persons,
as ends and not as means.   Where such a spirit is found, an
industrial group can be said to be Christian.

More controversial is the teaching of the early Christian (iii) in the
code with regard to the " subordination " of wives to their relation-
husbands.   Reference to a later section of this volume [1] will husbands
shew that this matter is the subject of much fuller treatment and
by St. Paul than by St. Peter ;   and it is to be noted also that, wives :
whereas the former has something to say on the reciprocal
duties of parents and children, the latter is silent on that topic.
The issue as a whole is therefore best discussed in connexion
with St. Paul's teaching.   Certain features in St. Peter's
handling of the matter here, however, are noteworthy.   First,
though his approach is from the side of subordination, St.
Peter does here balance his teaching about the duties of wives
by teaching about those of husbands.   The obligations of
married persons, that is to say, are reciprocal.   Secondly, he
still further emphasizes the spiritual equality of the sexes by iii.
his allusion to the prayers of husband and wife, and by making
this allusion in his address to husbands.   Prayers — and the
plural here, as in iv. 7, points to definite acts or habits of

[1] Essay II, pp. 432-5, and Table XIII.

prayer — are to be regulative of conduct in this most intimate relationship of life, providing conjugal intercourse with its rule of temperance and its true basis of fellowship. Husband and wife are " both alike heirs of the grace of life ", and must so live together that their " prayers be not hindered ". The author shews himself here a profound psychologist, lifting the sexual side of life on to the high level of the spiritual relationship between man and wife, and associating it with the religious impulse. If husbands do not treat their wives as spiritual equals and respect them accordingly, the activity of prayer can have no free course in them ; and, conversely, the absence of any such barrier to prayer is symptomatic of a sexual life that is healthy. Nothing could be further from the idea, common among eastern cults and peoples, that women are by nature inferior to men, or even devoid of souls altogether.

Finally, and in the light of these considerations, it is plain that for St. Peter the " subordination ", which the Apostle enjoins upon wives, is a matter of practical adjustment rather than of ethical principle. Their obedience is to be to their iii. 1, 6 " own husbands ", a phrase twice used ; there is no question of a general subordination of women to men ; and indeed, in iii. 7 so far as woman is the " weaker vessel ", the fact gives her a special title to consideration and respect. Further, being a rule of adjustment rather than a principle of ethics, the command to the wife to " obey " is changeable with changing circumstances. St. Peter wrote for a society where the husband was both the protector of the wife and the breadwinner for the family. In the economic order of the western world to-day, these conditions often do not prevail ; the wife secures equal protection with the husband at the hands of the law, and she is sometimes the main financial support of the family. Yet the second of these conditions is relatively rare, even in the west; and where it does not prevail, the domestic rule inculcated in the early Christian code is a matter of commonsense. For the fact of differentiation of function between husband and wife remains, even if it is not easily defined. The New Testament code provides a rough-and-ready rule, which experience shews normally to work well in practice, and to be capable of modification where needed.

And the interpretation which St. Peter gives here to the rule—
chaste conduct in the wife and " the inviolability of a gentle
and quiet spirit " — reveals him as one well aware of the real
truth of the matter.

Reasons are given elsewhere for believing that the early (iv) in the
Christian code contained a section dealing with the reciprocal life of the
duties of different orders in the Church, though the traces of Church
it are less clear in this Epistle than in some others.[1]   Here it
suffices to observe the way in which St. Peter enjoins humility v. 1-5
upon all alike, pastors no less than people.   Calling himself
" fellow-presbyter " with the clergy whom he addresses, he
sets before them an ideal of authority in Church life which
abjures the imperious or self-seeking spirit and is exemplary
and pastoral.   The young may be expected to catch the infec-
tion of such a spirit — such is the force of ὁμοίως in v. 5 — and
thus all can be enjoined to shew humility towards one another.
All alike have gifts, and they are to use them in one another's service, " as stewards of the manifold grace of God ". iv. 8-11
Throughout these sections the dominating idea is the connexion between humility and grace, pride being the great obstacle to grace, and grace the very life-blood of the Church.

So far we have been considering the social code which is Ethical
found in this Epistle as a sociological document, comprising principles
a discipline rather than an ethic, laying down in the first tions in
instance norms of conduct within certain concrete spheres of the
relationship.   The social code, however, is very far from Epistle
representing the whole of the Apostle's ethical teaching.   We
have already observed to what broader issues he turns the rule
of subordination in each case ; how civic duty becomes the
raw material of loyalty, freedom, and respect for human
personality, the slave's patience a meekness which is " grace
in God's eyes ", the wife's obedience the expression of inward qualities precious in His sight, and subordination in
the life of the Church the key to reciprocal humility, itself
an indispensable condition of grace.   In these interpretations
we pass from practical adjustments to valuations.   For adjustments are not enough.   " The justification of a type of
behaviour as being an efficient piece of adjustment to a given
situation does not yet determine its being right or wrong from

[1] Cf. below, Essay II, pp. 415 ff. and Table VIII c.

a Christian or a non-Christian point of view." [1]   There are
needed also valuations or ethical principles.   In this Epistle
these are supplied in the detailed interpretations which St.
Peter gives of the injunctions of the social code.   But they do
not stand alone.   Thus, he concludes the code with an ethical

iii. 8, 9   summary which is wholly composed of valuations.   " Finally,
be ye like-minded, sympathetic, filled with brotherly love,
good-hearted, humble of mind, not rendering evil for evil,
or railing for railing, but contrariwise blessing. . . ."   Here
are principles which are always and everywhere valid.   They
sum up, moreover, not only the teaching of the social code,
but also much else in the Epistle, not least the principles of

i. 13–ii. 12   holiness, especially charity, honesty, and temperance, enunciated in an earlier passage, together with the tougher virtues
of courage, stedfastness, persistence in well-doing, and hope,
which are emphasized throughout.

The theo-   Nor is this all.   Both the particular teachings of the code
logical   and the general ethical teaching are intimately associated with
frame-   ideas, events, images, and religious ordinances which con-
work   stitute the *Weltanschauung* of Christianity.   The Christian's
and back-   civic obligations are linked with the will of God and the
ground   reverence due to Him ;   the conduct of slaves leads into the
great passage on the *imitatio Christi* and the Atonement;
that of wives is to be a following of the example of Sarah and

iii. 17–iv. 1   other holy women of old.   The principle of the dying life,
again, is closely linked both with baptism and with Christ's
passion, death, and resurrection, which provide the context

i. 6 ff.   also for Christian rejoicing in suffering.   Christian stedfastness is based upon faith in God the Creator and on His call.

iv. 19,   Christ, the Good Shepherd, is at once the guarantee of sin's
iii. 9, v. 10   cure and of man's conversion and also the Giver of eternal life
ii. 25, v. 4   and reward at the last.   Few things are more striking in the
work of modern writers [2] who see the tremendous choice con-
fronting civilization to-day than their insistence, from many
angles and on many grounds, on the vital importance of this
theological background to ethical thought.

To sum up.   The Epistle presents us with a threefold

[1] Mannheim, *op. cit.* p. 133.
[2] Cf. Mannheim, *op. cit.* pp. 131-42;
also Lewis Mumford, *Faith for Liv-*   *ing*, especially pp. 65-79, and Walter
Lippmann, *A Preface to Morals*,
chapters ix., x.

structure of ethico-religious teaching. The raw material of The re-sulting unity much of its form is supplied by a discipline or pattern of be- haviour, based upon earlier Jewish and perhaps Gentile models, and expressed in rules or maxims. This pattern is expanded into, and amplified by, what is more properly called a Christian ethic, based upon the Old Testament and the teaching of Christ and expressed in statements of principle or valuation. The third element is strictly religious and theological, based upon the facts of the Christian Gospel and its proper *cultus* and expressed in what came afterwards to be known as dogma. All these elements, moreover, are organically united; none stands alone or is dissociable, ex- cept in a superficial sense, from the other two. The result is to supply the moral life with a basic vision, and to require of faith a practical fruit, which give to the Christian ethic a peculiar strength and vitality, and thus enable it to exercise a formative influence on human society through every kind of vicissitude and change.

8. THE DIRECTION OF THE CHURCH'S LIFE

The Godward movement of the Church's life and the The goal of life expressed in terms of: spiritual motives which are its inspiration are brought out in this Epistle in the frequent references to God's glory as the final cause of conduct, in the place given to prayer, and in the emphasis laid upon the hope of eternal life at Christ's appearing.

The glory of God is set before us as the governing aim of the glory of God; the Church's life in general (ii. 9), and as the motive for the brotherly love, mutual consideration, and meekness in suffer- ing which are the marks of the Christian calling (ii. 12, iv. 11, 16). Moral theologians have been accustomed to find the final cause of human action either in charity or in the glory of God, the Schoolmen on the whole preferring the former definition,[1] Anglican (and Scottish) divines the latter. But they do not really differ; for the reference of all actions to the glory of God does not mean that His glory is thereby

---

[1] Cf. Peter Lombard, *2 Sent. Dist.* xxxviii. 1, from which it passed into scholastic theology generally. Cf. my edition of *The First Book of the Irenicum of John Forbes*, pp. 170, 204 f.

augmented (since that is impossible), but that it is published and shewn forth ; and the great means to that end is charity. Just as St. Paul names charity first among the fruits of the Spirit, so St. Peter enjoins it " before all things " (iv. 8, i. 22) ; it is a κατάλληλον φάρμακον, a "reciprocal medicine", to use St. Chrysostom's expressive phrase,[1] and " hides a multitude of sins " (iv. 8).[2]

of prayer ; Closely connected with the idea of Christian conduct as shewing forth God's glory is the regulative position which the Apostle assigns to prayer. Baptism admits the believer into an open and unimpeded access to God, which is founded in purity of conscience and gives assurance of answer to prayer (iii. 21, 12). There is nothing strictly mystical in this teaching ; the conceptions of the vision of God and of union with God which were to play so large a part in later theology are not found in this Epistle ; but the author's teaching is wholly in keeping with the words of his Master, " Blessed are the pure in heart, for they shall see God ". For him, prayer is a crowning activity of the Christian life. Thus, he says not only, " Be sober, be vigilant " (v. 8), but also, " Be sober and watch unto prayers " (iv. 7) ; and he bases the injunction upon the nearness of the End of all things. This is very close to a *logion* of Jesus recorded by St. Mark (xiii. 33), and in a developed form by St. Luke (xxi. 36), though the words used for " watch " and " prayer " are different : " Watch ye therefore, and pray always, that ye may be accounted worthy to escape all these things that shall come to pass, and to stand before the Son of man ". Moreover, both in iv. 7 and iii. 7 he uses the plural προσευχάς, as though he thought of prayer as consisting in definite acts and occasions, to be numbered among the " sacrifices acceptable to God " which it was the Church's privilege and function to offer.

and of hope ; Nowhere in the New Testament can we see more clearly than in I Peter how the eschatology of the Gospel becomes the teleology of the Church's life. Hope is one of the keynotes of this Epistle, as faith is of St. Paul's Epistle to the Romans and love of the first Epistle of St. John. It is a light which shines all the more brightly in the Church in times of calamity ;

---

[1] On Gal. v. 22 f.

[2] St. Peter's teaching about the glory of God is more fully discussed below in Add. Note B, pp. 253 ff.

it embraces the dead as well as the living, and in that sense the past as well as the future ; and it concentrates the energies of the Christian mind upon a supernatural and supertemporal end.   To an age like our own which is filled with the idea of planning, the Christian hope is of peculiar relevance ; for to the questions, " To what end, and after what design, are we to plan ? ", it proposes an answer.   It insists that, for whatever new world men may essay to build, the first need is for an Architect and a plan.   By proclaiming that man's " end " is supramundane and only to be fully realized beyond the grave, it forearms the Christian believer against too much trust in human contrivance, and therefore against the disillusionment which follows hard on human failure : by contrast with the hopes that play men false, the Christian hope is a " living " hope.   By associating the " end ", moreover, with Christ's appearing, and by teaching that it has already been realized, though not yet fully realized, in the Incarnation, it provides men with a pattern for the guidance of their common life.   Out of the Christian conception of the last things is thus born a practical motive for conduct.   It is no accident that some of Christendom's most vigorous practical reformers — St. Francis, Savonarola, Elizabeth Fry, Wilberforce, Shaftesbury — have been men and women whose otherworldly interests were intense.

If we should say that St. Peter teaches the immediacy of the End of all things, we should do less than justice to his thought ; for, as already indicated, he conceives of the End as organically linked with what has already taken place, in the case both of Christ and of the Church.   " The end of all things ", he says, " has drawn near " (iv. 7).   He does not say " draws near ", but " has drawn near " ; and the perfect tense implies that events have occurred in which it is already represented.   The Greek word, indeed, might almost be translated " has begun ".   The grace in which Christians stand is of a piece with the crown of glory they shall have at the end.[1]   It is not a question of the speedy occurrence of

and gathered up into the End of all things

i. 13, v. 4

---

[1] Cf. Hooker's quaint words : " In meriting, our actions do work with two hands : with the one they get their morning stipend, the increase of grace; with the other, their evening hire, the everlasting crown of glory " (*Serm.* ii. 33).

something wholly novel but of the culmination of something already known. The situation is similar to that which meets us not only in Acts but also in the Synoptic Gospels, where the Kingdom of God is conceived of as both present and future : from a historical or chronological point of view, the present is a preparation for, and indeed a foretaste of, the future ; but from a theological standpoint, the future governs and conditions the present. The idea of immediacy is therefore both necessary and irrelevant ; necessary, in order to express the organic connexion between present and future, which. is theologically vital ; irrelevant, because the " when " of the fulfilment is unknown to all save God alone. We are dealing here not with dial time, but with moral time. For St. Peter the historical manifestation of Christ to reconcile believers to God by His sacrificial life and death was the beginning of the End, the point at which the eschatological hope began to be fulfilled, and the transcendent order entered history ; and the proof of it was His resurrection and exaltation to God's right hand. Nor is that the only sign that the End is near : the trials which believers are suffering, rising at times at any rate to a severe ordeal, are to be regarded as part of the birthpangs of the Messianic Kingdom (i. 11 and note, and 1 Pet. i. 5 Add. Note J, pp. 300-03). Meanwhile Christians are guarded in the power of God through faith until they inherit the salvation which is ready to be revealed. The metaphor is a fine one, similar to that in Ps. cxxvii. 1, " Except the Lord keep [1] the city, the watchman waketh but in vain ", with the added thought that in the city of the Christian Church the divine power is met by the response of faith. And this faith is shot through with hope and looks to an end, namely, salvation. The word " salvation " [2] occurs only twice in 1 Peter, and in one of the two passages it is not certain that it is used in an eschatological sense. The Apostle's favourite phrase. when speaking of the End is " the revelation of Jesus Christ " —a phrase which occurs elsewhere in N.T. only in 2 Thess. i. 7 and 1 Cor. i. 7. " Parusia " [3], on the other hand, which is so

[1] The words differ in the Greek, but in the Vulgate *custodire* is used in both places.
[2] For a fuller discussion of the terms salvation, revelation, and glory in

1 Peter cf. Add. Note B, pp. 250 ff.
[3] Cf. Milligan, *St. Paul's Epistles to the Thessalonians*, Note F, for a discussion of this and kindred words.

common in the rest of N.T. as to be almost a technical term, does not occur in our Epistle. The author's preference for the word " revelation " in this context is of a piece with his description of the Lord as One " whom not having seen, ye i. 8 love ; in whom, though now ye see him not, yet believing, ye [shall] rejoice ", etc. There is a personal note in it. " Revelation " was the mode in which St. Peter had experienced crisis. It was by divine " revelation " that the Apostle had first grasped the truth of Christ's Messiahship (Matt. xvi. 17) ; and it was through " a vision in ecstasy " (Acts xi. 5), which was commonly accepted as a means of revelation, that he came to realize the catholicity of the Church. He writes, in fact, as one to whose mind the Master is always present, though hidden for a time from sight, just as God, at whose right hand He is, is hidden. But the ceiling which divides the heavenly world from this is a thin one, and not distant. Hope already penetrates it from this side, and grace from the other (i. 13) ; its removal will be the moment of the Lord's appearing.

And He will be revealed *in glory*.[1] In Jewish thought, and especially in the apocalyptic writings, glory is one of the characteristics of the advent of the Messiah and the Messianic age. In St. Paul's Epistles this glory is freely transferred to the Christian Church as already embodying the Kingdom ; in 1 Peter, as in St. Mark, it normally denotes the final revelation of Christ at the End. Thus, the Apostle speaks of " the revelation of His glory " (iv. 13) and of " the glory that is to be revealed " (v. 1). In this latter case, he describes himself as a sharer in the glory ; though it is probable that the reference in this phrase is not merely to the future, but contains an allusion to what he himself had experienced on the mount of the Transfiguration, and perhaps also to his vision of the risen Lord ; for the glory that was then for a moment revealed is no other than the glory which all will behold in the final revelation. In that day there will be " glories " or triumphs for believers which will more than compensate them for their sufferings in Christ's service now : to the faithful shepherd

---

[1] Lancelot Andrewes' words in his Paraphrase of the Lord's Prayer reflect the Petrine theology exactly : " Let thy kingdom come to me here in the state of grace, that I may come to it in the state of glory ".

of His flock is promised " the unfading crown of glory " — a crown which some of the Rabbis used to say was woven out of prayer. Into this eternal glory which is " in Christ " believers have been called by the God of all grace.

At the same time the End will involve a Judgment — or rather the culmination and completion of the Judgment which has already begun in the separation of believers and un-believers, and of which the trials through which the Church is already passing are premonitory signs. True, St. Peter does not go so far as St. John, nor even as St. Paul, in identify-ing the Judgment with the moment of men's choice between accepting or rejecting the Gospel ; nor does he dwell, like the authors of Jude and 2 Peter and the Apocalypse, upon the details of the overthrow and punishment of evil. But he leaves no doubt that, while Christians who are faithful to their calling will be rewarded, unbelievers and persecutors must expect just retribution at the hands of God or of Christ. In that day the wicked shall render an account of their doings, and those who have lived rightly and humbly will be vindi-cated. Meanwhile, therefore, they can commit themselves to God and go about their work in serene and humble con-fidence, for He has created them and will not fail them : they can trust His impartial justice.

Of the nature of this new and transcendent order the Apostle says little ; but what he does say is important. The references to glory signify that it will be a realm of light, radiant with the divine presence. And it is an " inheritance ", something that we are to possess and use and share with others ; a country of which we are to be citizens, which no invading army can ravage, no sin or infidelity can desecrate, no lapse of time or caprice of nature can bring to dissolution or decay. The name of the Holy Land is not mentioned, but there can be little doubt that it was in St. Peter's mind ; for the three points in which he contrasts the new order with the old — military aggression, religious and moral apostasy, and economic impoverishment — are written on page after page of the nation's history. And the passage, in consequence, glows with the purest patriotism. All his readers who had Jewish blood in their veins would have been stirred by it. Plato could paint the realm of the Ideas in words of noblest poetry,

ii. 8
i. 11 (cf. note)

ii. 12, iv. 5, 17, 18

iv. 5, v. 4, 6

iv. 19, i. 17

but in the last resort the pattern laid up in heaven " for him
who desires to behold it, and beholding found a city in himself " [1] is not a matter of certainty ; and " it makes no difference whether it does exist or ever will exist anywhere ".
About the " inheritance " of which the Apostle speaks, on the
other hand, there is nothing abstract or contingent.   It has
been implied in the pilgrimage of God's people from the
earliest times; seeking " a better country, that is an heavenly",
they have been sustained by a hope which has solid grounds,
for " God has prepared for them a city " [2] ; and now all who
are born again through Christ's resurrection are to find this
hope a reality and their title to the promised inheritance
secure.   More than a century ago a great English statesman
claimed that he had " called the New World into existence to
redress the balance of the Old ".   But the words might be
used with even greater truth and significance of the realm of
light and truth and peace which God has given us through the
resurrection of Christ.   For this world that He has opened up
for us is one that knows no war, no conflict of races, no false
or degrading creed, no famine, no counting of economic loss or
gain.   It is the world of spirit and of life — of the spirit of Love
and of Life Eternal.

[1] *Rep*. 592 B.   Adam's translation.   The Greek is, ἐν οὐρανῷ ἴσως παράδειγμα
ἀνάκειται τῷ βουλομένῳ ὁρᾶν καὶ ὁρῶντι ἑαυτὸν κατοικίζειν.
[2] Heb. xi. 13-16.

ΠΕΤΡΟΥ ΚΑΘΟΛΙΚΗ ΕΠΙΣΤΟΛΗ

ΠΡΩΤΗ

ΠΕΤΡΟΣ ἀπόστολος Ἰησοῦ Χριστοῦ ἐκλεκτοῖς παρεπιδήμοις

1, 2. The form of the Salutation, which is common also in St. Paul's Epistles, conforms to the ancient usage of first-century correspondence. Cf. R. Harris, *The Expositor*, vol. viii. (Sept. 1898).

1. Πέτρος] The Greek form of the Aramaic name Kephas given to St. Peter at his call to discipleship by our Lord Himself (Jn. i. 42), and that by which he is usually designated in N.T. It is significant that, though this form of the Apostle's name (with or without "Simon") is overwhelmingly preponderant in the Gospels and in Acts, St. Paul uses it only twice (Gal. ii. 7, 8), whereas he uses "Kephas" eight times, all in Galatians and 1 Corinthians. The reasons for this usage seem to deserve study. Was it that the Aramaic term persisted in circles which felt themselves to be in a special sense custodians of the primitive tradition, and that St. Paul therefore used it in order to commend himself and his message to such circles? It was the name our Lord Himself had given to Simon; and, while it would have been inappropriate here in addressing mixed Greek-speaking communities, St. Paul may well have felt that by using it he would show that, despite criticisms and disagreements, his personal relations with St. Peter were still those of affection and esteem.

ἀπόστολος Ἰησοῦ Χριστοῦ] descriptive of his office, and therefore of his title to address the churches concerned. The Apostolate is the only order of ministry in N.T. which is followed by this genitive, indicating the unique relationship in which it stood to the historic Christ. For "Apostles" in the Jewish Church see Harnack, *Expansion of Christianity*, i. pp. 409 ff.; and for the tendency of the term to supersede "The Twelve" in the primitive Church cf. Burton, *Galatians* (I.C.C.), pp. 376 f. St. Peter was Christ's apostle in a special sense, cf. Mk. i. 17, Matt. xvi. 16 ff., Lk. xxii. 32, Jn. xxi. For a criticism of Loisy's view that Apostolic authority did not exist in the primitive Church see Jackson and Lake, *Beginnings*, v. pp. 211 ff. Plummer on 2 Cor. viii. 23 rightly points out the distinction between "apostles of Christ" and "apostles of Churches"; but it is also worth observing that St. Paul in the exordium of his Epistles always accompanies the term ἀπόστολος [Χριστοῦ] with some conditioning phrase or adjective, cf. Rom. i. 1, 1 and 2 Cor. i. 1, Gal. i. 1, Eph. i. 1, Col. i. 1, 1 and 2 Tim. i. 1, Tit. i. 1. Its use here without such a qualification would be unique in N.T. unless κατὰ πρόγνωσιν below be taken with it as well as with ἐκλεκτοῖς.

ἐκλεκτοῖς] Divine election was a characteristic of the people of Israel as a whole (Deut. iv. 37, vii. 6, xiv. 2, Is. xlv. 4, Ps. cv. 6, 43) now transferred to the Christian Church as the inheritor of Israel's calling (cf. ii. 9 below).

Election is one of a number of terms (foreknowledge, predestination, creation, calling, etc.) used in Scripture to denote the transcendent relationships which give to men their true status as persons. For a discussion of the terms cf. Dorner, *System of Christian Doctrine*, iv. pp. 165-87. They describe different moments in the divine

διασπορᾶς Πόντου, Γαλατίας, Καππαδοκίας, 'Ασίας, καὶ Βι-

action and initiative on which the relationship rests. As between " election" and " calling", the former is prior, being the ground of the latter, which is experienced at a point or points in time. For the contrast between the Christian κλῆσις (vocation) and the Greek τέχνη (profession or trade) cf. Jaeger, *Paideia*, i. pp. 290 ff.

παρεπιδήμοις] *sojourners*. The term is closely akin to πάροικοι, with which it is used in ii. 11 below, as in Gen. xxiii. 4 and Ps. xxxix. 13 (LXX). ξένοι is used with πάροικοι in the same sense in Eph. ii. 19, Heb. xi. 13. Zahn (*Einleitung*, ii. p. 4) points out that both words were common in secular writings in N.T. times; and says that παρεπίδημος emphasized the transitoriness of the sojourner's stay in a place, πάροικος his legal status as a non-citizen (cf. μέτοικος). These are the two points emphasized by Lightfoot in his masterly note on παροικοῦσα and cognate words in 1 Clem. *ad Cor.* i. Cf. 2 Clem. v. 1 and *Ep. ad Diogn.* v. The idea of Christians as sojourners in the world came to be felt as so expressive of their condition that παροικία became a common term for a Christian community in a place: hence our word " parish ". The earliest example of this usage is in Ps. Sol. xvii. 19, where Ryle and James' note should be consulted. And cf. Ps.-Plat. *Axiochus*, 365, τὸ κοινὸν δὴ τοῦτο καὶ πρὸς πάντων θρυλούμενον, παρεπιδημία τίς ἐστιν ὁ βίος, with Blakeney's note and references *in loc.* Moffatt (*Comm., in loc.*) takes the word in this general sense here, but the context is against it.

διασπορᾶς] *in the Dispersion*. The genitive after παρεπιδήμοις might express the sojourners' place of origin (as in P. Oxy. iii. 473. 2, cited by MM), or the place or people where they sojourned (as in 2 Clem. v. 1, τὴν παροικίαν τοῦ κόσμου τούτου). Though ἐν or κατά is more commonly used in such cases, one (or both) of these meanings is to be preferred here. Hort takes

the genitive in a kind of qualifying sense, as almost equivalent to " dispersed sojourners"; and Ryle and James seem to support this in the note already cited where they write of Jewish sojourners in foreign lands: " As ἡ διασπορά they are described in their relation to their fatherland; as ἡ παροικία they are described in their relation to the countries in which they sojourned for a time until the day of Israel's restoration". The distinct connotation of the terms is well brought out; but Hort's rendering of St. Peter's phrase here does not follow from it, nor does it tally well with the view that the Epistle was addressed primarily to Gentile Christians; and it is not grammatically the most direct rendering. It is easiest to take it as the genitive of time and place, which derives from the genitive of possession, cf. Moulton, *Grammar*, i. p. 73 — the same genitive, in fact, as occurs immediately afterwards in Πόντου, etc.; with which cf. Jn. vii. 35, τὴν διασπορὰν τῶν Ἑλλήνων, " the Dispersion among the Greeks ".

It may be observed that this genitive would have a different *nuance* according as the Jewish or the Gentile elements in a mixed church were in view: if of Jewish origin, Christians were sojourners *from* the Dispersion (cf. the first sense given above) like οἱ ἐπιδημοῦντες Ῥωμαῖοι in Acts ii. 10; if Gentiles, they were sojourners *in* the Dispersion. Further, each term in this phrase adds something to the description of those addressed: ἐκλεκτοῖς denotes the theological basis and ground of their position; παρεπιδήμοις points to an occasion or period when circumstances were emphasizing their transitory and non-privileged outward status; while διασπορᾶς points to their position as heirs of the O.T. promises (cf. ii. 1-9) and to a unity binding them which transcended their geographical dispersion.

It is probable that **the technical**

θυνίας, ²κατὰ πρόγνωσιν Θεοῦ πατρός, ἐν ἁγιασμῷ Πνεύματος,

use of διασπορά for the Jews outside Palestine, which is clear in Jas. i. 1 and Jn. vii. 35 as well as here, was due to Christian influence; for it had no Hebrew equivalent, and is not found in O.T., Philo, or Josephus. Cf. Jackson and Lake, *Beginnings*, i. pp. 137 ff. But the way was prepared for it by such passages as Deut. xxviii. 25, Is. xlix. 6, Jer. xv. 7, 2 Macc. i. 27. Ps. Sol. viii. 34, ix. 2, xvii. 20 (ὁ σκορπισμὸς αὐτῶν) are also relevant, with Ryle and James' notes there and on Ps. xi.

Πόντου κτλ.] For the order in which these provinces are named see Additional Note III in Hort's edition : his hypothesis, viz. that the names occur in the order in which the bearer of the letter planned to visit the provinces, seems still to be without adequate rival. We need not, however, suppose that the whole of each province was to be visited ; and copies of the letter may well have been made at the chief centres *en route* for regional distribution. Cf. Introd. pp. 45-7.

2. κατὰ πρόγνωσιν Θεοῦ πατρός] Most commentators regard this and the following prepositional clauses as governed by the verbal noun ἐκλεκτοῖς. But ἀπόστολος is also virtually a verbal noun ; and a fuller meaning is given if we reckon the clauses to be governed by this also. The primary import of the three clauses is to open up clearly at the outset of the Epistle the transcendent origin, nature, and purpose of the Church and its life. The Apostle's readers are the heirs of all the ages. They also focus three " moments " in God's redemptive activity towards man — His knowing or taking note of those whom He will choose, His gift of sanctifying grace, and His finished work in their obedience and pardon. For the bearing of this passage on Trinitarian doctrine see Add. Note A, pp. 247 f., and Lebreton, *Histoire du Dogme de la Trinité*, i. p. 6 (1927). The doctrine of Providence ex-

pressed in the phrase κατὰ πρόγνωσιν Θεοῦ πατρός is well illustrated in Judith ix. 5, 6, where LXX uses the word πρόγνωσις. The preposition in the compound denotes the fact that God's " knowledge " is part of His eternal counsel, cf. the προ- in πρόθεσιν and προώρισε in Rom. viii. 28, 29. And the knowledge is with a view to choice and calling, as in Amos iii. 2, 2 Tim. ii. 19, Justin, *Dial.* 42 (261 B), *Apol.* i. 71 B (even if, as in this last passage, the calling is delayed). For the Hebraic idea of the wisdom of God in creation and history see Kohler, *Jewish Theology*, ch. xxii.

ἐν ἁγιασμῷ Πνεύματος] ἐν might be instrumental here, as often in Hellenistic Greek, " in virtue of ", cf. Moulton, *Grammar*, i. p. 61 ; but it is simplest to take it as a slight extension of the ordinary local sense, meaning " in the sphere of ". The phrase would then be analogous to ἐν Χριστῷ and to ἐν δυνάμει in verse 5 below. We may also compare 1 Cor. vi. 11, ἐδικαιώθητε ἐν τῷ ὀνόματι τοῦ κυρίου Ἰησοῦ Χριστοῦ καὶ ἐν τῷ πνεύματι τοῦ θεοῦ ἡμῶν, and Ignatius, *Eph.* iii., ἐν Ἰησοῦ Χριστοῦ γνώμῃ, *Smyrn.* xii., ἀσπάζομαι . . . τοὺς συνδούλους μου διακόνους . . . ἐν ὀνόματι Ἰησοῦ Χριστοῦ καὶ τῇ σαρκὶ αὐτοῦ καὶ τῷ αἵματι κτλ. Cf. Deissmann, *Die Formel. in Christo Jesu*, pp. 97 f.

Πνεύματος is a subjective genitive, " by the Spirit ", as in 2 Thess. ii. 13, Tit. iii. 5 (cf. Rom. xv. 16). Lightfoot's disinclination to choose between a subjective and an objective genitive in his note on Phil. i. 19 is not relevant here, as he is using the terms in a different sense, i.e. to distinguish between the Giver and the gift. The word ἁγιασμός, " hallowing ", occurs also three times in 1 Thess. iv. and may perhaps be regarded as a mark of Silvanus' style: cf. Essay II, pp. 372 f., 382 ff.

Hallowing by the Spirit represents the inward part of the sacrament of

εἰς ὑπακοὴν καὶ ῥαντισμὸν αἵματος Ἰησοῦ Χριστοῦ· χάρις ὑμῖν

baptism, which may be in the Apostle's mind here. Cf. Jeremy Taylor, *Life of Christ*, I. ix. §§ 20-4 (*Works*, ii. pp. 240-4, ed. 1847), and especially: " And therefore as our baptism is a separation of us from unbelieving people, so the descent of the Holy Spirit upon us in our baptism is a consigning or marking us for God, as the sheep of His pasture, as the soldiers of His army, as the servants of His household ". Paulinus' words (*Ep.* 32) are in point :

> Sanctus in hunc coelo descendit
> Spiritus amnem,
> Coelestique sacras fonte maritat
> aquas :
> Concipit unda Deum, sanctamque
> liquoribus almis
> Edit ab aeterno semine progeniem.

εἰς ὑπακοὴν καὶ ῥαντισμὸν αἵματος Ἰησοῦ Χριστοῦ] *in order that we may be obedient, and forgiven through the blood of Christ*. For ὑπακοή used absolutely for " the obedience of one who conforms his conduct to God's commands " (Grimm-Thayer) cf. 1 Pet. i. 14. Windisch's coupling of ὑπακοήν with Ἰησοῦ Χριστοῦ as an objective genitive, though grammatically paralleled from 2 Cor. x. 5 and 1 Pet. i. 22, is thus not necessary, and it would involve Ἰησοῦ Χριστοῦ in being at once possessive and objective genitive. At the same time the whole phrase has an inner connexion of thought, both its terms, " obedience " and " reconciliation through Christ's blood ", referring to the Covenant-sacrifice described in Ex. xxiv. Cf. Hort, *in loc.* The *rationale* of animal sacrifice in ancient times distinguishes two principal elements in it, the victim's death and the ritual or sacerdotal acts concerned with the disposal of its blood. The death represented the absoluteness of the gift ; it was thus wholly and irrevocably given. Cf. Westcott (on Heb. ix. 14-17, Notes and Additional Notes), who suggests that the victim's death in the Covenant-

sacrifice meant no more than " the covenanter's abandonment of all freedom of movement or change in regard to the matter of the covenant ". Cf. also Spens, *Essays Catholic and Critical*, pp. 433-6. The sacerdotal acts declared the aim and meaning of the sacrificial action, and gave it its sacrificial character. The nature of the Covenant-sacrifice in Ex. xxiv. is thus described by Dr. Vincent Taylor : " In this narrative (Ex. xxiv. 1-11) a distinction is drawn between the blood sprinkled upon the altar and that which is sprinkled upon the people. The former is the symbol of the people's obedience ; it is their offering to God, confirmed by the words : ' All the words which Yahweh hath spoken will we do ' (cf. the ' obedience ' in St. Peter's phrase). The latter, the blood sprinkled upon them, is dedicated blood which Yahweh has accepted, and the sprinkling means that the people now share in the blessings and powers which it represents and conveys. It is this blood which is described as ' the blood of the covenant' " (*Jesus and His Sacrifice*, p. 137).

It is not easy to say how far forgiveness or remission of sins was directly or indirectly included among the blessings conferred by this sacrifice; though Hort regards the idea of purification, if not of atonement, as one of " the essential points of the narrative in Exodus ". But forgiveness figures clearly in the " new covenant " foretold by Jeremiah as destined to replace the old (Jer. xxxi. 31-4, especially verse 34) ; and it is not surprising, therefore, to find them prominent when in N.T. the Covenant-sacrifice was used to illustrate the meaning of the death of Christ. According to St. Mark, indeed, this aspect was emphasized by our Lord Himself : cf. V. Taylor, *The Atonement in N.T. Teaching*, pp. 40 f. For, unlike St. Paul (1 Cor. xi. 25), St. Mark records our Lord as explicitly fusing the ideas

καὶ εἰρήνη πληθυνθείη.

³Εὐλογητὸς ὁ Θεὸς καὶ πατὴρ τοῦ Κυρίου ἡμῶν Ἰησοῦ Χρι-

of covenant and of atonement (τὸ αἷμά μου τῆς διαθήκης τὸ ὑπὲρ πολλῶν ἐκχυνόμενον), thus interpreting Ex. xxiv. in the light of Is. liii. ; and St. Matthew underlines the teaching still further by adding εἰς ἄφεσιν ἁμαρτιῶν. From the fact, again, that St. Mark was the " interpreter " of St. Peter, we may infer that it was in this sense that the Apostle understood the new covenant in Christ's blood. The usage is well exemplified, moreover, in early Christian thought. Cf.

Heb. x. 29, τὸ αἷμα τῆς διαθήκης . . . ἐν ᾧ ἡγιάσθη . . .
Heb. x. 22, ἐρραντισμένοι τὰς καρδίας ἀπὸ συνειδήσεως πονηρᾶς, καὶ λελουμένοι τὸ σῶμα ὕδατι καθαρῷ.
Heb. xii. 24, διαθήκης νέας μεσίτῃ Ἰησοῦ καὶ αἵματι ῥαντισμοῦ κρεῖττον λαλοῦντι παρὰ τὸν Ἄβελ (for the blood of Christ pleads with God, not like Abel's, for vengeance but for forgiveness, and speaks peace to men. Cf. Westcott, in loc.).

And even more precise is Ep. Barn. v. 1, ἵνα τῇ ἀφέσει τῶν ἁμαρτιῶν ἁγνισθῶμεν ὅ ἐστιν ἐν τῷ αἵματι τοῦ ῥαντίσματος αὐτοῦ.

The fact is that in their allusions to Christ's blood, the N.T. writers " are simply making use of the vocabulary of the earliest preaching and worship " (V. Taylor, The Atonement in N.T. Teaching, p. 34). Moreover, both the human and the divine sides of the covenant undergo a change, when we pass from the old religion to the new. The phrase as a whole sums up the nature of the Church's life, as St. Peter envisages it.

χάρις ὑμῖν καὶ εἰρήνη πληθυνθείη] a slightly amplified form of the conventional greeting. In Greek letters the sender began by bidding the recipient χαίρειν, or εὐψυχεῖν, or πλεῖστα χαίρειν. The last-named wish can be equally well expressed by χάρις πληθυνθείη. The nearest biblical parallel is in Dan. iv. 1 (Nebuchadnezzar's letter), Εἰρήνη ὑμῖν πληθυνθείη. For

the idea of peace as " abounding " cf. Ps. xxxvii. 11, lxxii. 7. As Rendel Harris (The Expositor, vol. viii. (Sept. 1898)) points out, the N.T. salutations are " either directly coincident with " those current in ordinary correspondence, " or derived from the Greek salutations, such as χαίρειν and τὰ πλεῖστα χαίρειν, by a reference to χάρις as underlying the expression in common use ".

3-12. First Doctrinal Section.
The author gives praise to God for the crowning mercy of Christ's resurrection, which he lays down as the ground of the new life and hope and spiritual inheritance now open to all believers. In the security which faith gives them for salvation, they rejoice in whatever trials they may suffer now; for such trials are a means of probation, their rejoicing is a foretaste of the unspeakable bliss which will be theirs when faith receives its ultimate reward. The flowing tide of grace now experienced by the Church is the answer to the earnest searchings of prophets through the ages; the sufferings of Christ's disciples and their destined recompense are part of the divine purpose now being fulfilled in the outpouring of the Spirit and the spread of the Gospel — events which arrest the awestruck gaze of the angelic host.

3. Εὐλογητὸς κτλ.] With this outburst of praise following the salutation cf. 2 Cor. i. 3 ff., Eph. i. 3 ff. The emphasis in 1 Peter, however, is more on the objective historical fact than in the Pauline writings.

The verbal adjective is not found in classical Greek, but εὐλογεῖν is common, meaning " to praise " : cf. Soph, O.C. 720, ἐπαίνοις εὐλογούμενον. εὐλογητός is the regular LXX word for " praised " or " blessed ", especially of God or God's Name. The blessing of God was a characteristic feature of Jewish prayer, and became focused in the Shemoneh 'Esreh or Eighteen

στοῦ, ὁ κατὰ τὸ πολὺ αὐτοῦ ἔλεος ἀναγεννήσας ἡμᾶς εἰς ἐλπίδα

Benedictions, which were recited thrice daily in the synagogue. (An English translation of them is given in Oesterley's *The Jewish Background of the Christian Liturgy*, pp. 58 ff.) The *berakha* or blessing was " invariably a thanksgiving *to* God *for* the specific content the formula expressed ", and thus appeared in Greek indifferently either as εὐλογία or εὐχαριστία, cf. Gavin, *The Jewish Antecedents of the Christian Sacraments*, p. 71, Dugmore, *The Influence of the Synagogue upon the Divine Office*, pp. 12, 16 f. The blessing in 1 Pet. i. 3 ff. is not a hymn but a Christian *Shema*.

The Christian benediction is richer than the Jewish both in its conception of God and in its idea of immortality. God is now revealed and known as " the God and Father of our Lord Jesus Christ"; not as God only, but as God revealed by relation to His only begotten Son, and not as His Father only, but also as His God, for the incarnation does not exhaust God's manifestation of Himself. And the Son is described in three ways ; in His relationship to us (" our Lord "), in His Person (" Jesus "), and in His divinely promised and world-wide office (" Christ "). The concept of immortality is likewise enlarged, both by being related to the concrete historical fact of Christ's resurrection, and also through being made part of an objective and concrete reality possessed by all who are redeemed. The contrast is clearly seen if we compare with this passage the jejune words of the Second Benediction, " Blessed art thou, O Lord, that quickenest the dead ".

κατὰ τὸ πολὺ αὐτοῦ ἔλεος] mercy to those who have nothing merited. Cf. Is. lxiii. 7-9, and the beautiful Rabbinic parable quoted in Abrahams, *The Glory of God*, pp. 46, 47.

ἀναγεννήσας] not found in classical Greek nor in LXX, nor elsewhere in N.T. except verse 23 below. MM

quote Reitzenstein, *Poimandres*, p. 339, 11, where however the true text is almost certainly ἐγεννήθη, connoting not rebirth but birth. The idea of regeneration (παλιγγενεσία) was nevertheless not uncommon in the Mystery Religions (see references given by Büchsel in Kittel's *Wᵇ.z.N.T.* pp. 671-4), being used like μεταμόρφωσις and μετατύπωσις to describe the change through which the initiated person passed on admission to the Mystery. For a discussion of Perdelwitz' theory as to the bearing of the Mystery Religions on this Epistle see Add. Note L, pp. 306-08.

Büchsel further cites Jos. *B.J.* iv. viii. 4, ἔτι δὲ κἂν τοῖς καρποῖς σποδιὰν ἀναγεννωμένην (*cineres renascentes*, of the ashes living again in the fruits on the site of ancient Sodom) and Philo[?], *Aet. Mund.* 8, οἱ δὲ Στωικοὶ κόσμον μὲν ἕνα . . . ἐξ ἧς πάλιν ἀναγέννησιν κόσμου συνίστασθαι (of the renewal of the world after the ἐκπύρωσις, called *ib.* 9 παλιγγενεσία), to show that the word was familiar and non-technical in meaning ; and we may add Jos. *Ant.* IV. ii. 1, τῶν ἐκ τοῦ στασιάζειν αὐτοῖς ἀναγεννωμένων (*quae exoriuntur*) δεινῶν, and Philo, *de Vit. Mos.* ii. 65 [II. 144 M], where it is said of Noah and his family, who were delivered from the Flood, that they παλιγγενεσίας ἐγένοντο ἡγέμονες καὶ δευτέρας ἀρχηγέται περιόδου. Philo also uses παλιγγενεσία of the life after death in *de Cherub.* 114 [I. 160 M]; εἰς παλιγγενεσίαν ὁρμήσομεν οἱ μετὰ ἀσωμάτων σύγκριτοι ποιοί. We are justified, therefore, in view of this variety of context in which ἀναγέννησις and παλιγγενεσία occur, in saying that the words were used in Graeco-Jewish circles to signify any decisively new stage in nature, history, or personal life.

A decisively new stage, both in world-history and in the lives of the converted, is precisely what the New Testament asserts to have been introduced by Christianity, and what indeed, so far as the personal life was concerned, the Jewish Rabbis claimed in the case of proselytes to Judaism ; and a writer so rich in expressive words as our author (cf. Bigg, *op. cit.* Introd. § 2) might well have applied the verb ἀναγεννᾶν to the change involved in conversion, even if the Jews had not done so before him. For we must remember that Judaism in the first century and earlier was not without its Hellenizing tendencies, and a theological terminology suitable to Christianity was in process of formation. For Rabbinic parallels cf. Add. Note L, pp. 306 f. Further, this use of ἀναγεννᾶν falls into line with much else in N.T. The *nidus* of the idea appears in the *verba Christi* in Mk. x. 14, 15, ἄφετε τὰ παιδία ἔρχεσθαι πρός με, μὴ κωλύετε αὐτά· τῶν γὰρ τοιούτων ἐστὶν ἡ βασιλεία τοῦ θεοῦ. ἀμὴν λέγω ὑμῖν, ὃς ἐὰν μὴ δέξηται τὴν βασιλείαν τοῦ θεοῦ ὡς παιδίον, οὐ μὴ εἰσέλθῃ εἰς αὐτήν ; while on the scale of cosmic history our Lord's use of παλιγγενεσία in Matt. xix. 28 (whatever may have been the Aramaic original) is equally relevant. Compare also, on the personal side, the conception of baptism found in Rom. vi. 5, Tit. iii. 5, the teaching about the new birth in our Lord's discourse with Nicodemus (Jn. iii., cf. i. 12, 13) also referring to baptism, and the ethical transformation described in St. John's words, " We know that we have passed from death unto life, because we love the brethren" (1 Jn. iii. 14) ; and again, on the cosmical side, the ideas of the new creation in Gal. vi. 15, 2 Cor. v. 17, and particularly Jn. xx. 22 (cf. Hoskyns' note).

[The above considerations go far, I think, to invalidate Burkitt's view (*Christian Beginnings*, p. 109) that the concepts of new creation and of rebirth belong to different circles of ideas : cf. for example, Philo's equation of ἀναγέννησις with παλιγγενεσία in the passage cited above ; also Hoskyns on Jn. i. 12, 13. The difference is one of context, the concept of new creation throwing into theological metaphor the truth represented in such a phrase as " The world has become a different place ", while that of rebirth arises from the experience expressed in " I have become quite a different person ".

Compare, for example, the words of one who has been converted to belief in immortality in Ps.-Plato, *Axiochus*, 370 (third century B.C.), ἔκ τε τῆς ἀσθενείας ἐμαυτὸν συνείλεγμαι καὶ γέγονα καινός.]

Justin, in his account of baptism in *Apol.* i. 61 (93 D–94 D), uses ἀναγεννᾶν, ἀναγέννησις repeatedly, substituting it for γεννηθῇ in his quotations from Jn. iii., and confining it to baptism (as also in *Dial.* 138 (367 D)), while he uses καινοποιηθέντες, which is almost " new creation ", to denote the Christian instruction which preceded it. E. H. B. cites also Clem. Alex. *Strom.* VII. 889 [P], τὸν πατέρα . . . τὸν ἀναγεννῶντα καὶ ἀνακτίζοντα . . . τὴν ψυχὴν τὴν ἐξειλεγμένην. Cf. also [Ambrose], *de Sacramentis*, iii. 1. 2.

If the question is asked whether baptism was directly in the Apostle's mind when these words were written, the answer must be that the evidence does not enable us to decide ; nor is the question of great importance, since conversion in the primitive Church was always followed by baptism. Büchsel's sharp rejoinder to Windisch on this issue need not therefore detain us. Like St. Paul, St. Peter regards the change involved in conversion as " summed up in one definite act of the past ; potentially to all men in our Lord's passion and resurrection, actually to each individual man when he accepts Christ, is baptized into Christ ". So Lightfoot, *On a Fresh Revision of the New Testament*, pp. 84 ff. (ed. 1871), who cites also 1 Pet. i. 18, ii. 21, iii. 9, and many Pauline passages. Cf. the discussion of νῦν and ἄρτι in this Epistle above, Introd. pp. 41-2.

ἡμᾶς] On " we ", " us ", " you " in this Epistle see Introd. p. 28.

ζῶσαν δι᾽ ἀναστάσεως Ἰησοῦ Χριστοῦ ἐκ νεκρῶν, ⁴εἰς κληρονομίαν ἄφθαρτον καὶ ἀμίαντον καὶ ἀμάραντον, τετηρημένην ἐν

ἐλπίδα ζῶσαν] a hope that is never extinguished by untoward circumstances, just as " living waters " are waters flowing fresh from a perennial spring. For an amplified statement of the idea cf. 1 Cor. xv. 12-19. The words have a special force if the author is St. Peter, who could remember being raised by his Master's resurrection from the despair that found utterance in his threefold denial to a hope that no changes of fortune could shake.

4. εἰς κληρονομίαν] The range of the writer's argument is increased, and sweeps on beyond the hope, which springs from the rebirth, to the trans-subjective reality which forms the content and substance of the hope. This is defined by a word regularly used in LXX of Canaan as Israel's possession, cf. Gen. xvii. 3 (the first promise of it), Ps. lxxix. 1, Ps. Sol. vii. 2. But, unlike Canaan, the promised possession of the Christians is not subject to the ravages of war or calamity (cf. φθείρω in 1 Chron. xx. 1, Is. xxiv. 3, 4, Dan. ix. 26), nor to idolatry and the sensual vices that accompanied it (cf. Jer. ii. 7, 23, iii. 2, Ezek. xx. 43, Hag. ii. 13, 14), nor to the wasting effects of time or unkind seasons (cf. Job xv. 30, Wisd. ii. 8). The three adjectives themselves all occur in the Book of Wisdom (to the vocabulary of which our author was partial), being used of God's Spirit and the light of the Law (ἄφθαρτος, xii. 1, xviii. 4), of the rewards of virtue (ἀμίαντος, iv. 2), and of Wisdom (ἀμάραντος. vi. 12); and they are well suited to describe an inheritance in which life is immortal, and worship pure and ethical, and the satisfactions offered beyond all the vicissitudes of time. For κληρονόμος as implying not merely expectation but real possession cf. Heb. xi. 7, with Westcott's note.

The succession of adjectives beginning with α-privative has abundant parallels in the philosophical writings

of the period, cf. Ps.-Plat. Axiochus, 370, ἔνθα ἄπονα πάντα καὶ ἀστένακτα καὶ ἀγήρατα (a description of heaven); but here it is more likely to have a poetical inspiration. We may compare Soph. Antig. 1071, ἄμοιρον, ἀκτέριστον, ἀνόσιον νεκύν; and in English, Shakespeare's " unhousel'd, disappointed, unanel'd ", or Milton's " unshaken, unseduced, unterrified ". It is to be noted that ἀμάραντος and ἄφθαρτος occur in the same sentence in Apoc. Pet. v., where the blessings of heaven are described, and were presumably borrowed from 1 Pet. i. 3.

τετηρημένην ἐν οὐρανοῖς] St. Paul (Col. i. 5) speaks of the hope, St. Peter of the inheritance, as laid up for Christians in heaven. When the Jew wished to designate something as predestined, he spoke of it as already existing in heaven (cf. Dewick, Primitive Christian Eschatology, p. 253). And the perfect tense brings out the thought that the custody of the inheritance has been from all time : cf. the perfect participles used of the " mystery " of the universal Gospel in Rom. xvi. 25, 1 Cor. ii. 7-9, Eph. iii. 9.

The whole passage recalls the striking passage in Lk. xii. 22-40, which probably underlies it, though not directly but mediately through the tradition. The context there is provided by the thought of the Kingdom as the highest object of a Christian's ambition and as God's promised gift to faith. Christians are to bend all their efforts towards the acquisition, not of earthly, but of heavenly goods, beyond the reach of thief or moth or time's decay ; for this spiritual aim is what determines character. The resemblances of thought and imagery between this passage and 1 Pet. i. 4 are notable enough in themselves to suggest dependence, especially when we observe that both passages lead to

οὐρανοῖς εἰς ὑμᾶς ⁵τοὺς ἐν δυνάμει Θεοῦ φρουρουμένους διὰ πίστεως εἰς σωτηρίαν ἑτοίμην ἀποκαλυφθῆναι ἐν καιρῷ ἐσχάτῳ. ⁶ἐν ᾧ ἀγαλλιᾶσθε, ὀλίγον ἄρτι, εἰ δέον ἐστί, λυπηθέντες ἐν

the practical exhortation to vigilance and hope:

Lk. xii. 35 f. ἔστωσαν ὑμῶν αἱ ὀσφύες περιεζωσμέναι . . . καὶ ὑμεῖς ὅμοιοι ἀνθρώποις προσδεχομένοις τὸν κύριον κτλ. I Pet. i. 13. διὸ ἀναζωσάμενοι τὰς ὀσφύας τῆς διανοίας ὑμῶν . . . ἐλπίσατε ἐπὶ τὴν φερομένην ὑμῖν χάριν ἐν ἀποκαλύψει κτλ.

St. Paul uses the *logion* to a different end in two passages. (i) In Rom. xiv. 17 he concludes his plea for mutual charity and toleration in the matter of food customs (on which see Lake, *Earlier Epistles of St. Paul*, p. 381) with the summary statement that " the kingdom of God is not eating and drinking, but righteousness and peace and joy in the Holy Ghost ". The negative part of his statement is a compendious interpretation of our Lord's words in Lk. xii. 29, μὴ ζητεῖτε τί φάγητε καὶ τί πίητε; its positive part may be regarded likewise as his interpretation of our Lord's command to give our earthly goods away as alms and to seek first the Kingdom of God. (ii) In Col. iii. 1 f., the injunctions—τὰ ἄνω ζητεῖτε . . . τὰ ἄνω φρονεῖτε, μὴ τὰ ἐπὶ τῆς γῆς—are connected with Christ's resurrection, with the new life of Christians in Him, and with their expectation of being later manifested with Him in glory. But the injunctions themselves may none the less derive ultimately from the passage in Lk. xii.

St. Peter retains more than St. Paul of the original imagery of the passage, while combining it with the familiar O.T. idea of the κληρονομία; but like St. Paul in Col. iii. he connects it with Christ's resurrection, with the new life of Christians in Him (ἀναγεννήσας), and with their expectation of glory (verses 5, 7, 13, etc.).

For a description of the pursuit of false values cf. T. Traherne, *Centuries*

of Meditations, i. p. 33, especially " The works of darkness are Repining, Envy, Malice, Covetousness, Fraud, Oppression, Discontent and Violence. All which proceed from the corruption of Men and their mistake in the choice of riches: for having refused those which God made, and taken to themselves treasures of their own, they invented scarce and rare, insufficient, hard to be gotten, little, movable and useless treasures."

ὑμᾶς τοὺς ἐν δυνάμει Θεοῦ φρουρουμένους κτλ.] For Christians as living " in " God's power cf. Ignatius, *Eph.* xi., ἐν δυνάμει Ἰησοῦ Χριστοῦ; xiv., ἐν δυνάμει πίστεως ἐάν τις εὑρεθῇ εἰς τέλος. " This power from without corresponds to the faith from within " (Hort). φρουρεῖν usually has military associations, but not always: cf. Soph. *O.T.* 1479; and here, as in Gal. iii. 23, Phil. iv. 7, it means simply " securely protected ".

5. σωτηρίαν . . . καιρῷ ἐσχάτῳ] The salvation in the sense of the actual possession of the inheritance, with its fulness of life and its open vision of God, is still future. It is ready to be revealed " in the last time ". The phrase is eschatological. Hort gives some examples from classical Greek to support his rendering, " in a season of extremity ", *in extremis*: but there is no instance of ἔσχατος bearing this meaning in N.T. The reference, when the word is combined with ἡμέρα, ὥρα, χρόνος, is either to the Christian dispensation as the final fulfilment of the historical process, as in I Pet. i. 20; or to the last period of extreme distress preceding Christ's Parusia, as in 2 Tim. iii. 1, I Jn. ii. 18, *Did.* xvi. 3; or, as here and often in the Fourth Gospel, to the time of the Parusia and final manifestation of Christ's power and glory itself.

6. ἐν ᾧ] *in which circumstance* (Bengel), *wherefore* (Lat. *quae cum*

ita sint) : the circumstance being that of a Church life divinely originated and governed by the imminence of the Parusia : equivalent to καὶ ἐν τούτῳ, " and meanwhile ". This relative beginning a sentence is followed by three others in verses 8, 10, 12. St. Peter is fond of a succession of relatives, cf. iii. 18-22. These are more striking than the reiteration of the relative in ii. 22-4, where, as in Rom. ix. 4 ff., the antecedent remains the same.

Three views are held as to the antecedent to this relative pronoun ; (1) Hort refers it to the θεὸς καὶ πατήρ or the Ἰησοῦς Χριστός of verse 3, there being abundant O.T. precedent for the thought of exultation in God ; (2) Bigg, with whom Windisch agrees, connects it with the immediately preceding καιρῷ ἐσχάτῳ, urging that ἀγαλλιᾶσθαι ἐν followed by the ground of the joy is not found elsewhere in N.T. ; (3) Bennett (*Century Bible*) supports Bengel, and renders, " in view of the considerations stated in verses 3-5, ' wherefore ' ". Kühl and von Soden give a subjective turn by translating " in which assurance ". Of these, (2) seems the least probable ; the grammatical reason alleged for it is unconvincing, and the words καιρῷ ἐσχάτῳ are scarcely a large enough element in the previous sentence to carry the weight of this rich and significant relative clause. Such a sense would be " very difficult to combine with the context " (Bennett), and the analogy of the opening words of verse 10 suggests that St. Peter would have written ἐν ᾧ καιρῷ, if that had been his meaning. Only if Origen's reading ἀγαλλιάσεσθε were right (on which see below) would Bigg's rendering be probable. As between (1) and (3) it is difficult to choose ; (1) connects verses 6-9 with the subject of the main clause, and expresses the Church's response to the divine initiative there proclaimed ; (3) makes the emphasis lie on the whole situation — rebirth, hope, inheritance, faith, imminence of the End—resulting from this initiative.

So Estius. Either provides a weighty antecedent for the weighty relative clause, (3) being the more inclusive.

ἀγαλλιᾶσθε] The two occurrences of this word in i. 6-8 involve questions of textual criticism, of grammar, and of theology. The first is discussed in Add. Note C, p. 258; but I have taken the usual reading as the basis of the exegetical notes here, though gravely doubtful as to its correctness in verse 8.

ἀγαλλιᾶσθαι is never found in the Pauline writings, but is common in LXX, especially in the Psalms, expressing the worshipper's exultation in God and in His mercy. The usual construction is ἀγαλλιᾶσθαι ἐν followed by the ground of the rejoicing, which would be ample authority for a similar usage here, if that were needed. In the present case, the circumstantial and the objective sense of ἐν seem to merge into one another, but the former is predominant.

Some commentators have taken ἀγαλλιᾶσθε here as imperative, like χαίρετε in iv. 13 : but the injunction would be premature at this point. It is true that the imperative occurs in the closely parallel passage in Jas. i. 2, but the note of exhortation governs the whole exordium of that Epistle. Others again in ancient times interpreted the present here as having a future meaning. Cf. Oecumenius, who writes τὸ γὰρ ἀγαλλιᾶσθε ἀντὶ μέλλοντος εἴληπται, ἢ καὶ κατὰ τὸ ἐνεστός. Alford agrees. The interpretation points to the difficulties of the passage, but is arbitrary as a way out of them. Moreover, the idea of rejoicing in, or on account of, tribulation is not uncommon in N.T., and occurs elsewhere in this Epistle ; and its expression in verse 6 does not present the same difficulties as in verse 8.

ὀλίγον ἄρτι, εἰ δέον ἐστί, λυπηθέντες] *at having now been distressed somewhat, it may be.* The same three problems occur here. (1) εἰ δέον without ἐστί is attested by אB, and Clem. Alex. *Strom.* IV. 622 [P]. ἐξόν is similarly used for ἔξεστί in Acts ii. 29, 2 Cor.

xii. 4. The meaning is equivalent to that of εἰ θέλοι τὸ θέλημα τοῦ θεοῦ in iii. 17, and implies that the trials alluded to were spasmodic rather than universal. λυπηθέντες has an important variant λυπηθῆναι, cf. 105, Vulg. and St. Augustine (*modicum nunc si oportet contristari*); while λυπηθέντας is found in Lא¹dfj(k ?)m, a reading which would require the infinitive ἀγαλλιᾶσθαι to be understood. Either variant supports the interpretation given below.

(2) ὀλίγον means here, as the context implies, "for a short time", as in Prov. xxiv. 33, ὀλίγον νυστάζω, ὀλίγον δὲ καθυπνῶ, ὀλίγον δὲ ἐναγκαλίζομαι χερσὶν στήθη. Wherever ἄρτι occurs in N.T. with a past tense, it refers to an action or event just begun or concluded. Cf. Grimm-Thayer, *sub voc.* (Rev. xii. 10 is not an exception, for the triumph acclaimed refers to the events just related as having occurred). Must we, therefore, understand that the distresses alluded to were at the moment in abeyance ? Not necessarily, unless we take the participle in a concessive sense, as in E.V. and most commentaries. The aorist participle, however, must not be translated as though it were a present or even a perfect : though it must refer to an event which was anterior, in one sense or another, to the action of the main verb. But such priority may be either (*a*) logical, as when one action is the *ground* of another, or (*b*) chronological, as when one action is earlier *in time* than another, or (*c*) a combination of the two. The last hypothesis is the most satisfactory here, and yields the translation, "at having been somewhat distressed, it may be, just now". This is a common construction in classical Greek after a verb expressing emotion, such as χαίρειν, ὀργίζεσθαι, αἰσχύνεσθαι. Cf. Blass, *Grammar of N.T. Greek*, pp. 245 f. A good N.T. example is Acts xvi. 34, ἠγαλλιάσατο . . . πεπιστευκὼς τῷ θεῷ, where the participle (as here) is in a tense anterior to that

of the main verb. Cf. also Goodwin, *Greek Grammar*, §§ 1563, 1580, 1581. The sentiment has an exact parallel in Acts v. 41. In other words, their situation being what it is (ἐν ᾧ), the Christians rejoice (ἀγαλλιᾶσθε), not despite their recent distresses, but *because of* them. For they were not only an experience (that would have called for the present or perfect participle) but an event, and an event pregnant with meaning.

(3) The meaning is to be found in the paradox of joy in suffering which is characteristic of N.T. thought. Three elements may be distinguished in it, which may be called moral, mystical, and eschatological, suggestive severally of probation, of privilege, and of reward or reversal of fortune through the advent of the Kingdom. (i) The idea of suffering as a necessary part of man's earthly *probation* is common in the Jewish Wisdom literature ; cf. Wisd. iii. 4-6, Ecclus. ii. 1, 5 ; also Prov. xvii. 3, xxvii. 21 ; and cf. Heb. xii. 11. St. Paul has the same thought in Rom. v. 3, 4 and 2 Cor. vi. 10, viii. 2, adding to it the idea of "boasting" (Romans) or of joy (2 Corinthians). So does St. James (i. 2-4), where the joy is to be found *in* the trials, not in spite of them. Cf. also *Ep. ad Diogn.* v. In pagan literature we may cite Seneca, *de Prov.* 4. St. Peter will dwell on the same point in a moment. The Christian exults in being tested and tried. (ii) The mystical element in the paradox lies in the Christians' possession of the Holy Spirit (1 Thess. i. 6), and in the share which suffering gives them in Christ's sufferings (Rom. viii. 17, and in this Epistle, ii. 19 and iv. 13). Cf. Ignatius, *Philad.* prooem., ἐκκλησίᾳ . . . ἀγαλλιωμένῃ ἐν τῷ πάθει τοῦ κυρίου ἡμῶν ἀδιακρίτως καὶ ἐν τῇ ἀναστάσει αὐτοῦ, πεπληροφορημένῃ ἐν παντὶ ἐλέει· ἣν ἀσπάζομαι ἐν αἵματι Ἰησοῦ Χριστοῦ ἥτις ἐστὶν χαρὰ αἰώνιος καὶ παράμονος. Rom. viii. 31-9 is also to the point. The teaching is similar to that of our Lord in Matt. x. 29,

30, where sacrifice of earthly goods and persecutions meets with abundant spiritual compensation now, and eternal life hereafter. A special form of the thought occurs in Acts v. 41, where the disciples went away " rejoicing that they were counted worthy to suffer dishonour for the Name ". In all these passages the note of *privilege* is emphasized — a note characteristic, at least in modern times, of Russian Christianity. Cf. Madame Gorodetsky, *The Humiliated Christ in Modern Russian Thought.* Cf. also 2 Macc. vi. 30, and 4 Macc. ix. 29 (of one of the Maccabean martyrs), " But he stedfastly enduring this agony said, ' How sweet is every form of death for the sake of the righteousness of our fathers ' ". And we may compare Pastor Niemöller's words in his last sermon, given on June 27, 1937, before his imprisonment : " There is indeed no hope except to hold firm to the Crucified One and learn to say in simple and therefore certain faith : ' In the bottom of my heart Thy name and Cross alone shine forth at all times and in all hours, and therefore I can be glad '. It may be a long road until we are truly glad, like those who, like the Apostles, were counted worthy to suffer harm for Jesus' name." The passage well illustrates the tension of the experience. It is noteworthy that Origen, *Exhort. ad Mart.* 22-6, quotes 2 Macc. vi. and vii. over and over again. The thought in 2 Macc. vii. 9, 16 may have been present to our Lord's mind in His charge to the Twelve, Matt. x. 28. (iii) The eschatological element occurs first on our Lord's own lips in the Sermon on the Mount ; cf. especially Matt. v. 11, 12, where the verbal parallels with 1 Peter are striking (μακάριοί ἐστε, ὅταν ὀνειδίσωσιν ὑμᾶς καὶ διώξωσι . . . ἕνεκεν ἐμοῦ. χαίρετε καὶ ἀγαλλιᾶσθε· ὅτι ὁ μισθὸς ὑμῶν πολὺς ἐν τοῖς οὐρανοῖς . . .). So St. Paul speaks of Christians as " boasting " or " rejoicing " in *hope* (Rom. v. 2, xii. 12). Further, trials (πειρασμοί) and distresses (λυπαί), and

in particular persecutions, were among those premonitory signs of the Parusia which our Lord had led His disciples to expect (Mk. xiii. 7-13, 28-37). They were part of the travail-pangs of the new order (ἀρχὴ ὠδίνων). [This metaphor from childbirth occurs more than once in O.T. to express sharp and sudden reversal of fortune ; and it is developed by our Lord in Jn. xvi. 20-24, where the abundant and lasting joy which the disciples will have in His resurrection will erase the memory of their grief meanwhile. Origen (*Exhort. ad Mart.* 39) touches on the point when quoting 1 Pet. i. 6, and cites Gen. iii. 16.] For the Messianic Woes cf. Ezek. xxxviii., xxxix., Hagg. ii. 6 f., Zech. xi., xii., *Jubilees* xxiii., *Test. XII Patr.*, Levi 10, Dan 5, *Apoc. Bar.* xxix. 2, 2 Esdr. v. 1-12, vi. 18-24 (vii. 30) ; and in N.T. Mk. xiii., 2 Thess. ii. 3 ff., Rev. viii., ix. Cf. Add. Note J, pp. 300-03.

The λυπαί and πειρασμοί of St. Peter's readers are thus part of an eschatological pattern which is now being unrolled to view. Yet it is instructive to compare and contrast the Christian pattern as we have it in Mk. xiii. and in 1 Peter with its Jewish analogues, as we find them, e.g., in the almost contemporary 2 Esdras. The great difference is in the " living hope ", and consequent joy, which the resurrection of Christ has imported into it. Milligan is not going too far (on 1 Thess. i. 6), when he speaks of " this union of suffering and joy as marking a new aeon in the world's history ". It is not merely that the new order is imminent, but that it is so real, the object of so vivid a hope, so fully manifested already to believers in Christ as to effect a transvaluation of values. One symptom of this is that the sufferings themselves tend to appear less onerous. Thus St. Paul speaks of τὸ παραυτίκα ἐλαφρὸν τῆς θλίψεως ἡμῶν (2 Cor. iv. 17), and says that " the sufferings of this present time are not worthy to be compared with the glory that shall be revealed

ποικίλοις πειρασμοῖς, ⁷ἵνα τὸ δοκίμιον ὑμῶν τῆς πίστεως πολυ-

towards us" (Rom. viii. 18); and a similar thought underlies Heb. xii. 9-13 (cf. πρὸς ὀλίγας ἡμέρας in verse 10). The teaching embodies sound psychology; for it appears to be a fact of common experience that men forget pain more easily than joy, which suggests that it goes less deep. It is in such a context that we shall best understand the ὀλίγον in 1 Pet. i. 6: the short duration of the distresses is relative to the promised glory. Cf. Origen, *Exhort. ad Mart.* 1, who interprets the ἔτι μικρόν, ἔτι μικρόν of Is. xxviii. 10 (LXX) in this sense. Cf. also 2 Clem. xix. 3. And we may recall Bacon's aphorism, "Prosperity is the blessing of the Old Testament; adversity is the blessing of the New, which carrieth the greater benediction".

Of the three elements in the paradox of joy in suffering as characteristic of Christians, the first and third are clearly shewn by the next clause to be in the Apostle's mind; the second is not developed until later in the Epistle, but is just glanced at in the ἀγαπᾶτε and πιστεύοντες of verse 8.

ἐν ποικίλοις πειρασμοῖς] *in trials o̱ many kinds.* ποικίλος, "diversified", is a good Platonic word, cf. Ast, *Lex. Platon. sub voc.*, and occurs in the Synoptic Gospels, the Pastoral Epistles, Hebrews, and James, as well as in this Epistle. The diversity of the tortures endured by the Maccabean martyrs was a commonplace of their story (cf. 4 Macc. xv. 8, 21, xvi. 4, xvii. 7, xviii. 21), and may have influenced the choice of words here and in Jas. i. 2, as it has undoubtedly influenced the substance of Heb. xi. 35-40. In 3 Macc. ii. 6 we have (of the Ten Plagues) Φαραὼ ποικίλαις καὶ πολλαῖς ἐδοκίμασας τιμωρίαις.

πειρασμοῖς, "trials", and so usually in N.T. according to Hatch, *Essays in Biblical Greek*, pp. 71 ff. Yet Mayor's caution on the point should be borne in mind, cf. his note on Jas. i. 2.

7. ἵνα τὸ δοκίμιον . . . Ἰησοῦ Χριστοῦ] Grammatically, ἵνα depends on the participle λυπηθέντες, expressing its purpose. But the distresses together with their purpose and result form a single whole, which is dependent in turn on the main verb ἀγαλλιᾶσθε. The joy is not merely in distress, but in distresses which are dominated by such a moral and eschatological end. So, similarly, in Jas. i. 2, 3 the rejoicing in trial is conditioned by the knowledge (γινώσκοντες) of its ethical end.

δοκίμιον] so WH in text. But they include it in their List of Suspected Readings, and regard it as "probably a primitive error for δόκιμον". Deissmann, however, has shown (*Bible Studies*, pp. 259 ff.) that the two words are interchangeable in Papyri of the first three centuries, where they are adjectives, almost equivalent to γνήσιον (cf. 2 Cor. viii. 8); and we may translate "the proven part ot your faith". Cf. 2 Cor. viii. 8, τὸ τῆς ὑμετέρας ἀγάπης γνήσιον, with Plummer's note (I.C.C.) (δοκιμή in Rom. v. 4, 5 has a kindred, though not identical, meaning, according to SH). The advantage of this rendering is that it gives a straightforward analogy between the probation of character and the refining of metals. The genuine element in their faith is proved by a process similar to that of metal-refining and is found to be something more precious than the precious metals. If, on the other hand, δοκίμιον means an "instrument of testing" as in Plato, *Timaeus*, 65 C, φλέβια, οἱόνπερ δοκιμεῖα τῆς γλώττης τεταμένα, Longinus xxxii. (E. H. B.), γλῶτταν γεύσεως δοκίμιον, Origen, *Exhort. ad Mart.* 6, δοκίμιον καὶ ἐξεταστήριον τῆς πρὸς τὸ θεῖον ἀγάπης [πειρασμός], then the word πολυτιμότερον could only be applied to it by a very circuitous method of reasoning, or, as B. Weiss calls it, "metonymically". The matter is further complicated by the relationship of this passage to Jas. i. 2, 3, and

τιμότερον χρυσίου τοῦ ἀπολλυμένου διὰ πυρὸς δὲ δοκιμαζομένου
εὑρεθῇ εἰς ἔπαινον καὶ δόξαν καὶ τιμὴν ἐν ἀποκαλύψει Ἰησοῦ

their joint or several relationships to O.T. passages, especially Prov. xvii. 3, xxvii. 21, Ps. xii. 6. On the former point cf. *Studia Biblica*, i. p. 137, where J. Wordsworth thinks that in Jas. i. 3 τῆς πίστεως was rightly omitted in the Corbey MS., τὸ δοκίμιον meaning simply *probatio* ; and on the questions of literary criticism involved see Essay II below, pp. 450 ff.

Plato makes deliberate provision in his educational system (*Rep*. 413 D, E, 503 A) for the testing of character by pleasures and pains (ὥσπερ χρυσὸν ἐν πυρὶ βασανιζόμενον) and for the reward of those who pass the test successfully.

πολυτιμότερον] For the scale of values which rates spiritual goods above gold, etc. cf. Ps. cxix. 127, Prov. viii. 11 ; Plato *Rep*. 336 E, δικαιοσύνην . . . πρᾶγμα πολλῶν χρυσίων τιμιώτερον ; Philo, de *Ebr*. 86 [I. 369 M], τὸν γὰρ σοφόν . . . δεῖ τῇ παντὸς τιμιωτέρᾳ χρυσοῦ φρονήσει κεκοσμῆσθαι.

χρυσίου . . . δοκιμαζομένου] In addition to the passages already cited cf. 1 Cor. iii. 13, Rev. iii. 18, Herm. *Vis*. IV. iii. 4.

εὑρεθῇ κτλ.] with πολυτιμ. as its predicate, rather than, as in A.V. and R.V., with the words that follow ; though the phrase εἰς . . . τιμήν is a kind of additional predicate explaining the direction or purpose of the verb. Cf. Moulton, *Grammar*, i. p. 76 n. The usage is not unlike that of λογίζεσθαι εἰς, on which see Blass, *Grammar*, pp. 85 f., and pp. 92 f. For the forward-looking use of εὑρεθῇ cf. 2 Pet. iii. 14.

εἰς ἔπαινον . . . τιμήν] Cf. Phil. i. 11. Primarily the praise, etc. bestowed by God upon man : even δόξα and τιμή, which are essentially divine attributes, can be imparted by God to man, as in Ps. viii. 5. And cf. Mattathias' exhortation to his sons in 1 Macc. ii. 51 ff. to emulate their forefathers and receive δόξαν μεγάλην

καὶ δόξαν αἰώνιον, and his chronicle of past leaders of faith and their rewards, which must have suggested much of Heb. xi. It is to be observed also that human actions which God approves do, in fact, redound to His glory, cf. iv. 11, ii. 9. ἔπαινος is very rare in LXX, but common in classical Greek. Aristotle defines it in *Rhet*. I. ix. 33, as " language exhibiting greatness in the case of virtue ", and claims it for inward principles and dispositions of character rather than isolated acts. It corresponds to ἀρετή (cf. Phil. iv. 8 ; and below, ii. 14). On ἔπαινος Hort aptly quotes Marc. Aur. *Comm*. xii. 11, μὴ ποιεῖν ἄλλο ἢ ὅπερ μέλλει ὁ θεὸς ἐπαινεῖν. We may compare J. S. Mill's well-known judgment that it would not be easy " to find a better translation of the rule of virtue from the abstract into the concrete than to endeavour so to live that Christ would approve our life " (*Three Essays*, p. 254).

ἐν ἀποκαλύψει Ἰησοῦ Χριστοῦ] The reference is to the Day of the Lord, when the Son of Man shall be revealed in power and great glory, as the Judge of quick and dead, cf. Lk. xvii. 30, Matt. xxv. 31-46, and shall award praise and condemnation, life and death, to all according to their works. For St. Peter's eschatology see Introd. pp. 111-15, and Add. Note B, pp. 250 ff. Comparable passages in this Epistle are i. 5, iv. 13, v. 1. For St. Paul cf. 1 Cor. i. 7, 2 Thess. i. 7, the latter being of special importance as Silvanus was part author of that Epistle. It is improbable that he should have used the phrase in different senses in the two Epistles in which he had a hand. In Rom. ii. 5-16 the judicial functions are ascribed not to Christ but to God ; in verse 7 " honour and glory " are mentioned among the ambitions of those whom God rewards, but the ambition is conditioned " by patient continuance in well-doing "

Χριστοῦ· ⁸ὃν οὐκ ἰδόντες ἀγαπᾶτε, εἰς ὃν ἄρτι μὴ ὁρῶντες πιστεύοντες δὲ ἀγαλλιᾶσθε χαρᾷ ἀνεκλαλήτῳ καὶ δεδοξασμένῃ,

(an Aristotelian touch). For the connexion of praise with the joy of Christ's
appearing cf. Matt. xxv. 21, 23.

8. ὃν οὐκ ἰδόντες ἀγαπᾶτε . . . μὴ
ὁρῶντες κτλ.] Moulton, *Grammar*, i.
p. 232, supports Hort (against Blass,
Grammar, p. 256) in regarding the
change in the negative particle as
significant, since none but a slovenly
writer would have made it otherwise.
μή is the usual negative with participles
in Hellenistic Greek (Blass, *op. cit.*
p. 253), so that it is the οὐ which needs
explaining. The simplest reason is
that St. Peter is here stating a past
historical fact, which he wishes to
emphasize. Moreover, the change of
negatives is appropriate, since, while
his readers' experience in past and
present remained the same, his own
changed. They did not see the Lord,
but he did, cf. 1 Jn. i. 3 : now neither
he nor they see Him. Windisch admits that the phrase points to the
author being an eyewitness, but thinks
that this is not so if εἰδότες be read for
ἰδόντες as in several MSS. and Fathers
(though against the best MS. authority).
But I cannot see why.

The N.T. distinguishes four stages
in men's apprehension of Christ. The
first is hope or desire, represented by
our Lord's words about " prophets and
kings " in Lk. x. 23 f., to which we
may add the allusion to angels in
verse 12 below. The second is physical
sight or eyewitness, referred to in the
present verse, with which cf. Acts x. 39.
The third is faith, contrasted with the
last in this passage, and more expressly
in our Lord's words to St. Thomas in
Jn. xx. 29, " Thomas, because thou
hast seen me thou hast believed :
blessed are they that have not seen
(οἱ μὴ ἰδόντες), and yet have believed ".
The fourth is the beatific vision, when
faith passes into a new kind of sight,
of which St. Paul speaks in his hymn
to Charity (1 Cor. xiii. 12) and St.
John in his First Epistle (iii. 2), saying

that " we shall be like him, for we
shall see him as he is ".

The passage may have inspired the
beautiful description of the Christian
confessors as " the followers of the true
Love " in Polycarp, *ad Phil.* i., for he
goes on to quote the verse in an abbreviated form (εἰς ὃν οὐκ ἰδόντες πιστεύετε
χαρᾷ κτλ.). Irenaeus (*adv. Haer.* v.
vii. 2) connects the phrase with 1 Cor.
xiii. 9, 12.

For Jewish teaching cf. Philo, *de
Praem. et Poen.* 27 [II. 412 M], with
its three stages of faith, joy, vision
of reality ; and Drummond, *Philo
Judaeus*, i. p. 26 and ii. p. 321 : also
4 Esdras vii. 98. From a different
angle some words of Napoleon afford
an apt comment : " An extraordinary
power of influencing and commanding
men has been given to Alexander,
Charlemagne, and myself. But with
us the presence has been necessary, the
eye, the voice, the hand. Whereas
Jesus Christ has influenced and commanded His subjects without His
visible bodily presence for eighteen
hundred years " (*Diary of Rev. F.
Kilvert*).

ἀνεκλαλήτῳ] *unspeakable, beyond
words*. Rom. viii. 26 (ἀλαλήτοις) is
often adduced as a parallel. More
germane, perhaps, is Is. lxiv. 4 quoted
in 1 Cor. ii. 9, with the addition of the
words ὅσα ἡτοίμασεν ὁ θεὸς τοῖς ἀγαπῶ-
σιν αὐτόν; which again are echoed in
Jas. i. 12, a passage closely similar in
sense to the one before us. Ignatius
(*Eph.* xix. 2) uses ἀνεκλάλητος of the
star of the Nativity. Philo, *de Virt.*
67 [II. 386 M], has ὑποπλησθεὶς ἀλέκτου
χαρᾶς. Note also Clement of Alexandria's definition of ἀγαλλίασις (*Strom.*
VI. xii. 789 [P]) as " cheerfulness which
arises from the consideration (ἐπιλογι-
σμόν) of true virtue, through a kind
of exhilaration and relaxation of
soul ".

δεδοξασμένῃ] *glorified, endowed with
glory from above*. Cf. 2 Cor. iii. 10,

⁹κομιζόμενοι τὸ τέλος τῆς πίστεως ὑμῶν, σωτηρίαν ψυχῶν.

" that which has been instinct with glory (δεδοξασμένον) has lost its glory ". On δόξα and its compounds in I Peter see Add. Note B, pp. 253-8. δοξάζω in classical Greek usually means " opine " or " reckon ", but sometimes =extol, hold in honour, e.g. Thuc. iii. 45, Polyb. VI. liii. 10; and so often in epitaphs (see MM, sub voc.). Milligan on I Thess. ii. 12 is worth consulting. Both joy and glory are commonly predicated of the Messianic age in Jewish thought (cf. Dalman, The Words of Jesus, E.T. p. 118). If ἀγαλλιᾶσθε (or ἀγαλλιᾶτε) is the true reading here, we may take St. Peter as meaning to emphasize the Messianic character of the Church as an expression of the presence of God's Kingdom. But another interpretation is not to be ruled out, according to which the language should be regarded as that of religious experience rather than of theology. For both joy and glory are common features of the experience of conversion : cf. William James, Varieties of Religious Experience, pp. 248-56, Starbuck, The Psychology of Religion, pp. 118-24. [In the Table on p. 121 of the last-named work, Joy is mentioned as the predominant feeling after conversion in 44 per cent of the cases analysed.] The following two sentences from descriptions of converts are illuminating : " there seemed to be . . . an appearance of divine glory in almost everything " ; and " in an instant the Lord made me so happy that I cannot express what I felt ". Such descriptions are, no doubt, coloured by familiarity with biblical language, but they are not the less spontaneous for that. Inexpressible joy and " glory " belong to the vocabulary of enthusiasm in all languages. If this psychological interpretation be allowed here, whether in place of or in combination with the theological one, the passage would become of importance for our view of the historical situation underlying the

Epistle ; and it has links with the allusion to " new-born babes " in ii. 2. See Introd. pp. 39-42.

9. κομιζόμενοι] winning for yourselves. κομίζεσθαι, middle, is a good classical word meaning " carry off for oneself ", with special reference to what is deserved or earned, e.g. Eur. Hipp. 432 (δόξαν ἐσθλήν), Plato, Rep. 615 B (τὴν ἀξίαν), ib. 621 D (τὰ ἆθλα αὑτῆς), the last passage being in the noble conclusion of the Republic, where Plato is speaking of salvation (cf. ἡμᾶς ἂν σώσειεν [ὁ μῦθος], ἂν πειθώμεθα αὐτῷ, ib. 621 C), and enjoins the pursuit of the upward way, " that we may be loved by one another and by the gods, not only during our stay on earth, but also when, like conquerors in the games collecting the presents of their admirers, we receive (κομιζώμεθα) the prizes of virtue. . . ." St. Paul uses the word in exactly this sense in 2 Cor. v. 10, Eph. vi. 8, Col. iii. 25, and so also St. Peter again in v. 4.

Hort says that the participle here states " an additional concomitant fact " : but there does not seem any adequate reason for excluding (as Hort does) the usual construction, whereby the participle gives the ground for the emotion.

τὸ τέλος τῆς πίστεως ὑμῶν] As Hort says, ὑμῶν is probably a very early interpolation. But the reading is not of great importance either way, since the πίστεως surely takes up the πιστεύοντες of the previous clause. Cf. τὴν πίστιν absolutely in Heb. xiii. 7, where the context supplies the genitive. The meaning is that the Christians by virtue of their faith and love towards Christ win the ineffable joy of personal salvation which is faith's guerdon and goal.

τέλος in N.T. is most commonly used of the temporal end or cessation. But the usage here conforms more closely to that which is normal in classical Greek, where τέλος =the logical end of a process or action, its

¹⁰περὶ ἧς σωτηρίας ἐξεζήτησαν καὶ ἐξηρεύνησαν προφῆται οἱ

issue, consummation, perfection, and thus (in philosophical writings) its ideal or chief good. This classical sense is found in 1 Tim. i. 5 (" the end of the commandment is love " etc.), whence it became one of the axioms of moral theology ; and probably Jas. v. 11 (on which see Mayor's note). Despite the contrary opinion of SH, I am inclined to follow Bengel and add Rom. x. 4 (τέλος γὰρ νόμου Χριστός) to these examples ; cf. Matt. v. 17, and Rom. xiii. 10. For both senses in Hellenistic Greek see MM, *sub voc.*

The doctrine of faith issuing in a salvation realized in part here and now is not uncommon in N.T., cf. Acts xiv. 9, xv. 11 (St. Peter's words ; and see Bengel's note), xvi. 31, Eph. ii. 8, and, generally, passages dealing with justification by faith ; cf. 2 Thess. ii. 13, 2 Tim. iii. 15, Heb. x. 39. At the same time the eschatological use of σωτηρία in verse 5, and the allusion to spiritual growth in ii. 2, suggest that here too there is an eschatological element ; see Add. Note B, pp. 252 f. For the combination cf. L. Andrewes, *Sermons*, ii. p. 201 : " Verily, here must the spirit rise to grace, or else neither the body nor it shall there rise to glory ".

σωτηρίαν ψυχῶν] as e.g. in Matt. xvi. 25 f. St. Peter uses the plural ψυχαί five times, sometimes with special reference to the spiritual side of men's lives (i. 22, ii. 25), sometimes quite broadly as almost=persons, selves (iii. 20, iv. 19), as in Acts xxvii. 10, Jas. i. 21.

St. Peter's thought in this whole passage offers an instructive comparison and contrast with St. Paul's in Gal. iii. 23. His mind is dwelling on a stage further in advance : for St. Paul addressing the Galatians the Jews were " guarded " under a law until faith came, while for St. Peter the Christians are " guarded " through faith until salvation comes.

The above notes are based on the

view that ἀγαλλιᾶσθε in verse 8 is the true reading. For an alternative view see Add. Note C, p. 258.

10-12. περὶ ἧς . . . παρακύψαι] For a full discussion of this difficult passage see Add. Note D, pp. 259 ff. The notes given here are mainly illustrative.

10. ἐξεζήτησαν καὶ ἐξηρεύνησαν] The two compounds occur together in 1 Macc. ix. 26, where the allusion is to the thorough search carried out by Bacchides' police in their efforts to track down the friends of Judas. Both words are common in LXX. ἐκζητεῖν is mainly used in two senses : (1) to " require " or " avenge ", especially with αἷμα, as in Lk. xi. 50, (2) to " seek " in a moral and devotional sense, especially with τὸν κύριον or θεόν, e.g. Deut. iv. 29, and repeatedly in 2 Chronicles and Psalms. The second sense is that implied here. We may illustrate it from Habakkuk ii. 1, ἀποσκοπεύσω τοῦ ἰδεῖν τί λαλήσει ἐν ἐμοί, καὶ τί ἀποκριθῶ ἐπὶ τὸν ἔλεγχόν μου. Cf. also 2 Esdr. iv. 51 f., and for popular surmise as to the time of fulfilment Ezek. xii. 27, 28. ἐξερευνᾶν expresses the " search " for something hidden, whether a person or a hidden truth or meaning, the object being either (1) the person or thing searched for (1 Sam. xxiii. 23, Prov. ii. 4) or (2) the area in which search is made (e.g. the land of Israel, Jud. xvii. 2, the Law, Ps. cxix. 69). Both ideas are relevant here, since prophets searched for light on God's gracious purpose and His time for its accomplishment, and the Christian prophets had the O.T. writings before them as the place to look for it. Cf. Josephus' use of ἀνακρίνειν in *Ant.* IV. vi. 2, for Balaam's enquiry of God's will. We might say that the process indicated here is one of intense search for an object or truth known to be discoverable, ἐκζητεῖν referring especially to its mystical side (cf. Heb. xi. 6, xii. 17, and the quotation of Amos ix. 12

περὶ τῆς εἰς ὑμᾶς χάριτος προφητεύσαντες, ¹¹ἐρευνῶντες εἰς τίνα

(LXX) in Acts xv. 17), ἐξερευνᾶν to its literary and theological side. The double process was preliminary to the utterance (προφητεύσαντες). ἐξερεύνησαν is spelt as in Souter's text; but Bigg and MM support WH's preference for ἐραυνάω.

προφῆται] In view of the author's apparent casualness about articles, the absence of the article here need not in itself excite comment. But the context gives it some significance. " Prophets who prophesied about the grace now shewn to you " is a phrase with a wider reference than to the O.T. prophets only, and embraces the whole prophetic tradition, including the Christian prophets. Interest in the time of fulfilment was a feature of apocalyptic, as the Book of Daniel shews. But the word ἐξηρεύνησαν suggests that it was the Christian prophets who were especially in our author's mind, since this activity does not correspond to what we are told in O.T. of the prophets nor to what Jewish thought ascribed to them. Cf. Philo, de Vit. Mos. ii. 1 [II. 135 M], where Moses is said to combine the gifts of philosopher and king, desired by Plato, with those of priest and prophet; and Quis Rer. Div. Her. 52-3 [I. 510-11 M], where Num. xii. 6, 8 and Deut. xxxiv. 6 are quoted to shew that the prophet receives the divine disclosures in a state of " ecstasy ", his reason being superseded as the divine afflatus seizes him. Cf. also de Praem. et Poen. 9 [II. 417 M]. Drummond's statement (Philo Judaeus, ii. p. 282) should be consulted. In the case of the Christian prophets, on the other hand, for whom the " searching " of the Scriptures (cf. Jn. v. 39) was an important part of their task, the reasoning powers must have been brought fully into play.

τῆς εἰς ὑμᾶς χάριτος] For the construction cf. 1 Cor. xv. 10, ἡ χάρις αὐτοῦ ἡ εἰς ἐμέ. Hort cites Acts xi. 23 and refers the phrase primarily to the grace shewn in the admission of the Gentiles to the Christian Church. And cf. J. Armitage Robinson, Ephesians, Add. Note on χάρις and χαριτοῦν; and Moffatt, Grace in N.T. p. 323. But should we not rather extend the reference to embrace the whole outpouring of grace which followed from this and issued in the " flowing tide " of spiritual life and expansion which clearly underlies St. Paul's Ephesians ? For χάρις as the central theme of the Gospel see Lightfoot's note on Col. i. 6. Among O.T. prophecies on the theme we may cite Is. xl., lv., Joel ii., Hab. ii. 14. We have a glimpse of the work of the Christian prophets in relation to the spread of the Gospel in Acts xiii. 1-3 ; and cf. Eph. ii. 20, iii. 5 f., Lk. ii. 32.

11. ἐρευνῶντες] For the omission of the preposition in the case of a second verb, where the same sense is intended, cf. Eur. Bacch. 1065, κατῆγεν, ἦγεν, ἦγεν . . . ; and in N.T. Rev. x. 10, κατέφαγον . . . ἔφαγον.

A good example of the searching of prophecy to discover an answer to a question is to be found in Acts xvii. 11. The decisive guidance of prophecy is exemplified by St. James' words in Acts xv. 15 f., and its evidential value by St. Paul's sermons alluded to in Acts xvii. 2 f. Cf. also Justin, Apology, i. 34 (75 D). Justin's theme in these chapters (32 ff.) is that (1) the events of Christ's life had been prophesied, (2) by consulting the prophecies the Romans can find the true doctrine about Christ and the nature of His authority and kingdom. The word is used in Rom. viii. 27 of God who " searcheth the hearts " (cf. Rev. ii 23), and of searching the scriptures in Jn. v. 39.

εἰς τίνα ἢ ποῖον καιρὸν] While the seeking and searching of the previous verse refer to the promised salvation generally, this question of the time of its fulfilment was that which was of special interest to St. Peter's contem-

ἢ ποῖον καιρὸν ἐδήλου τὸ ἐν αὐτοῖς Πνεῦμα Χριστοῦ, προμαρ-

poraries, whether prophets or hearers; just as the grace which his readers had lately received was the point in the prophecies of the past and present which concerned them most nearly. The question of when (τίνα) and in what circumstances (ποῖον) salvation should come arose in our Lord's life-time (Lk. xvii. 20, 21), and was pressed by the disciples after His resurrection (Acts i. 6, 7).

In LXX, as in classical Greek, καιρός means a period of time charac-terized by some feature either stated or implied in the context, i.e. "time charged with opportunity" (E. H. B.). Outstanding passages referring to the salvation of the Messianic age are Is. xlix. 8 ff., lx. 22, Jer. iii. 17, Dan. vii. 22, ix. 26, 27, Zeph. iii. 16-20 (four times). It is used also of God's visita-tions in judgment, Jer. vi. 15, x. 15, xxviii. 18, l. 27, 31, Ezek. vii. 7, 12. In Dan. xii. 1 καιρός refers to the Mes-sianic Woes which precede the End, which is also spoken of as a καιρός (ib. 4, 9). Passages like Zeph. iii. 16-20, with its allusions to "that time" were bound to raise the question, "What time?"; and Ezek. xii. 27, Dan. ix. 1, 2, shew how the question of the time of fulfilment was canvassed by those who heard the prophetic utterances. Cf. also 4 Esdras ix. 1-9, though unfortunately the Greek is missing. Distinct "seasons" are re-cognized in N.T. as referred to in prophecy, cf. Acts (i. 7) iii. 19, 21 (St. Peter's words). Of special import-ance for our present purpose is Heb. ix. 6-10, where the argument turns on the distinction between "the time then present" (τὸν καιρὸν τὸν ἐνεστηκότα), of which the Holy Place was repre-sentative and to which its ordinances were appropriate, and "the time of reformation" (καιροῦ διορθώσεως), i.e. the Christian order, indirectly pre-figured by the Holy of Holies and its ritual. Moses was reckoned as a prophet, indeed the greatest of them

(Lk. xvi. 29, xxiv. 27, Jn. v. 45, 46, Acts iii. 22, cf. Acts xxvi. 22), and the writer of Hebrews here answered the question, ποῖος καιρός, when asked about the Temple ordinances, by saying that they referred prophetically to the priestly work of the ascended Christ.

ἐδήλου] The word is used in a similar sense of what the Holy Spirit was "indicating" or "pointing to" in some ordinance or utterance of O.T. prophecy in Heb. ix. 8 (the passage cited above), xii. 27. But I cannot find any example in classical Greek or LXX of δηλοῦν εἰς, though the phrase is not ill-found.

τὸ ἐν αὐτοῖς Πνεῦμα Χριστοῦ] It was a commonplace of Jewish teaching that prophets spoke under the inspira-tion of God's Spirit (2 Sam. xxiii. 2, Is. lxi. 1); and this doctrine was taken over by the Christian Church, cf. 2 Pet. i. 21, "prophecy came not in old time by the will of man: but holy men of God spake as they were moved by the Holy Ghost". Cf. also Ign. Magn. viii. (on which Lightfoot observes that in 1 Pet. i. 10 f. "there are several ideas in common with it"), οἱ γὰρ θειότατοι προφῆται κατὰ Χριστὸν Ἰη-σοῦν ἔζησαν. διὰ τοῦτο καὶ ἐδιώχθησαν, ἐμπνεόμενοι ὑπὸ τῆς χάριτος [αὐτοῦ], Magn. ix., Justin, Apol. i. 32 ff.; Iren. adv. Haer. IV. xxxiii. 9. Various words were used to describe the in-spiration, e.g. ἐμπνεόμενοι, θεοφορού-μενοι.

For the pronoun αὐτοῖς referring to the subject of the main verb, where the reflexive would be more usual in classical Greek, see Lightfoot's note on Col. iii. 21, and Hort, N.T. in the Original Greek, Appendix p. 144. The usage is further justified here, where the allusion is to prophetic circles and a prophetic tradition rather than to specific individuals.

The phrase "the Spirit of Christ" occurs in only one other N.T. passage (Rom. viii. 9); but cf. also Phil. i. 19,

τυρόμενον τὰ εἰς Χριστὸν παθήματα καὶ τὰς μετὰ ταῦτα δόξας.

Acts xvi. 7, and Gal. iv. 6, which are similar. In connexion with the inspiration of Christian prophets its use is natural enough, and is implied in such passages as Jn. iii. 34, 1 Cor. xii., and Eph. iv.; with which compare Ign. *Magn.* viii. and *Ep. Barn.* v. cited above. As applied to the O.T. prophets, it should either be rendered " the Messiah-Spirit ", or else regarded as a deduction from the revelation of the identity of the " Holy Spirit " active in the Church with " the Spirit of God " alluded to in O.T. ; an identity affirmed in e.g. Heb. iii. 7, ix. 8, x. 15, 2 Pet. i. 21. For a similar " proleptic " phrase cf. Heb. xi. 26, where Moses is said to have esteemed τὸν ὀνειδισμὸν τοῦ Χριστοῦ more highly than the treasure of Egypt. Much has been made of it as implying the doctrine of the pre-existence of Christ,[1] and even Windisch adopts this view. That doctrine would not be foreign to the mind of the writer of 1 Pet. i. 20 : but if any development of doctrine is to be discerned here, it belongs to the doctrine of the Spirit rather than to Christology.

προμαρτυρόμενον] not in classical Greek nor LXX, and ἅπαξ λεγόμενον here in N.T. The simple μαρτύρομαι is used in Plato, *Phileb.* 47 c, of a solemn declaration, as in the sight of God or man, the thing declared (as here) being the object and in the accusative. St. Paul uses it in Acts xx. 26 and xxvi. 22, the latter passage referring to the fulfilment of prophecy. The προ- in such compounds may mean " beforehand " or " publicly ", " forth ", cf. Lightfoot on Gal. iii. 1 (προεγράφη), where it has the latter signification. The former is illustrated in Melito, p. 9, ll. 35 ff. (*S.D.* xii. 125), οὕτως δὴ καὶ τὸ | τοῦ κυρίου πάθος ἐκ μακροῦ προδηλωθὲν | διά τε τύπον ὁραθὲν σήμερον οὕ|τως τυγχάνει τετελεσμένον.

τὰ εἰς Χριστὸν παθήματα] the suffer-

ings of the Christward road. The primary meaning of εἰς is " direction towards ", after a word expressing or implying motion, cf. Col. ii. 22 (εἰς φθοράν), Philem. 6 (εἰς Χριστόν). From this it is a short step to the meaning of purpose, after any noun or verb, cf. εἰς αὐτόν in Rom. xi. 36, 1 Cor. viii. 6, Col. i. 16, 20. The sense of the passage may be illustrated by St. Paul's words to the Ephesian elders at Miletus (Acts xx. 22 f.), when he spoke of not knowing what would befall him, πλὴν ὅτι τὸ πνεῦμα τὸ ἅγιον κατὰ πόλιν διαμαρτύρεταί μοι λέγον ὅτι δεσμά με καὶ θλίψεις μένουσιν. Such a statement was itself a προμαρτυρία, given by Christian prophets. Cf. also 2 Tim. i. 8, συγκακοπάθησον τῷ εὐαγγελίῳ κατὰ δύναμιν θεοῦ κτλ.; Melito, p. 10, ll. 32-34, (*Studies and Documents.* xii. 129), πολλὰ μὲν οὖν καὶ ἕτερα | ὑπὸ πολλῶν προφητῶν ἐκηρύχθη εἰς | τὸ τοῦ πάσχα μυστήριον, ὅ ἐστιν Χριστός . . .; and Origen, *Exhort. ad Mart.* 42, οἱ κοινωνοὶ τῶν παθημάτων, κατὰ τὴν ἀναλογίαν τῶν παθημάτων ὧν εἰσι κοινωνοὶ πρὸς Χριστόν, κοινωνοὶ ἔσονται καὶ τῆς παρακλήσεως.

The inevitability of these sufferings and their place in the eschatological pattern were clearly taught by our Lord, cf. Matt. x. 17-25, xxiv. 7-12, Mk. xiii. 9, Lk. xii. 11, 12, xxi. 23 f. They were part of the Messianic Woes, which included also war, apostasy, false teaching, widespread affliction, and natural disorders, cf. Mk. xiii., Lk. xxi., 2 Thess. ii. 3-12, 2 Tim. iii. 1, and which had been expressly foretold in such prophecies as Zech. xi.–xiv., and formed a regular feature of Jewish apocalyptic teaching. (For a fuller discussion and references see below, Add. Note J, pp. 300-03. The inclusion of persecution among the Messianic Woes was possibly due to our Lord Himself.)

Hort observes that the word " suffer "

---

[1] For a thorough application of this doctrine to O.T. history cf. Melito, *Homily on the Passion*, pp. 13, 14 (*Studies and Documents*, xii. pp. 143-51). The O.T. miracles are regarded as Christ's no less than those of the Gospels.

¹²οῖς ἀπεκαλύφθη ὅτι οὐχ ἑαυτοῖς ὑμῖν δὲ διηκόνουν αὐτά, ἃ νῦν
ἀνηγγέλη ὑμῖν διὰ τῶν εὐαγγελισαμένων ὑμᾶς ἐν Πνεύματι Ἁγίῳ

or "suffering" occurs no less than
eight times in 1 Peter with respect to
Christ, whereas in all St. Paul's
Epistles it occurs only twice and then
with reference to the participation of
Christians in Christ's sufferings. It is
used in 1 Peter of the sufferings of
Christians also eight times, exclusive
of this passage.

δόξας] *triumphs*. The plural is ἅπαξ
λεγόμενον in N.T. in this sense: in
Jude 8, 2 Pet. ii. 10 the meaning is
different. But in LXX we have Ex.
xxxiii. 5, where God bids the Israelites
ἀφέλεσθε τὰς στολὰς τῶν δοξῶν ὑμῶν,
i.e. "of your triumphs", and Ex.
xv. 11 (Song of Moses), δεδοξα-
σμένος ἐν ἁγίοις, θαυμαστὸς ἐν δόξαις,
ποιῶν τέρατα, where δόξαις = " glorious
deeds ", " triumphs ", especially the
conquest of Pharaoh. (See Add. Note
B on δόξα and its cognates, pp. 253 ff.).
Had the allusion been to Christ's
resurrection and ascension, the singular δόξαν would have been almost
certainly used, as in verse 21 below.
As it is, the phrase finds its best commentary in Rom. viii. 18-39.

12. οἷς ἀπεκαλύφθη κτλ.] ἀποκαλύπτειν followed by ὅτι does not appear
to occur in classical Greek, LXX, or
elsewhere in N.T. But this fact
scarcely lends support to the rendering
of ὅτι by " because " (E. C. Selwyn,
St. Luke the Prophet, p. 119). The
dependent clause gives the content of
the mystery now revealed, and it is
good Greek.

οὐχ ἑαυτοῖς ὑμῖν δὲ] The dative is
perhaps, as Hort says, " for " rather
than " to ", since a διάκονος is one
who serves a primary giver — in this
case, God — rather than the recipient
of the gift. The distinction between
the plain and immediate meaning and
the hidden and more distant meaning
of a prophecy is often alluded to, and
became in later ages the theme of the
system of Antiochene exegesis known
as θεωρία (cf. article by A. Vaccari, in

Biblica, Jan. 1920). In O.T. we have
Hab. ii. 1-3, though here the oracle's
immediate meaning is lost in the truth
which would ultimately appear; from
the Pseudepigrapha, *Enoch* i. 3 and
4 *Esdras* iv. 33 ff. offer examples; and
in N.T. we have Acts ii. 25-36 (especially verse 34), xiii. 24-6, Rom. iv. 23,
24 (and cf. xv. 4, xvi. 26), 1 Cor. ix. 9,
10, x. 11 (and cf. *ib.* xiv. 4). Justin,
Apol. i. 35 (76 B) is also relevant. St.
Paul nowhere speaks more in the vein
of a Christian prophet than in Acts
xiii. 26 ff. So, indeed, did John the
Baptist in his recognition of the Lamb
of God, in Jn. i. 29.

διηκόνουν αὐτά] Rendel Harris'
emendation διενοοῦντο is ingenious,
and is adopted by Moffatt (*The Moffatt
N.T.* p. 344), who translates, " to
them it was revealed that they got this
intelligence not for themselves⸱", etc.
R. Harris quotes *Enoch* i. 2, οὐκ εἰς
τὴν νῦν γενεὰν διενοούμην ἀλλ' ἐπὶ
πόρρω οὖσαν ἐγὼ λαλῶ. But it is not
required by any intrinsic difficulty in
the words; for διακονεῖν is used in
similar senses elsewhere, e.g. iv. 10
below, 2 Cor. iii. 3, viii. 19, 20. For
αὐτά, " their findings ", " the results of
their search ", cf. iv. 10 (αὐτό), and
Hab. ii. 2 (LXX), Γράψον ὅρασιν καὶ
σαφῶς εἰς πυξίον, ὅπως διώκῃ ὁ ἀνα-
γινώσκων αὐτά — a close parallel. The
meaning is determined by the context.

ἃ κτλ.] the " findings " alluded to
in αὐτά, which is the antecedent to this
relative. νῦν: as Perdelwitz observes
(pp. 18, 19), this " now " runs " like a
scarlet thread " through the Epistle.
For a discussion of the circumstances
denoted by it see Introd. pp. 41-2.

ἀνηγγέλη] The primary meaning of
ἀναγγέλλειν in LXX is " to tell ", as
when one man " tells " another what
has happened. In the Psalms and the
prophetic literature it is often used for
" tell openly, declare, proclaim " (cf.
Ps. xix. 1, Is. xlviii. 3, 5), especially
when some solemn declaration is

138   FIRST EPISTLE OF ST. PETER   [I. 12

ἀποσταλέντι ἀπ' οὐρανοῦ· εἰς ἃ ἐπιθυμοῦσιν ἄγγελοι παρακύψαι.

denoted. There are also about fifty places where the preposition in the compound verb seems to express the idea of bringing *back* information that has been asked for; and the number is increased, if we include those passages where a prophet " reports " what he has seen or heard by divine inspiration. This idea of bringing news *back* from an authoritative source underlies many passages where the word occurs both in N.T. and in classical Greek, and seems more characteristic than the note of " telling in successive particulars " which Hort finds in the compound. Thus we have Acts xiv. 27, xv. 4, xix. 18, 2 Cor. vii. 7, 1 Jn. i. 5, and even (I think) Jn. xvi. 13, 14, 15; and in classical writers we may note Aesch. *P.V.* 661 (from an oracle), Eurip. *I.T.* 761 (implying that the friends have been sent to enquire), Thuc. iv. 122 (cf. Classen *in loc.*), Polyb. 1. lxvii. 11. [A very good example. Anno wished to make a communication to his large polyglot army : he decided eventually to do it through the generals, " some of whom did not catch what was said, while in other cases, though they expressed agreement, they sometimes *gave out* (ἀναγγέλλειν) to the multitudes the opposite of what the general said, either through ignorance or through malice ". Naturally the result was that ἦν ἀσαφείας, ἀπιστίας, ἀμιξίας ἅπαντα πλήρη.]

LXX usage forbids us to say that the reference to an authority behind the ἄγγελος or announcer of the news is always implied in the verb ; but it is very often present. It would be fair to say that while a newspaper correspondent ἀπαγγέλλει, a B.B.C. announcer ἀναγγέλλει.

εὐαγγελισαμένων ὑμᾶς] This construction is not found in LXX, where the accusative after εὐαγγελίζεσθαι always denotes the content of the preaching, the recipients of it being put in the dative. So, too, usually in

N.T. But Acts viii. 25 and Gal. i. 9 shew parallels to the construction here. St. Peter is elastic in his usage, cf. i. 25 and iv. 6 below. For the " preachers " alluded to, and the content of their message, cf. Introd. pp. 18 ff., 45 f.

ἐν Πνεύματι κτλ.] On ἐν see note on i. 2. Eph. iii. 5 affords a close parallel to this passage : cf. also Eph. ii. 22, v. 18, vi. 18 and Armitage Robinson's note on the last-named. The statement that the Holy Spirit was " sent down from heaven " is especially in point if a well-known occasion or period of religious expansion or revival was referred to.

εἰς ἃ κτλ.] The sentence means that the circumstances of the Church and the progress of its redemptive work are such as excite the rapt attention of the angels. The source of the idea is probably the *verbum Christi* in Lk. xv. 10, " I say unto you, there is joy in the presence of the angels of God over one sinner that repenteth " — a word that might quickly have been adapted to baptismal use. See Add. Note D, pp. 267 f.

Windisch cites passages from O.T., N.T., and Philo to illustrate the normal Jewish view of angels as knowing, and even mediating, God's revelations to men ; but says that here we have to do with God's refusal of such knowledge, as in *Enoch* xvi. 3, *Slav. Enoch* xxiv. 3, Mk. xiii. 32, 1 Cor. ii. 6, Ign. *Eph.* xix. So too Bennett in *Century Bible*. But whenever in N.T. ἐπιθυμεῖν signifies an unfulfilled desire, the absence of fulfilment is either stated or directly implied in the context, the verb in such cases often being put in the past tense (as in Lk. xxii. 15); and there is no such suggestion here. Classical usage is the same. Moreover, this distinction is irrelevant : we have not to do here with the angels' knowledge or lack of it, but with their intense interest in something occurring on earth. And this cannot be a past

¹³Διὸ ἀναζωσάμενοι τὰς ὀσφύας τῆς διανοίας ὑμῶν, νήφοντες,

occurrence, but something contemporary or future.

παρακύψαι] to stoop down to look. For this, which is the primary meaning of παρακύπτειν, cf. Theocr. iii. 7, Lucian, Pisc. 30. It is used of the disciples stooping to peer into the sepulchre (Lk. xxiv. 12, Jn. xx. 5), and Mary Magdalene (Jn. xx. 11). And so metaphorically in Jas. i. 25. It is used of the angels in Enoch ix. 1 (παρέκυψαν ἐπὶ γῆν ἐκ τῶν ἁγίων τοῦ οὐρανοῦ). B. Weiss (Manual, i. p. 355) quotes Eph. iii. 10 to illustrate "the contemplative share of angels in the work of redemption". Cf. Moffatt, Introduction, p. 382, n. Charles Wesley's words give a true interpretation :

Angels in fix'd amazement
Around our altars hover,
  With eager gaze
  Adore the grace
Of our Eternal Lover.

But those who believe the Epistle to have baptismal associations might fairly adduce this passage as the earliest expression of the belief, found later in the Church, that the angels took an attentive interest in baptisms, and might say that "fonts" would be a better illustration than Wesley's "altars". Thus, Cyril of Jerusalem, Cat. i. 3, speaks of the gift of baptism as "the wondrous, saving seal, which demons tremble at and angels recognize"; and St. Ephraim's "Hymn of the Baptized" (fourth century) contains the verse, "Watchers and Angels, joy over the repentant : they shall joy over you, my brethren, that unto them ye are made like". The mediaeval artists, e.g. Raphael, Botticelli, Titian, and perhaps most of all Benozzo Gozzoli in his "Paradise", seem to have known intuitively what the words meant, and often portrayed it. The Vulgate translates by prospicere = "see from afar", as in Seneca, (infanti) nihil amplius contingit quam prospicere vitam. But it is not a good translation of the Greek. The

passage is carelessly quoted by Hippolytus, 120 (Lagarde, 1858).

13-25. First Ethical Section.

Having laid bare the theological basis of the life of the Christian communities addressed and set it in relation to the realities opened up by the Gospel, the author proceeds to exhort his readers to holiness, reverence, and mutual charity. Each of these also has a doctrinal motive ; holiness in the character of God who has called them (a traditional Jewish injunction), reverence in the costliness of their redemption, and charity in the transcendent nature of their regeneration. But the emphasis throughout the passage is on the ethical demands which follow from the Christian faith.

13. Διό] the usual particle when an author passes from statement to inference.

ἀναζωσάμενοι] here only in N.T., and only rarely in sub-classical Greek. But cf. Lk. xii. 35, ἔστωσαν ὑμῶν αἱ ὀσφύες περιεζωσμέναι, καὶ οἱ λύχνοι καιόμενοι ; Eph. vi. 14, στῆτε οὖν περιζωσάμενοι τὴν ὀσφὺν ὑμῶν ἐν ἀληθείᾳ. Bishop Creighton (The Mind of St. Peter, pp. 13 f.), who connects the phrase with the Lucan logion, justly observes that the compound ἀναζ. expresses not the safety (περιζ.) but the activity of the Christian mind, and the concentration of energy needed for power ; and he considers that the λύχνοι καιόμενοι are represented by νήφοντες, which denotes restraint and wisdom in the use of power. For the metaphor cf. Seneca, ad Polyb. 11, in procinctu stet animus. The English phrase "pull yourselves together" would express the meaning. The phrase ἀναζ. τὰς ὀσφύας is quoted in conjunction with Ps. ii. 11 by Polycarp (ad Phil. ii. 1), who also quotes part of 1 Pet. i. 21. The quotation of Ps. ii. 11 was probably suggested by ἐν φόβῳ in 1 Pet. i. 17, which St. Peter himself may have derived from the Psalm.

τελείως ἐλπίσατε ἐπὶ τὴν φερομένην ὑμῖν χάριν ἐν ἀποκαλύψει
Ἰησοῦ Χριστοῦ, ¹⁴ὡς τέκνα ὑπακοῆς μὴ συσχηματιζόμενοι ταῖς

νήφοντες] *keeping sober.* νήφειν denotes abstinence from wine, as νηστεύειν from food, cf. Soph. *O.C.* 100, νήφων ἀοίνοις. The word is common in Plato, when it is usually contrasted with μεθύειν, as in *Laws*, i. 640 D; and cf. Arist. *Metaphys.* I. iii. 16, ['Αναξαγόρας] οἷον νήφων ἐφάνη παρ' εἰκῇ λέγοντας. Hence it comes to mean sobriety generally in conduct, speech, and judgment, cf. Plut. ii. 800 B, νήφων καὶ πεφροντικώς. "Be sober" (A.V.) or "Live soberly" is therefore the best translation : Moffatt's "Keep cool" is too narrow, for actual intemperance (cf. iv. 3, οἰνοφλυγίαι, κῶμοι, πότοι) was a pressing temptation in pagan surroundings, and is here, no doubt, present to the author's mind. At the same time, the possibility should not be forgotten that νήφοντες may be a marginal gloss on the preceding phrase which has erroneously crept into the text (cf. Milligan, *The Epistles to the Thessalonians*, pp. 126, 127).

τελείως] *unreservedly.* Hort takes this with νήφοντες, "with a perfect sobriety", extending to all their thoughts and ways. But it is unusual for an adverb to follow the verb which it qualifies (cf. Blass, *Grammar of N.T. Greek*, p. 289) ; and a better sense is given if τελείως is taken with ἐλπίσατε.

ἐλπίσατε ἐπὶ] *set your hope upon.* This is one of many aorist imperatives in 1 Peter, cf. i. 17, 22, ii. 2, 17, iv. 1, v. 2. It may be little more than a trait of individual style ; for, " in general, the aorist imperative is considered more forcible and urgent than the present" (Winer, *Grammar of N.T. Greek*, p. 395). With such an urgent injunction τελείως, "up to the hilt", "without reserve" is fully in keeping : cf. Judith xi. 6, τελείως πρᾶγμα ποιήσει μετὰ σοῦ ὁ θεός. For ἐλπίζω with a preposition cf. Jn. v. 45 (εἰς), Rom. xv. 12 (ἐπί with dative) ; Ps. xxxvii. 3, ἔλπισον ἐπὶ κύριον, and

Ep. Barn. vi. 9, ἐλπίσατε ἐπὶ τὸν ἐν σαρκὶ μέλλοντα φανεροῦσθαι ὑμῖν Ἰησοῦν. The construction is common in LXX. For an example of the place of hope in contemporary Jewish thought the fine passage in Philo, *de Praem. et Poen.* 10-14 [II. 410 M] should be consulted.

τὴν . . . Ἰησοῦ Χριστοῦ] χάριν φέρειν τινί, to confer a kindness or boon on anyone, is a phrase common in Attic Greek, and must control the meaning of this passage, indicating it to be " the blessing that is being conferred on you in the Lord's appearing". [The equivalent phrase in LXX, fairly common in Psalms and Ecclesiasticus (two favourite books with our author), is χάριν διδόναι.] The only difficulty in the phrase is the use of the present, and not the future, participle. But (1) the future, οἰσθησομένην, is so cumbrous that a periphrasis would have been almost necessary, (2) the present is in keeping with the thought of our author who regards the object of hope as already virtually possessed ; cf. i. 3, 4 ; iv. 7 (ἤγγικε). The Church in this Epistle " lives by a hope which bears within itself the power and certainty of its realization " (Hofmann). For the connexion of grace with the Lord's advent cf. *Did.* x. 6, ἐλθέτω χάρις καὶ παρελθέτω ὁ κόσμος οὗτος.

14. ὡς τέκνα ὑπακοῆς] The phrase is Hebraic in character, though rare in LXX ; cf. Hos. x. 9, Is. lvii. 4, τέκνα ἀπωλείας (cf. 2 Thess. ii. 3), 1 Macc. ii. 47, τοὺς υἱοὺς τῆς ὑπερηφανίας, *Enoch* xci. 3, xciii. 2, cv. 2, "children of righteousness". For its use by our Lord cf. Lk. xvi. 8, Jn. xii. 36, "children of light", a phrase reproduced in 1 Thess. v. 5, Eph. v. 8. Matt. xi. 19, " Wisdom is justified of all her children", is also relevant. Commenting on οἱ υἱοὶ τῆς βασιλείας in Matt. viii. 12, xiii. 38, Dalman points out that the word " sons (or children) of " may have two meanings : (1) "heirs to",

πρότερον ἐν τῇ ἀγνοίᾳ ὑμῶν ἐπιθυμίαις· ¹⁵ἀλλὰ κατὰ τὸν καλέ-

and therefore having a right to the possession of, something; (2) of like nature with, deriving their character from. As Alford says (on Eph. ii. 3), "That of which they are sons is the source and spring of their lives, not merely an accidental quality belonging to them".

The mention of obedience here as determining the quality of the Christian life is in keeping with the note of dependence upon God, and with the subordinationist character of the ethical teaching, which run through the Epistle. St. Paul speaks of the mystery of the Gospel being opened to all the Gentiles for the purpose of their obedience (εἰς ὑπακοὴν πίστεως). For the Jew the first duty of man had always been to keep God's commandments and to do His will (cf. Lev. xviii. 4, 5); and it receives re-statement, and in no sense reversal, on Christ's lips in the Sermon on the Mount. Montaigne writes as a good Christian moralist, when he says (II. xii.) : "To obey is the proper office of a rational soul". Cf. Introd. pp 66, 84 ff. and Essay II, pp. 389 ff.

συσχηματιζόμενοι] following the capricious guidance of (Lightfoot). For σχῆμα as denoting something changeable, fleeting, and unstable, cf. Lightfoot's note in his Philippians, pp. 127 ff. The word also occurs in Rom. xii. 2, and may have belonged to a primitive baptismal form : cf. Essay II, p. 404. With the negative command here preceding the positive cf. i. 18, 23, iii. 3. For the probability that this " is a common catechetical opening, based on Lev. xviii. 1-5, 24-30", see Carrington, The Primitive Christian Catechism, p. 16. Whether συσχηματιζόμενοι here and ἔχοντες in ii. 12 are examples of the imperatival participle it is not easy to say, but the context makes it not unlikely : cf. Moulton, Grammar, i. p. 181, and Dr. Daube's Appended Note below, p. 487.

ταῖς . . . ἐπιθυμίαις] The combination of "lusts" with "ignorance" seems to indicate Gentile readers, but cf. Introd. pp. 43-4. For ignorance as marking the heathen world cf. Acts xvii. 30 (St. Paul at Athens), and Eph. iv. 18, where its ματαιότης is also mentioned, as below, verse 18. The picture given is of a society where men are without knowledge of God (ἄγνοια), without objective moral standards (ἐπιθυμίαι), and without any plan or purpose which they expect to be able to fulfil (ματαιότης). Out of a life so characterized Christians have now been called.

15, 16. ἀλλὰ . . . ἅγιοι] On this use of κατά see note on iv. 6 : the construction is well paraphrased in E.V. For the place of this fundamental principle of the Jewish Law of Holiness (Lev. xvii.–xxvii., especially xix. 2) in Jewish education see Bishop Carrington, op. cit. pp. 16-21. We may also note that the command to " be holy unto your God " (Num. xv. 40) was part of the central core of the Jewish liturgy known as the Shema. The injunction here anticipates the ethical teaching of the Epistle, and controls it, as the original utterance in the Law of Holiness controls that (cf. Lev. xix. 2, xx. 7, 26). And so Clement of Rome seems to have understood it; for in his Epistle, ch. xxx., he begins with the same principle, " Seeing then that we are the special portion of a Holy God, let us do all things that pertain unto holiness ", and expands it with prohibitions (καταλαλιάς, μέθας τε καὶ . . . ἐπιθυμίας), injunctions (ὁμόνοιαν, ταπεινοφρονοῦντες), and the citation of Prov. iii. 34 found also in 1 Pet. v. 5 and Jas. iv. 6, which suggest that he had in mind our Epistle or some source behind it. It is instructive to compare the biblical doctrine with Plato's. In the great passage in Theaetetus, 176 B, Plato says of " assimilation to God " that it is δίκαιον καὶ ὅσιον μετὰ φρονήσεως

σαντα ὑμᾶς ἅγιον καὶ αὐτοὶ ἅγιοι ἐν πάσῃ ἀναστροφῇ γενήθητε·
¹⁶διότι γέγραπται, Ἅγιοι ἔσεσθε, ὅτι ἐγὼ ἅγιος. ¹⁷καὶ εἰ πατέρα

γενέσθαι. But he shews his difference from the Hebraic and Christian teaching in describing this as a " flight " from mortal nature. For the Apostle, on the other hand, it means the transformation of human nature through the acceptance of the cross. Escapism is foreign to the ethical teaching of N.T.

ἀναστροφῇ] *behaviour, conduct*: cf. Tob. iv. 14 (a stock passage in Jewish catechetical teaching), 2 Macc. vi. 23; and in N.T. Gal. i. 13, Jas. iii. 13, and frequently in this Epistle. Mayor, on Jas. iii. 13, quotes Polyb. IV. lxxxii. 1 and Epict. *Diss*. i. 22. 13; and cf. Deissmann (*Bible Studies*, pp. 88, 194), who shews that the ethical use of the word was common both before and after the probable date of 1 Peter. The verb corresponding to it in N.T. is ἀναστρέφεσθαι, or περιπατεῖν (St. Paul and St. John), or πορεύεσθαι (Luke, Acts, 1 and 2 Peter, Jude); a Hebraic metaphor exemplified in *halakhah* ("walking"), the name given to the legal and preceptual part of Jewish oral tradition.

17-21. The first mark of conformity to the holiness of God in believers will be their godly fear (verse 17, ἐν φόβῳ); and it rests upon the revelation of God's Fatherhood revealed in Christ.

17. πατέρα ἐπικαλεῖσθε] *invoke, pray to, as Father*. ἐπικαλοῦμαι has two meanings in N.T.: (1) " call ", " surname ", e.g. Acts x. 18, Σίμων ὁ ἐπικαλούμενος Πέτρος, (2) " invoke ", " appeal to ", e.g. Acts xxv. 11 ff. (I appeal unto Caesar), 1 Cor. i. 2, τοῖς ἐπικαλουμένοις τὸ ὄνομα τοῦ Κυρίου, and more simply " pray to ", Acts vii. 59, Rom. x. 12, 2 Tim. ii. 22. This second use is common in LXX and in the papyri.

Hort and Windisch emphasize the O.T. character of the passage, quoting Ps. lxxxix. 26, Jer. iii. 19 (and cf. Is. lxiii. 16), though Kohler, *op. cit.*

p. 258, says that the doctrine of God's Fatherhood only occurs seven times in O.T.; and both reckon that the weight of the protasis lies not on the thought of God's Fatherhood but on His impartial judgment. Hort says that πατέρα ἐπικαλεῖσθε may be taken together, " as only a more precise ἐπικαλεῖσθε ". But this is surely to miss the very emphatic place given to πατέρα: the sense cannot be, " if the Father you invoke is the impartial Judge of every man's work ", but conversely " if you invoke the impartial Judge as Father ". A question arises, however, as to the meaning of εἰ, which may be (1) concessive, " even if ", (2) conditional, " if it is the case that (as it is) ". In the first case, the καί would not join the sentence to the previous one, but would be taken with εἰ, as in 1 Pet. iii. 1, 14, where καί has an " ascensive " force (cf. Winer, *Grammar*, pp. 554, 555); and the clause would then be a warning against allowing the revelation of God's fatherly love to obscure the truth of His awful majesty and righteousness. But, apart from the artificial asyndeton thus created between this verse and the last, the meaning of πατέρα is still not fully brought out. For (2) in making his exhortation to reverence rest upon the revelation of God as Father, the author is wholly within the circle of traditional Jewish ideas. Reverence for father and mother was one of the primary principles of the *tōrah* (cf. Lev. xix. 3, Ecclus. iii. 1-16), and belonged to the First Table of the Decalogue; and in the hierarchy of Jewish society, the father ranked higher, and was a more " numinous " figure, than the judge; for it was the father's function *par excellence* to command and to teach, which was held to be a more august function than the judge's of giving rewards and punishment. It is noticeable that in the passage from the Law of Holiness

ἐπικαλεῖσθε τὸν ἀπροσωπολήπτως κρίνοντα κατὰ τὸ ἑκάστου
ἔργον, ἐν φόβῳ τὸν τῆς παροικίας ὑμῶν χρόνον ἀναστράφητε,

quoted in verse 16 the command to "fear" mother and father follows immediately upon the command to be holy. The ground of Christian as of Jewish piety is less that God is the impartial Judge than that He is known as Father. At the same time this idea is enriched and illuminated by the specific revelation of God, and especially of His forgiving love, which has been given in Christ, so that God's Fatherhood has for Christians a special character. This is expressed in the clause beginning with εἰδότες (verses 18 ff.), which is thus linked up with the main clause. For the idea of reverence as the true response to God's mercy and forgiveness cf. Ps. cxxx. 4, "For there is mercy with thee, therefore shalt thou be feared", Jer. xxxiii. 9, 1 Kings viii. 39, 40. God forgives in order that men may fear Him; the cost of this forgiveness is the cross of Christ; and its result is that believers call on God as their Father. The Jew, or indeed the devout heathen, could fear God as the impartial Judge of all: the Christian has the added motive that he is aware of the riches of God's mercy to all who repent and will accept it (cf. Rom. ii. 1-11).

The phrase "invoke as Father" recalls Gal. iv. 6, Rom. viii. 15. In view of the fact that "Abba, Father" was probably already a liturgical formula (cf. Lightfoot on Gal. iv. 6; also Kirk on Rom. viii. 15 in the Clarendon Bible), we may reasonably regard St. Peter's words here as referring likewise to Christian worship, and especially to the use in it of the Lord's Prayer. Cf. F. H. Chase, in Texts and Studies, vol. i. No. 3 (1891), pp. 23, 24, though he does not mention 1 Pet. i. 17.

ἀπροσωπολήπτως] here only in N.T.; but St. Paul three times says that God and His judgment are without προσωπολημψία (Rom. ii. 11, Eph. vi. 9,

Col. iii. 25), and St. Peter, in an utterance recorded in Acts which we have seen reason to regard as primitive (cf. Introd. p. 33), is reported to have said, "Of a truth I perceive that God is no respecter of persons (προσωπολήπτης): but in every nation he that feareth him, and worketh righteousness, is accepted with him" (Acts x. 34). The idea of God's impartiality was Hebraic (cf. Deut. x. 17); but St. Peter was the first to apply it to the equality of Jew and Gentile in relation to the Gospel. The word would have been specially relevant here if the readers of the Epistle were a "mixed" church. In 1 Clem. i. 3 ἀπροσωπολήπτως is used of the attitude of the Christian Church towards visitors, and in Ep. Barn. iv. 12 we have ὁ κύριος ἀπροσωπολήπτως κρινεῖ τὸν κόσμον, which may be an echo of Acts x. 34 or of 1 Pet. i. 17.

ἐν φόβῳ] reverently. This is preferable to Souter's "diffidently" (Pocket Lex. of N.T. Greek, sub voc.). The word reverence has suffered through being almost confined in common parlance to behaviour at worship: it has its focus in worship, but, as this passage shews, should govern the whole conduct of life and every thought of men. The allusion to God's fatherly authority and forgiving love, moreover, shews that the whole sentiment or emotional attitude of reverence is here implied. The thought of God as Judge would evoke awe, which is compounded of three instincts, fear, wonder, and "negative self-feeling" (cf. McDougall, Social Psychology, pp. 128-32); reverence is formed, when to these is added the tender emotion aroused by God's mercy. And reverence, as McDougall says, "is the religious emotion par excellence". For the teaching generally cf. Phil. ii. 12, with Lightfoot's note, where 2 Cor. vii. 15, Eph. vi. 5, and 1 Cor. ii. 3 are also cited, and the phrase μετὰ φόβου

¹⁸εἰδότες ὅτι οὐ φθαρτοῖς, ἀργυρίῳ ἢ χρυσίῳ, ἐλυτρώθητε ἐκ τῆς

καὶ τρόμου is interpreted as "a nervous and trembling anxiety to do right". The teaching is characteristically Jewish, cf. Ps. cxi. 10, "The fear of the Lord is the beginning of widsom"; also Ecclus. xl. 26, and the Rabbinic saying given in *Pirqe Aboth*, iii. 13, "Whosesoever fear of sin precedes his wisdom, his wisdom stands", and Pereq R. Meir, 1, [*tŏrah*] "clothes him (i.e. man) with meekness and fear". Leighton, in a fine piece of exposition, speaks of this fear as begetting "true fortitude and courage to encounter all dangers, for the sake of a good conscience and the obeying of God". It is the clue, we may add, to the clause in the Lord's Prayer: "Lead us not into temptation".

τὸν . . . ἀναστράφητε] τὸν χρόνον is accusative of duration. "The time of your sojourning" takes up the description of the readers in the address as παρεπίδημοι (i. 1), and prepares the way for its reiteration in ii. 11. Their lack of real place in the society of Asia Minor is not allowed to be forgotten, and conditions their life. The "time" alluded to corresponds to τὸν ἐπίλοιπον ἐν σαρκὶ . . . χρόνον of iv. 2, in contrast with ὁ παρεληλυθὼς χρόνος of their pre-Christian estate.

For the idea of life as a pilgrimage cf. Seneca, *Ep.* cxx. 597 B, *nec domum esse hoc corpus sed hospitium et quidem breve hospitium*.

18. εἰδότες] Christian reverence rests upon the knowledge of redemption, four aspects of which are now enumerated : (1) its cost in the death of Christ, (2) its transcendent origin, (3) its certification in Christ's resurrection, (4) its fruit in the Church's faith and hope in God. This last point recalls the πατέρα ἐπικαλ. of verse 17.

φθαρτοῖς] Cf. verse 23 below. Incorruptibility is one of our author's favourite concepts : he predicates it of the inheritance to which believers are entitled (i. 4), of the sanctuary of the meek and quiet spirit (iii. 4), of the

seed of grace by which believers are begotten again (i. 23), and here of the price paid for redemption. Cf. also i. 6 and notes there. The word φθαρτός and its cognates ἄφθαρτος, ἀφθαρσία, are rare in LXX, and are almost confined to the apocryphal books, especially the Book of Wisdom. They were, however, the natural words for our author to use, if he had in mind our Lord's teaching in Matt. vi. 19-21, Lk. xii. 33, 34, where the perishableness of this world's goods is placed in sharp contrast to the imperishableness of spiritual goods. Writing to people who were cut off from worldly securities and privileges, it is natural that the author should have felt, and wished to convey to his readers, this side of Christ's teaching. For an illustration of this teaching in practice we may mention St. Peter's sharp rebuke of Simon Magus in Acts viii. 20.

ἐλυτρώθητε] *you were redeemed.* Cf. Tit. ii. 14, Heb. ix. 12. λυτροῦσθαι, λύτρον (usually plural, λύτρα), λύτρωσις occur in two contexts in LXX : (1) the redemption of property from mortgage, λύτρα being the price payable, e.g. Lev. xxv., xxvii., (2) the deliverance of a person or a nation from bondage, e.g. Deut. vii. 8, Pss. *passim*, and Acts vii. 35 (λυτρωτής of Moses). In view of the idea of the Christian inheritance as the new Canaan in i. 4, it is reasonable to see here a reference to Christian baptism as a new Exodus, all the more in view of the allusion to the lamb "without blemish and without spot" which immediately follows. Readers of Jewish origin would have been quick to seize the point. A further indication of a LXX background is the use of the instrumental dative for the redemption-price instead of the genitive of price more usual in Gentile parlance. At the same time, the word would have had ample significance for readers who knew nothing of Judaism; for, as Deissmann

ματαίας ὑμῶν ἀναστροφῆς πατροπαραδότου, ¹⁹ἀλλὰ τιμίῳ αἵματι

has shewn (*L.A.E.* pp. 322 ff.), this group of words was in common use in connexion with the ransoming of slaves. Cf. also MM, *sub voc.* Under Hellenistic law, the manumission of a slave necessitated the price of his ransom being deposited at the shrine of a god, who returned it, less the commission, to the master. Many slaves saved enough to buy their own freedom ; but a kinsman or friend could provide the money, just as in the Levitical law a kinsman could redeem a man who had sold himself or his stock for debt (Lev. xxv. 47 ff.). Contemporary custom thus probably provides the clue to the meaning of λύτρον in Mk. x. 45, Matt. xx. 28 : Vincent Taylor, following Hort, notes it as one of the points of affinity between 1 Peter and Mark in their teaching on the Atonement (*The Atonement in N.T. Teaching*, p. 40) ; and cf. Tit. ii. 14, *Ep. ad Diogn.* ix. 2. St. Paul's metaphor in 1 Cor. vi. 20, vii. 23, τιμῆς ἠγοράσθητε, is not quite identical, as it implies the slave's transference from one owner to another, from man's service to Christ's ; where λυτροῦσθαι is used, the idea is of ransoming from slavery into freedom. Further, the rite of sacral manumission was often accompanied, or completed, by a sacrifice ; and the Gentile, therefore, no less than the Jew, would have felt that the term ἐλυτρώθητε prepared the way for the sacrificial reference in the following verse.

ἐκ τῆς ματαίας . . . πατροπαραδότου] This was the Egypt from which St. Peter's readers had been delivered, cf. Eph. iv. 17, ἐν ματαιότητι τοῦ νοὸς αὐτῶν (of the Gentiles). Like "lies", "vanities" in O.T. often means idols, as in Lev. xvii. 7, Jer. viii. 19, x. 15 ; and cf. Acts xiv. 15. More broadly, it describes the ways of those who are without the worship of the true God, either because they have never known it or because they have fallen into apostasy from it. The latter sense is

the more common. In the present case, however, the use of πατροπαραδότου, "traditional", makes it probable that the reference is to Gentile paganism. For πατροπαραδ., "inherited" cf. Dion. Halic. *Ant. Rom.* v. xlviii., ἀλλ' ἐπὶ τῇ μικρᾷ καὶ πατροπαραδότῳ διέμεινεν οὐσίᾳ, and with reference to worship Diod. Sic. iv. 8. 5, πρὸς τὸν θεὸν μηδὲ τὴν πατροπαράδοτον εὐσέβειαν διαφυλάττειν, and the Pergamene inscription quoted by MM, *sub voc.* Had our author here been writing to Jewish Christians, he would have been transgressing the Rabbinic rule that "one must not reproach a descendant of proselytes with his sinful ancestry" : cf. W. G. Braude, *Jewish Proselyting*, pp. 14 f. We do not know the extent of apostasy in the Dispersion of Asia Minor, nor of how long standing it was, and B. Weiss makes a case for referring the phrase to apostate Jews. But on the whole πατροπαραδ. suggests that the author has in mind readers who had been brought up in the varied and longstanding tradition of Gentile paganism. Cf. Theophilus' allusion to idolaters in *ad Autolycum*, ii. 34. 3 (ed. Otto, 1881) as πειθόμενοι δόγμασιν ματαίοις διὰ πλάνης πατροπαραδότου γνώμης ἀσυνέτου. On the whole question of the recipients of the Epistle see Introd. pp. 42-7.

19. ἀλλὰ τιμίῳ . . . Χριστοῦ] The phrase expresses the nature of the ransom-price (blood, not money), its costliness (precious, not perishable), and its religious significance (sacrificial and Messianic). Cf. Greg. Naz. *Orat. Theol.* iii. 20, πωλεῖται καὶ λίαν εὐώνως, τριάκοντα γὰρ ἀργυρίων, ἀλλ' ἐξαγοράζει κόσμον, καὶ μεγάλης τιμῆς, τοῦ ἰδίου γὰρ αἵματος κτλ. The whole passage is a fine example of the pulpit rhetoric of the period. For redemption in or through or by Christ's blood conceived as the price cf. Acts xx. 28, Eph. i. 7, Rev. i. 5, v. 9, xiv. 1-5. ἄμωμος, "without blemish", is the word used in the general directions

ὡς ἀμνοῦ ἀμώμου καὶ ἀσπίλου Χριστοῦ, ²⁰προεγνωσμένου μὲν
πρὸ καταβολῆς κόσμου φανερωθέντος δὲ ἐπ᾽ ἐσχάτου τῶν χρόνων
δι᾽ ὑμᾶς ²¹τοὺς δι᾽ αὐτοῦ πιστοὺς εἰς Θεὸν τὸν ἐγείραντα

given in Lev. xxii. 17-25 as to the quality required in sacrificial victims ; together with the rare, vernacular ἄσπιλος, which is not found in LXX, it is equivalent to the τέλειον of Ex. xii. 5, which St. Peter no doubt avoided owing to having written τελείως in verse 13. The reference is to the Paschal lamb, which was connected *par excellence* with Israel's redemption ; and it belongs to a series of " redemption formulae " based on the traditional Jewish exegesis of Ex. xii.–xxiv., and interwoven - with the " consecration formulae " derived ultimately from Lev. xvii.–xxvi. (cf. Carrington, *op. cit.* pp. 6, 7, 28, note 1; and Essay II below, p. 374). As Clement of Alexandria says (*Adumbrationes*, 1006 [P]), *Hic tangit leviticas et sacerdotales antiquas celebrationes.* The extent to which the narrative of the Exodus (Ex. xii.) was used in the Church of the second century is well illustrated in Melito's *Homily on the Passion* published in 1940 ; though on this point (p. 2, ll. 30, 31, *Studies and Documents*, xii. p. 93) Melito uses the language of 1 Peter, λήμψῃ ἄσπιλον ἀμνὸν καὶ ἄμωμον, the phrase of Ex. xii. 5 was evidently in his memory. On St. Peter's doctrine of the Atonement see Introd. pp. 90 ff.

20. προεγνωσμένου] Cf. note on πρόγνωσιν in verse 2. The καταβολὴ κόσμου is the Creation, the beginning of history, cf. Lk. xi. 50, Heb. iv. 3 ; and history is thus measured ἀπὸ καταβολῆς κόσμου. The preposition πρό carries the thought back to a stage anterior to the Creation, i.e. to the transcendent sphere, cf. Jn. xvii. 24, Eph. i. 4. For the teaching cf. *Odes of Solomon*, xli. 16, and Melito, p. 13, ll. 26 ff. (*S.D.* xii. 143), ὅτι οὗτός ἐστιν ὁ πρωτότοκος τοῦ θεοῦ, ὁ πρὸ ἑωσφόρου γεννηθείς . . . φανερωθέντος. Cf. also

Rom. xvi. 25, 26 (of the " mystery " of the Gospel), χρόνοις αἰωνίοις σεσιγημένου φανερωθέντος δὲ νῦν . . ., 1 Cor. ii. 6, 7, 10, Eph. iii. 9, Tit. i. 2, 3.

ἐπ᾽ ἐσχάτου τῶν χρόνων] *at the end of the times*, or aeons (as in Rom. xvi. 25 above), i.e. the significant periods which make up time as seen in God's eyes. ἔσχατον, without article, is frequently used in LXX, especially in Isaiah and Jeremiah for " the end of ", both in a local and a temporal sense. The phrase, like ἐπ᾽ ἐσχάτου τῶν ἡμερῶν in Heb. i. 2, and ἐπὶ συντελείᾳ τῶν αἰώνων in Heb. ix. 26, shews how the Incarnation was regarded as an eschatological event. On the construction see Blass, *Grammar*, p. 156.

δι᾽ ὑμᾶς] St. Peter thus focuses the whole divine counsel of redemption upon his readers, and sets them, strangers and pilgrims as they are, in the forefront of the drama of history. The fact would help them to realize the love of God and the privilege of their calling, and so would strengthen them in the midst of the world's indifference and cruelty.

21. τοὺς δι᾽ αὐτοῦ πιστοὺς εἰς Θεὸν] *who through him believe in God.* As Bigg says, no other meaning will suit the context. In a long note Hort shews that (1) πιστός in LXX always means " trustworthy ", " worthy of credence ", as in iv. 19, v. 12 below ; (2) the word is used in an active sense by some classical authors, chiefly poets, cf. Soph. *O.C.* 1031, ἀλλ᾽ ἔσθ᾽ ὅτῳ σὺ πιστὸς ὢν ἔδρας τάδε, and Jebb's note giving several examples of the active sense of verbal adjectives in -τος ; (3) πίστις in N.T. is normally active, and prepared the way for the active use of πιστός, as in Gal. iii. 9, 2 Cor. vi. 15 and six times in the Pastoral Epistles, though in none of these cases is the object expressed. The construction here is grammati-

αὐτὸν ἐκ νεκρῶν καὶ δόξαν αὐτῷ δόντα, ὥστε τὴν πίστιν ὑμῶν

cally a classicism, while theologically it emphasizes the *status* of those addressed, just as we speak of "the faithful". If Lietzmann (*H.z.N.T.*) is right, the latter usage is illustrated by πιστός (=a Christian) in 1 Cor. vii. 25, which has some support from the use in Syrian inscriptions of πιστός as a title.

At the same time, the term is enriched by the addition of δι' αὐτοῦ and εἰς Θεόν κτλ. The first emphasizes the redemptive work of Christ as the ground and instrument of Christian faith (cf. iii. 18), the second shews this faith to be theistic, God's power being vindicated by the resurrection: the first differentiates Christianity from Judaism, the second from heathenism. An almost exact parallel to this use of δι' αὐτοῦ occurs in Acts iii. 16, ἡ πίστις ἡ δι' αὐτοῦ (St. Peter's words), though in that place, as Page observes, "Jesus gives the faith, and is also the object of it". The coincidence of phrase is the more striking, since, everywhere else in N.T. where πιστεύειν διά with genitive occurs, the instrumentality is human.

The double occurrence of εἰς Θεόν here and in the following clause hardly constitutes a tautology, for the words are required for different purposes in the two cases : in the first occurrence they point to the divine Author of the resurrection, in the second they lay the emphasis on God as the supreme object of faith and hope. This last point is again emphasized in iii. 21, where the allusion is to the baptismal confession of faith, ἐπερώτημα εἰς Θεόν, which is also connected, as here, with Christ's resurrection and exaltation. The words have a special significance, if the author were St. Peter and remembered the restoration of his own faith through Christ's resurrection; and they would come home to his readers with particular force, if they were intended to be read at the Easter festival.

τὸν ἐγείραντα] The resurrection of Jesus is regularly spoken of in St. Peter's speeches in Acts as owing to God's "raising" of Him ; cf. ἐγείρειν in Acts iii. 15, iv. 10, v. 30, x. 40 (and cf. 1 Thess. i. 10), and ἀνίστημι in Acts ii. 29, 32. St. Paul also commonly uses this form, and the passive ἐγήγερται in 1 Cor. xv. 4 suggests that it was the usage in the earliest credal formulae of the Church. Cf. *Essays Catholic and Critical*, pp. 291, 292 (article "The Resurrection", by the present author), and A. M. Hunter, *Paul and his Predecessors*, p. 33. For the revealing effect of Christ's resurrection cf. Rom. iv. 24 ; though, as Wand observes, St. Paul's custom is to connect the resurrection not with hope but with justification.

δόξαν αὐτῷ δόντα] Cf. Acts iii. 13 (St. Peter's words), ἐδόξασεν τὸν παῖδα αὐτοῦ Ἰησοῦν. Hort sees here a probable allusion to Is. lii. 13, the beginning of the oracle of the Suffering Servant. On δόξα in this Epistle see Add. Note B, pp. 253 ff.

ὥστε . . . εἶναι] Two questions are involved here. (1) Moffatt follows Kühl in taking ἐλπίδα as predicate, and rendering " and thus your faith means hope in God ". But the emphatic position of εἰς Θεόν, and still more the fact that throughout this Epistle faith and hope are so closely intertwined, are against this : the author would be unlikely to make such a point of what elsewhere he takes for granted. (2) More difficulty attaches to the meaning of ὥστε . . . εἶναι, many commentators, e.g. Hort, Bigg, Wand, taking it as stating a fact, " so that your hope and faith are towards God ". I cannot but think, however, that the E.V. and the older commentators are right in regarding the construction of ὥστε with the infinitive as expressing the intended or contemplated result : as Blass observes (*Grammar*, p. 224), " the boundary-line which separates these sentences from sentences of design almost disappears ". Cf. also Moulton, *Grammar*, i. p. 209, who, however, justly criticizes Blass on certain points. It may be true, as he says, that " the construction with the infinitive has a wider range than in Attic "; but the construction with the indicative occurs twenty-one times in N.T., and it is distributed over many books, while the construction with the imperative, which is similar in principle, is also not rare. In the only other case where ὥστε is used in this Epistle, iv. 19, the imperative follows. We may say, therefore, that, had the author desired simply to state a consequential fact, there is no reason why he should not have used the indicative.

The classical constructions of ὥστε are discussed in a celebrated note by Shilleto (Dem. *de Fals. Leg.*, App. B). After saying that, in general, the indicative after ὥστε expresses the *real* result or consequence, while the infinitive expresses the *natural* consequence, he proceeds : . . . " an energetic speaker, wishing to express that the result (was not only of a nature to follow, but) actually did follow, would employ the *indicative* : whereas in ordinary and unimpassioned language the *infinitive* would imply all that was necessary, *the natural consequence* supposing *the real* ". [In the former case the negative was οὐ, in the latter usually μή; though Shilleto notes certain passages which do not seem to conform to this rule. I cannot think, however, that Euripides, *Hel.* 108, should be reckoned among these, since the words οὐδ' ἴχνος constitute a single idiomatic phrase.] Goodwin (*Greek Grammar*, §§ 1449-52) follows Shilleto, and adds that " the infinitive with ὥστε may express a purpose like a final clause ": the difference between expressing a natural result and expressing an intended result is obviously very small. This usage is also well attested in N.T., cf. Matt. xxvii. 1, Lk. iv. 29, ix. 52, xx. 20,

Rom. vii. 6 (see SH, *in loc.*), 2 Cor. ii. 7. It is true that in N.T., as indeed even in the classical authors, the two constructions sometimes seem to overlap ; but reasons need to be adduced, before we assume that in any particular case the ordinary rule has been abandoned.

Finally it may be urged that the *flair* for the true meaning which is one of the principal characteristics of the translators of A.V. has not deserted them here. The insertion of a sentence stating a fact about the present spiritual condition of the readers would be incongruous and out of place in this strongly hortatory passage (i. 13-25), where every main verb is in the imperative. The first of these imperatives, moreover, is a command to hope ; and such an injunction would surely be unneeded, if the hope asked for were already an evident fact of their condition. Again, the whole rhythm of the passage is purposive, culminating in the highest of all spiritual fruits in the Church, sincere mutual charity ; and the long sentence on the Atonement is absorbed into the movement of thought and feeling if the consecutive clause at the end is likewise purposive. The place of εἰς Θεόν, moreover, at the close of the sentence is emphatic, and there was good reason for it ; for it served to distinguish Christianity from the contemporary pagan cults. They, too, professed to know of divine beings — Dionysus, Attis, Horus — who had been raised from the dead and glorified, and who became themselves the object and term of their worshippers' faith ; Christianity, while it encouraged the worship of Christ and was therefore Christocentric, yet worshipped Him in the context of the Blessed Trinity, and His exaltation was that men's faith might rest *there* — in God. We may conclude, therefore, that consideration of the context tells, like the grammar, in favour of the translation given in E.V.

καὶ ἐλπίδα εἶναι εἰς Θεόν. ²²τὰς ψυχὰς ὑμῶν ἡγνικότες ἐν τῇ
ὑπακοῇ τῆς ἀληθείας εἰς φιλαδελφίαν ἀνυπόκριτον ἐκ καρδίας

22. τὰς ψυχὰς] The asyndeton is less abrupt if we remember that the tenour of the whole passage is hortatory.

ἡγνικότες] *having cleansed*. Cf. Jas. iv. 8, ἁγνίσατε καρδίας, δίψυχοι. ἁγνός, ἁγνίζω are common in classical authors, and usually have a moral sense ; even where physical cleansing is the immediate meaning, it is as the symbol of moral cleansing, as in Ajax's resolution of repentance :

ἀλλ' εἶμι πρός τε λουτρὰ καὶ παρ-
ακτίους
λειμῶνας, ὡς ἂν λύμαθ' ἁγνίσας ἐμὰ
μῆνιν βαρεῖαν ἐξαλύξωμαι θεᾶς.
(Soph. *Ajax*, 654-6).

In LXX ἁγνίζω generally has a ceremonial reference, though ἁγιάζω is far more common in that sense, especially in the Pentateuch. (ἁγιάζω is not found in classical authors, nor in the vernacular of the papyri, etc.) The phrase here may be reckoned among the " consecration formulae " of this passage, but both the word chosen (ἁγνίζω) and the words which follow shew how the idea of consecration, which is one of the most " numinous " in religion, has here been moralized. Cf. Otto, *The Idea of the Holy*, ch. ii., and also ch. xx. pp. 175 ff.

The perfect participle is significant and implies that the personal cleansing of the soul through conversion and baptism is antecedent to the warm spirit of churchmanship described as " love of the brethren ".

ἐν τῇ ὑπακοῇ τῆς ἀληθείας] The words take up ὑπακοή in verses 2, 14, as ἡγνικότες takes up ἁγιασμῷ in verse 2 and ἅγιοι in verse 15, and ἀναγεγεννημένοι takes up ἀναγεννήσας in verse 3. But something is added in each case : sanctification is not only effected by the Holy Spirit, but is consummated in obedience : the obedience itself is defined as obedience to the truth ; and the regeneration, which in the earlier passage is described as to its efficient

(ὁ Θεός) and its final (εἰς ἐλπίδα κτλ.) causes, is now defined as to its material cause (σπορᾶς κτλ.).

On " the amicable and, indeed, inseparable agreement betwixt " obedience and faith cf. J. Lightfoot, *Works*, vii. pp. 251 f. [ed. 1822].

For ἁγνίζειν ἐν cf. 2 Chron. xxxi. 18, ὅτι ἐν πίστει ἥγνισαν τὸ ἅγιον, where ἐν πίστει means " in the faithful discharge of their office ", and so is closely analogous to this. For ἐν here means " in the sphere of ", or almost " in the practice of ", cf. note on verse 2. The general meaning is well illustrated by Jn. xvii. 17 (cf. 19), " Sanctify them in the truth : thy word is truth ", where the association of consecration, truth, God's word, presents a close analogy to this passage.

τῆς ἀληθείας] *to the truth*, i.e. the Gospel. Bengel aptly compares Acts xv. 9 (St. Peter's words), οὐδὲν διέκρινε μεταξὺ ἡμῶν τε καὶ αὐτῶν, τῇ πίστει καθαρίσας τὰς καρδίας αὐτῶν. The parallel is still closer if with several ancient MSS. (Syr., Eth., O.L.) διὰ πνεύματος be inserted after ἀληθείας ; for in Acts xv. 7 the opening of " the word (λόγον) of the Gospel " to the Gentiles is connected with the gift of the Holy Spirit. But even without this insertion there seems no reason to discover here, as Wand does, traces of " a binitarian character " in this exhortation. ἀλήθεια does not occur elsewhere in this Epistle ; but it occurs three times in 2 Thessalonians as equivalent to the Gospel (ii. 10, 12, 13) and often elsewhere in N.T. It is peculiarly appropriate here (1) as pointing the contrast between the truth of Christianity and the falsehoods of heathenism (cf. ἀγνοίᾳ, verse 14, ματαίας, verse 18), (2) as summing up under one head the truths of God's fatherhood and of the incarnation, cross, resurrection, and ascension of Christ expounded in the preceding verses. For the objective genitive after

ἀλλήλους ἀγαπήσατε ἐκτενῶς, ²³ἀναγεγεννημένοι οὐκ ἐκ σπορᾶς

ὑπακοῇ Windisch cites 2 Cor. x. 5, εἰς τὴν ὑπακοὴν τοῦ Χριστοῦ; with which cf. Eph. v. 21, ἐν φόβῳ Χριστοῦ. [Hort interprets 2 Cor. x. 5 otherwise, but see Plummer, I.C.C. *in loc.*] The idea of obedience (to the Gospel, Rom. x. 16; to the faith, Rom. i. 5, xvi. 26) as underlying faith is confined to St. Paul's earlier Epistles (SH on Rom. xvi. 26, quoting Hort), and points to a time when the adhesion of the Gentiles to the Church appeared predominantly as an act of submission, both in itself and in its consequences in the acceptance of the " subordinationist " ethic of Christianity which was so sharply at variance with heathen life. Cf. also Acts vi. 7, ὑπήκουον τῇ πίστει, 2 Thess. i. 8, τοῖς μὴ ὑπακούουσι τῷ εὐαγγελίῳ, Clem. Alex. *Strom.* VII. 886 [P], ζῶντας ἡμᾶς κατὰ τὴν τοῦ εὐαγγελίου ὑπακοήν.

εἰς φιλαδελφίαν ἀνυπόκριτον] The relation of love of the brethren, i.e. for fellow-members of the Church, to charity which is universal is well illustrated in 2 Pet. i. 7, ἐν . . . τῇ φιλαδελφίᾳ τὴν ἀγάπην. The spirit of general benevolence is nursed in the particular affection which unites Church-people as in a family. In Rom. xii. 9, 10 the adjective ἀνυπόκριτος is joined with ἀγάπη, not φιλαδελφία; cf. also 2 Cor. vi. 6. It is a warning both against the jealousies and selfishnesses which may still lurk in the Church, and also against the sentimental professions which often do duty for brotherly love ; and we may well suppose that the new fusion of Jews and Gentiles in the Church made it specially opportune when St. Peter wrote. St. Peter's teaching finds apt illustration in Lord Lister's statement of the two great requisites for the medical profession : " First, a warm, loving heart, and secondly, Truth in an earnest spirit " (*Lord Lister*, by Sir Rickman John Godlee, Bt., p. 91 : Lecture at Glasgow, 1860), and again in his *Graduates' Address*, 1876 (*ib.*, frontispiece) : " It

is our proud office to tend the fleshly tabernacle of the immortal spirit, and our path, if rightly followed, will be guided by unfettered truth and love unfeigned ".

ἀλλήλους ἀγαπήσατε] This injunction to mutual love occurs three times in the Epistles to the Thessalonians, of which Silvanus was a joint author, 1 Thess. iii. 12, iv. 9, 2 Thess. i. 3 ; and three times in addition to this passage in 1 Peter: ii. 17, iii. 8, iv. 8. It is based on the " new commandment " given by our Lord at the Last Supper, Jn. xiii. 34 f., xv. 12, 17, and reiterated in St. John's First Epistle. Through the place given it as the climax of this whole passage, the author shews that love is the fulfilment of the new faith as of the old law.

ἐκτενῶς] *with heart and soul*: cf. Lk. xxii. 44, Acts xii. 5, where the reference is to prayer, as in Joel i. 14, Jon. iii. 8, Judith iv. 12, 3 Macc. v. 9. In all these cases the word is used with words which imply highly energetic activity in prayer. It is used again with ἀγάπη in 1 Pet. iv. 8. Suidas interprets by ὁλοψύχως.

23. ἀναγεγεννημένοι] See note on ἀναγεννήσας in i. 3, and Add. Note L, pp. 306 f.

σπορᾶς] *sowing*, i.e. " origin ", as in Aesch. *P.V.* 871, σπορᾶς γε μὴν ἐκ τῆσδε φύσεται θρασύς ; and cf. Soph. *Ajax*, 1298. Windisch also cites *Corp. Herm.* xiii. 1, ἀγνοῶ, ὦ τρισμέγιστε, ἐξ οἵας μητρὸς ἀνεγεννήθης, σπορᾶς δὲ ποίας, and *ib.* 2, ἡ σπορὰ τὸ ἀληθινὸν ἀγαθόν. This gives a satisfactory sense, and does justice to the distinction between the prepositions ἐκ and διά which lie so close together. The supernatural origin or source from which believers have been begotten again is here not the Word (which will be alluded to in a moment) but God's creative *grace*, the Word being the means of their regeneration. St. Peter's own name Bar-jona or Barjohanan, " Son of the Grace of God "

φθαρτῆς ἀλλὰ ἀφθάρτου διὰ λόγου ζῶντος Θεοῦ καὶ μένοντος.

may have fostered this idea, as he thought on it. His readers were children of nature and have now become children of grace. As Sir Edwyn Hoskyns says, commenting on Jn. i. 13, " Beyond the whole process of nature, beyond every Jewish or other genealogy, beyond the action of the body, and beyond every act of human will, there are children who have been brought into being by the creative power and will of God ", i.e. by grace. And such a procreation may rightly be called, by a metonymical use of the epithet, " not corruptible but incorruptible ". This seems better than to take it as seed (vulg. *satio*) " in a quasi-collective sense " (Hort), though this can be illustrated from Eur. *Andr.* 636-8,

πολλάκις δέ τοι
ξηρὰ βαθεῖαν γῆν ἐνίκησε σπορά,
νόθοι δὲ πολλοὶ γνησίων ἀμείνονες,

and Philo, *de Praem. et Poen.* 10 [II. 410 M], quoted by Hort; and MM cite a parallel from the papyri. Bigg, moreover, sees an allusion to the parable of the Sower, and to the Sowing (*satio*) initiated by our Lord and now carried on by His disciples. Such a Sowing could be called " incorruptible ", as resulting in people endued with eternal life in contrast with a harvest which lasts but a few months. This interpretation, however, is much less simple than the other, and blurs the distinction between ἐκ and διά in the text.

διὰ λόγου . . . μένοντος] We pass from the source of the new birth to God's instrument for its communication. This is said to be " God's living and abiding word ". Two questions present themselves : (1) do the participles belong to λόγου or to Θεοῦ ? (2) what is the meaning of λόγου here, and what is its relation to the ῥῆμα of verse 25 ?

(1) Bengel, Bigg, and (less confidently) Windisch connect the participles with λόγου. On the other side

it is urged, e.g. by Hort, that the combination of μένων and ζῶν with θεός in Dan. vi. 26 probably underlies this passage, and that this interpretation best suits the context. His argument is subtle, but I do not find it convincing. Linguistically, it seems to me that, if Θεοῦ were meant to carry the weight of two such significant adjectives, it would have been placed immediately after λόγου or at the end of the sentence : coming as it does between the two adjectives it looks as though it were not intended to be emphatic. Cf. Winer, *Grammar*, pp. 657, 659 (section lix. 2) and pp. 238, 239 (section xxx. 3, par. 2, citing Eph. ii. 3, τέκνα φύσει ὀργῆς).

(2) The use of λόγος and λόγος θεοῦ in N.T. has been illuminated by the Detached Note in Hoskyns, *op. cit.* i. pp. 152-64, and he regards this passage as one of those which shew " how deeply the phrase *The Word of God* was embedded in the primitive Christian vocabulary and how steadily and consistently it was pressed to describe the work of Christ ". Further examples of how " both the Gospel and the word of God are drawn into the orbit of [Christ's] person " are Lk. i. 2, αὐτόπται καὶ ὑπηρέται γενόμενοι τοῦ λόγου, Mk. i. 1, τοῦ εὐαγγελίου Ἰησοῦ Χριστοῦ, 1 Jn. i. 1-4, 10, Col. i. 25-8, where an equation is asserted between " the word of God ", " the mystery ", " the riches of this mystery ", " Christ in you ", and Jas. i. 18, ἀπεκύησεν ἡμᾶς λόγῳ ἀληθείας, εἰς τὸ εἶναι ἡμᾶς ἀπαρχήν τινα τῶν αὐτοῦ κτισμάτων. We have not yet reached the explicit identification of the Word (of God) with Christ which we find in Rev. xix. 13 (cf. also Rev. i. 2, 9, vi. 9, xx. 4) and in the Prologue of the Fourth Gospel and which is the subject of striking doctrinal development in *Ep. ad Diogn.* xi. ; but N.T. thought is already on the way there. And this explains why St. Peter uses λόγος here in preference to ῥῆμα, although ῥῆμα

²⁴διότι Πᾶσα σὰρξ ὡς χόρτος, καὶ πᾶσα δόξα αὐτῆς ὡς ἄνθος
χόρτου. ²⁵ἐξηράνθη ὁ χόρτος, καὶ τὸ ἄνθος ἐξέπεσε· τὸ δὲ ῥῆμα
Κυρίου μένει εἰς τὸν αἰῶνα. τοῦτο δέ ἐστι τὸ ῥῆμα τὸ εὐαγγελισθὲν εἰς ὑμᾶς.

is in his quotation from Isaiah. For in N.T. usage the λόγος is more than the ῥῆμα : it is the ῥῆμα, the promise of Jehovah, *fulfilled* and therefore (verse 25) preached, τὸ ῥῆμα τὸ εὐαγγελισθέν being equivalent to τὸ γενόμενον ῥῆμα καθ᾽ ὅλης τῆς Ἰουδαίας of Acts x. 37. And this last passage, which is part of a speech of St. Peter's, makes clear that the promise fulfilled was none other than the Incarnation and the universal salvation offered with it. The διὰ λόγου Θεοῦ, indeed, though less explicit than the δι᾽ αὐτοῦ of verse 21, is not fundamentally different from it ; nor does it differ, if thus interpreted, from the δι᾽ ἀναστάσεως Ἰησοῦ Χριστοῦ which is said in verse 3 to be the instrument of regeneration. Again, of the two words, λόγος and ῥῆμα, used in LXX for the Word of God active in the creation of the world, it was λόγος which was taken up into the quasi-technical vocabulary which was forged in the primitive Church. Finally, this significance of God's word is brought out still further in the participles which qualify it : it is " living " and " abiding ". It is " living " because it is the instrument of God's creative grace, cf. Is. lv. 10, 11 ; the fact of Christ, the word fulfilled, is not simply brute fact but fact that is full of generative power, and so able to re-create the character of men ; it has in itself " energies of action " (Westcott on ζῶν γὰρ ὁ λόγος τοῦ θεοῦ, Heb. iv. 12). And it is " abiding " because the Kingdom of Christ is abiding (cf. Ps. lxxxix. 36, 37; especially τὸ σπέρμα αὐτοῦ εἰς τὸν αἰῶνα μένει, i.e. the regenerate Israel of the Messianic age), in contrast with the transiency of all human things.

24, 25. Πᾶσα . . . αἰῶνα] From Is. xl. 6-8 (LXX). The deviations from LXX are unimportant, and may

have been in the text used by the author (Hort), or he may have quoted from memory. The first part of the quotation (verses 24, 25a) does not illustrate the phrase just used, but is highly relevant to the context as a whole. The prophecy, which opens II-Isaiah, was addressed to a people exiled and oppressed, and offers them hope and comfort ; God promises deliverance to those who are repentant and receptive, and His promise — in contrast to all else in human life — remains sure (cf. Driver, *Isaiah*, p. 138) ; ideal messengers are bidden spread the good news (ὁ εὐαγγελιζόμενος (*bis*), verse 9) ; Jehovah will come in might, but also as a Shepherd (ὡς ποιμὴν ποιμανεῖ τὸ ποίμνιον αὐτοῦ, verse 11, cf. 1 Pet. ii. 25) ; and the whole context is governed by the thought of His grace (cf. the beautiful interpretation of verses 1, 2 in G. Adam Smith, *The Book of Isaiah*, pp. 74-80, especially " Thus God adventures His Word further by nameless and unaccredited men upon no other authority than the Grace, with which it is fraught for the heart of His people "). Every leading thought here fits in with what our author has been saying. He too is addressing readers who are exiled (παρεπιδήμοις, παροίκους τε καὶ παρεπιδήμους, i. 1, ii. 11) and oppressed ; and he has the same message for them, the contrast between the perishability of all mortal things (cf. φθαρτός in verses 18, 23) and the incorruptibility of the Christian inheritance and hope (cf. i. 4, 21, v. 4, etc.) ; and this good news is also published by " evangelists " (i. 12, 25b). The passage quoted is, therefore, the focal point of a much longer passage which must have been often present to the Apostle's mind.

τὸ ῥῆμα τὸ εὐαγγελισθὲν εἰς ὑμᾶς]

II. ¹'Ἀποθέμενοι οὖν πᾶσαν κακίαν καὶ πάντα δόλον καὶ ὑποκρίσεις καὶ φθόνους καὶ πάσας καταλαλιὰς ²ὡς ἀρτιγέννητα

taking up the διὰ τῶν εὐαγγελισαμένων ὑμᾶς of i. 12, and thereby bringing the whole section to a close in the events of the contemporary scene.

ii. 1-10. Second Doctrinal Section.

A brief transitional passage leads into a statement of the nature and function of the Church. Believers are to grow up to salvation not in isolation, but as a community, where members are fastened to Christ as the stones of a temple to the cornerstone. And this cornerstone has been laid by God. Those who were first called to join in the building rejected the calling. But a new world, the Gentile world, has been called in to redress the balance of the old ; and the Christian Church which has supervened upon this act of divine judgment, and which is built upon Christ, has inherited the whole vocation of Israel ; its priestly calling to represent man in his approach to God, and its prophetic calling to represent God to man. The result is a company of people whose life shines brightly amid the surrounding darkness, and who have found in the common experience of God's mercy a new loyalty and a new source of pride.

1, 2. These verses summarize the preceding passage of exhortation in preparation for an eloquent unfolding of the meaning of the Church's life.

1. 'Ἀποθέμενοι] For the place of this renunciation in primitive Christian catechetical teaching and its parallels in N.T. see Introd. pp. 19, 98 f., and Essay II, pp. 393-400. It is the parent of the renunciations at the beginning of the Church Catechism.

πᾶσαν κακίαν] The words seem to embrace the whole wickedness of the pagan world. Contemporary philosophers were equally aware of it : cf. the words of the contemporary Stoic, Musonius, quoted by Stobaeus, Florileg. xxix. 78, οἱ δὲ φιλοσοφεῖν ἐπιχειροῦντες, ἐν διαφθορᾷ γεγενημένοι

πρότερον πολλῇ καὶ ἐμπεπλησμένοι κακίας, οὕτω μετίασι τὴν ἀρετὴν κτλ. Cf. also Sext. Math. ix. 90, quoted in Zeller, Stoics, Epicureans, and Sceptics [E.T. ed. 1870], p. 255, note 2.

πάντα δόλον] the repetition of πάντα here, but not again, suggests that a different class of sins is here in view, namely those which threatened the life of believers in spite of, or even in consequence of, their conversion ; and πάντα is probably meant to cover all. These sins were δόλος, "deceitfulness" —a fault most difficult to outgrow ; ὑποκρίσεις, i.e. the temptation to join the Church from false motives, or with mental reserves (like those of Ananias and Sapphira in Acts v.) —a fault which is not unknown to-day in the mission field ; φθόνοι, which are a constant plague of all voluntary organizations, not least religious organizations, and to which even the Twelve themselves were subject at the very crisis of our Lord's ministry (Lk. xxii. 24 ff.) ; and καταλαλιαί, " evil speakings ", " backchat ", which is usually the fruit of envy.

καταλαλιὰς] detractions (Bengel). In classical Greek καταλαλεῖν means to " run down ", " disparage " ; and it is the habit of disparagement rather than open slander which the author here denounces. The verb is fairly common in LXX, especially in the Psalms ; but the noun occurs only once, Wisd. i. 11, ἀπὸ καταλαλιᾶς φείσασθε γλώσσης. Cf. also Clem. Rom. ad Cor. xxx. (bis) and xxxv., where the word's association with ψιθυρισμός suggests that Rom. i. 30 is in mind ; and Ep. Barn. xx., where ὑπόκρισις, δόλος, and κακία occur as marks of " the way of the Black One ", and among those who walk in it are men who are εὐχερεῖς ἐν καταλαλιᾷ. The injunction would have been specially in place here, if the Epistle were addressed to mixed communities, where the tendency would have been for the

βρέφη τὸ λογικὸν ἄδολον γάλα ἐπιποθήσατε, ἵνα ἐν αὐτῷ αὐξη-

jealousies and contempts of those who before their conversion had belonged to rival cults and sects to continue in the new life, unless checked.

2. ὡς ἀρτιγέννητα βρέφη] as newborn babes. ἀρτιγέννητα (a word found in Lucian and other sub-classical authors) has been pressed into the service of rival theories affecting the chronology of the Epistle. Cf. Introd. pp. 41-2. But as Hort points out, the weight of the sentence as a whole lies on the λογικὸν ἄδολον γάλα which Christians are to desire ; and, since this is no way contrasted, as is the case in 1 Cor. iii. 2 f. and Heb. v. 12 ff., with any stronger diet such as would be suitable to later years, we need not suppose that there is any allusion to the length of time during which the readers had been Christians. The purpose of the adjective is to make the imagery of the passage more vivid ; and we may compare ὡς λέων ὠρυόμενος in v. 8. What the author wants to express is the ardour of the suckled child. A very human illustration of the same point occurs in 1 Thess. ii. 7 where St. Paul likens himself and his colleagues, Silvanus and Timothy, to a nurse fostering her children ; with which cf. Origen, in Evang. Matth. xv. 17 (quoted by Milligan), ὁ ἀπόστολος ἐγένετο νήπιος καὶ παραπλήσιος τροφῷ θαλπούσῃ τὸ ἑαυτῆς παιδίον καὶ λαλούσῃ λόγους ὡς παιδίον διὰ τὸ παιδίον.

βρέφη] For the innocence of infants cf. 2 Macc. viii. 4, ἀναμαρτήτων νηπίων, Hermas, Mand. ii. 1, τὰ μὴ γινώσκοντα τὴν πονηρίαν, Sim. IX. xxix. 1 ; and Strack-Billerbeck, i. pp. 773 ff.

τὸ λογικὸν ἄδολον γάλα] i.e. the divinely-given nourishment supplied by the Gospel. There is no need to refer to the Mystery Cults for light on the metaphor (cf. Add. Note L, pp. 308-09), when it can be so readily interpreted from Jewish or independent Christian sources. Cf. Montefiore and Loewe, A Rabbinic Anthology,

pp. 163, 164, 189, 190, especially the passage on p. 163 beginning, " The words of the Law are compared with water, wine, oil, honey, and milk ". In the Christian dispensation all these metaphors are transferred from the Law to the grace which comes through the Gospel. For water cf. Jn. iv. 10-15, vii. 37-9, Rev. xxi. 6, Ep. Barn. xi.; for wine, 1 Cor. xi. 25, Jn. ii. 1-11 ; for oil, 1 Jn. ii. 20, 27, 2 Cor. i. 21 ; for honey, Rev. x. 9, Ep. Barn. vi. 17 (cf. Ps. xix. 9, 10) ; and for milk, this passage and Ep. Barn. vi. 17. Water, milk, and wine represent fundamental sources of human nourishment, as in Is. lv. 1 (Heb.) ; and milk is combined with honey in Cant. iv. 11 as symbolic of sweetness (cf. Theocr. Id. xx. 26 f.). The sustinence given by the Gospel, which causes growth, is the property relevant here ; its sweetness, which charms the taste, is alluded to in the following clause.

For the use of " milk " in this sense in the Church of the early centuries pertinent illustrations occur in the Odes of Solomon, e.g. viii. 17, " I (sc. God) fashioned their members : My own breasts I prepared for them that they might drink My holy milk and live thereby " ; and xix. 1-4, " A cup of milk was offered to me : and I drank it in the sweetness of the light of the Lord. The Son is the cup, and He who was milked is the Father : and the Holy Spirit milked Him : because His breasts were full, and it was necessary for Him that His milk should be sufficiently released ; and the Holy Spirit opened His bosom and mingled the milk from the two breasts of the Father. . . ." I quote from Dr. Rendel Harris' translation. Dr. Bernard (J.T.S. xii. No. 5, Oct. 1910), who believes the Odes to be baptismal hymns of about the middle of the second century, cites also iv. 7-10, which end with the prayer, " Distil Thy dews upon us ; and open Thy rich fountains that pour forth to us milk and honey " ; with which may be compared *Ep. Barn.* vi. 17, where the "milk and honey" of Canaan are regarded as types of "our faith in the promise and . . . the word " ; Clem. Al. *Paed.* I. 124 [P], "the milk of the Father by which only the babes (νήπιοι) are suckled ", and *ib.* 127 [P], εἰ γὰρ ἀνεγεννήθημεν εἰς Χριστόν, ὁ ἀναγεννήσας ἡμᾶς ἐκτρέφει τῷ ἰδίῳ γάλακτι, τῷ λόγῳ, and Narsai, *Hom.* xxi (c), p. 52, "As milk he (sc. the newly baptized) sucks the divine mysteries, and by degrees they lead him, as a child, to the things to come ". There is ample evidence, according to Bernard, that from the second century onwards milk and honey were administered to the newly baptized. This verse in 1 Peter suggests how the rite might have arisen.

λογικὸν] *spiritual* : so R.V. The word has been variously interpreted. Thus Kühl, Perdelwitz, Bigg render "flowing out of the Word of God ", connecting it with λόγος in i. 23 (cf. A.V. "of the word "); Usteri, "nonmaterial"; Hort, "rational", "reasonable " (cf. Vulg. *rationabile*, v.l. *rationale*). Kittel (*Th. W*[b].*z.N.T.*, *sub voc.*), who renders "geistig ", "übersinnlich ", connects it with οἶκος πνευματικός in ii. 5, and believes St. Peter to be pointing the contrast with the animal sacrifices of Judaism and paganism, which Christianity had superseded by a spiritual worship; and he thinks that the word is borrowed here, though not in Rom. xii. 1, from the terminology of the Mystery Religions. Hort notes the prominence of the word in the Stoic philosophers for that which appertains to reason, and regards it as taking up the ἀναζωσάμενοι τὰς ὀσφύας τῆς διανοίας and νήφοντες of i. 13. Cf. also Philo, *de Migr. Abr.* 185 [I. 465 M], where it is contrasted with ἄλογον. Even in the philosophers, however, the word connoted something of spiritual exaltation as well as of rational thought, cf. Epictetus, *Dissert.* i. 16, εἰ γοῦν ἀηδὼν ἤμην, ἐποίουν τὰ τῆς ἀηδόνος, εἰ

κύκνος, τὰ τοῦ κύκνου· νῦν δὲ λογικός εἰμι, ὑμνεῖν με δεῖ τὸν θεόν.

The rendering of λογικός by "spiritual " may be illustrated from Chrysostom's comment on Rom. xii. 1 (E. H. B.), τί δέ ἐστι λογικὴ λατρεία; ἡ πνευματικὴ διακονία, ἡ πολιτεία ἡ κατὰ Χριστόν. In view of ii. 5 below, Rom. xii. 1 may have been in St. Peter's mind, or both may be drawing on common material, based on Jewish sources. Cf. *Test. Levi* iii. 6, προσφέρουσι τῷ κυρίῳ ὀσμὴν εὐωδίας λογικὴν καὶ ἀναίμακτον προσφοράν, with Charles' note — a passage earlier at any rate than A.D. 50. A prophecy such as Is. xxviii. 9 would have facilitated the imagery here : "Whom shall we teach knowledge? and whom shall we make to understand doctrine ? Them that are weaned from the milk, and drawn from the breasts."

MM give examples to illustrate the meaning "metaphorical", and F. H. Chase, in an unpublished letter to E. H. B., wrote of "what is not literally but according to a spiritual analogy γάλα ". But in view of the lavish use of metaphor in N.T. without any explanatory adjective, this seems improbable. Windisch, as well as Kittel, refers to parallels in the Mystery Religions, on which see Add. Note L, pp. 308 f. below, and also A. D. Nock in *Essays on the Trinity and the Incarnation*, pp. 116 ff.

ἄδολον] *unadulterated*, i.e. uncontaminated by alien matter. Cf. Aesch. *Ag.* 94, 95, φαρμασσομένη χρίματος ἁγνοῦ μαλακαῖς ἀδόλοισι παρηγορίαις ("with all-pure smooth bewitching spell" (Walter Headlam)). The word is common in the papyri for unadulterated wheat ; and cf. Philo, *de Decal.* 58 [II. 190 M], ἀδόλου καὶ καθαρᾶς εὐσεβείας. The accurate determination of this word is important here, since it could scarcely have been used, if St. Peter had supposed that there was any infiltration into Christianity of ideas or customs characteristic of the Mystery Religions.

ἐπιποθήσατε] a strong word, indica-

θῆτε εἰς σωτηρίαν, ³εἰ ἐγεύσασθε ὅτι χρηστὸς ὁ Κύριος· ⁴πρὸς

tive of strong desire (ἐπί-) and vigorous action (aor. imp.), such as are seen in a child being suckled. The word is common in LXX, especially the Psalms, and expresses intense and yearning desire (usually with a preposition, ἐπί, εἰς, or πρός), cf. Ps. xlii. 1, " As the hart panteth after (ἐπιποθεῖ ἐπί) the water-brooks, so panteth my soul after thee, O God", and cxix. 174, "I have longed for thy salvation, O Lord ". Intensity of desire is also indicated by its use in classical authors, e.g. Herod. v. 93, Plato, *Protag.* 329 D. Intensity rather than addition seems to be the force of ἐπί in verbs compounded with it.

ἵνα ἐν αὐτῷ αὐξηθῆτε] *that you may thrive on it and grow up.* αὐξάνεσθαι is a common word in Greek for the growth of children ; cf. Herod. v. 92. 5, μετὰ ταῦτα ὁ παῖς ηὐξάνετο, Eur. *Suppl.* 323, ἐν γὰρ τοῖς πόνοισιν αὔξεται [sc. σὴ πατρίς], "your country thrives on trouble ", a passage which likewise illustrates the use of ἐν after αὐξάνεσθαι. I have added the words "and grow up" in order to provide a link with the εἰς σωτηρίαν which follows. Hort thinks that St. Peter's words are "founded on" Eph. iv. 15, but the hypothesis seems unnecessary. The image of the suckled child still governs the passage.

εἰς σωτηρίαν] omitted in some late MSS., but probably genuine. For the connexion of this passage with Jas. i. 21 see Essay II, pp. 389 ff. The words support the view taken above that γάλα represents the grace of God, for there is no suggestion (as in 1 Cor. iii. and in Heb. v. 12, vi. 2) that the milk is a diet to be outgrown. Bigg's note on the contrasted uses of the milk †mage by St. Peter, St. Paul, and the Epistle to the Hebrews respectively is instructive.

3. εἰ ἐγεύσασθε . . . Κύριος] The

present tense of γεύομαι is never found in N.T., though the future occurs once ; in all other passages the word is in the aorist tense, indicating a single or initial act of some kind. The verb governs a dependent clause introduced by ὅτι once in LXX (Prov. xxxi. 18), but never in N.T. except here, nor apparently ever in classical authors. The construction is to be explained here by the fact that the phrase is adapted from Ps. xxxiv. 8, γεύσασθε καὶ ἴδετε ὅτι χρηστὸς ὁ κύριος, the καὶ ἴδετε not being used owing to its not being required by the imagery of the suckled child,[1] or having fallen out in liturgical use. The meaning of the passage hardly lies on the surface. If the fact of the quotation is ignored, the passage would be an admonition to " go on growing in grace, provided your first taste of the Christian life has proved satisfactory " — a qualification which one cannot imagine coming from the pen of a N.T. writer. The emphasis must, therefore, lie on the ἐγεύσασθε rather than on its object, the meaning being, " go on growing in grace, now that you have once begun", and the form of the clause is due to the fact that it is a quotation. In that case, the underlying idea is closely similar to that of Heb. vi. 4-6, " For it is impossible for those who were once enlightened, and have tasted (γευσαμένους) of the heavenly gift, and were made partakers of the Holy Ghost, and have tasted (γευσαμένους) the good word of God, and the powers of the world to come, if they shall fall away, to renew them again unto repentance ". The first γευσαμένους governs the genitive, the second the accusative, and the order of the words (καλὸν γευσαμένους θεοῦ ῥῆμα) is such that they might fairly be translated, " having tasted that the word of God is good ". We may compare also St.

---

[1] If Rendel Harris is right in seeing in Acts xxvi. 23 (εἰ παθητὸς ὁ Χριστός, εἰ πρῶτος κτλ.) the titles of *catenae* of O.T. proof-texts, this phrase εἰ ἐγεύσασθε κτλ. might be in the same category. Or it may have been the title of a hymn.

Bernard (letter to Prior Guiges), " So having tasted how sweet the Lord is he [sc. the Christian] passeth to the third stage and loveth God not for his own sake, but for the sake of God Himself ". The three stages are (i) love of self, (ii) love of God for self's sake, (iii) love of God for God's sake.

The force of the passage would be best brought out, therefore, if we rendered it by, " if you have responded to the Psalmist's words, ' taste and see that the Lord is good ' ", i.e. if you have taken the initial step of adherence to Christ. εἰ then means " seeing that " (Lat. *siquidem*), as in i. 17, a usage recognized by Winer, *Grammar*, p. 562, who gives a number of classical and N.T. examples. Cf. also St. Paul's similar argument in Eph. iv. 17-24, especially verse 20, ὑμεῖς δὲ οὐχ οὕτως ἐμάθετε τὸν Χριστόν· εἴγε αὐτὸν ἠκούσατε καὶ ἐν αὐτῷ ἐδιδάχθητε. And this is rendered the more likely, in view of the fact that " the whole Psalm was present to St. Peter throughout the Epistle " (Bigg); cf. verse 10 with i. 15-17 ; verse 5 with i. 17 and with πρὸς ὃν προσερχόμενοι in ii. 4 ; verses 13-17 quoted *verbatim* in iii. 10-12 ; verse 23, λυτρώσεται . . . ἐλπίζοντες ἐπ' αὐτόν with i. 18, 13 ; and verse 20 with the Epistle *passim*. We may perhaps conjecture that the Psalm was already in use in the Church in Asia Minor, perhaps as part of a " catechumen-document " or of a " persecution-document ", or as a baptismal hymn.

It is interesting to observe that Ps. xxxiv. came into regular use in the early Church at the Eucharist ; cf. the passages quoted in Bingham, *Antiquities*, Book XV, ch. v. § 10, e.g. *Apost. Const.* VIII. xiii., Cyril, *Cat. Myst.* v. 17 (who shews that it was verse 8 which brought this about), Jerome, *Epist.* xxviii. (who adds Ps. xlv.). If baptism was already in the first century connected with the great Feast of the Redemption, which culminated in the Eucharist, the " first communion " of the converts may have been present to the author's mind here. For γεύσασθαι in this connexion cf. Acts xx. 11. Lohmeyer (*Theol. Rundschau* (1937), p. 296) is not prepared to rule out a Eucharistic reference in this verse itself : cf. Add. Note H, pp. 295-7.

χρηστός] used of things tasted in Jer. xxiv. 3 (figs), Lk. v. 39 (wine). ὁ Κύριος] i.e. Christ, as shewn by the next verse ; cf. iii. 15, Κύριον δὲ τὸν Χριστὸν ἁγιάσατε. In the Psalm it means God (Jehovah), as usual in LXX. The application of the title to Christ probably comes from the language of the original community at Jerusalem, i.e. Aramaic, and was none the less acceptable owing to the fact that the Hellenistic world was familiar with the word in a religious connotation. Cf. A. D. Nock, in *Essays on the Trinity and the Incarnation*, p. 85.

4. πρὸς ὃν προσερχόμενοι] The words effect a swift transition from the individual to the institutional aspect of religion, which is nevertheless kept personal throughout. For a general discussion of verses 4-10 see Add. Notes E, F, G, H, pp. 268-98. This opening phrase recalls Matt. xi. 28, δεῦτε πρός με ; with which cf. various forms of ἔρχομαι πρός in Jn. vi. προσέρχεσθαι in N.T. takes the dative, cf. Heb. iv. 16, vii. 25, xi. 6. But it is used absolutely in Heb. x. 1, 22, and the construction with πρός is quite common in classical Greek. Hort thinks that the root of the word present in προσήλυτος may have been in St. Peter's mind ; but Philo (*de Monarchia* i. 7 [II. 219 M]) in this connexion uses the dative. His suggestion that Ps. xxxiv. 6, προσέλθατε πρὸς αὐτὸν καὶ φωτίσθητε has influenced the expression is perhaps more probable, as (1) the Psalm has just been quoted, (2) φωτίσθητε was germane to a baptismal context, and may have suggested the allusions to φῶς in verse 10, (3) the second part of the verse, καὶ τὰ πρόσωπα ὑμῶν οὐ μὴ καταισχυνθῇ is very like Is. xxviii. 16b

ὃν προσερχόμενοι, λίθον ζῶντα, ὑπὸ ἀνθρώπων μὲν ἀποδεδοκι-

quoted immediately below in I Pet. ii. 6. I should be inclined to say that the force of the double πρός is to connote " coming to stay ", i.e. as an adherent.

λίθον ζῶντα] λίθος is the usual word for a worked stone, whether a stone used in a building or a precious stone ; and it is to be distinguished from πέτρος, a loose stone lying on field or roadside, and from πέτρα, a rock, or simply rock in contrast with e.g. sand or metal.

ζῶντα is one of a number of adjectives used in these verses to point the contrast between the Christian Church and the pagan temple ; and they serve the purpose at the same time of shewing that the substantive is used in a non-literal sense. The latter usage is common in Aeschylus ; cf. Sept. 64, κῦμα χερσαῖον, P.V. 880, ἄρδις ἄπυρος, ib. 803, ἀκραγεῖς κύνας, Choeph. 493, πέδαις ἀχαλκέντοις, ib. 600, ἀπέρωτος ἔρως ; cf. also Pindar, Ol. vi. 78 [46], ἀμεμφεῖ ἰῷ μελισσᾶν. In the passage before us the stones are living people, as opposed to the dead stones of the temples of cults now superseded ; it forms a " spiritual house ", where " spiritual sacrifices " are offered, in contrast to the centres of idolatrous heathen worship ; and its priesthood is " holy ", because resting (like the Aaronic priesthood in its time) on divine appointment ; and its sacrifices are acceptable "through Jesus Christ" and not through any merit in the worshipper. On the positive side, Alford sums up the argument well : " Spiritual, because as the temple, as the priests, as the God, so the offering ".

In what sense was Christ " a (the) living stone " ? He was a Stone in the sense that He had applied to Himself, and claimed to fulfil, the passage about the Stone in Ps. cxviii. 22. The Stone there, as in Is. xxviii. 16, stands for the Jewisht heocracy, God's chosen people. (Cf. Briggs, I.C.C., on Ps. cxviii., Driver, *Isaiah : His Life and*

Times, p. 52. Even if W. E. Barnes and Oesterley are right in taking Ps. cxviii. 22 as referring primarily to the Psalmist himself, it undoubtedly contained the wider reference from the first.) The conception was not in these passages Messianic ; but Dan. ii. 31-45 shews that by the second century B.C. it had come to be applied to the Messianic *kingdom*, though not to the Messiah himself : " the proud empires engaged in building up the fabric of universal history had ignored or cast aside little Israel, which should yet become the central factor in the religious development of the human race, by virtue of its unique vocation to witness to the true God " (Edghill, *The Evidential Value of Prophecy*, pp. 386 f.). Our Lord uses it as a familiar illustration of the principle, abundantly verified in the history of Israel, that God often does His most wonderful works by instruments which the world rejects ; and he hints that it will receive a yet more striking application in Himself (Edghill, *op. cit.* p. 421). Such a use of Ps. cxviii. 22 is wholly in line with His use of Is. liii., which embodied a similar reversal of values ; and in neither case have we evidence that the application to Messiah personally was already current in His day. It is probable that the application was first made by the Lord Himself, who as Messiah represented in His own Person both the Davidic kingdom and the ideal remnant of Israel. At the same time, two passages in Justin Martyr (*Dial.* 34 (251 D), 36 (254 C), ed. Otto) imply that Jewish circles had by the second century given a direct Messianic interpretation to the O.T. passages about the Stone ; and this may well have been suggested to them by the destruction of Jerusalem in A.D. 70. So far as Christian theology is concerned, the idea that Jesus was the Stone of Ps. cxviii. 22 (and of Is. xxviii. 16 and viii. 14) rested on His

μασμένον παρὰ δὲ Θεῷ ἐκλεκτόν, ἔντιμον, ⁵καὶ αὐτοὶ ὡς λίθοι
ζῶντες οἰκοδομεῖσθε οἶκος πνευματικός, εἰς ἱεράτευμα ἅγιον,

own word, and needed no further introduction : the term is hardly yet a title. St. Peter carries the idea one stage further ; for in speaking of the Lord as the λίθος of Scripture, he had in mind not only the reversal of human judgment by God's judgment implied in prophecy and revealed in Christ's exaltation, but also the relation of Christ as cornerstone to the other stones of the Christian Church.

Further, this Stone is " living " because personal, and able to enter into vital relations with men. In the majority of cases in N.T. where the participle of ζάω is used as an adjective, it occurs as an attribute of God. The remaining instances are Jn. iv. 10 f., vii. 38, ὕδωρ ζῶν; vi. 51, ὁ ἄρτος ὁ ζῶν; Acts vii. 38, λόγια ζῶντα; Rom. xii. 1, θυσίαν ζῶσαν ; Heb. x. 20, ὁδὸν πρόσφατον καὶ ζῶσαν; and 1 Pet. i. 3, ἐλπίδα ζῶσαν, with the two occurrences in ii. 4, 5. The interpretation " full of vitality and force " will suffice in Acts vii. 38 and 1 Pet. i. 3 ; but it takes on a richer meaning when applied to persons, and still more when applied to Christ or to His gifts. When applied to persons, as it is in Rom. xii. 1 and 1 Pet. ii. 5, it connotes all that we mean by human vitality — the power of will and feeling and thought, and of entering into relationship with God and with one another. When applied to Christ or to His gifts, it adds to the idea of " living " that of life-giving. The " living water " which He gives becomes in the believer " a fountain of water welling up to life eternal " (Jn. iv. 14). He is " the living bread which came down from heaven ", and to eat of it is to have eternal life (Jn. vi. 51). His blood, shed upon the cross, constitutes a " new and living way " by which believers have access to God. So here, where Christ is called " the living stone ", the Apostle has in mind both the fact that He is now a living Person

and the fact that He communicates life to those who come to Him in faith.

ὑπὸ ἀνθρώπων . . . ἐκλεκτόν, ἔντιμον] In anticipating the passage which he is going to quote in verse 7, the author gives it a wider range, abundantly justified by the experience of the Church of his day, by substituting " men " for " the builders " of the original Scripture cited by the Lord. In ἐκλεκτόν, ἔντιμον, LXX differs from the Hebrew which gives " proven " and " precious " respectively. But the Greek suited our author well ; for ἐκλεκτόν was used of the Servant of the Lord in Is. xlii. 1, and ἐκλελεγμένος in the Lucan version of the voice from heaven at the Transfiguration (with which Hort compares the Western reading in Jn. i. 34, ὅτι οὗτός ἐστιν ὁ ἐκλεκτὸς τοῦ θεοῦ) ; while ἔντιμος is the regular Greek word for " esteemed ", held in honour ". Cf. Plato, *Rep.* 554 B, χρήματα γοῦν μάλιστα ἔντιμα . . . παρὰ τῷ τοιούτῳ.

5. καὶ αὐτοὶ ὡς λίθοι ζῶντες] Note the ὡς inserted here, but not before λίθον ζῶντα in the previous clause. Christ is in His own right the living Stone of prophecy, which He fulfils ; and that function of His is not limited to His relation to the Church and its members. Their position as stones, on the other hand, is derivative from His and is doubly metaphorical.

οἰκοδομεῖσθε] are being built up. Bigg, following Alford, takes the verb as imperative. But, though οἰκοδομεῖν is often used in a figurative sense in LXX, the second person imperative passive never seems to occur, and indeed it would involve straining the metaphor to breaking-point. Nor does the context here support it ; for in verse 4 we pass from exhortation to doctrine. The reading ἐποικοδομεῖσθε (A²C𝔑bdo 36 vulg. Cyr) is probably due to assimilation to Eph. ii. 20.

οἶκος πνευματικός] a spiritual house. Though οἶκος can mean " household ",

ἀνενέγκαι πνευματικὰς θυσίας εὐπροσδέκτους Θεῷ διὰ 'Ιησοῦ

its proximity to οἰκοδομεῖσθε shews that " house " is the meaning here; and the context is not domestic but religious and sacerdotal. The use of οἶκος for a shrine or temple is well established both in classical Greek and in LXX; e.g. Eur. *Phoen.* 1372 f., Παλλάδος χρυσάσπιδος βλέψας πρὸς οἶκον, ηὔξατ'·, Ps. cxvi. 19, ἐν αὐλαῖς οἴκου κυρίου, cxviii. 26, ηὐλογήκαμεν ὑμᾶς ἐξ οἴκου κυρίου, lxix. 10, ὁ ζῆλος τοῦ οἴκου σου καταφάγεταί με. The last passage is quoted in Jn. ii. 17 as having recurred to the minds of the disciples in connexion with the Cleansing of the Temple.

More important still, as giving the clue to the meaning of the word πνευματικός, are the words of Is. lvi. 7 which our Lord quoted on that occasion in combination with Jer. vii. 11. For a full discussion see Add. Note H, pp. 286 ff., where it is suggested that the phrase might be rendered " God's true temple ". Cf. *Ep. Barn.* iv. 11, " Let us become spiritual, let us become a temple perfect unto God ".

εἰς ἱεράτευμα ἅγιον] The previous words have defined the nature of the Church : these describe its vocation. For this " accusative of the predicate (of destination) " cf. Winer, *Grammar*, pp. 285-6, who cites Acts xiii. 22, ἤγειρεν αὐτὸν τὸν Δαβὶδ εἰς βασιλέα, i.e. " to be a king ". Cf. also 1 Clem. xlii. 4, καθίστασαν τὰς ἀπαρχὰς αὐτῶν . . . εἰς ἐπισκόπους καὶ διακόνους κτλ. But a closer analogy is to be found in Eph. ii. 21, 22, where we have αὔξει εἰς ναὸν ἅγιον and συνοικοδομεῖσθε εἰς κατοικητήριον κτλ. in consecutive verses. The usage is found in LXX and in the later Greek writers. Hort's rendering," act of priesthood ", though it would make good sense, will not do ; for (1) the word is used immediately below for " body of priests ", " priesthood ", where it is quoted from Ex. xix. 6, xxiii. 22 ; (2) this makes a better transition to the infinitive of

purpose (cf. note on verse 8) which immediately follows ; (3) the use of substantives ending in -μα in this personal and active sense can be abundantly illustrated from Greek literature, e.g. Soph. *Ant.* 756, δού-λευμα=slave, Aesch. *Ag.* 1439, μεί-λιγμα=solace (the usual meaning of the word), Eur. *Suppl.* 173, *Rhes.* 936, πρεσβεύματα=ambassadors. Jebb, on Soph. *Ant.* 650 (παραγκάλισμα), suggests that " the neuter gives a contemptuous tone " ; but this will not apply to the instances of πρεσβεύματα. The usage seems commoner in verse than in prose ; but for the latter we may cite Plutarch, *Timoleon*, ix. 4. 1, ὡς οὖν . . . οἱ Κορίνθιοι τοῖς τε πρεσβεύμασι τούτοις ἐνέτυχον καὶ τοὺς Φοίνικας . . . κατεῖδον. ἱεράτευμα meaning a priesthood or body of priests is on all fours with πρέσβευμα, and presents no real difficulty. For vernacular usage MM quote τεχνίτευμα=body of craftsmen, from an inscription of the third century B.C. The priesthood is "holy" in contrast with the heathen priesthoods of Asia Minor, which were at best idolatrous and therefore false, and at worst immoral. And the Christian Church is a priesthood, because it bears the same relation to mankind as a whole as the Jewish priesthood bore to the whole people of Israel. For further discussion of this passage see Add. Note H, pp. 291-4.

ἀνενέγκαι] ἀναφέρειν occurs in three other places in N.T. for the offering of sacrifice, Heb. vii. 27 (*bis*), xiii. 15 (sacrifice of praise), Jas. ii. 21 (offering of Isaac). In Heb. vii. 27b the reading is not certain. In Heb. ix. 28, 1 Pet. ii. 24, ἀναφέρειν is used with ἁμαρτίας, cf. note on last-named passage. Westcott thus distinguishes between ἀνα-φέρειν and προσφέρειν, both of which are common in LXX. " In ἀναφέρειν (*to offer up*) we have mainly the notion of an offering made to God and placed upon His altar, in προσφέρειν (*to offer*) that of an offering brought to God

In the former the thought of the destination of the offering prevails : in the letter that of the offerer in his relation to God. ἀναφέρειν therefore properly describes the ministerial action of the priest, and προσφέρειν the action of the offerer (Lev. ii. 14, 16 ; iv. 33, 35); but the distinction is not observed universally " [1] (on Heb. vii. 27). Here the word is used in its proper sense of a sacerdotal act. It would be specially appropriate if the Eucharist were in the author's mind, as the focus of the prayers and praises, alms, and brotherly love [2] and self-surrender of the people ; the whole constituting the " spiritual sacrifices " or acts of self-oblation which they offer. See Add. Note H, pp. 285-98.

A similar distinction of terms is found in Christian liturgical literature, where προσφορά is the usual word for the Offertory, ἀναφορά for the liturgy as a whole and finally for the central part of it, or " Prayer of Consecration " said by the celebrant. Cf. W. H. Frere, *The Anaphora*, pp. 27 f.

πνευματικὰς θυσίας] as distinct from the material sacrifices of Jewish and heathen religion. Prophets and psalmists were fully alive to the distinction, sometimes pressing it to extreme lengths as in Hos. ix. 4, Is. i. 11-15, where the sacrificial system is wholly rejected owing to the wickedness of the worshippers, at others emphasizing the superiority of righteousness to sacrifice as in Hos. vi. 6, Mic. vi. 6-8, Ps. l. 13, 14, at others again teaching that the spiritual sacrifice is the pre-condition of the other's acceptance as in Ps. li. 19. Moreover, the diversity of significance attaching to a Jewish sacrifice [3] and expressed in the different rites prescribed for it prepared the way for the various ways in which spiritual sacrifice was conceived : cf. Lev. vii. 11 ff., where the " sacrifice of peace-offerings " is adapted to express thanksgiving (αἰνέσεως) or a vow or voluntary

offering (εὐχὴν ἢ ἑκούσιον). Accordingly we find the language of sacrifice used in O.T. of prayer (Ps. cxli. 2), praise and thanksgiving (Ps. l. 14, 23, cvii. 22 : cf. W. E. Barnes, who on the last-named passage points out that in Ps. xix. 14, lxix. 30, 31, the Psalmists speak as though they regarded their songs as in themselves sacrifices), penitence (Ps. li. 19, cf. Song of the Three Children, 15, 16), and more generally righteousness (Ps. iv. 5, cf. Deut. xxxiii. 19).

In N.T. some of these figurative uses of sacrificial language recur, cf. Rev. viii. 3, 4 (prayer), Heb. xiii. 15 (praise and thanksgiving) ; the " sacrifice of righteousness " is broadened out into the complete surrender of the self to God, " the spiritual service and sacrifice of the soul " (Rom. xii. 1, 1 Pet. ii. 5) ; and this general meaning is applied in particular directions, such as faith (Phil. ii. 17), the conversion of the Gentiles (Rom. xv. 16), the apostle's labours (*ib.*), martyrdom (2 Tim. iv. 6), almsgiving (Phil. iv. 18, cf. Acts x. 4) and works of brotherly love and kindness (Heb. xiii. 16, cf. Eph. v. 2). None of these can be ruled out in the case of 1 Pet. ii. 5, though his emphasis on the *imitatio Christi* in ii. 21 ff., iii. 18 ff., and on brotherly love as the highest expression of holiness in i. 13 ff., and his exposition of the social code governing the relationships of Christians towards one another and towards their non-Christian neighbours in ii. 11–iii. 12, suggest that the sufferings incidental to the Christian life and the duties of meekness and ἀγαθοποιΐα were chiefly in his mind.

Chrysostom's exposition of Rom. xii. 1, 2 is worth consulting. How can we present our bodies as a sacrifice, he asks ? By righteousness : the eye must not see evil, nor the tongue speak it, nor the hand do it ; but conversely, τῆς τῶν ἀγαθῶν ἡμῖν ἐργασίας δεῖ, ἵνα ἡ μὲν χεὶρ ἐλεημοσύνην ποιῇ, τὸ δὲ

[1] ἀναφέρειν is used, for example, of the offerings of the congregation (ἡ ἐκκλησία) in 2 Chron. xxix. 31, 32.
[2] Cf. Taylor's note on " kindness " in *Pirqe Aboth*, i. 2.
[3] Cf. W. H. Frere, *The Anaphora*, p. 17.

στόμα εὐλογῇ τοὺς ἐπηρεάζοντας, ἡ δὲ ἀκοὴ θείαις σχολάζῃ διηνεκῶς ἀκροάσεσιν. The offering of our bodies to God means that they are no longer ours but His, and so must be kept free from impurity and luxury. The whole of our lives must be made an act of worship: ἔσται δὲ τοῦτο, ἐὰν καθ' ἑκάστην ἡμέραν προσφέρῃς αὐτῷ θύματα, καὶ ἱερεὺς τοῦ οἰκείου σώματος γίνῃ, καὶ τῆς κατὰ ψυχὴν ἀρετῆς· οἷον, ὅταν σωφροσύνην προσενέγκῃς, ὅταν ἐλεημοσύνην, ὅταν ἐπιείκειαν καὶ ἀνεξικακίαν. Similar teaching is found also in Clem. Alex. *Strom.* VII. vi. 34 [850 f. P], where the sacrifice of corporate prayer and praise is accompanied by the incense that is " brought together in praises, with a pure mind, and just and right conduct, from holy works and righteous prayer". [E. H. B. also cites Minuc. Fel. xxxii., Origen, *con. Cels.* viii. 21, and Lactantius vi. 25 (e.g. " His offering is innocency of soul; His sacrifice praise and a hymn "), and adds: " It was common among the philosophic schools to enjoin *words* of praise rather than material offerings, e.g. in *Hermetica*, δέξαι λογικὰς θυσίας (of speech alone); cf. Cic. *de Nat. Deor.* ii. 71. Some went so far as to consider even verbal worship needless, e.g. Porphyry, διὰ σιγῆς καθαρᾶς . . . θρησκεύομεν αὐτόν."] Cf. also *The Apostolic Tradition of Hippolytus*, iii. 6, with B. S. Easton's note (p. 68) and longer note entitled " The Christian ' Sacrifices ' ", pp. 65 f., and *Poimandres*, pp. 339-48 quoted by Kennedy, *St. Paul and the Mystery Religions*, pp. 107 ff.

εὐπροσδέκτους Θεῷ διὰ 'Ιησ. Χρ.] εὐπρόσδεκτος is not in LXX, but is a word of literary Greek (cf. Plut. 2. 801 C), which is used four times by St. Paul; cf. especially Rom. xv. 16, where it refers to the offering (προσφορά) he has collected for the Church at Jerusalem. δεκτός (Phil. iv. 18), ἀποδεκτός (1 Tim. ii. 3), and εὐάρεστος (Rom. xii. 1, Heb. xiii. 16) are synonyms for it. The acceptability of a sacrifice was a matter of great

moment with the Jews and with the ancients generally ; and it was symbolized in the fire which descended upon the victim in certain sacrifices (Gen. xv. 17, Lev. ix. 24), in the fire perpetually kept burning upon the altar (Lev. vi. 9), and in the " sweet smoke " (ὀσμὴ εὐωδίας) which ascended from the burnt-offering or the incense accompanying it. Cf. Gen. viii. 21, Lev. ii. 2, Ps. cxli. 2 (with Kirkpatrick's note). The portion of the meal-offering mixed with oil burnt with incense on the altar was also called the " Memorial " (ἀνάμνησις), and is probably referred to in the titles of Pss. xxxviii. and lxx. The ὀσμὴ εὐωδίας was so closely connected with acceptable sacrifice as to become before the Christian era virtually a synonym for it ; cf. *Test. Levi* iii. 6 (of the sacrifices offered by angels on men's behalf), quoted above, in the note on λογικόν. St. Paul employs the term in 2 Cor. ii. 15, 16 to denote the fragrance of the missionary work of the ministry (where mention of Christ manifesting τὴν ὀσμὴν τῆς γνώσεως αὐτοῦ is followed by : ὅτι Χριστοῦ εὐωδία ἐσμὲν τῷ θεῷ ἐν τοῖς σωζομένοις καὶ ἐν τοῖς ἀπολλυμένοις· οἷς μὲν ὀσμὴ ἐκ θανάτου εἰς θάνατον, οἷς δὲ ὀσμὴ ἐκ ζωῆς εἰς ζωήν) ; in Phil. iv. 18 (where the reference is to the Philippians' contributions to the Apostle's collection) ; and in Eph. v. 2 (where Christ is said to have offered Himself for us προσφορὰν καὶ θυσίαν τῷ θεῷ εἰς ὀσμὴν εὐωδίας).

In the case of the Christian sacrifice, the proof of its acceptance lies in Christ's resurrection. The point has been well worked out by P. de la Taille, S.J. in *The Mystery of Faith*, pp. 14 f.

The Church's sacrifices are acceptable *through Jesus Christ*, because and in so far as they are brought into the ambit of His own perfect and sufficient sacrifice offered on the cross. The means of this union of the Church's sacrifices with His is faith : and its outward expression, both on God's

Χριστοῦ. ⁶διότι περιέχει ἐν γραφῇ, Ἰδού, τίθημι ἐν Σιὼν λίθον ἀκρογωνιαῖον, ἐκλεκτόν, ἔντιμον· καὶ ὁ πιστεύων ἐπ᾽ αὐτῷ οὐ

side and on man's, is the Eucharist. Without this relationship of the Church's sacrifices to Christ's, the former would be "works", which could not obtain merit. Thus, Bengel, quoting Is. lvi. 7, αἱ θυσίαι αὐτῶν ἔσονται δεκταὶ ἐπὶ τὸ θυσιαστήριόν μου, adds : " Christ is both *precious* in Himself, and makes us accepted ; for He is the altar ".

6. διότι περιέχει ἐν γραφῇ] *wherefore it stands in writing* ; or, *and that is why it says in the hymn.* For περιέχει in this sense cf. Jos. *Ant.* XI. iv. 7, τὸ ἀντίγραφον ὑμῶν τῆς ἐπιστολῆς, ἐν τοῖς ὑπομνήμασιν εὑρὼν τοῖς Κύρου, ἀπέσταλκα· καὶ βούλομαι γίνεσθαι πάντα, καθὼς ἐν αὐτῇ περιέχει (rendered in Hudson-Havercamp (1726), *voloque ut omnia fiant quemadmodum in eis prescriptum est*). Hort also quotes Orig. *in Gen.* vi. 9, and MM give several examples of its use, sometimes with the subject added, at others intransitively, in the papyri.

ἐν γραφῇ can hardly mean " in the passage from Scripture ", which would be ἐν τῇ γραφῇ (cf. Mk. xii. 10, Lk. iv. 21, Acts i. 16, Jas. ii. 8), nor " in Scripture ", which all N.T. writers render by ἐν ταῖς γραφαῖς. But ἐν γραφῇ is used in LXX for " in writing ", cf. 2 Chron. ii. 11, xxi. 12, Ecclus. xxxix. 32, xlii. 7, xliv. 5. The last-named passage — ἐκζητοῦντες μέλη μουσικῶν, διηγούμενοι ἔπη ἐν γραφῇ — is particularly relevant, if the allusion here is to a hymn. The phrase proves, at any rate, that St. Peter was here quoting from a documentary source other than the text of Scripture itself.

Is an allusion to similar documentary sources to be discerned in the phrase διὰ γραφῶν προφητικῶν in Rom. xvi. 26 ?

Ἰδού, τίθημι κτλ.] adapted from Is. xxviii. 16, combined in the next verse with Ps. cxviii. 22 and Is. viii. 14. See Add. Note E, pp. 268 ff.

ἀκρογωνιαῖον] *designed for the corner*,

cornerstone ; not " chief cornerstone ", because the word is the κοινή equivalent of the Attic γωνιαῖος ; cf. Armitage Robinson on Eph. ii. 21, who gives examples. As he observes, " ἀκρογωνιαῖος stands to γωνιαῖος as ἐπ᾽ ἄκρας γωνίας stands to ἐπὶ γωνίας ". For the same reason, we may reject the view that a top stone, i.e. at the head of a gable, is intended, as in Zech. iv. 7 (cf. Kirkpatrick, in C.B.S., on Ps. cxviii. 22, Cadbury, *Beginnings*, v. p. 374). Both the ἀκρο- in ἀκρογωνιαῖον (Is. xxviii. 16) and the κεφαλήν in κεφαλὴν γωνίας (Ps. cxviii. 22) mean no more than the extremity of the angle : extremity and not height is the point connoted. The chief features of a cornerstone are that it controls the design of the edifice and that (unlike a foundation stone) it is visible. The old hymn of the Sarum Dedication office combines the two :

Angulare fundamentum lapis Christus missus est,
qui compage parietum in utroque nectitur,
quem Syon sancta suscepit, in quo credens permanet.

The position of a foundation stone is assigned in N.T., where the metaphor of a building is used, both to Christ Himself (1 Cor. iii. 11) and to " the apostles and prophets " (Eph. ii. 20). And Christ is indeed both " cornerstone " and " foundation stone " : the former " clearly emphasizes the cohesion of believers in the Body of Christ ", as the latter " implies their dependence on His work and strength " (Swete, on Mk. xii. 10). The " Petrine text " is not strictly germane ; for it deals, not with any part of the building, but with the nature of the sub-soil (i.e. rock) on which the building stands, as in Matt. vii. 24. Yet the Jews had curious ideas about the unity of the Rock and those, like Abraham, who were built on it ; and these ideas seem to have

μὴ καταισχυνθῇ. ⁷ὑμῖν οὖν ἡ τιμὴ τοῖς πιστεύουσιν· ἀπιστοῦσι δὲ Λίθος ὃν ἀπεδοκίμασαν οἱ οἰκοδομοῦντες, οὗτος ἐγενήθη εἰς κεφαλὴν γωνίας, ⁸καὶ λίθος προσκόμματος καὶ πέτρα σκανδάλου, οἳ προσκόπτουσι τῷ λόγῳ ἀπειθοῦντες, εἰς ὃ καὶ ἐτέθησαν.

influenced Origen (cf. E. A. Abbott, *The Son of Man*, § 3596 and notes, quoting Orig. *in Evang. Matth.* xii. 10, *con. Cels.* vi. 77).

ἐκλεκτόν, ἔντιμον] See note on verse 4.

7. ὑμῖν οὖν ἡ τιμὴ τοῖς πιστεύουσιν] a *midrashic* note on the preceding promise to the faithful, which it links up with the description of the Stone as "held in honour". The meaning is that the honour which Christ has by virtue of God's choice is imparted to, and shared by, the faithful. Hort objects to this as "a weak and superfluous statement", because it repeats in a positive form what was said negatively in the previous clause. But the interpretation was needed at this point, if the main theme of the Church's relation to Christ were to be sustained throughout. καὶ αὐτοὶ ὡς λίθοι ζῶντες ... ὑμῖν οὖν ἡ τιμή ... ὑμεῖς δὲ γένος ἐκλεκτόν form a connected series, strong enough to carry the allusion to unbelievers without the main sense being lost. The alternative rendering of τιμή as "preciousnesss", though supported by many great names in the sixteenth and seventeenth centuries, is effectively criticized by Bigg.

ἀπιστοῦσι ... κεφαλὴν γωνίας] See notes on λίθον ζῶντα and ἀκρογωνιαῖον above.

8. λίθος προσκόμματος] *a stone to stumble over*, such as would be any chance stone lying in the way. It is not true to say that Christ is everything or nothing, and can be taken or left; for to those who refuse belief He is a constant anomaly, meeting them in unexpected places and challenging their indifference. His own words, "He that is not with me is against me" (Matt. xii. 30), illustrate the truth: cf. also Lk. ii. 34, Jn. ix. 39. And it is verified in the stumbling ways, the confusion and lack of direc-

tion, which characterize ages of unbelief. The theme is powerfully set forth by L. T. Mumford in *Faith for Living*.

οἱ προσκόπτουσι κτλ.] The fundamental cause of their stumbling on the word is unbelief (ἀπιστοῦσι being the antecedent of οἵ), its proximate cause is the disobedience (ἀπειθοῦντες) which is inseparable from unbelief. τῷ λόγῳ is governed by both verbs. For disobedience in this sense cf. iv. 17 below, τῶν ἀπειθούντων τῷ τοῦ Θεοῦ εὐαγγελίῳ. The word is indicative of more than the suspense or refusal of intellectual assent; it connotes a revolt of the will corresponding to the fact that the Gospel is addressed to the heart and conscience of man and not only to his mind. This is the case wherever sin is placed in the forefront of Christian teaching and preaching. A good example of this occurs in the story of the man healed at the Pool of Bethesda (Jn. v. 1-16). He obeyed Jesus' command to take up his bed and was cured, and stoutly pleaded that injunction when charged with contravening the sabbath rules. But when Jesus met him later and spoke of sin, he rebelled, and went and informed against Jesus. When it was a question simply of his own physical cure, he could be bold enough; but when its spiritual lesson was underlined, he turned traitor. As Leighton says (*op. cit.* p. 253), "Besides all the opposition that meets faith within, in our hearts, it hath this without, that it rows against the great stream of the world's opinion".

εἰς ὃ καὶ ἐτέθησαν] i.e. ordained by God: cf. Is. xlix. 6, 1 Tim. ii. 7, 2 Tim. i. 11, and especially 1 Thess. v. 9, οὐκ ἔθετο ἡμᾶς ὁ θεὸς εἰς ὀργήν, ἀλλ' εἰς περιποίησιν σωτηρίας. Bigg would restrict this *praedestinatio in*

⁹ὑμεῖς δὲ γένος ἐκλεκτόν, βασίλειον ἱεράτευμα, ἔθνος ἅγιον, λαὸς

malam partem to the divine decree that stumbling follows inevitably upon disobedience. Hort, more profoundly, sees a connexion between τίθημι in verse 6 and ἐτέθησαν here, and urges that both the redemptive mission and work of Christ and its rejection and rejectors were within the counsel and purpose of God. On the other hand, it is not stated here that this rejection is final and irretrievable. The primary reference here is probably to the rejection of Christ by the Jews (Hort, Windisch), and St. Paul in Rom. ix.–xi. emphasizes both how their " stumbling " (xi. 11) was over-ruled to the blessing of the Gentiles and also that it could be retrieved by their repentance (xi. 23 ff.). But there is nothing here to suggest that St. Peter was borrowing from St. Paul, nor that he had the Jews only in mind. Moreover, St. Paul's argument in Rom. ix.–xi. will apply, *mutatis mutandis*, to the heathen world generally. Work in the mission field is often checked along one line, only to develop along another; as in India, for instance, the stiffness of the Brahmin resistance to Christianity has led the Church to turn to the outcaste populations, with very fruitful results. St. Peter's teaching brings both Brahmin and outcaste within the range of God's purpose, and thereby prompts us to a patient and reverent interpretation of history. For, as Archbishop Leighton observes, " Here it were easier to lead you into a deep, than to lead you forth again ".

Erasmus and many other commentators followed Bede in referring εἰς ὅ to *faith*, as being the general subject of the passage. Estius surveys and criticizes these views well.

9. ὑμεῖς δὲ κτλ.] For a discussion of this passage see Add. Note F, pp. 277-81. Cf. H. Newton Flew, *Jesus and His Church*, p. 220, " all the titles of privilege can be applied to them which were applied to Israel of old ".

γένος ἐκλεκτόν] taking up the ἐκ-

λεκτοῖς of the Salutation. As Newton Flew observes, the idea goes back to the *verba Christi*, cf. Matt. xxii. 14, Mk. xiii. 20, 22, 27, Lk. xviii. 7. And St. Peter's language seems clearly influenced by Is. xliii. 20, 21, ποτίσαι τὸ γένος μου τὸ ἐκλεκτόν, λαόν μου ὃν περιεποιησάμην τὰς ἀρετάς μου διηγεῖσθαι, where the collocation of γένος ἐκλεκτόν, λαός, περιεποιησάμην (περιποίησις), ἀρετάς (in the plural) is repeated in too marked a way to be accidental.

βασίλειον ἱεράτευμα] For ἱεράτευμα see the note on verse 5. βασίλειον may be either a substantive or an adjective. (1) As a substantive, βασίλειον never seems to be equivalent to βασιλεία, " kingdom ". In LXX it means " sovereignty " (Dan. iv. 32, vii. 22, Wisd. i. 14), or " monarchy " (2 Macc. ii. 17), or palace, king's place (Prov. xviii. 19 (sing.), Esth. i. 9, Dan. vi. 18, Nah. ii. 6 (plur.)). In the last-named sense the word is also usually plural in classical Greek, cf. Herod. i. 30, 178, Xen. *Cyr.* ii. iv. 3, Plato, *Critias*, 115 C, 116 A, 117 A, *Axiochus*, 371 A. Polybius (iii. xv. 3) uses it in the singular of a " royal city ", " capital ". The connotation of the word in the Greek of 400–100 B.C. is important as throwing light on the meaning it had for the LXX translators ; for, while the Hebrew of Ex. xix. 6 gave them " a kingdom of priests ", they rendered it by two substantives, βασίλειον and ἱεράτευμα, in apposition. That this was so is rendered almost certain by 2 Macc. ii. 17, where God is described as ἀποδοὺς τὴν κληρονομίαν αὐτοῦ πᾶσιν καὶ τὸ βασίλειον καὶ τὸ ἱεράτευμα καὶ τὸν ἁγιασμόν, καθὼς ἐπηγγείλατο διὰ τοῦ νόμου, and by Philo, *de Sobr.* 66 [I. 402 M] τῶν δώδεκα . . . φυλῶν, ἃς οἱ χρησμοὶ βασίλειον καὶ ἱεράτευμά φασιν εἶναι. Rev. i. 6, v. 10, ἐποίησας αὐτοὺς τῷ θεῷ βασιλείαν καὶ ἱερεῖς also bears out this view. But, while all these passages take βασίλειον ἱεράτευμα in Ex. xix. 6 as two substantives in apposition, they give βασίλειον different meanings : for the author of 2 Maccabees it means " the institution of monarchy ", for Philo " palace " (βασίλειον γὰρ ὁ βασιλέως δήπουθεν οἶκος, ἱερὸς ὄντως καὶ μόνος ἄσυλος), for the Seer of Patmos " kingdom ".[1] In the only other place where the word occurs in N.T. (Lk. vii. 25), it is a substantive meaning " king's house " or " palace ". And βασίλειον is nearly always a substantive in the Fathers (except when quoting this passage, as e.g. Aug. de Civ. Dei xvii. 5, plebs sancta, regale sacerdotium), cf. Eus. V.C. iii. 38, xxxvi. 2, Greg. Nys. Or. Cat. 18 (M 45. 36 A) (palace) ; 2 Clem. vi. 9, Just. Apol. i. 32 (73 C), Eus. V.C. ix. 5, xxix. 4 (119 C) (kingdom, empire); 2 Clem. xvii. 5 (sovereign authority) ; Ath. Ep. ad Jov. 4 (M 26. 821 C) (majesty). [I owe the references to the courtesy of the editor of the forthcoming Patristic Lexicon.] (2) βασίλειος as an adjective meaning " royal " is not rare in the Greek tragedians, but seems to connote a more intimate and personal relationship than βασιλικός, and to be almost equivalent to τοῦ βασιλέως. If St. Peter took βασίλειον in Ex. xix. 6 as an adjective, he would have meant by it " a priesthood in the service of a king ", i.e. God. Such priesthoods, moreover, were widely spread throughout the Roman Empire in the first century A.D. in connexion with the worship of the Emperor, who was often called βασιλεύς (cf. 1 Pet. ii. 17) ; though I cannot find evidence for the phrase βασίλειον ἱεράτευμα with this reference in the secular literature of the period. Had Tacitus written in Greek he might have used such a phrase to describe the sodalium Augustalium sacerdotium whose foundation by Tiberius in A.D. 15 he records in Ann. i. 54. Both at Rome and Athens, moreover, the chief religious

official went by the name of rex and βασιλεύς respectively. There was good reason, it might be argued, why St. Peter, before quoting the words βασίλειον ἱεράτευμα, should be at pains to forestall any misunderstanding by saying that the Christians form a ἱεράτευμα ἅγιον.

Three reasons seem to turn the scale in favour of the former of the two views just described. There is first the testimony of 2 Maccabees and Philo to current exegesis of Ex. xix. 6. Secondly, there is the order of the words : if βασίλειον were an adjective, it would most naturally follow ἱεράτευμα as ἐκλεκτόν follows γένος and ἅγιον follows ἔθνος. And, thirdly, there is the interpretation of βασίλειον which appears to be implied in πνευματικὸς οἶκος. The extent to which in verses 4, 5 St. Peter is interpreting the O.T. phrases which he will quote immediately in verses 6-10 is discussed at length in Add. Note E on pp. 268-77. And βασίλειον, " a king's house ", would need no less interpretation than βασίλειον, " royal " : if the latter suggested a priesthood analogous to the Augustales, the former had implications of splendour and wealth which might easily be misleading, to the unbeliever no less than to the Christian. When the Apostle says that Christians are " built up a spiritual house ", it is as though he said, " You constitute a real ' king's house ', but it is the house of God the invisible King, who is worshipped in spirit and truth ".

λαὸς εἰς περιποίησιν] a people for God's own possession (cf. Aug. in loc., haereditas acquisita, and Jerome, in peculium). This is the rendering St. Peter's source gives of Ex. xix. 5, λαὸς περιούσιος (" special ", " peculiar ") ἀπὸ πάντων τῶν ἐθνῶν· ἐμὴ γάρ ἐστιν πᾶσα ἡ γῆ ; and a very good paraphrase it is. The original LXX phrase (Ex. xix. 5, Deut. vii. 6, etc.) occurs in Tit. ii. 14. But the same Hebrew

---

[1] So apparently Melito, Homily on the Passion, p. 11, l. 17 [Studies and Documents, xii. p. 133].

εἰς περιποίησιν, ὅπως τὰς ἀρετὰς ἐξαγγείλητε τοῦ ἐκ σκότους

word is translated by some part of περιποιεῖσθαι, περιποίησις, in I Chron. xxix. 3, Mal. iii. 17, and especially Is. xliii. 21. The nearest N.T. parallel is Acts xx. 28, τὴν ἐκκλησίαν τοῦ θεοῦ, ἣν περιεποιήσατο διὰ τοῦ αἵματος τοῦ ἰδίου. περιποίησις would describe the action of a boy who collects curios, gadgets, knives, etc., which become his special treasures. Israel had been the object of God's special affection in a similar way, and this affection was now transferred to the Christian Church.

The substantive περιποίησις is used both actively and intransitively in N.T. It is intransitive in Eph. i. 14 and here, but active and governing a genitive in Heb. x. 39, εἰς περιποίησιν ψυχῆς. In I Thess. v. 9, εἰς περιποίησιν σωτηρίας and 2 Thess. ii. 14, εἰς περιποίησιν δόξης, the construction is doubtful. Commenting on the former verse Milligan claims that the active sense is preferable, because "in the only other passages where the word occurs in N.T. (2 Thess. ii. 14, Heb. x. 39) the active sense is alone suitable". But this is doubtful, in view of I Pet. ii. 9 and Eph. i. 14. Lightfoot discusses the phrase in On a Fresh Revision of the New Testament, pp. 237, 241 f. (1871), and Notes on the Epistles of St. Paul, p. 76 and p. 121 ; and seems to favour the intransitive use in these two passages of Thessalonians, owing to "the almost technical sense which the words περιποιεῖσθαι, περιποίησις bear in the New Testament". He adds that περιποίησις is almost equivalent to ἐκλογή. And MM cite a second-century papyrus for the phrase τὸ τῆς περιποιήσεως δίκαιον = "the claim of ownership". In that case σωτηρίας and δόξης are descriptive or qualifying genitives, and the phrases would be rendered by "for a redemptive possession" and "for our Lord's glorious possession" respectively. A further important point is that the idea of "acquiring"

the glory of our Lord Jesus Christ is one without parallel in N.T. : it is imparted to Christians, but not acquired. As we shall see (Essay II, pp. 382-4), 2 Thess. ii. 13-17 is a passage which presents a specially close affinity in language and ideas with I Peter, and this use of εἰς περιποίησιν may be regarded as a characteristic of Silvanus.

τὰς ἀρετὰς] excellencies, noble acts. As Hort observes, the word ἀρετή connotes both excellence in any sphere of activity and also the prestige which such excellence acquires ; and this double usage is particularly common in the Greek poets of the fifth and earlier centuries B.C. Though ἀρετή came increasingly to be used by the philosophers of moral excellence only, its earlier variety of meaning is clearly implied in Aristotle's definition of happiness as ψυχῆς ἐνέργεια κατ᾿ ἀρετὴν ἀρίστην ἐν βίῳ τελείῳ (Eth. Nicom. I. vii.). So too Plato, Rep. 618 B, where ἀρεταί means "noble deeds", as probably also in Ps.-Plato, Axiochus, 365 ; and cf. Dion. Halic. Ant. Rom. I. lxx. 177, οἷς τὸ εὐγενὲς αἱ ἀρεταὶ μὴ ἀπιστεῖσθαι πάρεσχον. The plural is very rare in LXX, but it would have appealed strongly to Greek ears, not only the intrinsic glory of God's character but also the "noble acts" (cf. Ps. cl. 2) by which He had revealed it throughout history. In the case before us, the author has in mind especially the redemption brought about by Christ's death and resurrection, and the divine wisdom, love, power, and mercy which lay behind it and in it.

ἐξαγγείλητε] advertise : a more striking word than διηγεῖσθαι, which is commoner in LXX. Cf. Ps. cvii. 22, καὶ θυσάτωσαν θυσίαν αἰνέσεως, καὶ ἐξαγγειλάτωσαν τὰ ἔργα αὐτοῦ ἐν ἀγαλλιάσει.

τοῦ ἐκ σκότους . . . φῶς] a description of the change from heathenism to Christianity, which the experience of

ὑμᾶς καλέσαντος εἰς τὸ θαυμαστὸν αὐτοῦ φῶς, ¹⁰οἵ ποτε οὐ λαός,
νῦν δὲ λαὸς Θεοῦ, οἱ οὐκ ἠλεημένοι, νῦν δὲ ἐλεηθέντες.

the mission field to-day abundantly justifies. St. Paul claimed (Acts xxvi. 17, 18) that he was sent to the Gentiles, " to open their eyes, and to turn them from darkness to light, and from the power of Satan unto God, that they may receive forgiveness of sins, and inheritance among them which are sanctified by faith " in Christ. Darkness often represents in Hebrew thought the sphere or condition of sin, cf. Prov. ii. 13, " Who leave the paths of uprightness, to walk in the ways of darkness ". So our Lord says, " If thine eye be evil, thy whole body shall be full of darkness " (Matt. vi. 23). And this darkness reached its climax in the sin of those who crucified Him : " this is your hour, and the power of darkness " (Lk. xxii. 53). The metaphor expresses the deceit and concealment which accompany evil, and the bewilderment and misery which it causes. Light, on the other hand, was thought of as from the Creation onwards the special characteristic of God, who dwells in it and imparts it to all who love truth and justice ; and thousands have made the Psalmist's words their own, " The Lord is my light and my salvation ; whom then shall I fear ? "

The words here are not a quotation from O.T.; but Is. lx., especially verses 1-3, 14, 15 may well have been in the writer's mind. The phrase reflects " that profound dualism which dominates the biblical history of humanity from Genesis to Revelation " (Godet).

The transition from darkness to light represents intellectual conversion in the great simile of the Cave in Plato's *Republic*. And cf. Bacon's *Essays* (E. H. B.) : " The first creature of God in the works of the days was the light of the sense ; the last was the light of reason ; and His sabbath work ever since is the illumination of His spirit ". And cf. Milton, *Par. Lost*, iii. ll. 1-12.

10. οἵ ποτε κτλ.] based on verses in Hos. i. and ii., cf. Add. Note F, pp. 277-81. The term λαός would have appealed at once to St. Peter's Jewish readers, many of whom must have felt that they had become dispersed morally as well as geographically through their distance from Palestine, and that their sense of being " the people of God " was hard to keep alive. But it would have had a meaning equally important for Gentiles of Greek upbringing. In Homer the word means people regarded as a community, whether defined by common allegiance to a prince or by pursuit of a common avocation ; cf. *Il.* xi. 676, *Od.* xiv. 28, and later Aesch. *Pers.* 383, ναυτικὸς λεώς, Ar. *Pax*, 920, ὁ γεωργικὸς λεώς. In the fifth century and later it was used of the people assembled as such in the theatre or other place of meeting, and also of any people, such as a tribe or nation, who were called by one name. In short, the term connotes in Greek *community*. In the mixed society of the Roman Empire, where freedom of association was suspect and subject to restrictive laws, as in modern despotic states, this sense of community must have worn very thin, and produced a widespread feeling of homelessness ; for experience does not suggest that, when men cease to say " Dear city of Cecrops ", they substitute for it " Dear city of mankind ". Old loyalties can wither and die, without larger ones taking their place, except in a superficial way. What St. Peter's words conveyed to people so placed was that they now once again belonged to a community which claimed their loyalty ; and it was something which could give all their instincts of patriotism full satisfaction.

ii. 11–iii. 12. Second Ethical Section.

Having established the unique calling and character of the Christian

¹¹'Αγαπητοί, παρακαλῶ ὡς παροίκους καὶ παρεπιδήμους
ἀπέχεσθαι τῶν σαρκικῶν ἐπιθυμιῶν, αἵτινες στρατεύονται κατὰ

community as the true Israel, the author proceeds to shew how the principles governing its membership are to be applied to the relationships of daily life. He begins with a short general paragraph which recalls the opening phrase of the Epistle and summarizes the law of holiness set forth in i. 13-25; and he goes on to deal in detail with the civil power and the duties of Christians as citizens, and then with their duties within the home, whether as slaves, as wives, or as husbands. The Apostle appears to be using here a domestic code which was familiar in outline to his readers and was used by other N.T. writers also; and he makes the slave-master relationship the occasion for a most striking passage of teaching on the *imitatio Christi*. For the primitive domestic code cf. Essay II, pp. 419-39, and Appended Note, pp. 467-88: it is probable that the content, but not the order, of the original is represented more closely in 1 Peter than in any other Epistle. The keynote of the ethical teaching of this Section is submission.

ii. 11, 12. Introduction to the Section, at once resumptive and prefatory.

11. 'Αγαπητοί] For the use of this vocative in N.T. at points where traditional teaching is again recalled to the readers' mind cf. Essay II, p. 388. The term is especially opportune here, since Love has been emphasized above (i. 22) as the characteristic quality of the holy community. ὡς παροίκους καὶ παρεπιδήμους] St. Peter has used both terms earlier, παροικ. in i. 17 and παρεπιδήμ. in i. 1. Though their meaning is almost identical, παρεπιδήμοις in i. 1 has special reference to the historical circumstances of the communities addressed, while τὸν τῆς παροικίας ὑμῶν χρόνον has a wider reference, connoting permanent conditions governing the life of a holy com-

munity, i.e. its detachment. This detachment is emphasized in the Law of Holiness (Lev. xvii.–xxvii.), where the fact that the Israelites were προσήλυτοι καὶ πάροικοι before God (Lev. xxv. 23) is given as a reason why land should not be sold as a freehold. πάροικος καὶ παρεπίδημος occur in conjunction in LXX only in Gen. xxiii. 4 (Abraham's description of himself, and the ground of his plea for a burial-place) and in Ps. xxxix. 13 (the ground of the Psalmist's prayer for God's help). In the present case the historical circumstances of St. Peter's readers were an outward expression of the detachment from the world which belonged to their calling as God's holy community; and their combination provides a strong ground for the ethical injunction which follows. They do not belong to the Gentile world around them, and they must not mix with it. They have a spiritual inheritance (i. 4, 5, cf. Heb. xi. 13) and calling, and they must shew it by the quality of their lives. For the detachment involved in the Christian pilgrimage we may compare Epictetus, " But while He allows thee to enjoy it [sc. thy property], use it as a thing which does not belong to thee, and as a traveller uses a hostelry ". Cf. also the end of *Piers Plowman*, with Skeat's comment.

ἀπέχεσθαι] For the place of this in the primitive Christian catechism and its connexion with the Jewish Law of Holiness cf. Essay II, pp. 369-75.

τῶν σαρκικῶν ἐπιθυμιῶν] i.e. the impulses which belong to the selfish and lower side of man's nature, and are characteristic of *l'homme moyen sensuel*. They carry on war against man's soul, which is his true self and marks him as a spiritual being; and they thus hinder his salvation (i. 9), and are incompatible with the " spiritual sacrifices " alluded to just above. The " lusts of our flesh " are alluded

τῆς ψυχῆς· ¹²τὴν ἀναστροφὴν ὑμῶν ἐν τοῖς ἔθνεσιν ἔχοντες καλήν,
ἵνα, ἐν ᾧ καταλαλοῦσιν ὑμῶν ὡς κακοποιῶν, ἐκ τῶν καλῶν

to in Eph. ii. 3 (cf. also Rom. xiii. 14, Gal. v. 16, 17, 24, 1 Jn. ii. 16); and the spiritual combat which they involve in men's inner life is referred to in somewhat different terms in Rom. vii. 22 f. and Jas. iv. 1. But, as Windisch observes, there is no reason to deduce from these parallels that our author was dependent upon any of these works, for the teaching and the imagery in which it is clothed were commonplaces of Jewish-Hellenistic-Christian education. Cf. Plato, *Phaedo*, 83 B, ἡ τοῦ ὡς ἀληθῶς φιλοσόφου ψυχὴ οὕτως ἀπέχεται τῶν ἡδονῶν τε καὶ ἐπιθυμιῶν καὶ λυπῶν καὶ φόβων, καθ᾽ ὅσον δύναται. Aristotle (*Eth. Nicom.* II. ii. 9) illustrates his discussion of virtuous habits with the sentence οὕτω δ᾽ ἔχει καὶ ἐπὶ τῶν ἀρετῶν· ἔκ τε γὰρ τοῦ ἀπέχεσθαι τῶν ἡδονῶν γινόμεθα σώφρονες, καὶ γενόμενοι μάλιστα δυνάμεθα ἀπέχεσθαι αὐτῶν. So too Sallust, *Catil.* 51, *Ubi intenderis ingenium, valet; si libido possidet, ea dominatur, animus nihil valet.* And for the inward conflict cf. Philo, *Leg. All.* ii. 106 [I. 85 M], μάχου δὲ καὶ σύ, ὦ διάνοια, πρὸς πᾶν πάθος καὶ διαφερόντως πρὸς ἡδονήν. Moral teaching of this kind had long been taught in the philosophical schools and gymnasia of the Graeco-Roman world, the former laying great stress (at least in the pre-Christian era) on the duty of submission to authority. Cf. Rostovtzeff, *op. cit.* ii. pp. 1078-87, and iii. p. 1379, n. 83. There is an echo of 1 Pet. ii. 11, Gal. v. 17, and perhaps Tit. ii. 12 (τὰς κοσμικὰς ἐπιθυμίας) in *Ep. Polyc.* v. 3, καλὸν γὰρ τὸ ἀνακόπτεσθαι ἀπὸ τῶν ἐπιθυμιῶν ἐν τῷ κόσμῳ ὅτι πᾶσα ἐπιθυμία κατὰ τοῦ πνεύματος στρατεύεται.

12. τὴν ἀναστροφὴν κτλ.] "St. Peter now passes from the inner purity to its visible fruits" (Hort). For ἀναστροφή see the note on i. 15 above. Careful regard to the *effect* of Christian life and conduct on the minds of con-

temporary society rested on the *verbum Christi* in Matt. v. 16, and was a prominent feature of early Christian teaching, cf. Essay II, p. 373. καλός and not ἀγαθός is the adjective used here, because it implies that the conduct in question not only is good, but also appears so. This point was of particular importance in a society which applied to the highest kind of human character the term καλὸς κἀγαθός, i.e. one whose intrinsic goodness is also beautiful in others' eyes.

ἔχοντες] For construction cf. note on συσχηματιζόμενοι in i. 14.

ἵνα κτλ.] But the motive for creating this impression is not self-regarding: its aim is the conversion of the unbelieving world through a juster view of Christian character to a belief in God which expresses itself in worship.

ἐν ᾧ] *whereinsoever, whenever*, i.e. almost "in the very act of". Bengel's interpretation of ἐν ᾧ in i. 6 (q.v.) fits this passage and the similar one in iii. 16, and above all iv. 4. It is more general than Hort's "in which matter", and therefore more easily adaptable to different contexts, such as e.g. Rom. ii. 1, xiv. 21, 2 Cor. xi. 12.

καταλαλοῦσιν] best expressed by our phrase "run down": the author is dealing here with malicious gossip and slander, not with legal charges: cf. Field, *Otium Norvicense*, p. 149 (on Jas. iv. 11).

κακοποιῶν] used quite generally of "wicked men", "evil-doers", in Prov. xxiv. 19, and cf. the adjective with γυνή in Prov. xii. 4. This general sense fits all the other occurences in 1 Pet. (ii. 14, iii. 17 (particularly) iv. 15, cf. 3 Jn. 11). The result of these slanders was that Christians acquired, or could be charged with having, a bad reputation, such as in Rome enabled Nero to make them the scapegoats of his crimes. Cf. Tac. *Ann.* xv. 44, *quos per flagitia invisos vulgus Christianos appellabat*; Suet.

ἔργων ἐποπτεύοντες δοξάσωσι τὸν Θεὸν ἐν ἡμέρᾳ ἐπισκοπῆς.
¹³Ὑποτάγητε πάσῃ ἀνθρωπίνῃ κτίσει διὰ τὸν Κύριον, εἴτε

Ner. 16, *Afflicti suppliciis Christiani,
genus hominum superstitionis novae ac
maleficae* ; and, for a later age, Tert.
Apol. 7.

ἐκ τῶν καλῶν ἔργων ἐποπτεύοντες] *as
a result of your good works, as they
watch them.* So too below, iii. 1, 2.
ἐποπτεύοντες is here present participle,
not aorist, as covering a longer period
of time than the actual good deeds,
and including the observers' memory
of them and reflexion upon them.
Classical usage supports the meaning,
" watch over a period ", cf. Aesch.
Choeph. 489, and ἐποπτής in *P.V.*
301, with which cf. 1 Clem. lix. 3.
There are, in fact, three moments in
the Apostle's purview : (1) the good
works are done, (2) the heathen watch
them and reflect upon them, (3) as a
result they end by glorifying God " in
the day of visitation ". For ἐποπτής,
ἐποπτεύειν in the Mystery Religions
cf. Add. Note L, p. 310.

δοξάσωσι] *end by glorifying.* Based
on the *verbum Christi* in Matt. v. 16,
ὅπως ἴδωσιν ὑμῶν τὰ καλὰ ἔργα, καὶ
δοξάζωσι τὸν πατέρα ὑμῶν τὸν ἐν τοῖς
οὐρανοῖς. The idea has an earlier
Jewish root in *Test. Naphth.* viii. 4,
" If ye work that which is good, my
children, both men and angels shall
bless you ; and God shall be glorified
among the Gentiles through you, and
the devil shall flee from you ". The
text was probably familiar in the early
Church, as the last phrase is quoted in
Jas. iv. 7: see Essay II, pp. 417 f..
For patristic echoes of the idea cf. Ign.
Eph. x., Hermas, *Mand.* iii. 1.

ἐν ἡμέρᾳ ἐπισκοπῆς] not " the day of
your trial ", or " verdict in court ",
though that would make a good sense,
but the day of divine inquest, when
God will search (ἐπισκέπτομαι) the conscience of the heathen, so that they
turn either to life or to death. For
ἐπισκοπή see Kittel, *Th.W⁰.s.N.T.*,
sub voc. In general, " ἐπισκοπή is not
exercised by men " in O.T. : a " day

of visitation " is usually a day of
punishment (cf. Is. x. 3, and ἐν καιρῷ
ἐπισκοπῆς in Jer. vi. 15, x. 15, ὥρα ἐπισκοπῆς in Ecclus. xviii. 20), but acquittal, pardon, and blessing are not
excluded (Gen. l. 24 f., Is. xxiii. 16,
Wisd. iii. 7, iv. 15). N.T. takes over
this eschatological connotation, cf.
Lk. xix. 44, a *verbum Christi* where
the day of visitation is identified with
Christ's offer of salvation to Israel.
On 1 Pet. ii. 12 Kittel says : " One
may understand this day as that on
which God will present to the slander-
ous heathen, with their conversion,
also the right insight into the morality
of Christian life ; for the ἐπισκοπή
is understood as the whole personal
experience of mercy in which Christ
becomes Lord over men ". If Kittel
is right, the phrase is eschatological,
but of a piece with that " realized
eschatology " in terms of which the
advent of salvation through Christ
was interpreted : it looks forward to
this crisis of conversion rather than to
final Judgment. Cf. Wisd. iii. 13, ἕξει
καρπὸν ἐν ἐπισκοπῇ ψυχῶν. E. H. B.
draws my attention to Cranmer's beautiful prayer : " Lord, we beseech thee,
give ear unto our prayers, and by thy
gracious visitation lighten the darkness of our hearts ; through Jesus
Christ our Lord ".

13-17. Christians and the Duties
of Citizenship. For the general teaching of this passage on the authority
and function of the State and the
relationship of Christians towards it
cf. Introd. pp. 87-90; and for the
probable source underlying it, Essay
II, pp. 429-31. Similar teaching
occurs in Romans, 1 Timothy and
Titus, but this Petrine passage appears
to be nearest to the original.

13. Ὑποτάγητε] St. Peter prefers the
aorist imperative (twenty-two times) in
commands to the present (six times) :
in marked contrast to St. Paul's usage
(Moulton, *op. cit.* i. p. 174). Yet here,

βασιλεῖ, ὡς ὑπερέχοντι, ¹⁴εἴτε ἡγεμόσιν, ὡς δι' αὐτοῦ πεμπο-
μένοις εἰς ἐκδίκησιν κακοποιῶν ἔπαινον δὲ ἀγαθοποιῶν· ¹⁵ὅτι

as in Jas. iv. 7, more than an idiosyncrasy of style may be involved, the
aorist pointing less to the continual
course of submission than to the act of
decision by which this policy of submission is adopted. What is inculcated, in that case, is an act of faith
rather than a rule of conduct. The
same cause probably accounts for the
imperative being used here, whereas
in ii. 18, iii. 1, 7, 9 the author uses the
imperatival participle: cf. Dr. Daube's
Appended Note, pp. 467-88.

πάσῃ ἀνθρωπίνῃ κτίσει] *to every fundamental social institution*, i.e. the State,
the household, and the family. κτίσις
was the regular Greek term for the
founding of a city (cf. Polyb. IX. i. 4),
and it is in this sense rather than the
usual O.T. sense of a divine creation
that it is employed here : though the
idea that such institutions were part of
God's plan for human life (cf. Ecclus.
vii. 15, of husbandry, xxxviii. 1, of
medicine) was not excluded. Whereas
St. Paul emphasizes the divine *origin*
of the State, St. Peter speaks rather of
its divinely ordained *functions* : the
institution itself, together with those
of the household and the family, he
takes for granted.

διὰ τὸν Κύριον] i.e. as deserving not
merely an outward submission, but
an inward loyalty. There may be an
allusion to the *imitatio Christi* here,
which is to be developed in the next
section ; for the Lord had shewn
complete submission before Caiaphas,
Herod, and Pilate, and His disciples
must do likewise. Further, the phrase,
like St. Paul's " for conscience' sake "
(Rom. xiii. 5, cf. 1 Pet. ii. 19, Tit. iii. 1),
provides a motive for civic duty very
different from that of Greek thought
which claimed as of right to sacrifice
the individual to the community. Cf.
Luigi Sturzo, *Church and State*, p. 23.

13, 14. βασιλεῖ] a word applicable
to any of the kings among the Diadochi
whom the Romans continued to allow

to reign, e.g. in Egypt, Syria, Palestine, or Pergamum ; but applied *par
excellence* to the Emperor, as here.
ἡγέμονες connotes both the *legati
Caesaris* and the proconsuls, who
governed the imperial and senatorial
provinces respectively.

ὡς ὑπερέχοντι . . ὡς δι' αὐτοῦ
πεμπομένοις] Note the contrast here
between the sovereign power (ὑπερέχοντι), on whose origin the Apostle is
silent, and the officials and ministers
who are sent to govern by his mandate
(δι' αὐτοῦ). Bigg seems to go too far
in ascribing to St. Peter and St. Paul
respectively the doctrines of sovereignty
which were distinguished in the English political thought of the late seventeenth century as Whig and Tory ;
and St. Peter's acceptance of the
sovereignty of the Emperor without
attempting to explain it recalls Montrose's famous words on its mysterious
nature. Cf. John Buchan, *Montrose*,
Appendix, pp. 397-406. For a discussion of mediaeval and later views
of sovereignty cf. Figgis, *The Divine
Right of Kings*.

εἰς ἐκδίκησιν κτλ.] On the statement
as a whole cf. Bishop Butler, *Analogy*,
I. ii. p. 37 (Oxford, 1849) : " The
annexing pleasure to some actions,
and pain to others, in our power to do
or forbear, and giving notice of this
appointment to those whom it concerns : is the proper formal notion of
government ". The negative side of
the statement is illustrated by *Pirqe
Aboth*, iii. 2, " Pray for the peace of
the kingdom, since but for fear thereof
we had swallowed up each his neighbour alive ". As Bigg points out,
quoting *Digest* i. 16. 9, a Roman
proconsul was concerned not only
with the suppression of crime but with
the promotion of deference on the part
of subordinates, e.g. children and
freedmen, to their elders and betters,
much as a colonial governor in British
territories is concerned with social be-

οὕτως ἐστὶ τὸ θέλημα τοῦ Θεοῦ, ἀγαθοποιοῦντας φιμοῦν τὴν
τῶν ἀφρόνων ἀνθρώπων ἀγνωσίαν· ¹⁶ὡς ἐλεύθεροι, καὶ μὴ ὡς

haviour to-day. St. Peter and St. Paul are at one in their teaching here, and what they teach is of great importance for Christian political philosophy; for they insist that the State is concerned not only with living (τὸ ζῆν), or as we say with men as economic units, but with the good life (τὸ εὖ ζῆν), i.e. with men as political and moral beings. In so doing, they give us the standard Christian interpretation of the *verbum Christi*, " Render unto Caesar " etc. Emil Brunner's statement (*The Divine Imperative*) that " in its reality the State is always organized selfishness " is true ; but since the alternative is anarchy in greater or less degree, its functions are necessary to the diffusion of the good life.

ἔπαινον δὲ ἀγαθοποιῶν] This positive side of the statement is exemplified in such recognition of meritorious service as is contained in the Honours Lists. For ἀγαθοποιός cf. Plut. *Mor.* 368 B, ὁ γὰρ Ὄσιρις ἀγαθοποιός, καὶ τοὔνομα πολλὰ φράζειν, οὐχ ἥκιστα δὲ κράτος ἐνεργοῦν καὶ ἀγαθοποιὸν [ὃ] λέγουσιν : and see note on ἀγαθοποιοῦντες, verse 20 below.

15. ὅτι οὕτως κτλ.] *because that is in accordance with God's will, who wills that by well-doing men should muzzle the ignorance of foolish men.* Hort seems to me to have fully established the fact that οὕτως is " habitually retrospective " in N.T. and always so in 1 Peter ; and the ἀγαθοποιοῦντας clause must therefore be taken as a pendant in apposition to τὸ θέλημα. We have first a reason given (ὅτι) for the moral function of civil government, and then a restatement of this reason in narrower terms, drawing out the implications of the general principle.

φιμοῦν] *put to silence,* as our Lord silenced the unclean spirit (Mk. i. 25), the storm (Mk. iv. 39), and the Sadducees (Matt. xxii. 34). For the sentiment cf. Seneca, *de Benef.* vii. 31, " Pertinacious goodness overcomes

evil men ". But the simple sense of " muzzle " need not be excluded, for it is better to prevent an ass from braying than to stop it when it has brayed.

τῶν ἀφρόνων ἀνθρώπων] The word ἄφρων is not common in N.T., but occurs more frequently in the Book of Proverbs than in the whole of the rest of LXX put together : it is also common in Ecclesiastes, Wisdom, and Ecclesiasticus. It is a characteristic word, in fact, of Jewish gnomic literature, which had a powerful influence on primitive Christian teaching (cf. Essay II, pp. 407-13, and for the influence of Proverbs especially pp. 413-15). Furthermore, it occurs in conjunction with φιμοῦν in two non-LXX translations of verses in Proverbs, namely, xvii. 28 (*Quinta*) and xxvi. 10 (Theodotion, " and he who muzzles a fool muzzles anger "), the latter being reflected also in the Latin " judgment decides causes, and he who imposes silence on a fool mitigates anger ". Theodotion was probably a native of Asia, perhaps of Pontus (cf. Swete, *Introduction to O.T. in Greek*, pp. 42 f.), and the possibility cannot be ruled out that he was quoting the proverb in a form in which it was familiar in Asia Minor. When we reflect on the long life which proverbs have, it seems to me not unlikely that in 1 Pet. ii. 15 the phrase φιμοῦν τὴν τῶν ἀφρόνων ἀνθρώπων ἀγνωσίαν, or in simpler terms φιμοῦν τοὺς ἄφρονας, was used in Jewish and early Christian ethical teaching in Asia Minor in the first century ; and that this appositional phrase is really, at least in part, a quotation —a fact which would help to explain our author's use of it here. ἀγαθοποιοῦντας may well have been part of it too ; but the note of pity which sounds in ἀγνωσίαν strikes one as decidedly Christian.

16. ὡς ἐλεύθεροι] resuming the subject of the verb ὑποτάγητε. The

ἐπικάλυμμα ἔχοντες τῆς κακίας τὴν ἐλευθερίαν, ἀλλ᾽ ὡς δοῦλοι
Θεοῦ. ¹⁷πάντας τιμήσατε· τὴν ἀδελφότητα ἀγαπᾶτε· τὸν Θεὸν
φοβεῖσθε· τὸν βασιλέα τιμᾶτε.

doctrine of the moral functions of the State in promoting the good life, as enunciated in verses 13-15, is further developed to embrace a liberal as distinct from an absolutist or totalitarian conception of the State. The idea that men are free and servants of God is the head and front of offence in the eyes of totalitarian political philosophy, and accounts for such modern attempts to suppress Christianity by various forms of persecution as have been seen in Russia and Germany. The Christian citizen's submission to the civil power is the act of a free man, for which he has good reasons in his knowledge of the true character of the State. And to this paradox is added another, that of his freedom being conditioned by his duty to God, whose servant he is. For St. Paul's similar doctrine cf. 1 Cor. vii. 22 ; and the phrase " whose service is perfect freedom " (cui servire regnare) in the Collect for Peace at Mattins. The paradox may be traced back to the striking verbum Christi in Matt. xvii. 26. Cf. Od. Sol. xlii. 26, " they are free men, and they are mine ". But fundamentally this freedom of the Christian man is a freedom from sin : indeed, " the whole New Testament rings with the sense of freedom from sin "[1]; and therefore St. Peter, like St. Paul (Rom. vi. 18-22, Gal. v. 13), adds a warning against abusing it as a cloke for license.

The connexion of freedom with virtue was well established in antiquity, cf. Ennius, Trag. fr. 340, ea libertas est, quae pectus purum et firmum gestitat ; Seneca, Ep. xcii. 433 B, nemo liber est, qui corpori servit, and Vit. beat. 15, deo parere libertas ; Plut. Cato min. 65, δούλους εἶναι τοὺς φαύλους ἅπαντας ;

Cicero, pro Cluentio, liii. 146, legum denique idcirco omnes servi sumus, ut liberi esse possimus ; and the fine passage, too long to quote here, in Epictetus, Diss. iv. 1. But the element of " escapism " so often found in the ancients' ideas of liberty is wholly obviated by the Christian insistence on the service of God : Christian freedom rests not on escape from service, but on a change of master.

ἐπικάλυμμα] cloke, veil, cf. Menander, Βοιωτ. 3, πλοῦτος δὲ πολλῶν ἐπικάλυμμ᾽ ἐστὶν κακῶν, Philo, de Decal. 172 [II. 208 M], τὸ μὴ ποιεῖσθαι προκάλυμμα πίστιν ἀπιστίας. Note also St. Paul's teaching in Gal. v. 13.]

17. πάντας τιμήσατε κτλ.] The aorist imperative, immediately preceding three present imperatives, if not due to euphony, again goes back to the moment of decision in the believer's mind, and might be rendered: "Let your motto be: Honour all men, etc.". In the first clause St. Peter lays down the obligation of the respect and courtesy due to human personality as such,[2] an obligation which is inconsistent, in the political sphere, with those principles of absolute or totalitarian government which sacrifice the individual wholly to the State, and in the economic sphere with all systems and methods which regard men as simply " hands ". In the second clause, St. Peter passes to the more limited sphere of the Christian brotherhood (cf. i. 22, φιλαδελφίαν, iii. 8, iv. 8, and also v. 9 below, with lexicographical note on ἀδελφότης), where a higher quality than respect and courtesy, namely love, is demanded. He closes with an injunction based upon Prov. xxiv. 21, a book so often drawn on in this Epistle, φοβοῦ τὸν θεόν, υἱέ, καὶ βασι-

---

[1] Hoskyns and Davy, The Riddle of the N.T. p. 253 ; and cf. Hoskyns, The Fourth Gospel, pp. 386 f.
[2] Cf. Pirqe Aboth, iv. 4, "Who is honoured ? He that honours mankind." For other examples of this universality in N.T. cf. Essay II, p. 428.

¹⁸Οἱ οἰκέται, ὑποτασσόμενοι ἐν παντὶ φόβῳ τοῖς δεσπόταις,
οὐ μόνον τοῖς ἀγαθοῖς καὶ ἐπιεικέσιν, ἀλλὰ καὶ τοῖς σκολιοῖς.

λέα, which, however, he modifies for
reasons of style, by repeating the
verb τιμᾶν in connexion with the
Emperor. The result is a fourfold
injunction which is itself intrinsically
well balanced, and affords a fitting
summary to the whole section on
Christian citizenship.

[Hort's commentary on the Epistle
ends at this point. Though we have
not always agreed with him, his
immense biblical knowledge and his
sober judgment make his work still
of the greatest value ; and we cannot
part from it without this brief word of
farewell.]

18-25. The duties of Christian
slaves. For the teaching on meekness, and especially on the duty of
the *imitatio Christi*, cf. Introd. pp.
90 ff., 103 f. ; and for the probable
source underlying it cf. Essay II, pp.
429-31. The section has parallels in
Colossians, Ephesians, 1 Timothy, and
Titus, and the more primitive order is
probably that found in Colossians-
Ephesians, St. Peter's deviation from
it being due to what he has said about
" freedom " and " servants of God "
in verse 16, cf. Essay II, pp. 429-31.

It is instructive to read St. Paul's
beautiful letter to ·Philemon in the
light of St. Peter's teaching. Philemon was a Christian householder, and
it seems probable that Onesimus had
behaved badly towards his master
(verses 18, 19) before running away.
That may have been one motive for
his flight ; but another was assuredly
the impression which St. Paul's personality and teaching had made on the
slave when he was a visitor in the
master's house. He was thus in a
similar psychological condition to the
Apostle himself shortly before his
conversion ; torn between evil and
good ; and his meeting with the
Apostle in prison at Rome led to his
becoming himself a Christian. St.
Paul is anxious to keep him for his
own service ; but his loyalty both to
Philemon and to the rule of subjection
leads him to send Onesimus back to
his master, with the plea that he will
treat him with generosity.

18. Οἱ οἰκέται] For the " articular
nominative in address " cf. Moulton,
Grammar, i. p. 70 : nearly sixty examples are found in N.T., but the
idiom is also classical.

οἰκέται] The choice of the word here
in preference to δοῦλος shews that the
author has the life and welfare of the
family in mind. He is thinking of
slaves not as members of a social class
(as e.g. in 1 Cor. vii. 21), but as members of something more fundamental,
i.e. the social *unit* of the οἶκος or home.

ὑποτασσόμενοι] For this use of the
participle as an imperative cf. ii. 12,
iii. 1, 7 (9), iv. 8-10, Rom. xii. 9-19,
Eph. v. 21, Col. iii. 16. The usage is
discussed in Essay II, pp. 387 f., and
Dr. Daube's Appended Note, pp.
467-88.

ἐν παντὶ φόβῳ] See note on i. 17, and
cf. *Did.* iv. 11, " But ye, slaves, shall
be subject to your masters, as to a type
of God, in shame and fear ", and the
saying ascribed to Antigonus in *Pirqe
Aboth*, i. 3.

οὐ μόνον . . . ἐπιεικέσιν] Cf. Suet.
Aug. 53, *O dominum aequum et
bonum !* The distinction here drawn
between different types of master
implies that St. Peter has in mind
mainly heathen householders. A curious commentary on the relationship
of masters and domestic slaves is
afforded by Philo's discussion of a
priest's relation to his servants in *de
Spec. Leg.* i. 126-8 [II. 231, 232 M],
where the priest is enjoined for three
reasons to provide for his slave out of
the first-fruits ; namely (*a*) he is the
one proper source (πόρος εἰς) of his
servant's livelihood, (*b*) the slave will
be tempted to steal, if he cannot count
on " perquisites ", thus committing
both sacrilege and theft, (*c*) fear of

¹⁹τοῦτο γὰρ χάρις, εἰ διὰ συνείδησιν Θεοῦ ὑποφέρει τις λύπας

his master (ὁ δεσποτικὸς φόβος) will suffice to keep him straight, if he is provided with his share.

σκολιοῖς] *harsh, unjust.* The word is rarely used of persons in classical Greek, but cf. Hes. *O. et D.* 7, [Ζεὺς] ἰθύνει σκολιόν. LXX gives us Deut. xxxii. 5, γενεὰ σκολιὰ καὶ διεστραμμένη, quoted in Phil. ii. 15, cf. Acts ii. 40.

19. τοῦτο γὰρ χάρις] Cf. next verse, τοῦτο χάρις παρὰ Θεῷ. χάρις is used in a quite naïve and untechnical sense here for a gracious act pleasing to God. The usage is classical, cf. Soph. *Ajax*, 522, χάρις χάριν γάρ ἐστιν ἡ τίκτουσ' ἀεί; and the addition of παρὰ θεῷ gives it a religious flavour. Accordingly, the answering gratitude or gracious act is likewise called χάρις, as in Lk. vi. 32-4, ποία ὑμῖν χάρις ἐστιν ;. This, at least, is the usual explanation, and accounts for the E.V. in Luke, "what thank have ye?", and here "thankworthy"; and 1 Pet. ii. 19, 20, which is surely dependent on the *verba Christi*, suggests that, perhaps, the Lucan phrase would be fairly paraphrased by, "In what sense are you doing a gracious deed?" Harnack (*The Sayings of Jesus*, p. 62) argues that μισθόν in Matt. v. 46 is more probably original than χάρις in Lk. vi. 32-4, because χάρις "is a specifically Lucan word" : it occurs eight times in the Gospels and seventeen times in Acts, but never in Matthew or Mark. But it is equally true that μισθός [1] is a characteristically Matthaean word, occurring ten times, but only once in Mark and thrice in Luke. Moreover, Matt. v. 43-8 does not stick to μισθός : τίνα μισθὸν ἔχετε ; in verse 46 is followed by τί περισσὸν ποιεῖτε ; in verse 47 ; while μισθός occurs in Lk. vi. 35. The facts seem best met by "the hypothesis of a summary of Christian teaching intended for catechetical instruction, current in oral tradition in more than

one form ".[2] At the same time we may urge that Luke and 1 Peter reflect the atmosphere of the *verba Christi* more successfully than Matthew ; for the context of μισθός in Matt. v. 43-8 shews no less clearly than its explicit interpretation in Lk. vi. 35 that the governing idea is the divine generosity, and the possibility of resembling God in being ourselves generous and forgiving.

A word may be added as to the relation of the Petrine to the Pauline usage of χάρις. Reference to the other passages where the word occurs in 1 Peter (i. 2, 10, 13, iv. 10, v. 10, 12) and to the notes on them shews that, except perhaps in i. 10, our author uses χάρις in ways that appear quite independent of Pauline influence. This is natural enough, if we bear in mind the difference in the life-histories of the two Apostles ; for in St. Peter's case the grace of God had come in gentler ways, and had had far less to overcome in inherited prejudice, argumentative propensity, and actual opposition to the Christian faith.

Pagan philosophers offer some parallels to St. Peter's teaching here, cf. εὖ μὲν πράττειν, κακῶς δ' ἀκούειν, βασιλικόν ("it is a roiale and kingly act patiently to suffer blame for well-doing" (Holland)), ascribed by M. Aurelius to Antisthenes, by Plutarch to Alexander. And Stobaeus cites Philemon (320 B.C.) for

ἥδιον οὐδὲν οὐδὲ μουσικώτερον ἔστ' ἢ δύνασθαι λοιδορούμενον φέρειν.

διὰ συνείδησιν Θεοῦ] *for conscience' sake before God,* or, as A.V. and R.V., "for conscience toward God". Commentators are divided in their interpretation of the phrase. Thus, (1) Calvin, Alford, Westcott (on Heb. ix 9), Bigg, von Soden, Windisch, Wand take it as meaning "on account of the consciousness of the presence and will of God", συνείδησις then connoting

---

[1] For references to scholastic and early Anglican discussions of the relations of merit, reward and grace, see my edition of *The First Book of the Irenicum of John Forbes* (of Aberdeen), p. 157 n
[2] Streeter, *The Four Gospels* pp. 252 f.

" spiritual awareness ", and Θεοῦ being objective genitive ; (2) Bengel and Bennett support the rendering of E.V., and Bengel paraphrases : " on account of the consciousness of a mind which does things good and pleasing to God, even though they please no man " ; and he notes the bearing on this of κλέος in the next verse. On this view, the genitive Θεοῦ expresses that " inner reference " of which Winer gives several examples (*Grammar*, pp. 235-7), e.g. Jn. v. 29, ἀνάστασις ζωῆς, κρίσεως, Mk. i. 4, βάπτισμα μετανοίας, Rom. vi. 6, σῶμα τῆς ἁμαρτίας, and cf. note on 1 Pet. i. 1, παρεπιδήμοις διασπορᾶς above, where the reference is more precisely one of place or sphere. Despite the weight of authority on the other side, the second alternative is to be preferred, as more consonant with N.T. usage, where the developed, almost technical meaning, " conscience ", is the normal one. For St. Paul cf. Rom. ii. 15, συμμαρτυρούσης αὐτῶν τῆς συνειδήσεως, ix. 1, συμμαρτυρούσης μοι τῆς συνειδήσεώς μου ἐν πνεύματι ἁγίῳ, xiii. 5, οὐ μόνον διὰ τὴν ὀργήν, ἀλλὰ καὶ διὰ τὴν συνείδησιν. Hence comes the phrase " good conscience ", as in Acts xxiii. 1, πάσῃ συνειδήσει ἀγαθῇ πεπολίτευμαι τῷ θεῷ, and twice in 1 Peter, iii. 16, συνείδησιν ἔχοντες καλήν, and iii. 21, συνειδήσεως ἀγαθῆς ἐπερώτημα εἰς θεόν. It may be observed that in the present passage certain MSS., including ab 36 syrr, substitute ἀγαθήν for Θεοῦ, and A¹ and 13 add it after Θεοῦ, which suggests that they interpreted the phrase in this sense.

The conscience of the Christian slave provides a fortifying motive for the patient endurance of injustice, and is also satisfied in it. We might almost translate " for God's sake ", cf. *The Imitation of Christ*, xix. 3, " For with God it is impossible that anything, how small soever, if only it be suffered for God's sake, should pass without its reward ".

Kirsopp Lake and Cadbury (*Beginnings*, Pt. I, vol. iv. pp. 286 f.),

commenting on Acts xxiii. 1, say that " the use of the word in N.T. is not to be understood as technically philosophical ", but this view does not seem to be borne out by the history of the term in Greek and Latin authors and LXX. συνείδησις occurs twice in Menander in our sense of " conscience ", cf. *Monost.* 654, βροτοῖς ἅπασιν ἡ συνείδησις θεός, which corresponds to Cicero's use of *conscientia* in e.g. *ad Fam.* VI. iv., *conscientiam rectae voluntatis maximam consolationem esse rerum incommodarum*, and *pro Mil.* xxiii. 61, *magna vis est conscientiae, iudices, et magna in utramque partem : ut neque timeant, qui nihil commiserint, et poenam semper ante oculos versari putent, qui peccarint*. In Cicero it is allied to the " unwritten law(s) " (cf. Soph. *Ant.* 454 ff., Xen. *Mem.* IV. iv. 19, Plato, *Laws*, 793, Dion. Hal. *Ant. Rom.* VII. xli.) or " natural law " (cf. Ar. *Rhet.* I. xiii. 2, κοινὸν δὲ [νόμον] τὸν κατὰ φύσιν, Cic. *de Rep.* iii. 22, *recta ratio naturae congruens*), implanted in the heart of man, and expounded by the Stoics. A more common form of συνείδησις in Greek was τὸ συνειδός, but it was inconvenient grammatically.

The classical usage is found in LXX in Eccl. x. 20, ἐν συνειδήσει σου (i.e. in your inner thoughts) βασιλέα μὴ καταράσῃ ; and (if the reading is right) in Ecclus. xlii. 18, ἔγνω γὰρ ὁ ὕψιστος πᾶσαν συνείδησιν (where συνείδησις is almost equivalent to τὸ πνεῦμα τοῦ ἀνθρώπου τὸ ἐν αὐτῷ of 1 Cor. ii. 11). A more definitely ethical signification occurs in Wisd. xvii. 11, πονηρία . . . προσείληφεν τὰ χαλεπὰ συνεχομένη τῇ συνειδήσει (i.e. by a "bad conscience"). The word was therefore ready to be baptized into Christian service, as it was in signal fashion by St. Paul (cf. SH on Rom. ii. 15). If conscience be defined as a kind of Reason which possesses objective validity, then its objective ground may be found either in a law, whether " natural " or human (as in Cicero and the Stoics), or in the will of God ; and it is at this latter

πάσχων ἀδίκως. ²⁰ποῖον γὰρ κλέος, εἰ ἁμαρτάνοντες καὶ κολαφιζόμενοι ὑπομενεῖτε; ἀλλ' εἰ ἀγαθοποιοῦντες καὶ πάσχοντες
ὑπομενεῖτε, τοῦτο χάρις παρὰ Θεῷ. ²¹εἰς τοῦτο γὰρ ἐκλήθητε,

point that the concept becomes specifically religious. Thus, for instance,
Sanderson (*Lectures on Conscience and
Human Law*, p. 31) speaks of " the
Passive obligation of the Conscience,
as she is a subject bound to conform to
the Divine Will ". That St. Peter
should mention this objective ground
is wholly in keeping with the Godward reference which pervades his
teaching : cf. Introduction, pp. 66,
76 f., 108 f. The point is one of importance in an age when conscience is
often invoked as though it meant no
more than a personal prejudice obstin-
ately held, e.g. by anti-vaccinationists.
St. Peter's phrase guards the word
from becoming thus emptied of its true
content.

The difference between the two
interpretations we have been discussing is not, however, absolute, but
corresponds to the distinction noted by
theologians of a later age between the
actual and the *habitual* reference of
actions to the will of God. The first
view assumes an actual, the second a
habitual reference, to be in the Apostle's
mind. Estius' exegesis of the phrase
— *Dei respectu, id est, ut Deo placeat,
quem animo gerit* — covers both kinds
of reference, and is worth recording.
[Estius also alludes to another interpretation, which however he rejects, as
premature at this point : *propter Dei
conscientiam, id est, quia veri Dei estis
cultores, videlicet eo nomine dominis
vestris exosi*. Had it stopped at *cultores*, this interpretation would be near
the mark, and would link the phrase
with membership of the " spiritual
house " and " holy priesthood " of
ii. 5.]

ἀδίκως] here only in N.T., but in
LXX and literary Greek : cf. Marc.
Aur. *Comm.* vi. 30, ἔφερεν ἐκεῖνος τοὺς
ἀδίκως αὐτῷ μεμφομένους, μὴ ἀντιμεμ-
φόμενος [E. H. B.].

20. κλέος] *credit*, whether with God
or man.

κολαφιζόμενοι] *when you are cuffed*.
The verb is used of the " buffeting "
of our Lord in Mk. xiv. 65 ; and cf.
the *verbum Christi* in Matt. v. 39. Its
use here is a fitting introduction to the
imitatio Christi which follows. Note
the contrast between the Christian
and the Stoic teaching as represented
by Seneca, *de Const. Sap.* 14 : " What
will the wise man do when he is
buffeted (*colaphis percussus*) ? He
will do as Cato did. . . . He did not
burst into a passion, did not avenge
himself, did not even forgive it, but
denied its having been done " (quoted
by Lightfoot, *Dissertations*, p. 264).

ἀγαθοποιοῦντες] *when you work
well*. Plummer, on Lk. vi. 33, suggests that this word in LXX, Matthew,
Luke, is used of helping others as
opposed to harming them, whereas in
I Peter (ii. 15, 20, iii. 6, 17) it connotes
doing what is right as opposed to doing
what is wrong. But the distinction is
unreal. The truth rather is, as Lightfoot observes (on I Clem. ii. 2), that
ἀγαθοποιΐα looks to the results of an
action and more especially to its effects
on others ; and this is so whether the
action is one that falls within or outside the normal sphere of duty : in
both cases a generous and cheerful
spirit is called for. In I Clem. xxxiv.,
for example, it is contrasted with sloth
and carelessness. The translation
given above, " when you work well ",
brings out the meaning in the present
context ; and it is important to emphasize that the Christian way of life
demands a spirit of beneficence even in
the discharge of " the trivial round,
the common task ".

21. εἰς τοῦτο] i.e. to patient endurance when suffering unjustly. For a
fuller exposition of verses 21-5 see
Introd. pp. 90-101. The passage

ὅτι καὶ Χριστὸς ἔπαθεν ὑπὲρ ὑμῶν, ὑμῖν ὑπολιμπάνων ὑπογραμμόν, ἵνα ἐπακολουθήσητε τοῖς ἴχνεσιν αὐτοῦ· ²²ὃς ἁμαρτίαν οὐκ
ἐποίησεν, οὐδὲ εὑρέθη δόλος ἐν τῷ στόματι αὐτοῦ· ²³ὃς λοιδορού-

develops the ideas implicit in διὰ συν-
ειδήσιν θεοῦ, for the Christian conscience is largely moulded by the
passion of Christ.

ὑπὲρ ὑμῶν] The addition of these
words shews that this influence of
Christ's passion is not merely exemplary, but touches a deeper chord
in the heart, that of gratitude. The
Christian calling and character are
grounded in Christ's deed of atonement, though no particular doctrine of
Atonement is at this point involved.
For the affinities between St. Peter's
emphasis on the vicarious aspect of
Christ's death and that which underlies St. Mark's Gospel (1 Pet. i. 20,
ii. 21, 24, Mk. x. 45, xiv. 24), see
V. Taylor, *The Atonement in N.T.
Teaching*, pp. 38 ff.

ὑπολιμπάνων] a rare word, not in
LXX nor elsewhere in N.T., meaning
" leaving behind " rather than simply
"leaving"; Thucydides (viii. 17) uses
καταλιμπάνω in this sense, and perhaps
the usage here is due to attraction by
the preposition in ὑπογραμμόν. In
Dion. Halic. *Ant. Rom.* I. xxiii. ὑπο-
λιμπάνειν is intransitive and used of
springs " failing " in summer. Bengel
rightly adds *in abitu ad Patrem.*

ὑπογραμμόν] *example.* Here only in
N.T., and very rare elsewhere, though
its two meanings are amply exemplified in the classical use of the noun ὑπο-
γραφή and the verb ὑπογράφω. They
are, (1) a " tracing " of letters for
children to write over or to copy, called
by Clem. Alex. *Strom.* v. 675 [P], ὑπο-
γραμμοὶ παιδικοί, cf. Plato, *Prot.* 326 D;
(2) an architectural outline or artist's
sketch, to be coloured or filled in by
others, cf. 2 Macc. ii. 28, ἐπιπορεύεσθαι
τοῖς ὑπογραμμοῖς τῆς ἐπιτομῆς (" to prepare an epitome ", Charles), analogous
to the use of ὑπογράφειν in Plato, *Rep.*
548 D, *Laws*, 803 D, Isocr. 99 D. Perhaps the closest parallel, in view of the

words which immediately follow, is
Aesch. *Choeph.* 209 f.,

πτέρναι τενόντων θ' ὑπογραφαὶ με-
τρούμεναι
ἐς ταὐτὸ συμβαίνουσι τοῖς ἐμοῖς στί-
βοις,

where Electra claims to recognize her
brother's footprints in the sand through
their resemblance to her own.
   1 Pet. ii. 22-4 are largely quoted,
though not in the correct order, in
Polycarp, *ad Phil.* viii.
   22. ὃς . . . στόματι αὐτοῦ] a quotation, slightly modified, from Is. liii. 9
(LXX), ὅτι ἀνομίαν οὐκ ἐποίησεν, οὐδὲ
δόλον ἐν τῷ στόματι αὐτοῦ. If Windisch is right in regarding verses 21-5
as part of a hymn about Christ (*Christuslied*), the modifications may well
have been due to the hymnodist. On
the presence of hymnal material in
this Epistle see Add. Notes E, F, pp.
268 ff. The sinlessness recalls the
" lamb without blemish and without
spot " of i. 19, the guilelessness the
teaching of ii. 1, 2.
   23. ὃς λοιδορούμενος κτλ.] This
verse lies very close to the Passion-
story. With λοιδορούμενος οὐκ ἀντελοιδόρει cf. Mk. xv. 29, Matt. xxvii. 39
(ἐβλασφήμουν αὐτόν), Matt. xxvii. 41
(ἐμπαίζοντες), 44 (ὠνείδιζον), Lk.
xxiii. 11 (ἐξουθενήσας . . . ἐμπαίξας),
35, 36 (ἐξεμυκτήριζον . . . ἐνέπαιζον);
with πάσχων οὐκ ἠπείλει cf. Mk. xiv. 65,
Lk. xxii. 63-5, Jn. xix. 1-5, and
contrast the behaviour of the impenitent thief, Lk. xxiii. 39 : for Christ's
silence cf. Mk. xiv. 61, xv. 5, Matt.
xxvi. 62, xxvii. 12, 14, Lk. xxiii. 9, Jn.
xix. 9 ; with παρεδίδου δὲ κτλ. cf. Lk.
xxiii. 46, πάτερ, εἰς χεῖράς σου παρατίθεμαι τὸ πνεῦμά μου.
   The implied object of παρεδίδου
may be His cause rather than Himself : Windisch cites Josephus, *Ant.*
IV. ii. 4, παραχωρῆσαι τὴν κρίσιν τῷ
θεῷ, VII. ix. 2, περὶ πάντων ἐπιτρέψαι

μενος οὐκ ἀντελοιδόρει, πάσχων οὐκ ἠπείλει, παρεδίδου δὲ τῷ
κρίνοντι δικαίως· ²⁴ὃς τὰς ἁμαρτίας ἡμῶν αὐτὸς ἀνήνεγκεν ἐν τῷ
σώματι αὐτοῦ ἐπὶ τὸ ξύλον, ἵνα ταῖς ἁμαρτίαις ἀπογενόμενοι

κριτῇ τῷ θεῷ; with which cf. Rom.
xii. 19, Heb. x. 30, Polycarp, ad Phil.
ii. 1 (end). Yet παρέδωκεν in Is. liii. 6
suggests that E.V. is probably right.
Cf. also Is. liii. 12, παρεδόθη εἰς θάνατον
ἡ ψυχὴ αὐτοῦ, with A. M. Hunter's
comments on the use of this word in
N.T., *Paul and his Predecessors*, p. 35
and notes. The whole verse is such as
we might have expected to be written
by an eyewitness who had also in mind
Is. liii. 7, 9. The O.T. rather than the
N.T. passage seems to lie behind
Odes of Solomon, xxxi. 7, 8 : " And
they made me a debtor when I rose
up, me who had not been a debtor :
and they divided my spoil, though
nothing was due to them. But I
endured and held my peace and was
silent, as if not moved by them."
E. H. B. points to a graphic English
rendering of 1 Pet. ii. 21-3 by Chaucer
in *The Tale of Melibeus*, 2691-3.
ἀντελοιδόρει] cf. Plut. *Mor.* 88 E,
γελοῖον δ' ὅλως ἐστὶ τὸ λοιδορεῖν καὶ
σκώπτειν ὁτιοῦν ἀντιλοιδορηθῆναι δυνά-
μενον.
24. ὃς . . . ἀνήνεγκεν] From the
fact that ἀναφέρειν is commonly used
in LXX of the priest's task of bringing
a sacrificial victim and laying it on the
altar (e.g. Lev. xiv. 20 ; and so, in
N.T., 1 Pet. ii. 5, Jas. ii. 21, Heb. ix. 28
(xiii. 15)), Bigg and others have
concluded that τὰς ἁμαρτίας is an
allusion to the " sin-offering " of the
Levitical rites. But, though in Lev.
vi. 25 the singular ἡ ἁμαρτία is used
for the sin-offering, which is described
in the next sentence as τὰ περὶ τῆς
ἁμαρτίας, this usage appears to be
unique ; and no Jew thought of the
sins being laid on the altar, seeing that
nothing which was not holy might
come into God's presence (cf. V.
Taylor, *op. cit.* p. 42, with quotation
from Denny in note 4). The ordinary
usage is accurately represented in

Heb. vii. 27 where the priests are
said ὑπὲρ τῶν ἰδίων ἁμαρτιῶν θυσίας
ἀναφέρειν, whereas Christ made atonement ἐφάπαξ ἑαυτὸν ἀνενέγκας. The
true source of St. Peter's expression is
to be found in Is. liii. 12, καὶ οὗτος
ἁμαρτίας πολλῶν ἀνήνεγκεν, where the
verb translates the same Hebrew
original as is found in Is. liii. 4, οὗτος
τὰς ἁμαρτίας ἡμῶν φέρει; though we
need not deny that St. Peter has preferred the word which had more
sacrificial associations. As V. Taylor
says (*op. cit.* p. 42), " In order to
express the meaning of Christ's death,
[1 Peter] draws upon underlying ideas
of the sacrificial system, rather than
the special associations of any one
rite ".
In what sense, we may ask, did
Christ " bear " our sins ? In the
sense that He took the blame for
them ; suffered the " curse " of them
(cf. Deut. xxi. 23, quoted in Gal. iii.
13), which is separation from God ;
and endured their penal consequences.
These are things which, though in
different measure, Christians can do
for their neighbours and so imitate
Christ ; for we have no reason to think
that the pattern which St. Peter bids
Christians follow was not intended to
include the " sin-bearing " as well as
the meekness of the Master.
For a full discussion of the various
strands of thought combined in this
passage of 1 Peter cf. *supra*, Introd.
pp. 91-7.
ἐπὶ τὸ ξύλον] Bigg, like Westcott
(*The Epistle to the Hebrews*, p. 32),
interprets this of Christ's carrying up
our sins " to the altar of the cross ",
being Himself at once both Priest and
Victim. But this is surely to read
into the passage ideas which belong to
other and more doctrinal contexts.
ξύλον is used of the cross by St. Peter
in Acts v. 30 and x. 39, the last a

τῇ δικαιοσύνῃ ζήσωμεν· οὗ τῷ μώλωπι ἰάθητε. ²⁵ἦτε γὰρ ὡς
πρόβατα πλανώμενοι, ἀλλ' ἐπεστράφητε νῦν ἐπὶ τὸν ποιμένα καὶ

passage which may probably be regarded as representing very primitive teaching (cf. Introd. pp. 33, 35), and by St. Paul in Acts xiii. 29. The word was used in classical Greek (cf. Aristoph. *Frogs*, 737) of the scaffold on which criminals were hung ; and it could also mean the stocks (cf. MM, *sub voc.*). The dominant implication in all these passages (including also Deut. xxi. 22, 23) is that of *criminality*; and the atmosphere of this Petrine text is dramatic and spectacular rather than doctrinal. The words are such as we might expect if they came from one who witnessed Christ's progress, with a malefactor on either hand, to Calvary ; and this would be so whether they were part of a hymn or were dictated by St. Peter himself. They portray " the Lamb of God which taketh away the sin of the world " of Jn. i. 29, and they give the idea a precision of time (aorist ἀνήνεγκεν), place (ἐπὶ τὸ ξύλον), and personal reference (plural τὰς ἁμαρτίας, and ἡμῶν) which bespeaks a primitive date.

ταῖς ἁμαρτίαις ἀπογενόμενοι] The effect of the atonement is described as an actual abandonment of sin rather than release from guilt, and a redirection of life towards righteousness. ἀπογίγνεσθαι in classical Greek means " to depart ", and is either used absolutely as in Herod. v. 4, and in a more developed sense in Thuc. ii. 34, where οἱ ἀπογενόμενοι=the departed, i.e. the dead, or with a genitive as in Thuc. i. 39, τῶν ἁμαρτημάτων ἀπογενόμενοι. For the dative of reference in ταῖς ἁμ. see Winer, *Grammar*, pp. 261-4; and cf. Rom. vi. 2, vii. 4, Gal. ii. 19, and after ζῆν Rom. vi. 10. But the similarity of construction (which is a common one in N.T.) must not lead us to impute to St. Peter here the mystical doctrine found in Rom. vi. : his thought is ethical and psychological rather than mysti-

cal, and the phrase is best translated " having ceased from " or " having abandoned ".

τῇ δικαιοσύνῃ ζήσωμεν] The goal and motive of the new life is described quite generally as righteousness, and the verb is ζῆν rather than (as in iv. 2) βιῶσαι, because this motive provides an integration and wholeness of life which goes beyond the mere spending of time. It gives a " life which is life indeed ".

οὗ τῷ μώλωπι ἰάθητε] derived from Is. liii. 5, τῷ μώλωπι αὐτοῦ ἡμεῖς ἰάθημεν. μώλωψ, here only in N.T., is a weal, such as many a slave's back in ancient times would shew ; and it recalls the scourgings of Jesus. Theodoret well summed up the paradox of this sentence : " A new and strange method of healing ; the doctor suffered the cost, and the sick received the healing ". On the αὐτοῦ found in some MSS. after μώλωπι cf. Moulton, *Grammar*, i. pp. 94, 237.

25. ἦτε γὰρ . . . πλανώμενοι] from Is. liii. 6, πάντες ὡς πρόβατα ἐπλανήθημεν, a thought which is more fully developed in Ezek. xxxiv. The words would have applied both to the lapsed Jews of the Dispersion and to the heathen, with their " gods many, lords many ", who had been brought into the Christian communities of Asia Minor.

ἐπεστράφητε] On this use of the aorist as a perfect, " the ordinary use in Sanskrit ", to express what has just happened, see Moulton, *op. cit.* pp. 134 ff. In classical and sub-classical Greek ἐπιστρέφειν means to " turn about " or " turn round " rather than to " return ", and this best suits the historical context here. See LS, *sub voc.* ἐπιστρέφω and ἐπιστροφή. The readers of the Epistle had not had any shepherd before (Mk. vi. 34).

νῦν] *now that you have become Christians*. Their baptism is no doubt implied, but no particular bap-

ἐπίσκοπον τῶν ψυχῶν ὑμῶν.

III. ¹Ὁμοίως, γυναῖκες, ὑποτασσόμεναι τοῖς ἰδίοις ἀνδράσιν,

tismal ceremony need be in mind. Cf. Introd. pp. 41·2.

τὸν ποιμένα . . . ψυχῶν] For Christ as the Shepherd cf. v. 4, Jn. x. 11 ff., Heb. xiii. 20, Rev. vii. 17. So much is implied also in Mk. vi. 34 and its synoptic parallels, and in Mk. xiv. 27, and the term would have appealed specially to St. Peter, in view of the threefold charge by the Lake (Jn. xxi.).

In O.T. the image of the shepherd and the sheep is found in Ps. xxiii., where God Himself is the Shepherd (cf. Is. xl. 11), and in Ezek. xxxvii. 24, where the " one shepherd " probably points to the Messiah, and in Ezek. xxxiv., where it is applied to those called to minister in the Jewish Church. The shepherd's task is that of care (cura pastoralis) in its widest sense, including searching for the lost, gathering the sheep together, tending those that are sick, guarding them from wild beasts or other enemies, and leading them to good pasture. Ps. xxiii. may well have been in the Apostle's mind, since in verses 1-3 we have ποιμαίνει, τὴν ψυχὴν μου ἐπέστρεψεν, and δικαιοσύνης, which are all found in 1 Pet. ii. 24, 25.

St. Paul does not apply the metaphor to our Lord, but uses it of the Church's ministry in Eph. iv. 11, and in Acts xx. 28, which is illuminating for our present passage, shewing that the words καὶ ἐπίσκοπον are an interpretation of τὸν ποιμένα rather than the introduction of a new idea : προσέχετε ἑαυτοῖς καὶ παντὶ τῷ ποιμνίῳ, ἐν ᾧ ὑμᾶς τὸ πνεῦμα τὸ ἅγιον ἔθετο ἐπισκόπους, ποιμαίνειν τὴν ἐκκλησίαν κτλ. A similar collocation of the terms is found in Ezek. xxxiv. 11, ἰδοὺ ἐγὼ ἐκζητήσω τὰ πρόβατά μου, καὶ ἐπισκέψομαι αὐτά, and we find it also below in 1 Pet. v. 2, 3, ποιμάνατε τὸ ἐν ὑμῖν ποίμνιον τοῦ θεοῦ, ἐπισκοποῦντες μὴ ἀναγκαστῶς ἀλλ' ἑκουσίως . . . τύποι γινόμενοι τοῦ ποιμνίου. In the following

verse Christ is described as the ἀρχιποίμην or chief shepherd ; but ἐπίσκοπος, not ποιμήν, became one of the titles of the Christian ministry, presumably because it was felt that ποιμήν was a term best reserved for the Lord Himself. ἐπίσκοπος, on the other hand, was a common classical word for a guardian or overseer, and came into use as the title for officers sent by the Athenians to manage the affairs of subject states.

Both terms are found in Philo, cf. de Agr. 50 f. [I. 308 M], 54 [I. 309 M], ἥτις δὲ ὑπὸ θεοῦ ποιμαίνεται ψυχή, and de Migr. Abr. 115 [I. 454 M], ὁ τῶν ἐν ψυχῇ ταμιευομένων ἐπίσκοπος. In the Martyrdom of Polycarp, xix. 2, our Lord is called " Shepherd of the world-wide Catholic Church ".

iii. 1-7. The duties of Christian wives and husbands.

For the teaching on conjugal duty and for the probable source underlying it cf. Essay II, pp. 432-5. The section has parallels in Colossians-Ephesians, 1 Timothy, and Titus, though in the last two there is no mention of husbands' duties. 1 Clem. i. 3 and Polycarp, ad Phil. iv. 2 contain what appear to be echoes of the same traditional material.

1. Ὁμοίως, γυναῖκες] Bigg thinks that ὁμοίως is meant to connect the section with ii. 18, wives having to honour their husbands as slaves do their master. But the keyword is subjection ; and it is not improbable that ὁμοίως, here and in verse 7 below, belongs to the Code of Subordination which underlies the passage.

ὑποτασσόμεναι] Cf. note on ii. 18.

ἰδίοις] This word delivers the passage from any charge of inculcating the " inferiority " of women to men, and shews that the subordination is one of function, within the intimate circle of the home. St. Peter's teaching implies that every institution must have a head for practical purposes,

ἵνα, καὶ εἴ τινες ἀπειθοῦσι τῷ λόγῳ, διὰ τῆς τῶν γυναικῶν ἀναστροφῆς ἄνευ λόγου κερδηθήσονται, ²ἐποπτεύσαντες τὴν ἐν φόβῳ ἁγνὴν ἀναστροφὴν ὑμῶν. ³ὧν ἔστω οὐχ ὁ ἔξωθεν ἐμπλοκῆς

and that in the home this should be the husband.

εἴ τινες κτλ.] This clause shews that the women St. Peter has in view are by no means only the wives of unbelieving husbands. Though the evangelist or teacher may fail to convince a heathen enquirer, yet the conduct of the wife may succeed by its silent witness, when the spoken word has failed. For a similar sentiment cf. Philo, *de Jos*. 86 [II. 54 M].

τῷ λόγῳ . . . ἄνευ λόγου] The word (ὁ λόγος) or Gospel message claims men's obedience, refusal of which is fatal, cf. ii. 8 ; but the presentation of it in the discourse (λόγος) by missionary or teacher is not the only means by which men may be won to render it.

κερδηθήσονται] Cf. Matt. xviii. 15, ἐκέρδησας τὸν ἀδελφόν σου, 1 Cor. ix. 19-22 (five times), where κερδαίνω means " win over to a point of view ", and so almost " convert ". For the future after ἵνα (ὅπως) cf. Dan. iii. 11, vi. 7, ἐμβληθήσεται, and Winer, *Grammar*, pp. 360, 361. [Some MSS. read κερδηθήσωνται, as in 1 Cor. xiii. 3, κανθήσωμαι.]

2. ἐποπτεύσαντες] As Windisch observes, this verse implies a recognition of the " natural law " as a factor operative in the heathen mind, without which the teaching of Christianity would have had no point of contact with it. The *locus classicus* for this in N.T. is Rom. ii. 14-16, with which cf. also Rom. i. 32, 1 Thess. iv. 12, Col. iv. 5, Phil. iv. 5. Sensitiveness to the effect of Christian conduct on public opinion is emphasized both by St. Peter and St. Paul : see Essay II, pp. 373, 428, and for St. Peter's teaching in particular Introd. pp. 89 ff., 97 f.

The aorist participle is used here, in contrast to the present participle in ii. 12, presumably because it states the

cause rather than the occasion of the change of attitude.

τὴν ἐν φόβῳ ἁγνὴν κτλ.] The chaste bearing of the Christian wife is intimately bound up with those instincts of reverence which are an essential ingredient of the Christian life in general (i. 17), and are exemplified also in the submission of slaves to their masters (ii. 18). In ὑμῶν the transition from the third person in τῶν γυναικῶν just above to the second person is noteworthy, seeing that the same persons are in view ; and it suggests that the whole phrase ὑποτασσόμεναι . . . κερδηθήσονται may be a quotation from an earlier written or oral source.

3. ὧν ἔστω] *And you Christian women must be marked by* . . ., not the ostentation of outward ornament, but the inward beauty of the heart.

ὁ ἔξωθεν . . . κόσμος] Bengel observes how the verbal nouns in this phrase " imply the labour bestowed on dress, which consumes much time ". The three kinds of outward ornament here specified are coiffure, jewellery, and dress. All are alluded to in the fine satire of Is. iii. 18-24, where, however, no positive counterpart to these gaudy and perishable things is put forward. We need not suppose that the prophet's words were in St. Peter's mind, for similar teaching was a commonplace among the poets and moralists of antiquity, cf. Ausonius, *Sept. Sapient. Sent.* i. 4 (*Quae dos matronae pulcherrima? Vita pudica*), Epict. *Enchir.* 40, Quint. *Instit.* viii. prooem. 20 (*cultus muliebris non exornat corpus*), and Diodor. xii. 21 (γυναικὶ ἐλευθέρᾳ . . . μηδὲ περιτίθεσθαι χρυσία μηδὲ ἐσθῆτα παρυφασμένην). Later Jewish teaching is represented by *Test. Reub.* v. 5, where the " wiles " used by women who " adorn their heads and faces to deceive the mind "

τριχῶν καὶ περιθέσεως χρυσίων ἢ ἐνδύσεως ἱματίων κόσμος,
⁴ἀλλ᾽ ὁ κρυπτὸς τῆς καρδίας ἄνθρωπος, ἐν τῷ ἀφθάρτῳ τοῦ
πραέος καὶ ἡσυχίου πνεύματος, ὅ ἐστιν ἐνώπιον τοῦ Θεοῦ πολυτελές. ⁵οὕτω γάρ ποτε καὶ αἱ ἅγιαι γυναῖκες αἱ ἐλπίζουσαι εἰς

are said to have lured the Watchers, called "sons of God" in Gen. vi., to their sin; though the converse view is expressed in *1 Enoch* viii. 1, and supported by Tertullian in *de Cultu Fem.* I. ii. Philo comments in *de Virtut.* 39 [II. 382 M] on the injurious social effects of feminine luxury (πολυτελέσιν ἐσθῆσι καὶ ὅρμοις καὶ οἷς ἄλλοις εἴωθε διακοσμεῖσθαι γυνὴ πᾶσιν ἀσκηθεῖσαι καὶ τὸ ἐκ φύσεως κάλλος εὐμορφότερον ταῖς ἐπιμελείαις ἀπεργασάμεναι).

For the similarity between this passage and 1 Tim. ii. 9 ff., and the probability of a common catechetical source, cf. Essay II, pp. 432-5. Fine dress is symptomatic of luxurious living in the description of Dives in Lk. xvi. 19, and of the wicked city in Rev. xvii. 4: and it is associated with sexual sin in *Apoc. Pet.* ix.

4. ὁ κρυπτὸς τῆς καρδίας ἄνθρωπος] The contrast with what is rejected is exact:

ὁ ἔξωθεν	ὁ κρυπτός
τριχῶν . . . χρυ-	τῆς καρδίας
σίων . . . ἱματίων	
κόσμος (shew)	ἄνθρωπος (self)

and the meaning of the latter phrase is still further developed by emphasis on its incorruptibility, its meekness and quietness, and its preciousness before God.

ἄνθρωπος] Cf. St. Paul's use of ὁ ἔσω ἄνθρωπος in Rom. vii. 22, 2 Cor. iv. 16, Eph. iii. 16. St. Peter's preference for κρυπτός here, where ἔσω would have pointed the contrast with ἔξωθεν so easily, points to his independence of St. Paul. Further, it is very close to such *verba Christi* as Matt. vi. 4, 6 (the duties of almsgiving and prayer ἐν τῷ κρυπτῷ), Matt. xii. 34-6, xv. 18, 19 (the heart as the seat of good and evil words and deeds), Matt. xi. 29 (meekness and lowliness characteristic of

Christ), Matt. v. 1-9 (the value of the hidden character in God's eyes). St. Peter's whole thought here is ethical rather than metaphysical (as in 2 Cor. iv. 16) or psychological (as in Plato, *Rep.* 589 A, ὁ ἐντὸς ἄνθρωπος).

τῆς καρδίας] genitive of definition: probably a Hebraism, cf. Blass, *Grammar*, p. 98.

ἐν] *found in, expressing itself in.* The usage is not easy to parallel, but cf. Eph. ii. 15, ἐν δόγμασιν (" consisting in ").

τῷ ἀφθάρτῳ] *the incorruptibility.* For the construction cf. Goodwin, *Greek Grammar*, § 933.

τοῦ . . . πνεύματος] πραΰτης is typical of Christ Himself, Matt. xi. 29, xxi. 5, and is regularly enjoined in the ethical code of primitive Christianity (cf. Essay II, pp. 425 ff.). " Quietness " is enjoined also in 1 Thess. iv. 11, 1 Tim. ii. 2, 11, 12. Bengel distinguishes " meekness " as an attribute of the character that does not cause disturbance, and " quietness " as that of one that bears with serenity the disturbances caused by others. But is it not rather the other way about? Both classical and N.T. usage seem to suggest so.

πνεύματος] *disposition*, cf. Lk. ix. 55, οἵου πνεύματός ἐστε ὑμεῖς, and (less nearly) 1 Cor. iv. 21, Gal. vi. 1, with Burton's Note in *Galatians* (I.C.C.), *in loc.*, and App. p. 490.

ὅ ἐστιν . . . πολυτελές] The direction to Samuel to choose David among the sons of Jesse (1 Sam. xvi. 6 ff.) is an illustration of this; " for the Lord seeth not as man seeth; for man looketh on the outward appearance (LXX, εἰς πρόσωπον), but the Lord looketh on the heart ".

5. αἱ ἅγιαι γυναῖκες] Cf. Eph. iii. 5, οἱ ἅγιοι ἀπόστολοι καὶ προφῆται, 2 Pet. iii. 2, οἱ ἅγιοι προφῆται. The words

Θεὸν ἐκόσμουν ἑαυτάς, ὑποτασσόμεναι τοῖς ἰδίοις ἀνδράσιν· ⁶ὡς
Σάρρα ὑπήκουσε τῷ Ἀβραὰμ κύριον αὐτὸν καλοῦσα, ἧς ἐγενή-
θητε τέκνα, ἀγαθοποιοῦσαι καὶ μὴ φοβούμεναι μηδεμίαν πτόησιν.

signify the women who pre-eminently represented the holiness of Israel's calling, i.e. its "saints", cf. Matt. xxvii. 52.

αἱ ἐλπίζουσαι] preferred to πιστεύουσαι, because every devout Jewish mother hoped that she might be the mother of the Messiah. Abraham similarly "hoped", Rom. iv. 18. [Sarah appears, however, as an example of faith in Heb. xi. 11, where the context would account for the change. And the v.l. αὐτῇ Σάρρᾳ may be right there, in which case Abraham is the subject of the sentence. Cf. Field, Otium Norvicense, p. 145.]

ἐκόσμουν ἑαυτάς] The Apostle implies that holiness has its own beauty and charm. Horace's simplex munditiis is not wide of the mark.

ὑποτασσόμεναι] The main clause of the paragraph is recalled by this repetition of the catechetical "text" from the Code of Subordination, which serves also to rule out any spiritual pride from the holiness of the Christian wife. Subordination, active well-doing, and serenity are the three qualities here inculcated by ancient example.

6. Σάρρα κτλ.] The mother par excellence of the Hebrew race as a chosen people, cf. Is. li. 2, which is perhaps our author's immediate source. The occasion alluded to here is that described in Gen. xviii. 1-15, when Abraham told her that they were to have a child, despite their age. Sarah laughed, and yet even amid her derision called Abraham "lord" (verse 12, ὁ δὲ κύριός μου πρεσβύτερος, "and my lord is too old"). But her laughter quickly died away, "for she was afraid".

ἧς . . . τέκνα] whose children you have become, i.e. by spiritual likeness and descent. Windisch considers that this phrase is a clear indication that the

Epistle was addressed to Gentiles, since Jewesses would already be Sarah's children by birth, and would not "become" so through their behaviour. But the metaphorical use of τέκνα and υἱοί to connote spiritual affinity was already too well established for this argument to be of weight: cf. Matt. v. 9, 45, xi. 19, xxiii. 15, 31, and the development of the idea in Rom. ix. 7, 8, Jn. viii. 39. Christian wives would be true daughters of Sarah through being in the spiritual tradition which derived from her. Soo too Philo, de Virtut. 195 [II. 438 M].

ἀγαθοποιοῦσαι] Cf. note on ii. 20.

καὶ μὴ φοβούμεναι κτλ.] The words may be a conscious echo of Prov. iii. 25, καὶ οὐ φοβηθήσῃ πτόησιν ἐπελθοῦσαν: and that chapter was in catechetical use in the primitive Church, cf. Essay II, pp. 408 ff., 413 f. St. Peter quotes verse 34 below at v. 5, as does St. James (iv. 6). And Prov. iii. 27-9 may have suggested ἀγαθοποιοῦσαι. The accusative μηδεμίαν πτόησιν is a cognate or epexegetic accusative (Goodwin, op. cit. §§ 1051 ff., Winer, op. cit. p. 291); and it is in place here, because, with the exception of iii. 14 and this passage, φόβος is always used in this Epistle in a good sense, meaning reverence or respect. [It is true, as Bigg points out, that in Prov. iii. 25, where πτόησιν is qualified by ἐπελθοῦσαν and correlated with another noun (οὐδὲ ὁρμάς), the accusative is probably the accusative of object. But in the way our author uses it here the construction seems to me to have changed to the cognate accusative.] Attempts to specify the ground of agitation and alarm which the author has in mind here are not very fruitful. Direct allusion to the danger of persecution, as in iii. 14, including efforts to intimidate the wife into leaving the

⁷Οἱ ἄνδρες, ὁμοίως, συνοικοῦντες κατὰ γνῶσιν, ὡς ἀσθενε-

Christian Church, seems out of place here. Nor is a reference to agitating experiences in Sarah's life like those recorded in Gen. xii. 11-20, xx. 1-16, or to the fear of bad temper on the husband's part, more convincing. On the other hand, Medea's speech in Eur. *Med.* 214-51 shews how widely the customs of behaviour in wedlock differed in the ancient world, and these differences probably prevailed equally in the mixed communities of Asia Minor addressed by St. Peter over four centuries later. Cf. especially ll. 235-43 :

κἂν τῷδ' ἀγὼν μέγιστος, ἢ κακὸν λαβεῖν
ἢ χρηστόν· οὐ γὰρ εὐκλεεῖς ἀπαλλαγαὶ
γυναιξίν, οὐδ' οἷόν τ' ἀνήνασθαι πόσιν.
ἐς καινὰ δ' ἤθη καὶ νόμους ἀφιγμένην
δεῖ μάντιν εἶναι, μὴ μαθοῦσαν οἴκοθεν,
ὅπως μάλιστα χρήσεται ξυνευνέτῃ.
κἂν μὲν τάδ' ἡμῖν ἐκπονουμέναισιν εὖ
πόσις ξυνοικῇ μὴ βίᾳ φέρων ζύγον,
ζηλωτὸς αἰών· εἰ δὲ μή, θανεῖν χρεών.

Evidently the risks of marriage for women were felt to be great by the best minds of antiquity. The words are best taken, I suggest, as a pendant to ἀγαθοποιοῦσαι with a meaning similar to that in iv. 19 below, the words being suggested by Prov. iii. 25. Let the Christian wives do good in serenity of spirit, and leave all else calmly in God's hands : then they will shew themselves true daughters of Sarah.

7. ὁμοίως] See note on verse 1. If the word is more than a mere connecting link and the point of similarity is to be emphasized, Bengel is probably right in finding it in " the foundation of love ". For the article before ἄνδρες see note on ii. 18, and for the participle used as imperative in συνοικοῦντες, Essay II, pp. 387 f., and Dr. Daube's Appended Note.

κατὰ γνῶσιν] *prudenter et cum ratione* (Estius). The meaning is well illustrated by 2 Cor. vi. 6, ἐν ἁγνότητι, ἐν γνώσει, ἐν μακροθυμίᾳ, and 2 Pet. i. 5, ἐν δὲ τῇ ἀρετῇ τὴν γνῶσιν, ἐν δὲ τῇ γνώσει τὴν ἐγκράτειαν κτλ. This

practical understanding and tact — *recte et scienter agendi peritia* (Calvin) — is to extend to the whole of married life ; for συνοικοῦντες, while it includes the sexual side of it, is by no means limited to that meaning : cf. Ecclus. xxv. 8, μακάριος ὁ συνοικῶν γυναικὶ συνετῇ, καὶ ὃς ἐν γλώσσῃ οὐκ ὠλίσθησεν, and still more generally Philo, *Quis Rer. Div. Her.* 265 [I. 511 M] (referring to the supersession of the prophet's reason by the divine Spirit), θέμις γὰρ οὐκ ἔστι θνητὸν ἀθανάτῳ συνοικῆσαι.

The intellectual element involved in γνῶσις must not be underestimated : indeed, it calls for and justifies such instruction for Christian marriage as is contained in much modern literature on the subject, and such hints of practical philosophy as are given in e.g. André Maurois' *The Art of Living.* The " knowledge " here spoken of finds expression especially in the due regard (τιμήν) paid by the husband to the wife ; and this regard is based on two grounds (for such is the force of ὡς) — first, the fact that woman (τὸ γυναικεῖον) is the weaker sex, and secondly, the fact that husband and wife are jointly and equally heirs of the gift of eternal life, i.e. on terms of complete spiritual equality. Finally, the verse concludes with the motive which must govern all conjugal relationships, that the prayers of both husband and wife may be unimpeded.

The spiritual equality of husband and wife is well represented in early patristic literature by Ign. *ad Polyc.* v. Marriage, moreover, is to be entered upon " with the bishop's consent ", an injunction which lays the foundation of future episcopal jurisdiction in matrimonial causes.

[Mr E. H. Blakeney suggests to me that κατὰ γνῶσιν may refer directly to the duty of sexual intercourse, cf. 1 Cor. vii. 5. But (1) there does not seem any evidence that St. Peter in this Epistle had encratite tendencies to combat amongst his hearers ; (2) the

στέρῳ σκεύει τῷ γυναικείῳ ἀπονέμοντες τιμήν, ὡς καὶ συγ-

text is not one of those quoted by
Clem. Alex. *Strom.* III. 547, 548 [P]
and III. 559 [P], where he discusses
sexual relationships, though it would
have served his purpose well ; and it
may be presumed, therefore, that he
did not take γνῶσις in this sense.]
ὡς ἀσθενεστέρῳ σκεύει] ὡς goes
with these words, not with ἀπονέμοντες.
For this commonplace that woman (τὸ
γυναικεῖον) is the weaker sex cf. Thuc.
ii. 45, " To a woman not to shew more
weakness than is natural to her sex is
a great glory " (Jowett), Plato, *Rep.* v.
455 D, ἐπὶ πᾶσι δὲ ἀσθενέστερον γυνὴ
ἀνδρός, *ib.* 457 A, τὰ ἐλαφρότερα ταῖς
γυναιξὶν ἢ τοῖς ἀνδράσι δοτέον διὰ τὴν
τοῦ γένους ἀσθένειαν, *Laws*, 781 A,
τὸ θῆλυ, διὰ τὸ ἀσθενές. How far
would this commonplace hold to-day ?
The great change which has taken
place since ancient times in the economic and legal position of women
has certainly narrowed its application :
it cannot be held to apply to character
or to ability, nor is it true of health or
physical endurance without many
reservations. And yet the Apostle's
phrase answers to some deep-seated
truth which both sexes alike still agree
to recognize. " Heavy " industry, for
example, such as calls for the handling
of great physical weights, is by common consent assigned to men ; and
the heavier responsibilities, such as are
involved in the initiation and manage-
ment of large business enterprises or
the conduct of war, are mainly confined to the male sex. In the present
passage the context from iii. 1-7 suggests that both ideas are present to the
author's mind. The husband is physically stronger in the sense of being
more muscular ; and his is the ultimate responsibility for the direction of
the home.
σκεύει] *body*, almost in the popular
Scottish sense, e.g. " puir body "=
person. For the body as the " vessel "
of the personality cf. Lucr. *de Rerum
Natura* iii. 554 ff. :

*sic animus per se non quit sine corpore
et ipso
esse homine, illius quasi quod vas
esse videtur,*

on which Munro quotes also *ib.* iii.
440 f., 793, and Cic. *Tusc. Disp.* i. 22,
*corpus quidem quasi vas est aut aliquod
animi receptaculum.* σκεῦος is used for
" body " in 1 Sam. xxi. 5 (probably) ;
in N.T. in 1 Thess. iv. 4, 2 Cor. iv. 7 ;
and later in Hermas, *Mand.* v. 1, *Ep.
Barn.* vii. 3, xi. 9, τὸ σκεῦος τοῦ πνεύματος, and xxi. 8, ἕως ἔτι τὸ καλὸν σκεῦός
(i.e. the good vessel of the body) ἐστιν
μεθ' ὑμῶν. Special importance attaches
to 1 Thess. iv. 4, 5, εἰδέναι ἕκαστον ὑμῶν
τὸ ἑαυτοῦ σκεῦος κτᾶσθαι ἐν ἁγιασμῷ
καὶ τιμῇ, μὴ ἐν πάθει ἐπιθυμίας, καθάπερ καὶ τὰ ἔθνη τὰ μὴ εἰδότα τὸν θεόν,
because it was probably written by
St. Peter's amanuensis, Silvanus (cf.
Introd. pp. 14-17) ; in which case
that passage would seem decisive
for its meaning here. [Lightfoot's
note in *Notes on Epistles of St. Paul*
is clear and forceful as usual ; but I
think his conclusion is wrong. Cf.
Milligan, *in loc.*] Further, just as
σῶμα is used in N.T. as almost equivalent to " person " (e.g. Rom. xii 1),
so σκεῦος need not be confined to a
purely physical connotation either.
The " vessel " here thought of is the
whole personality of the wife regarded
as a representative of her sex. We
might translate the phrase " rendering chivalrous respect to the woman
in them, as the weaker sex ".
Wand says that " both husband and
wife are weak pieces of furniture in the
house of the Holy Spirit, but in view
of her physical constitution the wife is
the weaker ", and alludes to Strack-
Billerbeck, iii. pp. 632 f. But if the
Holy Spirit is in mind at all, it is best
thought of as something of which the
σκεῦος is the container (so Lightfoot
on 1 Thess. iv. 4). I cannot, however,
see any reason to postulate any reference to the Holy Spirit.
τῷ γυναικείῳ] almost " das ewig-

κληρονόμοι χάριτος ζωῆς, εἰς τὸ μὴ ἐγκόπτεσθαι τὰς προσευχὰς
ὑμῶν.
⁸Τὸ δὲ τέλος, πάντες ὁμόφρονες, συμπαθεῖς, φιλάδελφοι,

weibliche ", i.e. " the woman in her ".
For this use of neuter adjective with
article to connote an abstract noun cf.
Goodwin, op. cit. § 933. For a somewhat contemptuous Jewish reference
to feminine " weakness ", very far
removed from St. Peter's teaching, cf.
Letter of Aristeas, 250 (probably of
first century B.C.).

ἀπονέμοντες τιμήν] 1 Clem. i. 3
uses the same phrase of the respect due
to older members of the Christian
community : Philo, de Spec. Leg. i. 65
[II. 222 M] uses the plural ἀπονέμειν
τὰς τιμάς, as not infrequently in Greek
drama, cf. Soph., Aj. 1351, τοῖς φίλοις
τιμὰς νέμειν. The plural signifies the
many acts of courtesy and consideration in which a due regard will shew
itself.

συγκληρονόμοι] Ignatius, ad Polyc.
v. 1, develops this by saying that those
who marry should do so μετὰ γνώμης
τοῦ ἐπισκόπου, ἵνα ὁ γάμος ᾖ κατὰ κύριον
καὶ μὴ κατ᾿ ἐπιθυμίαν.

ἐγκόπτεσθαι] hinder. Cf. Polyb.
XXIV. i. 12. [The v.l. ἐκκόπτεσθαι
would mean " made an end of " rather
than " interrupted " ; but the textual
weight is on the side of ἐγκόπτεσθαι.]
Where hardening of heart is caused by
lack of understanding in the highest
and most delicate of all human relationships, the relationship with God expressed in prayer is subject to serious
impediment. Cf. 1 Jn. iv. 18-20. At
the same time access to God in prayer
is at once the goal and the test of
human affection. Far more is implied
here than the tempus amplexandi, et
tempus longe fieri ab amplexibus of
Eccl. iii. 5, quoted by Estius, or even
than the developed form of it quoted
by Windisch from Test. Napth. viii. 8,
καιρὸς γὰρ συνουσίας γυναικὸς καὶ καιρὸς
ἐγκρατείας εἰς προσευχὴν αὐτοῦ, though
that is not excluded. St. Peter cuts
deeper, and reaches to the roots of the

affective life and its contact with the
divine Life.

iii. 8-12. General summary of
ethical teaching, based on the verba
Christi and on Ps. xxxiv., which
was probably already in catechetical
use.

For a comparison of this summary of
the Catechumen Virtues, as regards
both its substance and its place in the
pattern of moral teaching, with that
in Col. iii. 8-15, and for its relation
to 1 Thess. v. 13-22 and Rom. xii.
9-19, see Essay II, pp. 407-13, and
Tables VIII A and B. It appears to
be closest, as we might expect, to
1 Thessalonians.

8. Τὸ δὲ τέλος] finally, moreover.
Cf. Plato, Laws, 740 E, καὶ δὴ καὶ τό
γε τέλος, " and what is more, finally ",
introducing a last and crowning consideration. τέλος or τὸ τέλος, in this
adverbial sense, always seems to introduce a fresh point, and not simply to
summarize what has gone before.
Here it effects the transition from
specific ethical duties to a general,
though summarized, statement of
Christian character.

The sentence has no main verb,
ὄντες (the participial imperative) being
understood.

ὁμόφρονες] For the vocabulary of this
verse see below, p. 412, n. 1. The
adjectives are all found in good literary Greek, except ταπεινόφρονες. For
ὁμόφρ. cf. Hom. Il. xxii. 263, ὁμόφρονα
θυμὸν ἔχουσιν; for συμπαθεῖς, Plato
Com. Incert. 19, οὐδεὶς ὁμαίμου συμπα-
θέστερος φίλος (the converse of Hom.
Od. viii. 585 f.,

ἐπεὶ οὐ μέν τι κασιγνήτοιο χερείων
γίγνεται ὅς κεν ἑταῖρος ἐὼν πεπνυμένα
εἰδῇ),

and Dion. Halic. Ant. Rom. II. xlv.,
μακρὰν καὶ συμπαθῆ διεξῆλθε δέησιν; for
φιλάδελφοι, Xen. Mem. II. iii. 17. εὔσπλαγχνοι occurs in Hippocr. 89 c in a

εὔσπλαγχνοι, ταπεινόφρονες, ⁹μὴ ἀποδιδόντες κακὸν ἀντὶ κακοῦ
ἢ λοιδορίαν ἀντὶ λοιδορίας, τοὐναντίον δὲ εὐλογοῦντες, ὅτι εἰς

physical sense. Our only guide to its previous meaning in a spiritual sense is the use of the substantive εὐσπλαγχνία in Eur. *Rhes*. 192, where it means " courage " ; and " good-hearted " would therefore seem the best rendering here. εὔσπλαγχνος, like σπλάγχνα, the seat of the feelings, changes its meaning according to its context: while " tender-hearted " is called for in *Ep. Polyc*. v., and " forgiving " in Clem. Alex. *Fragm*. 1018 [P], and " affection " is signified by εὐσπλαγχνία in *Pass. S. Perp*. iii., " good-hearted " suits very well in *Ep. Polyc*. vi. ταπεινόφρων and its cognate verb occur in LXX rarely, and are also used in a good sense in Epictetus and the Sibylline Oracles ; but the associations of ταπεινός in classical Greek are always of debasement (cf. Plutarch, *Mor*. 336 E, εἴπωμεν οὖν, ὅτι μικροὺς ἡ τύχη ποιεῖ καὶ περιδεεῖς καὶ ταπεινόφρονας : and Trench, *Synonyms* (ed. 1865), pp. 145 f. See note on v. 5 below), and the Christian use of the word is one of the plainest examples of the transvaluation of values achieved by Christianity. [Cf. Nock, *Conversion*, p. 206 quoting Orig. *con. Cels*. iii. 59, " Let us hear whom these people invite : *Whosoever*, they say, *is a sinner, whosoever is unwise, whosoever is foolish,* — in a word, *whosoever is a wretch — he will be received into the Kingdom of God* ".] The whole passage, verses 8 and 9, is a beautiful summary of the ethical and spiritual qualities required of members of the Church in their relations one with another and in their attitude to their non-Christian and often hostile neighbours. They are to be in their common life (1) in outlook, like minded, as sharing a common heritage of faith and ethical tradition; (2) in feeling, full of sympathy ; (3) in action, kind ; and that not in any sparing way, but (4) out of the fulness of brave hearts. [The nature of φιλα-

δελφία is one of the questions answered in the *Epistle to Diognetus*, chs. i., v., vi. (cf. edition by E. H. Blakeney), the others being the nature of the God whom Christians believe in, and the nature of the Christian Church.] This good-heartedness is a quality that knows no frontiers, and so prepares the way for those qualities which especially face towards the outside world, of which (5) humility and (6) the forgiveness of injuries stand in the foreground. To lives so lived attaches the divine blessing promised in Ps. xxxiv. The Church's inner cohesion and its members' meek and unprovocative conduct towards others rest on a theological foundation, springing from a knowledge of God and God's ways which enables Christians to be in the world though not of it, and to live in detachment from current secular habits and standards, as those whose life is hid with Christ in God.

9. μὴ ἀποδιδόντες κτλ.] For the parallels in 1 Thess. v. 15 and Rom. xii. see Essay II, pp. 412 f. and Table VIII A, p. 408. The injunction is probably part of the primitive catechism, and rests on *verba Christi* in the Lord's Prayer and the Sermon on the Mount. λοιδορίαν] Cf. *supra*, ii. 23, of Christ's meekness, and St. Paul's claim in 1 Cor. iv. 12, λοιδορούμενοι εὐλογοῦμεν. The Lucan version of the Sermon on the Mount (Lk. vi. 27 f.) is verbally closer to this than the Matthaean. On the contrast between this teaching and that of Aristotle (*Anal. Post*. II. xii. 21) on this point of the right reaction to insult cf. Robertson and Plummer on 1 Cor. iv. 12 ; Aristotle's teaching in *Eth. Nicom*. IV. iii. 30 is somewhat different, in the sense that ὁ μεγαλόψυχος is not μνησίκακος. But Epictetus, *Ench*. 42, approaches the Christian standpoint : ἀπὸ τούτων οὖν ὁρμώμενος πραέως ἕξεις πρὸς τὸν λοιδοροῦντα.

τοῦτο ἐκλήθητε, ἵνα εὐλογίαν κληρονομήσητε. ¹⁰Ὁ γὰρ θέλων
ζωὴν ἀγαπᾶν, καὶ ἰδεῖν ἡμέρας ἀγαθάς, παυσάτω τὴν γλῶσσαν
ἀπὸ κακοῦ, καὶ χείλη τοῦ μὴ λαλῆσαι δόλον· ¹¹ἐκκλινάτω δὲ ἀπὸ

εὐλογοῦντες] "speaking well of" would be the ordinary classical sense; but the occurrence of εὐλογίαν immediately below, and the *verba Christi* in Matt. v. 44 and Lk. vi. 28, shew that the religious sense common in LXX is present here also: intercession for enemies, beneficence towards them, and speaking well of them, are all comprised in the term.

ὅτι εἰς τοῦτο κτλ.] i.e. "freely ye have received, freely give". The Christian's attitude of goodwill towards those who inflict personal insult or injury is grounded in a thankful realization of God's mercies and promises to himself.

10-12. A quotation, with slight modification, from the LXX of Ps. xxxiv. 13-17a. For the use of this Psalm by St. Peter, here and in 1 Pet. ii. 3, 4, see Essay II, pp. 413 f., and Table VIII A, pp. 408-10, where the view is expressed that Prov. iii. and Ps. xxxiv. were both drawn upon in a section of the early Christian catechism dealing with the Catechumen Virtues; and for the possibility that part of the Psalm was already in use as a hymn, Add. Note E, pp. 268 ff. But, whether this be so or not, the choice of the passage is masterly and is St. Peter's own ; for it gathers up in convincing fashion the simple, positive ethic he has been teaching, and does so in a way that reveals the personality of the author.

Kirkpatrick (C.B.S.) points out that in this Psalm "thought and style are those of the Book of Proverbs", and apparently of a later age than David, i.e. post-exilic. It was one of the Eucharistic psalms of the early Church; cf. Bingham, *Antiq.* v. p. 460, Oesterley, *The Psalms, in loc.*

The principal verbal differences between 1 Peter and Ps. xxxiv. here are the change of form in the first verse

from an interrogative

Ps. xxxiv. 13	1 Peter
τίς ἐστιν ἄνθρωπος ὁ θέλων ζωήν, ἀγαπῶν ἰδεῖν ἡμέ- ρας ἀγαθάς;	ὁ γὰρ θέλων ζωὴν ἀγαπᾶν, καὶ ἰδεῖν ἡμέρας ἀγαθάς,

to a participial clause, and the use of the third person imperative instead of the second person imperative in the main verbs following. Alford says that in LXX "all is plain: whereas θέλων ζωὴν ἀγαπᾶν is hardly intelligible". Admittedly the phrase is unusual ; but it is far from unintelligible, if St. Peter intended to indicate that he was quoting the Psalm *with a difference*, and, so far from being content with the original meaning, "life on earth" (so Wand and others), had in mind the true, abiding life, as in 1 Jn. v. 12, 16 (cf. also the *verbum Christi* in Jn. x. 10 and ὁδοὺς ζωῆς in Acts ii. 28), which belongs to the "incorruptible inheritance (i. 4) of Christian hope. Jas. iv. 14 and 2 Tim. iv. 8 are not irrelevant here. Bengel aptly quotes Eccl. ii. 17, ἐμίσησα τὴν ζωήν, the cry of the frustrated and disillusioned soul, which is oppressed by life's tedium ; the opposite of which is the zest for life imparted by a grasp of its eternal ends and issues. It is this that makes the Christian's days on earth "good days".

10. ἡμέρας ἀγαθάς] Cf. Tobit iv. 5, 6, "Do uprightly all thy life long, and follow not the ways of unrighteousness. For if thou deal truly, thy doings shall prosperously succeed to thee, and to all them that live justly." This is typical of the Jewish view.

παυσάτω] Why is the second person imperative of the LXX changed to the third person ? It is sufficiently accounted for by the author's abandonment of the interrogative in the previous verse ; though an additional reason may be that it appeared in this

κακοῦ, καὶ ποιησάτω ἀγαθόν· ζητησάτω εἰρήνην, καὶ διωξάτω
αὐτήν· ¹²ὅτι ὀφθαλμοὶ Κυρίου ἐπὶ δικαίους, καὶ ὦτα αὐτοῦ εἰς
δέησιν αὐτῶν· πρόσωπον δὲ Κυρίου ἐπὶ ποιοῦντας κακά.
¹³Καὶ τίς ὁ κακώσων ὑμᾶς, ἐὰν τοῦ ἀγαθοῦ ζηλωταὶ γένησθε;
¹⁴ἀλλ' εἰ καὶ πάσχοιτε διὰ δικαιοσύνην, μακάριοι· Τὸν δὲ φόβον

form in his catechetical source.

11. καὶ ποιησάτω ἀγαθόν] i.e. red-
dens bona pro malis, et benedictionem
pro maledictione (Estius).

ζητησάτω . . . καὶ διωξάτω] The
words enjoin the same active and persistent effort on behalf of peace as is
enjoined in the Beatitude in Matt. v. 9.

12. πρόσωπον . . . Κυρίου] the face
being the divine Presence in manifestation, whether in wrath and dis-
favour (Ps. xxi. 10, cf. Ex. xiv. 24) or
in blessing (Num. vi. 25, 26).

iii. 13–iv. end. Third Doctrinal
Section.

This section is comparable to the
first (i. 3-12) in depth and richness, and
it also breathes a note of confident
gaiety which must spring from the
author's character. The basic theme,
emphasized in the first and in the last
verses of the section, is the pursuit and
practice of goodness, and its power of
triumphing through suffering. For
suffering, and suffering in the form of
persecution for Christianity's sake,
becomes now a dominant issue. It is
still, as previously in i. 6, a contingency
rather than a universal fact ; but that
it has occurred in some of the communities addressed may reasonably be
inferred.[1] Yet that constitutes no
ground for alarm or fear : rather
for serene confidence and sublime
joy. And the reason is doctrinal.
Christ also suffered unjustly; but His
death had redemptive efficacy even
beyond the confines of the Christian
Church, and it was crowned by His
resurrection and exaltation in glory.
The cross at once transmuted suffering
and conquered sin ; and the suffering
of Christians, accepted at baptism
in the same spirit, may do the like.
Certainly the persecution bodes crisis

and climax, for them as it did for
Him ; but in that hour of judgment
they can commit themselves without
reserve into God's hands.

13. Καὶ τίς κτλ.] Besides, who is it
who, etc. ? The resumption is rapid,
after the quotation from Ps. xxxiv., and
effects a swift and easy entrance to the
new theme. [E. H. B. suggests that
there is a note of indignant protest here
that anyone should think otherwise, as
in Dem. de Fals. Leg. 232, καὶ τίς,
ὦ ἄνδρες 'Αθηναῖοι, τοῦτ' ἰδὼν τὸ
παράδειγμα δίκαιον αὐτὸν παρασχεῖν
ἐθελήσει ; and cf. the Latin quis
tandem ?]

κακώσων] harm, damage. Cf. Aesch.
P.V. 976, ὅσοι παθόντες εὖ κακοῦσί μ'
ἐκδίκως. The verb takes up the ποιοῦντας κακά of the end of the Psalm,
and applies it to the actual situation of
the readers.

τοῦ ἀγαθοῦ ζηλωταὶ] enthusiasts for
goodness. This phrase, similarly, takes
up the ὁ θέλων ζωὴν ἀγαπᾶν and the
ποιησάτω ἀγαθόν of the first two verses
of the quotation. Cf. Tit. ii. 14,
ζηλωτὴν καλῶν ἔργων, Eph. ii. 10 ; and
in classical Greek Isocr. 4 B, ζηλωτὴς
τῆς ἀρετῆς. We may recall Sir John
Seeley's words : " No heart is pure
that is not passionate, no virtue safe
that is not enthusiastic "

γένησθε] you have become, i.e. by
your adhesion to Christianity.

14. ἀλλ' εἰ καὶ πάσχοιτε] but if indeed
you should suffer. For εἰ καί in this
sense cf. Soph. O.T. 305, with Jebb's
note in the Appendix to his edition.
Note the optative, which envisages a
contingency not immediately pressing
or obvious. It is consistent with a risk
which has become an actuality in
certain cases, but not more.

διὰ δικαιοσύνην, μακάριοι] The words

---

[1] For a fuller discussion of the historical background implied see Introd. pp. 52-6.

αὐτῶν μὴ φοβηθῆτε, μηδὲ ταραχθῆτε, ¹⁵Κύριον δὲ τὸν Χριστὸν

are, no doubt, based on the *verbum Christi* in Matt. v. 10, μακάριοι οἱ δεδιωγμένοι ἕνεκεν δικαιοσύνης, also quoted in Polyc. *ad Phil.* ii. 3. μακάριος is one of three words in Greek connoting happiness : (1) εὐλογητός always has a religious meaning, and is used constantly in LXX of God and of those whom God sends or blesses ; and so too in N.T. (2) εὐδαίμων is the word for the man who is happy or fortunate in the ordinary secular sense, though Aristotle in the *Ethics* invested the word with a high ethical and intellectual significance. (3) μακάριος, while it connotes " happy and successful prosperity " (McNeile, on Matt. v. 3), commonly has, if not a religious, at least a " numinous " meaning, as the Homeric use of οἱ μάκαρες for the gods indicates ; and it is distinguished by Aristotle in *Eth. Nicom.* 1. x. 14 from εὐδαίμων as connoting a higher state, namely felicity rather than happiness. As regards LXX and N.T. the case is admirably put by Montefiore (on Matt. v. 3) : " . . . neither ' happy ' nor ' blessed ' is quite accurate or adequate. The happiness implied is of a particular type. It is religious happiness. But, moreover, it may be doubted how far the meaning is that the persons described as happy experience acute feelings of delight. At any rate, this is not the only, and probably not the chief, meaning. The main meaning probably is that they are religiously fortunate, that they enjoy, or will enjoy, a peculiar divine blessing or favour." Pss. i. 1, ii. 12 afford good examples of the usage.

Τὸν δὲ φόβον αὐτῶν . . . ταραχθῆτε] The construction is difficult, but the meaning clear : " be not afraid of them ". It is based on Is. viii. 12, 13, τὸν δὲ φόβον αὐτοῦ οὐ μὴ φοβηθῆτε οὐδὲ μὴ ταραχθῆτε· κύριον αὐτὸν ἁγιάσατε, καὶ αὐτὸς ἔσται σου φόβος, where αὐτοῦ probably (i.e. if the Hebrew is to be followed) means " the fear felt by the people ". But φόβος can take

either a subjective genitive (fear felt *by* someone) or an objective genitive (fear felt *of* someone) ; and, even if the former was the construction in Is. viii. 12, St. Peter was fully entitled to use the latter construction here. Cf. Blass, *Grammar*, p. 166. It is then exactly parallel, as Estius observes, to the usage in Ps. lxiv. 2, ἀπὸ φόβου ἐχθροῦ ἐξελοῦ τὴν ψυχήν μου. The accusative φόβον is the cognate accusative as in χαίρειν χαρὰν μεγάλην (Matt. ii. 10), and in iii. 6 above, μὴ φοβούμεναι μηδεμίαν πτόησιν. Had St. Peter not been quoting, he could have written μὴ φοβηθῆτε αὐτούς. Winer, *op. cit.* p. 281, lays it down that this construction " is only used when the notion of the verb is to be extended ", either by an objective genitive or by an adjective ; or, we may add, as in iii. 6 above, where the notion of the verb is rather defined with greater accuracy than extended.

On the use of Is. viii. in this Epistle and in Rom. ix. see Add. Note E, pp. 268 ff., where it is urged that Is. viii. 14 was already part of an early Christian hymn. Did verses 12 and 13 also form part of the hymn ? It seems to me probable enough.

15. Κύριον δὲ τὸν Χριστὸν ἁγιάσατε] St. Peter substitutes τὸν Χριστόν for the αὐτόν of Is. viii. 13, but again changes the meaning. Bigg takes τὸν Χριστόν as appositional, but the predicative use of κύριον, i.e. " as Lord ", surely gives a better sense, and does more justice to the order of the words. ἁγιάζω is a word with several shades of meaning in N.T. (cf. Wilke, *Clavis Novi Testamenti, sub voc.*) ; but here it=*venerandum facio vel agnosco, pie colo*, i.e. " acknowledge as holy ", as in Is. xxix. 23, Ezek. xx. 41, Ecclus. xxxvi. 4, and in the Lord's Prayer, Matt. vi. 9. We may also mention Ezek. xi. 16 f., a passage which St. Peter's words may well have recalled to the minds of Jewish Christians amongst his readers, especially in view of ii. 11. Ecclus.

ἀγιάσατε ἐν ταῖς καρδίαις ὑμῶν· ἔτοιμοι ἀεὶ πρὸς ἀπολογίαν
παντὶ τῷ αἰτοῦντι ὑμᾶς λόγον περὶ τῆς ἐν ὑμῖν ἐλπίδος, ἀλλὰ

xxxvi. 4 is especially to the point, as the " consecration " of God in the Jewish people (ἐν ἡμῖν) is before the face of the Gentiles, and leads to His being " magnified " among them (ἐν αὐτοῖς) ; just as here the " consecration " of Christ as Lord in the hearts of Christians leads on to the success of their defence of their faith before the Gentiles and the convincing of the latter. Further, on this interpretation, the allusion to Christ here anticipates what is to follow in verses 18 ff. The Christ whom they are to consecrate as Lord is the Christ who, though guiltless, suffered for sinners : what is enjoined is not merely a devotional love of Christ, but such a love inspired by a right theology, which at once invests Christ with the O.T. attributes of Jehovah as " Lord " and Christ's death, which was outwardly a judicial murder, with atoning significance. On the transference of the O.T. attributes of Jehovah to Jesus as Messiah in the Gospels cf. Hoskyns and Davey, *The Riddle of the New Testament*, *passim* ; and on the application to Eucharistic theology of the idea of the " consecration " of Christ's death, as investing it with its sacrificial significance, see W. Spens, *Essays Catholic and Critical*, Essay xiii., and *Theology*, vol. xv. No. 88 (Oct. 1927), p. 231.

The doctrinal implications of this passage are far-reaching, as regards both the Incarnation and the Atonement ; but St. Peter sticks close to the original *nidus* of Christian doctrine, namely the O.T. Scriptures and the historical events of the Gospel, and there is nothing here which is not simple and does not bear the marks of being primitive.

Some MSS. give Θεὸν instead of Χριστὸν, but the weight both of Greek and Latin texts is against it. Wand suggests that the alteration was made by certain early copyists who feared

that the passage went doctrinally too far.

ἐν ταῖς καρδίαις ὑμῶν] i.e. in the seat of the instinctive and affective life, where fear would reside, if it were present. Cf. Seneca, *Fragm.* 123, in Lactant. *Div. Inst.* vi. 25, " Temples are not to be built to God of stones built on high : He must be consecrated in the heart of each man ".

ἔτοιμοι ἀεὶ πρὸς ἀπολογίαν] *ready always to offer explanation and defence.* The swift, terse, style (where ὄντες or ὡς might have been expected with the adjective) is in keeping with the spirit of constant readiness required. The whole passage recalls Lk. xii. 1-12 (cf. Lk. xxi. 14, 15), with its teaching as to what to fear in persecution and what not to fear, and its promise of the Holy Spirit's guidance when confronted with the question πῶς ἢ τί ἀπολογήσησθε. Cf. also Col. iv. 6. ἀπολογία and its cognates are used both of public self-defence (as in Lk. xii. and xxi., Acts xix. 33, xxii. 1, xxvi. 1, 2, 24) and of more private and less formal utterances (as in 2 Cor. vii. 11). Its application to written treatises such as Plato's *Apology* does not seem to occur in Christian literature before the second century, where we have the Apologies of Justin, Aristides, and the anonymous author of the *Epistle to Diognetus*. The first sense is not excluded here, but the second must be chiefly in mind, for αἰτοῦντι is a quite informal term, and indicates conversation rather than police enquiry.

Similar teaching was given by the Jewish Rabbis, as in *Pirqe Aboth*, ii. 18. For a fine modern exposition of this theme see Maritain, *Redeeming the Time*, ch. v., especially p. 110.

λόγον περὶ] *a rational account of.* Cf. Plato, *Polit.* 285 E, ὅταν . . . τις βουληθῇ τῷ λόγον αἰτοῦντι περί του . . . ἐνδείξασθαι. Our author is using a good classical Greek phrase here, which it is not easy to parallel else-

μετὰ πραΰτητος καὶ φόβου· ¹⁶συνείδησιν ἔχοντες ἀγαθήν, ἵνα, ἐν
ᾧ καταλαλεῖσθε, καταισχυνθῶσιν οἱ ἐπηρεάζοντες ὑμῶν τὴν
ἀγαθὴν ἐν Χριστῷ ἀναστροφήν. ¹⁷κρεῖττον γὰρ ἀγαθοποιοῦντας,

where in N.T. λόγον ἀποδιδόναι, and
even λόγον διδόναι (Rom. xiv.
12) have a juridical flavour which is not implied,
I think (despite Windisch), in the text
before us. The verse is quoted with
effect at the beginning of Eunomius'
Ἔκθεσις Πίστεως written for the
Emperor Theodosius.

περὶ τῆς ἐν ὑμῖν ἐλπίδος] Cf. i. 3, 21
and notes there. ἐν ὑμῖν means that
the hope inspires the whole Christian
community ; and it was all the more
notable in an age when the sense of
frustration was widespread. Cf. Eph.
ii. 12 ; and Blakeney, Ep. ad Diogn.
pp. 10 f.

ἀλλὰ μετὰ . . . φόβου] The confidence of Christians in their position
and their readiness to speak up for it
must not be accompanied by any over-
bearingness of manner, or lack of
respect, or failure of reverence before
the divine mystery entrusted to them.
The injunction of gentleness is illustrated by Pirqe Aboth, ii. 14, " Let the
honour of thy friend be dear unto thee
as thine own ; and be not easily provoked ". It seems unlikely that St.
Peter had his own denials of our Lord
in mind, for they were chiefly prompted
by fear in quite another sense.

16. συνείδησιν] Cf. note on ii. 19.
ἐν ᾧ] Cf. note on ii. 12. Here the
phrase might be translated, amidst the
obloquy you suffer. But several good
MSS., including ℵAC, read καταλαλοῦσιν (-ῶσιν) ὑμῶν ὡς κακοποιῶν, as
in ii. 12 ; and this is followed by A.V.
R.V., on the other hand, follows the
text in WH (and Souter), and since it
is the more difficult reading, and
might therefore easily have been
assimilated to ii. 12, it would on normal principles be preferable. It has,
however, difficulties of its own ;
for, though καταλαλεῖν is occasionally
found with an accusative of the personal object both in Polybius and in

epigraphic Greek, and there is one
instance of the passive in Polybius
(XXVII. xii. 2), the genitive is the only
construction found in N.T. (Jas. iv. 11
(tris), 1 Pet. ii. 12). In LXX moreover the personal object of καταλαλεῖν
is always in the genitive, with or without κατά ; and the passive καταλαλεῖ-
σθαι does not occur. Cf. also 2 Clem.
iv. 3, Herm. Mand. ii. 2, where the
direct personal object is in the genitive. Further, we are not tied up to
the choice between these two readings ;
for the Vulgate has in eo quod detra-
hunt de vobis without the words tamquam de malefactoribus found in ii. 12.
If the original were simply ἐν ᾧ καταλαλοῦσιν ὑμῶν, assimilation to ii. 12
would account for the addition of ὡς
κακοποιῶν, while the form ἐν ᾧ καταλαλεῖσθε might be due to a scribe who
thought that the main verb was to be
in the active voice, i.e. καταισχύνητε
τοὺς ἐπηρεάζ. κτλ. The meaning
would then be, in the very act of
running you down.

οἱ ἐπηρεάζοντες] abuse, treat spite-
fully. It is a good classical word,
usually governing the dative ; but the
accusative object is found, e.g. Ar.
Pol. v. viii. (x.) 9. Cf. also Rhet.
II. ii. 4, where ἐπηρεασμός is defined
as a form of ὀλιγωρία, and " a thwart-
ing another's wishes, not that anything
may accrue to the person himself who
so impedes, but in order that something may not accrue to that other ".
The verb more often connotes spiteful
actions than spiteful speech, as probably in Lk. vi. 28. τὴν . . . ἀναστροφήν, however, may be the direct object
of καταισχυνθῶσιν as in Isocr. 60 E, κατ-
αισχυνθέντες τὴν ἀρετὴν αὐτῶν (" feeling
shame at "), and ἐπηρεάζοντες would
then mean " your persecutors ".

ἐν Χριστῷ] Cf. v. 10, 14. Christ was
in their hearts (verse 15), and they
were also " in Christ ", now (as in this

εἰ θέλοι τὸ θέλημα τοῦ Θεοῦ, πάσχειν ἢ κακοποιοῦντας. ¹⁸ὅτι καὶ Χριστὸς ἅπαξ περὶ ἁμαρτιῶν ἔπαθε, δίκαιος ὑπὲρ ἀδίκων,

verse and in v. 14) and to eternity (v. 10). The *locus classicus* for this reciprocal indwelling is Jn. xv. and xvii. The origin of the phrase is as much theological and historical as mystical, and is to be traced to the corporate idea involved in the concept of " the Son of Man ". Cf. the present author's earlier book (1915) *The Teaching of Christ*, pp. 186 ff., expecially : " The figure of the vision [sc. of " one like unto a Son of Man " in Daniel] had taken flesh and blood in Jesus, and was now brought near to the Ancient of Days. But likewise it had taken body in the saints of the Most High, who were the Church ; so that members of the Church might be most aptly spoken of as ' in Christ '." For the importance of our Lord's Ascension, and of St. Stephen's vision and St. Paul's conversion, for the translation of that teaching into religious experience, see *The Approach to Christianity* by the present author, ch. v., especially pp. 110-18.

The beautiful Greek of the participial clause in this verse is noteworthy, and bespeaks a cultured amanuensis.

17. ἀγαθοποιοῦντας] See note on ii. 20.

εἰ θέλοι] Cf. εἰ καὶ πάσχοιτε, *supra*, verse 14, with note, and i. 6. A similar *contingency* in regard to suffering was felt by our Lord even on the very threshold of His passion, Matt. xxvi. 39, 42.

For a similar sentiment in classical authors, E. H. B. cites Plato, *Gorg.* 508 B, τὸ ἀδικεῖν τοῦ ἀδικεῖσθαι . . . κάκιον ; with which cf. also *Laws*, 829 A.

18 ff. On this passage (iii. 18-iv. 6) see Essay I, pp. 317-39. Windisch regards iii. 18-22 as a baptismal hymn to Christ. This seems to me unlikely, since (1) it does not fall easily into verse form, (2) it cannot properly be detached from iv. 1-6 which follow.

That a hymn on the " harrowing of hell ", comparable to *Odes of Solomon*, xlii., may underlie it, is not impossible ; but the passage as it stands is doctrinal rather than liturgical in character. Völter regarded it as an interpolation ; but it fits closely into its context both before and after, and is almost essential to the main argument.

18. ὅτι καὶ Χριστὸς] A new application of the *imitatio Christi* : we pass from the *Christus patiens* to the *Christus victor*. In ii. 21 ff. the emphasis was on Christ's meekness, here it is on His courage and triumph ; in both His passion is thought of as vicarious (ὑπὲρ ἀδίκων, verse 18, and ὑπὲρ ὑμῶν, ii. 21) and atoning (περὶ ἁμαρτιῶν, verse 18, and ὃς τὰς ἁμαρτίας ἡμῶν κτλ., ii. 24). In both cases, also, the doctrinal passage is introduced by ὅτι, Christ's death in its atoning efficacy, its motive (ἵνα . . . ζήσωμεν, ii. 24, ἵνα . . . τῷ θεῷ, iii. 18, ἵνα . . . ζῶσι . . . πνεύματι, iv. 6), and its achievement (οὗ . . . ἰάθητε, ii. 24, νῦν σώζει, iii. 21) being the ground of Christian conduct. At the same time this later passage goes further than the earlier, in its emphasis on (1) the utterness of Christ's sacrifice (ἅπαξ, iii. 18), (2) its infinite range (καὶ τοῖς ἐν φυλακῇ πνεύμασι, iii. 19, καὶ νεκροῖς εὐηγγελίσθη, iv. 6), and (3) the completeness of His victory through the resurrection (θανατωθεὶς . . . πνεύματι, iii. 18, δι' ἀναστάσεως Ἰησ. Χρ., ὅς ἐστιν κτλ., iii. 22). The keystone of the whole doctrinal arch is in iv. 1a, Χριστοῦ οὖν παθόντος σαρκὶ καὶ ὑμεῖς τὴν αὐτὴν ἔννοιαν ὁπλίσασθε.

ἅπαξ κτλ.] Christ's death is supremely able to bring illumination and courage to those who suffer innocently, because (1) it was the conclusive and definitive embodiment in history (ἅπαξ, cf. Heb. ix. 26, 28, x. 10, 14) of the principle of the transformation of suffering and death, (2) it was invested with sacrificial and redemptive

ἵνα ἡμᾶς προσαγάγῃ τῷ Θεῷ, θανατωθεὶς μὲν σαρκὶ ζωοποιηθεὶς

significance (περὶ ἁμαρτιῶν . . . δί-καιος ὑπὲρ ἀδίκων), and (3) it revealed the victory of good (ζωοποιηθεὶς δὲ πνεύματι). Wheeler Robinson, Re-demption and Revelation, chs. xii., xiii., develops this theme with great force.

περὶ ἁμαρτιῶν] as in Heb. v. 3, x. 26, 1 Jn. ii. 2. περὶ (τῆς) ἁμαρτίας is used in Lev. v. 6, 7, vi. 30, Ezek. xliii. 21 of the sin-offering, which was propitia-tory : in Ps. xl. 7, quoted in Heb. x. 6, περὶ ἁμαρτίας is used as a substantive, sin-offering. The plural in 1 Peter makes the phrase less technical, i.e. "in respect of sins". In Ezek. xliii. 22, 25, xliv. 29, xlv. 17, xlvi. 20 [τὰ] ὑπὲρ ἁμαρτίας is used in the same sense, as in 1 Cor. xv. 3, Gal. i. 4 ; but St. Peter prefers to reserve the preposition ὑπέρ for the persons benefited, as here and in ii. 21.

There are some variant readings in this passage, which are not, however, of great importance for the meaning. (a) After ἁμαρτιῶν some Latin and Syriac texts, and Cyprian, Augustine, and Bede, add ἡμῶν (nostris) ; while Lℵ c 13 33 add ὑπὲρ ἡμῶν, and A abo copt add ὑπὲρ ὑμῶν. (b) For ἔπαθεν some good MSS., including Aℵ ák 13 vulg. syrr, read ἀπέθανεν. This is a formidable convergence of testimony, and justifies WH in regarding ἀπέ-θανεν as "primary" ; and the repeated occurrence of parts of πάσχειν in the context would account for its being altered in some MSS. to ἔπαθεν. But the meaning is not seriously affected, for ἔπαθεν undoubtedly refers to Christ's death. Cf. Ign. Smyrn. ii., καὶ ἀληθῶς ἔπαθεν, ὡς καὶ ἀληθῶς ἀνέστησεν ἑαυτόν, and Ep. Barn. vii. 11. And the word was used for dying in literary Greek : cf. [Plato], Axiochus, 369, where εἴ τι πάθοις means " if you should die ". We can, however, say that ἀπέθανεν makes it more probable than ἔπαθεν that the author was en-visaging a form of persecution which might issue, and in some cases perhaps

already had issued, in martyrdom. (c) ἡμᾶς has the better support among Greek and Latin MSS. ; but ὑμᾶς is read by B abjmo syrr arm. The second person plural occurs, however, often enough in the context, both before and after, to account for it.

προσαγάγῃ] Classical Greek would have the optative, but that mood is never found in N.T. in final clauses. On its obsolescence even in literary Greek see Moulton, op. cit. i. pp. 196 f. Various technical meanings have been found in, or read into, προσαγάγῃ, as that it refers to the bringing of men before God to be made priests, as in Ex. xxix. 4 (Kühl), or to the bringing of the sacrificial victim before the Lord, as in Lev. iii. 12, iv. 4, viii. 14 (cf. Vulgate, ut nos offerret Deo), or to the mystagogos bringing the neophytes to the Mysteries (Perdelwitz, cf. Add. Note M, p. 310). But elsewhere in N.T. the word is used quite simply for " bringing to ", and the indirect object is in the dative as here. There seems no reason to see in the word any further significance than is involved in the access to God spoken of in Eph. ii. 18, iii. 12, Heb. iv. 16, vii. 25, x. 22, xii. 22, which is, after all, the be-all and end-all of religion. As so often, the simplest interpretation is the most profound : Christ's atoning sacrifice brings us to God.

θανατωθεὶς . . . πνεύματι] The datives σαρκί and πνεύματι are " datives of reference ", cf. note on ii. 24, and are rightly paraphrased by Alford as quod ad carnem and quod ad spiritum. The usage is classical, cf. Xen. Mem. II. i. 31, τοῖς σώμασιν ἀδύνατοι . . . ταῖς ψυχαῖς ἀνόητοι. For this double con-trast both of verbs and nouns cf. Rom. i. 3 f. and 1 Tim. iii. 16 (ἐφανερώθη ἐν σαρκί, ἐδικαιώθη ἐν πνεύματι). The contrast recurs in iv. 6, where it is transferred from Christ to those who believe in Him. 1 Tim. iii. 16, 17 are probably part of an early credal hymn (cf. Essay I, pp. 325 f., Parry, The

δὲ πνεύματι, ¹⁹ἐν ᾧ καὶ τοῖς ἐν φυλακῇ πνεύμασι πορευθεὶς

Pastoral Epistles, in loc.); and this gives colour to the view that the language of St. Peter here reflects the thought of the primitive community. But what is that thought? Though the language is simple and untechnical, it is not without doctrinal bearings. θανατωθεὶς μὲν σαρκί refers to the reality of Christ's physical death; and the invariable connotation of the word in the Gospels, i.e. "put to death", makes it probable that the violence of Christ's death is also in the Apostle's mind here. In the natural and physical order (σαρκί), He was the victim of a judicial murder. But He was "quickened in spirit", i.e. in that part of His nature which belonged to the supernatural and spiritual order. Bengel, who is followed here by Wand and Windisch, distinguishes between this "quickening", which was for the purpose of preaching to the spirits in prison during the "three days" of the entombment, and Christ's resurrection; but the phrase clearly embodies a familiar N.T. contrast between Christ dead and Christ living (cf. Rom. xiv. 9, 2 Cor. xiii. 4, 1 Tim. iii. 16); and the patristic view (Epiphanius, Augustine, Oecumenius), which is followed by Estius, Bigg, Bennett, is to be preferred. [Clement of Alexandria has a characteristic interpretation in his *Adumbrationes* (Ὑποτυπώσεις) on 1 Peter (ed. Klotz, iv. p. 54, 1007 [P]), *Hoc est, in nostris vivificatus est spiritibus.* Cf. also the curious passage about the waters which engulf "the kings and the mighty", etc., "for the healing of the body, and for the punishment of the spirit" in *1 Enoch* lxvii. 8 ff.] Though we may distinguish between this quickening and the resurrection on the third day, it is unlikely that this distinction was present to the Apostle's mind.

Alford's note on this whole phrase is excellent. "His flesh was the subject, recipient, vehicle, of inflicted death: His spirit was the subject,

recipient, vehicle, of restored life. . . He, the God-man Christ Jesus, body and soul, ceased to live in the flesh, began to live in the spirit; ceased to live a fleshly, mortal life, began to live a spiritual resurrection life." At the same time, emphasis on the persistence of Christ's *ego* throughout these catastrophic changes, illustrated by His saying in Jn. x. 17, 18, must not make us blind to all that is meant by the fact that He *really died*. There is a point here where the Platonic and the Hebraic conceptions cannot be reconciled; and the thought of this passage, as of N.T. generally, is on the Hebraic side.

Shakespeare, in Sonnet CXLVI, shews himself a deep ponderer on this matter:

> Then, Soul, live thou upon thy servant's loss,
> And let that pine to aggravate thy store;
> Buy terms divine in selling hours of dross;
> Within be fed, without be rich no more;
> So shalt thou feed on death, that feeds on men,
> And death once dead there's no more dying then.

19. ἐν ᾧ] *in which state* or *circumstance*, i.e. of spirit quickened after physical death, or better and more broadly, "in which process", *in the course of which*, referring to Christ's passion and resurrection generally. The antecedent cannot be πνεύματι, for there is no example in N.T. of this dative of reference, or adverbial dative as I should prefer to call it, serving as antecedent to a relative pronoun. The antecedent to ἐν ᾧ lies in the preceding context, which here may be the phrase immediately before it (θανατωθεὶς . . . πνεύματι) or the whole process described in verse 18. Cf. note on i. 6. For the important bearing of this grammatical point on the exegesis of the passage see Essay I, p. 315.·

Rendel Harris' emendation ἐν ᾧ καὶ

Ἐνώχ (*Exp.* vi. iv. pp. 346 ff., v. pp. 317 ff.), supported by Schültz and Moffatt, is celebrated but most improbable ; for, in addition to the point already mentioned, (1) the allusion to Enoch would be abrupt and quite unprepared for ; (2) Enoch is represented in the *Book of Enoch* and elsewhere as proclaiming doom and nothing else on the fallen angels. Further, the antecedent to ἐν ᾧ, even if it were πνεύματι alone, is too intimately bound up with Christ to admit of Enoch being regarded as " in " it. If any emendation were made, I should suggest ἐν ᾧ καὶ Νῶε, citing 2 Pet. ii. 5, where Noah is described as δικαιοσύνης κήρυκα. But this would involve assuming still further corruption, e.g. the omission of a line ; and the text does not appear to be corrupt.

καὶ] *even* rather than *also*, and to be taken with the words immediately following, τοῖς . . . πνεύμασι.

τοῖς ἐν φυλακῇ πνεύμασιν] Are these " spirits in prison " angelic beings, or human, or both ? (i) Writers of the anthropological school (e.g. Gunkel, Bousset, etc.) take the phrase as referring to the fallen angels of Gen. vi., *Enoch*, and *Jubilees*, in which they find Persian and other non-Jewish influences. In favour of this view is the fact that the word πνεύματα is a phrase used of angelic beings, both good and evil, not only in Jewish apocalyptic (cf. *Enoch* xviii., lxix., and the repeated attribution to God of the title " Lord of Spirits "), where they are also sometimes identified with planets or falling stars, but also in N.T. itself. Thus the angels are described in Heb. i. 14 as λειτουργικὰ πνεύματα (cf. also Rev. i. 4, iii. 1), and τὰ πνεύματα occurs in Lk. x. 20 on our Lord's lips as connoting demons. According to *1 Enoch* xv. 8 ff., liv. 5, *Jubilees* x., these evil spirits were the progeny of the angels whose sin is described in Gen. vi., and whose punishment had been imprisonment. Cf. Kohler, *Jewish Theology*, p. 192 : " The whole world of demons is regarded as alienated from God by the

rebellion of the heavenly hosts, as if the fall of man by sin had its prototype in the celestial sphere ". The facts that the word πνεύματα is used absolutely of supernatural beings, that Jewish tradition spoke of such beings, under the names of angels, watchers, stars, or spirits, as disobeying God and transgressing their due order (cf. especially *Enoch* xiv. 4–xvi. 1, *Apoc. Bar.* lxi. 12, 13, *Test. Reub.* v., *Test. Napth.* iii.), and being punished by imprisonment (cf. *1 Enoch* x., xviii. 13-15, xxi., lxvii. 4, *Jub.* x.), that the period of this transgression was always reckoned as immediately prior to the Flood ; and that these beliefs are undoubtedly alluded to in 2 Pet. ii. and Jude 6, 7— these facts tell strongly in favour of this interpretation here.

(ii) On the other side it is contended that the use of πνεύματα to connote spirits or souls of the departed is justified by the extent to which πνεύματα and ψυχαί had become interchangeable terms by the Christian era (cf. *Enoch* xxii. 3, 4), and that the phrase before us is sufficiently illustrated by Heb. xii. 23, καὶ πνεύμασι δικαίων τετελειωμένων. Cf. also Song of the Three Holy Children 64, and for the obverse, Josephus' mention of " those called demons which are no other than πονηρῶν ἀνθρώπων πνεύματα " (*B.J.* vii. vi. 2). Further, *Enoch* ix. 3, 10 (Syn. Gk.), which gives us τὰ πνεύματα καὶ αἱ ψυχαὶ τῶν ἀνθρώπων, and τὰ πνεύματα τῶν ψυχῶν τῶν ἀποθανόντων ἀνθρώπων, belongs to a chapter which has already suggested to our author the παρακύψαι of 1 Pet. i. 12. This language indicates that πνεύματα could mean human beings, as in Num. xvi. 22, xxvii. 16, θεός, θεὸς τῶν πνευμάτων καὶ πάσης σαρκός, a phrase echoed apparently in Heb. xii. 9, τῷ πατρὶ τῶν πνευμάτων, and in Clem. Rom. lviii., lix. *Enoch* xxii. is of particular importance, for after " the prison of the angels " has been described in ch. xxi., it sets forth the various divisions in which the dead are assembled in Sheol, the first being for those who like Abel were martyred (verses 5-7), the second for the souls of those righteous persons who had not been killed by violence (verse 9), the third where sinners who had lived prosperously and been honourably buried without incurring punishment in their lifetime (verses 10, 11) are now "bound", and the fourth for sinners who suffered in their life and are therefore less severely punished in Sheol. Linguistically, however, when these illustrations are examined, they do not quite prove their case : in most of them πνεύματα is followed by a qualifying genitive, and wherever such a genitive is absent, πνεύματα connotes either persons now living on earth or the supernatural beings, or possibly (as in Heb. xii. 9) both. There is no trace of πνεύματα being used absolutely to connote "departed spirits"; and it is noteworthy that de Witt Burton (*Galatians*, I.C.C. p. 491) gives no other N.T. example besides 1 Pet. iii. 19 of πνεύματα connoting the spirits of men in Sheol, though πνεῦμα means a "ghost" in Lk. xxiv. 37, 39, and possibly in Acts xxiii. 9. On the other hand, it is to be observed that τὰ πνεύματα is not used quite absolutely here, but is qualified by ἐν φυλακῇ; and that point is of great importance for those who identify the "spirits in prison" of 1 Pet. iii. 19, in whole or in part, with the "dead" of iv. 6.

(iii) Windisch, who here as often is followed by Wand, solves the problem by the view that "the spirits in prison" is a phrase embracing both the fallen angels and the wicked men of Noah's day, though he does not give any examples in which angelic beings and the dead are thus lumped together under the one term πνεύματα. This interpretation, however, has something to commend it, if we have regard to the phrase τὰ ἐν φυλακῇ πνεύματα *as a whole*; though it is more attractive in the form given it by Loisy, who says (*Remarques sur la littérature épistolaire du N.T.*, p. 130) that the preaching to the dead referred to in 1 Pet. iv. 6 was given " on the occa-

sion when " Christ preached to the fallen angels. Cf. also his *Les Origines du N.T.*, p. 186. Linguistically, there is far more authority for τὰ πνεύματα without a qualifying genitive connoting supernatural beings than departed human beings, nor is ἐν φυλακῇ the kind of term which indicates that the dead are being referred to. *Apoc. Bar.* lxi. 13-15, moreover, speaks of "those who dwelt on the earth" perishing together at the same time as, or shortly after, the punishment of the fallen angels ; but they are not comprised together under one name. Strack-Billerbeck, iv. ii. p. 1076, says that the Rabbis often speak of hell as a prison or dungeon ; and Josephus (*Ant.* xviii. i. 3) says that it was part of Pharisaic doctrine that the souls of the wicked were to be detained in an everlasting prison. The idea, indeed, is common to many religions. But that would not in itself account for the phrase before us. The whole phrase, in fact, is unlike our author in its periphrastic style, unless he drew it from familiar literary sources. But such sources do exist in Jewish tradition, as shewn above : *Enoch* especially speaks of the fallen angels (cf. references above) and of the dead (cf. *1 Enoch* xxii. 3, 4, 11 ff., and perhaps x. 14) as being bound or kept in prison until the final judgment. And Is. xxiv. 21-3, Hos. xiii. 14, Zech. ix. 12 may have seemed to justify the thought. The importance of the point will be variously estimated according as 1 Pet. iii. 19 f. is connected with iv. 6 or not. In view of the meaning of τὰ πνεύματα in Lk. x. 20, Rev. i. 4, iii. 1, and of the allusions to the fate of the fallen angels in Jude 5, 6, 2 Pet. ii., I cannot doubt that the primary reference is to such supernatural beings ; but *Enoch's* descriptions of the wicked dead as well as the fallen angels being bound or in prison make it possible that the former also were included in St. Peter's mind, if not in the phrase itself.

A further point arises as to whether

ἐκήρυξεν, ²⁰ἀπειθήσασί ποτε, ὅτε ἀπεξεδέχετο ἡ τοῦ Θεοῦ μακρο-

these " spirits in prison " may include the spirits which were believed to inhabit the abysses (cf. Rom. x. 7), penned there until they are finally destroyed, and which appear in Scripture under various names, Tehom, Leviathan, Rahab, the Serpent, and the Dragon. Cf. Oesterley, *The Evolution of the Messianic Idea*, chs. v. and vii., and Bernard, *Texts and Studies*, vol. viii. No. 3, pp. 32 ff. The question is discussed below in Essay I, pp. 317-36.

ἐν φυλακῇ] For Sheol regarded as a prison-house cf. Rev. xviii. 2, xx. 1-7, and 2 Pet. ii. 4, with Mayor's note. In 2 Pet. ii. 9 the false teachers of Christianity are described as guarded in a place of punishment until the day of judgment. Jewish eschatology comprised many different views as to Sheol or Hades ; but those who thought of it as a temporary abode of spirits awaiting a final judgment would think of these spirits as meanwhile " under ward ". Thus *Apoc. Bar.* xxiii. 4 speaks of a place being prepared where " the living might dwell and the dead might be guarded " (the righteous by angels, as in *Enoch* c. 5, and the wicked by " the guardians of the gates of Hades ", as in *2 Enoch* xlii. 1 (Charles)). Similar conceptions underlie the *verbum Christi* in Matt. xvi. 18, πύλαι ᾅδου οὐ κατισχύσουσιν αὐτῆς, and the description of Christ Himself in Rev. i. 18, καὶ ἐγενόμην νεκρός, καὶ ἰδού, ζῶν εἰμι εἰς τοὺς αἰῶνας τῶν αἰώνων, καὶ ἔχω τὰς κλεῖς τοῦ θανάτου καὶ τοῦ ᾅδου. The more usual idea as to the future state of the wicked, once moral discriminations had been introduced into the conception of Sheol, was that they " wandered about " in pain, cf. 2 Esdras vii. 80 ff.

πορευθείς] Cf. verse 22 *infra*, where the reference is to the Ascension, as repeatedly in Jn. xiv., xvi. As the word there connotes a definite " going " of Jesus to heaven after His resurrection, so it must connote here an equally

definite " going " to Hades at the time of His death. A mystical " going ", such as was imagined by Augustine and Bede, is excluded. On the possible allusion to this passage in Ignatius, *Magn.* ix. see Essay I, pp. 340, 343.

ἐκήρυξεν] *made proclamation.* The verb is usually followed by its object in N.T., cf. Mk. i. 4 (βάπτισμα μετανοίας), 14 (τὸ εὐαγγέλιον τοῦ θεοῦ), Lk. ix. 2 (τὴν βασιλείαν τοῦ θεοῦ), Acts viii. 5 (τὸν Χριστόν) ; but it is sometimes used absolutely, when the context makes clear what is proclaimed or preached. The dative of the indirect object is found in the Synoptic Gospels only in Mk. xvi. 15, and in the quotation from the LXX in Lk. iv. 18 ; elsewhere in N.T. in Acts viii. 5 (αὐτοῖς), x. 42 (τῷ λαῷ), 1 Cor. ix. 27 (ἄλλοις) : the usual construction, especially when the indirect object is a substantive noun, is with εἰς or ἐν (Mk. xiii. 10, Lk. iv. 44, Gal. ii. 2, Col. i. 23, 1 Tim. iii. 16). The commonest reference is to the Gospel and its offer of salvation, to which the appropriate response is repentance. But in Rev. v. 2 the word is used of an angel's proclamation, and this neutral meaning is the more probable here. Christ's work of redemption was achieved : it still needed to be proclaimed, even to the disobedient angels who could not, in the ordinary sense of the term, repent, but who could be brought into subjection (cf. verse 22). In so far as angelic beings are referred to in τὰ . . . πνεύματα, we might find the substance of this proclamation in the judgment pronounced on " the prince of this world " in Jn. xii. 31, xvi. 11. In the parts of Asia Minor affected by the Colossian heresy, spiritual agencies were believed to be in rivalry with Christ, and their subjection was therefore a vital feature of the Christian faith (cf. Lightfoot, *Colossians*, p. 150). Belief in spirits, indeed, and not least evil spirits, was universal in the first cen-

θυμία ἐν ἡμέραις Νῶε, κατασκευαζομένης κιβωτοῦ, εἰς ἣν ὀλίγοι,

tury A.D. (cf. Lake, *Earlier Epistles of St. Paul*, pp. 192 ff.), and Jewish aetiology traced them to the disobedience of angels before the Flood. The belief of the early Church that Christ had dealings with the world of spirits is expressed in the early credal formula in 1 Tim. iii. 16 (ὤφθη ἀγγέλοις). In so far as the dead of Noah's generation are concerned, quickening rather than instruction would perhaps have been in the Apostle's mind : cf. the hymn quoted in Eph. v. 14, ἔγειραι, ὁ καθεύδων, καὶ ἀνάστα ἐκ τῶν νεκρῶν, καὶ ἐπιφαύσει σοι ὁ Χριστός.

20. ἀπειθήσασί] See note on ii. 8. It is noticeable that in Gen. vi. the wickedness which led to the Flood is ascribed to men only : the story of the descent of angelic beings (" sons of God ") and their intercourse with human women is a piece of aetiology designed to account for an age of giants. The idea that human sin derived from this miscegenation was a product of much later Jewish thought, cf. Essay I, pp. 328 f.

ποτέ] *once upon a time, long ago,* as in iii. 5 *supra.* Classical authors use it in this sense when telling a story, cf. Plato, *Phaedr.* 237 B, Ar. *Vesp.* 1182. In N.T., when ποτέ refers to the past, it is always used either in this sense, or to point a contrast between past and present conditions of affairs (as in 1 Pet. ii. 10). The Apostle is drawing on ancient lore here exactly as he did in iii. 5, 6.

ἀπεξεδέχετο] *waited eagerly.* Elsewhere in N.T. (for Rom. viii. 25 is no real exception) the verb is transitive, as also in late Greek writers ; and the object of the expectation is the Parusia or some feature of it.

ἡ τοῦ Θεοῦ μακροθυμία] The idea of God's long-suffering patience, the purpose of which was to give man time for repentance, was based on Gen. vi. 3, " And the Lord said, My spirit shall not always strive with man, for that he also is flesh : yet his days shall be

an hundred and twenty years " ; and it was so interpreted by Rabbinic teachers. Cf. Bennett's note on 1 Pet. iii. 20. The thought was developed both by Jewish and by Christian writers. For the Jewish teaching we have *Pirqe Aboth*, v. 2, " Ten generations were there from Adam to Noah, to shew how great was His longsuffering ; for all the generations were provoking Him, till He brought the deluge upon them " (cf. Taylor's note); and cf. also *1 Enoch* lxvi. The Christian teaching is represented by 2 Pet. iii. 5-9, where the delay in God's judgment on the wicked is explained as due to His long-suffering desire that they should have time for repentance. Cf. also Acts xiv. 16, xvii. 30, Rom. iii. 25. If any object of God's expectant waiting is to be understood, it would be men's repentance. The majority, however, did not repent, but ignored the existence of God and His claims upon men's worship and obedience ; and His judgment fell swiftly and suddenly upon them.

ἐν ἡμεραῖς Νῶε] For the prominence of Noah in Jewish hagiography cf. Essay I, pp. 328 ff. Heb. xi. 7 and 2 Pet. ii. 5, iii. 5-9 shew the interest of the early Church in the application of the story of the Flood to Christian teaching, practice, and experience ; and these various allusions, together with the marked compactness of the passage before us, suggest that the story was the subject of midrashic interpretations in the Christian community akin to that which we find in regard e.g. to the stories of Abraham and of Moses in St. Paul's Epistles (e.g. 1 Cor. x.). And this theology had its basis in the *verba Christi* recorded in Matt. xxiv. 37, 38 (Lk. xvii. 26), ὥσπερ δὲ αἱ ἡμέραι τοῦ Νῶε, οὕτως ἔσται ἡ παρουσία τοῦ υἱοῦ τοῦ ἀνθρώπου. ὥσπερ γὰρ ἦσαν ἐν ταῖς ἡμέραις ἐκείναις ταῖς πρὸ τοῦ κατακλυσμοῦ τρώγοντες καὶ πίνοντες, γαμοῦντες καὶ ἐκγαμίζοντες, ἄχρι ἧς ἡμέρας

τοῦτ᾽ ἔστιν ὀκτὼ ψυχαί, διεσώθησαν δι᾽ ὕδατος· ²¹ὃ καὶ ὑμᾶς

εἰσῆλθε Νῶε εἰς τὴν κιβωτὸν κτλ. The aim of the *verba Christi* was to drive home the suddenness of the divine judgment and the peril of careless and secular living ; but the N.T. writers developed the lesson in different directions. In I Peter the emphasis is on the scope of God's victorious redeeming power, which has reached even to the fallen angels of Noah's days, as it reaches the heathen to-day. In Hebrews the emphasis is on Noah's faith, which made him alive to the spiritual meaning of life as his contemporaries were not. In 2 Peter the emphasis is both on the certainty of divine judgment which will overtake false teachers and their adherents in the Church, despite appearances being to the contrary, and also, and even more markedly, on the triumph of God's mercy to the righteous.

κατασκευαζομένης] used of the ark in Heb. xi. 7, and of the tabernacle in Heb. xi. 2, 6. The building of the ark is ascribed to angels in *I Enoch* lxvii. 2, but elsewhere (including *I Enoch* lxxix. 1) to Noah himself.

ὀλίγοι . . . ὀκτὼ ψυχαί] The word ὀλίγος recalls the *verba Christi* in Matt. vii. 14, " strait is the gate and narrow the way that leadeth unto life ; and few there be that find it ", and in Matt. xxii. 14, " many are called, but few chosen ". The question addressed to our Lord in Lk. xiii. 23, " Lord, are there few that be saved ? " may well have occurred to many of St. Peter's readers, as they realized their minority position in the pagan society around them.

The eight souls are those enumerated in Gen. vii. 13, namely Noah, his wife, his three sons, Shem, Ham and Japheth, and their three wives. So Justin, *Dial.* 138 (367 C). (For other interpretations see J. B. Mayor's note on 2 Pet. ii. 5.)

For ψυχαί in this sense of " persons " cf. Acts ii. 41, vii. 14, xxvii. 37. In all these examples, as in Gen. xlvi. 15,

Ex. i. 5, the noun is accompanied by a cardinal numeral. Was this the usage in formal documents, such as census-rolls, of the period ? That the tradition of the number of persons in the ark was eight became well established is shewn by the curious discussion of the story of Noah in Theophilus, *ad Autol.* ii. 19.

διεσώθησαν] *were brought safely through*. Cf. Plato, *Rep.* 540 A, Thuc. iv. 113 ; and, most significantly, Wisd. xiv. 5 f.

δι᾽ ὕδατος] Commentators differ as to whether διά is here local or instrumental. (1) In favour of the former view it is urged (Bigg, Wand) that the words εἰς ἥν shew Noah's passage through, and escape from, the rising waters of the Flood to be in mind ; and the lesson is that, as Noah passed through water to safety in the ark, so the baptized pass through water to safety in the Church. (2) On the other hand, it is urged (Alford, Plumptre) that the allusion to baptism in verse 21, in which the water is the instrument of salvation, requires us to take διά as instrumental here, and the meaning is that the water of the Flood carried the ark to safety, as the water of baptism carries the Christian. εἰς ἥν is not a decisive objection to this, for a participle like ἰόντες may be regarded as implied in διεσώθησαν (cf. Goodwin, *Greek Grammar*, § 1225 ; Winer, *op. cit.* pp. 516 f.). Further, the narrative in Gen. vii. speaks of Noah entering the ark seven days before the Flood-waters broke : he went εἰς τὴν κιβωτὸν διὰ (because of) τὸ ὕδωρ τοῦ κατακλυσμοῦ. The truth, however, seems to be that the two views are not mutually exclusive. The difficulty arises from the fact that our author is at one and the same time abbreviating the story of the Flood and making it serve as the type of Christian baptism. The tradition was that Noah went into the ark and got safely away in it, and this is expressed succinctly by εἰς ἥν διεσώθησαν ; and he was brought safely away through water, both directly in the local sense of διά and indirectly in the instrumental sense. The more obvious fact that the water destroyed the rest of mankind is ignored here, since the author's interest, as the next verse indicates, was in those who were saved, who were the type of the Christian Church. So we find in Hermas, *Vis.* III. iii. 5, ἡ ζωὴ ὑμῶν δι᾽ ὕδατος ἐσώθη καὶ σωθήσεται: and cf. *Odes of Sol.* vi. 17, *Clem. Recog.* IV. xii. For similar ambiguity in the use of διά cf. 1 Cor. iii. 15, σωθήσεται οὕτω δὲ διὰ πυρός, 1 Tim. ii. 15, σωθήσεται διὰ τῆς τεκνογονίας.

21. ὃ καὶ ὑμᾶς . . . βάπτισμα] *And water now saves you too, who are the antitype of Noah and his company, namely the water of baptism. . . .* The reading ὃ is attested in every type of textual evidence (cf. Alford, *in loc.*). Yet Hort (*The New Testament in Greek*, App. p. 102), following Erasmus and Beza, and supported in modern times by Bernard (*The Expositor*, vol. viii. No. 69, pp. 241 ff.), upholds the dative ᾧ unreservedly. His words are worth quoting : " The order of the words renders it impossible to take ἀντίτυπον with βάπτισμα, whether in apposition to ὃ or to the sentence ; and it is hardly less difficult to take ἀντίτυπον with ὃ, as though it were either ἀντίτυπον ὄν or ἀντιτύπως. Accordingly ὃ seems to be a primitive error for ᾧ, the force of which might be hidden by the interposition of καὶ ὑμᾶς before ἀντίτυπον: this deviation from the more obvious order is justified by the emphasis on καὶ ὑμᾶς. Both by sight and by sound the interchange of letters would be easy."

Hort's support for an emendation, which involves so drastic a departure from the accepted canons of textual criticism, is at least an indication of the acute grammatical difficulties besetting the usual interpretations of this passage, difficulties which are fully reflected in the Vulgate version, *Quod et vos nunc similis formae salvos facit baptisma* ; indeed, if the text be at

fault, it would be better to regard ἀντίτυπον as an early scribe's marginal gloss, which had crept in error into the text. At any rate the difficulties may be taken to justify a new attempt to construe it. The rendering I have given is that which seems to me demanded by the rhythm of the Greek sentence (an important point when translating from so good a stylist as our author) ; it gives a simple and straightforward sense ; and it avoids the difficulties which arise from taking ἀντίτυπον in apposition with ὃ and with βάπτισμα. [Even if ᾧ were the right reading, I should prefer to take ἀντίτυπον as in apposition with ὑμᾶς, the antecedent to ᾧ being then Noah. With the rendering I have suggested, the order of words is not forced or unnatural, and the appositional βάπτισμα is removed to the end of the clause, to prevent confusion with ἀντίτυπον, and to provide the transition to the baptismal doctrine which follows.]

In the " type-theology " of the early Church — a form of theology which goes back in principle to such *verba Christi* as Lk. xi. 29-9, xvii. 26-9, 32 ; Matt. xi. 14, xvii. 12 — the parallels were as much between persons as between events or things ; and in the case before us Noah and his company were as much a type of the Christian community as the Flood-water was of the water of baptism. Though τύποι and τυπικῶς in 1 Cor. x. 6, 11 are not quite parallel with the usage here, owing to the examples being summarized under the pronoun ταῦτα, the use of the plural verb following ταῦτα indicates that persons were mainly in St. Paul's mind (cf. Winer, *op. cit.* pp. 646 f. ; also Rom. v. 14). Further, the singular ἀντίτυπον (rather than ἀντιτύπους) is to be explained by the fact that St. Peter's readers are thought of as a community : cf. the use of τύπον in 1 Thess. i. 7, with Milligan's note, and the singular number in Phil. iii. 17, 2 Thess. iii. 9, *Did.* iv. 11. Finally, it is significant that the point of comparison which Cyprian em-

ἀντίτυπον νῦν σώζει βάπτισμα, οὐ σαρκὸς ἀπόθεσις ῥύπου ἀλλὰ

phasizes on each of the three occasions when he quotes 1 Pet. iii. 19 in connexion with baptism (*Epp.* lxxiii. 11, lxxiv. 15, lxxv. 2) is the parallel between the company associated with Noah and the Christian Church. " The one ark of Noah ", he says, " was a type of the one church " : i.e. conversely, the Church — the ὑμᾶς of 1 Pet. iii. 19 — was the antitype. And Justin's interpretation in *Dial.* 138 is similar : the Church is " another race, regenerated by Christ through water and faith and wood, which contained the mystery of the cross, as Noah too was brought safe in wood, floating on the waters with his family ".

καὶ] with the word that follows, as in iii. 5, 19, iv. 1.

ὑμᾶς] There is considerable authority for reading ἡμᾶς here, which, as Estius observes, though not in the Vulgate, is called for by the Vulgate's addition after *qui est in dextera Dei* in verse 22 of the words, *deglutiens mortem ut vitae aeternae heredes efficeremur.*

ἀντίτυπον] ἀντίτυπος is an adjective in Soph. *Phil.* 693, 1460, and Lucian, *De domo*, 3, and means " echoing " ; while elsewhere it connotes the exactness of correspondence between the stamp and the die, this being probably the fundamental connotation ; cf. *Or. Sib.* i. 33, ἀντίτυπον μίμημα. MM cite Polybius VI. xxxi. 8, τοῖς δ' ἱππεῦσι τούτοις ἀντίτυποι τίθενται, where ἀντίτυποι means " opposite ", and in Esth. iii. 8 (Swete, LXX, xiii. 4), ℵA give τοῖς νόμοις ἀντίτυπον πρὸς πᾶν γένος, " diverse in its laws from every race ". In the verse before us, if ᾧ were read, the word would no doubt be adjectival, and may be so in any case. On the other hand, in Heb. ix. 24, " the only other occurrence in N.T., " the holy places made with hands " into which Christ has entered are described as ἀντίτυπα τῶν ἀληθινῶν, and here the word is undoubtedly a substantive, for

otherwise it would be followed by the dative. As Lightfoot points out in his note on 2 Clem. xiv. 4, τὸ ἀντίτυπον can be used as the " copy " in two senses, either as the earthly expression or embodiment of heavenly reality (in which sense it is used of the elements in the Eucharist (*Const. Apost.* v. 14. 4, vi. 30. 1)) or as the fulfilment of that which was only adumbrated in earlier times (as here).

It is worth noting that John Lightfoot took the view here advocated. The Apostle's purpose, he says, " to shew that as Noah and his family were then saved by water, so Ἀντίτυπον ἡμᾶς, they that had received baptism, were the antitype to that " (*Works*, iii. p. 322, ed. 1822).

For a fuller discussion see Add. Note I, pp. 298 f. below.

βάπτισμα] Cf. Melito in Routh's *Reliquiae Sacrae*, i. p. 124, δύο γὰρ συνέστη τὰ ἄφεσιν ἁμαρτημάτων παρεχόμενα, πάθος διὰ Χριστὸν καὶ βάπτισμα.

οὐ σαρκὸς κτλ.] *not a fleshly putting-away of dirt*, i.e. the cleansing in baptism is not physical but sacramental. The broad meaning is simple but the details are more difficult. The rhythm of the sentence is in favour of taking σαρκός as an objective genitive governed by ἀπόθεσις ῥύπου, a periphrasis for "washing" or "cleansing" probably suggested by the fact that ἀποθέσθαι was a keyword in the primitive Christian catechism. Cf. ii. 1, with notes there, and Essay II, pp. 393-400, where the *Deponentes* clause of the catechism is discussed. Jas. i. 21, ἀποθέμενοι πᾶσαν ῥυπαρίαν καὶ περισσείαν κακίας, states the ethical renunciation involved in baptism, and is often quoted as a parallel ; but it reflects a slightly later stage of thought, when the literal σαρκὸς ῥύπον has become the metaphorical ῥυπαρία κακίας. 1 Peter, further, distinguishes between an outward and an inner side to the sacramental action ; and the inward side which he mentions is not

συνειδήσεως ἀγαθῆς ἐπερώτημα εἰς Θεόν, δι' ἀναστάσεως Ἰησοῦ

the divine grace given in baptism, but the eliciting or pledging of the human faith which makes it efficacious. A more significant illustration is afforded by Col. ii. 10-12, where Christ is spoken of as ἡ κεφαλὴ πάσης ἀρχῆς καὶ ἐξουσίας· ἐν ᾧ καὶ περιετμήθητε περιτομῇ ἀχειροποιήτῳ, ἐν τῇ ἀπεκδύσει τοῦ σώματος τῆς σαρκός, ἐν τῇ περιτομῇ τοῦ Χριστοῦ, συνταφέντες αὐτῷ ἐν τῷ βαπτίσματι, ἐν ᾧ καὶ συνηγέρθητε διὰ τῆς πίστεως τῆς ἐνεργείας τοῦ θεοῦ τοῦ ἐγείραντος αὐτὸν ἐκ τῶν νεκρῶν. Here we have (a) an allusion to Christ's subjection of angelic powers, as in 1 Pet. iii. 19, 22, (b) a contrast between the outward and the inward, as in 1 Pet. iii. 21, (c) an allusion to the power of faith in Christ's resurrection, which recalls 1 Pet. iii. 21, 22. St. Paul's language takes its colour from the point he is making to the effect that baptism is the Christian counterpart of circumcision, which it supersedes. Is it possible that that idea is present also to St. Peter's mind, and that in the words οὐ σαρκὸς ἀπόθεσις ῥύπου he is implicitly contrasting Christian baptism both with Jewish circumcision and with pagan lustration-rites?

St. Basil, who quotes 1 Pet. iii. 21 in *de Spiritu Sancto*, § 35, uses it to illustrate a similar contrast between the inward and outward sides of the sacrament : " if there be any grace in the water, it is not from the nature of the water, but from the presence of the Spirit " ; and he continues in instructive fashion, πρὸς οὖν τὸν ἐξ ἀναστάσεως βίον καταρτίζων ὑμᾶς ὁ κύριος τὴν εὐαγγελικὴν πᾶσαν ἐκτίθεται πολιτείαν, τὸ ἀόργητον, τὸ ἀνεξίκακον, τὸ φιληδονίας ἀρρύπωτον, τὸ ἀφιλάργυρον τοῦ τρόπου νομοθετῶν — a sentence which well summarizes the ethical teaching of the Apostolic age.

ἀλλὰ . . . εἰς Θεόν] a *pledge to God proceeding from a clear conscience*. This rendering by G. C. Richards (*J.T.S.* No. 125, Oct. 1930) seems on the whole the most satis-

factory. MM cite P. Cairo Preis 1[16] (second century A.D.), ἐὰν γὰρ μηδὲν ἐπερώτημα ᾖ ἐνγεγραμμένον, for the view that ἐπερώτημα, called in Latin *stipulatio*, was used for the clause in a contract containing the formal question and consent (ὁμολογία) of the contracting parties. It was thus suitable to a rite which included the Christian's ὁμολογία of his faith (cf. Rom. x. 10). Words such as ἐπερωτηθέντες ὡμολόγησαν occur frequently in contracts from the third century A.D. onwards, but earlier instances are rare. On the other hand ἐπερώτημα δήλων (*v.l.* ἐρώτημα δικαίων), which properly means " enquiry of Urim ", in Ecclus. xxxiii. 3, is an example of how the word was stretched to include the answer as well as the enquiry itself ; for it was the answer of the Urim when consulted which provided the parallel to the reliability of the Law there spoken of. The whole context Ecclus. xxxii. 23–xxxiii. 4 is germane to our passage. ἐπερώτημα also occurs in Theodotion's version of Dan. iv. 14, where according to Greeven (Kittel, *Th.Wb.z.N.T.*) it means " judgment " or " decision ", a sense which, if it could be established, would be very suitable here. Note also Oecumenius' paraphrase of ἐπερώτημα as οἷα ἀρραβὼν καὶ ἐνέχυρον (*pignus*) τῆς πρὸς θεὸν ἀγαθῆς συνειδήσεως ; and Grotius' comment : ἐπερώτημα (*stipulatio*) *est vox Juris*. Grotius connects it with the Renunciations of the early baptismal rites and with Tertullian's use of *sponsio*.

The idea that baptism was a seal of contract given by a good conscience towards God is not far removed from that which led to the application of the word *sacramentum*, " military oath ", to Baptism and the Eucharist. This gives us, moreover, a good antithesis to the " putting-off of the filth of the flesh " with which our author contrasts it. ἐπερώτημα is used in Herod. vi. 67 and Thuc. iii. 53, 68 of a test-

Χριστοῦ, ²²ὅς ἐστιν ἐν δεξιᾷ τοῦ Θεοῦ, πορευθεὶς εἰς οὐρανόν,

question, and so was suitable both to juristic language and to the solemn interrogatories preceding baptism in early times, out of which the Creeds arose. We have an example in the Western addition to the text of Acts viii. 37, namely, εἶπεν δὲ αὐτῷ, εἰ πιστεύεις ἐξ ὅλης τῆς καρδίας σου [, ἔξεστιν]; ἀποκριθεὶς δὲ εἶπεν, πιστεύω τὸν υἱὸν τοῦ θεοῦ εἶναι τὸν Ἰησοῦν [Χριστόν]. Cf. also Acts xvi. 31 ff. Armitage Robinson believes that the ῥῆμα referred to in connexion with baptism in Eph. v. 26 was such a formula, and observes that the context of 1 Pet. iii. 21 " contains phrases which correspond with the second division of the baptismal creed of the second century ". The procedure is thus described by Tertullian (de Cor. Mil. iii.), Denique . . . aquam adituri, ibidem sed et aliquanto prius in ecclesia, sub antistitis contestamur nos renuntiare diabolo et pompae et angelis eius. Dehinc ter mergitamur, amplius aliquid respondentes quam Dominus in evangelio determinavit. Cf. also Tert. de Pudic. ix., where the return of the Prodigal Son is likened to the reception in baptism of the ring, quo fidei pactionem interrogatus obsignat. Similarly, Origen, in Num. Hom v. 1, speaks of τῶν ἐπερωτήσεων καὶ τῶν ἀποκρίσεων; and E. H. B. adds Tert. de Res. Carn. xlviii., Anima enim non lavatione sed responsione sancitur (" is sanctified "). See Turner, The Use of Creeds, pp. 11 ff., and Blenkin, op. cit. p. 81.

Current baptismal practice thus provides the context (" selbstverständlich folgender Bejahung ") which Windisch finds lacking here. His own rendering of ἐπερώτημα, " prayer for a good conscience ", seems, however, to have no linguistic support elsewhere. The frequent use of ἐπερωτᾶν for " consult " in LXX, followed by accusative, ἐν, or διά of the personal object, and the accusative or περί of the theme of the enquiry, has classical and patristic parallels (Herod. ix. 44, Thuc. iv. 38, Hermas, Mand. xi. 2); and the object may be an oracle (as in classical literature), or soothsayers, witches, etc. (cf. 1 Chron. x. 13), or, as most commonly in O.T., God. If this is the association of ideas here, the phrase could only mean " an enquiry of a good conscience after God ", the convert's seeking after God being thus contrasted with the pagan's address to his favourite oracle (cf. F. W. H. Myers' essay on " Greek Oracles " in Essays Classical, especially pp. 33-9, 60-8). This would give us a possible sense, but one that does not arise out of the context, and is not specially applicable to baptism.

δι' ἀναστάσεως] recalling what is said of Christ's resurrection, and its connexion with regeneration, in i. 3, and also the ζωοποιηθείς of verse 18. There is also perhaps a contrast with δι' ὕδατος in verse 20. Taken in conjunction with σώζει these words draw out the sacramental significance of baptism.

22. ὅς κτλ.] As the last verse recalled Jn. vi. 63, so this recalls Jn. vi. 62, " What and if ye shall see the Son of Man ascend up where he was before ? " The whole context of Christian baptism has now been unfolded, as the Passion (verse 18), Descent (verse 19), Resurrection (verse 21), and Ascension and Heavenly Session of Jesus Christ. The phrase ὅς . . . τοῦ θεοῦ occurs verbatim in Rom. viii. 34; the idea of His session being added in Col. iii. 1, Eph. i. 20, Heb. i. 3, viii. 1, x. 12, xii. 2. Cf. Mk. xvi. 19. " It is not a dead Christ on whom we depend, but a living. It is not only a living Christ, but a Christ enthroned, a Christ in power " (SH).

πορευθεὶς εἰς οὐρανόν] The phrase echoes the πορευθείς of verse 19, and shews how the scope of the redemption reaches to both spiritual realms, that below and that above. The theme is developed by St. Paul in somewhat

ὑποταγέντων αὐτῷ ἀγγέλων καὶ ἐξουσιῶν καὶ δυνάμεων.

different language in Eph. i. 21, iii. 10, vi. 12, Phil. ii. 9-11, Col. ii. 15. Such *verba Christi* as Matt. xvi. 18 (addressed to St. Peter himself) and Mk. iii. 27, Lk. xi. 21, 22 may well have prompted this belief.

ὑποταγέντων . . . δυναμέων] The spiritual hierarchy is listed in N.T. in various ways, which are set out synoptically below.[1] The exact order in which St. Peter names these powers, ἄγγελοι, ἐξουσίαι, δυνάμεις is found in *Asc. Is.* i. 3, which may, however, be based on reminiscence of the Petrine text (E. H. B.).

The domination of Christ over the supernatural orders is asserted in 1 Cor. xv., Eph. i., Col. ii., being in in Eph. i. and Col. ii. regarded as an accomplished fact, in 1 Cor. xv. as an element in the End of all things. The subordination of the supernatural hierarchy to Christ is asserted in 1 Peter and Phil. ii. as an accomplished fact resulting from the Incarnation, the Cross and the Ascension; and in Col. i. it is said to derive from Him through its creation, and to have been reconciled (i. 20) to God through Christ and the blood of His Cross.

In Rom. viii. 38 the supernatural powers are said to be impotent to separate Christians from the love of God in Christ. In Eph. vi. 12 all the spirit-powers mentioned are powers of evil, with which Christians have to wrestle ; and in 1 Cor. xv. 24-8, where ἀρχαί, ἐξούσιαι, and δυνάμεις are specified, they are all regarded as hostile to God and His Kingdom (cf. πάντας τοὺς ἐχθρούς in verse 25). It may be noted that the " reconciliation " spoken of in Col. i. 20, 21 embraces both the spirit-powers of evil [2] and the alienated world of the Gentiles.

In 1 Cor. xv. 24 f. and Eph. vi. 12 the supernatural hierarchy in question is undoubtedly evil (cf. 2 Thess. ii. 8); in Rom. viii. 38, Col. i. 16, ii. 15, Eph. iii. 10 it at least includes evil powers, who need to be enlightened (Eph. iii. 10) or reconciled (Col. i. 20) or triumphed over (Col. ii. 15) or swept aside (Rom. viii. 38 f.). The method by which Christ's supremacy over them is established is not consistently set forth. In 1 Cor. xv. they are destroyed : in Col. ii. they are shaken off and triumphed over : in Col. i. (cf. Eph. iii. 10, Phil. ii.) they

1 Pet.	1 Cor. xv. 24	Rom. viii. 38	Phil. ii. 10	Col. i. 16	Col. ii. 15
ἀγγέλων καὶ ἐξουσιῶν καὶ δυναμέων	πᾶσαν ἀρχὴν καὶ πᾶσαν ἐξουσίαν καὶ δύναμιν	οὔτε ἄγγελοι οὔτε ἀρχαί . . . . οὔτε δυνάμεις	πᾶν γόνυ . . . . ἐπουρανίων καὶ ἐπιγείων καὶ καταχθονίων	εἴτε θρόνοι εἴτε κυριότητες εἴτε ἀρχαί εἴτε ἐξουσίαι	τὰς ἀρχὰς καὶ τὰς ἐξουσίας

Col. ii. 10	Eph. i. 21	Eph. iii. 10	Eph. vi. 12
ὅς ἐστιν ἡ κεφαλὴ πάσης ἀρχῆς καὶ ἐξουσίας	πάσης ἀρχῆς καὶ ἐξουσίας καὶ δυνάμεως καὶ κυριότητος καὶ παντὸς ὀνόματος	ἵνα γνωρισθῇ νῦν ταῖς ἀρχαῖς καὶ ταῖς ἐξουσίαις ἐν τοῖς ἐπουρανίοις διὰ τῆς ἐκκλησίας ἡ πολυποίκιλος σοφία τοῦ θεοῦ	οὐκ ἐστὶν ἡμῖν ἡ πάλη πρὸς αἷμα καὶ σάρκα, ἀλλὰ πρὸς τὰς ἀρχάς, πρὸς τὰς ἐξουσίας, πρὸς τοὺς κοσμοκράτορας τοῦ σκότους τούτου, πρὸς τὰ πνευματικὰ τῆς πονηρίας ἐν τοῖς ἐπουρανίοις

---

[1] I owe the term to Canon Deane's *St. Paul and his Letters*, p. 216, which here as so often hits the happy phrase.

IV. ¹Χριστοῦ οὖν παθόντος σαρκὶ καὶ ὑμεῖς τὴν αὐτὴν ἔννοιαν

are reconciled. [Cf. Lightfoot's note on the force of ἀποκαταλλάξαι in Col. i. 20, suggesting the ἀποκατάστασις of Acts iii. 21.] St. Peter's choice of the neutral term ἐκήρυξεν in 1 Pet. iii. 19 reflects his caution of statement.

Allusion may also be made to Heb. i. where Christ's superiority to the angels by virtue of His " more excellent name ", i.e. that of Son, is asserted, and the context implies that its realization follows upon His finished work of atonement culminating in His heavenly session. Cf. also Heb. ii. 5-9, where the paradox of Christ's inferiority to the angels as Man and His superiority to them as a result of His victorious death is set forth.

One of the sources of the primitive Christian nomenclature for the spiritual hierarchy may be *Enoch* lxi. 10 ; and the phrase there, "all the angels of power, and all the angels of principalities", suggests perhaps, as Bigg observes, that we should translate St. Peter's words here " angels both of authorities and of powers ". For in view of the evidence given above, the most natural reference in St. Peter's phrase here is to *evil* supernatural agencies. Why else, indeed, should their " subjection " be spoken of ? The spirit-powers of good have never ceased to be obedient.

Note how the word ὑποταγέντων applies to the superhuman realm the rule of subordination already so freely applied in the Epistle to man's social life on earth. 1 Cor. xv. 24-8 dwells equally on the fact of the subordination (ὑποτάσσειν) of the spirit-powers of evil, but thinks of it in terms of the future, not the present.

iv. 1 ff. A practical application of the doctrine of Redemption just enunciated is now made ; and verse 1 is one of the most important, as it is one of the most difficult, verses of this whole section.

1. οὖν] resumptive from iii. 18a,

ὅτι καὶ Χριστὸς ἅπαξ περὶ ἁμαρτιῶν ἔπαθε, the intervening passage 18b-22 being, despite its richness of teaching, parenthetic to the main argument, which is concerned with the *imitatio Christi*.

σαρκὶ] There is strong textual evidence, namely AKLℵ³ rel syrr copt Ath₃ Epiph Jer Aug, in favour of the insertion of ὑπὲρ ἡμῶν (ℵ¹bmo ὑπὲρ ὑμῶν) after σαρκί, BC vulg sah being the chief authorities for omitting the words ; and it seems to me probable that the words are original, and were early omitted, partly because the vicarious element of Christ's sufferings was one which was felt to be beyond the scope of believers' imitation, partly because (as the *varia lectio* ὑπὲρ ὑμῶν shews) there was felt to be a discontinuity between ὑπὲρ ἡμῶν and ὑμεῖς immediately following. But the vicarious element is in any case implied by the way in which οὖν resumes 18a. And the point is important, for, as Leighton observes, it reminds us that Christ's death is not only an example to stir the imagination, but also an appealing motive which awakens gratitude and love.

Athanasius, *Orat. adv. Arianos*, iii. 34, has an eloquent passage on the meaning of σαρκί and its bearing on the doctrine of the Incarnation.

ἔννοιαν] *principle, counsel, mind*, as in Prov. i. 4, iii. 21, xxiii. 19. Wilke's paraphrase *cogitandi et sentiendi ratio* hits the mark accurately. Philo, *de Praem. et Poen.* 42 [II. 415 M], uses it of the temper of mind induced by the spectacle of the cosmic order, which leads us to infer purpose and not chance as its Cause. The only other occurrence is in Heb. iv. 12, on which see Westcott's note. The principle of thought and feeling here referred to is that of the dying life voluntarily accepted and put on as armour, and finding expression in the meek and courageous pursuit of the spiritual life.

ὁπλίσασθε, ὅτι ὁ παθὼν σαρκὶ πέπαυται ἁμαρτίας, ²εἰς τὸ μηκέτι

ὁπλίσασθε] The accusative object is due to the idea of "put on as your armour", which the verb connotes. Cf. Soph. *El.* 995, ὁπλίζεσθαι θράσος. For the thought of the Christian armour in St. Paul cf. Essay II, pp. 396-400, 456-8. Even in his dying life, and indeed most of all then, the Christian is a soldier.

ὅτι ὁ παθὼν σαρκὶ πέπαυται ἁμαρτίας] *Enoch* lxvii. 9 contains similar teaching as to the purifying effect on the spirit of bodily suffering, with which cf. 2 Macc. vi. 12-16, *Apoc. Bar.* xiii. 10, lxxviii. 6. St. Paul is applying the same thought in 1 Cor. v. 5, where he speaks of delivering a wrongdoer "unto Satan for the destruction of the flesh, that the spirit may be saved in the day of the Lord Jesus"; and cf. the passage from Melito quoted in the note on βάπτισμα above. For the idea developed by the Rabbis, that suffering and sickness, no less than death itself, are in themselves means of atonement, cf. *Sifre* 73b, *Bereshith Rabba* 5a, quoted by Box and Oesterley on Ecclus. xviii. 20 (Charles' *Apocrypha and Pseudepigrapha*, vol. i.); also Ecclus. ii. 11. St. Peter's words are thus paraphrased by Archbishop Leighton: "Although affliction simply doth not, yet affliction sweetly and humbly carried, doth purify and disengage the heart from sin, wean it from the world and the common ways of it". This is, no doubt, the meaning, though it depends on the relation being firmly established between παθὼν σαρκί — Χριστοῦ οὖν παθόντος σαρκί (iv. 1) — Χριστὸς ἅπαξ περὶ ἁμαρτιῶν ἔπαθε, δίκαιος ὑπὲρ ἀδίκων . . . θανατωθεὶς μὲν σαρκὶ ζωοποιηθεὶς δὲ πνεύματι (iii. 18); for suffering in itself often hardens and embitters men, and makes them more resolute in evil courses. This difficulty probably led to the genitive singular ἁμαρτίας being substituted for the dative plural ἁμαρτίαις; but, as Bigg observes, the textual evidence for the latter, which includes Bℵ³ vulg syr aeth, is reinforced by the fact that in 1 Peter ἁμαρτία is always used in the concrete sense of a sinful act: only once, indeed, in ii. 22, is the singular number used. The dative is the dative of reference, as in ii. 24, to which it is closely parallel in sense. παύεσθαι does not elsewhere occur in N.T. with the dative, but neither does it occur with the genitive. The succeeding verses, moreover, bear out this interpretation: the meaning is that he who innocently and meekly suffers persecution rather than join in the wickedness of the world around him "can be trusted to do right" (Bigg). For a somewhat similar sentiment in regard to the intellectual life we may compare [Plato], *Axiochus*, 369, τὰ δὲ παθήματα σοφισμάτων (tricks of sophistry) οὐκ ἀνέχεται (ed. E. H. Blakeney).

Those who can see little in this Epistle except Paulinism naturally regard this phrase as an echo of St. Paul's baptismal teaching in Rom. vi. 3-11. It is true that both Apostles, like the primitive Church generally, regard the ethical obligations of baptism in the same light. But the mysticism of Rom. vi. is conspicuously absent from St. Peter's teaching about baptism here, which in its firm historical reference is far more like that in 1 Cor. x. 1, 2; and the Pauline idea of justification, essential to the argument in Rom. vi. 6, 7, nowhere occurs in 1 Peter.

Few verses in this Epistle are more characteristic of it than iv. 1. The reality of Christ's sufferings, their atoning significance, and His meekness in bearing them, gathered up from ii. 21-5 and iii. 18; the Christians' main duty, namely the *imitatio Christi*, gathered up from ii. 21-5 and iii. 14-18; the emphasis on baptism as involving a conscious ethical change and redirection of life, already implied in the allusion to the ἐπερώτημα in

ἀνθρώπων ἐπιθυμίαις ἀλλὰ θελήματι Θεοῦ τὸν ἐπίλοιπον ἐν
σαρκὶ βιῶσαι χρόνον. ³ἀρκετὸς γὰρ ὁ παρεληλυθὼς χρόνος τὸ
βούλημα τῶν ἐθνῶν κατειργάσθαι, πεπορευμένους ἐν ἀσελγείαις,

iii. 21 and to be illustrated in iv. 2-5 : all these thoughts are present in this verse, and represent the quintessence of the doctrinal, ethical, and sacramental teaching of the Epistle as a whole. Lancelot Andrewes finely expounds the passage, with reference also to Rom. vi. (*Sermons*, vol. ii. pp. 202 f.) : " To cease from sin, I say, understanding by sin, not from sin altogether — that is a higher perfection than this life will bear, but as the Apostle expoundeth himself in the very next words, *Ne regnet peccatum* (Rom. vi. 13), that is, from the dominion of sin to cease. For till we be free from death itself, which in this life we are not, we shall not be free from sin altogether ; only we may come thus far, *ne regnet*, that sin ' reign not ', wear not a crown, sit not in a throne, hold no parliament within us, give us no laws ; in a word . . . that we serve it not. To die to the dominion of sin — that by the grace of God we may, and that we must account for."

2. εἰς τὸ μηκέτι κτλ.] This beautifully constructed sentence illustrates what the author means by ceasing from sins. The baptized will conduct their lives (βιῶσαι) in future (τὸν ἐπίλοιπον ἐν σαρκὶ . . . χρόνον) not by sharing in the haphazard desires, whether of groups or individuals, which dominate the secular world around them (μηκέτι ἀνθρώπων ἐπιθυμίαις), but under the guidance of a single principle, namely, the will of God. For the general idea cf. Eph. iv. 17, Herm. *Mand.* iv. 1, *Sim.* VI. i. 4 : μηκέτι is characteristic of all the passages.

ἀνθρώπων ἐπιθυμίαις] a term wider than " the fleshly lusts " of ii. 11, and including all forms of purely individual desire such as spring from covetousness, envy, pride, or even simply fashion. The Johannine phrase in

1 Jn. ii. 16 illustrates it : " all that is in the world, the lust of the flesh, and the lust of the eyes, and the pride of life ".

The datives, ἐπιθυμίαις and θελήματι, are " datives of the rule by which " (T. E. Page), as in Acts xv. 1, ἐὰν μὴ περιτμηθῆτε τῷ ἔθει Μωϋσέως. Cf. Winer, *op. cit.* p. 270. Cf. also Lancelot Andrewes again, *ib.* p. 203 : " And then live we according to Him, when His will is our law, His word our rule, His Son's life our example, His Spirit rather than our own soul the guide of our actions ".

ἐν σαρκὶ] In the conditions of the flesh, i.e. on earth ; with a meaning distinct from that of the dative of reference as twice in the previous verse, and in verse 6.

3. Though no doubt the moral condition here described would have been applicable to many lapsed Jews in Asia Minor, as to lapsed Jews in Palestine a generation earlier, the language used is more natural if the readers of the Epistle had been heathen before their conversion.

ἀρκετὸς] elsewhere in N.T. only in Matt. vi. 34, x. 25. In all these passages there is a touch of irony in the word. Isocr. *Paneg.* 167, has a similar phrase when speaking of the hardships of military service which come with adult life : ἱκανὸς γὰρ ὁ παρεληλυθώς, ἐν ᾧ τι τῶν δεινῶν οὐ γέγονεν. For the sentiment cf. *Apoc. Bar.* lxxxiii. 6, " And let us not now look unto the delights of the Gentiles in the present, but let us remember what has been promised to us in the end ".

τὸ βούλημα τῶν ἐθνῶν] The " desires of men " (verse 2) are here regarded as falling under a single principle contrasted with " the will of God " just mentioned. We are on the way to the Johannine conception of " the world ".

πεπορευμένους] Used here for the

ἐπιθυμίαις, οἰνοφλυγίαις, κώμοις, πότοις, καὶ ἀθεμίτοις εἰδωλο-

perfect of the usual N.T. word περιπατεῖν, which does not occur. For the
ethical use of πορεύεσθαι cf. Jude 11,
16, 18, 2 Pet. ii. 10, iii. 3, and frequently
in O.T. ethical writings (LXX), e.g.
Ps. i. 1, μακάριος ἀνὴρ ὃς οὐκ ἐπορεύθη
ἐν βουλῇ ἀσεβῶν.

ἐν ἀσελγείαις κτλ.] For the " catalogue " method in Jewish and Hellenistic moral teaching cf. Essay II,
p. 421, and Tables II, XIV (g),
where the parallels to this passage in
Lk. xxi. 34, 1 Thess. v. 7, Rom.
xiii. 13, and Eph. v. 18 are set out.
The verbum Christi in Lk. xxi. 34
indicates that drunkenness and revelry
were not uncommon in Palestine in
our Lord's time. It is noticeable that
the only one of these parallel " catalogues " in which idolatry occurs is
that in Gal. v., addressed like 1 Peter
to communities in Asia Minor. The
use of plurals throughout points
both to the variety and the frequency
of the vices named. For similar
" catalogues " in Orphic and Neo-
platonist teaching cf. Kirk, The Vision
of God, p. 120.

On ἀσέλγεια Lightfoot says (on Gal.
v. 20),-" a man may be ἀκάθαρτος and
hide his sin; he does not become
ἀσελγής, until he shocks public de-
cency ". Cf. also Wisd. xiv. 25, 26,
where ἀσέλγεια occurs as part of a
catalogue of the evil results of idolatry,
and in immediate collocation with
μοιχεία.

ἐπιθυμίαις] The repetition of the
word here after its occurrence in verse
2 is curious, and suggests that St.
Peter or his amanuensis may be drawing on some catalogue already familiar
to the readers.

οἰνοφλυγίαις] Cf. [Plato], Eryxias,
405 E, ὅσοι τῶν ἀνθρώπων τυγχάνουσι
κυβευταὶ ὄντες, οἱ δὲ οἰνόφλυγες, ἕτεροι
δὲ γαστρίμαργοι — ἅπαντα γὰρ ταῦτα
οὐδὲν ἕτερον τυγχάνει ὄντα ἢ ἐπιθυμίαι.
The context shews that the word means
" habitual drunkards ", " topers ";
and so in Arist. Eth. Nicom. III. v. 15,

οἰνοφλυγία is reckoned as a form of
ἀκολασία or " excess ". MM cite
Musonius, p. 14[15], λιχνεῖαι (gourmet
ways) καὶ οἰνοφλυγίαι καὶ ἀλλὰ παρα-
πλήσια κακά, and Philo, de Vit. Mos.
ii. 185 [II. 163 M], οἰνοφλυγίαι καὶ
ὀψοφαγίαι καὶ λαγνεῖαι (sexual immor-
alities) καὶ ἄλλαι ἀπλήρωτοι ἐπιθυμίαι.
The verb οἰνοφλυγέω occurs in Deut.
xxi. 20 with the same connotation.
οἰνοπότης (Matt. xi. 19, Lk. vii. 34),
on the other hand, conveyed in itself
no such stigma.

κώμοις] festal gatherings, revels,
whether private and domestic, or
public and religious. In Homeric
times the word had no objectionable
associations : the May-day festival or
the annual fête in a country parish to-
day is a κῶμος. Xenophon, indeed,
speaks of a city as being ἐν κώμῳ, en
fête. But already by Plato's time (Rep.
573 D) κῶμος had come to be regarded
as a form of dissipation; and the
public κῶμοι associated with the cult
of certain gods, especially Dionysus,
lent themselves easily to licence.
Demosthenes gives a graphic description of Aeschines' part (which he
regards as per se discreditable) in the
initiation rites of Dionysus Sabazius
in de Corona, 259, 260 ; and in view
of the Phrygian origin and vogue of
Sabazius-worship, these rites may well
be in St. Peter's mind here. For the
derivation of Σαβάζιοι from Σαβοῖ
cf. Harvard Theological Review,
xxxiii. 3 (July 1940), pp. 173 f.
Horace alludes to the licence associated with the rites of Bacchus and
of Cybele in Od. i. 1. 11-16, and
Od. iii. 19. 18 f. The debased music
of Roman revelry came from these
exotic sources.

πότοις] In classical Greek the word
means " drink ", usually as distinct
from food, and carries with it no moral
connotation whatever. It is used,
however, for a " feast " in Gen. xix. 3,
and in the Letter of Aristeas, 262, and
such feasts might easily become

λατρείαις· 4ἐν ᾧ ξενίζονται μὴ συντρεχόντων ὑμῶν εἰς τὴν αὐτὴν

" drinking-parties " ; cf. Aristoph. *Vesp.* 1253 ff. :

κακὸν τὸ πίνειν· ἀπὸ γὰρ οἴνου γίγνεται
καὶ θυροκοπῆσαι καὶ πατάξαι καὶ
βαλεῖν,
κἄπειτ' ἀποτίνειν ἀργύριον ἐκ κραι-
πάλης,

and Alexis 286, ἐχθὲς ὑπέπινες, εἶτα νυνὶ κραιπαλᾷς.

Among the Romans the *comissatio* which followed the *cena* often degenerated into a drunken orgy, cf. *Companion to Latin Studies*, p. 207.

So Wetstein quotes Appian, *Bell. Civ.* i. 700 (of Sertorius), τὰ πολλὰ ἦν ἐπὶ τρυφῆς, γυναιξὶ καὶ κώμοις καὶ πότοις. Add also Dion Chrys. *Euboean Discourse*, § 152, τοῖς ἄγαν φιλοπότοις καὶ οἰνόφλυξι.

ἀθεμίτοις] *abominable, unrighteous* : " by which the most sacred law of God is violated " (Bengel). The word usually seems to have reference to some religious law or tradition, cf. Acts x. 28, *Did.* xvi. 4 ; but it is used quite broadly in Clem. Rom. lxiii. 2.

4. ἐν ᾧ] as in i. 6 (cf. note *supra*), ii. 12, iii. 19 : *in which circumstance, wherefore.*

ξενίζονται] ξενίζειν means (1) to entertain, e.g. strangers, as often in Homer ; (2) to astonish, surprise. The first meaning occurs often in N.T., the second here and verse 12 below in the passive, and in Acts xvii. 20 in the active. The last-named passage shews how the word " entertaining " came in Greek, as in English, to have a new meaning. The word occurs in Polybius, and the meaning ranges from being surprised or entertained by the novelty of a thing in I. xxiii. 5 to being surprised or upset at a new turn of events in III. lxviii. 9 ; and the restricted scope of the term seems indicated by the way it needs to be strengthened, in III. cxiv. 4, ξενίζουσαν ἅμα καὶ καταπληκτικὴν συνέβαινε γίνεσθαι τὴν πρόσοψιν. E. H. B. compares M. Aur. *Comm.* viii. 15, μέμνησο ὅτι ὥσπερ αἰσχρόν ἐστι ξενίζεσθαι εἰ ἡ συκῆ

σῦκα φέρει, οὕτως εἰ ὁ κόσμος τάδε τινὰ φέρει ὧν ἐστι φόρος· καὶ ἰατρῷ δὲ καὶ κυβερνήτῃ (helmsman) αἰσχρὸν ξενίζεσθαι, εἰ πεπύρεχεν οὗτος ἢ εἰ ἀντίπνοια γέγονεν (if a man has a fever or if the wind is unfavourable). For a careful lexicographical discussion of the word cf. R. J. Walker, *Sophocles' Ichneutae*, pp. 87-9. It contains no suggestion of panic. In 1 Pet. iv. 4 " surprised " is the best rendering, in verse 12 " upset ". The prejudice evoked by the moral standards of a distinctive religion are well illustrated in Wisdom ii. 12-16, the difficulties of conscience imposed on believers in Tert. *ad Uxorem*, II. iv.-vi. In 1 Jn. iii. 12 Cain is said to have murdered Abel " because his own works were evil, and his brother's righteous ". And cf. the heathen hatred of Christianity expressed in Rev. xi. 10. And in modern times we may take the following testimony from the diocese of Damaraland (*Quarterly Paper of the Ovamboland Mission*, 1939) : " The Church has to prohibit the attendance of Christians (cf. μὴ συντρεχόντων ὑμῶν) at the heathen marriage and initiation rites, and so immediately tests the obedience and loyalty of the people. For some years the sense has been growing among the people that, although conscience is technically free, yet the Government looks with favour on participation in these rites — a feeling strengthened by the fact that *Efundula* takes place in the winter when many visitors from the South are led by curiosity to be present. Also the dance is performed as a welcome to all official visitors. The pull of paganism is thus immensely strengthened."

For the possibility that ξενίζεσθαι should also be read in 1 Thess. iii. 3 cf. Essay II, p. 451, and Table XIV.

συντρεχόντων] used of crowds gathering in Mk. vi. 33, Acts iii. 11. The word exactly describes the way in which people run from all directions to

τῆς ἀσωτίας ἀνάχυσιν, βλασφημοῦντες· ⁵οἳ ἀποδώσουσι λόγον τῷ
ἑτοίμως ἔχοντι κρῖναι ζῶντας καὶ νεκρούς. ⁶εἰς τοῦτο γὰρ καὶ

see e.g. a procession pass, and suggests that the author has public ceremonies mainly in mind. This is good Greek (cf. Lycurgus 149. 40, with εἰς τὴν ἐκκλησίαν) and depicts better than the legal formula coire, convenire licet, the gathering of worshippers or pilgrims at a pagan temple; and it is more probable than the meaning "consort with" found in Ps.l.18, Ep.Barn.iv.2, where the indirect object is expressed. συνδρομή and σύνδρομος have a kindred meaning; and so in Latin concurrere, concursus, and concursatio. The cults of Artemis (cf. Acts xix.) and Demeter, centred in Ephesus, and of Dionysus (Sabazius) and Cybele in Phrygia and at Pergamum, afforded ample occasions for these gatherings. Cf. Introd. pp. 49-50.

ἀσωτίας] profligacy, used of the Prodigal Son's "riotous living" in Lk. xv. 13 (cf. Prov. xxviii. 7); and associated with drunkenness by St. Paul in Eph. v. 18. The adjective occurs in Soph. Aj. 190, and the substantive in Plato, Rep. 560 E, a passage which aptly illustrates this verse; for it describes, according to James Adam, the aftermath of the Eleusinian mysteries, and how they ended in ὕβριν καὶ ἀναρχίαν καὶ ἀσωτίαν καὶ ἀναίδειαν λαμπράς, all of which were exalted by the revellers as virtues. And if that were so in civilized Athens, how much more must it have been so among ᵗhe excitable peoples of Asia Minor! Aristotle discusses ἀσωτία in Eth. Nicom. IV. i. 3, saying that it is a comprehensive term of reproach for those who spend their substance upon profligate living.

ἀνάχυσιν] excess, effusion. Strabo, III. i. 9, p. 206 a, says that the word was used of the rock-pools filled up by the sea at high tide. Cf. also Strabo, II. v. 24, τοιαύτη μὲν ἡ πρὸς ἄρκτον τοῦ Αἰγαίου πελάγους ἀνάχυσις καὶ τοσαύτη. But the origin of the term may be medical, as Aretaeus, a medical writer

of the latter part of the first century, uses it of an "effusion".

βλασφημοῦντες] used in classical authors, with εἰς, κατά, περί, of speaking evil both of sacred persons or things and of other people. It is found in vernacular Greek with the accusative object, as in Matt. xxvii. 39, and in the passive in 1 Cor. x. 30. The verba Christi in Matt. xii. 31-6 may well have been in St. Peter's mind here, in view of the sentence which immediately follows and of the fact that the blasphemy consisted in calling good evil and evil good.

5. οἳ ἀποδώσουσι λόγον κτλ.] closely parallel to Matt. xii. 36, ἀποδώσουσι περὶ αὐτοῦ λόγον ἐν ἡμέρᾳ κρίσεως The mockings of the heathen were likely to have been "idle" enough.

τῷ ἑτοίμως ... νεκρούς] For ἑτοίμως ἔχοντι cf. Acts xxi. 13, 2 Cor. xii. 14; and in LXX Dan. iii. 15. The phrase occurs in Demades, an Attic orator of Demosthenes' time; cf. Goodwin, § 1092. The phrase κριτὴς ζώντων καὶ νεκρῶν occurs on St. Peter's lips in Acts x. 42, and suggests that the reference here too is to Christ (in contrast to Rom. xiv. 10, where the judgment-seat is God's), as also in 1 Cor. iv. 5 and 2 Tim. iv. 1. Cf. too Ep. Barn. viii. 7, 2 Clem. i. 1. The doctrine rests on such verba Christa as Mk. viii. 38, xiii. 33-7, Matt. xxv. 31 ff., Lk. xxi. 34-6, xiii. 24-30, xii. 35-46, and upon Messianic prophecy. At the same time this judgment which Christ executes is one committed to Him by the Father, cf. Jn. v. 22, 27, Acts x. 42, xvii. 31, Rom. ii. 16; and in that sense the Judge is God Himself, as in Rom. iii. 6; and in yet other verba Christi, e.g. Matt. x. 32, 33 (cf. Lk. xii. 8, 9), as also in 1 Pet. i. 17, ii. 23, the judgment is assigned to the Father. For a discussion of our Lord's teaching as to His own function of Judge cf. Wendt, The Teaching of Jesus, vol. ii. pp. 274 ff., 280 n. 1, where the view is

νεκροῖς εὐηγγελίσθη, ἵνα κριθῶσι μὲν κατὰ ἀνθρώπους σαρκί,

expressed that " He attributes to Himself the judicial function with reference
to the peoples *living at His return to
the earth* and gathering about Him
there, and He declared His judicial
decree to apply with reference to the
conduct which these peoples shall have
manifested *indirectly towards Himself*". See also the discussion by
T. W. Manson in *The Teaching of
Jesus*, ch. viii., and the same author's
development of his theme, especially
as regards Matt. xxv. 31 ff., in *The
Mission and Message of Jesus*, pp.
541-4. Dr. Manson's point is that
" the Son of Man " in the latter
part of Christ's ministry is a title
connoting a corporate entity, namely,
the Church or " the saints " (cf. 1 Cor.
vi. 2), which takes over the attributes
of the Remnant in Jewish prophecy,
and which is the executant of Judgment, in the sense — and only in
the sense — that it gives the testimony
which secures acquittal or condemnation. It is certainly the case that
Christ's office of Judge in no way
derogates from the powers of universal
judgment which Hebrew thought
always ascribed to God, cf. e.g. Ps.
cxliii. 1, Amos iii. 2, 2 Esdras xvi. 61-7;
but in the passage before us (in contrast to i. 17, ii. 12) the attitude of the
heathen world towards Christ and His
Church is so much to the fore that the
phrase is best understood as referring
to the judicial function of Christ.

6. εἰς τοῦτο γὰρ] εἰς τοῦτο, here as
in iii. 9, refers forward and is the
antecedent to ἵνα; γάρ refers back-
ward, and shews that the sentence
supplies a reason or explanation for
something that has gone before.
Here the reference is to the statement
in the preceding sentence that Christ's
judgment extends to dead as well as
living. Chase (*DB*, article on 1
Peter) and Blenkin assume some such
sentence as " And His judgment is
just " as the antecedent to γάρ; but
this seems very far-fetched.

καὶ νεκροῖς] For a full discussion of
the interpretations of this passage see
Essay I, pp. 337-9. νεκροί in this verse
must have the same meaning as in the
preceding verse, and mean people
actually dead in the common acceptance of the term. It is tempting to
see here a reference to the universality
of Christ's judgment corresponding to
the universality of His redemption
asserted in iii. 18 ff.; but no such
reference is required by the text. It
is simpler, indeed, to suppose that
St. Peter in verse 5 has in mind past
and present members of the Church
and their persecutors, and in verse 6
the first of these only. See Essay I,
pp. 337 f.

εὐηγγελίσθη] He (*Christ*) *was
preached*, cf. i. 12. The word εὐαγγελίζεσθαι is applied to the preaching
given by Jesus Himself only by Luke
among the evangelists, and by him
(including the quotation of Is. lxi. 1 in
Lk. iv. 18) only four times. Evidently
St. Luke liked the word, for it is
frequent in the Acts, where it always
refers to preaching given by the
Apostles. On the other hand, Christ is
the object of εὐαγγελίζεσθαι (middle) in
Acts v. 42, viii. 35 (Ἰησοῦν), xi. 20 (τὸν
κύριον Ἰησοῦν), xvii. 18 (τὸν Ἰησοῦν),
Gal. i. 16 (αὐτόν); and he is the subject of κηρύσσεσθαι (passive) in 1 Cor.
xv. 12, 2 Cor. i. 19. Bigg says that
εὐηγγελίσθη here is impersonal, but
examples of this construction in N.T.
are exceedingly rare. Blass, who
observes this fact (*op. cit.* p. 75), gives
a few references, but only Rom. x. 10
is a true impersonal passive of the
type illustrated by Goodwin (*Greek
Grammar*, § 1240). Hermas, *Mand.*
iii. 3, ἐπιστεύθη τῷ λόγῳ μου, is not
germane either, for πιστεύειν governs
the dative, and therefore a direct passive construction was impossible. On
the other hand, we get a perfectly
normal construction by taking Christ
as the subject of εὐηγγελίσθη; and if,
as on other grounds we have seen to

ζῶσι δὲ κατὰ Θεὸν πνεύματι.

be probable, τῷ ἑτοίμως ἔχοντι refers
to Christ, there is no difficulty in so
taking it.

ἵνα κριθῶσι μὲν κτλ.] that, though
they have been judged humanly speaking in the flesh, they may live in God's
likeness in the spirit.

κριθῶσι] For the importance of distinguishing between κρίνειν and its
derivatives compounded with prepositions cf. Lightfoot, On a Fresh
Revision of the New Testament (ed.
1871), pp. 62-7. κρίνειν connotes acts
of judgment which are temporary and
thus corrective and remedial, or else a
final judgment of which the issue is
open until the verdict is given : the
word for " condemn " is κατακρίνειν.
The context here shews that the contrast is between the difficult lot of
believers in this life, and their restoration and vindication in another life.
κριθῶσι does not refer to legal sentences
upon men, which would require κατα-
κριθῶσι ; and the trials and persecutions of the faithful, whether Jews or
Christians, frequently involved no judicial procedure at all. But it may well
refer to these trials and persecutions
themselves, as in 1 Cor. xi. 32, and
particularly to death ; for, humanly
speaking (κατὰ ἀνθρώπους), men are
"judged" at death in the sense that
a decision is reached then as to the
value of their life here. Cf. the maxim
" Call no man happy until he is dead ";
or, " Home hath gone and ta'en his
wages ". In Is. xxvi. 16 death is
spoken of as " thy discipline ", and in
Wisd. iii. 4 we have a passage which
may have been in St. Peter's mind
here : " For though they be punished
in the sight of men, yet is their hope
full of immortality ". Between κατὰ
ἀνθρώπους and ἐν ὄψει ἀνθρώπων there is
but little difference. For the contrast
between " judgment " and " life "
here we may compare Jn. v. 20-9, discussed in Essay I, pp. 346 ff.

For a parallel contrast in Greek
literature cf. Lysias, Funeral Oration,

79-80, καὶ γάρ τοι ἀγήρατοι μὲν αὐτῶν αἱ
μνῆμαι, ζηλωταὶ δὲ ὑπὸ πάντων ἀνθρώπων αἱ τιμαί· οἳ πενθοῦνται μὲν διὰ τὴν
φύσιν ὡς θνητοί, ὑμνοῦνται δὲ ὡς
ἀθάνατοι διὰ τὴν ἀρετήν.

μὲν . . . δὲ] The μέν clause is parenthetic, the δέ clause providing the
true final clause to εἰς τοῦτο. 1 Peter
is partial to this antithesis, cf. iii. 18 ;
but Blass observes that it only occurs
with any frequency in Acts, Hebrews,
1 Peter, and some of the Pauline
Epistles, and in many of these passages
it indicates little more than mere
correspondence (Grammar, pp. 266 f.).

κατὰ ἀνθρώπους] κατά expresses conformity to some standard, model, rule,
or will ; cf. i. 15, and Winer, op. cit.
pp. 500 f. St. Paul uses the singular
κατὰ ἄνθρωπον frequently (Rom. iii. 5,
1 Cor. iii. 3, ix. 8, xv. 32, Gal. i. 11,
iii. 15), and in every case it refers to the
subject of the sentence, even when (as
in 1 Cor. iii. 3) the subject is plural.
The plural in St. Peter's phrase is less
adverbial and more concrete, as though
the " men " in question were envisaged
as real persons, whose opinions rather
than actions were in mind : he does
not mean that the dead have been
judged as men are judged, which
would call for κατὰ ἄνθρωπον, but that
they have been according to human
standards judged. Phrases like κατὰ
Χριστόν in Col. ii. 8, Rom. xv. 5 are
closer parallels than κατὰ ἄνθρωπον.
The exact shade of meaning of such
phrases governed by κατά depends on
the context : " in men's estimation "
would be a fair paraphrase here.

κατὰ Θεόν is rarer. It occurs in
4 Macc. xv. 3 (a work not later than
1 Peter) in the phrase τὴν εὐσέβειαν
μᾶλλον ἠγάπησεν τὴν σώζουσαν εἰς
αἰώνιον ζωὴν κατὰ θεόν, which affords
a close parallel to our present passage.
St. Paul uses it three times in 2 Cor.
vii. 9-11 of the sorrow (λύπη) which is
" godly " in contrast to " the sorrow
of the world "; and in Rom. viii. 27
the Spirit is said to " make interces-

⁷Πάντων δὲ τὸ τέλος ἤγγικε· σωφρονήσατε οὖν καὶ νήψατε
εἰς προσευχάς· ⁸πρὸ πάντων τὴν εἰς ἑαυτοὺς ἀγάπην ἐκτενῆ

sion for the saints according to the will of God ". In Eph. iv. 24 St. Paul speaks of καινὸν ἄνθρωπον τὸν κατὰ θεὸν κτισθέντα, and the meaning " in the likeness of God " is drawn out in Col. iii. 10 where we have κατ' εἰκόνα τοῦ κτίσαντος αὐτόν. Here in 1 Pet. iv. 6 κατὰ Θεόν is best translated " in God's likeness " or " as God lives ", i.e. eternally. Though the phrases κατὰ ἀνθρώπους . . . κατὰ Θεόν are correlative, the parallelism is not exact, and it is better to express this difference in the translation. What St. Peter is contrasting is judgment in the flesh, of which death is commonly regarded by men as the supreme sign and example, and life in the spirit, which is, like God's life, eternal.

With the general sentiment of the passage we may compare 2 Macc. vii. 14, " So when he was ready to die he said thus, It is good, being put to death by men, to look for hope from God to be raised again by him : as for thee, thou shalt have no resurrection to life ", and 4 Macc. vii. 19, (xvi. 25), οἱ πιστεύοντες ὅτι θεῷ οὐκ ἀποθνήσκουσιν, ὥσπερ γὰρ οἱ πατριάρχαι ἡμῶν Ἀβραάμ, Ἰσαάκ, Ἰακώβ, ἀλλὰ ζῶσιν τῷ θεῷ — words recalling Mk. xii. 27.

7. δὲ] moreover. Cf. Winer, op. cit. p. 552 [Part III, Sect. liii. 7 (b)]. St. Peter presses home his point : the judgment of which he speaks is no vague or distant matter ; it is at the door. On the association of prominent Jewish saints with eschatology cf. Charles, Apocrypha and Pseudepigrapha, ii. p. 314, G. H. Boobyer, St. Mark and the Transfiguration Story, pp. 70 ff. ἤγγικεν is the word regularly used in our Lord's words about the Kingdom of Heaven, the perfect tense connoting immediacy, and such immediacy that the kingdom may be said in certain senses to have actually come (cf. Dodd, The Parables

of the Kingdom, pp. 44 f.) : it is part of the immediate perspective of life. Usage in LXX is similar, cf. Lam. iv. 18, Ezek. vii. 7. So too Jas. v. 8, ἡ παρουσία τοῦ κυρίου ἤγγικε, where the imminence of the End is made the ground for patience and courage, as here for sobriety and love, and in Ign. Eph. xi. 1 for reverence and fear.

On the connexion of this passage with 1 Thess. v. 1 ff. and 2 Thess. ii. 1 ff. see Essay II, pp. 375 ff., 450 ff., and Tables II, XIV.

σωφρονήσατε] keep your heads. σωφρονεῖν connotes the cool head and balanced mind which is the opposite of all μανία or undue excitement, whether this be inspired by a divine spirit (Plato, Phaedr. 244 A) or by evil spirits (Mk. v. 15, Lk. viii. 35), or by love (Plato, loc. cit.), or by pride (Rom. xii. 3, cf. Aesch. Pers. 829, P.V. 982) or success (Thuc. viii. 24). It is expressed negatively in 2 Thess. ii. 2, εἰς τὸ μὴ ταχέως σαλευθῆναι ὑμᾶς ἀπὸ τοῦ νοὸς μηδὲ θροεῖσθαι.

νήψατε] See note on i. 13.

εἰς προσευχάς] See note on iii. 7; and for the urgency of prayer in time of crisis cf. the verbum Christi in Matt. xxvi. 41.

8. πρὸ πάντων] In Jas. v. 12, which is part of a passage (v. 7-12) presenting many analogies with 1 Pet. iv. 7-11, the pre-eminent position is given to abstention from swearing; here to charity. For the parallels with James see Essay II, p. 407, and Tables VIII A, XIV (e).

τὴν εἰς ἑαυτοὺς ἀγάπην] i.e. the φιλαδελφία enjoined in i. 22, iii. 8. As Bengel says, the adjective ἐκτενῆ (on which see note on i. 22) is here predicative. The charity " is already presupposed to exist": the injunction is, that it be made fervent. For the relationship of this passage to Rom. xiii. 8-10 and Jas.

ἔχοντες, ὅτι ἀγάπη καλύπτει πλῆθος ἁμαρτιῶν· 9φιλόξενοι εἰς

ii. 8 cf. Essay II, p. 413, and Table VIII A. Behind these parallels lie such *verba Christi* as Mk. xii. 30-3, Jn. xiii. 34 f.

ὅτι ἀγάπη . . . ἁμαρτιῶν] Commentators differ as to whether the sins thus " covered " are those of the Christian who shews charity or those of others who receive it ; Oecumenius, Estius, Bengel, Bigg, Bennett, Wand preferring the latter view, Windisch the former, in support of which he adduces the allusions in 1 Pet. i. 14, ii. 1, 11 f., iv. 1-4, to the sins of the readers' pre-Christian manner of life. Tertullian, *Scorp.* vi. and Origen, *in Lev. Hom.* ii. 5 (ii. p. 190), refer it also to the covering of a man's own sins, but only because they interpret ἀγάπη as love for God or for Christ. Clement of Alexandria uses the proverb to illustrate the love of God in " covering " or " forgiving " sins (as in Ps. xxxii. 1) in *Strom.* II. xv. 463 [P], and of love's power to win forgiveness for others (*pace* Lightfoot on 2 Clem. xvi. 4) in *Quis Div. Salv.* 38, 956 [P]. If, however, the proverb was already in circulation in the Church, as its appearance in a different context in Jas. v. 20 suggests, and still more if, as Resch maintains (*Agrapha*, pp. 310 f.), it was a *verbum Christi* unrecorded in the Gospels, we are not called upon to decide between these views ; for they are not mutually exclusive. The proverb lays down the broad principle of the " covering " effect of charity upon sin : its application may be self-regarding, as in 1 Clem. xlix. 5, l. 5, 2 Clem. xvi. 4 (and cf. Lk. vii. 47), or other-regarding, as the mind of each writer may prefer. And its other-regarding application carries with it its correlative ; for, as Oecumenius says, ὁ μὲν γὰρ εἰς τὸν πλησίον ἔλεος, τὸν θεὸν ἡμῖν ἱλέων ποιεῖ : Christ made our hope for forgiveness of our own sins depend on our readiness to forgive others.

And in what sense does charity

" veil " sins ? Not, surely, in the sense of " hushing up " or " condoning " as in *Test. Jos.* 17, καὶ ὑμεῖς οὖν ἀγαπᾶτε ἀλλήλους καὶ ἐν μακροθυμίᾳ συγκρύπτετε ἀλλήλων τὰ ἐλαττώματα — an injunction which could never of itself have given rise to our proverb. Our forgiveness of others' sins, which even Lightfoot thinks is here St. Peter's primary meaning, could never be the *ground* of fervour of charity, but rather its consequence : its ground must be something weightier and wider than itself. *For wherever the causal ὅτι occurs in 1 Peter, it introduces the theological ground of an ethical injunction*, cf. i. 16, ii. 15, 21, iii. 9, 12, 18, iv. 1, 14, 17, v. 5, 7. The idea must be that of veiling or covering *before God* ; and the word is found in this sense in Ps. lxxxv. 2, ἐκάλυψας τὰς ἁμαρτίας αὐτῶν, and xxxii. 1, μακάριοι . . . ὧν ἐπεκαλύφθησαν αἱ ἁμαρτίαι. Bigg sees a reference here to the propitiatory sacrifices which according to Jewish ideas " covered " (*kippēr*) sins ; and, if this were so, it would tally well with the " spiritual sacrifices " alluded to in ii. 5. But the sacrificial reference in Ps. xxxii. 1 is doubtful (cf. Briggs in I.C.C.), and cannot be pressed here. What is true is that charity has effects like those of propitiatory sacrifices in reconciling men to God ; and this idea is common both to St. Peter here and to Jas. v. 20. Origen, *in Lev. Hom.* ii. 4, traces the saying, perhaps rightly, to the *verbum Christi* in Lk. vii. 47. Prov. x. 12 is often assumed to underlie the phrase in both N.T. places ; but both words and sense are very different in LXX, though not in Hebrew, and, as 1 Peter invariably quotes from LXX, it seems best to trace the phrase to a proverb, if not a *verbum Christi*, current in the Church. The idea is represented in Ecclus. xvii. 20-2.

For a classical illustration cf. Thuc. ii. 42. 3 (Pericles' speech), " For even where life's previous record showed

ἀλλήλους, ἄνευ γογγυσμοῦ· ¹⁰ἕκαστος καθὼς ἔλαβε χάρισμα, εἰς
ἑαυτοὺς αὐτὸ διακονοῦντες, ὡς καλοὶ οἰκονόμοι ποικίλης χάριτος

faults and failures, it is just to weigh the last brave hour of devotion against them all. There they wiped out evil with good and did the city more service as soldiers than they did her harm in private life " (tr. Livingstone).

9. φιλόξενοι κτλ.] Cf. Rom. xii. 13, Heb. xiii. 2, 1 Tim. iii. 2 and the *verbum Christi*, which was the ultimate authority for this injunction, in Matt. xxv. 35. Commentators (e.g. Bigg, Blenkin, Wand) point out that the work of the Christian mission carried out by itinerant apostles, prophets and preachers would have been impossible without the generous hospitality of the members of local Christian communities. Moreover, such hospitality must sometimes have been burdensome — hence the words ἄνευ γογγυσμοῦ, "without grumbling" (cf. 2 Cor. ix. 7, Phil. ii. 14) ; and in *Did.* xi.–xiii. we see how this hospitality came to be abused by charlatans. But it is doubtful whether this is the primary meaning of St. Peter's words here, which, in view of the context and of the words εἰς ἀλλήλους, appear to have a more intimate and domestic reference. The Apostle is thinking rather of ordinary social life in the Christian communities, where constant intercourse and meeting were essential to preserve the Church's cohesion and distinctive witness, and where the Christians' households, in default of church buildings, were the local units of the Church's worship (Rom. xvi. 5, 1 Cor. xvi. 19, Col. iv. 15). This reference of the phrase to house-churches provides further an easy transition to the specific allusions to two of the main activities of the worshipping body — teaching and ministering — which occupy verses 10, 11. The injunction in *Did.* iv., " Daily shalt thou seek out the persons of the saints (i.e. thy fellow-Christians), that thou mayest find rest in their words ", presupposes a willingness to keep open house (the modern

application of the point is well brought out by Professor John Foster, in *Then and Now*, ch. iii.) ; and this would often have entailed provocation to grumbling.

10. ἕκαστος κτλ.] When life is governed by the grace of God, there should be no room for grumbling, but only for graciousness. For His grace takes many forms, and Christians are its " stewards ", dispensing its several gifts (χάρισμα) as each has received them.

οἰκονόμοι recalls Lk. xii. 42 ff., " Who then is that faithful and wise steward ? ", etc., a *verbum Christi* addressed, in St. Luke's version, to St. Peter personally, and in a strongly eschatological context. In any case, 1 Peter here indicates that Lk. xii. 42 ff. was not a " Petrine text ", but was of general application ; and that the Apostle's question in Lk. xii. 41, " Lord, speakest thou this parable unto us, or even to all ? " was meant to be answered as in Mk. xiii. 37, " What I say unto you I say unto all, Watch ". The steward was responsible to the master of the house for distributing to the other members of the household their shares of his stores, cf. Hatch, *Essays in Biblical Greek*, p. 62 ; and in the " spiritual house " (ii. 5) each member has this responsibility of distribution. But what each is to distribute differs according to his or her gifts and calling : it is not the same for the lay member as for the apostle (1 Cor. iv. 1) or the " bishop " (Tit. i. 7). But whatever it be, it is in origin a gift (χάρισμα) of God's grace (χάρις).

Bigg thinks that the wherewithal to entertain is one of the gifts in St. Peter's mind, in which case we have an illuminating glimpse of the Apostle's attitude to money as something to be spent on others rather than hoarded or spent on oneself.

ποικίλης] See note on i. 6.

Θεοῦ· ¹¹εἴ τις λαλεῖ, ὡς λόγια Θεοῦ· εἴ τις διακονεῖ, ὡς ἐξ ἰσχύος
ἧς χορηγεῖ ὁ Θεός· ἵνα ἐν πᾶσι δοξάζηται ὁ Θεὸς διὰ Ἰησοῦ
Χριστοῦ, ᾧ ἐστιν ἡ δόξα καὶ τὸ κράτος εἰς τοὺς αἰῶνας τῶν
αἰώνων. ἀμήν.

11. εἴ τις λαλεῖ κτλ.] The writer
passes from the hospitable household
to the worshipping community generally, and he illustrates his point from
two of the Church's activities, teaching
and practical ministry. λαλεῖν is used
frequently in N.T. of teaching or
preaching, and even of God speaking
through His prophets (e.g. Acts iii. 21).
For the connexion of this passage with
Rom. xii. 6-8 cf. Essay II, pp. 415-
17, and Table VIII c.

ὡς λόγια Θεοῦ] as the spokesman of
God's holy words. λόγια sometimes
means Scripture (cf. Rom. iii. 2), but
is by no means confined to Scripture
(cf. Heb. v. 12). As in classical and
Hellenistic Greek it means any divine
utterances, such as oracles (cf. Thuc.
ii. 8, Aristoph. Eq. 122), so here : the
speaker in the congregation should
reckon himself to be charged not with
his own opinions but the utterances of
God. The principle is that which our
Lord said governed His own teaching,
cf. Jn. vii. 16-18. For the wider use
in sub-apostolic literature cf. Polyc.
ad Phil. vii., and for the narrower, i.e.
Scripture, which arises from the other,
1 Clem. xix., liii. Lightfoot, Essays
on Supernatural Religion, pp. 172 f.,
is worth consulting.

Bigg takes λόγια here as nominative,
translating " let him speak as Scripture speaks ", i.e. with sincerity and
gravity. But apart from the fact that
λόγια are always things spoken (even if
afterwards written down) and not
things speaking, the parallelism with
the next phrase requires the accusative
here. All is of grace : the teacher or
preacher is not to be the purveyor of
his own notions, but the transmitter of
the utterances of God ; the minister
must not be setting forth his own
competence or importance, but regard
himself as acting from resources which

God supplies.

εἴ τις διακονεῖ κτλ.] " διακονία was
used either generally of all Christian
ministrations (so Rom. xi. 13, 1 Cor.
xii. 5, Eph. iv. 12, etc.) or specially of
the administration of alms and attendance to bodily wants (1 Cor. xvi. 15,
2 Cor. vii. 4, etc.) " (SH on Rom.
xii. 7). The contrast with εἴ τις λαλεῖ
suggests that here, as in Rom. xii. 7,
the narrower meaning is in mind.
Comparison with Rom. xii. and with
1 Cor. xii. indicates that St. Peter is
reflecting here a very primitive differentiation of function in the Church,
such as meets us in Acts vi. rather than
in the Pauline Epistles. Windisch
goes beyond the evidence when he says
that the Church leaders alluded to are
" not officials or in any sense dele-
gates " ; rather St. Peter lets the
organized work of the Church fall into
two simple categories, those of teaching and of practical ministry.

ὡς ἐξ ἰσχύος] i.e. "in humble dependence upon God " (Bidding Prayer) ; a
spirit which inspires at once humility
and vigour.

χορηγεῖ] χορηγεῖν meant initially " to
be a chorus leader " ; then, since actor-
managers became more common, " to
supply a chorus " and so produce a
play at one's own risk ; and finally,
as in Aristotle, Polybius, Diodorus
Siculus, simply to furnish or supply
anything. For a full discussion of the
term see Armitage Robinson's note on
Eph. iv. 16. The word is not uncommon in LXX, cf. 1 Kings iv. 7,
1 Macc. xiv. 10, Ecclus. xxxix. 33,
xliv. 6 ; and E. H. B.'s note on Ep.
ad Diogn. i. 2.

ἵνα κτλ.] See notes on ii. 12 ; and
cf. the verbum Christi, Matt. v. 16.
The final clause depends not only on
the two preceding injunctions to a
humble spirit of dependence on God's

12 Ἀγαπητοί, μὴ ξενίζεσθε τῇ ἐν ὑμῖν πυρώσει πρὸς πειρασμὸν

grace in teaching and in service, but on the general law of charity governing the whole passage; as in Rom. xv. 5, 6. Charity and humility are closely allied; and the power and effective-ness which accompany them have the effect of shewing forth the glory of God, which is man's true end. Cf. the Synagogue liturgy, "Blessed be our God that has created us for his glory"; the Larger Scottish Catechism, "Man's chief and highest end is to glorify God and fully to enjoy him for ever"; and the Benedictine motto IOGD, ut in omnibus glorificetur Deus.

Westcott enumerates sixteen N.T. doxologies in The Epistle to the Hebrews [1909], pp. 466 f., and points out their variety. The following points may be noted. (1) Only in three cases, Rom. xvi. 27, Jude 25, 2 Pet. iii. 18 does the doxology conclude an Epistle; so that the occurrence of this doxology here affords no kind of presumption that the Epistle ended here, and that iv. 12–v. 11 or 14 was originally a distinct document. The occurrence of a doxology in an Epistle, in fact, is determined by the moment at which there flashes on the author's mind, as he writes, the vision of man's true end. (2) Glory is given to God through Christ in three doxologies, Rom. xvi. 27, Jude 25, and 1 Pet. iv. 11. (3) Glory is given to Christ in Rom. xvi. 27 (where the reading is questionable); Rev. i. 6, and (together with the Father), v. 13, vii. 10; 2 Pet. iii. 18; and perhaps 2 Tim. iv. 18 (cf. Ellicott, citing Theophylact) and Heb. xiii. 21. Rev. i. 6 contains the exact phrase ἡ δόξα καὶ τὸ κράτος εἰς τοὺς αἰῶνας τῶν αἰώνων· ἀμήν ascribed to Christ. Commentators have differed as to whether ᾧ in this doxology in 1 Pet. iv. 11 is referable to Christ; but the order of the words strongly favours it, and the above parallels, especially Rev. i. 6, support it. It has, moreover, Christ's own warrant, Jn. xvii. 5. At the same time, it is then the only

example in N.T. (if we except Rom. xvi. 27) of glory being ascribed to Christ and through Christ in the same doxology. Yet 1 Clem. xx. 11, 12 is very similar, and its two parts are also found separately in 1 Clem. lviii. 2 (through Christ) and l. 7 (to Christ). The ἀμήν indicates liturgical use which is commonly both diverse and endur-ing; and 1 Clement may well have taken the form in xx. 11, 12 from the same liturgical source as St. Peter.

At a later date sharp controversy ensued in the Church over the wording of doxologies, and it was the purpose of St. Basil's treatise de Spiritu Sancto to shew that orthodox doctrine could be preserved in more than one formula. On the "binitarian" tendency noticed here by Windisch and Wand see Add. Note A, p. 248 n.; and on the con-nexion of doxologies with doctrine cf. Hooker, L.E.P. v. xlii. 7-11. Hooker has some weighty words also on their value : "the glory of all things is that wherein their highest perfection doth consist. . . . God is glorified when such his excellency above all things is with due admiration acknowledged".

On the meanings of δόξα in N.T. cf. Add. Note B, pp. 253-8, and on the attempts to divide the Epistle at this point Introd. p. 32.

12-19. The section which began at iii. 13 is here concluded in a passage which recapitulates much that has been said — on persecution, on Christ's sufferings, on Christian duty, on the imminence of the End and of divine Judgment — and which reflects the intensity of the author's eschatological faith.

12. Ἀγαπητοί] See note on ii. 11 and Essay II, p. 388.

μὴ ξενίζεσθε] See note on iv. 4. Windisch makes the good point here that the Gentile Christians, unused to persecution as from their history the Jews were, and having been newly con-verted and made heirs of the Messianic kingdom, would have found persecu-

ὑμῖν γινομένῃ, ὡς ξένου ὑμῖν συμβαίνοντος· ¹³ἀλλὰ καθὸ κοινωνεῖτε τοῖς τοῦ Χριστοῦ παθήμασι, χαίρετε, ἵνα καὶ ἐν τῇ ἀπο-

tion peculiarly daunting and hard to
bear. This refusal to be troubled by
persecution is one of the points Origen
sums up in the phrase, τὸ ἀμέριμνον
τῆς σοφίας πνεῦμα ἀναλάβωμεν, *Exhort.
ad Mart.* xlix.

τῇ ἐν ὑμῖν κτλ.] Field, *Otium Norvicense*, observes that the order should
be τῇ πυρώσει (τῇ) γινομένῃ ἐν ὑμῖν πρὸς
πειρασμὸν ὑμῖν (ὑμῶν). This gives the
meaning clearly, but is not so polished
as what the text has : cf. Appian,
Basil. 1, Κρεούσης τῆς Πριάμου τῆς
ἐν Ἰλίῳ γενομένης αὐτῷ γυναικός. On
the nature of the persecutions alluded
to here cf. Introd. pp. 52-6, and on
the connexion of the passage with
i. 6, 7 and Jas. i. 2, 3 and the probability that both are dependent upon
a primitive Persecution-document cf.
Essay II, pp. 450 ff., and Table XIV.

πυρώσει] *ordeal*. πύρωσις means
(1) a burning, (2) exposure to the
action of fire, e.g. in baking (Ar.
Probl. xxi. 12) or boiling (Ar. *Meteor.*
IV. iii. 11), (3) testing by fire (Hesychius). And so Oecumenius says that
τῇ . . . πυρώσει stands ἀντὶ τοῦ δοκι-
μασίᾳ. The last meaning would follow
naturally from the practice of sub-
mitting metals to fire for the purpose
of testing them. And in view of i. 6, 7
(where see notes on πειρασμοῖς and
τὸ δοκίμιον κτλ.) there can be little
doubt that this is the meaning here :
a process of refining by fire is going on
amongst them for their testing. The
word πύρωσις is rare, but occurs in
Prov. xxvii. 21, δοκίμιον ἀργύρῳ καὶ
χρυσῷ πύρωσις; cf. Ps. lxvi. 10, ἐδοκίμασας ἡμᾶς, ὁ θεός, καὶ ἐπύρωσας ἡμᾶς
ὡς πυροῦται τὸ ἀργύριον; and *Did.*
xvi. 5, τότε ἥξει ἡ κτίσις τῶν ἀνθρώπων
εἰς τὴν πύρωσιν τῆς δοκιμασίας. The
eschatological context of the persecution envisaged both in *Did.* xvi. 5 and
here in 1 Peter may well have prompted
the use of the word πύρωσις; for fire
played a large part in Jewish expectations of the end (cf. *Enoch* cii. 1,

cviii. 3, 5, and the discussion by E. C.
Selwyn, *St. Luke the Prophet*, pp.
133 ff.). Nor can the possibility be
ruled out that Christians in Asia Minor
may have suffered, like the Jews in
modern Germany, from acts of deliberate incendiarism.

An alternative rendering, based on
the transference of πυροῦσθαι to connote a person's feelings, would be
" the harassing experiences " : cf.
1 Cor. vii. 9 (unsatisfied desire), 2 Cor.
xi. 29 (shame and distress), 2 Macc. iv.
38, x. 35, xiv. 45 (anger) ; and the
word would then be a more picturesque
term for the λυπή referred to in i. 6.
But the first rendering seems preferable.

συμβαίνοντος] Cf. Acts xx. 19, δου-
λεύων τῷ κυρίῳ μετὰ . . δακρύων καὶ
πειρασμῶν τῶν συμβάντων μοι ἐν ταῖς
ἐπιβουλαῖς τῶν Ἰουδαίων.

13. καθὸ] *in the measure in which*.
Cf. the *verba Christi* in Matt. x. 24, 25,
Jn. xiii. 16, and especially Jn. xv. 20.

κοινωνεῖτε κτλ.] In Rom. viii. 17
St. Paul speaks of Christians " suffering with (συμπάσχειν) Christ ", and in
2 Tim. ii. 11 of " dying with " Him
(συναπεθάνομεν), the latter passage
being probably part of a hymn. Phil.
iii. 10, τοῦ γνῶναι αὐτόν . . . καὶ
κοινωνίαν τῶν παθημάτων αὐτοῦ, gives
a closer parallel. Cf. also 2 Cor. i. 5,
and Polyc. *ad Phil.* ix., παρὰ τῷ κυρίῳ
ᾧ καὶ συνέπαθον. St. Peter's words are
fully in keeping with what he has said
of the *imitatio Christi* in ii. 20 ff.,
iii. 17 ff. His own designation of
himself in v. 1 below as ὁ καὶ τῆς
μελλούσης ἀποκαλύπτεσθαι δόξης κοινωνός may warn us against interpreting
the passage in terms of Christ-mysti-
cism. Cf. V. Taylor, *Forgiveness and
Reconciliation*, pp. 131-4. Christians
share in Christ's sufferings through
the experience of a like persecution and
opprobrium, and through " arming
themselves " with the same temper of
meekness and patience.

καλύψει τῆς δόξης αὐτοῦ χαρῆτε ἀγαλλιώμενοι. ¹⁴εἰ ὀνειδίζεσθε
ἐν ὀνόματι Χριστοῦ, μακάριοι· ὅτι τὸ τῆς δόξης καὶ τὸ τοῦ Θεοῦ

χαίρετε] See note on i. 6, with N.T.
references there given.

χαρῆτε ἀγαλλιώμενοι] *rejoice with
rapture.* The emphatic use of ἀγαλλιώμενοι here to express the exultation
which will be felt in the day of the
revelation of Christ's glory is one
of the considerations which suggest
that ἀγαλλιάσεσθε should be read in
i. 8.

14. εἰ ὀνειδίζεσθε κτλ.] The reference to the *verbum Christi* in Matt.
v. 11 is clear. No more need be
involved in the addition of ἐν ὀνόματι
Χριστοῦ than was foreseen by the Lord
Himself in such sayings as those recorded in Matt. x. 22, Mk. xiii. 13,
Lk. xxi. 17, and was realized in many
incidents occurring from Pentecost
onwards, cf. Acts iv. 17. The converse, i.e. kindness in Christ's name,
was also foretold, Mk. ix. 41 (though
the phrase here is less direct). On
" Persecution for the Name " see the
admirable study by E. G. Hardy,
Studies in Roman History, ch. vii.
Ramsay's contrary view is discussed
above, Introd. p. 54.

τὸ τῆς δόξης καὶ τὸ τοῦ Θεοῦ
Πνεῦμα] *the Presence of the Glory, yea
the Spirit of God, rests upon you.* For
a fuller discussion of the context and
interpretation of this phrase see Add.
Note B, pp. 256-7. The A.V. " the
spirit of glory and of God resteth
upon you " is improbable in view of
the second τό ; unless we may suppose
that our author intended to write πνεῦμα
after δόξης, and then amplified it by
identifying it with the Spirit of God.
" The spirit of (the) glory " does not
occur in N.T. ; but we may compare
Ezek. xliii. 5, ἀνέλαβέν με πνεῦμα καὶ
εἰσήγαγέν με εἰς τὴν αὐλὴν τὴν ἐσωτέραν,
καὶ ἰδοὺ πλήρης δόξης κυρίου ὁ οἶκος
(a relevant passage in view of the
allusion to the Church as the house ot
God in 1 Pet. ii. 5, iv. 17), and also
2 Cor. iii. 18. I take τὸ τῆς δόξης,
however, to mean the presence or

reflection of the glory, i.e. the *Shekinah.*
So, on the whole, Huther and Blenkin.
For this construction cf. in LXX Lev.
vii. 7 τὸ τῆς πλημμελίας = the trespass-
offering, 1 Sam. vi. 4, τὸ τῆς βασάνου =
the [offering for] the plague (cf. Hatch,
op. cit. p. 17) ; and in N.T. Matt. xxi.
21, τὸ τῆς συκῆς = the action in regard
to the fig-tree, Jas. iv. 14, τὸ τῆς αὔριον
= the conditions of to-morrow, 2 Pet.
ii. 22, τὸ τῆς ἀληθοῦς παροιμίας = the
situation contemplated in the true
proverb (with which Wetstein compares
Lucian, *Dial. Mort.* viii. 1, τοῦτο ἐκεῖνο
τὸ τῆς παροιμίας, ὁ νεβρὸς τὸν λέοντα).
Mayor on 2 Pet. ii. 22 quotes also
Xen. *Oecon.* xvi. 7, τὸ τῶν ἁλιέων =
the case of the fishermen, and Plato,
Phaedr. 230 C, τὸ τῆς πόας = the lush-
ness of the grass. In all these cases
the substantive to be understood is
internal to the substantive in the genitive, and its precise meaning is determined by the context. Here the
periphrasis was preferred because ἡ
δόξα had just been mentioned (verse 13)
in connexion with the final revelation
at the end of all things ; and what rests
upon the Church meantime, amidst its
persecutions, is not quite that glory but
its communicable part or presence (τὸ
τῆς δόξης), which the Apostle goes on
to explain as " the Spirit of God ". It
would be possible, as Blenkin says,
to understand ὄνομα from ἐν ὀνόματι
Χριστοῦ immediately preceding ; and
[τὸ] ὄνομα [τῆς] δόξης [αὐτοῦ] occurs in
Ps. lxxii. 19, lxxix. 9, Neh. ix. 5,
Dan. iii. 52, Judith ix. 8, 1 Macc. xiv.
10, 3 Macc. ii. 9. Judith ix. 8 is
particularly to the point, since the
tabernacle is there spoken of as τὸ
σκήνωμα τῆς καταπαύσεως τοῦ ὀνόματος
τῆς δόξης σου, i.e. where the name of
thy glory rests ; the periphrasis being
preferred to the plain τῆς δόξης, as so
often with the divine Name, from
motives of reverence. Cf. Kohler,
Jewish Theology, p. 197. Yet on the
whole it seems best here not to seek too

Πνεῦμα ἐφ᾽ ὑμᾶς ἀναπαύεται.   ¹⁵μὴ γάρ τις ὑμῶν πασχέτω ὡς

great precision : the " lustre " of the glory (as in Targum on Is. vi. 3, with which cf. Ezek. x. 4, τοῦ φέγγους τῆς δόξης κυρίου, Baruch v. 9, τῷ φωτὶ τῆς δόξης, Ps. Sol. ii. 5, τὸ κάλλος τῆς δόξης αὐτοῦ, Heb. i. 3, ἀπαύγασμα τῆς δόξης (cf. Wisd. vii. 26)) would fit the context equally well.

τῆς δόξης] i.e. the glory just spoken of as belonging to Christ (iv. 11) and soon to be revealed (iv. 13). "The rabbis kept the direct revelation of God for the hallowed past or the desired future, but at the same time they needed a suitable term for the presence of God ; they therefore coined the word Shekinah — 'the divine Condescension' or 'Presence' — to be used instead of the Deity Himself. Thus the verse of the Psalm (lxxxii. 1): 'God standeth in the congregation of God', is translated by the Targum, 'the divine Presence (Shekinah) resteth upon the congregation of the godly'. . . . Thus in the view of the rabbis Shekinah represents the visible part of the divine majesty" (Kohler, op. cit. pp. 197 f.). An alternative view, on the other hand, is that Shekinah " denotes the inner source and cause of the outward, glorious manifestation " (Boobyer, St. Mark and the Transfiguration Story, p. 80), and the rabbinic phrase, "the glory of the Shekinah" is cited in its support. But in any case, Shekinah, like Barnashā (Son of Man), was almost untranslateable into Greek ; but τὸ τῆς δόξης would have been intelligible in this sense to any Greek-speaking Jew, and its use here may be taken to indicate that St. Peter envisaged Jewish Christians amongst his readers. Whether ἡ δόξα by itself ever means the Shekinah in N.T. except in Rom. ix. 4 is doubtful ; Bengel and Mayor support this meaning in Jas. ii. 1, regarding it as a title of Christ, but the instances they cite, though numerous, are none the less unconvincing. τὸ τῆς δόξης on the other hand, especially in the

present context, is another matter. And Tertullian may so have understood it, for he translates, quod gloria et dei spiritus requiescit in vobis (Scorp. xii.).

Passages such as 1 Kings viii. 21, Is. lx. 1, 2, 7, Hag. ii. 7, with their allusions to God's glory rising upon Jerusalem and God's house of prayer being glorified and full of His glory, would have been suggested to the minds of Jewish Christian readers. And cf. the prayer in Ps. xc. 17. The converse is expressed in 2 Esdras vii. 112, " The present age is not the End ; the glory of God abides not therein continuously ". The idea that the glory of God is manifested specially in those who suffer in His Name was an essential part of our Lord's teaching about His Passion (Jn. xii. 23, xiii. 31, cf. also 2 Cor. iv. 17, Phil. ii. 9, Heb. ii. 9), and embodied in the concrete event of the Transfiguration ; and it was not without Jewish parallels (cf. Abrahams, The Glory of God, p. 86). What St. Peter means here is that the Shekinah, which was manifested in Christ's Transfiguration and Passion, was manifested likewise in the sufferings of His Church when rightly borne. St. Paul is perhaps expressing the same idea in 2 Cor. xii. 9, ἥδιστα οὖν μᾶλλον καυχήσομαι ἐν ταῖς ἀσθενείαις μου, ἵνα ἐπισκηνώσῃ ἐπ᾽ ἐμὲ ἡ δύναμις τοῦ Χριστοῦ.

Lebreton, History of the Dogma of the Trinity, i. pp. 86-9 has a useful discussion of this passage. And cf. J. Lightfoot's comment (Works, v. p. 330 [ed. 1822]): " We need not dispute what this 'Spirit of Glory' is ; take it for the spirit of holiness, and it gives but its right title ".

καὶ τὸ τοῦ Θεοῦ Πνεῦμα] He passes from the language of Jewish piety and hope to that of Christian experience, which was the true fulfilment of the other and was familiar to Gentile members of the communities addressed. If the Shekinah represented the institutional side of religion, the Spirit represented its personal and mystical side. An important parallel to the sequence of thought in this passage is to be found in 2 Cor. iii. 17, 18, where δόξα and πνεῦμα are brought into connexion with one another. St. Paul speaks of Christians reflecting (cf. Plummer, I.C.C. *in loc.*) as in a mirror the glory of the Lord, and being changed into the image there mirrored from glory to glory, i.e. by a continual process of glorification — καθάπερ ἀπὸ κυρίου πνεύματος, " as is natural under the influence of the Lord the Spirit " (cf. Goudge, Westminster Commentary on 2 Corinthians for the exegesis of this passage). The Spirit, that is to say, is the transforming agency who causes the hearts of believers to be conformed more and more to the glory of the Lord and to express it in their lives. It is evident that both Apostles are thinking of the relationship of the glory of God to the Holy Spirit. For St. Paul in 2 Cor. iii. and iv., the Gospel is the gospel of the glory of the Messiah (iv. 4, cf. Abrahams, *op. cit.* ch. ii.) ; Christ is the image of God, and in His face is revealed so much of the divine glory as is communicable to men, and this is made known by the Apostles, and produces illumination in the hearts of believers (iv. 6) ; believers are like a mirror reflecting this glory, and being transformed into the likeness of the image they reflect (iii. 18) ; and the Holy Spirit is the source and agent of this transformation (iii. 18), and engraves Christ upon believers' hearts, as letters were engraved upon the stone tablets of the Law (iii. 2, 3). Throughout the two chapters the metaphors are difficult and have given rise to various interpretations ; but it seems clear that St. Paul thinks of the glory as (1) expressed in the face of Christ (iv. 6), (2) reflected in the lives of believers, because imparted to their inward being (iii. 18), and of the Spirit as the agent of this communication and of the process of increased transforma-

tion which it sets up. St. Peter, on the other hand, seems to represent a more primitive and inchoate type of thought. The glory of God (1) is already Christ's (iv. 11), and (2) will soon be revealed in all its majesty ; meanwhile (3) its presence rests on the persecuted Church, as the *Shekinah* did on the Israelites and the tabernacle and the temple ; and (4) in the glory there rests also on the Church the Spirit of God, which is neither fully identified with it (καὶ τό) nor fully differentiated from it (singular ἀναπαύεται).

For similar doctrinal development of the Wisdom of God in connexion with Christ and with the Word and the Spirit cf. Rendel Harris, *The Prologue to St. John's Gospel.*

ἐφ' ὑμᾶς] The accusative expresses the *motion* of the Spirit, i.e. " comes to rest upon ".

ἀναπαύεται] used of the Spirit in Num. xi. 25, 26, ἐπανεπαύσατο τὸ πνεῦμα ἐπ' αὐτούς (the 70 elders), Is. xi. 2, ἀναπαύσεται ἐπ' αὐτὸν (the Davidic Messiah) πνεῦμα τοῦ θεοῦ. Elsewhere in LXX, with very few exceptions, ἀναπαύεσθαι means to " cease ", " have rest ". Cf. also Is. xi. 10, καὶ ἔσται ἡ ἀνάπαυσις αὐτοῦ τιμή. Jewish rabbis (*Berakoth*, 31 A) maintained that the glory of God could not rest on man except in joy. Thus, the *Shekinah* rested on students of the Law, both corporately and individually (Abrahams, *op. cit.* pp. 80, 81) ; and we find it stated of Hillel in the Talmud (*Sanh.* 11a), " There is one here fit that the *Shekinah* should rest on him, but the generation is unworthy ". Irenaeus evidently has 1 Pet. iv. 14 in mind in *A.H.* iv. xxxiii. 9, where after quoting Matt. v. 12 to shew the continuity of the Church's sufferings with those of the Hebrew prophets, he concludes : *quoniam nove quidem, sed idem Spiritus requiescens super eam, ab his qui non recipiunt Verbum Dei, persecutionem patitur.*

15. μὴ γάρ τις κτλ.] For the curiously cynical attitude of Basilides to

φονεύς, ἢ κλέπτης, ἢ κακοποιός, ἢ ὡς ἀλλοτριοεπίσκοπος· ¹⁶εἰ
δὲ ὡς Χριστιανός, μὴ αἰσχυνέσθω, δοξαζέτω δὲ τὸν Θεὸν ἐν
τῷ ὀνόματι τούτῳ. ¹⁷ὅτι ὁ καιρὸς τοῦ ἄρξασθαι τὸ κρῖμα ἀπὸ

this passage cf. Clem. Alex. *Strom.*
IV. xii. 600 [P].

κακοποιός] Cf. ii. 12 note. But
Tertullian (*Scorp.* xii.) translates it
here by *maleficus*, " magician " ; and
since other specific types of crime have
just been mentioned, this is possibly
right. Tacitus, *Ann.* ii. 69, speaks
of *alia malefica, quis creditur animas
numinibus infernis sacrari*; and
Furneaux (on Tac. *Ann.* ii. 27) observes that the magicians of Tiberius'
day " were often neither more nor less
than professional poisoners ".

ἢ ὡς ἀλλοτριοεπίσκοπος] *or as a
busybody*; for which Zahn and
Windisch aptly quote Epict. *Enchir.*
III. xxii. 97 (of the Cynics), διὰ τοῦτο
οὔτε περίεργος οὔτε πολυπράγμων ἐστὶν
ὁ οὕτως διακείμενος, οὐ γὰρ τὰ ἀλλότρια
πολυπραγμονεῖ, ὅταν τὰ ἀνθρώπινα ἐπισκοπῇ, ἀλλὰ τὰ ἴδια. Cf. also Terence,
Heaut. I. i. 23, 24 (E. H. B.), and Soph.
Trach. 616, 617 (Deianira speaks),

ἀλλ᾽ ἕρπε, καὶ φύλασσε πρῶτα μὲν
νόμον,
τὸ μὴ ᾽πιθυμεῖν πομπὸς ὢν περισσὰ
δρᾶν.

The famous definition in Plato, *Rep.*
433 A, τὸ τὰ αὑτοῦ πράττειν καὶ μὴ
πολυπραγμονεῖν δικαιοσύνη ἐστί, which
becomes in a sense the theme of the
Republic, is likewise to the point. The
repetition of ὡς between ἢ and ἀλλο-
τριοεπίσκοπος indicates that our author
has passed from his catalogue of legal
crimes to the social nuisance of inter-
fering in other men's business ̄and
professing to put them to rights. Tact-
less attempts to convert neighbours, or
to improve those who are already converted, are faults not confined to the
Church of apostolic days. Nor were
they unknown to the Jews, cf. Ecclus.
iii. 23, ἐν τοῖς περισσοῖς τῶν ἔργων σου
μὴ περιεργάζου (also *ib.* xi. 9, 10), and
Test. Iss. v. 1, μὴ περιεργαζόμενοι τοῦ
πλησίον τὰς πράξεις ; and the warning

may have been specially needed in
mixed churches of Jewish and Gentile
Christians. Tertullian's translation
(*Scorp.* xii.), *alieni speculator*, seems
to bear out this interpretation. Other
interpretations, such as *alieni* (*argenti*)
cupidus (Calvin, Beza, Estius), *delator*
(Jülicher), conformity to heathen customs (Bigg), have little to support
them.

16. εἰ δὲ ὡς Χριστιανός] On the deductions drawn by Ramsay from this
sentence see Introd. p. 54. Since
Christians in Antioch were already
called by that name some years before
the middle of the first century (Acts
xi. 26), there is no difficulty in
supposing that the name was also
current in Asia Minor some years
later, as it was in Rome (Tac. *Ann.*
xv. 44, Suet. *Nero*, 16). Whether the
term as St. Peter uses it is still rather
a nickname than a title, we cannot
say ; but it was an accepted title by
the time of Ignatius (*Eph.* xi. 2, *Rom.*
iii., *ad Polyc.* vii.). On the alternative reading in ℵ Χρηστιανός cf.
Bigg and Blenkin : Suet. *Claud.* 25,
impulsore Chresto, shows that that
form was current in Rome. With the
termination -ιανός cf. Ἡρωδιανοί in
the Gospels.

ἐν τῷ ὀνόματι τούτῳ] *by virtue of
bearing this name*, i.e. the name of
Christian. ἐν is possibly instrumental
(cf. Moulton, *op. cit.* pp. 12, 61), but
more probably connotes " the sphere
in which ", as in i. 2, iii. 16 ; and here
the sphere is twofold, outwardly one of
obloquy, and inwardly one of privilege,
providing the environment and opportunity for glorifying God, cf. ii. 12,
iv. 11, 16. Grammatically, parallels
are afforded by Acts ii. 38, iv. 10 ; but
a much commoner phrase in N.T. is
ἐπ τῷ ὀνόματι, on which see Winer,
op. cit. p. 490. εἰς ὄνομα in Matt. x. 41
has the same meaning as ἐν ὀνόματι in

τοῦ οἴκου τοῦ Θεοῦ· εἰ δὲ πρῶτον ἀφ᾿ ἡμῶν, τί τὸ τέλος τῶν
ἀπειθούντων τῷ τοῦ Θεοῦ εὐαγγελίῳ; ¹⁸καὶ Εἰ ὁ δίκαιος μόλις
σώζεται, ὁ ἀσεβὴς καὶ ἁμαρτωλὸς ποῦ φανεῖται; ¹⁹ὥστε καὶ
οἱ πάσχοντες κατὰ τὸ θέλημα τοῦ Θεοῦ πιστῷ κτίστῃ παρα-

our passage, and cf. also Matt. xxviii.
19, Acts viii. 16, where εἰς ὄνομα is constructed with βαπτίζεσθαι. MM quote
from Deissmann a first-century inscription where the dative τῷ τῆς
πόλεως ὀνόματι (without preposition)
means " as representing the city ",
an illustration more pertinent to Mk.
ix. 41 than to this passage. The
variant reading (KLP al.) ἐν τῷ μέρει
τούτῳ, " on that account ", has little
authority and looks like a gloss.
[E. H. B. suggests that the gloss may
none the less be instructive, and point
to the correct translation being " on
his account ", i.e. because he suffers as
a Christian. Swete gives ὄνομα this
meaning in Mk. ix. 41, i.e. " on the
score that ", and cites Thuc. iv. 60,
ὀνόματι ἐννόμῳ ξυμμαχίας, " under the
fair name of alliance " (Livingstone).
But a closer parallel is to be found, I
think, in the Latin *hoc nomine*, and the
Marcan phrase may be a Latinism.]

17-19.· The climax of the section.
Judgment is beginning at the house of
God. If it is so severe there, what will
it be for unbelievers ? (Cf. Lk. xxiii.
31, " If they do these things in a green
tree, what shall be done in the dry ? " ;
Jer. xxv. 29, Ezek. xxi. 3, 4.) But
Christians can commit themselves into
God's hands in perfect serenity.

For the parallels both of thought
and phrase between this passage and
2 Thess. i. 4-12 (also 1 Thess. v.)
cf. Essay II, pp. 450-2, and Table
XIV (*f*). The indications point to a
Persecution-*tōrah* underlying both.

17. ὁ καιρὸς] Cf. note on i. 11.
With ὁ καιρός sc. ἐστί, " now is ".

τὸ κρῖμα] For this form cf. Acts
xxiv. 25, Heb. vi. 2, Rev. xx. 4.

ἀπὸ τοῦ οἴκου τοῦ Θεοῦ] i.e. as
prophesied e.g. in Mal. iii. 1-5, where
the Lord suddenly comes to His
temple " as a refiner's fire " (cf. πύρω-

σις in verse 12 above), and begins by
purifying the sons of Levi. Two ideas
are combined in these verses : (1) that
the divine Judgment begins at the
house of God, an idea expressed by
our Lord in the concrete action of the
Cleansing of the Temple, (2) that it is
already operative in the trials suffered
by the Christian community. For a
fuller discussion cf. Add. Note J,
pp. 299-303.

E. C. Selwyn's view (*St. Luke the
Prophet*, pp. 141 ff.) that St. Peter is
drawing here on *Enoch* xci. and that
ἀπὸ τοῦ οἴκου means " with the building
of the house of God ", as in 1 Pet. ii. 5,
is well summarized by Blenkin (*op. cit.*
pp. 109, 110 note) ; and his criticisms
of it are, I think, convincing.

εἰ δὲ πρῶτον] an *a fortiori* argument,
as in Lk. xxiii. 31. " The judgment,
which is more tolerable at the beginning, gradually becomes more severe "
(Bengel).

18. καὶ Εἰ ὁ δίκαιος κτλ.] The author
clinches his point by a quotation from
Prov. xi. 31 (LXX). In the application to the Christian Church, the
righteous is " hardly ", i.e. only with
difficulty, saved, owing to the severity
of the trials which he has to endure.
Cf. the *verba Christi* in Mk. xiii. 19, 20.

19. ὥστε καὶ] *wherefore also.* For
ὥστε meaning *quare, itaque* cf. Winer,
op. cit. p. 377. καί introduces a new
thought : the certainty of divine
justice being exercised is a call to a
complete serenity of faith in God.
The ἄνεσις promised at the last in
2 Thess. i. 7 is to have its counterpart
now in the serenity of trust in God.
Had St. Peter in mind our Lord's
word from the Cross, πάτερ, εἰς χεῖράς
σου παρατίθεμαι τὸ πνεῦμά μου (Lk
xxiii. 46, citing Ps. xxxi. 5) ? Cf. also
St. Stephen's words, Acts vii. 59 ; and
1 Clem. xxvii. 1.

τιθέσθωσαν τὰς ψυχὰς αὐτῶν ἐν ἀγαθοποιΐᾳ.

V. ¹Πρεσβυτέρους οὖν ἐν ὑμῖν παρακαλῶ ὁ συμπρεσβύτερος

κατὰ τὸ θέλημα τοῦ Θεοῦ] Cf. iii. 17, a verse which has just been given a fuller meaning in iv. 17. Note that the outcome of this suffering according to God's will, and the self-committal which it must lead to, is not resignation, but active well-doing (ἀγαθοποιΐα).

πιστῷ κτίστῃ] For κτίστῃ, which is ἅπαξ λεγόμενον here in N.T., cf. 2 Sam. xxii. 32, 2 Macc. i. 24, 1 Clem. xix. 2 : E. H. B. adds *Hermet.* xiii., (let us praise God) τῷ πάσης φύσεως κτίστῃ. In literary Greek the word means "founder" or "colonizer", cf. Dion. Halic. *Ant. Rom.* I. i. 126. He is faithful in that He will abide by His covenant, cf. 1 Thess. v. 24, 2 Thess. iii. 3, 1 Cor. i. 9, x. 13. "The epithet πιστός is selected, because of the trust implied in παρατιθέσθωσαν, the title Creator, because it involves power which is able, and love which is willing, to guard His creatures" (Bigg).

παρατιθέσθωσαν] παρατίθεσθαι, παραθήκη were used in classical Greek of anything deposited with a friend for safe-keeping. But the word did not always have prudential associations, cf. *Od.* iii. 74, where ψυχὰς παρθέμενοι is used of the willingness of pirates to "stake their lives" on their enterprises. For the meaning in N.T. cf. especially Lk. xxiii. 46 (Ps. xxxi. 5), Acts xiv. 23, xx. 32 ; also 1 Tim. i. 18, 2 Tim. ii. 2.

ἐν ἀγαθοποιΐᾳ] a keyword of this Epistle : cf. ii. 14, 20 (with note), iii. 6. 1 Clem. ii. 2 (cf. Lightfoot's note), 7, xxxiii. 1, xxxiv. 2, fully bear out the meaning " active well-doing ".

v. Third Ethical Section, and concluding greetings.

An intimate personal note runs through this section, the author alluding to himself and his own experience and standing more directly than heretofore, and addressing his readers, especially those in the ministry, with primary regard to their pastoral relationship to one another in the Church.

Earlier themes, such as the need for humility and wakefulness, and the promise of grace to stand firm in persecution and of glory at the last, are repeated. His colleagues and disciples in the Church at Rome join in his greetings ; and the Epistle closes with the *Pax vobiscum.*

1. Πρεσβυτέρους] The word is used here in its official connotation, while in verse 5 below it refers to those who are " older " in years, as in 1 Tim. v. 1. Cf. Essay II, pp. 435-7. The term is not further defined, but probably includes all who have any kind of authorized pastoral office and function. Cf. the προϊστάμενοι of 1 Thess. v. 12, Rom. xii. 8, and the ἡγούμενοι of Heb. xiii. 7. Not all local churches would be served by the same type of minister, but the local minister most commonly found exercising pastoral care in the Christian communities was the " presbyter " : cf. Acts xiv. 23, xx. 17. The term was taken over by the Church from the synagogue, and Deissmann has shewn that its use both in Judaism and in the Church may have been facilitated by the fact that in Egypt and in Asia Minor πρεσβύτεροι was the technical term for the members of civil corporations : in some cases, indeed, as at Pergamus in the middle of the first century A.D., it appears that the authority of these officers, who constituted the Γερουσία of a city, was sacred as well as civic. Cf. Deissmann, *Bible Studies* (Engl. Tr.), pp. 154 f., 233 f. We may note also that those chosen for the office of πρεσβύτερος, whether in the civic life of the Hellenistic cities or in the religious life of the Hellenistic churches, would usually have been of some age. On the functions and place of the presbyterate generally in the primitive Church cf. Armitage Robinson in *The Early History of the Church and Ministry*, pp. 82 ff., A. C. Headlam, *The Doctrine of the Church and Re-*

καὶ μάρτυς τῶν τοῦ Χριστοῦ παθημάτων, ὁ καὶ τῆς μελλούσης

union, pp. 64 ff. For a criticism of the inferences derived by Streeter from this verse cf. Wand, *op. cit.* pp. 126 f.

οὖν] Some authorities omit οὖν, Cod. Sin. reads οὖν τοὺς ἐν ὑμῖν, Vulg Copt Syr omit οὖν but insert τοὺς before ἐν ὑμῖν. The text printed above is that of AB and is accepted by WH and Souter. The meaning is not affected whichever reading is followed.

ὁ συμπρεσβύτερος] The word, which seems to be coined for the occasion (though MM give an example of συμπρεσβευτής of date 120 B.C.), expresses not only the Apostle's modesty (Windisch) but still more his sympathy with the presbyters addressed : he knew the measure of their responsibility at first hand, and like Ezekiel (Ezek. iii. 15) identifies himself with them. The function which he and they had in common was that of pastoral care and government, just as that which led Ignatius (*Eph.* ii., *Magn.* ii., *Philad.* iv., *Smyrn.* xii.) to speak of the deacons as his σύνδουλοι was ministration. Cf. the words used by a bishop in the institution of a parish priest, *accipe curam tuam et meam* ; also Lightfoot, on Col. iv. 7 and Ign. *Eph.* ii., and, for examples of bishops addressing their clergy as " compresbyteri ", *Philippians*, p. 230 (ed. 1908). The definite article preceding συμπρεσβύτερος is not without significance, and signifies either the way in which St. Peter was thought of, and wished to be thought of, in the Church generally, or the particular memories which the churches of northern Asia Minor had of him. Thus Lightfoot writes (*Philippians*, p. 198), " The title ' fellow-presbyter ', which he applies to himself, would doubtless recall to the memory of his readers the occasions when he himself had presided with the elders and guided their deliberations ".

καὶ μάρτυς . . . παθημάτων] The writer thus claims to have been an eyewitness of Christ's passion. Eyewit-

ness was of the essence of the Apostolic office and function ; but why does not St. Peter speak of himself rather as an eyewitness of the resurrection (cf. Lk. xxiv. 12, 34, Acts i. 22) or of the passion and resurrection combined (cf. Acts i. 8, v. 32, x. 39) ? The reason may lie partly in the special relevance of the theme of the Passion to the hardships being endured by his readers ; but it is equally attributable to the collocation of παθήματα with δόξα in the verse as a whole, which is characteristic of this Epistle. Cf. i. 11, iii. 18-22, iv. 13, 14, v. 10. And here, as in v. 10 and Rom. viii. 18, it is not so much the resurrection as the ultimate glory which provides the balance to the earthly sufferings, whether of Christ or of Christians.

ὁ καὶ . . . κοινωνός] *who have also had experience of the glory that is to be revealed.* For the last phrase cf. Rom. viii. 18. But in what sense was the author a " sharer " in that final glory ? Commentators, almost without exception, extend the future tense expressed in μελλούσης to cover κοινωνός as well, as though ἐσόμενος were to be understood with it ; and the phrase is then interpreted as deriving from a definite promise made by Jesus to the Apostle such as those recorded in Matt. xix. 28, Jn. xiii. 36. Both Estius and Alford, however, allude to the view held by some scholars that the reference here is to St. Peter's experience at the Transfiguration ; and I cannot doubt that this view is correct. For, (1) κοινωνός, with its correlatives, is a word that normally connotes in the New Testament some kind of *concrete experience.* [Cf. V. Taylor's discussion of the word and its cognates in *Forgiveness and Reconciliation*, pp. 131-4.] Only here in N.T. is it used with δόξα, though there are places where it might have seemed suitable. (2) The phrase ὁ . . . κοινωνός is simple and correctly formed, the article being divided from its noun by

ἀποκαλύπτεσθαι δόξης κοινωνός· ²ποιμάνατε τὸ ἐν ὑμῖν ποίμνιον

the object of the noun; and the definite article, as in the case of ὁ συμπρεσβύτερος, would recall something which the readers already knew. Evidence of the currency of the narrative is supplied by Lk. ix. 36 (note especially ἐν ἐκείναις ταῖς ἡμέραις). Had the author been referring to his own future destiny, he could have written κοινωνήσων; though the statement would scarcely be in keeping with the author's spirit as this Epistle reveals it. (3) Fresh light of great importance has recently been thrown on the meaning of the Transfiguration by Mr. G H. Boobyer, in his *St. Mark and the Transfiguration Story* (1942). After pointing out the difficulties in the view that the Transfiguration-narrative was either a resurrection story or an ascension story, or that the Transfiguration itself was a prediction of either the resurrection or the ascension, Mr. Boobyer gives reasons which, to my mind, are overwhelming for believing that the true meaning of the experience was eschatological, and that it gave a foretaste of the glory of the Parusia. As Kittel says (*Th.W*[b].*z.N.T.*, article δόξα, ii. p. 152), " seine Verklärung ist Vorwegnahme seiner Eschatologie ", a statement fully borne out by the N.T. use both of ἀποκαλύπτειν and of δόξα. Kittel's words give us exactly the background needed for the interpretation of ὁ καὶ τῆς μελλούσης ἀποκαλύπτεσθαι δόξης κοινωνός. He had experienced, and was known to have experienced, a special revelation of the glory which had been restored to Jesus at the ascension (1 Pet. i. 21) and would be manifested to all when He came again at the End. The phrase is thus a development of the idea contained in μάρτυς: he was their fellow-presbyter, bound to them in sympathy through sharing their pastoral care; he had the authority of an Apostle which derived from having been an eyewitness of Christ's passion; nay more, he had been one of those three who

were specially privileged to have had experience, during Christ's life on earth, of His ultimate glory. And this title to address them as he does is stated not as the assertion of a claim, though a very high claim is in fact involved, nor as implying any personal merit, but quietly and humbly, as the statement of facts with which they were familiar, even if they had not fully realized before their cumulative weight.

If this interpretation be correct, the much more overt allusion to the Transfiguration in 2 Pet. i. 16-18 is a later development of the theme, as 2 Pet. ii. 4 ff. is of the theme of the *Descensus* in 1 Pet. iii. 19, 20. Loisy (*Remarques sur la Littérature épistolaire du N.T.*, pp. 130 ff.) regards the *Apocalypse of Peter* and the Apocryphal *Gospel of Peter* as the sources of the two ideas respectively in both Epistles. But the assumption is quite arbitrary, and the priority of 1 Peter to all the other " Petrine " documents accounts for the facts satisfactorily.

2. ποιμάνατε] *tend*: by discipline and doctrine (Bengel). Cf. *supra*, ii. 25. So Hilary interprets ποιμαίνειν (*in Ps.* ii. 9) as *pastoraliter regere*. The word is classical (Homer, Hesiod, Euripides, Plato, Theocritus), and includes the whole of a shepherd's care for his flock, and not feeding only. So too throughout Ezek. xxxiv., which underlies our Lord's teaching in Mk. vi. 34, Matt. xviii. 11-14, Lk. xv. 3-7, Jn. x. 1-16. Note how, in recording the Lord's threefold pastoral charge to St. Peter in Jn. xxi. 15 ff., St. John uses the word βόσκε of the lambs and ποίμαινε of the sheep, the latter needing a more general care than the former, for the ewes do much of this as well as of the feeding. The charge to the elders here derives a special poignancy from the charge which St. Peter himself had received, if he were the author. For similar words on St. Paul's lips cf. Acts xx. 28.

τοῦ Θεοῦ, ἐπισκοποῦντες μὴ ἀναγκαστῶς ἀλλ' ἑκουσίως κατὰ
Θεόν, μηδὲ αἰσχροκερδῶς ἀλλὰ προθύμως, ³μηδ' ὡς κατακυρι-

τὸ ἐν ὑμῖν ποίμνιον τοῦ Θεοῦ] The
flock is God's, as in Ezek. xxxiv. 31,
Ps. c. 3, and it is distributed in the
different localities where the presbyters
live and work (ἐν ὑμῖν). Erasmus and
Calvin render τὸ ἐν ὑμῖν as "to the
best of your power"; but the sequence
of the words is against this.

ἐπισκοποῦντες] *exercising your pastoral care.* The word connotes the
function of the ruler or "guardian" in
Plato's ideal state (*Rep.* 506 B). For
the LXX cf. 2 Chron. xxxiv. 12.
Only here in N.T. is the verb ἐπι-
σκοπεῖν used in this sense, its meaning
in Heb. xii. 15 not being parallel. The
noun ἐπίσκοπος is used of various kinds
of overseership in LXX, cf. Num.
xxxi. 14, Neh. xi. 9, 14, 22, 1 Macc.
i. 51, and always connotes administrative responsibility, and it has this
sense in St. Paul's address to the
Ephesian elders at Miletus, Acts xx.
28; whence it becomes in N.T. a term
synonymous at first with πρεσβύτερος;
cf. Lightfoot's essay on the Ministry
in his *Philippians.* The office itself is
expressed by ἐπισκοπή, 1 Tim. iii. 1, cf.
Ps. cix. 8 quoted in Acts.i. 20.

ἀναγκαστῶς] here only in N.T. St.
Paul writes ἐξ ἀνάγκης, 2 Cor. ix. 7,
where the reference is to almsgiving,
and the contrast is with a course freely
and cheerfully chosen, and κατ' ἀνάγκην
in Philem. 14, where he solicits his
reader's willing co-operation (κατὰ
ἑκούσιον) in the release of Onesimus.
What is the nature of the "necessity"
which St. Peter has here in mind?
Presumably the moral necessity which
attaches to the discharge of the duties
of an office. That, however, is not
enough without the right spirit and
motive: there is all the difference,
especially in spiritual matters, between the man who does his work for
no other reason than that he has to do
it, and the man who does it willingly,
as being in God's service. The words
κατὰ Θεόν are omitted by B and some

other MSS., followed by WH, but the
weight of textual evidence is in their
favour (ℵ am 13 vulg syr copt); and
they serve to make ἑκουσίως sparkle
with the motive of religious vocation.
On the phrase κατὰ Θεόν cf. note on
iv. 6 *supra.*

μηδὲ αἰσχροκερδῶς] The accusation
of making money out of religion was
brought against Samuel and against
St. Paul, and was vigorously rebutted
by both, cf. 1 Sam. xii. 3-5, Acts xx. 33.
St. Paul upheld the principle of a paid
ministry, on the strength of the *verbum
Christi* in Matt. x. 10, "the labourer is
worthy of his hire", though he took no
payment himself, 1 Cor. ix. 7-12,
2 Cor. xii. 13-17. We may infer from
1 Tim. iii. 8, v. 17, 18 that the presbyters and deacons were usually paid,
though the repeated warnings against
covetousness in the ministry, as in
1 Tim. iii. 3, 8, Tit. i. 7, 11, Polyc. *ad
Phil.* xi. 1, suggest that the remuneration was small and probably uncertain
in amount. What is forbidden is not
the desire for fair remuneration, but
the *sordid* love of gain. Cf. the charge
and countercharge in Soph. *Ant.*
1055 f. :

KP. τὸ μαντικὸν γὰρ πᾶν φιλάργυρον
        γένος.
TE. τὸ δ' ἐκ τυράννων αἰσχροκέρδειαν
        φιλεῖ.

Aristotle, *Eth. Nicom.* IV. i. 43, describes as αἰσχροκερδεῖς those who make
profit from illegitimate sources. For
their meanness cf. Theophr. *Char.* 26.

προθύμως] *with enthusiasm*: since
"the enjoyment consists in feeding the
flock, and not in the pay" (Bengel).
The word is not found elsewhere in
N.T., but is in LXX and literary
Greek, cf. Dion. Halic. *Ant. Rom.*
I. lviii. 148, and frequently in Dion
Chrysostom.

3. κατακυριεύοντες] *domineering
over*: cf. Ps. x. 10, κύψει καὶ πεσεῖται
ἐν τῷ αὐτὸν κατακυριεῦσαι τῶν πενήτων.
The word in LXX means to "master"

εὐόντες τῶν κλήρων ἀλλὰ τύποι γινόμενοι τοῦ ποιμνίου. ⁴καὶ
φανερωθέντος τοῦ ἀρχιποίμενος κομιεῖσθε τὸν ἀμαράντινον τῆς

or to "rule", as a stronger over a weaker. The *verbum Christi* in Mk. x. 42 ff. may well be in the author's mind ; οἴδατε ὅτι οἱ δοκοῦντες ἄρχειν τῶν ἐθνῶν κατακυριεύουσιν αὐτῶν, καὶ οἱ μεγάλοι αὐτῶν κατεξουσιάζουσιν αὐτῶν. οὐχ οὕτω δέ ἐστιν ἐν ὑμῖν κτλ., all the more as it closes with a statement of the example set by our Lord Himself of the opposite spirit and practice.

τῶν κλήρων] *your appointed portions*, or *assignments*, cf. Acts viii. 21, xxvi. 18, Col. i. 12. On the last passage Lightfoot quotes Chrysostom, διὰ τί κλῆρον καλεῖ; δεικνὺς ὅτι οὐδεὶς ἀπὸ κατορθωμάτων (" good works ") οἰκείων βασιλείας τυγχάνει. The responsibilities of the presbyters were not due to their innate gifts of leadership, but to God's call. In classical Greek κλῆρος was an allotment of land assigned to a citizen by the civic authorities (cf. Ar. *Pol.* II. iii. 7, 1265 b 15), the distribution frequently being made by lot, as in Thuc. iii. 50. The term was therefore familiar to Gentile readers ; while Jewish members of the Church would have found in it a still richer meaning owing to its association with κληρονομία, a word already used in i. 4. The κλῆροι or spheres of pastoral care were the several parts of the spiritual κληρονομία into which Christians had entered. The word " clergy " is derived from this, though this sense is not found before Tertullian (Blenkin). Bigg may be right in seeing here an allusion to Deut. ix. 29 (where Moses speaks of Israel as God's λαός and κλῆρος), seeing that God's mighty hand (ἐν τῇ χειρί σου τῇ κραταιᾷ) is alluded to there and also here in verse 6.

τύποι γινόμενοι] *shewing yourselves examples.* For τύπος in this non-classical sense of " example " cf. I Thess. i. 7 and other examples given in the note on iii. 21 *supra*. The usage is rare in LXX, but cf. 4 Macc. vi. 19,

καὶ αὐτοὶ μὲν ἡμεῖς γενοίμεθα τοῖς νέοις ἀσεβείας τύπος, ἵνα παράδειγμα γενώμεθα τῆς μιαροφαγίας. The root idea is a " pattern " or " model ", of which casts or copies were taken. γινόμενοι means more than ὄντες, since it suggests the length of time which is normally needed to shew the exemplary character of a priest or pastor.

4. φανερωθέντος] Cf. i. 20, where the reference is to the Incarnation, as in I Tim. iii. 16. For its application to the Second Coming cf. Col. iii. 4, I Jn. iii. 2 (Mk. iv. 22).

ἀρχιποίμενος] a beautiful word, ἅπαξ λεγόμενον in Scripture, but probably in the vernacular of the period. Cf. MM, *sub voc.*, and Deissmann, *Light from the Ancient East* (Engl. Tr. 1911), pp. 97-9. Symmachus uses it in place of the strange word νωκήθ, meaning " sheep-master ", in his version of 2 Kings iii. 4, and, still more significantly, it occurs in the Greek version of *Test. Jud.* viii. 1. The words are ἦσαν δέ μοι κτήνη πολλά, καὶ εἶχον ἀρχιποίμενα Ἱερὰμ τὸν Ὀδολομήτην ; and the date of this version is almost certainly before A.D. 50. Cf. Charles, *The Greek Versions of the Test. XII Patr.* p. ix. The Hebraic *nidus* of the image in O.T., illustrated in the note on verse 2 above, and our Lord's use of it in the Gospels, make the attempts of some scholars (cf. Perdelwitz, *op. cit.* pp. 99 ff.) to connect it with the ἀρχιβούκολος of the Mystery religions appear strangely far-fetched. The " good shepherd " of Jn. x. 11, 14 and " that great shepherd of the sheep " in Heb. xiii. 20, which fulfil the Messianic prophecy of Is. xl. 11, shew how the image had caught hold of Christian imagination. The Johannine phrase brings out the intrinsic quality of Christ's pastoral care and work ; that in Hebrews its all-embracing relationship to the universal Church ; while St. Peter's word ἀρχιποίμην underlines its relationship to

those who have pastoral charge in the
Christian ministry. In relation to
them Christ is the *chief* shepherd, set
over them yet sharing their function.
κομεῖσθε] See note on i. 9. κεκο-
μίσμεθα occurs with τὸν στέφανον τὸν
χρυσοῦν in 1 Macc. xiii. 37, meaning
" we have safely received ".

τὸν ἀμαράντινον . . . στέφανον] This
graceful phrase would have appealed
to Jewish and to Gentile Christians
alike. As well as being the emblem
of royalty (Ps. xxi. 3), crowns were
worn by bridegrooms at Jewish
weddings (Cant. i. 11, Is. lxi. 10,
lxii. 3); and from these sources, and
also from the Greek usages illustrated
below, which belonged to the Alex-
andrian environment of the Wisdom
literature, the word gathered round it,
and came to express, a number of
emotions and ideas. The element of
ostentation is seen in Is. xxii. 17, 21,
xxviii. 1, 3 (ὕβρεως); of legitimate
pride in Prov. xvii. 6, στέφανος γερόν-
των τέκνα τέκνων, cf. Prov. iv. 9 (Phil.
iv. 1); of success in Prov. xvi. 31, στέφανος καυχήσεως γῆρας, cf. Ezek. xvi.
12, xxiii. 42, 1 Thess. ii. 19, and especially Wisd. iv. 2, (ἀρετὴ) στεφανηφοροῦσα
πομπεύει, τὸν τῶν ἀμιάντων ἄθλων ἀγῶνα
νικήσασα, where the reference to Greek
games is clear; of grace and beauty in
Prov. iv. 9, Is. lxii. 3, Ezek. xxviii. 12
(κάλλους); of rejoicing in Ecclus. i. 11,
vi. 31, xv. 6 (ἀγαλλιάματος), cf. Lam. ii.
15 (εὐφροσύνης). Our present phrase,
"the crown of glory", occurs in
Jer. xiii. 18, καθῃρέθη ἀπὸ κεφαλῆς
ὑμῶν στέφανος δόξης ὑμῶν, and Is.
xxviii. 5, τῇ ἡμέρᾳ ἐκείνῃ ἔσται κύριος
σαβαὼθ ὁ στέφανος τῆς ἐλπίδος ὁ πλεκεὶς
τῆς δόξης τῷ καταλειφθέντι τοῦ λαοῦ.
In most of these cases the genitive
(ὕβρεως, καυχήσεως, ἐλπίδος, χαρίτων,
κάλλους, ἀγαλλιάματος, δόξης) is a
genitive of definition, as here and in
Jas. i. 12, Rev. ii. 10 (τὸν στέφανον τῆς
ζωῆς), 2 Tim. iv. 8 (ὁ τῆς δικαιοσύνης
στέφανος).

For Rabbinic uses of the metaphor
cf. *Pirqe Aboth*, iv. 19, i. 13, together
with Abrahams, *The Glory of God*,

pp. 697 f., where Hillel's insistence on
the need of humility before God gives
the crown is illustrated. Some Rabbis
spoke of the crown as woven out of
prayer.

But St. Peter's Gentile readers, who
were acquainted with the Greek *gymnasia* and the Greek games and
festivals, would have found his phrase
equally significant, and for them too
it would have religious, or at least
sacral, associations. For the four Pan-
hellenic festivals, famed in Greek
tradition and celebrated by Pindar
and Bacchylides, " were distinctively
the sacred meetings (ἱεροὶ ἀγῶνες) and
the games of the crown (στεφανῖται)",
in contrast with the numerous games
where prizes of value were given. Cf.
E. N. Gardiner, *Greek Athletic Sports
and Festivals*, p. 67. The primary
idea symbolized by the crown in Hellenistic society was that of victory.
Thus Pindar, *Ol.* viii. 99, extols the
achievement of the Blepsiad family,
ἔκτος οἷς ἤδη στέφανος περίκειται φυλλοφόρων ἀπ' ἀγώνων. And from this it
came to connote more generally a
crown of glory, an honour or distinguished reward, as in Soph. *Aj.* 464 f.,

τῶν ἀριστείων ἄτερ,

ὧν αὐτὸς ἔσχε στέφανον εὐκλείας μέγαν,
a passage apposite to our present purpose, for, as Jebb observes, στέφανον
εὐκλείας is an example of the genitive
of definition, like τῆς δόξης here, and
may be translated "glory-crown".
In a famous passage St. Paul combines the literal and the metaphorical
crowns, where he writes, ἐκεῖνοι μὲν
οὖν ἵνα φθαρτὸν στέφανον λάβωσιν,
ἡμεῖς δὲ ἄφθαρτον (1 Cor. ix. 25).

Enough has been said to illustrate
the various associations of the crown in
ancient life, both Jewish and Gentile.
The dominant idea is that of the reward
of victorious achievement, and closely
allied with it are the pride and honour
and rejoicing which the achievement
evokes. That Christ's crown of thorns
would have given to the Christian use
of the term a special significance is
probable enough; but it is unlikely

δόξης στέφανον. ⁵ὁμοίως, νεώτεροι, ὑποτάγητε πρεσβυτέροις.
πάντες δὲ ἀλλήλοις τὴν ταπεινοφροσύνην ἐγκομβώσασθε· ὅτι

that J. B. Mayor is right when, in commenting on Jas. i. 12, he says that the crown denotes the royalty of the Christian life. Such an idea was not foreign to St. Peter, as we can see from ii. 9 ; and our Lord's promise to the Twelve in Matt. xix. 28 was of an almost royal position. Cf. also 2 Tim. ii. 12. But there is no reason to narrow its reference here : rather, there lie behind it all the joyous and sacral associations of victorious achievement and its reward, which the word brought to the society of St. Peter's day.

ἀμαράντινον] The victor's crowns, as well as the garlands worn on festal occasions, were usually of leaves and flowers, such as myrtle, roses, oak, and ivy. Cf. φυλλοφόρων ἀπ' ἀγώνων in Pind. *Ol.* viii. 99 quoted above. In contrast to these crowns that of the victor in the Christian ministry was one that did not fade. Bigg rightly observes that ἀμαράντινος is not identical with ἀμάραντος of i. 4 or ἄφθαρτος of 1 Cor. ix. 25, but means " made of amaranths, or immortelles ". Immortelles are used to decorate graves in France to-day, and were presumably so used in seventeenth-century England : cf. Milton, *Lycidas*, 149 ff. :

> Bid Amarantus all his beauty shed,
> And Daffadillies fill their cups with tears,
> To strow the Laureat Herse where Lycid lies.

But these flowers were so named because they do not fade ; so that the meaning is the same.

τῆς δόξης] genitive of definition, as in many of the passages cited above. The crown of glory has for the Christian a special significance, when, as here, the idea of the unveiling of Christ's glory at the Parusia is present to the mind. The reward of the faithful and humble minister is that he will be given a share in the glory and joy of his Lord. Cf. Matt.

xxv. 21, 23. For similar phrases cf. Jas. i. 12 (crown of life), 2 Tim. iv. 8 (crown of righteousness). David is said in Ecclus. xlvii. 6 to have been given by God a διάδημα δόξης.

5. ὁμοίως] perhaps, as in iii. 1, 7, an original suture of the catechetical material current in the Church. Cf. note on iii. 1.

νεώτεροι] *ye younger people.* The reference here and in πρεσβυτέροις is to age and not official rank. Cf. Acts v. 6, 10, 1 Tim. v. 1, Tit. ii. 6. So Bengel, Bigg, Blenkin. Windisch's view that νεώτεροι means the " sheep ", i.e. the laity, has some support in Polyc. *ad Phil.* v. 3 ; but the probability that the phrase was in the early catechetical patterns points to the younger members of the Church being in St. Peter's mind. The transitions of thought are not difficult : the official " elders " of v. 1 suggests those who are senior in years (v. 5), from whom the presbyters would usually (though not always, 1 Tim. iv. 12) be drawn ; and the thought of them suggests the duty of deference (ὑποτάγητε) owed to them by the young. For a similar transition of thought, though with different words, cf. 1 Clem. i. 3 (with Lightfoot's note on τοῖς ἡγουμένοις), iii. 3, xxxi. 6. The application of the primitive Catechism to the position of the ministry in the Church in these passages, and even to the healing of schism in ι Clem. lvii. 1, calls for more attention than it has yet received.

πάντες δὲ] The author passes from the particular to the general : humility is incumbent on all members of the Church alike in their intercourse with one another. On the construction of ἀλλήλοις see below on ἐγκομβώσασθε.

ταπεινοφροσύνην] Cf. ταπεινόφρονες in iii. 8, and note there. Trench (*Synonyms* (ed. 1865), pp. 146 f.), after observing that in Greek writers ταπεινός almost always has a servile significance, yet maintains that Aristotle (*Eth. Nicom.* IV. iii. 4) is really a supporter of the Christian view, seeing that he advocates, or at least allows, a humble estimate of oneself, when that estimate is the true one. Plato (*Laws*, 716 A) pays a similar tribute to the well-balanced mind (ταπεινὸς καὶ κεκοσμημένος) which cleaves to justice. No doubt some of the rudiments of the humility, which St. Bernard describes as *virtus qua quis ex verissima sui cognitione sibi ipsi vilescit*, are here; but neither Plato nor Aristotle could have written St. Peter's ἀλλήλοις. Thomas Carlyle's comment in a letter to J. S. Mill is worth quoting: "'Walk humbly in well-doing'—there is no other road for one. It is long years since I first saw the meaning of humility (of self-killing, of Entsagen, as the Germans call it), and it came on me like water on one dying of thirst, and I felt it and still feel it to be the beginning of moral life." Creighton (*Life and Letters*, i. pp. 106-08) gives a similar testimony, based on Goethe; but it is the Greek rather than the Christian form of humility that is in question there, a knowledge of one's own capacities and their limits rather than a principle of reciprocal relationship.

ἐγκομβώσασθε] *bind unto yourselves*, as in "St. Patrick's Breastplate", "I bind unto myself to-day", etc. Suidas quotes Apollodorus Carystius (third-fourth century B.C.), τὴν ἐπωμίδα | πτύξασα διπλῆν ἄνωθεν ἐνεκομβωσάμην, and Epicharmus 4, εὖγε μὲν ὅτ' ἐπωμὶς ἐγκεκόμβωται καλῶς; and LS (1940) translate "bind a thing on oneself", "wear constantly". κόμβος was used especially of the fasteners of the sleeve-ends which served as gloves; and this usage is borne out by the A text of Gen. xlii. 35, where κόμβους appears for δεσμούς, and by τὰ ἐγκομβώματα in the Marchalianus text of Is. iii. 20. So Hesychius interprets κόσυμβος by δεσμός, ἀνάδεσμα, ἢ ἐγκόμβωμα. Bauer is therefore right (*G.D.Wᵇ.z.d. Schriften d.N.T.*) in rendering it

"to tie or put something on oneself", though the firmness of the clasp or fastening implied in the word must not be missed.

Such being the meaning of κόμβος, ἐγκόμβωμα could be used of any garment which was so "bound or fastened on" (cf. Suicer, *sub voc.*), whether the small white garment which a slave wore over his ἐξωμίς or sleeveless tunic, or a garment of some dignity (as in Is. iii. 20 (Qᵐᵍ)). The latter interpretation is supported by Bigg, the former by Wand. The Rev. A. W. Hopkinson writes to me to suggest that the garment in St. Peter's mind was the λέντιον, or towel used by slaves, with which our Lord girded Himself before washing the disciples' feet (Jn. xiii. 4, cf. Hoskyns, *in loc.*). The suggestion derives some support from the discourse that follows that incident (*ib.* 12-20, especially ἀλλήλων in verse 14), which in any case very aptly illustrates St. Peter's meaning. But we need not, in fact, connect the verb ἐγκομβώσασθε here with any particular kind of ἐγκόμβωμα. "Fasten firmly on" gives sufficient meaning in itself.

A further point arises with regard to the construction of ἀλλήλοις. Delling in Kittel's *Th.Wᵇ.z.N.T.*, following Suicer, Erasmus, Beza, and some MSS., would carry the sentence in 5a down to ἀλλήλοις and punctuate there, on the ground that the construction of the dative with ἐγκομβώσασθε is strange. The difficulty, however, is surely imaginary: the *dativus commodi* and the dative of relation, as e.g. in Plato, *Rep.* 598 D, ὑπολαμβάνειν δεῖ τῷ τοιούτῳ ὅτι εὐήθης τις ἄνθρωπος, give us all that we need, and the meaning is, "all of you, in your relations one with another, bind unto yourselves humility". ἀλλήλοις is constructed both with πάντες and with the verbal phrase: were it with the latter only, ἀλλήλοις would follow ἐγκομβώσασθε, cf. verse 14.

ὅτι κτλ.] As so often in this Epistle, ὅτι introduces the theological ground for an ethical injunction: cf. ii. 21, iii 18. E. H. B. observes that this

ὁ Θεὸς ὑπερηφάνοις ἀντιτάσσεται, ταπεινοῖς δὲ δίδωσι χάριν. [6]ταπεινώθητε οὖν ὑπὸ τὴν κραταιὰν χεῖρα τοῦ Θεοῦ, ἵνα ὑμᾶς

sentence was St. Augustine's favourite text.

ὁ Θεὸς κτλ.] cited from Prov. iii. 34, with the substitution, here as in Jas. iv. 6, of ὁ θεός for κύριος. Cf. 1 Clem. xxx. 2, where θεός is anarthrous. On the literary relation of this verse to Jas. iv. 6 see the discussion in Essay II, pp. 417 f. The interpretation of the O.T. passage is easier in 1 Peter than in James. In James it follows the well-known crux in Jas. iv. 5. Hort (The Epistle of St. James, in loc.) suggests that the γραφή alluded to there, not being any known O.T. passage may be " some intermediate source now lost to us ", and continues: " There are other reasons for supposing the N.T. writers to have used Greek paraphrases of the O.T. resembling the Hebrew Targums, and the words may have come literally from one of these ". It is precisely such paraphrases as these that we may conjecture the Jewish and the primitive Jewish-Christian community would have used for catechetical purposes; and Prov. iii. 34 may have been attached to one of these, in the form in which 1 Peter and James quote it. (We may compare Ecclus. iii. 18, ὅσῳ μέγας εἶ, τοσούτῳ ταπεινοῦ σεαυτόν, καὶ ἔναντι κυρίου εὑρήσεις χάριν.) In other words, the contrast between the friendship of the world and the friendship of God, which is the theme of Jas. iv. 4 and indeed of verses 1-3 also, is continued into verse 5. The sentiment is then aptly illustrated by Prov. iii. 34. Cf. 1 Clem. xxx. 8, θράσος καὶ αὐθάδεια καὶ τόλμα τοῖς κατηραμένοις ὑπὸ τοῦ θεοῦ· ἐπιείκεια καὶ ταπεινοφροσύνη καὶ πραΰτης παρὰ τοῖς ηὐλογημένοις ὑπὸ τοῦ θεοῦ. The sequence of thought in 1 Peter, on the other hand, is simple and straightforward. He is inculcating humility, and the passage from Proverbs — ἡ πανάρετος σοφία, as Clement of Rome names it (lvii. 3)—comes in to reinforce

his plea. And the meaning is not substantially different from that which the passage has in Jas. iv. 6, though differently approached: " the absolute self-surrender demanded of the Christian is rewarded by richer supplies of divine grace than he could otherwise receive " (Mayor, on Jas. iv. 6. Cf. also Knowling, The Epistle of St. James, p. 101. Unlike Mayor and Hort, however, I am inclined to interpret the sentence beginning πρὸς φθόνον ἐπιποθεῖ as expressing the contrast between human aspiration and divine grace : " jealousy of motive infects the aspirations of the human spirit, but God's gift is grace in prevailing measure ".)

6. ταπεινώθητε] St. Peter gives still further range to his teaching on humility. Beginning with the deference due from the younger to the older members of the Church, he has already extended it to a general principle of reciprocal relationship. But it is more than that : it is a general principle of their relationship to God, who not only gives grace to the humble, but will also vindicate them. ταπεινώθητε means not simply " humble yourselves " but " allow yourselves to be humbled, accept your humiliations " — those, namely, which the circumstances of the time brought so frequently upon Christian believers. The contrast between ταπεινοῦν and ὑψοῦν is an echo of such verba Christi as Matt. xxiii. 12, Lk. xiv. 11, xviii. 14; and Lk. i. 52 (Magnificat), recalling 1 Sam. ii. 7 (ταπεινοῖ καὶ ἀνυψοῖ). The sentiment is thoroughly Hebraic, cf. Pesiḳta R. p. 2a, cited by Abrahams, op. cit. p. 68, " Who seeks no glory here is fit for glory there ".

τὴν κραταιὰν χεῖρα] common in O.T., cf. especially Deut. ix. 26, 29, xxvi. 8, and note on κλήρων above. The deliverance from Egypt was the great example of God's mighty arm in history ; and that may well be in

ὑψώσῃ ἐν καιρῷ, ⁷πᾶσαν τὴν μέριμναν ὑμῶν ἐπιρρίψαντες ἐπ'
αὐτόν, ὅτι αὐτῷ μέλει περὶ ὑμῶν. ⁸νήψατε, γρηγορήσατε· ὁ
ἀντίδικος ὑμῶν διάβολος, ὡς λέων ὠρυόμενος, περιπατεῖ ζητῶν

St. Peter's mind here. The ταπείνωσις and θλιμμός of the Israelites in Deut. xxvi. 7 had their counterpart in the trials now threatening the Christians; and they too could trust in God to deliver them.

ἐν καιρῷ] *in His good time*: cf. Matt. xxiv. 45. ἐν καιρῷ in classical Greek means " at the propitious time " (Thuc. iv. 59, vi. 9), and therefore frequently, in relation to particular actions or events, " in good time " (Aesch. *P.V.* 381, Thuc. v. 61). In Thuc. i. 121 ἐν καιρῷ means " in due course ", or " in our own good time ". The rendering given above, therefore, seems to be that which tallies best both with classical and with N.T. usage. At the same time, in the context of the thought pervading this section of the Epistle, God's good time is the Parusia, described in i. 5 as καιρὸς ἔσχατος and in ii. 12 as ἡμέρα ἐπισκοπῆς; though the addition of ἐπισκοπῆς in A 33 and some other texts here is probably secondary. But for this eschatological context, we might interpret " God's good time " by reference to such passages as 1 Cor. x. 13.

7. πᾶσαν τὴν μέριμναν . . . περὶ ὑμῶν] Cf. iv. 19. The words recall the *verba Christi* in the Sermon on the Mount, Matt. vi. 25-32, Lk. xii. 22-31, μὴ μεριμνήσητε . . . οἶδε γὰρ ὁ πατὴρ ὑμῶν . . . ὅτι χρῄζετε τούτων ἁπάντων (cf. Lk. xii. 11, 12), and no doubt are based upon them. μέριμνα means " anxiety" or " worry". The language of the first clause is drawn from Ps. lv. 23, ἐπίριψον ἐπὶ κύριον τὴν μέριμνάν σου; and with the second clause cf. Wisd. xii. 13.

8. νήψατε, γρηγορήσατε] *be sober, be wakeful.* Cf. i. 13, iv. 7 and notes there, and on the collocation of these words, as in 1 Thess. v. 6, Essay II, pp. 452-6. Bengel observes the close connexion between the duties of

trusting God and wakefulness in Lk. xii. 22, 37.

ὁ ἀντίδικος ὑμῶν διάβολος] Both words translate the original Hebrew word " Satan ", which means " adversary ". In Num. xxii. 22 this word is translated by the periphrasis ἐνδιαβαλεῖν αὐτόν : σατάν occurs in 1 Kings xi. 14, 25, and ἐπίβουλος in 2 Sam. xix. 22, 1 Kings v. 4. The translation in Num. xxii. 22 was probably influenced by the fact that in the later Jewish literature, notably in Job i., ii., διάβολος, " accuser" or " calumniator ", was the normal translation of Satan, who was the adversary *par excellence*. Cf. the collocation of ἐνδιαβάλλειν and διάβολος in Ps. cix. 4, 6, where διάβολος is not used as a title but means " a false accuser ". The earliest example of ὁ διάβολος meaning the Devil is in Zech. iii. 1, 2 (*c.* 520 B.C.), where it is followed by τοῦ ἀντικεῖσθαι αὐτῷ. Persian influence is perhaps responsible for the development of the title, cf. Perowne, *The Books of Haggai and Zechariah*, App., Note B, pp. 153 ff. In Job i., ii. Satan seems to be more under divine control than in Zech. iii. 1, 2 or the still later 1 Chron. xxi. 1; and this aspect of his position appears in Lk. xxii. 31, 1 Cor. v. 5, 2 Cor. xii. 7, and also indeed in the introduction to our Lord's temptation, Matt. iv. 1. In Jn. xiii. 2, 2 Cor. iv. 4, Eph. vi. 16, 1 Thess. ii. 18, the Devil appears as the rebellious Prince of Evil *tout court*, the great Adversary of God's purpose, Jn. xii. 31, 2 Thess. ii. 8, 9, Rev. xii. 9, 10; the Father of lying and deceit, Jn. viii. 44, Acts v. 3, 2 Thess. ii. 10, Rev. xii. 9; the great Accuser or Slanderer, Rev. xii. 10. On this last see an illuminating article by R. O. P. Taylor, *Expository Times*, liii. 3 (Dec. 1941), who brings out the biblical idea of the Devil as the Sower of suspicion.

τινὰ καταπιεῖν· ⁹ᾧ ἀντίστητε στερεοὶ τῇ πίστει, εἰδότες τὰ αὐτὰ

St. Peter's use of more than one title for the Devil here is illustrated by Rev. xii. 9, 10, where no fewer than five titles are piled up for the sake of what we may call fulness of theological identification. But the two titles with which St. Peter is content are each appropriate to the context, ὁ ἀντίδικος expressing the hostility of the Devil to every aspect of the Christian life and the resulting temptation to apostasy, to which the response is stedfastness of faith in resistance, while διάβολος points to the favourite method of contumely and calumny (cf. ii. 12, iii. 16, iv. 4) resorted to by the Church's persecutors. That persecution is specially in mind is shewn by the allusion to τὰ αὐτὰ τῶν παθημάτων in the same verse, and cf. the echo of this passage in the Epistle from the Churches of Vienne and Lyons in Eus. H.E. v. i. 5, ii. 6. But Windisch goes too far in inferring that the verse presupposes some " general edict " for the harrying of the Christians : the picture of the lion ranging at will for his prey suggests the action of swirling tides of irrational prejudice used by a Gestapo rather than the deliberate imperial law ; and they might have been in operation at any time after A.D. 44. Cf. Mommsen, The Provinces of the Roman Empire, ii. pp. 160 ff., " the persecution of the Christians [sc. in the first century] was a standing matter as was that of robbers ; only such regulations were put into practice at times more gently or even negligently, at other times more strictly, and were doubtless on occasions enforced from high quarters ". On the possible connexion of 1 Pet. v. 9 ff. with Jer. li. 34-8 see Add. Note K, pp. 303-05.

ὡς λέων ὠρυόμενος] a graphic simile depicting the strength, ubiquity, and destructiveness of evil. Cf. Ps. xxii. 14, ἤνοιξαν ἐπ' ἐμὲ τὸ στόμα αὐτῶν, ὡς λέων ὁ ἁρπάζων καὶ ὠρυόμενος. This Psalm would have been specially fami-

liar in the early Church through its association with our Lord's passion, cf. verses 1, 8, 9, 16-19, 24. Hermas' vision of the "huge monster" (Vis. IV. i., ii.), which was a type of the great tribulation impending and threatening to overwhelm the Church, appears to have been partly prompted by this passage. Cf. also Ecclus. xxi. 2, where sin is depicted as having teeth like lion's teeth ἀναιροῦντες ψυχὰς ἀνθρώπων.

περιπατεῖ] like Satan in Job i. 7.

τινὰ] Souter gives this reading, which is based on אKLP and several versions : WH follow B and give καταπιεῖν without τινὰ. But Bengel and Windisch are surely right in reading τίνα, with A and Vulg. καταπιεῖν is seriously challenged by the future indicative καταπίεται of 13 (jkl), but I can find no other instance of the future active of πίνειν. The construction of the infinitive here, "whom to devour", is sufficiently unusual to account for καταπίει, and for καταπίῃ in A ; but the Greek language is so supple an instrument that we need not rule it out on that score. Cf. δοῦναι πιεῖν in Matt. xxvii. 34, Jn. iv. 7. Gregory of Nazianzus evidently found no difficulty in the construction, as he paraphrases it in Orat. Theol. ii. 2, εἴτε λέων ἁρπάζων καὶ ὠρυόμενος καὶ ζητῶν ἤν τινα βρῶσιν ποιήσεται τῶν ἡμετέρων ψυχῶν. The construction would seem to derive from the infinitive of purpose, which our author was not averse to using, cf. ii. 5, ἀνενέγκαι. Thumb (quoted by Moulton, Grammar, i. p. 205) shews that this use of the infinitive is much commoner in the Κοινή than in Attic, and is found in the Pontic dialect of Modern Greek ; and there, as in N.T., it usually follows verbs of a certain type — a usage to which this passage and ii. 5 fully conform. The reading τινὰ favoured by Lachmann, WH, Souter, Moffatt, gives a weak and colourless meaning, whereas the interrogative τίνα ex-

τῶν παθημάτων τῇ ἐν κόσμῳ ὑμῶν ἀδελφότητι ἐπιτελεῖσθαι. ¹⁰ὁ

presses the fell and deliberate purpose of the malignant Power of Evil.

9. ᾧ ἀντίστητε] Cf. Eph. vi. 13, ἵνα δυνηθῆτε ἀντιστῆναι ἐν τῇ ἡμέρᾳ τῇ πονηρᾷ καὶ ἅπαντα κατεργασάμενοι στῆναι. Dr. Carrington (*The Primitive Christian Catechism*, pp. 52 ff.) points out that the command to " resist the devil " occurs in Eph. vi. 11-13, Jas. iv. 7, 1 Pet. v. 9 and nowhere else in N.T. [though it is implied in *Test. Dan* vi. 1 and the devil's " flight " is found in *Test. Iss.* vii. 7, *Dan* v. 1, etc., and cf. Hermas, *Mand.* xii. 5, ἐὰν οὖν ἀντισταθῆτε αὐτῷ, νικηθεὶς φεύξεται ἀφ' ὑμῶν (recalling Jas. iv. 7), and ὅσοι οὖν πλήρεις εἰσὶν ἐν τῇ πίστει, ἀνθεστήκασιν αὐτῷ ἰσχυρῶς (recalling also 1 Pet. v. 9)] ; that ἀντιστῆναι is used by St. Paul, St. James, and St. Peter in this figurative sense nowhere else but in these passages ; and that Eph. vi. and 1 Pet. v. have both ἀντιστῆναι and στῆναι in that order and in this context. The conclusion is irresistible that the command to " resist the devil " was " a familiar phrase in the. catechetical literature of Greek Judaism ", whence it passed early into the Christian Church ; though whether as part of a baptismal manual or of a Persecution-manual may be debated. Cf. Essay II below, pp. 453-8.

στερεοὶ τῇ πίστει] *stedfast in your Christian faith*. Cf. Col. i. 23, εἴγε ἐπιμένετε τῇ πίστει τεθεμελιωμένοι καὶ ἑδραῖοι, this condition being expressed in 1 Peter by the one word στερεοί, " compact ", " solidly built ". στερεός is not used directly of persons in classical Greek or LXX, and usually has a bad connotation (harsh, cruel, obstinate) ; but Is. l. 7 f. is much to the point here, κύριος βοηθός μοι ἐγενήθη· διὰ τοῦτο οὐκ ἐνετράπην, ἀλλὰ ἔθηκα τὸ πρόσωπόν μου ὡς στερεὰν πέτραν, καὶ ἔγνων ὅτι οὐ μὴ αἰσχυνθῶ. ὅτι ἐγγίζει ὁ δικαιώσας με· τίς ὁ κρινόμενός μοι ; ἀντιστήτω μοι ἅμα. στερεὰ πέτρα was a phrase not likely to be lost on the Apostle whose Lord had named him

Kephas. A flint-like resolution is what he calls for here. For τῇ πίστει in this context cf. Acts xvi. 5, ἐστερεοῦντο τῇ πίστει, Ign. *Eph.* x. ἑδραῖοι τῇ πίστει. It is improbable that ἡ πίστις here means *fides quae creditur*, which would require ἐν τῇ πίστει : even in the Pastoral Epistles that meaning is very doubtful, cf. Parry, *The Pastoral Epistles*, pp. ciii ff. On the other hand we could not rightly translate the words " in faithfulness ", and Lightfoot's suggestion (on Col. i. 23) " your faith " seems to meet the case. For the faith in question is the definite Christian faith, which presupposes, and holds as it were in solution, a certain amount of Christian belief in the sense of doctrine. Cf. Hort, *The First Epistle of St. Peter*, pp. 47 f., 81 ff.

τὰ αὐτὰ τῶν παθημάτων] an unusual construction connoting " the same kinds of sufferings ". E. H. Blakeney writes : " τὰ αὐτά would be regarded as a noun-equivalent. Herodotus could write τὰ πολλὰ τῶν χωρῶν, but I have not seen anything exactly parallel to the Petrine phrase. Something akin may be found in Ovid, *Fasti*, i. 46 :

> *non habet officii Lucifer omnis idem.*

(So the best MSS.: the *v.l. officium* is surely the attempted correction of a scribe who was puzzled by the genitive.) " For the accusative and infinitive after εἰδέναι instead of the usual ὅτι cf. Lk. iv. 41. There is nothing to require the rendering " how to " with ἐπιτελεῖσθαι, with the various strained interpretations to which it leads. Cf. Blenkin's note *in loc.*

The effect of the motive here alluded to is observed by Thucydides, who, in his account of the misery of the Athenians after the naval defeat at Syracuse (vii. 75. 6), speaks of ἡ ἰσομοιρία τῶν κακῶν, ἔχουσά τινα ὅμως τὸ μετὰ πολλῶν κούφισιν : he adds, however, that οὐδ' ὡς ῥᾳδία ἐν τῷ παρόντι ἐδοξάζετο.

δὲ Θεὸς πάσης χάριτος, ὁ καλέσας ὑμᾶς εἰς τὴν αἰώνιον αὐτοῦ

τῇ ἐν κόσμῳ ὑμῶν ἀδελφότητι] *your brethren in the world at large.* The dative is the *dativus incommodi.* St. Peter uses ἡ ἀδελφότης as a collective noun for οἱ ἀδελφοί also in ii. 17 ; and cf. φιλαδελφιά in i. 22, and φιλάδελφοι in iii. 8. In 1 Macc. xii. 10, 17 ἀδελφότης means " brotherly affection", (as in Hermas, *Mand.* viii. 10), in 4 Macc. x. 3, xiii. 26 the bond of actual brotherhood, and in 4 Macc. ix. 23 the bond of brotherhood which consists in a common courage. But the collective noun occurs in 1 Clem. ii. 4, cf. *Ep. Polyc.* x. 1 (*fraternitatis*), Dion Chrys. ii. 137 ; and Suicer cites Nestorius' letter to Cyril of Alexandria (*Act. Eph.*, p. 11), πᾶσαν τὴν σύν σοι ἀδελφότητα ἐγώ τε καὶ οἱ σὺν ἐμοὶ προσαγορεύομεν. I suggest that St. Peter's fondness for this term for the Church may owe something to the Lord's charge to him in Lk. xxii. 32, καὶ σύ ποτε ἐπιστρέψας στήριξον τοὺς ἀδελφούς σου. Perdelwitz adduces no linguistic evidence to support the notion that the word was suggested by the φράτραι, φρατρίαι, or συμβιώσεις of the Mystery religions (*op. cit.* p. 80).

ἐν κόσμῳ] *the world at large.* ἐν τῇ οἰκουμένῃ might perhaps have been expected, as in Acts xvii. 6, xix. 27. But cf. Jn. xii. 19, ἴδε, ὁ κόσμος ὀπίσω αὐτοῦ ἀπῆλθεν, and 1 Jn. iv. 3. 1 Tim. iii. 16, ἐπιστεύθη ἐν κόσμῳ, would offer a close parallel, if the reference is not to the invisible as well as the visible world : cf. Essay I, p. 326. This seems better than to take it, with Blenkin, as " in the same worldly surroundings as yourselves ". What St. Peter wants them to understand is that the churches in Asia Minor are not alone in their sufferings.

ἐπιτελεῖσθαι] *are being accomplished, are taking their course.* Cf. Vulg. *fieri.* ἐπιτελεῖν means " to accomplish, complete ", and can be used of any task in hand, religious or otherwise. Cf. 2 Cor. viii. 6. Lightfoot **thinks** that in Gal. iii. 3, Phil. i. 6 the word

may carry a sacrificial nuance, but in both cases the cult word ἐνάρχεσθαι also occurs. If there is any ulterior meaning in the word in the verse before us, an eschatological reference seems more probable than a sacrificial one ; for the persecution of Christians was regarded as one of the premonitory signs of the End.

10, 11. Both in their general tenour and in the details of their phraseology (e.g. χάριτος, καλέσας, αὐτός, αἰώνιον, καταρτίσει, στηρίξει) these verses present close affinities with 1 Thess. v. 23-8, 2 Thess. ii. 13-17, Heb. xiii. 21, 22, and point to the pen of Silvanus. On the parallels between 1 Peter and the Thessalonian Epistles cf. Essay II, pp. 369-84, and on those between Heb. xii., xiii. and this Epistle, *ib.* pp. 463-6. Were they also part of a Crisis- or Persecution-document which Silvanus helped to shape ? Cf. *ib.* pp. 453-8, and Table XIV. The resemblances can hardly be accidental, and point to common authorship by Silvanus, or to use of common underlying material, or to both. In all cases alike they serve to round off the eschatological crisis-teaching of preceding passages ; and here they gather up a number of ideas which have been interwoven with the Epistle from the beginning — a fact which is relevant to the integrity of the letter as a whole.

10. δέ] *moreover* : as in iv. 7 (see note).

πάσης χάριτος] i.e. of grace sufficient for every occasion and need. Cf. 2 Cor. i. 3 (θεὸς πάσης παρακλήσεως), xii. 9. In iv. 10 God's ποικίλη χάρις is seen in the diverse variety of particular gifts and callings ; here πᾶσα χάρις brings out the comprehensiveness and universality of His activity towards believers, from the time of their baptism (καλέσας, cf. i. 15, ii. 9) onwards.

αἰώνιον . . . ὀλίγον παθόντας] On the contrast between the relative slight-

δόξαν ἐν Χριστῷ, ὀλίγον παθόντας αὐτὸς καταρτίσει, στηρίξει,
σθενώσει· ¹¹αὐτῷ τὸ κράτος εἰς τοὺς αἰῶνας τῶν αἰώνων. ἀμήν.

ness of the sufferings and the eventual
glory cf. the notes on i. 6-9.

δόξαν] the glory already alluded to
in verses 1, 4 above. God's eternal
glory brings out the full range and
objective of the Christian calling, and
the sufferings which it involves are thus
set in perspective.

ἐν Χριστῷ] Bengel takes this with
καλέσας, Hofmann with δόξαν. Bigg
and Wand point out that the dilemma
is not unavoidable, and this is surely
right. Their calling and its ultimate
issue are alike " in Christ ", in the
sense that He is the atmosphere or
climate of the whole Christian life.
Cf. 1 Cor. vii. 22, ὁ ἐν κυρίῳ κληθεὶς
δοῦλος.

ὀλίγον παθόντας] Cf. Rom. viii. 18,
2 Cor. iv. 17.

αὐτός] as in 1 Thess. v. 23, 2 Thess.
ii. 16. It is no merely fortuitous or
instrumental helps that are promised,
but God's own active intervention and
personal presence. αὐτός is rare with
ὁ θεός (ὁ πατήρ, ὁ κύριος, τὸ πνεῦμα)
in N.T. outside this Epistle ; only
nine times, indeed, of which five are in
1 and 2 Thessalonians. And it always
connotes a special intimacy and tenderness of relationship on God's part, cf.
Jn. xvi. 27, Rom. viii. 16, 26, Rev.
xxi. 3. In 1 Pet. ii. 24, as here, the
word gives special force and poignancy
to what is said.

καταρτίσει] will re-establish, make
whole. Latin redintegrare, resarcire.
To make whole (ἄρτιος) is the fundamental connotation of καταρτίζειν, the
precise nuance depending on the stage
at which the action of καταρτισμός
begins in each case, from " making
good" that which is weak (Ezra iv. 12,
Ps. lxviii. 10), torn (Matt. iv. 21), or
defective (1 Thess. iii. 10) to " perfect-
ing" that which is in course of preparation (Lk. vi. 40, Heb. xiii. 21).
Hence it means also " prepare " in a
quite neutral sense (Rom. ix. 22). The
use of the word in literary Greek is

identical : in the vernacular (cf. MM,
sub voc.) the neutral sense appears to
predominate. Lightfoot (on 1 Thess.
iii. 10, and Ign. Eph. ii.) lays special
stress on " two technical uses " of the
word, (1) to reconcile factions, Herod.
v. 28, 2 Cor. xiii. 11, (2) to set bones,
Galen, Op. xix, p. 461 (ed. Kühn).
The past participle in the verse before
us (ὀλίγον παθόντας) indicates that the
idea of re-establishment is to the fore
rather than that of perfection, as in
A.V. and Vulg. (perficiet). The experiences through which the Christian
communities had passed (cf. iv. 12 f.)
had evidently surprised and shaken
them : there may well have been some
mutual recrimination ; they would
certainly have wondered what the upshot was to be, for themselves and for
the Christian cause generally. This
verse gives the answer : God will
Himself re-establish their common life
and make it whole. Bengel's comment
ne quid vos labefactet aptly brings out
the meaning.

Some MSS. add ὑμᾶς after καταρτίσει,
but the great weight of textual authority is against it ; and the verbs are
more impressive without it. They
were the sufferers ; but the re-establishment which God was to effect
would embrace more than their personal fortunes. Some later MSS.,
again, give the optative instead of the
future indicative of the verbs ; but
assimilation to the optative in 1 Thess.
v. 23, 2 Thess. ii. 17, Heb. xiii. 21 will
explain this. What St. Peter gives his
readers is not a prayer but a promise.

στηρίξει] make stable, stablish : i.e.
making them στερεοὶ τῇ πίστει, as
above, verse 9. Cf. Lk. xxii. 32 (our
Lord's words to St. Peter), 2 Thess.
ii. 17, iii. 3, Jas. v. 8.

σθενώσει] ἅπαξ λεγόμενον here in
the Greek Bible. The verb is not
found in classical Greek either, but
σθένειν, " to be strong ", is common,
especially in Sophocles.

¹²Διὰ Σιλουανοῦ ὑμῖν τοῦ πιστοῦ ἀδελφοῦ, ὡς λογίζομαι, δι'

Some MSS., including ℵ, Syr, Copt, Arm, followed by Oecumenius and Theophylact, add θεμελιώσει (v.l. -αι), perhaps under the influence of Col. i. 23.

11. τὸ κράτος] The doxology affords an additional reason for faith and fortitude : power belongs to God, now and to eternity. The word occurs also in the doxology (which is addressed to Christ) in iv. 11 above ; in one of St. Paul's doxologies, 1 Tim. vi. 16 ; and in Jude 25, Rev. i. 6, v. 13. See note on iv. 11. For κράτος as one of the attributes of God in O.T. and Apocrypha cf. Job xii. 16, Judith ix. 14 (a verse which appears to provide the basis for the curious response in the Book of Common Prayer, " Because there is none other that fighteth for us, but only thou, O God "), 3 Macc. i. 27. Note also Ps. Sol. xvii. 3, ἡμεῖς δὲ ἐλπιοῦμεν ἐπὶ θεὸν τὸν σωτῆρα ἡμῶν, ὅτι τὸ κράτος τοῦ θεοῦ ἡμῶν εἰς τὸν αἰῶνα μετ' ἐλέου. The occurrence of ἐστιν in iv. 11 suggests that that word rather than ἔστω is to be understood here.

These verses, which conclude the Epistle proper, are characteristically Petrine in their emphasis and proportion. Though the eschatological motif has been so prominent from iv. 7 onwards, and though an eschatological promise might well have been expected after ὀλίγον παθόντας, the conclusion that we actually have is wholly appropriate. The Church not only has the hope of the next world, but is the hope of this world, and it is for that purpose that it is to be re-established and strengthened ; and such a this-worldly note fittingly crowns the ethical and practical aim which permeates the Epistle. At the same time, history, which is the subject of verse 10, is no secular field, independent of God's will and purpose : its events are unfolded before His eyes, and its issues guided and determined by His Providence, until time itself shall pass into the illimitable horizons of eternity.

12. Διά] i.e both as draftsman and as bearer of the Epistle. Cf. Bigg, op. cit., Introd. pp. 5 f. If he were the bearer only, ἔπεμψα would have been the more natural word. Cf. Acts xv. 22, 23, where πέμψαι is followed by γράψαντες διὰ χειρὸς αὐτῶν. Windisch draws attention to Papias' statement (Eus. H.E. iii. xxxix. 15) that St. Peter employed a ἑρμηνευτής, and infers that Silvanus played a real part in the composition (Konzipierung und Stilisierung) of the Epistle. Cf. Introd. pp. 9-11 on the position of the amanuensis in ancient times. That Silvanus was also the bearer of the letter is rendered probable by the order of the provinces in i. 1, which points to a fixed route settled beforehand, cf. Hort, op. cit., Add. Note III.

Σιλουανοῦ] On the identity of this Silvanus with that of 1 Thess. i. 1, 2 Thess. i. 1, and of the latter with the Silas of Acts see Introd. pp. 9-17, and cf. Lightfoot, Notes, etc., on 1 Thess. i. 1 : in the latter case, as Lightfoot observes, the identity " appears from the identity of situation ascribed to the two in the historical narrative and the allusions in the Epistle ". The etymology of the word is more doubtful. But Windisch agrees with Deissmann in deriving it from the Aramaic name Sili or Sch'l'iach, meaning " sent " (cf. the explanation of Siloam given in Jn. ix. 7 : the name still survives as Silwan, the village on the E. slopes of the valley of the Kidron, cf. Hastings, DB, article " Siloam "), this name being Graecized as Silas and Latinized as Silvanus : St. Luke preferred the former, St. Paul the latter. This view, which derives from St. Jerome, seems better than the usual opinion, viz. that Silas is simply a contraction of Silvanus ; for in that case we should have expected Silvas, and the accentuation of Σίλας in Acts does not suggest a contraction.

ὑμῖν] the position of this pronoun, which belongs grammatically to ἔγρα-

242 FIRST EPISTLE OF ST. PETER [V. 12

ὀλίγων ἔγραψα, παρακαλῶν καὶ ἐπιμαρτυρῶν ταύτην εἶναι ἀληθῆ

ψα, suggests that there was already a close link between Silvanus and the recipients of the Epistle.

τοῦ πιστοῦ ἀδελφοῦ, ὡς λογίζομαι] *that brother known to you all, in whom I have complete confidence*, i.e. whom I reckon I can rely upon implicitly to interpret my message and meaning faithfully. Similar light is thrown on Silvanus' character in Acts xv. 27, καὶ αὐτοὺς διὰ λόγου ἀπαγγέλλοντας τὰ αὐτά. Cf. Col. iv. 7, Τύχικος ὁ ἀγαπητὸς ἀδελφὸς καὶ πιστὸς διάκονος καὶ σύνδουλος ἐν κυρίῳ. In all the other passages in N.T. where πιστός is used of a particular individual, 1 Cor. iv. 17, Col. i. 7, iv. 7, 9, Eph. vi. 21, Heb. ii. 17, iii. 2, it means " to be relied on for a particular mission or purpose ". Elsewhere it means either (1) " reliable ", of God or of His word, or (2) " believing ", e.g. of Christians. λογίζομαι is " an auditor's term " (Lancelot Andrewes, *Serm.* ii. pp. 190, 200 f.) : Latin *reputare*.

δι' ὀλίγων] *briefly*, i.e. in relation to the greatness and variety of its subject-matter, on which Silvanus will be able to enlarge by word of mouth. Cf. Heb. xiii. 22, διὰ βραχέων ἐπέστειλα ὑμῖν. ἔγραψα is the epistolary aorist : in Latin both the perfect and the imperfect are used in this way.

παρακαλῶν] *exhorting*. Exhortation is the purpose of the Epistle. On παρακαλεῖν cf. Essay II, p. 388.

ἐπιμαρτυρῶν] here only in N.T., though συνεπιμαρτυρεῖν occurs in Heb. ii. 4. The word is classical, cf. Plato, *Crat.* 397 A, where the meaning is " supply evidence that " followed by accusative and infinitive. Cf. also Plut. *Alex.* 42 (quoted by Windisch), καὶ οἱ ἄνδρες ἐπεμαρτύρουν ὅτι ἀληθῆ λέγουσιν, where the meaning is " confirmed the fact by evidence ". In LXX the verb always occurs in the middle voice, and means " give testimony ", against someone or of some fact, cf. Neh. ix. 29, 30. The words have here the same ring as those of

Jn. xix. 35, καὶ ὁ ἑωρακὼς μεμαρτύρηκε, καὶ ἀληθινὴ αὐτοῦ ἐστιν ἡ μαρτυρία· κἀκεῖνος οἶδεν ὅτι ἀληθῆ λέγει, ἵνα κτλ., and Jn. xxi. 24, οὗτός ἐστιν ὁ μαθητὴς ὁ μαρτυρῶν περὶ τούτων, καὶ γράψας ταῦτα· καὶ οἴδαμεν ὅτι ἀληθής ἐστιν ἡ μαρτυρία αὐτοῦ. In both those cases the Jewish requirement of two witnesses (cf. Jn. viii. 17) was fulfilled; the testimony in the first case being given by the disciple and the Lord Himself (κἀκεῖνος, cf. Hoskyns, *in loc.*), in the second by the disciple and the Church. So, too, in the verse before us St. Peter adds his Apostolic testimony to the teaching of the prophet Silvanus, and the truth is thus established. As Estius says, he writes *tamquam testis et Apostolus Christi*. Such witness was the Apostle's primary function, cf. Acts i. 8 ; and the whole clause seems to sum up exactly what we conceive to have been the case with the authorship of this Epistle. Cf. Introd. pp. 27-33. It was the joint work of Silvanus and St. Peter, the former supplying the literary composition, much of it gathered from the common tradition, the latter providing the Apostolic testimony to the underlying facts of the Gospel and their application to the readers' condition.

ταύτην κτλ.] *that this is God's veritable grace*. But to what does ταύτην refer ? Usteri takes it of the persecutions, which are a form of divine favour, cf. note on 1 Pet. i. 6 *supra* ; but such an allusion would be obscure. Bigg thinks the reference is to " the whole of the contents of the Epistle ". Blenkin recalls the other uses of χάρις in this Epistle, with special reference to the universalism of the Messianic prophecies (i. 10) and expectations (i. 13), and to the grace promised to those who are humble (v. 5) and endure persecution (v. 10). This has the advantage of going behind the Epistle to the whole dispensation of the divine blessing which is its theme. " The

χάριν τοῦ Θεοῦ· εἰς ἣν στῆτε.   ¹³ἀσπάζεται ὑμᾶς ἡ ἐν Βαβυλῶνι

grace which they had experienced in conversion, and in the blessedness and progress of Christian life, was no delusion, as they were tempted to suppose by their troubles, but the genuine grace of God " (Bennett).

εἰς ἣν στῆτε] *wherein stand fast.* For this use of εἰς for ἐν cf. Moulton, *Grammar*, i. pp. 63, 234 f., Blass, *op. cit.* p. 123.

13, 14. Concluding greeting.

13. Βαβυλῶνι] a *soubriquet* for Rome. Papias, according to Eusebius, *H.E.* II. xv., so understood it, and this interpretation was universal both in east and west until the Reformation. The objection to the Mesopotamian Babylon being intended is that there is no local tradition of any Apostle other than St. Thomas being associated with those parts ; and the earliest Syriac tradition connects St. Peter not with Babylon but with Rome (Chase, Bigg). Still less likely is it that St. Peter is referring to the Roman military station named Babylon on the site of the modern Cairo. [It is not irrelevant to note, perhaps, that the Roman legionaries' custom of naming places after military stations where they had previously been on duty shews how easily names were transferred from one place to another : thus Happisburgh and perhaps Aspatria point to Roman legionaries having been there who had picked up the worship of Apis the Egyptian bull-god ; and Cocum Farm near Bullington in Hampshire similarly takes its name from a centre of Apis-worship in the Nile valley.]

Rome is called Babylon in Rev. xvii., xviii., and it does not appear to be used there for the first time : the word " Mystery " which introduces the title in xvii. 5 points to a hidden truth now known to Christians, and known first of all, no doubt, through the researches of the Christian prophets. For a possible source of the *soubriquet* in Jer. li. cf. Add. Note K, pp. 303-05. Babylon

is found for Rome in *Apoc. Bar.* xi. I and *Or. Sib.* v. 158, which, however, may be later than Rev. xvii., xviii. In the Apocalypse, again (xi. 8), Jerusalem is called " spiritually " Sodom or Egypt, just as in Gal. iv. 25 Sinai represents Jerusalem. A somewhat similar use of a historical name to denote a type not of place, but of person occurs in *Pirqe Aboth*, ii. 18, " R. La'zar said, Be diligent to learn *Thorah*, wherewith thou mayest make answer to Epicurus ", where Epicurus denotes a heretic or unbeliever. Windisch's observation that the idea of Rome as embodying the anti-religious world-power would scarcely have been intelligible to Christians before the Neronian persecution is unconvincing. *In Tiberim defluxit Orontes*, and the flaunting wealth and oriental vices of Rome were sufficient to recall Babylon, as soon as the hostility of the imperial régime to Christianity had become in any way evident. In the case of 1 Peter, reasons of prudence may have dictated the use of the symbolic name, as the letter might have to pass the censorship of police officers.

συνεκλεκτή] i.e. the Christian body in Rome, elect like the Christian communities of Asia Minor mentioned in the Address, i. 1. Though St. Peter was married (Matt. viii. 14, 1 Cor. ix. 5), it is improbable that his wife is alluded to here. There is no difficulty in understanding ἐκκλησία; for the feminine adjective with the article is often used in Greek by itself, where the context makes the meaning obvious ; cf. ἡ πολιτική, where either τέχνη or ἐπιστήμη can be understood according to the subject-matter in hand. A close parallel is afforded by ἐκλεκτῇ κυρίᾳ καὶ τοῖς τέκνοις αὐτῆς and τὰ τέκνα τῆς ἀδελφῆς σου τῆς ἐκλεκτῆς of 2 Jn. 1, 13, where the reference is almost certainly to churches : cf. Brooke, *The Johannine Epistles*, Introd. pp. lxxix ff., and *in loc.* : Dom Chapman, indeed (*J.T.S.*, July 1904),

συνεκλεκτή, καὶ Μάρκος ὁ υἱός μου. ¹⁴ἀσπάσασθε ἀλλήλους ἐν
φιλήματι ἀγάπης.
Εἰρήνη ὑμῖν πᾶσι τοῖς ἐν Χριστῷ.

believed that 2 John, like 1 Peter, was
addressed to the Church in Rome.
Blenkin suggests that ἡ συνεκλεκτή
may denote the Bride of Christ, ὁ
ἐκλεκτός being used of the Messiah
in *1 Enoch* xl. 5, xlv. 3, 4. Sufficient
warrant for the metaphor would lie in
the *verba Christi* in Mk. ii. 19, Jn.
iii. 29, which themselves recalled O.T.
prophecies such as Hos. ii. 19, 20 ; but
there is nothing in the context to
suggest that it is in St. Peter's mind
here, and συνεκλεκτή is a natural echo
of ἐκλεκτοῖς in i. 1.

Μάρκος ὁ υἱός μου] i.e. the Evangelist. His mother's house in Jerusalem was the place to which St. Peter
turned when released from prison
(Acts xii. 12 ff.), and he was working
with St. Paul in Rome during his
captivity (Col. iv. 10, Philem. 24).
Eusebius alludes to this verse in *H.E.*
II. xv., on the authority of Clement of
Alexandria (*Adumbrat.* 1007 [P]) and
Papias, and takes it as a matter of
course that St. Peter is referring to the
Evangelist and that by Babylon he
meant Rome. On his traditional connexion with St. Peter cf. Swete, *The
Gospel according to St. Mark*, Introd.
pp. xx ff., Rawlinson, *The Gospel according to St. Mark*, Introd. pp. xxx f.
" My son " is a natural expression of
affection between Apostle and pupil.
The chronological problems concerning the presence of St. Mark in Rome
at this time are discussed in the Introduction, pp. 60-2.

14. ἐν φιλήματι ἀγάπης] St. Paul
prefers ἐν φιλήματι ἁγίῳ, cf. 1 Thess.
v. 26, Rom. xvi. 16, 1 Cor. xvi. 20, or
ἐν ἁγίῳ φιλήματι, 2 Cor. xiii. 12. On
the kiss of peace see Lightfoot, *Notes
on the Epistles of St. Paul*, pp. 90 f.,
and Robertson and Plummer on 1 Cor.
xvi. 20. Cabrol (*Dict. d' Arch. chrét.*,
II. i. pp. 118 ff.) quotes Lk. vii. 45,
φίλημά μοι οὐκ ἔδωκας· αὕτη δέ, ἀφ' ἧς

εἰσῆλθον, οὐ διέλιπε καταφιλοῦσά μου
τοὺς πόδας, to shew how our Lord
valued this token of affection, and
suggests that Judas' choice of the kiss
to enable his company to identify Jesus
points to its having been in frequent
use between Jesus and His disciples.
By the middle of the second century it
was in regular use in the liturgy at the
conclusion of the prayers and immediately before the offertory, cf. Justin,
Apol. i. 65 (97 C, D), ἀλλήλους φιλήματι
ἀσπαζόμεθα παυσάμενοι τῶν εὐχῶν.
ἔπειτα προσφέρεται τῷ προεστῶτι τῶν
ἀδελφῶν ἄρτος καὶ ποτήριον κτλ.; and
Cabrol points out that this is the regular
place of the kiss of peace in all eastern
liturgies, and in liturgies, like the Galli-
can, Mozarabic and Celtic rites, influenced by the East. In the Roman
Church it occurs after the canon and
immediately before the communion.
Tert. *de Orat.* xviii. calls it *osculum pa-
cis, quod est signaculum orationis*, and
Cyril, *Cat. Myst.* v. 3, says, ἀνακίρνησι
τὰς ψυχὰς ἀλλήλαις καὶ πᾶσαν ἀμνησι-
κακίαν αὐταῖς μνηστεύεται. R. Seeberg, quoted in Hastings, *DAC*,
ii. p. 443, thinks that the evidence
of 1 Cor. xvi. 20-2 points to the kiss
of peace having been from St. Paul's
time connected with the Lord's Supper, and concludes that St. Paul
" expects that his Epistle will be
read immediately before the Supper ".
This would tally with second-century
usage, and the suggestion is attractive.
There was no other occasion when so
many members of a Christian community would be gathered together as
at the weekly celebrations of the
Eucharist ; and 1 Pet. ii. 3-10 would
have come home with special force if it
had been read at that point in the
liturgy. Cf. Add. Note H, pp. 294-8.

εἰρήνη] recalling i. 2, χάρις ὑμῖν καὶ
εἰρήνη πληθυνθείη. St. Paul normally
uses " grace " in these concluding

salutations, but speaks of " peace " in 2 Cor. xiii. 11, immediately before alluding to the kiss. In Rev. i. 4 we have " grace and peace " together. The salutation of the risen Lord was " Peace ", Lk. xxiv. 36, Jn. xx. 19, 21, 26, and these *verba Christi* may well account for St. Peter's preference.

τοῖς ἐν Χριστῷ] *id est, Christianis* (Estius), Christ being the environment of the Christian life. Cf. note on iii. 16

ADDITIONAL NOTES

A. *The Trinitarian formula in i. 2*

Issues both of a critical and a doctrinal character are raised by the rudimentary Trinitarian formulae in 2 Thess. ii. 13, 14 and 1 Pet. i. 2 ; and these should be studied in relation to the formula of blessing in 2 Cor. xiii. 14 and to the baptismal charge in Matt. xxviii. 19.

2 Thess. ii. 13, 14	1 Pet. i. 1, 2	2 Cor. xiii. 14	Matt. xxviii. 19
. . . εἵλετο ὑμᾶς ὁ θεὸς ἀπ᾽ ἀρχῆς εἰς σωτηρίαν ἐν ἁγιασμῷ πνεύματος καὶ πίστει ἀληθείας· εἰς ὃ ἐκάλεσεν ὑμᾶς διὰ τοῦ εὐαγγελίου ἡμῶν, εἰς περιποίησιν δόξης τοῦ Κυρίου ἡμῶν Ἰησοῦ Χριστοῦ.	. . . ἐκλεκτοῖς . . . κατὰ πρόγνωσιν θεοῦ πατρός, ἐν ἁγιασμῷ πνεύματος, εἰς ὑπακοὴν καὶ ῥαντισμὸν αἵματος Ἰησοῦ Χριστοῦ.	ἡ χάρις τοῦ Κυρίου Ἰησοῦ Χριστοῦ καὶ ἡ ἀγάπη τοῦ θεοῦ καὶ ἡ κοινωνία τοῦ ἁγίου πνεύματος μετὰ πάντων ὑμῶν.	. . . μαθητεύσατε πάντα τὰ ἔθνη, βαπτίζοντες αὐτοὺς εἰς τὸ ὄνομα τοῦ πατρὸς καὶ τοῦ υἱοῦ καὶ τοῦ ἁγίου πνεύματος, διδάσκοντες αὐτοὺς τηρεῖν πάντα ὅσα ἐνετειλάμην ὑμῖν. . . .

The Thessalonian and Petrine passages differ from the Pauline blessing and still more from the Dominical charge in being less *stylisés* and formal than they , but there are a number of cross-resemblances between the four passages which render their relationship difficult to determine. Thus, 2 Thessalonians and 2 Corinthians are alike in alluding to the Holy Trinity under the three terms God, Holy Spirit, Lord Jesus Christ, though in different order, whereas 1 Peter and St. Matthew are alike in naming the Father, though differing in the terms used for the Son and also in the order in which the three " Persons " are mentioned. Again, while the Corinthian passage is highly formal, falling into three phrases with a nominative followed by a genitive in each, it resembles the Thessalonian and Petrine passages in admitting of being regarded as a summary of the most essential things in the spiritual life and experience of the Christian community as a whole. Were it dependent directly upon the Matthaean charge, it would presumably have been verbally closer to it.

From the standpoint of literary criticism, the facts would seem most easily explained by the view that, though the baptismal formula of Matt. xxviii. has not influenced 2 Thessalonians or 2 Corinthians, it has had some influence upon 1 Pet. i. 2. This would be not unnatural if the Matthaean passage were first written as the concluding section of a collection of *verba Christi* — a place which consorts well with the injunction to the disciples to teach all that Christ had commanded them. I suggest that the resemblances between 2 Thess. ii. 13, 14 and 1 Pet. i. 2 are due to the fact that Silvanus drafted both, and the differences between them partly to St. Peter's special devotion to our Lord's passion and partly to the fact that between the writing of 2 Thessalonians (and 2 Corinthians) and 1 Peter the *verba*

Christi, containing the baptismal formula, had been published. The interest of this Epistle in baptism would have made the assimilation to the terms of the formula natural.

On the doctrinal side we are still in the period before formal statement has been developed. 1 Peter no less than 2 Thessalonians sets before us the divine origin, sphere, and purpose of the Christian life — its origin in God's initiative, will, and choice, its sphere in the Spirit's sanctifying power, its purpose a share in Christ's atoning work and glory. In both Epistles we cannot help observing the strongly functional character of the doctrine they contain. The Trinitarian ideas arise quite naturally out of the Church's experience of God's grace in its threefold activity of choice and foreknowledge, of sanctification, and of salvation through Jesus Christ. In 2 Thess. ii. 14, salvation is conceived eschatologically as consisting in a share of Christ's glory (a thought also expressed, but elsewhere, in 1 Peter) : in Pet. i. 2 the goal of the Christian life is conceived rather in terms of practical religion, and as the result, already within reach, of Christ's work as author of the new Covenant, which conveyed forgiveness through His sacrificial death and demanded obedience to God's will. Every feature here mentioned of the spiritual background of the Christian life is found later on in the Epistle, to which the whole clause thus forms a most appropriate preamble.

With regard to the Father, St. Peter's teaching is obviously cradled in the Hebraic revelation of God and in Jesus' interpretation of it. When the author is thinking of God's transcendent functions — His "foreknowledge" of those whom He elects to salvation, His power and mercy in the historical redemption, and His impartial judgment of men's deeds — it is natural that he should use that title of God which was characteristic of Christ's revelation of Him ; and he makes the invocation of the Father's Name, familiar to his readers from the Lord's Prayer, the ground of an appeal for reverence in the conduct of daily life (i. 17). But we should not be entitled to suppose that he might not equally well have spoken of " the Father " in several other passages where he does in fact speak of " God ". For him, as for the orthodoxy of a later date, the Father was the ἀρχὴ τῆς θεότητος ; and he would have been entirely at home with the standard forms of Christian liturgy in which prayer is addressed, entirely or at least predominantly, to the Father. The salutation of the Epistle indicates, no doubt, the presence of a distinction in the Apostle's mind between Father, Christ, and Spirit ; but it is a distinction of function rather than of " Person ".[1]

When we turn to Christology, we note that St. Peter does not use the title " Son " of Christ at all, though His unique Sonship to God is a necessary corollary of the blessing in i. 3 ; and there are no traces of the Pauline doctrine of the adoption of Christians as " sons ". Nor are we entitled to say that he was familiar with the idea of Christ's pre-existence with the Father before

---

[1] The rudimentary nature of much N.T. doctrine needs to be borne in mind when we are asked to describe it as frequently "binitarian". The so-called "binitarian" forms can be quite simply accounted for partly by the fact that Christian thought had not yet been called upon to define its philosophy of the Godhead in precise terms, and partly by the contexts in particular cases. Thus, the formula "Blessed be the God and Father of our Lord Jesus Christ", which opens up the argument of Ephesians and 1 Peter, or the phrase "God our Father and the Lord Jesus Christ", which occurs in the salutation of no fewer than thirteen Epistles, ceases to offer a doctrinal problem, if we reflect that what the writers intended to emphasize was the concrete, historical origin of the Christian religion and of the author's own authority within it, along with its derivation from God above. The authors were writing not as formulators of doctrine, but as Apostolic witnesses. In the case of 1 Peter, the formula which is alleged to be "binitarian" follows immediately upon a salutation which is plainly, though in rudimentary fashion, "trinitarian".

the Incarnation. For this idea is not necessarily implied in his description of Christ as " foreknown before the foundation of the world ", since Christians also are the objects of God's foreknowledge : all that we can say is that the phrase πρὸ καταβολῆς κόσμου affirms for Christ's office and work a supramundane range and importance. Nor, again, are we justified in seeing in his use of the term " the Spirit of Christ ", when speaking of the inspiration of the prophets, an assertion of belief in Christ's pre-existence.[1] The truth is that St. Peter was not approaching the matter from the theological, but from the pastoral side : it is with Christ as his and their Lord rather than God's Son that he is concerned. On the other hand, the position which St. Peter assigns to Christ is one which needs the doctrine of the Incarnation to set it forth. The title of " Lord ", which is normally used in the Old Testament for God, the inclusive relationship which binds Christ to believers so that they live " in " Him, the allusions to their suffering and glorifying God " in Christ's Name ", and the ascription to Him of eternal power and glory, recalling His own claim (Matt. xi. 27) that all authority had been given Him in heaven and on earth — these things are inconsistent with any belief which falls short of His divinity ; while, if the allusion to His exaltation in iii. 22 might seem consonant with some form of Adoptionism, this hypothesis is ruled out by what is said of the joy open to believers of sharing in His sufferings and in the glory of His Second Coming (iv. 13). For the Christ whom St. Peter sets before us is not two, but one ; not divided into the Jesus of history and the Christ of faith, but the one Lord Jesus Christ, who suffered in the flesh and rose again and shall return in glory.

The Christology of the Epistle, therefore, contains the roots of later Catholic doctrine, but not yet its flower, so far as conscious formulation is concerned : in particular, its metaphysical implications are not considered.

When we turn to the doctrine of the Spirit, we meet with a difficulty of a different kind : that of knowing whether St. Peter thought of the Holy Spirit as personal. Four passages fall to be considered, and none of them is without ambiguity. They are :

(i) i. 2, ἐν ἁγιασμῷ πνεύματος. The context of the phrase, both here and in 2 Thess. ii. 13, is in favour of the view that πνεύματος is a subjective genitive ; in which case its collocation with πατρός and Ἰησοῦ Χριστοῦ, both personal, suggests that πνεύματος is personal too. Lightfoot[2] goes so far as to say that in this passage " the mention of the three Persons of the Holy Trinity cannot fail to be noticed ".

(ii) i. 11, τὸ ἐν αὐτοῖς πνεῦμα Χριστοῦ. For parallels to " the Spirit of Christ" cf. Acts xvi. 7, " the Spirit of Jesus ", Rom. viii. 9, " Spirit of Christ ", Gal. iv. 6, " the Spirit of His Son ", Phil. i. 19, " the Spirit of Jesus Christ ". In the Pauline passages it is possible that " Spirit " may be thought of as an impersonal influence, but scarcely in Acts xvi. 7, where the meaning is determined by " the Holy Spirit " in the previous verse, personal action being envisaged in both cases. This is also the case in 1 Pet. i. 11, where the Spirit is regarded as Revealer to the prophets.[3] The Spirit is " the Spirit of Christ " in that He derived from Christ His mission to the Church, which was part of the Messianic fulfilment. If the reference in the verse is to the

[1] See the note on i. 11.
[2] On 2 Thess. ii. 13 (*Notes on Epistles of St. Paul*).
[3] For a number of similar passages, which argue likewise a personal Spirit, cf. Lebreton, *History of the Dogma of the Trinity*, i. p. 281 (Engl. Trans.).

O.T. prophets, the phrase implies the pre-existence as well as the personality of the Spirit; but if to the contemporary Christian prophets, His pre-existence is not in point.

(iii) i. 12, ἐν πνεύματι ἁγίῳ ἀποσταλέντι ἀπ᾽ οὐρανοῦ. The reference is to the outpouring of the Holy Spirit which accompanied and confirmed the evangelization of northern Asia Minor with the good news of the universality of the Gospel. If Hort and others are right in omitting ἐν, the idea of impersonal influence is not ruled out. But with the preposition, which means " in the power (or sphere) of ", the Spirit's personality seems implied.

(iv) iv. 14, τὸ τῆς δόξης καὶ τὸ τοῦ θεοῦ πνεῦμα ἐφ᾽ ὑμᾶς ἀναπαύεται, sc. if you suffer reproach in Christ's name. The passage is partly based on Is. xi. 2, καὶ ἀναπαύεται ἐπ᾽ αὐτὸν πνεῦμα τοῦ θεοῦ : and here, as in other O.T. passages where the Spirit of God is connected with Messiah or with Israel, it must be admitted that " the personality proper of the Spirit is . . . faint ".[1] It is less faint, however, when the whole phrase is considered, whatever be its correct interpretation.[2]

This survey of the evidence afforded by this Epistle bears out what Lebreton says of Apostolic Christianity generally, that it shews " the intimate union of God the Father and Jesus Christ in prayers, doxologies, hymns, and, generally, in the various expressions of the Christian faith and religion ", but that " the Holy Spirit is very rarely associated with them ".[3] One of these rare examples, however, is provided by the salutation in 1 Peter, and there is nothing in what is said elsewhere in 1 Peter of Christ or of the Holy Spirit which does not fit into that trinitarian framework. At the same time, the doctrine is still in an undeveloped stage ; the materials are there, but they have not been theologically co-ordinated. The author has not extended his belief in Christ's divinity to an affirmation of His pre-existence : his Christology is more like that of the early chapters of Acts than of St. John or even of St. Paul. His conception of the Holy Spirit, moreover, is still primitive and based on experience of His converting and sanctifying power rather than on thought about the nature of God. There is nothing in these facts to surprise us, seeing that the place of the Spirit in doxologies was still disputed until the time of St. Basil in the fourth century, and that the implications of Christ's unique Sonship were as yet only beginning to be realized. St. Peter's teaching marks a stage in the growth of the doctrine of the Trinity out of a firmly realized belief in the Father as the ἀρχὴ τῆς θεότητος ; and its primitive character is consonant with the early date to which on other grounds we have assigned the letter.

B. Revelation — Salvation — Glory

The three terms ἀποκάλυψις, σωτηρία, and δόξα and their correlative verbs, which occur with some frequency in this Epistle, are so closely associated with the language of early Christian eschatology, yet admit of so many different shades of meaning, that they seem to call for some more comprehensive treatment than was possible in the exegetical Notes.

1. REVELATION (ἀποκάλυψις, ἀποκαλύπτειν).

In N.T. usage generally Revelation is a matter both of present (and past)

<hr/>

[1] Lebreton, op. cit. p. 88.
[3] Op. cit. p. 280.
[2] Cf. note on this verse.

experience and of future hope. Our Lord used the term of the apprehension of the meaning of His message and mission which God gave to simple people in the course of His ministry, and which He Himself as the Son was Matt. xi. entitled to communicate to whom He would ; and He said that the truth 25, 27

His Messiahship, which St. Peter was the first of His disciples to grasp Matt. xvi. and to affirm, was revealed to him by His Father in heaven. This idea of 17 Revelation as a continuing feature of the progress of the Gospel was taken over by St. Paul and expanded. God's hidden wisdom and counsel of 1 Cor. ii. redemption for the world, which was for untold ages wrapped in silence, 7-10, Rom. has now in Christ been revealed, and made known to believers through the xvi. 25, Spirit. Faith itself is spoken of as " waiting to be revealed " during Israel's Eph. iii. 5 period of education under the Law ; and so intimate was the revelation when Gal. iii. 23 it came that St. Paul speaks of God as " revealing His Son in me ". On a Gal i. 16 broader scale, the Gospel represented the revelation both of God's righteous- (cf. Eph. ness and of His wrath — of His righteousness in the faith which accepted it iii. 3) and grew in the understanding of it, and of His wrath in the growing wicked- Rom. i. 17, ness of those who rejected it, a wrath which would culminate in a final judg- 18 ment of divine doom. (cf. Phil. iii. 15)

The truth is that the knowledge that men have through faith, of God's Rom. ii. 5 will and ways, comes through His own revelation of Himself. It may be Eph. i. 17 given through visions or other mystical experiences, or through the special Gal. ii. 2 gifts of insight and intuition possessed by prophets, who were a regular 2 Cor. xii. feature of the primitive Church. It is to this prophetic gift that St. Peter 1, 7 refers in i. 12. Rev. i. 1 1 Pet. i. 12

Of the five remaining passages, however, where St. Peter uses the term, four belong certainly, and the fifth probably, to a different category. Our Lord says that " there is nothing hid which shall not be revealed ", and the Matt. x. context both in St. Matthew and in St. Luke shews that the reference is 26 eschatological. St. Luke, again, makes Jesus describe the Parusia as the Lk. xii. 2 Day " when the Son of Man is revealed ". It is significant that ἀποκαλύπτειν Lk. xvii.30 does not occur in St. Mark, its place being taken by φανεροῦν ; but the word Mk. iv. 22 was in Q, and may be regarded as one of the verba Christi which so largely influenced St. Peter's thought and vocabulary. When we turn to St. Paul, we find the concept of Revelation frequently occurring in an eschatological context. In 2 Thessalonians he speaks of the revelation of the " Man of 2 Thess. ii. Sin " as the decisive portent of the End, " when the Lord Jesus shall be 3-8 revealed from heaven with his mighty angels ", in judgment upon His ad- 2 Thess.i.7 versaries. He addresses the Corinthians as " eagerly expecting the revela- 1 Cor. i. 7 tion of our Lord Jesus Christ " ; and he encourages the Christians of Rome in their present trials with the thought of " the glory that is to be revealed towards us " and of " the revelation of the sons of God " which is to be the Rom. viii. crown at once of the creative process and of human expectation. 18, 19

It is in keeping with these ideas that St. Peter writes of " the salvation 1 Pet. i. 5 ready to be revealed in the last time ", of Christ's Advent as " the revelation i. 7, iv. 13, of Jesus Christ " or " the revelation of his glory ", and of " the glory that shall v. 1 be revealed " as something in which the Apostle himself had been a sharer. There remains only the difficult phrase where the author exhorts his readers to set their hopes without reserve ἐπὶ τὴν φερομένην ὑμῖν χάριν ἐν ἀποκαλύψει i. 13 Ἰησοῦ Χριστοῦ. Hort maintained that there was no eschatological reference here, but that the " revelation " referred to was the day-by-day unfolding of the truth of Christ as that is implied in Rom. i. 17 and Phil. iii. 15. It is to be observed, however, that in both those passages St. Paul uses the verb, not the noun ; and that there is no other passage in 1 Peter which would afford a parallel to this usage. The collocation of the Parusia with the " on-rushing grace which you have " is admittedly difficult ; yet it reflects a fact of Christian experience, often exemplified in Christian history and expressed also by St. Paul in 1 Cor. i. 7, namely that the expectation itself is productive of advance in grace and knowledge.[1] And, conversely, grace (like the Holy Spirit) is an " earnest " or first instalment of the Kingdom of God. I cannot doubt, therefore, that here as elsewhere in 1 Peter (with the exception of i. 12) revelation is a term of eschatological meaning.

2. SALVATION (σωτηρία, σώζειν).

A similar double usage is found in N.T. in the words connoting salvation. On the one hand, it is regarded as a present fact distinctive of the Christian status and experience. Sometimes it is traced back to the time of believers' acceptance of Christ, or more precisely to their baptism ; and in these cases the aorist or perfect tense is used. More commonly it is a characteristic of their present condition. Christians are those who are " in course of salvation " (σωζόμενοι) ; the " day of salvation " has dawned for them ; the Gospel which they have received and in which they stand is the means of their salvation ; they are to work it out with fear and trembling. It is in this context that we should understand St. Peter's allusion to baptism as " now saving us " ; and the same thought is present in his quotation of Prov. xi. 31, where the note of realized eschatology is strongly brought out.

A passage of special interest, as linking the present and the future meanings of salvation, is St. Paul's phrase, " By hope (or in hope) we were saved ". However we interpret τῇ ἐλπίδι, the existing fact of Christians' salvation is associated with the future which is the content of Christian hope. The process of salvation was begun at conversion ; but it was governed then, as it is governed now, by the End to which it looks and which will only be accomplished in " the last time " when God's purpose for all things is complete.

Equally common, however, in N.T. is the purely eschatological conception of salvation. A good example from the Gospels is the disciples' reply to our Lord's teaching about the danger of riches : " who then can be saved ? " In the Epistles, it is characteristic of the two Thessalonian letters, where (as Milligan observes) the whole outlook on the subject is eschatological.[2] Similarly, in Romans, St. Paul can say quite simply, " now is our salvation nearer than when we believed ", and speak of the purpose of discipline in the Church as being " that the spirit may be saved in the day of the Lord Jesus ". It is to this category that we must assign St. Peter's allusion to " salvation ready to be revealed in the last time ", and his injunction to his readers to desire the spiritual milk, that they " may grow thereby unto salvation ". Hort, on this latter verse, quotes Jas. i. 21, and adds : " Salvation in the fullest sense is but the completion of God's work upon men, the successful end of their probation and education ".

St. Peter's use of σωτηρία in i. 9, and by consequence its use in i. 10, present, however, a more difficult problem. Taking the latter verse first, we

Side notes (left margin):
Eph. ii. 5, 8 (cf. Lk. xix. 9), Tit. iii. 5 Acts ii. 47, 2 Cor. ii. 15, vi. 2 (cf. Is. xlix. 8) 1 Cor. xv. 2, Phil. ii. 12, 1 Pet. iii. 21, iv. 18

Rom. viii. 24

Mk. x. 24-26

Rom. xiii. 11 1 Cor. v. 5

1 Pet. i. 5 ii. 2

(cf. 2 Tim. iv. 18)

---

[1] Cf. Lightfoot, *Notes on Epistles of St. Paul*, p. 149.   [2] *St. Paul's Epistles to the Thessalonians*, p. lxix.

note that, whether the " prophets " mentioned be Jewish or Christian prophets, the whole context is Messianic, and σωτηρία in this sense " covers the whole range of the Messianic deliverance ",[1] both that part of it which is already realized and that which is still to come. At the same time there is a special reference to the acceptance of the Gentiles into the Messianic order then taking place (τῆς εἰς ὑμᾶς χάριτος), though the grace operative in it is shortly after (i. 13) seen to have an eschatological setting and background. The word is used, that is to say, in its most comprehensive signification.[2] In i. 9, on the other hand, various facts point to the eschatological sense being uppermost. Thus, the word κομίζεσθαι is normally used in Greek for the winning of a reward or prize at the end of some activity and to mark its consummation ; and this meaning is made doubly probable here by the description of the " salvation of your souls " as " the end (τέλος) of your faith ". Further, if this salvation were thought of as an already accomplished result of faith, little room would be left for the " increase unto salvation " mentioned in ii. 2. The facts seem best explained by the view that the " salvation of souls " referred to in i. 9 is identical with the " salvation " already mentioned in i. 5, i.e. the final salvation effected by the Parusia ; that (as is argued elsewhere [3]) κομιζόμενοι takes its time-meaning from the future in ἀγαλλιάσεσθε ; and that the mention of this σωτηρία in verse 9 prompted an expansion of the thought to embrace the whole Messianic deliverance, present as well as future, which is the subject of verses 10-12.

3. GLORY (δόξα, δοξάζω).

The word δόξα and its derivatives are so characteristic of this Epistle, as the subjoined Table shews, that they seem to call for separate discussion.

N.T. Book or Books	No. of Pages in WH Greek Text	No. of occurrences of δόξα	No. of occurrences of δοξάζω	Total No. of occurrences
St. Matthew	68	8	4	12
St. Mark	41	3	1	4
St. Luke	73	13	9	22
St. John	52	18	22	40
Acts	70	4	5	9
St. Paul's Epistles to Churches	110	67	11	78
Hebrews	21	7	1	8
Revelation	36	17	2	19
1 Peter	6¾	10	4	14

It will be observed that the use of δόξα, δοξάζω in 1 Peter is very much more frequent than in any other book or group of books in N.T. The case is not altered if we add 2 Peter, where two of the five occurrences of δόξα (in four and a half WH pages) refer to the Transfiguration and δοξάζω does not occur at all. Nor does δοξάζω occur in the Johannine Epistles or Ephesians or Jude ; and it occurs only once in St. Mark. On the other hand, δοξάζω is relatively common in St. Luke, who uses it to connote the praise and thanks-

---

[1] Cf. SH on Rom. i. 16. The whole note should be consulted.
[2] Cf. Add. Note D, pp. 260-3. And note the allusion to the gift of hope in grace in 2 Thess. ii. 16.
[3] Add. Note C, pp. 258-9 below.

giving offered by those whom our Lord had healed. δόξα, δοξάζω, again, never occur in the Johannine Epistles, though they are common in the Fourth Gospel, where however they are without the eschatological signification often found in the Synoptic Gospels ; δόξα having this signification in all three of its occurrences in St. Mark, in five of its eight occurrences in St. Matthew, and in two of its thirteen occurrences in St. Luke. In 1 Peter five of the ten occurrences of δόξα are eschatological, which gives a proportion only slightly in excess of the Synoptic Gospels. But we are concerned rather with a broad view of the facts, which indicate clearly that δόξα and its correlatives form a distinctive feature of this Epistle.

(1) δοξάζω. It will be convenient to begin this study of N.T. usage with the verb, since its meaning is simpler than that of the noun and raises fewer doctrinal issues. The normal connotation of δοξάζειν is to glorify in the sense of giving thanks or praise to God, or of manifesting the glory of God or of Christ in action. And the question which we may most profitably ask is :

What are the things which in the teaching of the N.T. writers glorify God and cause men to worship and praise Him ? They fall broadly into three categories.

(a) The first consists of events and works of healing in which the power and mercy of God are so overwhelmingly felt that men are moved to praise Him. The thought is attested in all the Gospels and in the Acts, but markedly so in the Lucan writings : the notes of glory that sound so clearly in the Infancy narrative are heard again in his records of several of our Lord's miracles (Lk. xiii. 13, xvii. 15, xviii. 43). In the case of cures, both the person cured and the onlookers are moved to praise God : in the Jewish view, such cures argued God's gracious visitation (Lk. vii. 16, Jn. ix. 24), and the popular instinct to glorify Him for them was too strong to be withstood (Acts iv. 21). Our Lord accepted this belief, and said that Lazarus' mortal sickness, from which He was to raise Him, was in order that God might be glorified in the work of His Son (Jn. xi. 4).

(b) The second category, which meets us especially in the Epistles and the Revelation, comprises grounds which have to do with the Atonement conceived in its most inclusive sense. For the first age of the Church the reconciliation of men with God, and of Gentile with Jew, in Christ was of all God's works of power and mercy the mightiest and most merciful. God was to be glorified for the holiness which was His prerogative alone (Rev. xv. 4), and never more than in the hour of His judgments (Rev. xiv. 6, 7). But it was the revelation of His mercy and forgiving love in Christ which was for Christian believers the most potent motive for praise. The Seer of Patmos brings this out with special force in the repeated pictures he gives of the worship which surrounds the Lamb (Rev. i. 6, v. 12, vii. 12, xix. 7) ; but it is emphasized equally in the writings of St. Paul, where it is instinct with his own experience of conversion (Gal. i. 5, 24, 1 Cor. vi. 20, 1 Tim. i. 17). God's redeeming love is the fundamental reason why men should glorify Him, both Jew and Gentile alike ; the Jew because the cross is the crowning demonstration of God's faithfulness to His promises (Rom. iii. 7, iv. 20, 2 Cor. i. 20), the Gentile because he was admitted to salvation on equal terms with the Jew. For St. Paul, indeed, as for the Apostolic Church generally, the doctrine of the universality of the Gospel is part and parcel of the doctrine of the Atonement ; the love revealed in the cross is a love that knows no barriers of privilege or tradition ; and the realization of this truth leads believers at once to the outpouring of praise (Acts xi. 18, xiii. 48, Rom. xv. 7-9, Eph. i. 6, 12, 14).

(c) There are other features, also, in the life of the Church which shew forth God's glory and evoke the spirit of praise. Among them we may note the generosity of the outlying churches to the mother-church of Jerusalem shewn in the collection of alms which lay so near St. Paul's heart (2 Cor. viii. 19, ix. 13) ; the conversion of many to the faith through the free course of the Word (2 Cor. ix. 13, Phil. ii. 11, 2 Thess. iii. 1) ; the work of the leaders of the churches (2 Cor. viii. 19) ; and the spirit of dependence upon God in the exercise of any gifts we have, which ensures dignity and grace in human inter-course (1 Pet. iv. 11). Foremost among all these features is to be reckoned the good lives of Christian believers. This emphasis on the ethical as the demonstration of religion, of character as the best advertisement of creed, goes back to the Sermon on the Mount (Matt. v. 16) ; and the Lord's words are echoed in many parts of the New Testament. All conduct is to be sub-ordinated to the end of shewing forth God's glory, and in comparison with that all ritual rules are indifferent (1 Cor. x. 31) ; innocency of life and free-dom from sin are its sure advertisement (Phil. i. 11, 1 Pet. ii. 12, Jude 24) ; and at the last the overthrow of evil will occasion a great diapason of praise (Rev. xix. 1 ff.). Finally, the pursuit of goodness may involve death for the disciple as it did for his Master. St. Luke tells us how the centurion at the cross, seeing the way in which Jesus bore His sufferings, " glorified God, saying, Certainly this was a righteous man " (Lk. xxiii. 47). And St. Peter teaches that the Christian believer may have the privilege, if he will, of glorifying God in the same way (1 Pet. iv. 16).

This grounding of God's glorification in the cross, considered both in itself and in its fruits, finds supreme expression in the Gospel according to St. John. Christ's death is at once His own glory and the Father's (Jn. xvii. 1), as were His mighty works [1] ; His own because it marked the climax of the work He came to do (Jn. xiii. 31, xvii. 1, xix. 30), the Father's because it represented the perfect obedience, which alone is perfect worship (Jn. xii. 28, xvii. 4) and constitutes the foundation of the Christian religion (cf. Heb. v. 7-10).[2] Moreover, both this glory and the opportunity which goes with it of glorifying God are imparted by Christ to His disciples (Jn. xvii. 10). In their fidelity to His teaching, in their unity with Him and with one another, in the fruitfulness of their lives, in the effectual prayer which they will offer in His name, and in the work of the Spirit in the Church, Christ's own glory will be declared and the Father likewise glorified (Jn. xvii. 10, xv. 8, xiv. 13, xvi. 14). As a corollary of this, martyrdom is regarded as a signal means of glorifying God (Jn. xxi. 19, cf. Rev. xi. 13), for it is the seal of the believer's faithfulness and obedience : " the martyr wins for himself the crown of glory ; but also by his death he gives glory to God ".[3] In all this the teach-ing of St. John's Gospel is more compact than that of the rest of the New Testament but it does not substantially go beyond it, except in the decisive-ness with which it identifies Christ's death with His glory. The things which glorify God are the same things as those we observe elsewhere ; the

---

[1] Hoskyns, *The Fourth Gospel*, ii. pp. 497 f., 528 ff., 585 ff.
[2] *Op. cit.* p. 497.
[3] W. Temple, *Readings in St. John's Gospel*, ii. p. 221.

cross as the supreme embodiment of the Father's universal love and of the Son of Man's obedience, and its fruits in the faith and unity of the Church and the lives and conduct of its members. The high-priestly prayer " is the solemn consecration of Himself in the presence of His disciples as their effective sacrifice ; it is His prayer for glorification in and through His death ; it is His irrevocable dedication of His disciples to their mission in the world, and His prayer that both they and those who believe through their teaching may be consecrated to the service of God ; and finally it concludes with the prayer that the Church thus consecrated may at the End behold the glory of the Son and dwell in the perfect love of the Father and the Son ".[1]

(2) δόξα. The noun δόξα is never used in N.T. in the classical sense of " opinion " ; but the connotations, which it has in secular literature, of " shew ", " glamour ", and so of social " honour " or " esteem ", are occasionally found, e.g. Matt. iv. 8, vi. 29, Jn. xii. 43, 1 Cor. xi. 15, xv. 40, 41, Phil. iii. 19, 1 Pet. i. 24 (quoting Is. xl. 6) ; and in Jude 8, 2 Pet. ii. 10 the plural occurs meaning " authorities ". The plural δόξας in 1 Pet. i. 11 is best taken as an extension of the secular usage, meaning " triumphs ". Normally, however, δόξα in N.T. means the glory of God, inherent or imparted to others. It is therefore emphatically what Otto would call a *numinous* word,[2] expressing the majesty and wonder of the divine nature and province. In LXX it often represents the *Shekinah* or manifested presence of God, and is closely associated with visible brightness or splendour, as in 1 Kings viii. 11, cf. Acts xxii. 11 ; and from this it comes to represent the wondrous majesty, power, and love of God as manifested to men.[3] Nowhere is this meaning of δόξα better set forth than in Is. lx. 1, 2 : " Arise, shine ; for thy light is come, and the glory of the Lord is risen upon thee. For, behold, the darkness shall cover the earth, and gross darkness the people ; but the Lord shall arise upon thee, and his glory shall be seen upon thee."

With such a background in Jewish thought, it is not surprising that glory should be one of the essential attributes of God in N.T. Phrases such as " the God of glory " on St. Stephen's lips, or " the Father of glory " used by St. Paul, and the frequent use of " glory " in doxologies, where the construction is an affirmation rather than a wish,[4] attest the doctrine. It is in the same vein that St. Peter writes, when he speaks of God having " called us unto his eternal glory in Christ ".

Acts vii. 2
Eph. i. 17
1 Pet. iv. 11

1 Pet. v. 10

But one of the most striking features of N.T. is the way in which " glory " has become likewise a distinctive attribute of Christ. The way had been prepared for this in the Messianic thought of the Jews both prophetic and Rabbinic [5] ; and, like the application to Christ of the title " Lord " (κύριος), it is one of the primary evidences of the Apostolic doctrine of the Incarnation. Glory is something which Christ shared with the Father " before the world was " : He " manifested forth his glory " during His earthly life by His mighty works and sacrificial death, and His disciples saw it and recognized in it " the glory as of the only-begotten of the Father " : and a still plainer manifestation of it was given through His resurrection and ascension, when God " raised him up from the dead and gave him glory " — a thought which has frequent echoes throughout N.T.[6] From this it was no great step to the

Jn. xvii. 5
Jn. ii. 11
Jn. i. 14

1 Pet. i. 21

---

[1] Hoskyns, *op. cit.* p. 586.
[2] *The Idea of the Holy, passim.*
[3] Cf. Lightfoot on Col. i. 11, SH on Rom. i. 23.

[4] Cf. Lightfoot on Gal. i. 5.
[5] Cf. Mayor, note on Jas. ii. 1.
[6] e.g. Acts iii. 13, Phil. ii. 9, Heb. ii. 7, 9 (cf. Jn. vii. 39).

virtual identification of Christ with the glory, as when He is said to be the
" effulgence " (ἀπαύγασμα) of the divine glory or when St. James (as some Heb. i. 3
think) entitles Him simply " the glory ".[1]   Jas. ii. 1

There remains however, a more decisive manifestation yet, and one on
which our Lord Himself had laid great stress. This is at the End of all
things, when He will come " in the glory of his Father with the holy angels ", Mk. viii.
or (as He is elsewhere reported to have said) " in the clouds with great power 38, xiii. 26
and glory ". Of this ultimate glory of Christ the chosen Three of the
disciples were given a foretaste at the Transfiguration[2]; and it is a part of 1 Pet. iv.
early Christian expectation which is characteristic of 1 Peter. Thus, St. 13 (cf. i
Peter speaks of the " revelation " of Christ's glory ; of being a sharer of 13),v.1,i.7
" the glory that shall be revealed " : and of the tested faith of Christians re-
dounding " to praise and honour and glory at the appearing of Jesus Christ ".
In all this St. Peter reflects primitive eschatological teaching which goes
back to our Lord Himself.

The divine glory is also an attribute of the Church in N.T. For this,
too, there was a long preparation in Hebrew thought.[3] Nor was the idea
Messianic : indeed, the belief in the Shekinah as characteristic of the actual
life of Israel was in a sense a compensation for the delay in Messiah's appearance ; and even when the renovated Israel of the Kingdom of God is in
mind, the expectation of the " glory " is independent of, and more frequent
than, the expectation of a personal Messiah. This non-Messianic usage is Rom. ix. 4
found also in N.T., as applied to the Jews. Yet in 2 Cor. iii. we have an 2 Cor. iii.
illustration of the ease with which it could be given a Messianic colour and 7, 18
transferred to the life of the Church. For in N.T. the " glory " which characterizes the Church and transfigures the life of believers is always Messianic,
in the sense that it is regarded as imparted by Christ or at least dependent
on the relation of believers to Him. " The glory which thou gavest me I
have given them " : these words represent the view which underlies all N.T.
teaching on the subject. Even in 1 Pet. iv. 14, where kinship with Jewish
thought seems unusually close, the affirmation of the privilege of the Shekinah
is made to depend on suffering " in the name of Christ ".

The glory which characterizes the Church, like that which characterizes
Christ Himself, is thought of both as something already enjoyed and as
something which is still future. God has already glorified those whom He Rom. viii.
has justified ; the riches of His glory are already available to all who are in 30
Christ and live by His grace ; and nowhere is this experienced more fully Eph. i. 18,
than in the mercy which has led to the reconciliation of the Gentiles and their iii. 16
inclusion in the new covenant.   Rom. ix.
                                                                                23 f., Col.
Further, as John Lightfoot (Works, v. p. 330) justly observes, the holi- i. 27
ness of Christians is styled glory. " A holy Christian hath a glory here, and
a glory hereafter. So that may be taken, 2 Cor. iii. ult. ' We are changed
into the image of God from glory to glory ' : that is, from holiness to happiness." He cites also 1 Pet. iv. 14 and Rom. viii. 30, on the latter passage
(" Whom he called, them he also justified ; and whom he justified, them he also
glorified ") adding: " Where is ' sanctified ' ? It is included in ' glorified '.
Those that he justified, he endued with the glory of holiness here, and shall
reward with eternal glory hereafter." The whole passage is a noble piece of
seventeenth-century theology.

[1] Cf. note on 1 Pet. iv. 14 above.   Boobyer's work.
[2] Cf. note on 1 Pet. iv. 14, and reference to   [3] Cf. note on 1 Pet. iv. 14.

Yet the full measure of this glory of the Church waits, as in Christ's case, for His second coming. This glory is the object of confident hope (Rom. v. 2), the destined reward of a good life (Rom. ii. 7, 10), and a more than sufficient compensation for every trial suffered in faith's service on earth (2 Thess. ii. 14, Rom. viii. 18, 1 Pet. i. 11, iv. 13). It will mark the risen body of the Christian no less than his Lord's; it is the light of the heavenly city, the new Jerusalem, which is to supervene at the last upon the temporal order; and " when Christ, who is our life, shall appear, then shall [we] also appear with him in glory ". The language of our Epistle often echoes the same thought. The " praise and glory and honour " to which the stedfast-ness of Christians in trial redounds will be not only God's but theirs; the exultation derived from faith will issue in a joy that is " instinct with glory "[1]; and the reward of a faithful ministry will be " the amaranthine crown of glory ", when the Chief Shepherd shall appear.

It will be observed that all the different types of meaning which δόξα has in N.T. are found in 1 Peter, with regard both to Christ and to Christian believers; but the cases where the reference is eschatological amount to at least half of the whole number. When we add to this the decided pre-dominance of the eschatological reference in St. Peter's idea of revelation, and also his usage in regard to the concept of salvation, we conclude that for him all three terms were part of the language of eschatology, and that, though he was aware of other meanings, the eschatological meaning was that which was primary in his mind.

[Marginal references: 1 Cor. xv. 43, Rev. xxi. 11, 23; Col. iii. 4; 1 Pet. i. 7; 1 Pet. i. 8; 1 Pet. v. 4]

C. On ἀγαλλιᾶσθε and its variants in i. 6 and 8

1. The reading ἀγαλλιᾶσθε is doubtful, both in verse 6 and in verse 8. In verse 6 exultabitis is found in several MSS. of the Vulgate; and Origen's quotation of the passage in Exhort. ad Mart. 39 suggests that he read ἀγαλλιάσεσθε there. This book belongs to Origen's Caesarean period, but no Caesarean type of text for the Epistles has yet been shown to exist. [The Leicester cursive 69 is so badly written that the indications of contraction-marks over the . . . αοθ . . . in both cases cannot be relied on as evidence.] Exultabitis is also found in syrsch are Fulg. Bed206. In verse 8 Irenaeus read the future, as is clear from A.H. IV. ix. 2, V. vii. 2, both of them eschato-logical passages. Polycarp, ad Phil. i., has the future in OL, but not in the Greek; though the Greek, εἰς ὃν οὐκ ἰδόντες πιστεύετε χαρᾷ ἀνεκλαλήτῳ καὶ δεδοξα-σμένῃ (thus omitting ἀγαλλ.) admits of the view that Polycarp had in the MS. before him a future verb which would not have suited his context, and which he therefore omitted. So, too the future occurs in Augustine (Pecc. Mer. 1), Bede, Peshitto, and the Armenian version. It is supported, moreover, by the connexion of joy with the final revelation of Christ's glory, in 1 Pet. iv. 13. On the other hand the principal Greek texts read the present tense in both verses (but note the variants in verse 8, (ἀγαλλιᾶσθε) אAC²KLP, (ἀγαλλιᾶτε) BCOr3.692).

2. How shall we best account for these discrepancies in the textual evidence? The prevailing view is that the present tenses were held to have a future meaning (as interpreted in the commentary of Oecumenius, cited in the note on i. 6), and that the text was altered in the early versions accordingly. This is Moffatt's view, who accordingly translates by the

[1] Cf. note on i. 8 and Add. Note C, below, for the eschatological view of this verse.

future tense in both verses (cf. *The Moffatt Bible, in loc.*, and his commentary in *The Moffatt N.T.*). But an alternative hypothesis is that the future is original in verse 8 and the present in verse 6. It is easy to see how copyists should have assimilated the two tenses, and the present ἀγαπᾶτε in verse 8 would have assisted the process. (Bigg, indeed, considers that ἀγαπᾶτε almost requires the present ἀγαλλιᾶσθε : but see below.) On the other hand, it is not easy to see why, if presents occurred in both verses, either or both of them should have been altered on so wide a scale. And it must be remembered that, as Moulton observes (*Grammar*, ii. p. 48), since patristic comments and early versions " go back to periods considerably antedating our best uncials, they have naturally the weight in many cases of a primitive tradition, which no wise exegete would ignore ". Hence, " we must always be careful to realize our freedom to take our own line on sufficient reason ".

3. Hort gives reasons for preferring the reading ἀγαλλιᾶτε in verse 8, but I cannot regard them as convincing. Dittography with ἀγαπᾶτε above, if both words occurred at the end of their respective lines in an early MS., might account for it. On the other hand, the late Dr. Darwell Stone informed me that the active form is not rare in the apocryphal Acts, e.g. *Act. Phil.* 16, *Act. Thom.* 1075.

4. Other reasons which tell in favour of ἀγαλλιάσεσθε in verse 8 are as follows : (*a*) In the closely parallel passage in iv. 13 exuberance of joy is connected with the life to come, and contrasted with the chastened joy of sharing Christ's sufferings : the conception is almost a Petrine trait. (*b*) δόξα, τέλος, and σωτηρία are in all comparable contexts in this Epistle used with an eschatological reference, cf. for δόξα i. 7, 11, iv. 13, v. 1, 4, 10 ; for τέλος iv. 7, 17 ; for σωτηρία i. 5, ii. 2. The τέλος in i. 9 is the climax of the process of αὔξησις εἰς σωτηρίαν alluded to in ii. 3. The difficulties of reconciling this with a present tense in ἀγαλλ. are seen in the confusion which is to be observed in Leighton's usually clear exposition at this point. (*c*) A better sense is given in verse 8 itself. So far from the main verbs ἀγαπᾶτε . . . ἀγαλλ. needing to be, as many commentators have claimed, in the same tense, the change of tense in the participles (ἰδόντες, *v.l.* εἰδότες . . . ὁρῶντες, πιστεύοντες) from aorist or perfect to present suggests a parallel change, from present to future, in the main verbs ; the sense being, " You did not see Him, but you love Him ; you do not see Him, but in virtue of your faith you shall, etc.". The thought of verses 6-8 would then be summarized again in verse 11, τὰ εἰς Χριστὸν παθήματα καὶ τὰς μετὰ ταῦτα δόξας.

D. *Exegesis of i. 10-12*

Though Hort's commentary on these verses is often baffling and his meaning obscure, there are two ways in which he has laid us especially in his debt. In the first place, he is far more aware than any other commentator of the acute difficulties of the passage · and secondly he insists that the clue to it lies in a fact of religious history, namely the admission of the Gentiles to the Christian covenant. Since Hort wrote, however, our knowledge of this fact has been amplified · in particular, Dr. Armitage Robinson's commentary on Ephesians has enabled us to clothe with flesh and blood much which before was little more than the skeleton of knowledge ; and the life and worship of the Church in the middle of the first century have been illuminated for us by N.T. scholarship in many countries, and by the parallels which are continually being presented by the younger churches in the mission field. The result is that we can form a more detailed and vivid conception of the contemporary facts underlying the Epistle, and therefore interpret in clearer outline some of its allusions and meanings.

1. That the primary reference of the passage is to the contemporary life of the Church is indicated by the opening words, " About which salvation ". For the salvation in question is clearly identical with the " salvation of souls " mentioned in the previous verse ; and this salvation can be regarded as something to which the Christians addressed already have a title, acquired as the result of their faith. Moreover, this is still the case, even if we read ἀγαλλιάσεσθε in verse 8 and refer the whole verse to the future ; for the salvation, even if future, is regarded as organically related to the faith and love which are dominating features in the Church's contemporary life.[1] The point is made still clearer by the emphatic νῦν in verse 12. The meaning of this " now " in 1 Peter is discussed in the Introduction : what is important here is to observe that the " now " clause — a clause intimately bound up with the rest and in no sense otiose — binds down the whole passage to con-temporary events on earth. It is not permissible to interpret the passage as though it applied to the past facts of Christ's death and resurrection by which men's salvation was initially procured, or as though it applied to any doctrine of salvation in abstraction from its realization in fact. The fact is something into which angels desire to gaze.

2. The salvation was the object of intense enquiry and research by " prophets " ; and since the view will be taken here that the allusion in this passage is to Christian prophets, it may be well, before proceeding further, to give a brief account of an order or ministry which played so large a part in the life of the primitive Church.[2]

Jewish prophecy combined two elements found originally in separation, and denoted by two different words, nabi and ro-eh. Nabi was an Arabian rather than a Hebrew word ; and the nebiim or " prophets " were a feature of religion common to all the Semitic peoples. They were commonly seen in groups, and a fanatical religious frenzy was one of their chief characteristics. It was such a group that Saul joined, to the surprise and perhaps the dismay of his countrymen, after he had been anointed king by Samuel (1 Sam. x.). The enthusiasm of their religion was of an intensely patriotic kind : in modern times the mad mullahs of Somaliland and the dancing dervishes of the Sudan are heirs of their tradition. The other kind of prophecy, denoted by the word ro-eh, or " seer ", was of a mystical and contemplative type, and is well represented in the early history of Israel by Samuel. Ecstasy and second sight were characteristic of the seer ; and he had a reputation for practical insight which made his counsel sought for by many in regard both to public and to private affairs. The predictive element in later prophecy — an element which has been too little recognized in modern theology — be-longed to this tradition ; and so did the still later apocalyptic.

---

[1] Cf. Hoskyns, Cambridge Sermons, p. 39 : " Our religion survived the disappointment [of the delay in the Parusia] because it was primarily a possession and only secondarily a hope ".

[2] The most detailed English study of Chris-tian prophecy known to me is in four books by my father, the late Dr. E. C. Selwyn. They are The Christian Prophets (1900) ; St. Luke the Prophet (1901) ; The Oracles in the New Testament (1911) ; and the posthumous First Christian Ideas (1919).

It is easy to note the fusion of these two elements in the prophets of the classical period ; but what is not so easy is to realize the persistence of the prophetic circles which were the background of the great prophets. And yet the evidence is not wanting. The position of Huldah the prophetess, in the reign of Josiah, is a case in point. She is a " religious ", a member of a " college " or religious community (2 Kings xxii.), and she is consulted by the king and the priests as soon as the momentous discovery of " the book of the law " has been made. There was, that is to say, a prophetic guild or circle in the very heart of the institutional life of the Jewish Church of that period. And there is nothing to suggest that this was unusual. Both Jeremiah and Ezekiel, we know, came out of priestly circles ; while Amos' disclaimer, that he was not the son of a prophet, implies that the prophetic gift often went in families. And when we ask further what the functions of these prophetic circles were, the answer is surely not far to seek. They nourished a particular form of the spiritual life, marked by pre-eminent devotion, and exercised in the collection and study of the utterances and writings of the prophets. If the scribes were the canonists, the prophets were the theologians of the Jewish revelation. It is precisely such a circle that meets us on the threshold of the Gospel story. We find there the priestly and the prophetic side by side and working in closest harmony. Zacharias was a priest, but we are told that after the birth of his son, he " was filled with the Holy Ghost and prophesied ", his utterance being the Benedictus. Simeon is not styled a prophet, but all that is told us of him — his conviction that he should see the Lord's Messiah, his waiting " for the consolation of Israel ", his coming " by the Spirit " into the temple — shews that he was one. Of Anna we are definitely told that she was a " prophetess " (Lk. ii. 36), devoted to the temple, supplementing its regular services by her own " fastings and prayers ", and surrounded by others who " looked for redemption in Jerusalem ". At the opening of the Christian era, there-fore, prophecy was (1) at the very heart of the institutional life of the Jewish Church, (2) marked by special piety and devotion, (3) concentrated on the advent of the Messiah and on the prophecies concerned with him, (4) given to expressing itself in psalmody, (5) a function of women no less than of men.

Now it is evident that the existence of this tradition of religion has very great importance for the understanding of Christian prophecy proper. The great development to be observed flows from the conviction that in Jesus the Messiah has already come. Preoccupation with the fact and faith of the Messiah was, indeed, the primary mark of Christian prophecy, whether this expressed itself in hymnody, preaching, or teaching. And this preoccupa-tion bore a twofold fruit, theological and moral. Theologically, it gave a powerful impulse to the study of the ancient Scriptures, with a view to finding prophecies of the Messiah and His Kingdom, and applying them to current events by way of interpretation or guidance. And closely connected with this theological function — a work at once of research and of synthesis — went the task of fortifying the faith of believers against moral temptation and outward persecution. A typical representation of Christian prophecy on this side is to be found in Barnabas, " a good man, and full of the Holy Ghost and of faith ", who was sent by the Apostles at Jerusalem to strengthen the faith of believers at Antioch. It was after this mission, which included a year of regular teaching, that the name of " Christians " first came into vogue. So, too, we find two prophets, Judas and Silas, chosen to accompany Paul and Barnabas to Antioch with the findings of the Council at Jerusalem ; and we are told that they " exhorted the brethren with many words and confirmed them ". This aspect of prophecy is well summarized in the word παράκλησις, which is used alike of the expectations of Simeon, of Joses for whom it provided a *soubriquet*, and of the influence at Antioch of those who brought the reply from the Church at Jerusalem. It means more than the " consolation " of our E.V., and signifies the moral strengthening which comes from the presence and guidance of those who are strong in the faith. If we look at this practical aspect of Christian prophecy, there is no more " prophetic " book in N.T. than 1 Peter ; and it is significant that some part in its composition was played by Silvanus the prophet.

3. The prophets here alluded to are said to have " prophesied about the grace towards you ". This " grace " is introduced in a way which indicates that St. Peter's readers would have known quite well what was in his mind : the language is natural if the allusion were to a time of spiritual expansion and revival lately experienced in the Church. Hort regarded ὑμᾶς as connoting especially the Gentiles : but we are not bound to interpret it so narrowly. The equality of the Gentile with the Jew after conversion to Christianity was a glorious thing, as St. Paul shews in Ephesians. But the reflex action of the discovery of this fact on Jew and Gentile alike was something equally glorious. If the Gentile lost his sense of inferiority to the " chosen people ", the Jew lost his narrowness of outlook and found the full universality of the Messianic hope of which his nation had been the repository. The coincident recognition by both parties of the universality of the Gospel was an event which quickened the pulse of the whole Church, and the consequent revival might well be called — whether Jew or Gentile or both together were being addressed — " the grace towards you ".[1]

But who were the " prophets " who prophesied about it ? It has been generally assumed by commentators that the prophets of O.T. are meant. The same assumption held good in regard to the " prophets " mentioned along with " apostles " by St. Paul in Eph. ii. 20, iii. 5, and iv. 11, until Alford showed that a more probable reference was to Christian prophets [2] ; and his interpretation has won general acceptance. The traditional view involves two difficulties in this passage of 1 Peter : (1) the " seeking and searching " mentioned in verse 10 are not easily identifiable with what we know of the activities of the O.T. prophets : the " searching ", in particular, suggests work on written materials as in Jn. v. 39, such as is far more easily connected with the Christian prophets than with their predecessors of the older dispensation. If Jewish prophets are meant, indeed, then it is probably Daniel and the apocalyptic writers who are in mind rather than the prophets of the earlier periods. (2) The phrase " the spirit of Christ " is without parallel if applied to the O.T. prophets. This is not a decisive argument (see below, and notes on verses 10, 11), but it has some weight. Both these difficulties disappear if " prophets " in verse 10 means Christian prophets, or at least the prophetic tradition down to, and including, the Christian prophets. Further, the absence of the article before προφῆται, though in

---

[1] This meaning of grace in Ephesians is the subject of an Additional Note by Dr. Armitage Robinson in his commentary.

[2] Commentary, *in loc.*, followed by Hort, note on 1 Pet. i. 2 (p. 22), and J. Armitage

Robinson. Moffatt (*Introduction*, p. 382 n.) holds that the *autor ad Ephesios* " changes the O.T. prophets into Christian prophets ", by way of correcting 1 Pet. i. 10-12.

keeping with the style of the Epistle, is more natural if the reference were to men whose activities were well known to the readers. It is significant, moreover, that they are spoken of here, exactly as in Eph. iii. 5, as the recipients of a revelation (ἀπεκαλύφθη), of which St. Paul says that it was given, and St. Peter that it was disseminated, at a definite time (νῦν in both writers) and in the power of the Spirit (ἐν πνεύματι in both places).

4. These considerations are reinforced when we pass on to verse 11.

(i) The prophetic activity alluded to is one of research into the fulfilment of prophecy. Our notes on the passage shew that there are not wanting in O.T. indications of interest in the time of fulfilment ; but there is nothing which would entitle us to speak of a "research" on the subject ; whereas the Songs of Zacharias and of Simeon in Lk. i., ii., and the Revelation of the Seer of Patmos, so different and yet both so steeped in the Hebrew Scriptures, shew that the Christian prophets were largely engaged in this activity.

(ii) A still greater difficulty besets the usual hypothesis in the phrase τὰ εἰς Χριστὸν παθήματα. It is, indeed, astonishing to find how few commentators have found this phrase disturbing, and how willingly they have accepted the translation " the sufferings of Christ " ; though the difficulty was felt as far back as Jerome, who rendered the phrase by eas quae in Christo sunt passiones. Hort, following Tyndale, translates " the sufferings destined for Christ ", and quotes Lk. xxiv. 26, 46, Acts iii. 18, xvii. 3, xxvi. 23. Heb. ii. 10 might also be added. Yet none of these passages has such a phrase as εἰς Χριστόν. On the other hand, the construction has a close parallel in 2 Cor. xi. 3, τῆς ἁπλότητος καὶ τῆς ἁγνότητος τῆς εἰς τὸν Χριστόν, where the meaning is " directed towards Christ ", " Christward ". Cf. also 1 Cor. xvi. 1. The point to be observed is that the word that governs the prepositional clause is external to the noun within the clause. And this is the case with all the patristic passages quoted by Hort to illustrate εἰς Χριστόν here : in all of them the subject of the verb governing εἰς Χριστόν or in Christum is other than Christ Himself.

MM, sub voc. εἰς, give two examples from papyri of the early second century where εἰς with the accusative appears to stand for the possessive genitive. But these are far outweighed in number by the examples given of the flexible use of εἰς in the Κοινή to represent " in the direction of ", " for ", and even " in the name of ". Further, εἰς sometimes stands for ἐν. Though perhaps none of the passages cited by MM affords an exact parallel to St. Peter's phrase, some of them go near enough to serve as illustrations of its supple and sensitive meaning. εἰς Χριστόν means not " Christ's " but " Christward ".

This interpretation must surely stand, however we interpret " prophets " in verse 10. If the reference is to Jewish prophets, here too we must say that it is the apocalyptists rather than the prophets proper who are in mind ; for it was they especially who developed the theme of the " Messianic Woes " — afflictions, that is, which were conceived, not as suffered by the Messiah Himself, but as befalling the whole world in immediate preparation for the advent of the Messiah Himself. But certainly the phrase is more natural, and admits of a larger reference, if it alludes to the testimony of Christian prophets. The " sufferings of the Christward road " were predicted not only obscurely by the apocalyptists, but definitely and directly by Christ Himself, who said that they would presage His coming in glory (Matt. v. 11,

12, x. 17 ff., 38, xvi. 24, Mk. x. 39, xiii. 9 f., Lk. xii. 11, xxi. 14 ff., Jn. xvi. *passim*) and their own deliverance. Further, the prediction is reiterated in the early church, cf. Acts xiv. 22 (δεῖ of the sufferings of Christians, as ἔδει of Christ in Acts xvii. 3), 1 Cor. iv. 9 ff., 2 Tim. iii. 12, and in this Epistle ii. 21. And St. Paul speaks of the Holy Spirit testifying (διαμαρτύρεται) persecution for himself in particular in Acts xx. 23 — a passage of special importance as evidence of the actual happening in particular circumstances of what St. Peter alludes to generally. The words κατὰ πόλιν rule out, as Alford observes, the inner voice of the Spirit in St. Paul's mind, and connote the findings of prophetic groups in each place.

We may further illustrate the passage by comparing it with Rom. viii., and with Heb. xii. 2 ff. (*a*) In Rom. viii. 18-32, St. Paul contrasts " the sufferings of the present time " with the " glory " that is to be revealed " towards us ", when the liberty of the children of God shall be manifested, as the crown of the creative process. Meanwhile, we have the comfort of the Spirit's intercession, and the assurance that, as we are united with Christ in His suffering, so also we shall be in His triumph. Cf. 1 Pet. iv. 13. The sufferings alluded to in verse 18 in fact are suffered εἰς Χριστόν. (*b*) In Heb. xii. the sufferings attaching to faith are described as a " chastening " which is part of the privilege of sonship ; and Christians are bidden to "run the race " set before them, ἀφορῶντες εἰς τὸν τῆς πίστεως ἀρχηγὸν καὶ τελειωτὴν Ἰησοῦν, who despised the shame of the cross for the glory that lay beyond. Cf. also Heb. xiii. 12, 13.

(iii) The plural, " glories " or " triumphs ", is more easily understood of the divers rewards of a number of Christians than of Christ's alone. It is true that Christ's triumph involves that of His disciples too, whether we think of them as part of His triumphal cortège (2 Cor. ii. 14), or as repeating through baptism His overthrow of the powers of evil (cf. Col. ii. 15, with Lightfoot's note ; and the discussion of 1 Pet. iii. 18-21 in this volume). But this unusual plural is more natural if the idea is such as is expressed in 1 Cor. ii. 9, Jn. xiv. 1, Rom. viii., 2 Tim. ii. 12.[1]

5. St. Peter goes on to say that it was revealed to the prophets of whom he has been speaking that they were ministering their findings for the benefit not of themselves but of the Asiatic churches ; and further that these findings had recently been reported to these churches by men whose evangelistic work among them had been blessed by a wonderful outpouring of the Holy Spirit, such as had engaged the rapt attention of the angels. We have here fresh light on the activities of the prophets and on the dissemination of their teaching, and the result is both to confirm and to amplify the view here taken.

(i) We have already been told that " prophets " prophesied about the grace seen in the recent quickening and expansion of the Church, and had made the salvation which it portended for its members the subject of exhaustive mystical enquiry and theological research, with special reference to

---

[1] There is a vigorous discussion of this passage by E. A. Edghill in *The Evidential Value of Prophecy*, pp. 546-51, where the traditional view is very ably expounded. Believing that " St. Peter was much influenced by our Lord's allusions to prophecy in His post-resurrection teaching ", Dr. Edghill illustrates the point by comparing 1 Pet. i. 11 with Lk. xxiv. 25, 26 :

ST. PETER. τὰ εἰς Χριστὸν παθήματα καὶ τὰς μετὰ ταῦτα δόξας.

OUR LORD. οὐχὶ ταῦτα ἔδει παθεῖν τὸν Χριστὸν καὶ εἰσελθεῖν εἰς τὴν δόξαν αὐτοῦ ; and he suggests that δόξας (plural) referred to the resurrection, ascension, exaltation, and second advent of our Lord. Dr. Edghill feels the difficulties, however, of the phrase τὸ ἐν αὐτοῖς πνεῦμα Χριστοῦ, though I cannot think that he meets them very successfully. It is with regret that I find myself dissenting from one who was so fine a scholar and so inspiring a friend.

the time or circumstances in which the sufferings of the Christward road and the triumphs following them were to be accomplished. The answer was " Now " ; but the author is not content simply to say that. Instead, he inserts a further fact about the " prophets " and what was revealed to them, namely the application to the Christians of northern Asia Minor of their prophetic activity and its fruits. The following points may be observed : (a) Whatever be the meaning of the ὅτι . . . αὐτά clause, it is not one which can be said to have been revealed to the O.T. prophets. Their messages were emphatically for their own times, even when the prophets felt them to have a further meaning ; they were aware of Spirit-given intimations of future redemption, but the future to which these referred was just what was never revealed to them. Their ministry was primarily to their contemporaries. (b) We need not suppose that the contrast between " themselves " and " you " is a contrast between different ages of history ; as Hort indicates, the use of ὑμῖν rather than ἡμῖν points to a contrast " of classes of men " ; for, if St. Peter had meant " the present generation ", ἡμῖν would have been the natural word to use. Moreover, if that were the meaning, we might have expected μόνοις with ἑαυτοῖς, as in Rom. iv. 23, 24 (οὐκ ἐγράφη δὲ δι' αὐτὸν μόνον . . ., ἀλλὰ καὶ δι' ἡμᾶς). Cf. also 1 Cor. x. 11. More relevant to the contrast here is 1 Cor. ix. 9, 10, where St. Paul interprets the Mosaic ordinance, " Thou shalt not muzzle the ox that treadeth out the corn ", as indicating the divine principle governing industry, namely the right of the worker to profit by his labour. This scripture, he says with some irony, was not written for the sake of oxen, but entirely for our sakes, for ploughman and thresher should do their work in hope. And this principle, once established, applies equally to Christian teachers and their right to the fruit of their labours. As Alford rightly points out, St. Paul does not say " for oxen only " : in this case the contrast is not between a direct and an indirect application of the scripture, but between a false and a true interpretation of it.

In what sense, then, could " prophets " be said to have been ministering their findings to or for themselves ? It would appear that we are dealing with a change of outlook and method, almost amounting to a conversion, which was brought about by a revelation at a definite moment or moments (ἀπεκαλύφθη). There was a former phase (represented by the imperfect tenses in ἐδήλου and διηκόνουν), when they were aware of a message in their tradition which was still unclear in its practical import, and of a ministry which was narrow and introverted ; but a time came when the obscure parts of the message became illuminated, and the full range of their ministry was disclosed. The question may be asked whether we should understand by " themselves " men of their own race, i.e. Jews, or men of their own class and type, i.e. prophets : in the former case, the allusion is to the discovery of the universality of the Gospel, in the latter to such a change of emphasis as St. Paul illustrates when he writes, " He that speaketh in an unknown tongue edifieth himself ; but he that prophesieth edifieth the church " (1 Cor. xiv. 4) — the change from a type of religious ministry which was cloistral, contemplative, and self-centred to one that was active, public, and missionary-hearted. But the issue is more apparent than real. For the prophetic circles of later Judaism, for all their piety, had been inclined to be somewhat subjective and aloof from common life, so that the advent of John the Baptist struck the men of his time as a fresh outpouring of the prophetic Word after centuries of silence (cf. 1 Sam. iii. 1) ; and the narratives of Acts ii., iii. indicate that Christian prophecy combined in itself both the extroversion which it learnt from the example of the Baptist and of the Lord Himself and the universality of range which it substituted for the peculiarly Jewish outlook of its forerunners. The latter, indeed, would have carried with it the release of an activity which had tended, under the pressure of persecution and marytrdom, to be driven in upon itself. In interpreting ἑαυτοῖς, therefore, as meaning " men of their own race " we shall not be excluding the more limited, psychological reference.

Further, in expounding the passage in this manner, we find ourselves at once able to fill in many of the details of the situation recalled by the author. It is that which underlies Ephesians (cf. Introd. pp. 39 f.), and especially Eph. ii. 19–iii. 7, already referred to in this note. What has happened is the healing of a great misunderstanding. Both St. Peter and St. Paul had from the earliest days proclaimed the universality of the Gospel, the former having learnt it at Joppa, the latter at Damascus, and each by divine revelation. But they had differed in policy and method ; and, though the Church at Jerusalem recognized them as having separate spheres of work, the difference blazed out into open controversy at Antioch. It is evident from Acts xiii. 1-3 that Antioch was a great centre of Christian prophecy. Among the prophets there Barnabas at least was drawn into the controversy, and sympathized — for so Gal. ii. 13 implies — with St. Peter ; though this did not prevent his accompanying St. Paul on his first missionary journey. There followed the Apostolic Council at Jerusalem, when an attempt was made to give formal shape to the agreement on principle which had always existed, and to prescribe rules for its application to the day-to-day life of the Church. It is often said that since we hear no more of the Council's decree, we cannot tell how far it was successful ; and it is true that rifts of this sort are not healed by decrees, but by the co-operation of leaders and the work of the Spirit. Such co-operation, however, existed, and we have endeavoured to trace it in some detail in Essay II below ; and in bringing it about we may surmise that Barnabas and Silvanus, both of them prophets, played a leading part, and that the prophetic circles, which equally with them were seized of the truth, were to the fore in fostering the spiritual revival which accompanied it. And the result was that joyful time of expansion of the Church in Asia Minor which prompted St. Paul to write Ephesians, and which was still fresh in the memory of the persecuted Christians whom St. Peter addressed a little later.

And may we not bring yet further N.T. material into the picture ? The immediate result of the great outpouring of the prophetic Spirit at Pentecost (Acts ii. 14-36 : St. Peter's speech) was a quickening of worship. Thus, we find a large number of baptisms, daily meetings in the temple, daily eucharists in the homes, and an ever-growing concentration of religious life around the Apostles. Similarly we are told of the " prophets and teachers " at Antioch (Acts xiii. 1-3) that they " ministered (λειτουργούντων) to the Lord ", a phrase which implies some form of ordered and regular worship. The same prophetic activity seems to be in St. Paul's mind when he bids the readers of Ephesians (v. 19, 20) " be filled with the Spirit ; speaking to yourselves in psalms and hymns and spiritual songs, singing and making melody in your heart to the Lord ". May we not reckon that the writers also of these hymns

— from one of which he quotes a verse or two earlier, " Awake, thou that sleepest, and arise from the dead, and Christ shall give thee light " — were prophets ? For it is precisely this form which prophecy takes when first we meet with it in the N.T. (cf. *supra* p. 261). The Church had, indeed, ready to hand a series of exquisite hymns in the Canticles reproduced in Lk. i., ii. We do not know when St. Luke gathered them, though their Hebraic colour points to a Palestinian origin, and suggests that the period of St. Paul's stay at Jerusalem and Caesarea before his journey to Rome may have provided the occasion. What a wealth of meaning would have been found by those who were working for Jewish-Gentile reconciliation, or rejoicing in its achievement, in the last verse of the Benedictus with its emphasis on peace, and in the description of " salvation " in the Nunc Dimittis as " *a light to lighten the Gentiles, and the glory of thy people Israel* " !

Nor need we regard these as the only " prophetic writings " available. If St. Paul in Rom. xvi. 26 is alluding to the writings of Christian prophets — and the contrast between the " silence " of past times and the present revelation seems to favour this view — the reference might include these canticles and also such early attempts at Gospel narrative as St. Luke mentions in his Preface.

6. Hitherto the Apostle has been dealing with the hidden side of the prophets' work — their seeking and searching, the intimations of the Spirit within them pointing to a time of fulfilment, their concern with the inevitability of suffering in Christ's name and with its triumphant issue, and finally the revelation given to them of the universality of the Gospel. He comes now to the publication of their findings which had been so largely responsible for his readers' present mood of exultation. These findings have lately been reported to them by mission-preachers whose itinerant labours have been the signal for an outburst of spiritual fervour. The words seem to give us a glimpse of the life of the Church behind the Epistle similar to those which St. Paul's letters so often provide. There are the prophets, forming centres [1] of common worship and corporate theological work, and a background for the conferences of Apostles and other leaders ; there are these Apostolic men themselves receiving and reviewing the prophets' deliverances, giving them the hall-mark of their authority, and deciding when and in what form they shall be applied to the life and needs of the Church ; and finally there are the evangelists charged with the dissemination of the message and carrying it far and wide among the scattered communities of Christians.

7. And the result is such an experience of salvation as St. Peter has already described in the earlier verses of this chapter. The Christians whom he addresses have a faith in and a love for Christ which enable them to rejoice in their afflictions, and to see in them the presage of Christ's final manifestation in triumph. The new-found unity of Jew and Gentile in the Church was part and parcel of this salvation, and in large part accounted for it. And it is a fact of cosmic significance. St. Paul had expressed the same idea in Ephesians, when he wrote of this unity being now made public " to the intent that now unto the principalities and powers in heavenly places might be known through the church the manifold wisdom of God " (Eph. iii.

---

[1] It is often asserted that the prophets formed part of the general or itinerant ministry of the Church, like apostles. I cannot find any support for this view in N.T. : indeed, nearly all that we hear of them in N.T. points to their being a local, or at least a *localized*, form of ministry. Cf. Dr. Armitage Robinson's warning in *The Early History of the Church and Ministry* (ed. by Swete), pp. 76, 77—a warning which, if anything, understates the case.

10). St. Peter pictures these same heavenly beings gazing down to watch the work of salvation going forward, just as in Heb. xii. 1 a similar interest in the Church on earth is attributed to the heroic martyrs of old. The picture affords a solemn and noble conclusion to the whole passage.

E. *Critical problems of ii. 4-8*

The purpose of this note is to examine afresh the problems of literary criticism presented by this passage, with special reference to its relationship to the O.T. citations and to other similar passages in N.T. The principal problems are three :

  1. To account for the combinations of O.T. citations common to 1 Pet. ii. 4 ff. and Rom. ix. 32 ff., and their common deviations from the LXX ;
  2. To determine the nature of the document, if any, to which these facts point ;
  3. To note the bearing of other N.T. passages, not usually brought into this discussion, upon the problem.

Questions of exegesis are, so far as possible, dealt with in the notes on the text, and in Additional Notes G and H below.

Though the enquiry is inevitably of an inductive character, it will be convenient to set down at this stage the hypotheses which will be advanced to account for the evidence. They are :

  1. The primary element in the combination of Is. viii. 11 ff., Is. xxviii. 16, Ps. cxviii. 22 ff. in 1 Pet. ii. 4 ff. is Psalm cxviii. 22 ff., though St. Paul omits it as not relevant to his purpose ;
  2. Both St. Peter and St. Paul are dependent upon a common document, which was not, however, a collection of *testimonia*, but an early Christian hymn or rhythmical prayer ;
  3. The ideas contained in this document were also used by the authors of Hebrews and John.

  1. The relationship between the Petrine and Pauline passages and their O.T. citations can be conveniently studied in tabular form (see Table on pp. 270-1).

The verbal parallelism between St. Peter and St. Paul has long been felt to indicate literary dependence or interdependence ; but opinion has been sharply divided as to its nature. Hort, for example, regarded it as " morally certain that St. Peter borrowed from St. Paul " ; while Kühl and others have asserted that the borrowing was the other way about. More recently, the view has been advanced in various quarters that both were using a common source. In the nature of the case, the question turns mainly on internal evidence ; and in this the primary factors are (*a*) the way in which a number of O.T. passages are combined, and (*b*) the deviations from the LXX which are common to St. Peter and St. Paul.

  (*a*) Starting from 1 Pet. ii. 6, 7, we notice that Is. xxviii. 16, Ps. cxviii. 22, and Is. viii. 14b are combined in that order. Which of these was the magnet to the others ? Since Is. xxviii. 16 and Is. viii. 14b have little verbal similarity beyond the fact that the word " stone " occurs in both, and since even that word is used differently in the two prophecies, being a very definite stone in Is. xxviii. and an indefinite one in Is. viii., it seems unlikely that they would have been brought together of themselves.[1] It is not difficult, on the other hand, to see how both should have been drawn into the ambit of Ps. cxviii. 22. For that verse may be regarded as one of the sheet-anchors of early Christian teaching. Not only did it come from the last of the " Hallel " Psalms (cxiii.-cxviii.), which were among the best-loved and most familiar hymns used in Jewish worship, and may well have been known by heart by the congregation in the synagogue (cf. Oesterley, *The Psalms*, i. p. 101) ; but its use by our Lord as His ministry drew towards its climax, and in connexion with a parable closely bound up with that climax, gave it a special place in the mind of the Church as one of the *verba Christi*. And according to Acts iv. 11, it was used by St. Peter to clinch the brief apology which he made before the Sanhedrin in Jerusalem. The supposition, more-over, that it is the lynch-pin of the whole combined quotation in 1 Pet. ii. is rendered probable by the verses which lead up to the quotation ; for in these (ii. 4 f.) the emphasis is on the Lord as the " living stone " who had been rejected of men, but approved of God — a passage which reads like a " mid-rash " on Ps. cxviii. 22, with balancing words brought in from Is. xxviii. 16.

And this verse of Ps. cxviii., which was now a *verbum Christi*, was a verse very pregnant with meaning.[2] To the original meaning of a radical reversal of fortune in the history of Israel, together with the radical change of values which that event portended, was added, when it was used by our Lord, the assertion that a similar reversal was now enacted in His own Person as the representative of all that Israel stood for ; and that this enactment was of crucial significance for the Jewish people, involving at once the divine vindica-tion of Jesus as Messiah and the divine judgment upon those who rejected Him. In Acts iv. 11 the divine vindication is the aspect emphasized ; in our Lord's utterance, and especially in St. Luke's version of it,[3] the weight lies on the aspect of warning. In 1 Pet. ii. both aspects are found, the first in the " midrashic " verse 4, the second in the addition, in verses 6 and 7, of words from Is. viii. 14b to the citation of Ps. cxviii. 22 ; and the scope of the latter is further enlarged by the addition of Is. xxviii. 16, which is inter-polated between the introductory verse 4 and the citation of Ps. cxviii. in verse 6. And that these prophecies cited in verses 5 and 6 had already been combined, and combined in that order, when St. Peter wrote, is rendered probable by the fact that both occur, though in reverse order, in the intro-ductory verse 4. The explanation which seems best to fit the facts is that the three passages which now appear in 1 Pet. ii. 6, 7 were already extant in that cohesion in a source known to St. Peter, and perhaps also to his readers ; and that the theme of the sequence as a whole was the theme of Christ as the embodiment of a divine Judgment in and through the suffering Messiah, with consequences of vital moment both for believers and for unbelievers. The Incarnation and the Cross, in short, were decisive acts of God in human history, leading on the one side to the faith on which the Christian Church was built, and on the other to the rejection of those in Israel, and by implica-tion of non-Jews also, who did not believe.

This conclusion is borne out, if we turn to Rom. ix. 33. To the difficulty, already mentioned, which attaches to the view that St. Paul here

---

[1] I differ here from my father, E. C. Selwyn (*St. Luke the Prophet*, pp. 198 f.), whose lucid exposition of the facts I have none the less found very helpful. Cf. Jackson and Lake, *Be-ginnings*, v. p. 373, n. 3.

[2] Cf. Trench, *Notes on the Parables of our Lord*, pp. 200 ff.
[3] The words in Lk. xx. 17b, 18 " may be, or may have been thought to be, an allusion to Is. viii. 14 " (Bigg).

———— = Is. viii. 10 ff.
———— = Is. xxviii. 15 ff.
·········· = Ps. cxviii. 19 ff., and verba Christi.

Is. viii. 10 ff.	Is. xxviii. 15 f.	Ps. cxviii. 19 ff.	1 Pet. ii.	Rom. ix.	Other N.T. Occurrences
10. μεθ' ἡμῶν ὁ θεός. 11. οὕτως λέγει Κύριος, τῇ ἰσχυρᾷ χειρὶ ἀπειθοῦσιν τῇ πορείᾳ τῆς ὁδοῦ τοῦ λαοῦ τούτου. . . . 12. τὸν δὲ φόβον αὐτοῦ οὐ μὴ φοβηθῆτε οὐδὲ μὴ ταραχθῆτε.	15. ὅτι εἴπατε, Ἐποιήσαμεν διαθήκην μετὰ τοῦ ᾅδου. . . .	19. ἀνοίξατέ μοι πύλας δικαιοσύνης, εἰσελθὼν ἐν αὐταῖς ἐξομολογήσομαι τῷ Κυρίῳ 20. αὕτη ἡ πύλη τοῦ Κυρίου, δίκαιοι εἰσελεύσονται ἐν αὐτῇ. . . .	4. πρὸς ὃν προσερχόμενοι, λίθον ζῶντα, ὑπὸ ἀνθρώπων μὲν ἀποδεδοκιμασμένον, παρὰ δὲ θεῷ ἐκλεκτόν, ἔντιμον, 5. καὶ αὐτοὶ ὡς λίθοι ζῶντες οἰκοδομεῖσθε . . .		1 Pet. iii. 14. τὸν δὲ φόβον αὐτῶν μὴ φοβηθῆτε, μηδὲ ταραχθῆτε, Κύριον δὲ τὸν Χριστὸν ἁγιάσατε ἐν ταῖς καρδίαις ὑμῶν.
13. Κύριον αὐτὸν ἁγιάσατε καὶ αὐτὸς ἔσται σου φόβος.	16. διὰ τοῦτο οὕτως λέγει Κύριος Κύριος, Ἰδοὺ ἐγὼ ἐμβάλλω εἰς τὰ θεμέλια Σειὼν λίθον πολυτελῆ ἐκλεκτὸν ἀκρογωνιαῖον ἔντιμον εἰς τὰ θεμέλια αὐτῆς,	22. λίθον ὃν ἀπεδοκίμασαν οἱ οἰκοδομοῦντες, οὗτος ἐγενήθη εἰς κεφαλὴν γωνίας.	6. Ἰδού, τίθημι ἐν Σιὼν λίθον ἀκρογωνιαῖον, ἐκλεκτόν, ἔντιμον· καὶ ὁ πιστεύων ἐπ' αὐτῷ οὐ μὴ καταισχυνθῇ· 7. ὑμῖν οὖν ἡ τιμὴ τοῖς πιστεύουσιν· ἀπιστοῦσι δὲ Λίθον ὃν ἀπεδοκίμασαν οἱ οἰκοδομοῦντες, οὗτος ἐγενήθη εἰς κεφαλὴν γωνίας,		Mk. xii. 10, 11 (cf. Matt. xxi. 42, Lk. xx. 17a). οὐδὲ τὴν γραφὴν ταύτην ἀνέγνωτε· λίθον ὃν ἀπεδοκίμασαν οἱ οἰκοδομοῦντες, οὗτος ἐγενήθη εἰς κεφαλὴν γωνίας·

14. κἂν ἐπ' αὐτῷ πεποιθὼς ᾖς, ἔσται σοι εἰς ἁγίασμα, καὶ οὐχ ὡς λίθου προσκόμματι συναντήσεσθε οὐδὲ ὡς πέτρας πτώματι. . . . 17. πεποιθὼς ἔσομαι ἐπ' αὐτῷ. 18. ἰδοὺ ἐγὼ καὶ τὰ παιδία ἅ μοι ἔδωκεν ὁ θεός.	καὶ ὁ πιστεύων οὐ μὴ καταισχυνθῇ.	23. παρὰ Κυρίου ἐγένετο αὕτη, καὶ ἔστιν θαυμαστὴ ἐν ὀφθαλμοῖς ἡμῶν.	καὶ λίθος προσκόμματος καὶ πέτρα σκανδάλου· 8. οἳ προσκόπτουσι λόγῳ ἀπειθοῦντες, εἰς ὃ καὶ ἐτέθησαν.	33. προσέκοψαν τῷ λίθῳ τοῦ προσκόμματος, καθὼς γέγραπται, Ἰδοὺ τίθημι ἐν Σιὼν λίθον προσκόμματος καὶ πέτραν σκανδάλου· καὶ ὁ πιστεύων ἐπ' αὐτῷ οὐ καταισχυνθήσεται.	παρὰ Κυρίου ἐγένετο αὕτη, καὶ ἔστι θαυμαστὴ ἐν ὀφθαλμοῖς ἡμῶν. Lk. xx. 17b, 18 (after γωνίας). πᾶς ὁ πεσὼν ἐπ' ἐκεῖνον τὸν λίθον συνθλασθήσεται· ἐφ' ὃν δ' ἂν πέσῃ, λικμήσει αὐτόν. Acts iv. 11 (St. Peter's words). οὗτός ἐστιν ὁ λίθος ὁ ἐξουθενηθεὶς ὑφ' ὑμῶν τῶν οἰκοδομούντων, ὁ γενόμενος εἰς κεφαλὴν γωνίας. Eph. ii. 20. ἐποικοδομηθέντες ἐπὶ τῷ θεμελίῳ . . . ὄντος ἀκρογωνιαίου αὐτοῦ Χριστοῦ Ἰησοῦ.

first combined Is. xxviii. 16 and Is. viii. 14b, must be added the way in which the prophetic teaching about the " stone " is short-circuited, the positive nature of the " stone " as " precious ", " chosen ", and " a corner-stone " being omitted, and its dangerousness to unbelievers being dovetailed in to the place so rendered vacant.   It is true that St. Paul in the context of Rom. ix. 33 is concerned with faith and unbelief, and not with Christology; but the workmanship, on this hypothesis, would be exceedingly rough.   If, on the other hand, he found the combined passages already existing in much the same form as we have them in 1 Pet. ii. 6, 7, he would have omitted what he did not need, and also altered the relative position of καὶ ὁ πιστεύων . . . καταισχυνθήσεται ; but he would not have interpolated.   Otherwise, indeed, it would have been far simpler for him to have quoted Is. viii. 14b more or less as it stands (substituting καὶ for οὐδέ), and have added, if he wished it, Is. xxviii. 16c.

(b) The second set of facts to be considered comprises the deviations from the LXX text common to St. Peter and St. Paul, which attract attention because there is no doubt that both normally quote from the LXX and not from the Hebrew.   We may note the following : (i) that both use τίθημι instead of ἐγὼ ἐμβάλλω ; (ii) that both write ἐν Σιών instead of εἰς τὰ θεμέλια Σειών ; (iii) the omission of πολυτελῆ ; (iv) the introduction of ἐπ' αὐτῷ after ὁ πιστεύων.   To some extent these deviations may be owing to the fact that the Apostles were using a recension of the LXX text which was current in Asia Minor [1] : Hort, for example, believes that in (iv) ἐπ' αὐτῷ had been inserted before the Christian era ; but, in any case, it would certainly have been acceptable to those who thought of Christ as the ever-present object of faith.   (iii) might be due to the fact that each writer felt πολυτελῆ to be otiose in view of ἔντιμον, though the meaning of the words is not actually identical.   But (i) and (ii) are on a different footing.   They are without MS. support in any known text of LXX ; and the claim that they can be " justi-fied by the Hebrew ",[2] even if it be well founded, would not account for the detailed identity of rendering in 1 Pet. ii. 6 and Rom. ix. 33.   Dependence of one Epistle on the other, or of both on a common source, seems required by the evidence.   We have already seen reason to reject the view that St. Peter took the phrases from St. Paul.   Is Kühl's view that St. Paul borrowed from St. Peter any more probable ?   Even if we confine ourselves to internal evidence alone — and there are, of course, other weighty considerations against it — we can hardly say that it is.   For Rom. ix. 33, like 1 Pet. ii. 6, 7, is intro-duced by a " midrashic " note, but of a quite different character, dealing not with the position of Christ and the building of the Church, but with the " stumbling " of unbelieving Israel.   This use of the same cento of O.T. texts in a different context is natural enough, if it already existed independ-ently ; it is another matter, if St. Paul had it before him only in its Petrine context.

These difficulties disappear, however, if we adopt the hypothesis that both were using a common documentary source.   There will still be ques-tions to be answered, notably why the source should have altered ἰδοὺ ἐγὼ ἐμβάλλω εἰς τὰ θεμέλια into τίθημι ἐν ; and it is true that the latter form was far more convenient, though for different reasons, both to St. Peter and St.

---

[1] Cf. Swete, *Introduction to O.T. in Greek*, p. 403.
[2] E. C. Selwyn, *op. cit.* p. 191.

Paul than the former. Yet the reasons which would have led St. Peter to write τίθημι ἐν might have influenced equally the author or compiler of his source : he, too, may have been concerned not with foundations, but with a cornerstone. And, indeed, if the dominant element in his cento of texts was Ps. cxviii. 22, that would certainly have been so. Other reasons, as we shall see, may have told in the same direction. But even without these, we may conclude that study of the deviations from the LXX text common to 1 Pet. ii. 6, 7 and Rom. ix. 33 confirms the result to which we were led by study of the peculiar combination of O.T. verses in the passages before us ; and that the facts are best explained by postulating a common written source underlying both. That it was a written, not an oral, source is clear, indeed, from the phrases with which our author introduces it : " wherefore it stands *in writing* " (cf. the note on ii. 6). It remains now to try and determine the nature of this source.

2. The hypothesis most commonly adopted by those who hold this view is that the source in question was a collection of Messianic proof-texts, compiled in the early Church for the purpose of establishing the truth of Christianity to all who recognized the authority of prophecy. (The fullest treatment of the argument for the early existence of such a compilation is still Rendel Harris' *Testimonies*. Cf. also Dodd, *The Parables of the Kingdom*, p. 128 n., Cadbury in *Beginnings*, v. p. 373, Bigg, *op. cit.* p. 20, who traces the idea to Volkmar, and especially Moffatt, *Introduction* (1912), pp. 23-5.) The currency of such documents in the second and third centuries is not open to much doubt ; and their existence as early as the first century is not improbable, if Hatch was right in supposing that the Jews before the Christian era used manuals of extracts from O.T. for teaching and devotional purposes.[1] Yet the existence of such manuals, whether Jewish or Jewish-Christian, is one thing ; their use in evangelistic work among communities largely gentile is another ; and it is here that the theory seems to me to need to be supplemented. Even if the author of 1 Peter were acquainted with a manual of proof-texts, it does not follow that it would have seemed to him suitable for quotation, as he envisaged the Christian converts of Asia Minor and their needs. There are differences of temperament also in different writers to be considered. St. Paul had been trained in the school of Gamaliel ; and there was a strong vein of Rabbinism in his mind which is absent from the minds of St. Peter and St. John. And it is worth observing that in the chapter of St. Cyprian's *Testimonia* (ii. 16), entitled *Quod idem et lapis dictus sit*, Is. xxviii. 16 and Ps. cxviii. 22-26a are quoted together, but there is no mention of Is. viii. 14.

In looking, however, for common sources behind the Epistles, we are not confined to compilations of proof-texts ; for there were writings of another kind for whose existence and use in the early Church we have direct, and not merely circumstantial, evidence. I refer to hymns. That they were well known in the Christian communities of the middle of the first century is evident from St. Paul's injunction in Col. iii. 16 : " Let the word of Christ dwell in you richly in all wisdom ; teaching and admonishing one another in psalms and hymns and spiritual songs,[2] singing with grace in your hearts to the Lord " — a passage which incidentally suggests that hymns rather

---

[1] *Essays in Biblical Greek*, p. 203.
[2] The chief difference between psalms and hymns seems to have been that the former had an instrumental accompaniment, the latter not. Both were spiritual songs. See Lightfoot, *in loc.*

than theological manuals were the most acceptable medium of teaching in the churches of Asia Minor. And this is exactly what is found in the mission field to-day. The following passage [1] from a modern missionary book, " *The Untouchables' Quest* ", by Godfrey Phillips (1936) is instructive :—

Vernacular equivalents of the old Scottish Metrical Psalms have been specially helpful. " In the United Presbyterian Church in the Pasrur area, lady members of the enquiry staff found that many humble village women knew as many as eight or ten of the Psalms. Their knowledge of this classic devotional literature was enriching their minds, helping to erase the conception of themselves as despised Chuhras, and to substitute one of themselves as Christians."

Sometimes whole Gospels are turned into simple poetic metre and fitted with tunes, and large parts of them are memorized by the congregations. You may hear the herd-boy chanting them as he watches the buffaloes and goats at pasture, singing his way to a knowledge of Scripture —a method which surely would have delighted Martin Luther.

Unless the new Christians' minds are stored in some such fashion, the service in the mud-and-thatch church is apt to resolve itself into their sitting quiet while the teacher worships God on their behalf, by reading Scripture which they cannot follow, offering prayer during which their minds wander, and preaching a sermon during which the wandering goes still further. In mass movement areas the liturgical element in worship is becoming more and more prominent, with good effect. This may be a reflection of the conditions in which liturgies first arose. The new converts seem not to realize their Christian life unless they learn at least the Lord's Prayer, some stories in the life of Christ, and a few simple hymns or lyrics.

Similar testimony comes from the Evangelical revival in our own country : witness the following in a letter from Berridge to Wesley of July 16th, 1759 [2] :

As soon as three or four receive convictions in a village, they are desired to meet together two or three nights a week, which they readily comply with. At first they only sing ; afterwards they join reading and prayer to singing ; and the presence of the Lord is greatly with them. Let me mention only two instances. At *Orwell* two people were broken down in one night, only by hearing a few people sing hymns. At *Grantchester*, a mile from Cambridge, seventeen people was seized with strong convictions, last week, only by hearing hymns sung. . . .

Can we suppose that the situation was greatly different in the Asia Minor of A.D. 50–60 ? That there was a strong emotional element in the popular cults of the interior, we know ; and, though the cities on the main highways of traffic contained highly educated circles in which religious and ethical ideas were seriously discussed, it would be arbitrary to suppose that the infant Christian communities did not also contain, as in India and indeed in our own cities to-day, many to whom the appeal of religion was emotional rather than rational. Further, the Church of the first century was well able to supply the demand, for it had the Jewish Psalter as a model, a companion, and an inspiration. Indeed, they may have borrowed the method itself from Judaism , for the Dispersion felt itself specially charged with missionary propaganda.[3] As the New Testament shews, the Church's services were charged with emotion,[4] and in that atmosphere, which might easily degenerate into disorderly excitement, hymns would have been psychologically the ideal instrument for controlling the religious feelings and sowing the seed of Christian faith. Sometimes these were improvised (1 Cor. xiv. 26) ; but

[1] pp. 53 f.
[2] Quoted in Smyth, *Simeon and Church Order*, p. 172, n. 3.
[3] Cf. Box, *J.T.S.* vol. xiii., No. 51, p. 325 Apr. 1912).
[4] Cf. Heiler, *The Spirit of Worship*, ch. ii.

more often, we may be sure, they came from those prophetic circles in which the tradition of hymn writing and hymnody was kept constantly alive. The Canticles in Lk. i. and ii. are outstanding examples.

Moreover we have considerable evidence as to the methods on which these hymns were constructed. It was with hymns as with other imaginative Hebraic literature : " the prophet's imagination — the faculty which, when the outer senses, as in an ecstasy, are dormant, is abnormally active — combines the materials with which, while in a waking state, observation or reflection had stored his mind, into a new form ".[1] The hymns of which we have examples are mosaics of earlier texts quite as much as original compositions. We may cite the following examples :

(i) Ps. xiv. 3a-c (LXX). These three verses, which were almost certainly not in the Hebrew Psalter, and yet are quoted continuously in Rom. iii. 13-18, contain no fewer than five quotations, all from other Psalms or from Isaiah.[2]

(ii) The Psalms of Solomon, of date about 40 B.C. Ryle and James in the Introduction (§ viii) to their edition shew the extent to which the Psalmists have drawn on the Jewish apocrypha and apocalyptic literature ; and their Index III, of passages in LXX referred to in the Psalms of Solomon, shews that the Psalms and Isaiah were the O.T. books chiefly quoted.[3]

(iii) The Canticles in Lk. i., ii. The lists of O.T. parallels to the Magnificat and Nunc Dimittis given in Plummer's edition of St. Luke shew how closely these, too, are built up out of O.T. phrases, to which the Psalter contributes a large proportion. The Nunc Dimittis also echoes passages of Isaiah : the last verse, in particular, contains a striking combination of Ps. xcviii. 2 with Is. xlix. 6.

(iv) Should we not also add Acts iv. 24-30 ? Commentators mostly assume that δεηθέντων αὐτῶν refers to this utterance, but the words would be otiose unless they recorded a new fact, such as καί commonly indicates, cf. Mk. xiv. 26. And the introductory words ὁμοθυμαδὸν ἦραν φωνήν are far more suggestive of a hymn in which all joined than of a prayer said by one apostle to which the others assented. Some scholars, on the other hand, have regarded this noble utterance as " the earliest recorded Christian hymn " (W. M. Furneaux (Dean of Winchester), The Acts of the Apostles (1912), p. 65). Meyer, in loc., takes the utterance as proof that there was " already a stated prayer of the Apostolic church at Jerusalem ". Ellicott discusses, but does not favour, the view that we have here an early hymn. Modern views as to the nature of the speeches recorded in Acts make it easier for us to regard this passage as a hymn than it was for earlier generations. But I should prefer myself to speak of it as containing hymnodic matter rather than as being itself a hymn : verse 27, and perhaps verse 28, strike me as midrashic interpolations rather than as part of the hymn. The textual difficulties of the passage are well known, but these and other problems are too complicated for discussion here.

Of such construction, it is reasonable to suppose, were the " psalms and hymns and spiritual songs " of which St. Paul speaks. Whether the hymn or hymns which St. Paul and Silas sang in the prison at Philippi were Jewish or Christian, traditional or improvised, we cannot say : the tradition of

---

[1] Driver, Introduction to the Literature of O.T. (1913), p. 280.
[2] Swete, op. cit. pp. 251 f.

[3] Perhaps we should also add Ecclus. li., Judith xvi. 2-17, Tobit xiii.

psalmody was continuous from the foundation of the second Temple, and the singing of the Hallel by our Lord and the Twelve at the Last Supper made the O.T. Psalter a Christian hymn-book from the beginning. At the same time, wholly original composition is evidenced by the tristich in Eph. v. 14, and by other passages such as 1 Tim. iii. 16, vi. 15, 16, Rev. v. 9, iv. 8, 11, which either cannot be traced to any known Jewish source, or use the Jewish source with complete freedom. In what we have in N.T., indeed, we can find the *nidus* of the two streams of development in the expression of prayer and praise which meet us on the threshold of the second century in the rhythmical prayer exemplified in *Didache* x. and 1 Clem. lix.–lxi., which springs from the communal heart and mind rather than that of any individual,[1] and in the highly individual poems of the *Odes of Solomon*.

It is in this setting, I suggest, that the cento of O.T. texts in 1 Pet. ii. 6, 7 may profitably be studied.[2] If the verses were part of a hymn already known to the recipients of the Epistle, they would have come home to them now with redoubled force ; and the introductory verse 4 would have been readily intelligible to them, since it would have appeared to them as based not on two widely distinct texts of Scripture but on the familiar stanzas of a hymn. And it is in the true line of Hebraic " strophes " — that is to say, " a group of verses, connected together by a certain unity of thought ".[3] Of the rules of rhythm governing Greek versions of Psalms or hymns we know next to nothing, and they are perhaps more properly called rhythmical prose than poetry.[4] But that attention was given to rhythm and cadence we may be sure ; for otherwise they could scarcely have been sung to the " cantillations " which were almost certainly used as their musical expression. The point is important ; for the claims of rhythm may account for some of the deviations from the LXX text which meet us in N.T.

The limits of the quotation from the hymn are more difficult to determine ; and hitherto we have considered only 1 Pet. ii. 6, 7. But there are facts which suggest that verse 8a should also be included. Chief of these is the use both there and in Rom. ix. 33 of the verb προσκόπτω. If some part of this verb was in the source, then St. Paul's introduction to the quotation is of a piece with St. Peter's : that is to say, it turns on anticipating certain words or phrases in the quotation, and using them to give the clue to its use. ἀπειθοῦντες, moreover, may be derived from ἀπειθοῦσιν in Is. viii. 11, which is in the context of the passage about the stone of stumbling (viii. 14). In a quotation which St. Peter has, no doubt, adjusted *currente calamo* to his purpose,[5] we cannot do more than hazard a conjecture how the stanza ended.

---

[1] Cf. C. S. Phillips, *Hymnody Past and Present*, ch. i.

[2] Windisch describes the whole passage, 1 Pet. ii. 1-10, as " a hymn on the holy destiny of Christendom, in four strophes, 1-3, 4 f., 6-8, 9 f.". He is presumably using the term "hymn" loosely ; for there is nothing hymnodic in structure in verses 4, 5, and the ancient Jewish and Christian hymns available to us, while using Scriptural passages freely, do not include such prosaic and matter-of-fact insertions as διότι περιέχει ἐν γραφῇ.

[3] Driver, *op. cit.* p. 366.

[4] In view of 1 Cor. xiv. 26, Col. iii. 16 we cannot doubt that Christian congregations in the first century knew and sang the Psalms in Greek. So probably did those of the Jewish Dispersion, from whom the Christian Church derived the practice: cf. Dugmore, *The In-fluence of the Synagogue upon the Divine Office*, p. 80. Even the *Shema* "was recited in Greek and other languages ", cf. Schürer, ii. ii. pp. 283 f., Chase, *The Lord's Prayer in the Early Church*, p. 16. G. Zuntz (*H.T.R.*, vol. xxxvi. No. 4, Oct. 1943), has recently urged that in second-century Christian worship the O.T. Lesson was read in Hebrew and followed by the LXX translation used as a Targum, just as in the Palestinian synagogues the Hebrew Lesson was followed by an Aramaic Targum. But such a practice, even if it prevailed in the case of the Lesson, could hardly have been transferred to the Psalms, for they were sung.

[5] For an O.T. example of this cf. Ezra iii. 11, quoting the probably contemporary Ps. cxxxvi. 1.

But I am inclined to think that some part of ἀπειθεῖν was in the quotation, and that ἀπιστοῦσι also belonged to it, though it could be explained as being an adjustment of ἀπειθοῦσι to a form which makes it more plainly adversative to ὁ πιστεύων. The question is further complicated by the fact that the antithetical δέ is very rare except after personal pronouns in the comparable literature (Psalms, *Psalms of Solomon*, Canticles), though it does occur (e.g. Ps. xi. 5, xxviii. 3) ; and it is also unusual to find a line beginning with a relative pronoun or an anarthrous participle, though we can cite *Ps. Sol.* xvii. 6, xiv. 4, Lk. i. 53.

Set out in hymnal form, therefore, and with the proviso that the closing tristich can be no more than conjectural, the passage yields us the following strophe :

Ἰδοὺ τίθημι ἐν Σιὼν λίθον ἀκρογωνιαῖον ἐκλεκτόν, ἔντιμον,
καὶ ὁ πιστεύων ἐπ᾽ αὐτῷ οὐ μὴ καταισχυνθῇ·
λίθος ὃν ἀπεδοκίμασαν οἱ οἰκοδομοῦντες
οὗτος ἐγενήθη εἰς κεφαλὴν γωνίας·
ἀπιστοῦσι δὲ λίθος προσκόμματος καὶ πέτρα σκανδάλου,
οἳ προσκόπτουσι τῷ λόγῳ ἀπειθοῦντες,
εἰς ὃ καὶ ἐτέθησαν.[1]

The hypothesis that a hymn containing such a strophe as this underlies both 1 Pet. ii. 6-8 and Rom. ix. 33 appears to account better than any other theory for their similarities and also for their deviations both from the LXX and from one another. It agrees, moreover, with the practical needs of the communities addressed, so far as we can conjecture these from the situation in the mission field to-day. It would be known orally to many who had not seen it in writing ; but the Canticles in Lk. i., ii. shew that such hymns did not long remain solely in oral tradition. Being formed, moreover, largely of Scriptural texts, they could be appealed to as authoritative. Of the authorship of this hymn we have no evidence ; but in view of the sensitiveness to the music of words which marks this Epistle, it would not be fanciful to attribute it to Silvanus.[2]

F. *Critical Problems of ii. 9, 10*

The problems presented by these verses are closely similar to those discussed in connexion with verses 6-8, though they are without the more

[1] The closing tristich would then provide an example of " climactic parallelism ", cf. Driver, *op. cit.* p. 363. And the last two lines would be almost what later Greek hymn-writers distinguished as examples of στιχηρὰ ἀπὸ στίχου, i.e. verses or lines appended to broken fragments of Psalms. Cf. Neale, *History of the Holy Eastern Church*, Part I, pp. 830 ff. (1850).

[2] The further question may be asked whether we can trace any other vestiges of hymnal material in 1 Peter. There are at least a few straws of evidence which deserve mention :

(1) Is. viii. 12, 13, which are in the immediate context of the passage about the "stone" quoted in 1 Pet. ii., are drawn upon later in the Epistle at iii. 14 ; and the deviations from the LXX are just such as we might expect if they formed part of a hymn :

τὸν δὲ φόβον αὐτῶν μὴ φοβηθῆτε μηδὲ ταραχθῆτε,
κύριον δὲ τὸν Χριστὸν ἁγιάσατε ἐν ταῖς καρδίαις ὑμῶν.

(2) Dr. Bigg has drawn attention to the quotations and echoes in the Epistle of Ps.

xxxiv., and the evidence can be studied in Essay II, pp. 413 f., and Table VIII A, below. I am inclined to think that 1 Pet. iii. 14 belonged to the hymn used in 1 Pet. ii. 6, 7 ; and also that Ps. xxxiv. 6, 9, 10, 13-17 had become part of a Christian hymn, though probably a different one.

(3) Windisch speaks of 1 Pet. i. 3-12 as an " Eingangshymnus ", ii. 21-5 as a " Christuslied " similar to i. 18-21, and iii. 18-22 as a " Taufhymnus ". Except in the last instance, a hymnodic origin for these passages seems to rest on little evidence beyond their rhythmical character, and that may be attributed to Silvanus' mind and style, a characteristic equally observable in 2 Thess. i. 3-12 ; though a comparison of 2 Cor. i. 3 ff., Eph. i. 3-14 with 1 Pet. i. 3 suggests that Christian forms of benediction were being elaborated at this time with some care. 1 Pet. iii. 18-22 is in a different category from these, and it is urged in Essay I, p. 325 below that, though the passage is not itself quoted from a hymn, it rests on the credal hymn which is quoted in 1 Tim. iii. 16.

intricate complications of that passage. But here too we have a number of O.T. scriptures interwoven into a flowing cento, introduced by midrashic interpretations of certain words and phrases in it which suggest that our author was not himself composing the cento as he wrote, but commenting on a document that lay before him ; there are also indications that the document in question was rhythmical in structure, as would have been the case with a hymn ; and in part of it there is a correspondence with an O.T. quotation in Rom. ix., which has led some commentators, notably Hort, to the view that 1 Peter is here dependent upon Romans.

The literary evidence is set forth in the accompanying table (p. 279), the verbal parallels between 1 Peter and O.T. being underlined with heavy lines, and those between Romans and O.T. with light lines.

The following points may be observed :—

1. In ii. 9 St. Peter weaves together phrases from Ex. xix. 5, 6, and Is. xliii. 20, 21, taking γένος ἐκλεκτόν, εἰς περιποίησιν, and τὰς ἀρετάς with slight modifications from Is. xliii., and the rest of 9a from Ex. xix. Since his purpose is to assert that the Christian Church has now inherited the peculiar character and privileges of Israel, Ex. xix., which records the divine establishment of Israel's status and call as a result of the deliverance from Egypt, is no doubt the ground-bass of the passage. The Isaianic phrases come from a prophecy of the Exilic period, which promised the deliverance from Babylon — an event which was only second in significance to the Exodus in Israel's history, and which was relevant to the danger and distress in which the Christian communities now found themselves : and such passages as these, indeed, would have fostered the use of Babylon as a pseudonym for Rome which we find in 1 Pet. v. 13, and in the Apocalypse. At the same time there are divergences in the order of words between 1 Peter and Ex. xix. λαὸς εἰς περιποίησιν, which is the Isaianic version of περιούσιος, appearing after βασίλειον ἱεράτευμα καὶ ἔθνος ἅγιον, and not before them as in Ex. xix., The copula between ἱεράτευμα and ἔθνος is also omitted in 1 Peter, an omission which falls in well with the view already reached on other grounds (see the note on βασίλειον) that βασίλειον in 1 Peter is a substantive and not an epithet of ἱεράτευμα. The theory which appears best to account for the literary data is that the choice and order of words, which have a far more rhythmical sequence in 1 Peter than in Ex. xix., are due to literary reasons, such as would have operated if they had been adapted for hymnody.

2. A similar conclusion is suggested by the words τὰς ἀρετὰς ἐξαγγείλητε. We have already seen (in the note on ii. 9) that ἀρετή, both in the singular and the plural, is a favourite word of the Greek poets, who use it in a variety of meanings. Similarly ἐξαγγέλλειν is a more vivid word than the διηγεῖσθαι of Is. xliii. 21, which it replaces ; and, though both alike are used in the LXX of the Psalms, ἐξαγγέλλειν is much commoner in literary Greek and especially in poetry. We have to remember that the authors or compilers of the first Christian hymns would have been alive to considerations of style, since they wished to commend their compositions to congregations which were often mainly Hellenic in their background and were more conversant with Greek literature than with the Hebrew classics even when these were in Greek dress. If they had to choose between two words, one of which

I Peter ii. 9, 10	Ex. xix.	Is. xliii.	N.T. Parallels
9. ὑμεῖς δὲ γένος ἐκλεκτόν, βασίλειον, ἱεράτευμα, ἔθνος ἅγιον, λαὸς εἰς περιποίησιν, ὅπως τὰς ἀρετὰς ἐξαγγείλητε τοῦ ἐκ σκότους ὑμᾶς καλέσαντος εἰς τὸ θαυμαστὸν αὐτοῦ φῶς·	5. ἔσεσθέ μοι λαὸς περιούσιος ἀπὸ πάντων τῶν ἐθνῶν. . . . 6. ὑμεῖς δὲ ἔσεσθέ μοι βασίλειον ἱεράτευμα καὶ ἔθνος ἅγιον.	20. τὸ γένος μου τὸ ἐκλεκτόν. 21. λαόν μου ὃν περιεποιησάμην τὰς ἀρετάς μου διηγεῖσθαι.	Rom. ix. 25. ὡς καὶ ἐν τῷ Ὡσηὲ λέγει, καλέσω τὸν οὐ λαόν μου λαόν μου, καὶ τὴν οὐκ ἠγαπημένην ἠγαπημένην. 26. καὶ ἔσται, ἐν τῷ τόπῳ οὗ ἐρρέθη αὐτοῖς, Οὐ λαός μου ὑμεῖς, ἐκεῖ κληθήσονται υἱοὶ θεοῦ ζῶντος.
10. οἱ ποτὲ οὐ λαός, νῦν δὲ λαὸς θεοῦ,		Hos. i, ii. i. 6. κάλεσον τὸ ὄνομα αὐτῆς, Οὐκ ἠλεημένη. . . . 9. κάλεσον τὸ ὄνομα αὐτοῦ, Οὐ λαός μου, διότι ὑμεῖς οὐ λαός μου. . . . 10. . . . καὶ ἔσται ἐν τῷ τόπῳ οὗ ἐρρέθη αὐτοῖς, Οὐ λαός μου ὑμεῖς, κληθήσονται καὶ αὐτοὶ υἱοὶ θεοῦ ζῶντος. ii. 1. εἴπατε τῷ ἀδελφῷ ὑμῶν, Λαός μου, καὶ τῇ ἀδελφῇ ὑμῶν, Ἐλεημένη.	
οἱ οὐκ ἠλεημένοι νῦν δὲ ἐλεηθέντες.		23. . . . καὶ ἐλεήσω (v.l. ἀγαπήσω) τὴν Οὐκ ἠλεημένην (v.l. ἠγαπημένην), καὶ ἐρῶ τῷ Οὐ λαῷ μου Λαός μου εἶ σύ. . . .	

would have conveyed more to the educated Gentile than the other, they would
have chosen that one.

3. We have already seen how in ii. 4 St. Peter anticipates and interprets
certain words in the O.T. passages which he will quote in verses 6, 7. He
appears to be doing likewise in verse 5, in reference to verses 9, 10, interpreting the " king's house " of verse 9 by the οἶκος πνευματικός and the
" priesthood " by the ἱεράτευμα ἅγιον of verse 5. It is also probable (see
Add. Note H, pp. 294-8) that the allusion to the offering of acceptable sacrifices in verse 5 is an interpretation, though less directly, of the final clause
in ii. 9b, 10.

4. The phrase, " who called us out of darkness into his marvellous
light ", embodies a thought often expressed in N.T., of which 1 Thess. v. 4, 5,
is a good example : " But ye, brethren, are not in darkness. . . . Ye are all
the children of light, and the children of the day : we are not of the night
nor of darkness." Cf. also Col. i. 12, 13 ; 2 Cor. iv. 6 ; Eph. v. 8 ; and
especially Acts xxvi. 18 (St. Paul's speech before Agrippa, εἰς οὓς ἐγὼ ἀπο-
στέλλω σε ἀνοῖξαι ὀφθαλμοὺς αὐτῶν, τοῦ ἐπιστρέψαι ἀπὸ σκότους εἰς φῶς καὶ τῆς
ἐξουσίας τοῦ Σατανᾶ ἐπὶ τὸν θεὸν κτλ. The belief that Christians belonged to
the light rested upon verba Christi (cf. Matt. v. 14-16 ; Jn. viii. 12, xii. 35, 46),
and these in turn marked the fulfilment of prophecy (Is. ix. 2). But the
wording of the phrase in 1 Pet. ii. 9b is without exact parallel elsewhere, and
is of a striking poetical quality. The phrase may be the author's own, or it
may be part of a Christian hymn which he is quoting.

5. In verse 10 St. Peter and St. Paul are both using Hosea i. and ii. ; and
Hort believed that " St. Paul's quotation suggested St. Peter's allusion ".
But this judgment takes no account of certain facts which point in a somewhat different direction. St. Paul is no doubt, as Hort says, directly quoting
from Hosea in Rom. ix. 25 he conflates phrases from Hos. i. 6, 9, ii. 23
(using the Vatican text), and in ix. 26 he quotes Hos. i. 10 with only one
verbal deviation. Even when in ix. 25 he inverts the order of son and
daughter [1] (" No-people " and " Not-beloved " respectively), he has such an
inversion in his source in Hos. ii. 1, quite apart from the natural propensity
of the human mind to mention the male first and the female second. But
St. Peter can hardly be said to quote ; he is standing further off from his
original than St. Paul ; and when their courses overlap, we notice that the
text which he is following is different from St. Paul's ; where the latter has
Οὐκ ἠγαπημένη as the name of Hosea's daughter, St. Peter has οὐκ ἠλεημένοι for
the Asiatics now converted, whom Hosea's daughter symbolized. If St. Peter's
allusion, therefore, were suggested by St. Paul's quotation, we should have to
admit that none the less he used a different version of the LXX. That is possible ; but the supposition is not necessary if we recognize that St. Peter's
approach to Hos. i., ii. is other and less direct than St. Paul's. In St. Peter's
case, indeed, the words used in verse 10 suggest a general rather than a
particular relation to the symbolic story of Hosea's two children, and Hos. i. 6,
9 and ii. 1 provide all that is needed to account for the verbal similarities.

6. The parallelism between the two clauses of 1 Pet. ii. 10, each clause
itself containing an antithesis, can be abundantly illustrated from Jewish
psalmody and from the Canticles in Lk. i., ii. (cf. the Magnificat, and the
last verse of the Nunc Dimittis), and is distinct from our author's normal

---

[1] The daughter is usually named first in Hosea, because she was the elder child.

style. Nor is it suggestive of a manual of " proof-texts ". In so far as Cyprian's *Testimonies against the Jews* can be used as evidence for any such collection in the first century, it is noticeable that he quotes Is. xliii. 18-21 in I. xii. to illustrate Christian Baptism, and Hos. ii. 23, i. 10 (as in Rom. ix. 25, 26) to illustrate the quite different point, " That two peoples were foretold, the elder and the younger ; that is, the old people of the Jews, and the new one which should consist of us ". The data are readily to be explained, on the other hand, on the hypothesis that St. Peter is quoting not directly from Hosea, but from a hymn into which the Hosean *motif* had already been incorporated.

We should thus have a strophe consisting of two tristichs and a distich, and it may well have followed on that which we have already isolated from verses 6-8. The first strophe presumably represents words placed in the mouth of God, as e.g. in Pss. l. and lxxxi. ; and if the second strophe followed immediately on the first, the second person plural in ὑμεῖς, ἐξαγγείλητε, ὑμᾶς would be original. Otherwise, the first person plural more probably stood in the hymn. Some support to the view that the two strophes stood together is given by Rom. xi. 30-2, when we have ὑμεῖς ποτε ἠπειθήσατε . . . νῦν δὲ ἠλεήθητε . . . ἠπείθησαν . . . νῦν ἐλεηθῶσι . . . ἀπείθειαν . . ἐλεήσῃ. The argument is quite different from that in I Pet. ii., but there is a striking identity of underlying words. The whole would read :

'Ιδοὺ τίθημι ἐν Σιὼν λίθον ἀκρογωνιαῖον ἐκλεκτόν, ἔντιμον,
καὶ ὁ πιστεύων ἐπ' αὐτῷ οὐ μὴ καταισχυνθῇ·
λίθος ὃν ἀπεδοκίμασαν οἱ οἰκοδομοῦντες
οὗτος ἐγενήθη εἰς κεφαλὴν γωνίας·
ἀπιστοῦσι δὲ λίθος προσκόμματος καὶ πέτρα σκανδάλου,
οἱ προσκοπτοῦσι τῷ λόγῳ ἀπειθοῦντες,
εἰς ὃ καὶ ἐτέθησαν.

ὑμεῖς δὲ γένος ἐκλεκτόν, βασίλειον,
ἱεράτευμα, ἔθνος ἅγιον,
λαὸς εἰς περιποίησιν,
ὅπως τὰς ἀρετὰς ἐξαγγείλητε
τοῦ ἐκ σκότους ἡμᾶς καλέσαντος
εἰς τὸ θαυμαστὸν αὐτοῦ φῶς·
οἱ ποτὲ οὐ λαός, νῦν δὲ λαὸς θεοῦ,
οἱ οὐκ ἠλεημένοι, νῦν δὲ ἐλεηθέντες.

G. On πνευματικός *in ii. 4, 5*

The word " spiritual " is of such importance, not only in this passage but in the New Testament and in Christian thought generally, that it seems worth while attempting to give some account of its origin, and to establish the meaning of the concepts which it connotes. The word as a factor in religious terminology is almost a Christian coinage : it is not found in the LXX, nor apparently in Hellenistic religious literature before A.D. 100 ; and in classical Greek, e.g. Aristotle, it is connected solely with the meaning of πνεῦμα as " wind " or " air ". Its non-occurrence in the LXX is particularly striking, seeing that πνεῦμα is constantly used there of the Spirit of God conceived of as His power manifested in nature or in the ethical and religious life of Israel. If it is true of πνεῦμα that its N.T. usage shews peculiarities of its own, " which were probably not derived from outside but developed within the circle of Christian thought ", this is still more true of the adjective formed from it.

The phrase just quoted comes from the classical discussion of πνεῦμα by Dr. Burton in his edition of Galatians (I.C.C. (1921)) ; and he points out that its most frequent use is with reference to the Spirit of God, called also the Spirit, the Holy Spirit, and the Spirit of Christ. The two most common contexts, moreover, in which it occurs, are those in which it is regarded as the source of extraordinary religious phenomena, such as prophecy, tongues, healings, and those in which it is regarded as operative in the human spirit for the production of ethical results. The most exact contrast to this use of πνεῦμα for the Spirit of God is presented by its use to connote demonic agencies ; but the most usual contrast is simply the Spirit's absence.

But πνεῦμα is also used of the human soul or of part of it. As Lightfoot points out (*Notes on the Epistles of St. Paul*, on 1 Thess. v. 23), human nature is most frequently spoken of in the New Testament as consisting of two parts — the flesh or body, and the soul or spirit — which we may distinguish as the visible and the invisible part. But sometimes the invisible part is sub-divided into a higher element (πνεῦμα or νοῦς), with which man is brought into touch with God, and a lower element (ψυχή) which represents the natural or physical vitality common to all living things, and is the seat of feelings, impulses, etc. Furthermore, σάρξ may be used in a purely physical sense (adjective σάρκινος) or in an ethical sense (adjective σαρκικός), where the σάρξ is thought of as primarily the seat of the lower desires (cf. Robertson and Plummer on 1 Cor. iii. 1 (I.C.C.)). We thus sometimes find (as in 1 Corinthians) a tripartite division similar to that in the myth of the chariot in Plato's *Phaedrus*, where human personality comprises νοῦς, τὸ θυμοειδές, and τὸ ἐπιθυμητικόν ; an idea reproduced in Philo, *Leg. Alleg.* i. 22, 23 [I. 47, 48 M]. In St. Paul, πνεῦμα is contrasted not only with σάρξ (e.g. Rom. viii.) and with ψυχή (e.g. 1 Cor. ii., xv., cf. Jude 19) but also with the Law (Gal. v. 18). In 1 Peter, however, we find only the simple traditional distinction between " flesh " and " spirit ", the former representing the visible,[1] corruptible part of man's nature, the latter its invisible, incorruptible part ; and thus the author speaks of Christ as θανατωθεὶς μὲν σαρκὶ ζωοποιηθεὶς δὲ πνεύματι (iii. 18), or of believers after death as " judged according to men in the flesh, but living according to God in the spirit " (iv. 6). This simple, twofold division is taken for granted by Ignatius, cf. *Eph.* x. 3, ἐν πάσῃ ἁγνείᾳ καὶ σωφροσύνῃ μένετε ἐν Χριστῷ Ἰησοῦ σαρκικῶς καὶ πνευματικῶς (with Lightfoot's note). And it is used, when applied to Christ, to express His human and His divine nature respectively (*ib.* vii.).

The adjective πνευματικός means " concerned with [the] spirit ", as πολιτικός means " concerned with the πόλις ". But the usage of πνεῦμα affords only a partial clue to that of πνευματικός ; for not only is its use with a subjective reference very rare ; but its commonest use corresponds to what we may call a " mixed " usage of πνεῦμα, of which Dr. Burton gives only four instances (Jn. iii. 6b, 1 Cor. xiv. 14, 15, 16). The occurrences of πνευματικός may be classified as follows :—

(i) Purely subjective, referring only or primarily to the human spirit :

1 Cor. xv. 46, οὐ πρῶτον τὸ πνευματικόν, ἀλλὰ τὸ ψυχικόν.

1 Cor. xv. 44, σπείρεται σῶμα ψυχικόν, ἐγείρεται σῶμα πνευματικόν, where

---

[1] We must be chary of saying " material " or " immaterial ", for the Hellenistic world seems to have thought of πνεῦμα as a highly rarefied kind of matter. Cf. Hatch, *Essays in Biblical Greek*, p. 129. Edwyn Bevan, however (*Symbolism and Belief*, pp. 156 ff., 192-205), maintains that in N.T. the materialistic ideas attaching to πνεῦμα in Gentile thought have been wholly discarded.

πνευματικόν means "formed to be the organ of the πνεῦμα in man". But this supremacy of the spirit of man is not achieved except when it is indwelt by the Spirit of God. And the same comment applies to :

1 Cor. ii. 14, πνευματικῶς ἀνακρίνεται, i.e. by the spirit of man.

(ii) Objective, referring only or primarily to the Spirit of God :

Rom. i. 11, ἵνα τι μεταδῶ χάρισμα ὑμῖν πνευματικόν.

1 Cor. ii. 13, [πνευματικοῖς] πνευματικὰ συγκρίνοντες, "suiting spiritual matters (cf. διδακτοῖς πνεύματος in the same verse) to spiritual hearers " : cf. Robertson and Plummer in loc.

1 Cor. xii. 1, περὶ δὲ τῶν πνευματικῶν ; ib. xiv. 1, ζηλοῦτε δὲ τὰ πνευματικά : with reference to gifts of the Holy Spirit.

1 Cor. xiv. 37, εἴ τις δοκεῖ προφήτης εἶναι ἢ πνευματικός, i.e. endowed with some special gifts of the Spirit.

(iii) A mixed usage, both subjective and objective, applied to persons, whose spirits are quickened and governed by the Spirit of God :

1 Cor. ii. 13, πνευματικοῖς [πνευματικὰ] συγκρίνοντες.

1 Cor. iii. 1, οὐκ ἠδυνήθην λαλῆσαι ὑμῖν ὡς πνευματικοῖς, ἀλλ' ὡς σαρκίνοις, ὡς νηπίοις ἐν Χριστῷ.

Gal. vi. 1, ὑμεῖς οἱ πνευματικοί.

(iv) A mixed usage, both subjective and objective, applied to things, and arising from the indwelling of the human spirit by the Spirit of God :

Rom. vii. 14, ὁ νόμος πνευματικός ἐστιν, i.e. coming from God who is Spirit and the Giver of spiritual gifts, and addressed to the spirit of man.

Rom. xv. 27, τοῖς πνευματικοῖς αὐτῶν ἐκοινώνησαν τὰ ἔθνη, i.e. the spiritual blessings vouchsafed to the Church of Jerusalem.

1 Cor. ix. 11, εἰ ἡμεῖς ὑμῖν τὰ πνευματικὰ ἐσπείραμεν, i.e. religious blessings, contrasted with material benefits (τὰ σαρκικά).

1 Cor. x. 3, 4, πνευματικὸν βρῶμα . . . πνευματικὸν πόμα . . . ἐκ πνευματικῆς ἀκολουθούσης πέτρας. "Sacramental" is the best translation of πνευματικός in these verses. In each case the reference is to supernatural food and drink deriving from Christ the Giver of eternal life, and mediated through the visible gifts of the manna and the water from the rock. The Fathers were quick to see the sacramental teaching contained here. Thus Chrysostom (in 1 Cor. Hom. xxiii.) writes : " St. Paul means that it was not the nature of the rock that sent up the water — it would have run dry long before — but there was another spiritual rock which was working it, namely Christ, who was present to them everywhere, the worker of all miracles ". And in the West St. Augustine (in Evang. Johan. Tract. xxvi. 12 and xlv. 9 ; con. Faustum, XIX. xvi.) claims that the thing signified, namely, Christ, has been the object of faith and the giver of grace in all ages of the Church, Jewish and Christian ; the signs or outward forms only, under which He has been apprehended, have varied — for the Jews the cloud, the Red Sea, the rock, for us the water of baptism, the bread and wine of the altar. And among modern expositors, F. W. Robertson (Lectures on the Epistles to the Corinthians, pp. 154 f.) interprets on similar lines : " Figuratively, therefore, it [the rock] followed ; the life of it streamed after them : they were never without its life-giving influence ; and therefore never destitute of a sacrament ".

Col. i. 9, ἐν πάσῃ σοφίᾳ καὶ συνέσει πνευματικῇ, i.e. sanctified by the Spirit and influenced by grace. The meaning is made plain by 2 Cor. i. 12, οὐκ ἐν σοφίᾳ σαρκικῇ ἀλλ᾽ ἐν χάριτι θεοῦ. Intellectual gifts are a snare unless the human spirit, in which they inhere, is subject to the Holy Spirit.

Col. iii. 16, Eph. v. 19, ᾠδαῖς πνευματικαῖς, i.e. religious songs. Cf. Eph. i. 3, ἐν πάσῃ εὐλογίᾳ πνευματικῇ.

(v) Two special uses may be mentioned, which do not fall under any of the above categories.

Eph. vi. 12, τὰ πνευματικὰ τῆς πονηρίας ἐν τοῖς ἐπουρανίοις, i.e. the spiritual powers or forces ; for there were evil πνεύματα (demons, etc.) as well as good (angels, etc.).

Rev. xi. 8, τῆς πόλεως τῆς μεγάλης, ἥτις καλεῖται πνευματικῶς Σόδομα καὶ Αἴγυπτος. Alford says πνευματικῶς means " allegorically ; in a sense higher than the literal and obvious one ". But it comes to mean this only because " the spirit of prophecy " (Rev. i. 10, iv. 2, xvii. 3, xix. 10) in the Seer so interpreted the allusions to Sodom in Is. i. 9, 10, Ezek. xvi. 46-9, and to Egypt in such passages as Ex. xvi. 3, Ezek. xx. 5-9. Sodom stood for wickedness and vice, Egypt for idolatry and oppression of God's people. The best translation of πνευματικῶς here would be " in the language of prophecy ".

It is clear from the above evidence that the third group is the *nidus* of most of the uses of the word πνευματικός in N.T. ; for several of the instances in the first two groups shade off into it very easily, and it governs most of the instances in the fourth group. It is clear also what importance must be attached, in the development of the word, to the period immediately prior to the writing of 1 Corinthians. It is such a development as we might expect towards the close of the three years of settled work and Church-building which St. Paul had at Ephesus between A.D. 52 and 55 — a far longer period of settled work than he had had since he embarked on his ministry to the Gentiles. He had passed now from the stage of Church-founding to that of Church-building ; he had become used to feeding his flock on meat and not merely on milk (1 Cor. iii. 1, 2) ; and he thus had an experience of the strengthening and sanctifying power of the Spirit in the lives of the members of the Church which made the word "spiritual" a natural one to use. Much of the disappointment and distress which the Corinthian Church caused him was due to the fact that this fruit — the characteristic fruit of the Christian life — was not forthcoming as might have been expected, while its place was often taken by other kinds of fruit which, though more spectacular and exciting, were of doubtful value and full of dangers of their own.

Once the term " spiritual " became a normal one to use of the mature Christians and the settled Christian community, its extension to the things which entered into their spiritual life was not likely to be long delayed : their hymns, their thought, their religious blessings generally were all entitled to the word, if they were part of their religious life or served its purpose. Even the Law was spiritual, seeing that it was read at their worship and quoted by their prophets and provided material for their catechetical teaching. And the manna in the wilderness and the water from the rock and even the rock itself could be called " spiritual " by virtue of their resemblance to the sacraments of baptism and the Eucharist which formed so vital a part of the Church's spiritual life. And it is in this context also that we must interpret the term in these verses of St. Peter. The house is spiritual, because it consists of spiritual persons and exists for spiritual purposes ; and their sacrifices are spiritual because they are proper to those who live in grace and worship in spirit and truth.

H. *The " Spiritual House ", its Priesthood and Sacrifices, in ii. 5-9*

In the preceding note we have considered the lexicography of the word πνευματικός in I Pet. ii. 4, 5. But, as so often, the lexicography leads on to a further set of problems, those of semasiology — of the meaning of the word, that is to say, not simply as a word in a language, but as a term in a context of thought and practice, pointing to associated ideas which are relevant to the determination of its meaning. Sir Edwyn Hoskyns and Mr. Davey have shewn how important this second stage is for the study of the Gospels [1] ; and it is not less essential to that of the Epistles, especially in the case of an Epistle which, like I Peter, reflects at unusually close quarters the mind and life of the early Christian community.[2] In the present passage the terms " spiritual house ", " holy priesthood ", and " spiritual sacrifices " all call for such treatment.

The root of practical religion for the writers of N.T. lies in the indwelling of the Spirit of God or of Christ in the spirit of man. But this spiritual communion and interpenetration by grace is no simple matter resting merely on the natural affinity between the divine and the human spirit ; for that natural affinity has been marred and disintegrated by sin. For the bridging of the chasm so caused there is needed on God's side redemption, and on man's repentance. That is why we find in the New Testament that the teaching about the Holy Spirit is throughout *historically conditioned* ; and all Christian mysticism must allow itself to be governed by this fact.[3] The Fourth Evangelist was never more true to primitive Christian tradition than when, commenting on our Lord's utterance about " rivers of living water ", he said that " the Holy Ghost was not yet given ; because that Jesus was not yet glorified " (Jn. vii. 38, 39). The connexion of the Holy Spirit with Christ Himself, and especially with His death, resurrection, and ascension, is made clear from the outset of the Church's history. St. Luke's insistence, in the opening chapters of Acts, that " the Pentecostal outpouring . . . was the ripe fruit of the Passion and Resurrection consummated and crowned by His Ascension into heaven ",[4] is borne out by every stream of New Testament thought.[5] Furthermore, this tying of the spiritual life to historical events is represented visibly as well as orally, in the ordinances of the primitive Church, its ministry and sacraments, no less than in its preaching. The Apostles are primarily witnesses of Christ's resurrection, and they and all other ministers of the Church derive their commission, and the spiritual endowments which enable them to discharge it, from tne ascended Christ. Baptism is " into " Christ's death, and its efficacy depends on His resurrection and exaltation. In the Eucharist, memorial is made of His death, and to partake of it is to share in His sacrifice which He offered for man's redemption. Both sacra-

---

[1] *The Riddle of the New Testament*, ch. i.
[2] Cf. Vincent Taylor, *The Atonement in N.T. Teaching*, pp. 35 ff.
[3] It is, I think, because the tradition represented by the Cambridge Platonists and their successors has tended to obscure this side of

N.T. teaching that their influence has not been more widespread.
[4] Swete, *The Holy Spirit in the New Testament*, p. 77.
[5] I do not exclude Jas. iv. 5.

ments belong to the new covenant in His blood, promised by the prophets and now established in the dispensation of the Spirit.

It is against this background of life and thought in the Apostolic Church that we must consider the ideas represented by the house, the priesthood, and the sacrifices, of which St. Peter speaks.

1. THE SPIRITUAL HOUSE.

The idea of Christian believers, individually and corporately, as constituting a house or temple of God is found in several strands of the early tradition, and is to be traced to our Lord Himself. St. John underlines the vital significance of the conception, in his view, by placing together at an early point in his narrative two sayings of Jesus which in the Synoptic record belong to the close of His Ministry. They are :

(i) The *logion* about His Father's house which He uttered in cleansing the Temple (Jn. ii. 13-17) ;

(ii) The saying, " Destroy this temple, and in three days I will raise it up " (Jn. ii. 18-22).

The first of these sayings is an abbreviated form of the Synoptic version (Mk. xi. 17, Matt. xxi. 13, Lk. xix. 46), which involved a conflation of Is. lvi. 7 and Jer. vii. 11 ; the second is authenticated by being one of the accusations recorded by the Synoptists (Mk. xiv. 58, Matt. xxvi. 61) as brought against Jesus by the Jews. In both cases, St. John implies that the sayings were the subject of much reflection in the Church (ἐμνήσθησαν in verses 17, 22), and that their meaning became clearer in the light of Christ's resurrection. At the same time, there are differences between Mk. xiv. 58 and Jn. ii. 19, which suggest that the original *logion* was pregnant with several meanings, only one of which St. John emphasizes here, though he will bring out the others later (cf. Jn. iv. 23, 24, vi. 50 ff.). Thus, in Mk. xiv. 58, Jesus speaks of " building another temple ", in Jn. ii. 19 of " raising " the present one after destruction ; in both cases in " three days ". And the striking word ἀχειροποίητον, which is echoed later by St. Stephen in Acts vii. 48 and by St. Paul in Acts xvii. 24 and 2 Cor. v. 1, is in Mark but not in John. It is probably authentic, and it is to be observed that, while its use in 2 Cor. v. 1 belongs to the " resurrection " circle of ideas which is uppermost in Jn. ii. 21, its occurrence in both the Acts passages has closer affinities with the ideas of a new mode of divine presence and of a transfiguration of worship adumbrated in Mk. xiv. 58.[1] At the same time, St. John, by linking the *logion* with the Cleansing of the Temple, as the ground of Christ's authority in that action, indicates his awareness of the new order of religion which the resurrection was to inaugurate, as though the argument were : " I claim to cleanse it now of a particular abuse ; but I will transform it radically hereafter " ; and, though this link is not in Mark, it has some Synoptic support in Matt. xii. 6, where Jesus claims that " in this place is one greater than the temple ".

The salient points of the evidence, therefore, are that Jesus, by a deliberate and public act, had condemned the profanation of the Jewish temple and asserted its true purpose to be a centre of worship for all peoples ; that He had, in language of high paradox, claimed authority to supersede the visible

---

[1] For another possible *verbum Christi* to the same effect cf. A. T. Cadoux, *The Sources of the Second Gospel*, p. 177, citing the addition to Mk. xiii. 2 found in D, W and OL, καὶ διὰ τριῶν ἡμερῶν ἄλλος ἀναστήσεται ἄνευ χειρῶν.

temple built of stone by a different embodiment of God's presence, namely His body, which was to be offered as a sacrifice for the world's purification and the feeding of His disciples, who would thus come themselves to constitute His body in another sense ; that the transfer of the term " house of God " from a building to a community of people was the work of Jesus Himself ; and that the meaning of these utterances had only gradually dawned on the mind of the Church. St. John does not develop these thoughts here, but " he has formulated his theme, the theme of the true and spiritual worship of God, by which the worship at Jerusalem has been fulfilled and superseded ".[1] As E. A. Abbott puts it (The Son of Man, § 3589), " the Temple, in the Gospel of Jesus, is seen to mean men and women, sinners many of them, built into the walls of a new House of God established on the Rock of Faith ".[2]

Before passing to the echoes of this theme in the Epistles, the prophecy of Isaiah which our Lord uses to interpret His action deserves to be noted. Is. lvi. 1-8 gives a glowing promise of the blessings of the restored temple and the conditions of admission to it. These conditions are the observance of the Sabbath and of the Jewish moral law ; and all who keep them, even though at present outcasts from Israel or Gentiles, will be gathered into the new worship at Zion. " Even them will I bring to my holy mountain, and make them joyful in my house of prayer : their burnt offerings and their sacrifices (θυσίαι) shall be accepted (δεκταί) upon mine altar ; for mine house shall be called an house of prayer for all people." The salient features of the promise are the universality of the new worship, involving the substitution of a religious and ethical criterion of admission for a racial one ; the emphasis on prayer as the purpose of the new temple ; and the fact that the sacrifices offered in it will be acceptable. The germs of St. Peter's " spiritual house " and " spiritual sacrifices " are already there.

When we turn to St. Paul, we find that the Epistles to the Corinthians are those which have most to say about the temple of God, as they have about the Spirit. Both corporately and individually, believers constitute a holy building or temple.

(i) The idea of the Church as corporately a temple is found in :

1 Cor. iii. 16, 17. Know ye not that ye are the temple of God (ναὸς θεοῦ), and that the Spirit of God dwelleth in you ? If any man defile the temple of God, him shall God destroy ; for the temple of God is holy, which temple ye are.

[In the previous verses (10-15), St. Paul has compared himself to a wise architect, who has laid the foundation, on which another builds ; and he goes on to say that the foundation is Christ Himself, and that the materials used in the building vary greatly. Events will test their worth. Each congregation of believers is a sanctuary, since the Spirit who dwells in them is the Holy Spirit.]

2 Cor. vi. 16, 17. And what agreement hath the temple of God with idols ? For ye are the temple of the living God ; as God hath

[1] E. C. Hoskyns, on Jn. ii. 22.
[2] Abbott also quotes the verbum Christi embodied in Matt. xviii. 20, " Where two or three are gathered together in my name, there am I in the midst of them", and observes that following as it does so closely on the reference to the Church in Matt. xviii. 17, it implies " that 'gathering' in a certain 'name' constitutes a 'place of worship'". Cf. Ex. xx. 24.

said, I will dwell in them, and walk in them ; and I will be their God, and they shall be my people. Wherefore come out from among them, and be ye separate, saith the Lord, and touch not the unclean thing ; and I will receive you.

[In this passage the Apostle is insisting on the necessity of the Christian community separating itself from the paganism around it, and especially from its religious customs ; and he urges, first, that they themselves *are* God's temple, and therefore need no other ; and secondly, that they are in a position similar to the Chosen People when they were called out of Egypt and Babylon. And he supports his claim with O.T. quotations which throw a significant light on the thought of the early Christians on the theme of the house or temple of God, all the more as each is accompanied by words from its context (cf. Plummer on 2 Cor. vi. 16). Thus we have : (*a*) καθὼς εἶπεν ὁ θεός, introducing Lev. xxvi. 12, καὶ ἐνπεριπατήσω ἐν ὑμῖν καὶ ἔσομαι ὑμῖν θεός, καὶ ὑμεῖς ἔσεσθέ μου λαός, from the closing chapter of the Law of Holiness, of which we have already observed traces in 1 Pet. i. 13 ff. (cf. Essay II, pp. 369-75) ; and though the sentiment, " I will be their God, and they shall be my people ", is common in O.T., especially in connexion with the ideas of Redemption and of the gathering of peoples to God (cf. Jer. xxxi. 33, Ezek. xi. 20, xxxvi. 28, xxxvii. 21 f., Zech. viii. 8, xiii. 9), the verbal parallelism in the case of Lev. xxvi. 12 is much more exact.

(*b*) λέγει κύριος, pointing to Is. lii. 5, which introduces the passage culminating in the command, ἀκαθάρτου μὴ ἅψησθε, ἐξέλθατε ἐκ μέσου αὐτῆς, ἀφορίσθητε, οἱ φέροντες τὰ σκεύη κυρίου (verse 11). The whole paragraph seems to have been as familiar to St. Peter as the Song of the Servant (Is. lii. 13–liii.) which immediately follows : cf. ἐν τοῖς ἔθνεσιν in verse 5 with 1 Pet. ii. 12, εὐαγγελιζομένου ἀκοὴν εἰρήνης in verse 7 with Acts x. 36 (St. Peter's words), 1 Pet. i. 12, ἐλεήσῃ in verses 8, 9 with 1 Pet. ii. 10, and ὄψονται πάντα ἄκρα τῆς γῆς τὴν σωτηρίαν τὴν παρὰ τοῦ θεοῦ in verse 10 with 1 Pet. i. 5, 9. A further point to be noted in St. Paul's quotation of Is. lii. 11 here is that its primary reference in the original prophecy was to priests and Levites; from which the priestly character of the Church might well be inferred.

(*c*) λέγει κύριος παντοκράτωρ, pointing to 2 Sam. vii. 8, which introduces the great promise imparted to David through Nathan of the settled kingdom which God will give to Solomon, and containing the words (verse 14), ἐγὼ ἔσομαι αὐτῷ εἰς πατέρα καὶ αὐτὸς ἔσται μοι εἰς υἱόν. In this case the prophecy is enriched by the thought of the reunion and deliverance of all God's people expressed in κἀγὼ εἰσδέξομαι ὑμᾶς, taken from such passages as Jer. xxiii. 3, Ezek. xi. 7, xx. 41, Zech. ix. 8, 10 ; and by the substitution of " sons and daughters " for " son " (cf. Is. xliii. 6). Though the promise in 2 Sam. vii. 8-18 is that Solomon shall " build a house for my name ", i.e. a temple, the emphasis is far more on the continuance and settled character of his kingdom and people ; and this aspect of the promise is often repeated in O.T. Cf. Kirkpatrick, *2 Samuel*, p. 234. A further interesting fact is that, in his *Testimonies against the Jews*, i. 15, under the heading " That Christ should be the house and temple of God, and that the old temple should cease, and the new one should begin ", Cyprian quotes 2 Sam. vii. 4, 5, 12-16 in full, and adds our Lord's words recorded in Matt. xxiv. 2 and Jn. ii. 19.

The notes of the Church as the temple of God which St. Paul underlines by these quotations are God's presence ; the close relationship which binds Him to the Church as His own people, and as Father to His children ; and the duty of a holiness which in its separation from the secular world is sacerdotal. At the same time, we observe that the significant phrase, ἐνοικήσω ἐν αὐτοῖς (2 Cor. vi. 16) is not, in fact, in LXX at all, though the thought is common (e.g. Ex. xxix. 45). ἐνοικεῖν is not rare in LXX, but the subject of the verb is always a plural or a collective singular (such as " the people "), and it connotes a quite literal " inhabiting ". Its use here by St. Paul is an example of the use of an old word in a new and Christian sense — of a new semasiology, in fact ; and the creative idea behind it is that of the Church as the οἶκος θεοῦ or οἶκος πνευματικός.]

Eph. ii. 19-22. Now therefore ye are no more strangers and foreigners, but fellow-citizens with the saints, and of the household of God (οἰκεῖοι τοῦ θεοῦ) ; and are built (ἐποικοδομηθέντες) upon the foundation of the apostles and prophets, Jesus Christ himself being the chief corner stone (ἀκρογωνιαίου) ; in whom all the building (πᾶσα οἰκοδομή, i.e. " all that is builded ") fitly framed together groweth unto an holy temple (αὔξει εἰς ναὸν ἅγιον) in the Lord : in whom ye also are builded together (συνοικοδομεῖσθε) for an habitation of God through the Spirit (εἰς κατοικητήριον τοῦ θεοῦ ἐν πνεύματι).

[If we had to choose between the view that St. Peter had read Ephesians, and the view (held e.g. by Moffatt) that St. Paul had read 1 Peter, there can be little doubt on which side the dependence would lie ; for St. Paul's treatment of the theme is altogether richer and more varied than St. Paul's. St. Peter's words about the spiritual house in ii. 3-8 do not read like the compression of another's more flowing periods. At the same time, the passage in Eph. ii. is not simply an embellishment of 1 Peter : it omits as well as adds, and seems to branch off from the same stem, indeed, but lower down the stalk. The stem of common ideas is represented by the Church as a " house of God ", or " holy temple ", built not of stones but of living believers ; by Christ as the " corner stone " ; and by the fact that God dwells there through the Spirit. Those are ideas which St. Peter expresses by his use of the phrase οἶκος πνευματικός — the spiritual temple in which believers are " built " as " living stones " — and by his quotation of the passage about the cornerstone found in Is. xxviii. 16. And they are all ideas which go back to our Lord's own words.]

(ii) For the idea of the body of the individual Christian as a " temple ", we have :

1 Cor. vi. 19. What ? know ye not that your body is a temple of the Holy Ghost which is in you, which ye have of God ? (. . . ναὸς τοῦ ἐν ὑμῖν ἁγίου πνεύματος, οὗ ἔχετε ἀπὸ θεοῦ;).

[The passage is best explained as the particularization of the general statement about the Church as a temple of God already enunciated in 1 Cor. iii. 16, 17.]

2 Cor. v. 1 ff. For we know that, if our earthly house (οἰκία) of this tabernacle were dissolved (καταλυθῇ), we have a building (οἰκοδομήν) of God, an house (οἰκίαν) not made with hands (ἀχειρο-

ποίητον), eternal in the heavens. . . . For in this we groan, earnestly desiring to be clothed upon with our house which is from heaven. . . .

[St. Paul's idea is that each Christian soul, now enveloped in an earthly body, has a heavenly covering, conceived (by a confusion of metaphors) both as a house and as a vesture, laid up for it in heaven. The metaphor of the body as a " house " or " tabernacle " of the soul is found both in Hippocrates (*Aph.* viii. 18) and Philo (*de Somn.* i. 122 [I. 639 M]), and is not far removed from the Orphic idea expressed in σῶμα σῆμα. But the form in which the metaphor is expressed is peculiar ; and when we observe that the striking words καταλυθῇ, οἰκοδομήν, and ἀχειροποίητον all have their counterparts in the *verbum Christi* recorded in Mk. xiv. 58 (cf. Matt. xxvi. 61, Jn. ii. 19), the conclusion forces itself upon us that this utterance of our Lord's was present to the Apostle's mind. The *point d'appui* is the equation between " temple " and " body ", and our Lord's reported promise that the destruction of the old temple (or body) would be the signal for His building of the new.]

(iii) Four further passages may be briefly mentioned :

(*a*) 1 Tim. iii. 15, where the " house of God " is said to be " the Church, the pillar and support of the truth ".

[But in this passage " house " is used in the sense of " household " or " family ", as frequently in O.T., and not in the sense of " temple ".]

(*b*) Heb. iii. 1-6. Consider the apostle and high-priest of our confession, Jesus, who was faithful to him that appointed him, as also Moses was faithful in all his [God's] house. For this man was counted worthy of more glory than Moses, inasmuch as he who hath established the house hath more honour than the house. For every house is established by some man ; but he that established all things is God. And Moses verily was faithful in all his [God's] house, as a servant . . . ; but Christ as a son over his own house ; whose house are we, if we hold fast the confidence and the rejoicing of the hope firm unto the end.

[It is questionable whether, despite the repeated mention of the οἶκος θεοῦ, this passage has any links with those which we have been considering : οἶκος probably connotes God's " household " or " family ", as in 1 Tim. iii. 15, and 1 Pet. iv. 17, i.e. in Westcott's words, " the organized society in which He dwells ". It is significant, moreover, that the distinctive architectural word οἰκοδομεῖν is avoided, and κατασκευάζειν, a much more general word covering equipment and administration as well as construction, is used instead. On the other hand, the association of the " house " with Christ as its high priest suggests that the idea of the Church as a divine sanctuary or temple is not far removed.]

This is borne out by two further passages in this Epistle :

Heb. viii. 1, 2. We have such an high priest, who is set on the right hand of the throne of the Majesty in the heavens ; a minister of the sanctuary and of the true tabernacle which the Lord pitched and not man.

Heb. x. 21, 22. And having an high priest over the house of God (τὸν οἶκον τοῦ θεοῦ), let us draw near (προσερχώμεθα) with a true heart in full assurance of faith, having our hearts sprinkled from an evil conscience (ἐρραντισμένοι τὰς καρδίας ἀπὸ συνειδήσεως πονηρᾶς) and our bodies washed with pure water.

[The high-priest's office was one of constant relationship both to the temple in which, and to the people on whose behalf, he ministered ; and in the light of that relationship the two meanings of the οἶκος θεοῦ as " temple " and as " household " become scarcely distinguishable. Affinities between Heb. x. 21, 22 and 1 Peter are observable in the use of προσερχώμεθα (cf. 1 Pet. ii. 4) and in the allusion to the cleansing power of Christ's sacrifice on the conscience (cf. 1 Pet. i. 2, iii. 21).]

We have suggested in the notes on 1 Pet. ii. 5 that οἶκος πνευματικός may be best rendered by " God's true temple ". The above discussion of the relations, both derivative and collateral, in which the phrase stands to similar N.T. teaching, indicates the reason. The allusions in the context to the priesthood and acceptable sacrifices of Christians, and the more veiled but still fairly clear allusion to the vindication of Christ by His resurrection, shew that the author has in mind the whole complex of ideas derived from the *verba Christi*, treated with differences of emphasis and details by St. Stephen, St. Paul, the Fourth Evangelist, and the author of Hebrews. In the immediate background of St. Paul and St. Peter, and probably also of Hebrews, stand the circles of the Apostles and prophets which first mused upon the *verba Christi* and their connexion with O.T. history and prophecy, and whose work is reflected both in the " memories " of which St. John speaks in Jn. ii. 17, 22 and elsewhere, and in the Lucan Canticles and the primitive hymns quoted in e.g. 1 Pet. ii. 6 ff. and Eph. v. 14. No better commentary on St. Peter's phrase could be desired than St. Paul's words in Eph. ii. 21, 22 : " . . . an holy temple in the Lord : in whom ye also are builded together for an habitation of God through the Spirit ".

2. THE PRIESTHOOD OF THE CHURCH.

We have already shewn in a previous note (pp. 268-81) how St. Peter chooses out of the many prerogatives of the Church indicated in the O.T. scriptures and the primitive hymns compiled from them, which he will quote in a moment, those on which he wishes especially to dwell ; and it is significant that his choice falls on those which are connected with *cultus* — the spiritual temple or house of the unseen King, the holy priesthood, the acceptable sacrifices. It is therefore important to determine how our author conceived of priesthood, both in itself and in its relation to those on whose behalf the priesthood ministers.

And first in itself. The holiness which he predicates of it is the first attribute of the Levitical priesthood which meets us in the Pentateuch. " The word ' holy ' (ἅγιος, not ἱερός or ὅσιος) describes the primary relation of belonging to Jehovah ",[1] for which purpose the holy person or thing is separated from the world and from secular uses, and consecrated to Him. And this sanctification involved elaborate rites : in the case of Levites, from

---

[1] Davidson, *The Theology of the Old Testament*, p. 153 ; cf. also pp. 242 f., 306 ff. Patristic references are given in Suicer : note especially Chrys. *in Joh. Hom.* lxxxii., κυρίως

ἅγια τὰ τῷ θεῷ ἀνακείμενα, Cyr. Alex. *ad Joh. x. 34*, ἅγια καλοῦνται τὰ ἀφοριζόμενα εἰς θυσίαν θεῷ. And cf. Trench, *Synonyms*, pp. 312 ff.

whom the priests were chosen, sprinkling with " water of purifying ", sacrifices, and dedication to God through laying-on of hands (Num. viii.), and in the case of priests, washing with water, robing, anointing, sacrifices and the application of the sacrificial blood to Aaron and his sons, etc. (Lev. viii., Ex. xxix.). The chief purpose of these rites is to fit Levites and priests for their primary task of " ministering ", that is, of serving the holy God in worship. Closeness of relation to God and the conduct of the worship of God are the main ideas. It is easy to see, moreover, how applicable these ideas were to the members of the Christian Church. They, too, were chosen and called by God (1 Pet. i. 1, 15) ; they had become Christians through baptism (1 Pet. iii. 21, cf. i. 22, ii. 1), which washed away the stains of sin, and had received the laying-on of hands (Heb. vi. 2) ; they had an " anointing " (1 Jn. ii. 20, 27) ; and they were sprinkled with the sacrificial blood (1 Pet. i. 2, 18-21, 1 Jn. i. 7, Heb. x. 22, xii. 24) of the new covenant established by Christ. In similar vein the Seer of Patmos speaks of Christians as " kings and priests " (Rev. i. 6, v. 10).[1] Seeing how many of these features of Levitical sanctification are mentioned by St. Peter and what emphasis he lays on the necessity of holiness (i. 16), we cannot but regard his description of the Church as " a holy priesthood " as organically connected with, and indeed in a very real sense summarizing, his whole conception of the Church. The ritual and the ethical aspects, moreover, are closely combined : from this passage about the Church's priestly functions, St. Peter passes at once to the fervent injunction (ii. 11) to " abstain from fleshly lusts, which war against the soul ".

Secondly, the Jewish priesthood was representative. It was " taken from among men " ; the laying-on of hands by the people on the Levites (Num. viii. 10, 11) was for the purpose of designating them as their representatives before God ; the high-priest bore on his breastplate the names of the twelve tribes. And in speaking of the Church as a priesthood, St. Peter means us to understand that the Christian community represents the nations of mankind in the same way as the Levitical priesthood represented Israel. To the Jewish mind there was no conflict between representation and sanctification : the meaning of the sanctification of the Sabbath, for example, was not that that day only was holy, but that, because that day was holy, so all time was God's and meant to be dedicated to Him. The idea of the Church as a priestly body carries with it, therefore, as Dr. Swete observes, the idea that " in the Christian body the commonest and least spiritual acts of daily life belong to the service of God ".[2] *Laborare est orare ;* for as George Herbert says :

> Who sweeps a room, as for thy laws,
> Makes that and the action fine.

But that is not all. It also implies a relation of the Church to the world which is of the utmost significance. In a deeper sense than that of the Roman poet, the Church must say : *homo sum, humani nihil a me alienum puto.* It is to bring all men to God and God to all men. No generous ideals, no honest searches for truth, no strivings for better things, fall outside

---

[1] B. S. Easton, *The Apostolic Tradition of Hippolytus,* p. 90, thinks, in view of these passages and of 1 Pet. ii. 9, that Tertullian (*de Bapt.* vii.) may be right in tracing to this idea the custom of anointing in connexion with baptism ; though other explanations of the ceremony are not impossible. For the relation of sacrifice to consecration cf. Prestige, *God in Patristic Thought,* pp. 21 ff.
[2] *The Holy Catholic Church,* p. 87.

the proper range of its sympathy and interest ; for its own separation from the world is that it may hallow the world. Nor is its activity limited to the hallowing of what is good in man's life : it has to do equally with what is evil, from which it offers redemption ; and indeed it is the universality of human sin and corruption which makes it necessary that there should be in the midst of the world a priestly body which can " stand on the Godward side " on behalf of men,[1] and so enable them to find access to Him who is the true object of men's worship. And it will have a special responsibility in regard to the religious cults and traditions of men, which even in their crudest and least enlightened forms are an attempt to deal with this very problem of reconciliation between men and God. Its aim must be to be " a light to lighten the Gentiles ", such as shall draw the non-Christian world to find in Christ and His teaching and sacrifice the crown, as well as the redemption, of its spiritual instincts.

But thirdly we must guard against the danger of supposing that the representativeness of the Church's priesthood, the ties which bind it to mankind at large, constitute of themselves its mediatorial function and capacity. It is one of its preconditions ; but divine selection and appointment are no less essential. Like salt, the Church must preserve the apartness of its priestly calling, if it is to do its work. The patience and meekness under suffering, the courtesy towards opponents, and indeed the whole imitation of Christ (cf. Introd. pp. 90-101) which St. Peter inculcates upon his readers, for the purpose of winning men to Christ and glorifying God, is part of the Church's work as a " holy priesthood ". This conception colours, indeed, all his ethical teaching : his ethics are grounded in the idea of Christ's example and atoning sacrifice. And the idea of priesthood took on a new connotation from the identification of Christ, which is so marked in this Epistle, with the Suffering Servant of Isaiah. The priest in Israel had a mediatorial rather than a redemptive function ; it is when this function is united with those of the Shepherd and of the Sufferer who is both priest and victim, that priesthood enters into its full meaning. St. Peter lays stress on both these aspects of Christ's work (ii. 25 ; 21-4) ; he shews that he regards the Church's ministry as a pastoral one modelled upon the Lord's (v. 1-4) ; and he enjoins on all the same spirit of patience in well-doing and of meekness under rebuff and contumely as had marked their Master. The Epistle marks, therefore, an important stage in the development of the New Testament idea of priesthood, towards that efflorescence of it which we find in the Epistle to the Hebrews.

At the same time, there are differences to be noted in the teaching of the two Epistles no less than affinities. Two stand out pre-eminently. One is that St. Peter shews no desire to disparage the Levitical priesthood. He is more Judaic — we might almost say, more old-fashioned in his Judaism — than the author of Hebrews. He regards the Levitical ordinances and teaching as prophetic or typical of the new dispensation, and dwells rather on those parts of them which are now fulfilled than on those which are now obsolete. Hebrews, on the other hand, finds in the Levitical priesthood " a grammar and vocabulary . . . a starting-point . . . an analogy ".[2] But that priesthood is essentially a fiction and a shadow, and one which has had its day : it could never develop into Christ's or Christian priesthood. The

---

[1] Heb. ii. 17 (Nairne's rendering).   [2] Nairne, *The Epistle of Priesthood*, p. 140.

other difference is that St. Peter shews no knowledge of the " natural priest-hood ",[1] such as was exemplified in Melchizedek, which Hebrews brings in to compensate for the fact that the Levitical priesthood was no more than a shadow. Both these contrasts mark out 1 Peter as more primitive, and more representative of a common rather than an individual mind, than Hebrews. And to these two points of contrast may be added the fact that St. Peter's main emphasis is on the priesthood of the Church, while that of Hebrews is almost wholly on the priesthood of Christ ; though the priest-hood of the Church is implied in such a phrase as " we have an altar " (Heb. xiii. 10).

Finally, attention may be drawn to the wider bearings of the idea of the Church's priesthood on the relations of the Church and the world. Many scholars have been struck by the apparent paradox involved in St. Peter's teaching about the honour due to the civil power and the imperial officials, at a time when these were forwarding, or conniving at, the persecution of Christianity. These injunctions are less surprising in the light of the priestly character of the Church ; and it is no accident that they follow close upon the great passage we have been considering. For they are part and parcel of that inward relation to the secular world which is characteristic of priest-hood : if the distinctiveness of the Church's holy way of life — its " salt " — is emphasized in 1 Pet. ii. 11, 12, its sympathetic and leavening influence under-lies the teaching of 1 Pet. ii. 13-17. This standpoint is not unconnected with a feature observed by Dr. Nairne [2] as common to the Johannine writings and Hebrews with this Epistle, namely, the tendency to deal with sin by " cleansing " rather than by repentance ; that is to say, by the priestly rather than the prophetic manner of approach. For cleansing is a more inward and intimate process than prophecy : we need only contrast the attitude of 1 Peter with that of the Apocalypse. And it needs a more settled and prolonged relationship, which takes for granted the permanent necessity of the world's civic institutions no less than the eternal vocation of the Church. Neither the idea of a theocracy nor that of " a free Church in a free world " would represent St. Peter's thought : " the Church the soul of the State " would come far closer to it. The words of Zechariah on the relations of the civil and hierarchical heads of the ideal community, though they do not seem to have been present to the Apostle's mind, would express his meaning : " the counsel of peace shall be between them both " (Zech. vi. 13).

3. THE SPIRITUAL SACRIFICES.

Hort opens his long note on πνευματικὰς θυσίας with the statement that " St. Peter cannot be thinking of any ritual acts whatever " ; and among more recent commentators, Windisch is equally emphatic : " in no event is the Eucharist in mind " (on 1 Pet. ii. 3). Hort interprets the sacrifices re-ferred to as " consisting in devotion of the life to social service, offered as to God in thanksgiving " ; and he quotes in support of his view Rom. xii. 1, Eph. v. 1, 2, Phil. iv. 18, and Heb. xiii. 15. Bigg accepts this interpretation with the proviso that, while the good works and prayers and praises of the Christian communities are chiefly in mind, " their gifts are not excluded " : he under-lines the prominence given to the almsgiving mentioned in Phil. iv. 18, and adds Acts x. 4 (prayers and alms), Phil. ii. 17 (faith), and Heb. xiii. 16 (kind

---

[1] For this phrase see Westcott, *Epistle to the Hebrews*, p. 140, and Nairne, *op. cit.* pp. 143 ff.
[2] *Op. cit.* pp. 164 f.

deeds and almsgiving) to weight the scale. And this has been the general drift of exegesis, both ancient and modern. Estius, for instance, comments as follows : *spirituales hostias, id est, opera virtutum ; quae quidem omnia, quatenus ad Dei referuntur honorem, ut auctoris ac Domini universalis, hostiae dicuntur ; spirituales autem ad differentiam carnalium hostiarum, quae in veteri lege offerebantur, et per quas mysticae fuerunt significatae ; vel generatim ad discrimen cultus externi, qui ad interiorem cultum in animo consistentem referri debet. Subest igitur in hac parte exhortatio tacita ad opera bona, tamquam ad spirituales hostias, ad quas Deo offerendas consecrati sint sacerdotes in baptismo.*

On the other hand, E. Lohmeyer,[1] in the course of a judicious discussion of the Eucharist in N.T., maintains that this exegesis is inadequate : " for the section ii. 1-10 is packed with pictures and ideas taken from *cultus*, seeing that it begins with baptism and ends with the living building of a ' spiritual house ' for the offering of spiritual sacrifices ". " In such a context ", he continues, " the Eucharist, one might almost say, has a necessary place ; also *Did.* xiv. calls it later a ' pure offering ' (cf. Mal. i. 11, cf. iii. 3). Further, one can get some idea of the nature of the religious action from the phrases used : for example, people ' taste ' (Ps. xxxiv. 9) that the Lord is χρηστός — a well-known play on words, often connected later with the Name of Christ; people ' draw near to Him ', so that here the meal is entirely a ceremonial act of divine worship ; and meanwhile, in this approach and meal, ' people build themselves up into a holy priesthood '." Lohmeyer claims that, on this interpretation, the phrases give a vivid intimation — though not more than that — of " the whole design and behaviour of the believers in their religious gatherings ".

This wide variety of interpretations, which are nevertheless by no means mutually exclusive, suggests that there is room for a new approach to the problem. Two points may be observed at the outset.

First, the author proceeds direct from the mention of the spiritual sacrifices to his quotation about the cornerstone which God lays in Zion ; and it is reasonable to infer, therefore, that there is a close connexion of meaning between the two. The stone must be highly relevant to the temple, priest-hood, and sacrifices which it is brought in to illustrate. The stone is Christ ; but it is Christ the " lamb without blemish and without spot " of 1 Pet. i. 19 and iii. 21 ff., the " Christ our passover " of 1 Cor. v. 7, the " Christ crucified, unto the Jews a stumbling-block, and unto the Greeks foolishness " of 1 Cor. i. 18, who is in the author's mind. The Christ set before us here as the basis and centre of the Christian sacrifices is the Christ who " his own self bare (ἀνήνεγκεν) our sins in his own body on the tree " (ii. 24). We may recall how, directly after our Lord had given Simon his new name of Peter (stone), He passed on to tell the disciples of His approaching suffering and death (Matt. xvi. 13-23).

Secondly, as we have seen in the literary criticism of this passage (*supra*, pp. 268-81), verses 4, 5 anticipate the principal points of the quotation in verses 6-10 ; and the evidence suggests that the final clauses in verse 5 and verse 9 — ἀνενέγκαι κτλ. and ὅπως τὰς ἀρετὰς κτλ. — are in the same category ; in other words, that the offering of the spiritual sacrifices alluded to is identical with, or at least one form of, the proclamation of God's excellencies.

We are thus led to the view that the sacrifices offered by the priestly body, the Church, are intimately connected with the atoning work of Christ, and also serve to shew it forth in all its rich and reconciling mercy. He is presented as the centre of a new sacrificial worship and a new sacrificial way of life. The sacrificial way of life is a fundamental element in the ethical teaching of the Epistle (cf. Introd. pp. 97 ff.) : Christians are to imitate Christ in His meekness, patience, and suffering, and they are to do it in order to win others to the faith — that is to say, to shew forth God's excellencies. Every walk of life, and every moment, offers occasion for the exercise of this spiritual activity (cf. the passages from Chrysostom quoted in the note on ii. 5) ; and it reaches its climax in martyrdom,[1] which is the high-watermark of faith (Phil. ii. 17) and the occasion when the disciple shares most fully in the sufferings of his Lord. The idea is already adumbrated in Wisd. iii. 6, a passage not far from our author's mind when he wrote i. 7 : " As gold in the furnace he found them, And as a whole burnt-offering (ὁλοκαυτώματα θυσίας) he accepted them ". Even more significant is the *verbum Christi* in Mk. ix. 49, where the uncompromising integrity required of the Christian is compared to the salt of the covenant-relation " which purifies, preserves and consummates sacrifice " (Swete *in loc.*).[2] The self-oblation entailed by the new covenant is expressed in this *logion* in different language from that employed by St. Paul, for instance, in Rom. xii. 1, 2, but it cannot be excluded from the " spiritual sacrifices " alluded to by St. Peter. Further, it is a fact abundantly attested in history that men have been most able and willing to recognize the excellencies of God, and most alive to the noble acts of His mercy, when they have seen them reflected in the dying life of the Church. The blood of the martyrs is the seed of the Church ; but so also are all generous acts of self-surrender, forbearance, and loving service done in Christ's Name and under the inspiration of His cross. And in that sense we can see the social implications of the passage. For a priesthood implies a community on behalf of which the priesthood offers sacrifice, the gift being provided by the community ; and the Church's task is here set forth as the offering to God, and therefore the hallowing, of the common life of the communities — village and city, school and factory, nation and world — in which it lives and works.

Moreover, all such acts are hallowed and gathered up in the Eucharist.[3] Temple — priesthood — sacrifices : we are not entitled to regard these terms as purely metaphorical. The ethics of the Apostolic Church are inseparably bound up with its worship, and the term " sacrifice " is used of the latter as freely as of the former. Thus, a close parallel to the present passage is to be found in Heb. xiii. 15, " Through him let us offer the sacrifice of praise to God continually, that is, the fruit of our lips giving thanks to his name " ; where we observe the same word for " offering " (ἀναφέρειν), which is the liturgical word *par excellence* (cf. Westcott, on Heb. vii. 27), the same reference to Christ's mediation (δι' αὐτοῦ), and the same ethical context (cf. Heb. xiii. 16, 1 Pet. ii. 11 f.), as here. And this usage has links both backwards and forwards — backwards, with Jewish phraseology (cf. Lev. vii. 12), and forwards with the language of the Fathers (cf. Origen, *in Lev. Hom.* ix. 1,

---

[1] Cf. Lohmeyer, *L'Idée du martyre dans le Judaisme et dans le Christianisme primitif* (vol. dedicated to M. Loisy, 1928), ii. pp. 121 ff., for Jewish ideas of the meaning of the martyrs for the nation.

[2] The additional or alternative reading, καὶ πᾶσα (πᾶσα γὰρ θυσία ἀλὶ ἀλισθήσεται, which has strong MS. attestation, brings out the meaning of the WH text more clearly, but does not materially alter it.

[3] Cf. Heiler, *The Spirit of Worship*, ch. ii.

Greg. Naz. *Orat.* ii. 95). Such prayers and praises were by no means confined to the Eucharist ; but the N.T. writers leave us in no doubt that the Eucharist was their chief focus and occasion for use. Moreover, the whole action of the Eucharist was one of praise and thanksgiving arising out of the redemptive sacrifice of Christ's death. " As often as ye eat this bread, and drink this cup, ye do shew the Lord's death (τὸν θάνατον τοῦ κυρίου καταγγέλλετε), till he come ", says St. Paul (1 Cor. xi. 26) ; and between St. Paul's " shewing the Lord's death ", and St. Peter's " shewing forth the noble acts of God ", there is little difference ; for of all God's noble acts none was nobler than Christ's death. We are not surprised, therefore, when we find this interpretation early appearing in Christian literature ; as where the *Didache* (xiv. 1, 2) speaks of the " pure offering " (θυσία) of Mal. i. 11 as fulfilled in the Eucharist, and bases on it a strong appeal for brotherly concord, or where Justin Martyr describes the praises, prayers, and thanksgivings which surrounded the consecration of the baptismal Eucharist (*Apol.* i. 65 f.) and the Sunday Eucharist (*Apol.* i. 67, cf. *Dial.* 41) in the second century.

In view of these facts, I think we must recognize that Lohmeyer has made a valuable contribution to the understanding of 1 Pet. ii. 1-10. The " spiritual sacrifices " of which St. Peter speaks have been correctly interpreted as consisting in righteousness, self-oblation, deeds of kindness and brotherly love, prayer and praise and penitence. But the background against which our author thought of these sacrifices, and out of which they arose, was the worshipping community gathered for the celebration of the Eucharist and in particular, perhaps, for the baptismal Eucharist of which we have evidence in later days. The Eucharistic allusions in the passage would thus seem to be comparable to those in Jn. vi., where also the background of early Christian *cultus* provides the language rather than the immediate meaning or purpose of the Discourse. At the same time, St. Peter's words throw back a reflex light on the way in which the Eucharistic sacrifice was conceived in the middle of the first century. We may summarize it as follows :

(i) The Eucharistic sacrifice consists in the Eucharist *as a whole* ; the entire Eucharistic service, with its prayers and praises, its almsgiving and social brotherhood no less than its strictly sacramental features, is included in the term ;

(ii) The sacrifice is offered by the Church *as a whole*, in its priestly capacity, and not by any group or circle within it. The officiants act in a representative capacity only ;

(iii) Since the whole Church is sacerdotal, its acts in offering the Eucharist are sacerdotal acts ; and the Eucharist is therefore best interpreted as bearing the same relation to Christ's death on the cross as the sacerdotal acts of the Jewish priesthood bore to the victims of the Jewish sacrifices. They invest it, that is to say, with its sacrificial significance, and apply its benefits to the people [1] ;

(iv) The context of 1 Pet. ii. 1-10 is baptismal as well as Eucharistic ; and this should be borne in mind when we speak of the passage as sacramental. The custom of keeping the two sacraments together, in time as

[1] For references to the exposition of this doctrine by Sir W. Spens and P. de la Taille, S.J., see the note on i. 2 (ῥαντισμὸν αἵματος).

well as in thought, which was characteristic of the Church in the early centuries, may well have had its origin in Apostolic times [1] ;

(v) The way in which Christian social duty and almsgiving, prayer and praise, priesthood and sacramental actions are connected in the N.T. writings, and alike given a sacrificial meaning and reference, suggests that this connexion is an original feature of the Church's outlook and way of life.[2]

It has seemed desirable to dwell at length on these points, because so much depends upon the Church's power to maintain the true synthesis between the three elements just mentioned. Within the Church itself the divorce between sacramental and non-sacramental ideals of worship has found expression in boundaries dividing Christian bodies from one another ; while the divorce between the instincts of worship and the instincts of social fellowship and service, which is the modern counterpart of the old opposition between faith and works, is one of the main causes of the estrangement of many good men and women from the Church. The passage in 1 Pet. ii. which we have been considering, with others similar to it, comes as a valuable corrective to these exclusive claims and tendencies, and shews that, in the mind of the Apostolic community as we see it in the New Testament, these distinct strands of feeling and thought were not regarded as mutually independent but were woven together into a single and convergent witness to the cross of Christ and the wonderful works of God.

I. *On ἀντίτυπον in iii. 21*

The meaning of ἀντίτυπα in Heb. ix. 24 is plain ; but it seems to lie somewhat aside from the normal usage of the first two centuries. According to that usage, τύπος denotes that which is one way or another secondary, whether as the outline sketch or cast to the completed work, or as parable to fact, or as image to archetype. An interesting discussion of the term occurs in Campbell Bonner's Introduction to the recently published Homily of Melito on the Passion (*Studies and Documents*, xii. pp. 68-72, 108-15). Melito there compares the Law and the institutions of the old dispensation to a sculptor's cast or pattern, which is made of wax or clay or some other cheap material, before he embarks on the work itself. This pattern he calls τύπος or εἰκών or προκέντημα, while that for which it is made he calls τὸ φύσει ἀληθές or ἡ ἀλήθεια ; and when the task is completed, the pattern is discarded as of no value. Thus the Chosen People, the Law, the Passover, the earthly Jerusalem are discarded now that the Church, the Gospel, the sacrifice of Christ, and the heavenly Jerusalem have come.

This use of τύπος as equivalent to εἰκών and as something which foreshadows or represents a reality of a higher order than itself is found also in Clement of Alexandria (*Fragm.* 33, Stählin, iii. p. 218, 3), Hippolytus (PG 59, 723 ; 59, 732-3) and Origen (*in Lev. Hom.* x.), though its connotation is not always identical in detail with that in Melito. From a different angle the contrast, common in Philo, between εἰκών and ἀρχέτυπος is equally instructive, as an indication that τύπος is the word used for what is secondary ; and its correlative is ἀρχέτυπος. Cf. also St. Basil, *de Spir. Sancto*, 47, ἐπειδὴ δὲ διὰ δυνάμεως φωτιστικῆς τῷ κάλλει τῆς τοῦ θεοῦ τοῦ ἀοράτου

---

* For a simple description of such a service see *An Outline of Church History*, pp. 97 ff.   by J. H. Srawley, *The Early Histo.y of the Liturgy*, p. 38.
[a] A cautious review of the evidence is given

εἰκόνος ἐνατενίζομεν, καὶ δι' αὐτῆς ἀναγόμεθα ἐπὶ τὸ ὑπέρκαλον τοῦ ἀρχετύπου θέαμα. At the same time, in N.T. τύπος is used both in this sense of something secondary, and also, as in Acts vii. 44, in the sense of ἀρχέτυπος ; and this equivocal connotation of the word accounts for the fact that ἀντίτυπον (ἀντίτυπος) is itself a *neutral* word which may either, as Lightfoot says, " depreciate relatively ", or " extol relatively ". The meaning, therefore, must be determined by the context : in itself it means " corresponding " or " the corresponding thing ". Cf. MM *sub voc.*, and Alford's note on 1 Pet. iii. 21.

The linguistic difficulties of this passage, however, are less than the grammatical, and here various interpretations are possible : (1) if ᾧ be read, we have a simple sentence, " corresponding to which (i.e. the water of the Flood) baptism now saves you also ". This is straightforward Greek, and it is not easy to see why it should ever have been altered : (2) ἀντίτυπον may be a predicative adjective added to the pronoun ὅ. This is Winer's view (*op. cit.* p. 663) ; and it can be illustrated by Rom. iii. 25, ὃν προέθετο ὁ θεὸς ἱλαστήριον, if SH are right in regarding ἱλαστήριον as an adjective. In this case " in its antitypal form ", " or by way of antitype " would be a fair rendering, meaning that what the Flood-water adumbrated was fulfilled in the water of baptism : (3) ἀντίτυπον may be a substantive as in Heb. ix. 24 ; and this appositional construction can be paralleled in Heb. x. 20, ἣν ἐνεκαίνισεν ἡμῖν ὁδὸν πρόσφατον καὶ ζῶσαν. One may add that ἀντίτυπον was a substantive which by its very connotation lent itself to appositional construction. On the other hand, the *double* apposition here of two substantives, ἀντίτυπον and βάπτισμα, to a relative pronoun is exceedingly clumsy Greek and quite unlike our author's style. (4) Blenkin takes ἀντίτυπον closely with ὅ, " which antitype ", meaning that both the Flood and Baptism were antitypes or representations of the same spiritual original, namely death to sin and new life to righteousness. This gives ἀντίτυπον the meaning which it has in Heb. ix. 24, 2 Clem. xiv., Iren. *A.H.* . v. 6, and notably Cyril of Jerusalem, *Cat. Myst.* ii. 6, where baptism is described as τῶν τοῦ Χριστοῦ παθημάτων ἀντίτυπον. The great objection to this view is that this construction of a relative pronoun with an epexegetic substantive introducing a new idea, although legitimate in English, does not appear to occur in Greek (in Acts xxvi. 7, Heb. vii. 14, x. 10, 1 Pet. i. 10 the substantive is simply repeating the antecedent) ; nor is this kind of Platonism elsewhere found in this Epistle, where the thought is always historical rather than metaphysical.

Of these four views the second is perhaps open to least objection ; but, if the interpretation given in the notes is accepted, we are not driven to choose between them.

J. *Persecution and the Judgment in iv. 17-19*

1 Pet. iv. 17-19 is too pregnant a passage to be fully discussed in the notes on the text ; and something is here added, therefore, on the two main ideas which are there combined.

1. The idea that God's judgments began with His house or household of Israel was often taught by the prophets. In Amos iii. 2 this fact is a result of His peculiar love for Israel. In Jer. vii. 8 ff., a passage which was

on our Lord's lips (verse 11, cf. Mk. xi. 17) when He cleansed the temple, God's house, i.e. the temple at Jerusalem, is to suffer as the sanctuary at Shiloh did, and the inhabitants of all Judah to be punished, for their wickedness. In Jer. xxv., as in Zeph. i. and ii., judgment begins with " the city which is called by my name ", and spreads outwards to the heathen nations. Zech. xiii. 7-9 gives teaching closely similar to that in Mal. iii. And we may also cite *Apoc. Bar.* lxxviii. 6, " Therefore, if ye consider that ye have now suffered these things for your good, that ye may not finally be condemned and tormented, then ye will receive eternal hope ; if above all ye destroy from your heart vain error, on account of which ye departed hence ". Ezek. ix. 6 is often quoted in this connexion, but it is improbable that it was in St. Peter's mind more than any other passage. What St. Peter does is to transfer this idea from the partial judgments of the past to the final Judgment now imminent, and from the Jewish Church to the Christian. Other prerogatives have been thus transferred in 1 Pet. ii. 4-10.

This belief in judgment beginning at the house of God was subject to the same tension between present and future as exists in the rest of the eschatological teaching of our Lord and His Apostles. That is to say, it was already partially a fact. As Hoskyns points out (*The Fourth Gospel*, i. pp. 207-12), the cursing and withering of the barren fig-tree, the parable of the Wicked Husbandmen, the teaching about the stone which the builders rejected (cf. Add. Note E, pp. 268-77) that follows it, and the statement concerning the irrelevance of animal sacrifice (Mk. xii. 32-4) provide a setting for the Cleansing of the Temple in the Marcan narrative which gives it special significance ; and this significance is underlined by St. John through the transference of that narrative to the beginning of our Lord's ministry. In the actions and in the sufferings of the Messiah Judgment had already begun at the house of God. But now a new house of God had been set up (1 Pet. ii.̈ 5-10) by divine selection and creation after the old had been rejected ; and it was subject to the same law of judgment and purification as that which the Lord had executed towards Judaism (cf. Jn. xv.). As Bengel says (on 1 Pet. iv. 17), " It is one and the same judgment from the time of the preaching of the Gospel by the apostles until the last judgment ". The Church, like the world, stands under the Judgment of God (cf. Jn. xvi. 8-11), until the End of all things is fully consummated, when the faithful shall be glorified and the Church's enemies, whether within or without the household of God, shall be condemned.

2. The belief that the trials of Christians in persecution were a kind of first instalment of the last Judgment has an instructive history and occurs elsewhere in N.T. For summaries of the evidence see Schürer, *op. cit.* II. ii. pp. 154 ff., Thackeray, *St. Paul and Jewish Thought*, pp. 105 f., Charles, *Eschatology*, etc., pp. 382-5, 329 f., Dewick, *Primitive Christian Eschatology*, pp. 30, 173 ff. In the prophetic writings the premonitory signs of the Judgment are commonly political events, of which the uprising of Gog and Magog (Ezek. xxxviii., xxxix.), and the gathering of the Gentiles to battle and defeat (Joel iii., Zech. xiv.) are the most spectacular examples. Our Lord's words in Matt. xvi. 3, τὸ μὲν πρόσωπον τοῦ οὐρανοῦ γινώσκετε διακρίνειν, τὰ δὲ σημεῖα τῶν καιρῶν οὐ δύνασθε, were in this tradition. The vision of the four beasts in Dan. vii. brings the rise and fall of world-empires into the category of " signs of the End ". The Apocalyptic writers develop the

theme by laying stress upon portents and disturbances in the natural and social order, already sometimes predicted by their prophetic predecessors (cf. Is. xiii. 9-11, Joel ii. 28 ff.) ; and these Messianic Woes, or travail-pangs of the Messiah, became a regular feature of Jewish eschatological expectation (cf. Dan. xii. 1, *Jub.* xxiii. 11-25, *Ass. Mos.* x. 3-6, *Apoc. Bar.* xxvii., 2 Esdras v. 1-12, vi. 18-24, ix. 1-9). But in none of these predictions, save possibly *Jub.* xxiii. 13, was persecution for the faith reckoned as one of these signs or woes. That was a distinctively *Christian* view, and represents a definite addition to the features of the Jewish eschatological expectation, and one that profoundly modified its spirit and structure. In Mk. xiii. (with Matt. xxiv. and Lk. xxi.) we have a clear combination of (*a*) persecution and (*b*) portents of natural and social disintegration as among the ὠδῖνες or birth-pangs of the Messianic age. Whether the second of these goes back to our Lord's authentic teaching or not is doubtful : Charles and many others give good grounds for the view that Mk. xiii. has conflated two independent series of sayings, only one of which consists of *verba Christi*. But that Jesus did foretell persecutions and trials for His disciples, and that He set these in an eschatological context, is not open to doubt (cf. Matt. x. 16-26, xvi. 24, Mk. viii. 34, xiii. 9-13, Jn. xv. 18-27, xvi. 1-3). The order of the narratives in Mk. xi., xii. is particularly significant in this connexion (cf. Hoskyns, *The Fourth Gospel*, i. pp. 208 f.).

The Apostles crystallized this belief into dogmatic form in the words διὰ πολλῶν θλίψεων δεῖ ἡμᾶς εἰσελθεῖν εἰς τὴν βασιλείαν τοῦ θεοῦ (Acts xiv. 22). This represented a great step forward in the philosophy of persecution. In the teaching of the Hebrew prophets, the calamities of Israel were always regarded as illustrations of God's righteousness (cf. Davidson, *The Theology of O.T.*, p. 136). The apocalyptists raised the scale of the calamities and made them signs of God's approaching vindication of His righteousness in Judgment. The Christian Church singled out persecution as the calamity *par excellence* which belonged to the eschatological pattern, though the old idea can be seen in the background, as in 1 Cor. vii. 26, 2 Tim. iii. 1 ff., and gave expression to the thought in various ways. Thus we have (1) St. Paul's command to examine ourselves before Communion, itself an action with an eschatological reference (1 Cor. xi. 28), on the ground that such self-judgment will forestall and prevent such " judgment " as sicknesses and deaths (a view which much modern psychological medicine would endorse), adding, " But when we do receive judgment (e.g. through sickness), we are being chastened by the Lord, in order that we may not be condemned (κατακριθῶμεν) with the world " (cf. Robertson and Plummer *in loc.*, who also cite 2 Macc. vi. 12).

(2) In 1 Thess. iii. 3, 4 St. Paul, in bidding his readers not be alarmed by their afflictions, reiterates the general truth asserted in Acts xiv. 22, which he says had been part of the teaching given them by himself and Silvanus and Timothy, ὅτι εἰς τοῦτο κείμεθα . . . ὅτι μέλλομεν θλίβεσθαι ; and in 2 Thess. i. 4 he speaks of their endurance and faith in all their " persecutions and afflictions ", and speaks of this situation as ἔνδειγμα τῆς δικαίας κρίσεως τοῦ θεοῦ, εἰς τὸ καταξιωθῆναι ὑμᾶς τῆς βασιλείας τοῦ θεοῦ, ὑπὲρ ἧς καὶ πάσχετε. The great majority of scholars (e.g. Ellicott, Lightfoot, Zahn, Milligan, Frame (I.C.C.)) hold the view that the " proof " of God's just judgment lies in the endurance and faith of the Thessalonians. Bicknell (West. Comm.)

is less confident of this ; and Plumptre (C.B.S.) and Jowett definitely connect the phrase with the persecutions themselves (*St. Paul's Epistles to the
Thessalonians, Romans, Galatians*, i. p. 148 (1855)). Alford, as so often
refusing the dilemma, finds the proof " manifested in you being called on
and enabled to suffer for Christ, and your adversaries filling up the measure
of their opposition to God ". I am inclined to think that Alford is right, and
that the afflictions of the Thessalonian Christians no less than their faith
and fortitude in them are in St. Paul's mind. It is difficult to see in what
sense faith and fortitude *in themselves* constituted a proof of God's just judgment : they did so only in the context of the whole eschatological pattern
(already taught to the readers), in which the outbreak of afflictions or " woes "
was a premonitory sign or first instalment of the Judgment. Judgment was
beginning, in fact, at the house of God (1 Pet. iv. 17) ; its certain outcome
was to be the vindication of the Christians' title to a place in the Kingdom,
for which they were suffering, and the punishment of their unbelieving
persecutors (verses 6-10, cf. 1 Pet. iv. 5).

This conclusion receives support, moreover, from the detailed eschatological teaching given by St. Paul in 2 Thess. ii. 2-12. The teaching of this
passage differs markedly in one particular from that of 1 Peter, for St. Paul
is concerned to insist that the Day of the Lord has *not* yet set in [1] ; but the
eschatological pattern is the same. A time of apostasy and of a great manifestation of evil — tyrannous, godless, and yet fascinating by its brilliant
secular achievement — must occur before God vindicates His cause in
Judgment.

(3) Phil. i. 28-30 contains similar doctrine. Again St. Paul urges his
readers not to be startled like " a timid horse " (Lightfoot) by anything
their adversaries do. Their situation is a proof (ἔνδειξις) of the destruction
destined by God for their enemies and of the salvation destined for themselves ; because they have had the privilege, not only of believing in Christ,
but also of suffering for Him. Here too Lightfoot and others connect the
" proof " with the fearlessness of the Philippians, but with far less reason ;
for the explanation given by St. Paul of the " proof " refers simply to the
fact of their suffering for Christ's sake.

(4) In the Johannine Apocalypse frequent allusion is made to the sufferings of the faithful as among the preliminaries of the End. Thus, in iii. 10
the angel of the Church in Philadelphia promises deliverance ἐκ τῆς ὥρας τοῦ
πειρασμοῦ τῆς μελλούσης ἔρχεσθαι ἐπὶ τῆς οἰκουμένης ὅλης (cf. Swete *in loc.*,
" In the foreshortened view of the future which was taken by the Apostolic
age this final sifting of mankind was near at hand, not clearly differentiated
from the imperial persecution which had already begun "). The vision of
the martyrs of the past (vi. 9 ff.), which follows the opening of the fifth seal ;
the death of the " two witnesses " in ch. xi. at the hands of the Beast, especially verse 18, " And the nations were angry, and thy wrath is come, and the
time of the dead, that they should be judged, and that thou shouldest give
reward unto thy servants the prophets, and to the saints, and them that fear
thy name, small and great, and shouldest destroy them which destroy the
earth " ; and the dragon's persecution of the Church, typified as " the woman
which brought forth the man-child ", in ch. xii. — these are outstanding

---

[1] The difference may be due to a change in
Christian thought brought about by changed
circumstances, or to the fact that St. Paul is
taking an individual line in 2 Thess. ii. 2-12.
Cf. Introd. p. 16.

features of the pattern of the Last Judgment and its preludes, as the Seer of Patmos saw them.

Such, in outline, is the context of thought which appears to underlie St. Peter's words in iv. 17-19. These words are an important part of his teaching on suffering and the spirit in which the Christian should meet it, and serve to fill in the picture already adumbrated in i. 5-9 (cf. the notes on those verses, and Add. Note C, pp. 258-9). The Christian rejoices to suffer for, and with, his Lord ; and this is a distinctive contribution made by Christianity to the philosophy of suffering. To this rejoicing St. Peter adds here the further quality of serenity ; and both alike have a theological ground in the eschatological hope which the Christian Church took over, revised by Christ Himself — by His teaching and by the facts of the Incarnation, Cross, and Resurrection — from Judaism. The sufferings themselves are a proof of the imminence of the End ; and, in the light of that faith, they satisfy both the moral and the religious impulses of believers. They satisfy their moral impulses, in that the divine Judgment which they betoken will infallibly involve the execution of justice upon the " ungodly and cruel men " who betray Christianity from within (cf. 2 Tim. iii. 1 ff.) or seek to destroy it from without ; and they satisfy the religious impulses in the sure and certain hope of a blessed immortality and a crown of life which they guarantee to those who cleave to their Redeemer (cf. Matt. v. 1-12, especially 11, 12, Jas. i. 12, 1 Pet. iii. 13–iv. 6, v. 4, Rev. ii. 10, vii. 14-17).

K. On Babylon in v. 13

If Babylon in v. 13 means Rome, this is presumably the earliest occurrence of this appellation or cryptogram in Jewish or Christian literature ; for though it is found in Or. Sib. v. 143, 152 and Apoc. Bar. xi. 1, and in N.T. in Rev. xiv. 8, xvi. 19, xvii. and xviii., there is little doubt that these passages are later than 1 Peter.

In itself the term represents a mixture of prophecy and metonym which is not without parallel in N.T. Thus, in the Gospels, we have the application to John the Baptist of the name Elijah (Mk. ix. 11-13). The Jews expected that Elijah would come as the Forerunner of the Messiah, and our Lord avails Himself of the current coin of popular expectation, and says that " Elijah has already come " in the person of John the Baptist, meaning that John was the prophesied Forerunner. A similar usage is found in the Epistles, as when St. Paul speaks of the Christian Church as " Jerusalem which is above " (Gal. iv. 26) and as " the Israel of God " — though in both these cases the allegorical term is qualified. Heb. xii. 22 is another case in point : " ye have come unto mount Sion and unto the city of the living God, the heavenly Jerusalem " ; where the unqualified metonym of the first phrase is interpreted in the fuller statement of the second. From another standpoint, the Seer of Patmos alludes to the earthly Jerusalem as called " spiritually " — i.e. in the language of prophecy — " Sodom and Egypt" (Rev. xi. 8). In all these examples the proper name, whether of place or of person, stands for certain well-known attributes — Elijah for Messiah's Forerunner, Israel for God's chosen religious community, Mount Sion for the place of His worship, Jerusalem for the place of His Presence on earth, Sodom for wickedness, and Egypt for materialism and worldliness. So here, we may conjecture, Babylon in 1 Pet. v. 13 stands for the place of *exile*. St. Peter has already addressed his readers as " strangers and pilgrims " ; now he writes himself down as an exile too. He writes from the capital of the great empire in which his fellow-Christians were domiciled, and he may properly call it " Babylon ".

The usage, however, must be more than a matter of personal idiosyncrasy. Its occurrence in four sources so distinct as 1 Peter, Galatians, Hebrews and Revelation points to a widespread way of thinking and writing ; and we may safely surmise that it was the result of the Christian prophets' work, and emerged from their circles. Their special concern was with fulfilments,[1] and all the proper names we have mentioned are in the nature of fulfilments. Babylon as *par excellence* the place of exile in Jewish history would have sufficed to account for its use in 1 Peter ; but it does not follow that other associations in the term must be ruled out. Two others come before us in the Apocalypse, Babylon's combination of wealth and wickedness, and Babylon's oppressiveness and fall. St. Paul's language in Rom. i. shews how easily the prophetic circles might come to see old Babylon embodied in contemporary Rome by dint of its wickedness and wealth : St. Peter's language perhaps shews traces of being influenced by the second idea. For there are certain words in the preceding verses, 5-11, and also elsewhere in the Epistles, which are found in some of the great O.T. prophecies about Babylon and its fall. We may note the following :

(i) In Is. xliii., which has given St. Peter or the hymn which was his source much material for his picture of the Church in ii. 9, 10, the very phrases which he quotes from verse 21 shew the contrast between God's blessing upon Israel and His forthcoming punishment of Babylon mentioned in verse 14.

(ii) Still more marked are the verbal parallels between 1 Pet. v. 5-11 and Jer. l. (xxvii.) and li. (xxviii.). The chapters are a prophecy of Babylon's overthrow, described as ἡ ἡμέρα αὐτῶν καὶ καιρὸς ἐκδικήσεως αὐτῶν (l. 27, 31). Again, in Jer. li. 34 ff., we have Nebuchadrezzar compared to a " dragon " which devours (κατέπιεν, verses 34, 44) and to " lions " ; he is Israel's " antagonist " (ἀντίδικος) ; and throughout the two chapters the words ἐκδικεῖν, ἐκδίκησις form almost a refrain, occurring indeed relatively more frequently here than in any other passage of O.T. This word does not occur in the same sense in 1 Peter ; but in 1 Thess. iv. 6, 2 Thess. i. 8 it does, and we have seen already what close links bind these Epistles with 1 Peter. Thus, in 1 Thess. iv. 6 God is said to be the " punisher " (ἔκδικος) of sins of sensuality and covetousness, and in iv. 8 we have the word ἀθετεῖν used very much as in Is. xxi. 2 (ὁ ἀθετῶν ἀθετεῖ), which is in an oracle against Babylon. 2 Thess. i. 8 occurs in a more formal passage of eschatological prediction, which speaks of God's just judgment, of His recompensing (ἀνταποδοῦναι, cf. 1 Pet. iv. 5) the Church's persecutors, and of His giving punishment (ἐκδίκησιν) to the unbelieving and disobedient.

The eschatology of 1 Peter and its connexion with persecution, especially in such a passage as iv. 17-19, suggest that such ideas as these were not strange to the author, or at least to his associate, the prophet Silvanus. Yet in this Epistle they are still held in solution. Babylon is still primarily the place of exile. But already more sinister aspects of its character, its oppressiveness and its destined fall, are coming into the foreground of prophetic thought ; and we can well understand that the Neronian or the Domitianic persecutions would have brought them to such active and torrential expression as we find in the Apocalypse.

L. *1 Peter and the Mystery Religions*

Examination of the influence on 1 Peter of ideas and usages found in the Mystery Religions is facilitated by the collection of material made by Perdelwitz. Perdelwitz published his *Die Mysterienreligion und das Problem des I. Petrusbriefes* in 1911, only a year after Reitzenstein's *Die Hellenistischen Mysterienreligionen* had appeared to bring a new factor of great importance into the field of New Testament study.[1] The claims made for the new material thus collected varied greatly, from the extravagant theories which traced not only the early Christian *cultus* but even the Gospel itself to Hellenistic sources, to the more modest view that the language at least, and through the language the thought, of St. Paul and other of the N.T. writers had been greatly influenced by the Mystery-cults of the day.[2] Since then more sober estimates have increasingly prevailed. The historical basis of primitive Christianity and the persistently Jewish character of N.T. thought, not least in St. Paul, have offered a stubborn resistance to the attempts to explain either as owing anything fundamental to contemporary heathenism. The most that we can say is that the literature of the Mystery Religions shews certain religious phraseology to have been current, and certain terms " in the air ", at the time when the Christian Church took its rise. Perdelwitz' theory, therefore, which goes far beyond this, might not seem to-day to call for attention ; nor should I deem it otherwise, were it not that his book had been popularized by the late Canon Streeter who based upon it his chapter on 1 Peter in *The Primitive Church*. And at the same time it is worth trying to see whether, amid much that we must reject in Perdelwitz' work, there is not some light to be thrown by it on our Epistle.

Perdelwitz' main thesis is that ideas and phrases in 1 Peter which are not traceable to O.T. or current Jewish sources, nor to any known teaching of Christ, but which are found in the literature of the Mystery Religions, should be regarded as borrowed from the latter. Such borrowing may be of two kinds, and he gives examples of both, though without drawing the distinction. One is positive, and occurs where the Christian *cultus* and the ideas associated with it are described in language which is intended to set forth Christianity as a form of Mystery Religion, though of a superior type. The other is negative, and is found where the author is openly contrasting Christianity with these contemporary cults : the clues to it are the negative particles (οὐ, μή) and adjectives compounded with a-privative. In some cases the two kinds of borrowing are combined, as when a supposed similarity in principle is balanced by contrasts in detail. It will be convenient to bear this in mind while examining Perdelwitz' thesis.

---

[1] Attention had been drawn to the question in this country long before by Dr. Hatch, in his *Hibbert Lectures* of 1888, ch. x.
[2] A powerful statement and criticism of the Mystery Religion hypothesis will be found in

Dr. N. P. Williams' essay entitled "The Origins of the Sacraments " in *Essays Catholic and Critical*. There is a brief, but excellent, summary of these cults in John Buchan's *Augustus*, pp. 266-71.

I. The Nature and Effect of Conversion.

1. Perdelwitz begins with the concept of Rebirth (1 Pet. i. 3, 23, cf. ii. 2): and he claims that the combination of this concept with *cultus* as it meets us in i. 3 (with which may be compared Tit. iii. 5, λουτροῦ παλιγγενεσίας, Jn. iii. 3, 5, 1 Cor. xv. 29) has no Jewish precedent and can only be accounted for by reference to the Mystery Religions. The idea of παλιγγενεσία, he says, belonged from the earliest times to the cult of Isis ; and it was found also in those of Mithras and Attis.[1] The idea was common, in short, that Rebirth was necessary before a votary could be fully initiated (cf. Reitzenstein, *op. cit.* pp. 27, 31 ; also Angus, *The Mystery Religions*, pp. 94 ff., and Kennedy, *St. Paul and the Mystery Religions*, pp. 107 ff., 209-11, 229 ff.).

Now, the fact that a change in the votary on initiation came to be variously described in the parlance of the Mystery Religions as ἀναγέννησις, παλιγγενεσία, μεταμόρφωσις, μετατύπωσις is true ; but it is far from being the case that we can therefore assume that this idea passed from these cults into the Christian Church. For it was, in fact, well established in Jewish thought, and appears in the recorded words of our Lord. Even if we assign to Hellenistic and Gentile influence the words ascribed to our Lord about the new birth in His talk with Nicodemus (Jn. iii.), and the term παλιγγενεσία (which seems to have no exact Aramaic parallel) in Matt. xix. 28, we are still left with contemporary Jewish evidence of the currency of the idea in strictly Jewish circles, and its application to the status of converts to Judaism. Thus, we find R. Yose saying, " A newly converted proselyte is like a new-born child " (*Yebamoth*, 48b), and R. Judah, in *Tractate Gerim* (ii. 6), says that a convert is " like a babe one day old ". According to Jewish ideas, " his conversion affects the proselyte's status in two respects — towards God and towards God's people Israel. After being received as a proselyte he is regarded as ' newly born ', with reference to any guilt as to his past sins and misdeeds, and to their punishment. This is the Godward relation of his new status. In regard to Israel, as a child newly born he is entirely cut off from his family after the flesh ; all social relations start anew ; he has a special and peculiar relationship legally to the fellowship of Israel."[2] It is, of course, difficult to assign exact dates to Rabbinic documents ; but even Rabbinic ideas which meet us first in the second century are more easily assigned to sources within their own consistent and tenacious tradition than to any borrowing from the Gentile world. The bearing of this concept of the proselyte as " reborn " upon the uses of ἀναγεννᾶν and ἀρτιγέννητα in 1 Peter is obvious.

Further, the Judaic idea of rebirth is closely connected with the rite of proselyte-baptism, and gives us therefore precisely that combination of idea with *cultus* which Perdelwitz believed could only be found in the Mystery Religions. Moreover, the combination has far closer affinities with what we find in 1 Peter than anything which can be gleaned from pagan sources. It derives ultimately from the injunctions of the Holiness Code in Lev. xvii. and xviii. as to the admission of the " stranger " to membership of Israel ;

[1] For references see Perdelwitz, *Die Mysterienreligion*, etc., pp. 42-4.
[2] Gavin, *The Jewish Antecedents of the Christian Sacraments* (pp. 51, 52). And cf. his references to Strack-Billerbeck and to Kohler, and Rabbinic passages quoted in Dalman, *The Words of Jesus* (Engl. ed., 1902), pp. 177-9; also W. G. Braude, *Jewish Proselyting*, pp. 74 ff.

and evidence is given elsewhere in this volume [1] of the influence of this tradition on our Epistle, which also reflects throughout the triple nature — dogmatic, ethical, and eschatological — of the instruction commonly given to the Jewish convert.[2] As Clemen points out,[3] the Regeneration alluded to in 1 Pet. i. 3, 23 is explicitly connected with the historical fact of Christ's resurrection and with the preaching of the Word. What the convert is instructed in is no secret myth or ritual, but the facts of a Gospel widely attested and openly declared and a sacramental rite which had been a well-known and public feature of Judaism in the Roman Empire. Nor are these the only differences. Both in Judaism and in Christianity, baptism may be properly called sacramental, whereas the baptisms or washings in Greek religion at this time were rather lustral, preliminary to initiation rather than a part of it [4] ; and if an exception must be made in the case of the blood-bath of the Mithraic *taurobolium*, the disgusting character of that rite should suffice in itself to deter us from connecting it in any way with Christian baptism. Finally, there is no suggestion in 1 Peter, as might be urged in the case of 2 Pet. i. 4 and 1 Jn. iii. 2, of Regeneration signifying a metaphysical change ; there is no idea of " union with a God " such as we find frequently in the Mysteries, and Perdelwitz claims (p. 93) to find here. The Regeneration of which St. Peter speaks is to a " living hope " — an idea far more Jewish than Greek or Oriental, and wholly consonant with Hebraic history and religion.

2. The clue given by the parallel ideas of Rebirth in the Mystery Religions and in our Epistle is followed up in a number of details.

(a) i. 2. ῥαντισμὸν αἵματος. The description of the initiated convert as *renatus in aeternum* belongs to the Mithraic *taurobolium*, in which the votary descended into a pit where the blood of a bull dripped from a grid upon him and Perdelwitz believes that our author is here contrasting the sprinkling of the blood of Jesus with this rite. But the language is amply accounted for by Jewish custom. The Law prescribed the sprinkling of the blood of a sacrifice for the cleansing of a leper (Lev. xiv. 14), for the consecration of the Aaronic priesthood (Ex. xxix. 20), and for the ratification of the Covenant of Sinai (Ex. xxiv. 8) ; and our Lord's allusion to " my blood of the Covenant " at the Last Supper leaves little doubt that that is the circle of ideas underlying St. Peter's phrase. See the note on this verse. The two passages from Apuleius (xi. 6, xi. 15) quoted by Perdelwitz to shew that " obedience " was connected with initiation into the mysteries of Isis have little in common (as even Gunkel felt) with our present passage, which is thoroughly Jewish in thought.

(b) i. 23. οὐκ ἐκ σπορᾶς φθαρτῆς ἀλλὰ ἀφθάρτου. Perdelwitz traces this phrase to the idea current in Egyptian Mysteries, as evinced by the Hermetic literature, that in union with the god man's soul received the σπέρμα θεοῦ, being impregnated by the divine creativity. The Greeks identified this σπέρμα with Hermes (καὶ ψυχοπομπὸς καὶ ψυχῶν αἴτιος) ; and he, in turn, was sometimes called λόγος. But, in fact, this far-fetched allusion is unnecessary. The phrase is most easily understood of the grace of God

[1] Cf. Introd. pp. 18 ff., and Notes on i. 13 ff. ; also Essay II, pp. 369-75.
[2] Cf. Gavin, *op. cit.* pp. 38, 39, and his references to the works of Seeberg and of Klein on the primitive Christian catechism, and to the testimony of the *Didache*, i.-vi., on this point.

[3] *Primitive Christianity and its non-Jewish Sources*, pp. 225, 226. Cf. also Büchsel in Kittel, *W⁰·ᶻ·N.T.*, *sub voc.* ἀναγεννάω.
[4] Cf. A. D. Nock, in *Essays on the Trinity and the Incarnation*, pp. 67 f., 113-17.

which Christians know by experience (cf. Jn. i. 13, and my note on 1 Pet. i. 23) ; and the way in which Hermes was commonly thought of in the first century is well illustrated in the scene at Lystra, where St. Paul is identified with him (Acts xiv. 12).

(c) i. 4. κληρονομίαν ἄφθαρτον κτλ. The use of the characteristic Jewish term κληρονομίαν, and the fact that all the adjectives in this phrase occur in the Book of Wisdom, should have warned Perdelwitz that borrowings from Hellenistic cults were not to be looked for here. But he regards each of these adjectives as expressing a contrast with the Mystery Religions. The Christian inheritance is ἄφθαρτος in contrast to that of the Mithraist,[1] for whom the effects of the blood-bath were widely supposed to expire and need renewal after twenty years[2] ; ἀμίαντος, and therefore unlike the blood-stained garb of the Mithraist coming out of the pit ; and ἀμάραντος, whereas the garland worn by the Gentile votary at his initiation was a fading one ; and finally it is " laid up in heaven ", whereas the sacred garb of the Mystery is laid up only in a temple. Of these alleged parallels, it is sufficient to point out that none of them, with the possible exception of the first, is in pari materia with the " inheritance " which the adjectives describe. It is as though we were to confuse a Christmas present with the crackers and the mistletoe that provide its environment. No child would be guilty of such a mistake !

(d) i. 5. φρουρουμένους. Perdelwitz has to resort to the expedient of taking this as a participle in the middle voice, in order to bring it under his theory : " the condition of your having this inheritance is that you keep yourselves on guard, etc.". So interpreted, he reckons the word to be an allusion to the κάτοχοι or " prisoners of the god " who were detained for long periods in the Serapeum, as novices waiting for their initiation. The suggestion need not detain us.

(e) ii. 2. τὸ λογικὸν ἄδολον γάλα. The notes on this verse give what seem to me the most probable meaning and filiation of the terms. But we may perhaps be touching Hellenistic ground here, for the administration of milk and honey to the newly baptized began to be practised in the second century ; and it was a part also of the initiation-rites of the votaries of Cybele. Thus Sallustius says[3] : " after this we are fed on milk as though being re-born ; and that is followed by rejoicings and garlands and as it were a new ascent to the gods ". This belongs to the fourth century A.D., but earlier evidence for the custom is said to be available, especially in the Isis-cult.[4] For λογικόν, moreover, Kittel cites Corp. Herm. i. 31 (Scott, i. pp. 130, 22 f.), δέξαι λογικὰς θυσίας ἁγνὰς ἀπὸ ψυχῆς καὶ καρδίας πρός σε ἀνατεταμένης, ἀν-εκλάλητε, ἄρρητε, σιωπῇ φωνεύμενε. The probability that contemporary Gentile custom was present to our author's mind is enhanced by the context where ἄδολον may be intended to point a contrast with the " adulterated " milk of the Mysteries (cf. Tertullian, de Praescr. Haer. xl.), and χρηστός in the quotation from Ps. xxxiv. 9 means " good to the taste ". Perdelwitz even claims that there is no quotation here from Ps. xxxiv. 9, because the καὶ ἴδετε of the original is omitted ; and he would (though without MS. support) read Χριστός for κύριος. But St. Peter may well have been quoting from an early

---

[1] Mithraism derived the taurobolium from the much older Phrygian cult of Cybele ; and there was syncretism also with the cults of Attis and of Isis. Cf. F. Legge, Forerunners and Rivals of Christianity, ii. p. 259. His whole account of Mithraism is most instructive.
[2] Though some Mithraists believed the effects to be permanent.
[3] De Diis et Mundo, iv.
[4] Perdelwitz, op. cit. pp. 57 f.

Christian hymn based on Ps. xxxiv., in which καὶ ἴδετε found no place (cf. Add. Note E, pp. 273-7). More serious objections to bringing the quotation into direct relation with the allusion to the " milk " are that its use in later Christian literature is always eucharistic, not baptismal, and that St. Peter would hardly allude to his readers *having tasted* the milk immediately after enjoining them to desire it.

Nevertheless, it is possible that this is one of those cases where an idea which was already " in the tradition " of Jewish and Jewish-Christian thought was expressed in phraseology which was intended to link it with customs which were " in the air " of the religion of Asia Minor in the first century ; and the drink of milk which came to be given after baptism at the end of the second century may owe something to the combination.

(*f*) i. 9. σωτηρίαν ψυχῶν. Reitzenstein and Wobbermin trace the use of σωτήρ, σωτηρία to the Mystery Religions (cf. Isis' title of *salutaris dea*), and Wendland to the worship of the Emperor as " Saviour ". But the conception of God as Saviour is far too strongly entrenched in Hebraic thought, not least in the Psalms which were familiar to all worshippers, for any such hypothesis to be needed.

II. The Religious Community, and the Process of Initiation into it.

1. Perdelwitz maintains that the picture of the Christian community drawn for us in 1 Pet. ii. 4-10 and in certain other passages owes much to the ideas current in Hellenistic circles about the institutional side of the Mystery Religions. Thus, the Mithraists, we are told, used to call each other " Brother " and address their priests as " Father ".[1] In Lydia inscriptions shew that the fellow-members of a Mystery-cult were accustomed to regard their communities as φράτραι, φρατρίαι, or συμβιώσεις, and it is suggested that the Petrine ἀδελφότης in ii. 17 may be derived thence. From these facts Perdelwitz concludes that the initiates of the Mystery Religions thought of themselves as forming a great " spiritual family " (οἶκος πνευματικός, ii. 5) ; and their highest aim was to be " fathers " or " priests " to the novices whom they attracted into the cult. This is the source of the " holy priesthood " which the Christian community is to aspire to be, and the " spiritual sacrifices " which they are to offer are the converts whom they have won.

When the evidence adduced by Perdelwitz is carefully examined, it is found to be of very various quality ; and, while it suffices to attest a strong community sense at least in some places and at some periods, the outstanding features of St. Peter's picture of the Church do not occur in it, at any rate with any frequency. On the other hand, they are all deeply embedded in O.T. tradition and in the *verba Christi*. That membership of the Mystery-cults might have prepared men's minds for St. Peter's teaching is possible enough, thus forming part of that *praeparatio evangelica* which from St. Paul's time onwards Christian thinkers have loved to discern in the Gentile world. But more than that we cannot say.

2. Perdelwitz buttresses this thesis too with further detail :—

(*a*) ii. 4. The " living stone " is, he thinks, unintelligible apart from a reference to the Mystery Religions, owing to the abruptness of the change

---

[1] Cf. F. Legge, *op. cit.* ii. pp. 260 f., and n. 1.

of metaphor from the milk of verses 2 and 3.   In itself, the " stone " metaphor might well be, as Clemen maintained, an echo of Ps. cxviii.
22, but the
introduction of a quotation from this Psalm — so Perdelwitz maintains — is
incoherent and arbitrary in the context where we find it.   The combination
of " stone " and " milk ", however, meets us in various places in the Mystery-
cult literature.   Thus, Aphrodite-Astarte was represented in the form of a
cone-shaped stone at Paphos.   Mithras, again, was represented in stone-
reliefs as πετρογενής.   And it was in these circles that the drink of milk was
part of the initiation ceremonies.

Apart from the fact that the evidence for this combination of " stone "
and " milk " in the Mystery-cults seems to be very slender, the need for any
such explanation of St. Peter's λίθον ζῶντα disappears if the sequence of the
Apostle's thought is what we have suggested in the notes on this passage,
and in the Additional Notes above, pp. 268-77, 295 ff.   A theory is not
commended by the process of creating difficulties for it to explain.

(b) ii. 4. προσερχόμενοι.   Perdelwitz quotes Apuleius xi. 26, *eram cultor
denique adsiduus, fani quidem advena, religionis autem indigena*, and also an
inscription from a Mithraeum to shew that " προσέρχεσθαι, προσήλυτοι had
become technical terms for adherence to a Mystery-cult ".   A broad
conclusion seems to be based on narrow premises ; whereas in Hellenistic
Judaism the words had a long history in this sense, and the verb occurs in
the Psalm (xxxiv.) just quoted.   And the *verbum Christi* in Matt. xi. 28 may
have been present to the author's mind.   At the same time the term would
have been specially suitable if ıt were current in Gentile as well as Jewish
circles.

(c) ii. 9. τοῦ ἐκ σκότους ὑμᾶς καλέσαντος εἰς τὸ θαυμαστὸν αὐτοῦ φῶς.
Perdelwitz adduces evidence to shew that " calling " was necessary before
the Mystes could approach the sanctuary of Isis (Apuleius xi. 21, Pausanias x.
32. 13) ; and in her ceremonies, as well as in those of Dionysus and of
Mithras, the votary had to pass through a darkened chamber into a place of
wonderful light.   In the dark chamber he experienced φρίκη καὶ τρόμος καὶ
ἱδρὼς καὶ θάμβος, and was as a *homo moriturus*.   As he ascended into the
light, he was greeted with songs of joy, and found festal garb and a crown
awaiting him.   In the new blaze of light he came to view (ἐποπτεύειν) the
ἄρρητον, and so earned the title of ἐπόπτης.

The evidence does no more than illustrate the well-known fact, amply
attested by comparative religion, that darkness and light are almost universal
religious categories.   Nowhere are they better attested than in the Hebraic
tradition.

III. The *Descensus ad Inferos* (III. 18–IV. 2).

Perdelwitz suggests that the phrase in verse 18, ἵνα ἡμᾶς προσαγάγῃ τῷ
θεῷ, shews that our author is thinking of Christ as akin to the μυσταγωγός
or ὁδηγὸς τῆς ψυχῆς of the Mysteries ; and he holds that there is special reference to Orpheus.   The passage is fully discussed in Essay I, below.

On the basis of these parallels Perdelwitz conjectures that 1 Pet. i. 3–iv. 11
was originally an address to Christian neophytes on the occasion of their
baptism.   Both the author and his hearers must have belonged previously

to a Mystery-cult, probably connected with Cybele, a goddess held in great esteem in Phrygia. The author cannot have been St. Peter ; for the document must belong to a period when we know that the Mystery Religions were very active ; and this condition is satisfied by the first half of the second century. The rest of our present Epistle, i.e. 1 Pet. i. 1, 2, iv. 12–v. 14, was a short letter written in a time of actual persecution. It was probably addressed to a community of people who had been gathered together from the five provinces mentioned in i. 1 to some social or trading centre in Asia Minor, and they were in that sense ἐκλεκτοί. And they were also παρεπί-δημοι in the same sense as Cicero was in the eyes of the votaries of Attis, when he was governor of Cilicia ; for Quintilian (xii. 10. 14 f.) says that they regarded him as *alienigenam et parum superstitiosum devinctumque legibus illis*, and *alienigena* is the equivalent of παρεπίδημος.

The questions of the integrity, date and authorship of the Epistle will have to be settled on less slender grounds than these, and they are discussed in the Introduction. But if we apply to the evidence Perdelwitz' own canon — namely, that ideas and phrases which cannot be accounted for out of O.T. and Jewish tradition and the recorded *verba Christi* may probably be traced to the influence of the Mystery Religions — the results amount to very little. For, in fact, the passages which cannot be so accounted for, and accounted for without any far-fetched interpretation, are exceedingly few. The *Descensus ad Inferos* is admittedly one of great difficulty, but even there the climate of thought is decidedly Jewish ; while all the other main ideas and phrases adduced have affinities in Jewish or primitive Christian thought and practice : they are, that is to say, " in the tradition ". In so far as similar ideas and phrases were " in the air " of contemporary religion in Asia Minor, our author may have been glad to use them as a kind of bridge, ready to hand, between his own thought and theirs : in one case—the description of the social and religious customs in iv. 3, 4, which the Christians had now abandoned — it is probable enough that we have an open allusion to features of the Mystery Religions ; if other Gentile ceremonies, such as the drink of milk or the neophyte's passage from the dark to light, were present at all to our author's mind, they were only on its circumference, and even that is very doubtful. The claim that the author owed any of his leading ideas to the Mystery Religions must be rejected as wholly unproven. In many cases, where the parallels are superficially closest, the theory of a direct historical connexion is impossible ; in many others it can be shewn to be quite unnecessary ; while in not a few instances the resemblances, however striking on the surface, must be condemned as illusory and fallacious.

ESSAY I

CONTENTS

ESSAY I

ON I PETER III. 18–IV. 6

INTRODUCTION

Com-
plexities
of the
problem

THERE are few passages in the New Testament which have exercised commentators more, or given rise to greater variety of interpretation, than I Pet. iii. 18-22 and its context, especially iv. 6 : one need only follow the repeated changes in Luther's mind on the subject to realize the complicated net-work of factors which have to be weighed and considered in attempting to reach a conclusion. We have endeavoured in the Notes to set out, as far as possible, the linguistic and grammatical factors in the problem ; but in many of these there is a margin of doubt where the scales may be tipped one way or another by exegetical or even doctrinal considerations. The last-named are not, indeed, of primary importance from an evidential point of view, for the passage before us was not appealed to for doctrinal purposes in the first two centuries, and none of the main lines of interpretation which have been followed bring the passages into conflict with any settled New Testament doctrine.[1] Nevertheless doctrines have been based upon it, not least in nineteenth- and twentieth-century Anglican theology, notably the doctrine of what has been called the " Larger Hope " ; and these doctrines have been warmly cherished in the Church and might seem to have much of their foundations cut away if this or that interpretation were adopted. The scholar's task is therefore one of unusual responsibility : though there are no canons of orthodoxy to bias his judgment, he will desire to be most careful lest any fragment of divine revelation may be omitted or misunderstood in the course of his enquiry. Both his freedom and his responsibility are borne in upon him by the weight and the variety of those who support the rival types of exegesis ; for they belong to every age of Christian theology, and every stream of ecclesiastical tradition.[2] The new-comer to the problem finds a field, therefore, which is still open, though well ploughed by those who have gone before him ; and his task must be to bring into the discussion any

---

[1] As Dorner wisely observes, " Dogmatic sobriety enjoins moderation on this point " (*System of Christian Doctrine*, § 124, Engl. Tr. iv. p. 130).

[2] The facts are set out with great thoroughness in Loofs' admirable article in *ERE*, vol. iv., entitled " Descent to Hades (Christ's) ".

new facts which may have recently come to light — and in this case they are not numerous — and to go over the old facts again to see whether he can find a hypothesis which seems to account for them adequately. I propose first to summarize the lexicographical and I grammatical evidence offered in the Notes, and to estimate its importance ; next, to examine the two passages, 1 Pet. iii. 18-22 II and iv. 6, both separately and in their relation to each other and to the context as a whole ; then to consider them in connexion with III the development of doctrine in the early centuries on the subject of Christ's Descent into Hell, and its possible roots in the New Testament ; and finally to attempt an evaluation of St. Peter's teaching IV in this great passage.

I. SUMMARY OF LINGUISTIC AND GRAMMATICAL EVIDENCE

The salient points on the linguistic and grammatical side are The these [1] : linguistic and grammatical

(*a*) In iii. 18 the datives σαρκί and πνεύματι are adverbial datives, matical and there is no example in N.T. of such a dative being the ante- evidence cedent to a relative sentence.

(*b*) In iii. 19 ἐν ᾧ is not, therefore, dependent on πνεύματι, but on the preceding statement as a whole, namely Christ's passion, death, and resurrection. This would not exclude the view of those who, like Huther in Meyer's Commentary, assign the *Descensus* to the period immediately following the resurrection, for no precise note of time is given ; but the ground they advance, viz. that ἐν ᾧ refers to the spiritual condition of Christ's risen life, is invalid.

(*c*) τοῖς ἐν φυλακῇ πνεύμασιν refers primarily to the fallen angels or spirit-powers of evil imprisoned, according to *Enoch* and other Jewish teaching, since their transgressions before the Flood.

(*d*) ἐκήρυξεν can mean " made proclamation " no less than " preached the gospel " ; and its construction with the dative of the indirect object in the latter sense is rare in N.T.

(*e*) In iii. 21 ἀντίτυπον is best taken in apposition to ὑμᾶς.

(*f*) In iii. 22 πορευθείς connotes a real journey, however spiritually conceived, and this suggests that πορευθείς in verse 19 does likewise.

(*g*) It is on many grounds probable that the phrase " angels and [or of] principalities and powers " connotes primarily evil agencies.

(*h*) In iv. 1 the ἔννοια in question is the principle of the dying

[1] For fuller discussion of these points the reader is referred to the Notes.

life crowned by triumph and glory which was supremely exemplified in the passion, death, resurrection, and ascension of Christ.

(*i*) In iv. 5 τῷ ἑτοίμως ἔχοντι refers to Christ, who is also the subject of εὐηγγελίσθη. In iv. 6 νεκροῖς are those who are physically dead, as in the preceding verse.

(*j*) εὐηγγελίσθη should mean, according to N.T. usage, " He was preached ".

(*k*) κριθῶσι does not mean " condemned " but " judged ", i.e. their life's account settled. The reference in ζῶσι is to the eternal life which the dead will enjoy in the resurrection.

has been interpreted along three main lines,
Now there have been three main lines of interpretation of I Pet. iii. 18–iv. 6, and on one of these the linguistic evidence seems to me almost strong enough by itself to be decisive. The three views are :

(i) That the reference in iii. 18 f. is to a preaching by Christ in the Spirit, or in a spiritual condition, by the lips of Noah and his predecessors, to the wicked generation of men who lived before the Flood. This is the view of Augustine (in one passage), Bede, Aquinas, John Lightfoot, Leighton, Bishop Pearson, and in more recent times C. H. H. Wright and Salmond. Loofs follows Spitta in an intermediate view, viz. that the pre-existent Christ is referred to, but that those to whom He preached are the disobedient angels of Gen. vi.

(ii) That the reference in iii. 18 ff. is to a preaching by Christ in person to the fallen angels alluded to in Gen. vi., *Enoch, Jubilees* and other Jewish literature. This view has the support of Gunkel, Bousset, Loisy, but of few English commentators. On this view, there is no direct connexion between the ἐκήρυξεν of iii. 19 and the εὐηγγελίσθη of iv. 6. Windisch's suggestion is an attempt to form a bridge between the two ; but it involves linguistic difficulties from which Loisy's less closely-knit interpretation is free.

(iii) That the reference in iii. 18 ff., as in iv. 6, is to the dead, the preaching to the impenitent of Noah's generation affording a particular example of a much larger truth. This is the view of the majority of English and English-speaking commentators, including Bishop Horsley, Alford, Plumptre, Chase, Blenkin, Bennett, J. H. Bernard,[1] Charles, Bigg, Stevens, Wand. It is also supported by Beyschlag, Clemen, Dorner, Spörri, and Strack-Billerbeck among modern German exegetes. Clement of Alexandria probably held

---

[1] Bernard notes the difficulty of regarding " the spirits in prison " as typical of impenitent sinners generally (*DAC*, i. 290b, 291a). C. H. H. Wright is most trenchant upon this line of interpretation, which he describes as " the last resort of an exegesis driven to despair " (*Biblical Essays*, p. 180).

this view ; and so did Calvin [1] and Bengel with differences of their
own.

Each of these main lines of exposition admits of differences in of which
regard to details ; but no adjustment of details can overcome the the first
can be
obstacles which beset the first of them.   The figurative use of confidently
πορευθείς in iii. 19 in contrast with its literal use in iii. 22 is one of rejected
these ; another is the dubiety which must exist as to whose were the
lips by whom this " Christ in the spirit " preached. If they were
Noah's (cf. 2 Pet. ii. 5), then we might conjecture that the true
reading at the beginning of the verse had been ἐν ᾧ καὶ Νῶε — the
proper name being attributed by an early scribe to dittography and
therefore excised — were it not for the phrase ἐν ἡμέραις Νῶε a little
lower down.   Yet a third obstacle is the assumption that " the spirits
in prison " are the ante-diluvian sinners [2] ; though it will be more
convenient to discuss that point later. Most serious of all is the
grammatical difficulty involved in making ἐν ᾧ depend on the
adverbial dative πνεύματι as its antecedent — a difficulty which is
fully reflected in the laboured attempts to expound the phrase ἐν ᾧ
on this basis. Add to these obstacles the fact that the historical and
theological course of the argument has to be interrupted to make
room for this idea, which has nothing to suggest it in the context and
is irrelevant to the drift and purpose of this passage of very practical
and urgent exhortation ; and we may regard the hypothesis, despite
the weighty voices supporting it, as one that may be confidently
rejected.

II. Context and Exegesis of 1 Peter iii. 18 ff. and iv. 6

Allusion has been made above to the context in which 1 Pet. iii. General
18 ff. and iv. 6 occur, and this point may now be developed more context of
1 Pet.

[1] *Comm., in loc.* Calvin's view is
of great interest. *Non dubito*, he
says, *quin generaliter dicat Petrus,
gratiae Christi manifestationem ad
pios spiritus pervenisse: atque ita
vitali spiritus efficacia esse perfusos.*
These holy dead of the Jewish faith
were said to be " in prison ", because
they had been " confined " (*constringi*)
by the Law during life, and after
death *solicito Christi desiderio.* St.
Peter alludes to the disobedient of
Noah's day because at that time the
unbelievers greatly outnumbered the
believers : *tunc quoque permixtos
fuisse incredulis puros Dei cultores :*

immo multitudine eorum fere opertos. iii. 18 ff.
From the triumph of the grace of God and iv. 6
in that case, therefore, the Christians
of later days should take heart when
they found themselves so small a
minority in an unbelieving world.
*Hoc modo solatur pios, ne propter
suam paucitatem fracto sint vel abiecto
animo.* In this last sentence we
have the clue to much else in Calvin's
theology.

[2] Even Usteri (*Hinabgefahren zur
Hölle*, p. 32), whose exegesis of the
passage turns on this rendering,
admits that an exact parallel is not
easy to find.

positively. The section of the Epistle to which both passages belong is devoted to the encouragement of the Christians whom St. Peter addresses in face of continual social persecution, which blazed up sometimes, perhaps, into more legal forms of persecution. He enjoins on them an earnest and unruffled devotional life, a readiness to give an intelligent account of their faith in a spirit of gentleness and reverence, and the determination to persist in well-doing, cost what it may. And he bases these injunctions, as in the previous chapter, on the *imitatio Christi*, which he here amplifies and expands. There he was concerned with the Cross alone, as the focus of Christ's sacrifice and the fulfilment of the sacrificial ideas of the Old Testament, notably of Is. liii. Here he underlines once again, and very plainly, the atoning efficacy of the passion ; but instead of drawing out the ethical aspects of Christ's actions and sufferings, he passes quickly to their redress in His resurrection and ascension. Whereas in ii. 22 ff. the subject is *Christus Patiens*, here it is *Christus Victor*. What Christ exemplified was not only the dying life, in which Christians must strive to follow Him, but the dying life triumphant on a cosmic scale — a scale which embraced in its redemptive scope all history back to the days of the Flood, and all reality, unseen as well as seen, beyond this earth as well as on it. And the crucial point at which it impinges upon men's lives is baptism. So much is common ground to those who uphold both the second and third of the main lines of interpretation outlined above ; and their agreement is of great importance. Further, this cosmic range of Christ's redemptive work once established, St. Peter proceeds to develop it in two directions : in iv. 1-4 he draws out the ethical, and in verses 5, 6 the eschatological, implications of the dying life so triumphantly vindicated in the case of Christ. And in verses 7-19, which bring the section to a close, he expounds the eschatological theme still further, dwelling on the imminence of the End and on the significance of this both for the Christians and for their persecutors.

Let us now turn to tne two passages separately.

(A) I PET. III. 18-22

Cosmographical ideas of the early Christian era

It has been truly said that in the early centuries of our era men believed in a three-storeyed universe, and universality was therefore often expressed by phrases that embraced all three.[1] Thus, when

---

[1] We may cite the great oath in Hom. *Od.* v. 184 ff.,

ἴστω νῦν τόδε γαῖα, καὶ οὐρανὸς εὐρὺς ὕπερθε,

καὶ τὸ κατειβόμενον Στυγὸς ὕδωρ, ὅς τε μέγιστος

ὅρκος δεινότατός τε πέλει μακάρεσσι θεοῖσι.

St. Paul wished to proclaim the universality of the worship due from creation to Jesus, he speaks of every knee bowing " of things in heaven, and things in earth, and things under the earth " (Phil. ii. 10 ; cf. Col. i. 23). So, too, in Rev. v. 13, the universal praise offered to the Lamb is described as coming from " every creature which is in heaven, and on the earth, and under the earth, and such as are in the sea, and all that are in them ". And similarly Ignatius speaks of Christ's crucifixion being witnessed by " things in heaven and on earth and under the earth " (*Trall.* ix. ; cf. 1 Cor. iv. 9, 1 Pet. i. 12). That St. Peter should have employed a similar thought to express the universality of Christ's redemptive work would not in itself occasion difficulty. At the same time the phraseology of the N.T. writers on these matters is not consistent. St. Peter does not, in fact, in this Epistle speak of Christ going to " Hades ", though his speech in Acts ii. suggests that he would have done so had he been asked the *locale* of " the spirits in prison ". Again, St. Paul more than once uses τὰ ἐπουράνια to denote the sphere in which evil spiritual agencies were active ; and he too would probably have agreed that if his picture-language were to be translated from theological into cosmographical terms, Hades was the proper home from which these powers of evil emerged. I mention these points because the phrase " Christ's descent into Hades " is a convenient one to use ; but the facts just mentioned shew how careful we must be not to impute to the Apostles a literalness which their flexible terminology indicates that they did not have.[1]

We have to deal here with two closely related ideas — the idea of a " going " and the idea of a " proclaiming " — of which the first is much easier to account for and to parallel than the second.

(i) *Christ's* Descensus ad Inferos

We must remember that St. Peter's mind was that of a godly, (1) Christ's *Descensus ad Inferos* simple, and unsophisticated fisherman, and we should expect him in a matter of this kind to reflect the outlook of his upbringing. And this is precisely what we find in the earliest of his recorded speeches after Pentecost (Acts ii. 14-36) in which he bases his exposition of recent events upon the prophetic utterances of Joel and of David. The outpouring of the Spirit which his hearers have just witnessed is a fulfilment of the eschatological predictions of Joel ii. 28-32 ;

---

[1] It is important to emphasize this in view of the stress laid by Usteri (*Hinabgefahren zur Hölle*, pp. 17 ff.) on the inseparable connexion between πνεύματι and ἐν ᾧ. Those who believe that πορευθείς in 1 Pet. iii. 19 connotes a real activity on Christ's part are not thereby committed to a literalist interpretation of the Descent into Hell.

the resurrection of Jesus fulfils the promise of David in Ps. xvi.
8-11; and His ascension was foretold in Ps. cx. 1. The second of
these points is elaborated with some care, and St. Peter claims that
David foresaw the future and " spake of the resurrection of Christ,
that his soul was not left in hell, neither his flesh did see corruption ". The natural inference from this passage of Acts (ii. 24-32)
is that St. Peter thought of Jesus as having gone after His death
on the cross to " Hades ", the traditional abode of the dead,
though He was not left there, nor was His body subject, like those
of other men, to decomposition. The fact is stated simply as one of
a series of facts, and its significance is absorbed into that of Christ's
resurrection, which is in itself some evidence of primitive origin.
But such a belief, attested by prophecy as well as by the prob-
abilities of the case, was not likely, when once accepted, to be
left unclothed with theology proper to itself; and it is clear
from St. Paul's Epistles that Christ's *Descensus ad Inferos* was,
in fact, early interpreted as bearing on the universality of His
redemptive mission. The following passages in particular are to
be noted :

Develop-
ment of
the idea
by St.
Paul

(a) Rom. x 6-8

(a) in
Romans

In Rom. x. 6-8 St. Paul adapts a passage about the Law in
Deut. xxx. 12-14 in order to illustrate what he has to say about
Christ as " the end of the law for righteousness to every one that
believeth ". For our present purpose the chief interest lies in his
treatment of Deut. xxx. 13 (LXX), where οὐδὲ πέραν τῆς θαλάσσης
ἐστίν, λέγων τίς διαπεράσει ἡμῖν εἰς τὸ πέραν τῆς θαλάσσης, καὶ λάβῃ
ἡμῖν αὐτήν . . . becomes in Rom. x. 7, ἤ, τίς καταβήσεται εἰς
τὴν ἄβυσσον; τοῦτ᾽ ἔστι, Χριστὸν ἐκ νεκρῶν ἀναγαγεῖν. St. Paul
chooses ἄβυσσος here because it connoted not only the deep sea
(Ps. cvii. 26) but also Hades or the Lower World, and even its
lowest part (Lk. viii. 31, Rev. ix. 1),[1] and was thus suitable for use
figuratively in relation to Christ's resurrection after His descent into
Hades. The Apostle is expressing, none the less really because the
language is " indefinite and untechnical " (SH *in loc.*), the same
belief as is recorded of St. Peter in Acts ii. 24 ff. St. Paul's theme
is the power of faith to apprehend the living Christ here and now in
a spiritual relationship which transcends all thought of place or
movement ; and it is significant that he alters his O.T. text in order
to secure an equation in thought between Christ's ascension and
His *Descensus ad Inferos*.

[1] Cf. *infra*, p. 335.

Rom. xiv. 9 is also sometimes quoted in this connexion, but it is not clear that a *Descensus ad Inferos* is implied.

(*b*) EPH. IV. 8-10

Eph. iv. 8-10 reveals the same equation, though in this case no part of it is prompted by the O.T. text which he is using. He is speaking of the universality of Christ's grace involved in His ascension, and after adapting Ps. lxviii. 18 to read, ἀναβὰς εἰς ὕψος ᾐχμαλώτευσεν αἰχμαλωσίαν, καὶ ἔδωκεν δόματα τοῖς ἀνθρώποις, he adds : τὸ δὲ Ἀνέβη τί ἐστιν εἰ μὴ ὅτι καὶ κατέβη εἰς τὰ κατώτερα μέρη τῆς γῆς; ὁ καταβὰς αὐτός ἐστιν καὶ ὁ ἀναβὰς ὑπεράνω πάντων τῶν οὐρανῶν, ἵνα πληρώσῃ τὰ πάντα. Some scholars take τὰ κατώτερα . . . γῆς here as meaning " the earth below " and interpret the " descent " of the Incarnation ; but in view of Pss. lxiii. 9 and cxxxix. 15 this is improbable (cf. Armitage Robinson, *in loc.*). There can be little doubt that the underworld is the region referred to. In that case it is to be noted that St. Paul is treating Christ's *Descensus ad Inferos* as a belief fully accepted in the Church, and necessary if the universal range of Christ's redemptive work is to be adequately grasped. Further, though the only words in the quotation from Ps. lxviii. on which St. Paul comments here are ἀναβάς and ἔδωκεν δόματα, the captives whom he pictures our Lord as leading in His triumphal procession (cf. Col. ii. 15) must have been Satan and his hosts ; and so Irenaeus, for example, and Chrysostom understood it. Irenaeus' comment (*Demonstr. Apost. Preaching,* 83) is particularly instructive : " by *captivity* ". he says, " he means the destruction of the rule of the apostate angels ". The bearing of this on 1 Pet. iii. 18 f. is important.

(b) in Ephesians

(*c*) PHIL. II. 10

Phil. ii. 10, though it makes no explicit allusion to Christ's " going " to the underworld, yet mentions " things under the earth " together with those in heaven and on the earth as bowing in adoration at the Name of the crucified and exalted Jesus. The universality of His power and glory, that is to say, is depicted in the terms of the cosmic topography of the day. The same expression occurs in Ign. *Trall.* ix.

(c) in Philip- pians

(*d*) REV. V. 13

In Rev. v. 13 the worship of the Lamb is said to be offered by " every creature which is in heaven, and on the earth, and under the

and (d) by the seer of Patmos

earth, and such as are in the sea,[1] and all that are in them ". The idea is similar to that in Phil. ii. 10. Earlier in the same book, moreover (i. 17, 18) Christ is represented as saying : " I am the first and the last, and the living One : and I was dead, and, behold, I am alive for evermore, and have the keys of death and of hell ". Again, as in Phil. ii. 10, it is not said that Christ went to the nether kingdom ; but the phrase is most easily intelligible if the belief expressed in Rom. x. 6-8 and Eph. iv. 8-10 is presupposed.

Relation of the *Descensus* to the Ascension   The beliefs, then, that our Lord immediately after His death went to the underworld, and that His redemptive work embraced that region as well as earth and heaven, is part of the current coin of N.T. teaching. Furthermore, particular importance attaches to the balance between the *Descensus* and the Ascension which is so strongly brought out by St. Paul ; for the same balance occurs in 1 Pet. iii. 18-22. If we omit the reference to Noah and his times and to the baptismal analogy, we have left a Christology which is identical both with that of St. Peter in Acts ii. and with that of St. Paul : Christ was done to death in the flesh but quickened in spirit, and so " went " to the underworld,[2] and rising again " went " to heaven, where He is in glory at God's right hand. The same pattern of faith is expressed by both Apostles, though in different language and contexts. The *Descensus* and the Ascension appear as two pillars of fact which upheld the belief of the early Church in the universality of Christ's redemptive work.

(ii) *Christ's " Preaching " in the Underworld*

(ii) Christ's " preaching " in the underworld   We must now turn to the idea which is peculiar in the Epistles to 1 Peter that Christ " preached " or " made proclamation " in the underworld. The belief may be an original thought of St. Peter himself ; but before we conclude that it is so, it is worth enquiring whether it had precursors in Jewish or Christian tradition, from which it might be derived either by inference or by interpretation.

[1] For the sea as a traditional home of evil spirits cf. Oesterley, *The Evolution of the Messianic Idea*, chs. iv.-vii.

[2] The concept of Sheol or Hades as the abode of the dead generally, without ethical or other distinctions, was later differentiated to admit of distinct regions for the righteous and wicked respectively, as in *Enoch* xxii. As late as the *Psalms of Solomon* (cf. xiv. 6, xv. 11, xvi. 2) Hades was used for the place of punishment of the wicked, which is normally termed in N.T. Gehenna. The abode of the righteous, on the other hand, when a special term other than Hades is used, is spoken of as " Abraham's bosom " (Lk. xvi. 23) or " Paradise " (Lk. xxiii. 43). Both terms reflect the current usage of the day, and must not be pressed for doctrinal purposes.

We have given reasons in the Notes for the belief that by " the spirits in prison " St. Peter means primarily, if not solely, the fallen angels and their progeny whose doings and destiny loomed so largely in Jewish apocalyptic literature ; and we will proceed at the outset on that assumption.

(a) His Conflict with Evil Spirits

The idea that the Messiah should have dealings with the fallen angels is not often found in Jewish literature. *Enoch* liv., lv. and *Jub.* v. 10, 14, teach clearly that the spirits of evil shall be condemned in the final judgment, but only in *Enoch* xc. 20-7 is the judicial act in their case definitely ascribed to the Messiah. On the other hand, the belief is well attested in N.T., if we extend our purview to embrace the whole kingdom of the demons which derived, in the popular view, from the apostate angels.[1] At the head of this kingdom was Satan, and our Lord repeatedly represents Himself as in conflict with him and his realm. He is the tempter whose onset upon our Lord supervenes at once upon His assumption of the Messianic office at His Baptism ; he is chief of the evil spirits which " possess " men and whose exorcism is one of the Messiah's chief tasks and a sign that the Kingdom of God has come (Matt. xii. 22-8) ; he is the " strong man " who must be bound and his house despoiled (Matt. xii. 29) ; Jesus said that He had seen " Satan as lightning fall from heaven ", when the Seventy reported that even the devils were subject to them in His name (Lk. x. 17, 18). And in this establishment of His authority over the evil spirits, Jesus was doing what the Messiah was expected to do, only He was doing it " before the time " (Matt. viii. 29) : that is to say, He was anticipating the final judgment, bringing it in before its time.[2]

(b) St. Paul's Teaching

In view of these widespread beliefs[3] of our Lord's day and of

Marginal note: (a) His conflict with evil spirits

Marginal note: (b) St. Paul's teaching

[1] The apparent inconsistency between the imprisonment of the evil spirits in the time of Noah and the evidences of their present malign activities on earth was resolved in *Jub.* x. by the doctrine that nine-tenths of them were then imprisoned but one-tenth left free to serve Satan on earth.

[2] The interesting suggestion is made by M. Dibelius (quoted by Anton Fridrichsen in an article in *Theology*, xxii. p. 128, March 1931, translated from the *Svensk Teologisk Kvartal-skrift*, Häfte 4, 1930) that the βιασ-ταί of Matt. xi. 12 were the spiritual powers of evil who were stirred to feverish activity by Christ's ministry and sought to ravage the Kingdom. Cf. Lk. xxii. 31. Chrysostom, on the contrary, paraphrases βιασταί as πάντες οἱ μετὰ σπουδῆς προσιόντες (*in Matth. Hom.* xxxvii., 417 D).

[3] Similar beliefs in evil spirits, of course, were widespread throughout the Greek-speaking world ; cf.

His own reaction to them, it is not surprising that we should find several allusions in the Apostolic writings to supernatural agents of evil and to their conquest by Christ. Thus, in Col. ii. 15 Christ is said by His death to have " stripped off and put away the powers of evil " (Lightfoot's paraphrase) and to have displayed them boldly, as a victor displays his captives in a triumphal procession. The vivid metaphors would have appealed to St. Paul's readers, and not least the word ἀπεκδυσάμενος ; for the ἀπέκδυσις of sin (cf. Col. ii. 11, iii. 9) formed part of the early catechetical teaching (cf. Essay II, pp. 396 ff.) and was an inherent part of baptism. As Lightfoot says, " the ἀπέκδυσις accomplished in us when we are baptized into His death is a counterpart to the ἀπέκδυσις which He accomplished by His death ".[1] This baptismal association is significant in view of the similar association of Christ's κήρυγμα to " the spirits in prison " with baptism in 1 Pet. iii. 18 ff. The converse of this idea, moreover, — the putting-on of the whole armour of God — which is likewise a baptismal metaphor, is very clearly stated in Eph. vi. 10 ff., where St. Paul exhorts his readers to stand " against the wiles of the devil " and reminds them that they are engaged in conflict not with flesh and blood but " with the principalities (ἀρχάς), with the powers (ἐξουσίας), with the rulers of this dark world, with the spiritual hosts (τὰ πνευματικά) of wickedness in the heavenly sphere ". In this unseen world behind the world of sense, great forces are believed to be at work: " forces which are conceived of as having an order and constitution of their own ; as having in part transgressed against that order, and so having become disordered : forces which in part are opposed to us and wrestle against us : forces, again, which take an intelligent interest in the purpose of God with His world (cf. 1 Pet. i. 12), and for which the story of man is an object-lesson in the many-sided wisdom of God : forces, over all of which, be they evil or be they good, Christ is enthroned, and we in Him ".[2]

Two points may be noted before we pass on to another Pauline

F. W. H. Myers' study of " Greek Oracles " in *Essays Classical*, pp. 71 f., 80, with the references to Hesiod, Heraclitus, and Plutarch.

[1] With Col. ii. 15 cf. also Col. i. 16, 1 Cor. xv. 24, Rom. viii. 38, 39. In all these places the ἀρχαί and ἐξουσίαι alluded to include spiritual agencies of evil as well as of good. Note also 1 Cor. vi. 3, where Christians are said to be destined to judge angels. Dodd (on

Rom. xi. 30-2, p. 185) suggests that the liberation of the whole material universe in Rom. viii. 21 is connected with the reconciliation of the hostile spiritual agencies which are alluded to in Rom. viii. 38, 39.

[2] Armitage Robinson, *Ephesians*, pp. 20, 21, summarizing allusions to the supra-sensual world of spiritual agencies, evil as well as good, in Eph. i. 3, 20, 21, ii. 6, iii. 10, vi. 10 ff.

passage. One is that in Ephesians, as in Lk. x. 18 and Rev. xii. 7 ff., the spiritual powers of evil are thought of as in the heavenly sphere rather than in Hades. They are denoted, that is to say, rather by their metaphysical nature than by their cosmic locality.[1] The other is that the conquest of these powers is associated with our Lord's ascension rather than with a *Descensus ad Inferos*. Both points need to be borne in mind when we are interpreting 1 Pet. iii. 18 ff.

(*c*) AN EARLY CREDAL HYMN (1 TIM. III. 16)

The remaining passage to be considered is 1 Tim. iii. 16 — a (*c*) An passage which, even if 1 Timothy is not as a whole by St. Paul,[2] is in early credal all probability part of an early credal hymn already familiar in the hymn Church.[3] Here the parallelism with 1 Pet. iii. 18 ff. is very close, as (1 Tim. can be seen if the two passages are set side by side. iii. 16)

1 Tim. iii. 16	1 Peter
ἐφανερώθη ἐν σαρκί	iii. 18. θανατωθεὶς μὲν σαρκί [iv. 6. ἵνα κριθῶσι μὲν κατὰ ἀνθρώπους σαρκί]
ἐδικαιώθη ἐν πνεύματι	ζωοποιηθεὶς δὲ πνεύματι [iv. 6. ζῶσι δὲ κατὰ θεὸν πνεύματι]
ὤφθη ἀγγέλοις	19. τοῖς ἐν φυλακῇ πνεύμασι πορευθεὶς ἐκήρυξεν 22. ὑποταγέντων αὐτῷ ἀγγέλων καὶ ἐξουσιῶν καὶ δυνάμεων
ἐκηρύχθη ἐν ἔθνεσιν ἐπιστεύθη ἐν κόσμῳ	iii. 21. ὑμᾶς νῦν σώζει βάπτισμα . . . συνειδήσεως ἀγαθῆς ἐπερώτημα εἰς θεόν
ἀνελήφθη ἐν δόξῃ	iii. 22. ὅς ἐστιν ἐν δεξιᾷ τοῦ θεοῦ, πορευθεὶς εἰς οὐρανόν

The first, second, and sixth articles of this statement of faith are so nearly paralleled in 1 Pet. iii. 18-22 as to point to dependence ; nor is there any chronological difficulty in this if the statement was already current in the Christian community by A.D. 60. The third article has been often interpreted as though it referred to the occasions in our Lord's life when angels appeared to Him. But ὤφθη

---

[1] Cf. Delitzsch's note on Is. xxiv. 21, 22, quoted by C. H. H. Wright, *op. cit.* pp. 167 f., where "the host of the high ones on high" is referred to the evil angels whose rebellion was the cause of human sin.

[2] Cf. Harrison, *The Problem of the Pastoral Epistles*.

[3] Cf. Sir Robert Falconer, *The Pastoral Epistles*, p. 138.

is a technical term in LXX for the manifestation of God[1]; and Parry is undoubtedly right when he says[2] that the allusion is to the effect of the Lord's ascension upon the spiritual hosts of heaven. Further, he cites Phil. ii. 10 and 1 Pet. iii. 22 as illustrations of the same thought. But should we not name verse 19 as well as verse 22 of 1 Pet. iii. in this connexion? In the sequence of St. Peter's thought it follows hard upon the allusions to Christ's death and resurrection; his ἐκήρυξεν carries with it a self-manifestation (ὤφθη); his reference to baptism, which was the seal of faith, answers to the " preaching " and " believing "[3] of the early formula (cf. 1 Pet. i. 12, 25, ii. 4, 7); and the whole passage closes, like that in 1 Timothy, on the theme of Christ's ascension. The form in which St. Peter presents the thought of the universality of Christ's triumph as the Redeemer of all things differs in certain details from what we find in St. Paul and elsewhere; and to those differences and the reasons for them we shall return in a moment. But that his mind is moving in the same realm of ideas seems to me overwhelmingly probable. The double " going " which we find in St. Paul (Rom. x. 6-8, Eph. iv. 8-10, cf. 1 Pet. iii. 19, 22), the triumphal processions of captives following Christ's conquest of the angelic powers (Eph. iv. 8 (Ps. lxviii. 19), i. 21, Col. ii. 15; cf. 1 Pet. iii. 22, ὑποταγέντων), the proclamation of Christ in the spiritual realm (Eph. iii. 10)—all these are ways of expressing the fundamental fact and the all-embracing range of Christ's victory over death and the powers of evil[4]; and they are all found in the Petrine passage before us, and were all relevant to the purpose of his Epistle. In its main lines, that is to say, St. Peter's teaching here is not something new or unfamiliar: what is peculiar is the form in which he presents it and the use which he makes of it.

---

[1] Falconer, op. cit. p. 138.

[2] The Pastoral Epistles, p. 23.

[3] On the fifth clause of this cento in 1 Tim. iii., Mr. Blakeney writes to me: " In this ' crescendo ' of quoted passages may not ἐν κόσμῳ imply more than the world (already sufficiently indicated by ἐν ἔθνεσιν)? Perhaps in the whole universe." This suggestion seems to me fully borne out by St. Paul's use of κόσμος in such passages as Gal. iv. 3, Col. ii. 8, 20, and κοσμοκράτορας in Eph. vi. 12. Cf. Armitage Robinson's note on Eph. ii. 12.

[4] One of the earliest upholders of this view in England, so far as I know, was the Rev. Dr. E. W. Bullinger, in a pamphlet entitled " The Spirits in Prison : An Exposition of 1 Peter iii. 17–iv. 6 in the Light of the Epistle as a whole ", to which Mr. E. H. Blakeney has kindly drawn my attention. The date is about 1890. Dr. Bullinger rests his case largely upon a careful analysis of the structure of the Epistle as well as upon linguistic considerations and upon a comparison of 1 Pet. iii. 17-22 with 1 Tim. iii. 16, 2 Pet. ii. 4-9, Jude 6, 7. It is the more striking because the evidence of Enoch and other Jewish apocalyptic literature was not then at his disposal.

(iii) *Peculiarities in St. Peter's Teaching*

We may now turn to these peculiarities. Some afford little
difficulty. Thus, in placing Christ's visit to the world of spirits *in*
the course of His death and resurrection, St. Peter departs from St.
Paul's explicit identification of it with the Ascension, but keeps close
to the order of the formula found in 1 Tim. iii. 16. Again, in verses
20, 21 St. Peter keeps to the order of the formula, but conflates its
fourth and fifth articles with a passage about baptism, bringing to
a concrete point and occasion, and one very relevant to his Epistle,
namely baptism, what the formula had expressed more generally.
In what he says, however, about the visit and " preaching " to " the
spirits in prison ", St. Peter departs more markedly from Pauline
ways of thought. Why, for instance, did he speak of " the spirits
in prison " rather than of the authorities and powers which he
mentions in iii. 22 ? And why did he speak of Christ preaching or
making proclamation ?

(*a*) The Author's Mind and Purpose

In attempting to answer these questions we must bear in mind
once more the quality of St. Peter's mind, so far as we know it from
the Gospels and the Acts. It was essentially a concrete, simple,
matter-of-fact mind, capable of far-reaching intuitions but without
interest in abstract principles and devoted rather to the more practical tasks of dealing with each situation as it arose, and of co-
ordinating the various strands of teaching which he found in the
Church around him. In the passage before us, moreover, he is
concerned with the worth-whileness of the dying life which was
supremely exemplified in the case of our Lord, and which was now
increasingly involved in the profession of Christianity, of which
baptism was the sign and seal. Further, the sacrament of baptism
was for St. Peter of central importance : it was through the command
to baptize a Gentile that St. Peter himself had come to realize the
Catholic scope of Christianity ; and it was of exceptional importance
here and now, when the barriers between Jew and Gentile were down
— as Ephesians shews — and when " one baptism ", superseding
old issues between circumcision and uncircumcision, ranked with
one body and one Spirit, one Lord, one faith, and one God and
Father of all as an *articulus stantis aut cadentis ecclesiae*. For a
" type " of the religious and moral issues raised by baptism St.
Peter turned to the story of Noah[1] as St. Paul frequently turned to

[1] For an interesting discussion of　the article by Dr. E. C. Selwyn in
the connexion of this story with St.　*The Expositor* for November 1910.
Peter's trance at Joppa (Acts x.) see

the story of Abraham. And, still sticking to historical tradition, he found in Genesis and in later Jewish literature dealing with the same story records of God's judgment upon the apostate angels and the wicked men of Noah's generation, who seemed to represent supremely and in classical fashion angelic and human rebellion against God and also God's unfailing mercy towards those who believed in Him. Both the judgment and the mercy were relevant, for they were fulfilled in the crisis of faith with which Christianity confronted men (cf. 1 Pet. ii. 7, 8), and their issues would soon be made plain (1 Pet. iv. 5, 6, 17-19). Meanwhile, Christ Himself had gone to the very fountain-head of cosmic and human evil, and had proclaimed His sovereignty, and God's, over the spiritual world, even over those typically rebellious spirits of Noah's day. St. Peter substituted ἐκήρυξεν for the ὤφθη of the common formula, for it was better suited to express the assertion of a claim ; and its intransitive use was in keeping with the mystery that must invest so mighty an action. The result of the action was seen in the subordination of all heavenly agencies to Him, thus summing up the whole gradation of " degrees ", to use Shakespeare's phrase, which for St. Peter was a cardinal principle of the Christian moral law.

(b) The Prominence of Noah

(b) The prominence of Noah in Jewish thought

Carrying still further our investigation of the place of Noah and the Flood in St. Peter's mind, we must recognize that Noah occupied a very prominent place in Jewish theology and philosophy of history, and one which grew with the growth of interest in eschatology. The salient features of the narrative in Gen. vi.–ix. were all worked up for various doctrinal and homiletic purposes. The story begins with the *connubium* of superhuman or demonic beings with the daughters of men, an occurrence which came in some of the later literature, notably the *Book* (or *Apocalypse*) *of Noah* which is extensively quoted in *Enoch* and in *Jubilees*,[1] to rival the story of the Fall as the origin of evil in the world. The result was an age of increasing wickedness which demanded punishment, though for 120 years God stayed His hand, " to shew how great was His long-suffering " (*Pirqe Aboth*, v. 2). Noah alone was found righteous

---

[1] Both books are probably to be dated in the second century B.C., and the Noah book must be earlier than 170 B.C. For the historical facts underlying the story of Noah and the Flood reference may be made to Sir Leonard Woolley, *Abraham*, to Skinner, *Genesis* (I.C.C.), pp. 147-81, to Sir William Willcocks, *From the Garden of Eden to the Crossing of the Jordan*, chs. i. and ii., and to Frazer, *Folk-Lore of O.T.*, I. ch. iv. Among patristic authors E. H. B. draws my attention to Justin, *Apol.* II. v., Tert. *Apol.* xxii., *de Idol.* ix., and Lactantius ii. 14, 15. Cf. Josephus, *Ant.* I. iii. I.

and deserving to be delivered. It is clear from **Ezek. xiv.** 19, 20, Ecclus. xliv. 17, 2 *Enoch* xxxv. 1 that Noah was already a figure of hagiology no less than history, a *representative* good man. He appears in *1 Enoch* as conversing with Enoch, whose saintly life had ended in his translation to heaven (*1 Enoch* lxv.) ; he is represented as preaching to his generation against the shedding or eating of blood (*Jub.* vii. 20-39), inculcating the sacrifice of the first-fruits and other ceremonial rules (*ib.* vii., xxi. 10), and laying down the inviolability of frontiers (*ib.* viii. 10, 11). He is said also to have prayed that his offspring might be delivered from the power of the wicked spirits (*ib.* x. 1-7), and to have introduced the use of medicines, about which he left instructions in a book (*ib.* x. 12, 13).[1] Such a founder of civilization might well be regarded as one who served

> To lay the foundation of the heaven,
> And to strengthen the earth,
> And to renew all the luminaries which are in the firmament
> (*ib.* xix. 24).

When the Flood came, this man of blameless life, " of· whom came all righteous men ",[2] was delivered, together with his family, in the ark. Most writers follow Genesis in making him the builder of the ark, but in *1 Enoch* lxvii. 2, it is said to have been built by angels. The Flood was at once an act of divine judgment and of divine mercy.[3] The destruction of those who were living on earth at the time was accompanied by an equally decisive retribution on the evil spirits and demonic angels who had seduced them, who were bound in the depths of the earth (*Jub.* v. 1 ff.) or imprisoned in the burning valley of Gehenna (*1 Enoch* x. 4 ff., lxvii.), until the final Judgment. Noah, on the other hand, was the signal recipient of God's favour and mercy. The " waters of Noah ", which destroyed the wicked, were for the author of Is. liv. 9 symbolic of the mercies of God which were then secured for ever to the righteous. He was preserved, like Lot, by Wisdom herself (Wisd. x. 4). His deliverance from the Flood was followed by a covenant of surpassing importance, of which the rainbow was the symbol (*Jub.* vi. 15, 16), and which was the origin, according to *Jubilees*, of the Feast of Weeks later called Pentecost (2 Macc. xii. 32, Tob. ii. 1, 1 Cor.

(margin note: The Flood, the Ark, and the Covenant)

---

[1] Cf. *Test. XII Patr.* App. ii. 57.
[2] 2 Esdr. iii. 11. Philo (*de Congr. Erud. Gr.* 90 [I. 532 M]) observes that Noah was the first man in O.T. to be called " righteous ".
[3] J. B. Mayor notes that Jude and 2 Peter differ here, the former emphasizing the element of judgment, the latter that of mercy (on 2 Pet. ii. 5).

xvi. 8). This covenant was not only the first covenant God made with man ; it was also of eternal duration, and the model for the later covenants that should follow (*Jub*. xiv. 20). Philo, it is true, contrasted Noah with Moses, to the disadvantage of the former (*Quod Deus immut*. 109 [I. 289 M]), owing to Moses' superior philosophical gifts ; but he recognizes none the less the stability of the covenant with Noah (*de Somn*. ii. 223 and 237 [I. 688 and 690 M]). The point is emphasized in *The Biblical Antiquities of Philo*, iii. 9, where it is said that there shall be no Flood again until " the years of the world shall be fulfilled ".

Noah, again, is one of those patriarchs who are expressly named as having a place in the general resurrection. Thus we read in *Test. Benj*. x. 6, " And then shall ye see Enoch, Noah, and Shem, and Abraham, and Isaac, and Jacob, rising on the right hand in gladness ", to be followed first by the sons of Jacob (*ib*. x. 7, *T. Sim*. vi. 7, *T. Zeb*. x. 2), and then by all men, some to honour and some to dishonour (*ib*. x. 8, *T. Jud*. xxv. 4), when the final judgment will come. The resurrection of the saints of old is put in more general terms elsewhere ; a late version of it (perhaps *c*. A.D. 100) occurs in the passage of *The Biblical Antiquities of Philo* already alluded to, where God says to Noah : " I will quicken the dead and raise up from the earth them that sleep [1] ; and Hell shall pay his debt and destruction give back that which was committed unto him, that I may render unto every man according to his works and according to the fruit of their imaginations ". Noah had the high privilege, therefore, of being informed of the events of the End of all things. It was possibly owing to some such belief about him as this that the Sibyl represented herself as Noah's daughter-in-law (*Or. Sib*. iii. 824).

There is a curious passage in 4 Macc. xv. 31 with which we may conclude this sketch of the homiletic use of the Noah story among the Jews. It occurs in an apostrophe addressed to the noble Jewish matron, who had watched her seven sons martyred by Antiochus : " O woman, nobler to resist than men, and braver than warriors to endure ! For as the ark of Noah, with the [whole living] world for her burden in the world-whelming deluge, did withstand the mighty surges, so thou, the keeper of the Law, beaten upon every side by the surging waves of the passions, and strained as with strong blasts by the tortures of thy sons, didst nobly weather the storms that assailed thee for religion's sake." 4 Maccabees is a work of philosophical rhetoric, of date probably between

[1] Cf. 2 Esdras ii. 16, 31, 32.

63 B.C. and A.D. 38, and written in good literary Greek ; and the passage is an interesting illustration of how the story of the Flood had passed into these circles and of the use there made of it. It is not improbable that it was known to our author or his amanuensis.

When we turn to the New Testament, we find that the allusions to the Flood are few, but significant. First in importance are the verba Christi in Matt. xxiv. 37-9 and Lk. xvii. 26, 27, words which in all probability stood in Q. The passage, which is reported in very similar language by the two Evangelists, is a warning about the nature of the Parusia : it will burst suddenly upon the routine of men's secular life, when they are least thinking of God, as the Flood swept upon the feckless and indifferent generation of the days of Noah. In Lk. xvii. this illustration is followed by another, drawn from the destruction of Sodom and Gomorrah in the days of Lot. It is clear that the Flood is alluded to as a representative act or stock example of divine judgment familiar to all ; though even here the thought of the mercy shown to Noah and those with him in the ark is not omitted. The event is appealed to much as a preacher in England to-day might appeal to the Armada, or the deliverance from Napoleon, or the Abolition of the Slave Trade, to illustrate the divine Providence and the divine vocation in our own history, or as Vergil[1] used the story of Aeneas to teach the calling of imperial Rome.

This central idea of the story of Noah is amplified in the other N.T. passages where it occurs, though the development is still within the compass of Jewish tradition. Thus, in Heb. xi. 7, Noah is introduced as one of a long series of Hebrew saints who illustrated the virtue of faith. It was by faith that, when warned by God of the impending judgment, though it was still without outward evidence, Noah paid reverent heed to the warning and built the ark, and thereby condemned the world and became heir, i.e. possessor, of " the righteousness which is proper to faith ". The ideas of judgment and mercy are correlated here as in Jewish tradition generally, but the personality of Noah is given more prominence than in our Lord's saying, and his righteousness is ascribed to faith, a point which may be due to the influence of St. Paul's teaching. Much fuller development is found in 2 Pet. ii. and iii. In 2 Pet. ii. the Flood is alluded to as one of three signal judgments in Hebrew story which reveal the certainty that God will punish the wicked. The first is the punishment of " the angels that sinned ", an event

Allusions to Noah in N.T. :

in the Gospels

and in the Epistles

---

[1] Cf. C. S. Lewis, *A Preface to Paradise Lost*, ch. vi.

drawn from *1 Enoch* and other apocalyptic books,[1] and mentioned also in Jude 6 ; the second is the Flood and the deliverance of Noah ; and the third, also alluded to in Jude, is the destruction of Sodom and Gomorrah and the deliverance of " just Lot ". It is to be noted that in 2 Peter the judgments of Noah's time and of Lot's time occur in the same order as in the *logia* of Matt. xxiv. and Lk. xvii., and also that God's mercy to the righteous is quite as prominent as His sternness towards the wicked — a point in which 2 Peter differs markedly from Jude. Noah is also described as a " preacher (κήρυκα) of righteousness ",[2] presumably because he warned his generation of the approaching judgment (unless the phrase is based on the preaching in *Jub.* vii. mentioned above) ; and he is said to have been " eighth ", i.e. probably one of eight, as in 1 Pet. iii. 20. In 2 Pet. iii. the Flood is again adduced, but without mention of Noah, as an example of divine judgment ; and this judgment is said to have been due to that same Word of God [3] to which the heavens and the earth owed their creation.

Distinctive features in 1 Pet. iii. 18 ff. It is in this context of traditional lore that the allusion to Noah and the Flood in 1 Pet. iii. 19 ff. must be studied. Certain differences from the usual treatment of the subject strike one at once. In the first place it is not brought in to point a warning, as in our Lord's saying and in 2 Peter ; though the Flood was a judgment upon a notoriously disobedient generation, that is not the aspect here emphasized.[4] The emphasis lies on the divine mercy, which waited long before acting and which delivered Noah and his family — eight in all — " through water ". It is clear that among the thoughts uppermost in the Apostle's mind are the smallness of the number of those who were saved, and the fact that they were saved through water ; and the reason is clear in both cases. The insignificant number of those saved in the ark was illustrative (ἀντίτυπον) of the smallness of the Church amid the heathen world, and the water of the Flood was the presage of the saving water of baptism. These

---

[1] Cf. Mayor, *The Epistle of St. Jude and the Second Epistle of St. Peter.* Introd., chs. ix., x., and note on 2 Pet. ii. 4. To *1 Enoch* and *Jubilees* should be added *2 Enoch* xviii. 4-6 and *Apoc. Bar.* lvi. 9-16.

[2] Cf. 1 Clem. vii. 6, Νῶε ἐκήρυξεν μετάνοιαν, καὶ οἱ ὑπακούσαντες ἐσώθησαν, and ix. 4, Νῶε πιστὸς εὑρεθεὶς διὰ τῆς λειτουργίας αὐτοῦ παλιγγενεσίαν κόσμῳ ἐκήρυξεν. The latter passage illustrates the connexion between the Flood and baptism, to which we shall

come in a moment.

[3] So J. B. Mayor, *in loc.*, reading δι' ὅν. If δι' ὧν be read, the reference is perhaps to the joint operation of the Word as efficient cause, and the water as material cause, of the creation. So Bennett in The Century Bible, *in loc.*

[4] Yet the element of judgment in the Flood, though touched on only indirectly in iii. 20, was probably not far from the author's mind in view of the warnings uttered in iv. 5, 6.

topics were of manifest relevance to the purpose of an author who was writing to a minority body pledged through the sacrament of baptism to a distinctive way of life amidst a hostile world.

(c) The Flood and Baptism : St. Peter's Vision at Joppa : Baptismal Rites

These things would be sufficient to account for the prominence given to Noah and the Flood in this passage of 1 Peter ; but the case is still further strengthened if we take into account the nature and circumstances of St. Peter's conversion recorded in Acts x. and xi.[1] The place St. Luke gives it in his narrative, even if not chronologically exact, shews that he regarded it as an event of the same kind as the conversion of St. Paul recorded in Acts ix. : though St. Paul was converted from active unbelief to faith in Christ, and St. Peter from a narrow to a broader faith, the author of Acts thought of both events as of decisive importance for the early growth of the Christian Church.   Both, moreover, took place though the instrumentality of ecstasy or trance.   Now it was a feature of prophetic trance, as the Johannine Apocalypse shews, that in it ideas and images which had been previously familiar to the mind of the prophet became divorced from their old contexts and connexions and re-associated in new ways.   The suggestion is made that fragments of the Noah story underlie the vision of St. Peter at Joppa. In particular, for example, we may note an echo of the " four corners " (εἰς τέσσαρας ἀρχάς), into which the river flowing from Eden to water Paradise is divided (Gen. ii. 10), in the " four corners " (τέσσαρσιν ἀρχαῖς) of the vessel let down from heaven ; of the conglomeration of animals in Noah's ark of Gen. vi. 19, 20 (ἀπὸ πάντων τῶν κτηνῶν καὶ ἀπὸ πάντων τῶν ἑρπετῶν καὶ ἀπὸ πάντων τῶν θηρίων . . . ἀπὸ πάντων τῶν ὀρνέων τῶν πετεινῶν) in the animals enumerated in Acts xi. 6 (εἶδον τὰ τετράποδα τῆς γῆς καὶ τὰ θηρία καὶ τὰ ἑρπετὰ καὶ τὰ πετεινὰ τοῦ οὐρανοῦ) ; and of the altar of sacrifice which Noah built when he came out of the ark in the command to St. Peter to " arise, sacrifice and eat " (Acts xi. 7).   We may observe further that the tale of living things saved in the ark is repeated over and over again in Gen. vi.–ix., so that no-one born and bred a Jew could fail to know it well.   The " vessel ", again, which St. Peter saw descend, was like a great sail (σκεῦός τι, ὡς

(c) The Flood and baptism

St. Peter's vision at Joppa,

and its connexion with the Flood-story

[1] I am much indebted here to the suggestive article of my father, the late Dr. E. C. Selwyn, in *The Expositor* for November 1910 already mentioned. For a discussion of the psychology of conversion, etc., cf. Thouless, *An Introduction to the Psychology of Religion*, chs. v., xiii.-xvi. ; and of prophetic vision, Skinner, *Prophecy and Religion*, ch. i.

ὀθόνην μεγάλην),[1] such as the Apostle may have seen that very day in the sea at Joppa. And the purpose and upshot of this vision was to convince St. Peter of the sufficiency of baptism, by itself and without circumcision, as the gateway into the Christian Church, in the case of everyone whom God had cleansed (ἐκαθάρισε, cf. 1 Pet. i. 22).

The idea of the fulfilment of O.T. types in Christianity

Now St. Peter makes clear in 1 Pet. iii. 18-22 that he thinks of the Christian Church as the " antitype " or fulfilment of the ark, and of the waters of Christian baptism as prefigured by those of the Flood. It is part of that conception of Christianity as presaging the " restitution (ἀποκατάστασις) of all things " (Acts iii. 21) which the Apostle voiced in his speech in Solomon's Porch. Thus, in this Epistle, the creation of Adam is " restored " in the regeneration wrought by Christ and His Word (i. 3, 23) ; the Promised Land of Canaan, despoiled and desecrated so often, is " restored " in the new inheritance offered to Christians (i. 4, 5) ; the havoc wrought by the rebellion of the angels before the Flood is " restored " through their subjection to the *Christus Victor* of the Passion. In the case of the ark and the Flood two further possibilities may be noted. One is that the dove which figures in the vision of Jesus at His baptism (Mk. i. 10) was understood by St. Peter as the antitype of the dove (Gen. viii.) which Noah sent out of the ark and which eventually returned to him no more — apt emblem of the divine Spirit which had at last come to rest on the Founder of the new Covenant, to which entrance was through baptism. The other is that Is. liv. 9, 10 played a part in St. Peter's mind, as we know that the preceding chapter did.[2] The LXX runs : ἀπὸ τοῦ ὕδατος τοῦ ἐπὶ Νῶε τοῦτό μοί ἐστιν, καθότι ὤμοσα αὐτῷ ἐν τῷ χρόνῳ ἐκείνῳ, τῇ γῇ μὴ θυμωθήσεσθαι ἐπὶ σοὶ ἔτι . . . οὕτως οὐδὲ τὸ παρ' ἐμοῦ σοι ἔλεος ἐκλείψει, οὐδὲ ἡ διαθήκη τῆς εἰρήνης σου οὐ μὴ μεταστῇ. Such a passage would obviously have provided food for thought

is reflected in early baptismal rites

to one whose mind was musing upon the efficacy and sufficiency of Christian baptism.

It must be admitted that the evidence given above falls short of proof, and indeed when we are dealing with the report of anything so subjective as a vision, proof can hardly be expected ; but the facts suggest at least the possibility, and some would say the probability, that there is a direct connexion between St. Peter's experience at Joppa (and his interpretation of it) and the association of Noah, the

---

[1] See LS ὀθόνη : and cf. Polybius, v. lxxxix. 2, ὀθονίων ἱστοὺς τρισχιλίους.
[2] With 1 Pet. ii. 21-4, iii. 18a cf. Is. liii. 4-12 ; and with 1 Pet. ii. 25 cf. Is. liii. 6, lv. 7, lx. 17. St. Peter's speech

in Acts x. is equally full of Isaianic references : thus x. 36 recalls Is. lii. 7 ; x. 38, Is. lxi. 1 ; x. 39, Is. xliii. 10 ; x. 42, Is. xliii. 9-12 ; x. 43, Is. lv. 7.

ark, the Flood, baptism, the Church in 1 Pet. iii. 18-22. The allusion to the fallen angels stands outside this *nodus* of ideas, except in so far as the renunciation of the spirit-powers of evil was already associated with Christian baptism. J. H. Bernard (*DAC*, i. pp. 291 f., article " Descent into Hades ") gives evidence from Christian writings of the second century to " shew that the folklore of the *Descent into Hades* is closely connected with the folklore of baptism " ; and he discusses the matter also in his edition of the *Odes of Solomon*.[1] The starting-point of the association of ideas is the word ἄβυσσος, i.e. the deep waters of the underworld, the source of all Earth's springs and of the sea, and the abode of demons and monsters.[2] Thus, for example, Origen commenting on Lk. viii. 31 speaks of *ea aqua, quae subtus est, id est, aqua abyssi, in qua tenebrae sunt, in qua princeps huius mundi, et adversarius draco, et angeli eius habitant.* At the creation the Spirit brooded upon these waters, and they were gathered together and shut up (Gen. i. 2, 9, Job xxxviii. 8, Ps. xxxiii. 7) ; and a similar brooding of the Spirit was affirmed in the baptismal *Ordo* of Severus of Antioch to have taken place over Jordan when Jesus was baptized. Coptic and Armenian rites contain the same idea. Further, on the strength of passages such as Pss. xxix. 3, lxxvii. 16, cxiv. 3, the early baptismal rites affirm that the waters were terrified at Christ's coming for baptism, Origen extending their terror to " the underworld powers " which inhabited them. Christ's baptism involved, that is to say, a kind of Harrowing of Hell.

The transference of these ideas to the baptism of Christians and to the *Descensus* which accompanied the Passion was not difficult; and it was aided by the use of texts such as Is. xlv. 2 and Ps. cvii. 16 which were equally applicable to the baptism of Christ. As Bernard observes, " the same kind of language was used about the effects of Christ's baptism (and also of the baptism of believers) that was used about the effects of His Descent to Hades ". The purpose of Christ's *Descensus* as of Christian baptism was the release of men's souls from bondage to the evil powers of sin : His " proclamation " to " the spirits in prison " was to advertise them that the day of their rule was ended, and that, as Noah had been delivered from destruc-

The folk-lore of Christ's baptism and Descensus was transferred to the baptism of Christians,

---

[1] *Texts and Studies*, vol. viii. No. 3 (1912). Cf. especially pp. 32-9. Also his article entitled " The Descent into Hades and Christian Baptism " in *The Expositor*, Series viii., No. 64 (April 1916), pp. 241 ff., and note especially his summary, " The Parallelism is be-

tween the Ministry of Christ in Hades and the Ministry of Christ in Baptism".

[2] Cf. Oesterley, *The Evolution of the Messianic Idea*, pp. 75 ff. The idea that the sea was the abode of evil powers may underlie Rev. xxi. 1.

tion to become the recipient of God's first covenant with men, so
now the Christian Church was redeemed through baptism into the
liberty of a new moral and spiritual life over which sin was no longer
to dominate, and of which Christ's resurrection was the guarantee.

which
was con-
ceived as
a release
from
bondage

The Church's custom of baptizing catechumens on Easter Eve was
the appropriate expression of these beliefs. Moreover, we may
note also that the bearing of 1 Pet. iii. 18 ff. on second-century Christian ideas, like those in *Odes of Solomon* xvii. 11, xxi. 1, xxiv.,
xxv., xxxi., of baptism as a release of prisoners through Christ's
descent into the abysses, is easier to decipher if τὰ ἐν φυλακῇ
πνεύματα be interpreted of the angelic spirits than if it be interpreted of the dead. This is not so of *O.S.* xlii., which seems to
have other roots ; but, in the other passages named, the powers
that held the Christian soul in bondage before conversion were
presumably those powers of evil of whom St. Paul had spoken, and
of whom our Lord spoke on one memorable occasion in reference to
St. Peter himself (Lk. xxii. 31 ; cf. *ib.* xiii. 16) — a *verbum Christi*
which was concerned directly with St. Peter's own conversion. It
was these supernatural powers of evil which St. Peter thinks of
Christ as visiting in the course of His atoning death and resurrection and reducing to subjection ; and it was they which St. Paul
thought of the Christians repudiating at baptism, now that Christ
his Master had triumphed over them.

The evidence of baptismal rites from Tertullian onwards tells
a similar tale ; for in all the principal families of rite both in East
and West the formal renunciation (*abrenuntiatio*, ἀπόταξις) of the
devil and his angels found a regular place. Thus we may cite Tert.
de Spect. iv., *Cum aquam ingressi Christianam fidem in legis suae
verba profitemur, renuntiasse nos diabolo et pompae et angelis eius
ore nostro contestamur*; and St. Cyril of Jerusalem, *Cat. Myst.* i. 4 ff.,
expounds a formula which ran, ἀποτάσσομαί σοι, σατανᾶ, καὶ πᾶσι
τοῖς ἔργοις σου, καὶ πάσῃ τῇ πομπῇ σου, καὶ πάσῃ τῇ λατρείᾳ σου.
This renunciation was made towards the West : συμβολικῶς πρὸς
δυσμὰς ἀποβλέποντες ἀποτάσσεσθε τῷ σκοτεινῷ ἐκείνῳ καὶ ζοφερῷ
ἄρχοντι. In some places, moreover, it was followed by the administration of the oil of exorcism. This widespread and firmly
established custom of renouncing the powers of evil in the course
of the baptismal rite is best explained as deriving from the Pauline
and Petrine sources described above.[1]

---

[1] For further evidence cf. Hastings, *ERE*, art. *Abrenuntiatio*, Cabrol, *Dict. d'Arch. Chrét.* ii. 1, col. 288, art. " Baptême ", Assemani, *Codex* I. cv. 140, Darwell Stone, *Holy Bap-tism*, pp. 164 ff.

(B) I PET. IV. 5, 6

We have given in the Notes detailed reasons for the belief that He who is referred to in verse 5 as " standing ready to judge quick and dead " is Christ Himself, and that He too is the subject of εὐηγγελίσθη in verse 6 ; in which case εὐηγγελίσθη can hardly allude to the same " preaching " as ἐκήρυξεν in iii. 19. The point is still further strengthened, if " the spirits in prison " are those spirit-powers of evil whose rebellion Jewish tradition associated with the age preceding the Flood; for the word νεκροί could never be used with that connotation. Windisch has endeavoured to bridge the gap by his view that " the spirits in prison " include the wicked *men* of Noah's day no less than the wicked angels who fomented their wickedness, both alike being bound in *Enoch's* Sheol, and by claiming that in iv. 6, as in iii. 19, " the hearers of the preaching in Hades are here too all the dwellers in Hades ". νεκροί, however, is not a term which could be stretched to so comprehensive a meaning, even if τὰ ἐν φυλακῇ πνεύματα allowed of it ; and Windisch does not, in fact, give any example of such usage. No Jew and no Gentile of the first century ever thought of the evil spirits as " dead ". Further, νεκροί in verse 6 cannot connote the Gentiles or other sinners who are spiritually dead, but must mean, as in verse 5, those who are physically dead. At the same time, we are not bound to believe that *all* the dead are in mind.[1] Importance attaches to the fact observed by Wendt (cf. note on iv. 5) that, when Jesus in the Gospels attributes the supreme judicial function to Himself, He does so with reference, and only with reference, to those living at the time of His return to earth and to their past conduct towards Himself and His disciples. As time passed, however, the question arose, as we know from I Thessalonians, how those Christians stood who had already predeceased Christ's return ; and persecution, such as that alluded to in that Epistle as well as in I Peter, made it more urgent. The question at issue, as it actually confronted the Christians in the thick of the conflict, was not one of eschatological theory, but of personal and practical importance, namely the vindication of God's justice through the punishment of the wicked and the oppressors and the deliverance of the faithful and the persecuted, whether or not they had died before Christ's coming.

Marginal note: No necessary relation between I Pet. iii. 18 ff. and I Pet. iv. 5 f.

[1] So Hofmann, Usteri, von Soden among others : also Griffith-Thomas in *The Expositor*, viii. 69 (September 1916). Spörri (*op. cit.* pp. 149, 180 f.) vigorously criticizes this view, and assumes throughout that iv. 6 and iii. 19 both refer to the dead generally. But nowhere does he really face the linguistic and other difficulties attaching to this view of iii. 19.

"The dead" in iv. 6 has been variously interpreted, as connoting
(1) all the dead, (2) those who died at the time of the Flood, (3) those
who have died in martyrdom, either in St. Peter's time or in previous
persecutions, (4) Christians who have died.   The last two of these
views are by no means exclusive, the problem of martyrdom being
not a different problem from that of the decease of Christians
generally, but rather the point at which this general problem became most acute.   As already indicated, St. Peter is touching on
the problem alluded to in 1 Thess. iv. 13-18, an Epistle which has
many close associations with 1 Peter (cf. Introd. pp. 13-16, 20, and
Essay II).   The problem there arose from the apparent advantage
which those who survived to the Parusia (ἡμεῖς οἱ ζῶντες οἱ περι-
λειπόμενοι) would have over those Christians who died beforehand (οἱ κοιμώμενοι, οἱ νεκροὶ ἐν Χριστῷ); and St. Paul and his
collaborators are at pains to make it clear that such Christians would
rise first at the Judgment and join the survivors in being "rapt into
the air" to meet the Lord.   Here the problem is at once modified
and accentuated by the fact of persecution and social ostracism at
the hands of men who lived wholly for the flesh and scorned all
idea of future retribution and eternal life.   "What good is your
Christianity", they said, "when like the rest of us you die?"
The answer is that the preaching of the Gospel to those who have
died, so far from being useless, was directed to this very end, that,
though in men's eyes, and as men said, they were judged in the
flesh (κριθῶσι μὲν κατὰ ἀνθρώπους σαρκί), in God's eyes they might
live in the spirit (ζῶσι δὲ κατὰ θεὸν πνεύματι).   The μέν . . . δέ
clause, that is to say, connotes a reversal of the world's judgments
at Christ's, and at God's, hands, which vindicates and sets the seal
on the reversal of ethical values, which already distinguishes the
behaviour of Christians in the world.   On this view, the idea of
divine judgment on quick and dead is narrowed and applied to the
particular conditions and problems of the Church at the time; but
from another standpoint the ethical demand on Christians expressed
in iv. 1 ff. is broadened and deepened by being based on the ultimate
ends to which God's government of the world is directed.   Further,
this interpretation links the sentence with the section as a whole in
two ways.   First, the contrast σαρκί . . . πνεύματι recalls the similar
contrast in iii. 18, and indicates that the experience of Christ is
reproduced in those who believe in Him; and secondly, the verse
takes up the allusion in iii. 19 to Christ's preaching to "the spirits
in prison", in that the scope and triumph of the work of redemption
there set forth are illustrated on this more limited, but not less

important, field of the immediate expectations of the Church in persecution.

Furthermore, this is the sense required by the context as a whole. Those who, with Chase and others, give to iv. 6 a universal application, are driven to interpolate some idea not present in the passage in order to account for its relation to the context ; and this is the real objection to Loisy's view as well. For the argument at this point is compact, swift-moving, and self-consistent, dominated by the immediate necessity of stedfastness of faith and life in face of contumely and persecution. In the actual experience of the Apostle's readers, wrong triumphs and right goes to the wall : what is his answer to the dilemma ? His answer is that the Judge stands at the door ; that the wrong-doers will have to give account to Him ; and that the very reason why Christians — even those who were already dead — had had the Gospel preached to them was that, whatever the world might say of their troubled and seemingly fruitless lives here on earth, they might live eternally after God's likeness in heaven. Moreover, this was no distant prospect, but one very near at hand. Many commentators have been misled by failing to see that the argument does not end at iv. 6 : the eschatological theme developed in iv. 7-19, with its emphasis on the vital import-ance of Christians' conduct and its expansion of the thought of the great Judgment which has already begun at the house of God, is its proper climax and completion. In iv. 1-6 St. Peter is still within the compass of the concrete situation of his readers, wrestling with their hopes and fears ; in the remaining verses of the chapter, while still keeping these in view, he passes on to the wider field of Theodicy as a whole and in an outline philosophy of history justifies the ways of God to man.

III. Early Patristic Doctrine of Christ's "Descensus", and its Relation to N.T.

The conclusion from the above examination of 1 Pet. iii. 18 ff. and iv. 5, 6 is that each of the two passages admits of a satisfactory explanation separately ; that the balance of lexicographical con-siderations inclines definitely in this direction ; and that each stands in simpler relation to the whole context, if it is not stretched into doctrinal association with the other. We have now to see how far this conclusion is borne out or otherwise by the teaching of Christian writers between St. Peter's day and Clement of Alex-andria's, and what other grounds than these two passages in N.T. can be adduced for the belief that Christ preached to the departed.

Early patristic Doctrine of Christ's *Descensus* and its relation to N.T.

(i) *Patristic Evidence*

(i) Patristic evidence   The outstanding fact in the Patristic evidence before A.D. 190 is that, despite the popularity of the doctrine of Christ's " harrowing of hell ", 1 Pet. iii. 18 ff. is never quoted as authority for it. "The conception of the *Descensus* current in the early Church proceeds on entirely different lines, and arose independently of 1 Pet. iii. 19 f. Prior to the time of Clement of Alexandria (*Strom.* vi. pp. 763 f. [P]) and Origen (*in Ev. Joann.* vi. 35), this passage, so far as we know, was never referred to in connexion with the *Descensus* " ; while Irenaeus, "who . . . regarded 1 Peter as authentic . . . never quotes the passage at all, nor, in dealing specially with the *Descensus*, does he even allude to it." [1] That fact needs to be remembered throughout the whole discussion; and, with the possible exception of Lightfoot,[2] there is a weighty consensus of opinion on it among scholars, whatever view they adopt as to the correct interpretation of the passage.

Early interpretation of Christ's descent into Hades   That Christ descended into Sheol or Hades is a well-attested belief in the Church of the second century [3]; and when Tertullian interpreted the *Descensus* as meaning *huic* (sc. *mortis*) *quoque legi satisfecit*,[4] he was not saying anything that would have been repudiated by a second-century Christian brought up with a back-

---

[1] Loofs, *ERE*, iv. p. 659b, article "Descent to Hades (Christ's)". The reference is to Irenaeus, *A.H.* v. xxxi. 1. The same point is made by Swete, *The Apostles' Creed*, p. 58, who adds: "The earliest quotation of 1 Pet. iv. 6 we have been able to find is in Cyprian's *Testimonia* (ii. 27)".

[2] Ignatius, *Magn.* ix. 3 n. To Lightfoot's name should be added that of Wright, *op. cit.* p. 164. Lightfoot is impressed by the resemblance of Ignatius' doctrine of prophetic inspiration in *Magn.* viii. to that in 1 Pet. i. 10-12, and by the use of the word παρών in *Magn.* ix. But the connexion of *Magn.* viii. with 1 Pet. i. 10 ff. seems to me very dubious, and I doubt also whether there is any allusion to the *Descensus* in παρών. Would not Ignatius have written πορευθείς, if he had had 1 Pet. iii. 19 f. in mind? Further, in relation to the "expectation" of the prophets just mentioned, Christ "appeared" (παρῆν) at the Incarnation. Perhaps Christ's raising

of the prophets from the dead was connected in Ignatius' mind with His descent into Hades at death ; but his source may equally well have been Matt. xxvii. 53, or Jn. v. 25. We may note that Clem. Alex. mentions Matt. xxvii. 53 in close proximity with 1 Pet. iii. 19 f in *Strom.* vi. pp. 763 f. [P].

[3] Cf. Loofs, *op. cit.*, Blenkin, *op. cit.*, Add. Note A, pp. 83 f. The earliest creed in which the *Descensus* appears is that of Aquileia, though it had been endorsed by the Synod of Sirmium about forty years earlier. Rufinus, commenting on the Aquileian version of the Apostles' Creed (*Comm. in Symbol. Apost.*) in about A.D. 390, says that even then it was not in the Roman version. In ch. 28 he quotes 1 Pet. iii. 18, with very cautious comment, but in ch. 29 reflects the traditional ideas when he says of our Lord's resurrection, *Rediit ergo victor a mortuis, inferni spolia secum trahens.*

[4] So too, in substance, the Scottish Catechisms.

ground of Jewish, Greek, or Roman ideas. For in the popular view
to die was to go to Hades ; and from the beginning this belief was
held about Christ. It is when we come to the ways in which this
bare statement of fact was filled in that we find differences of
opinion. Two strands of teaching can be distinguished :

(a) THE OVERTHROW OF SATANIC POWERS

According to the first, represented by *The Ascension of Isaiah* (a) The
(which is probably of first-century provenance [1] and contains large over-
Christian elements), by the *Odes of Solomon* (xvii. 9, xxxi. 1), by Satanic
the *Gospel of Nicodemus* (a fourth-century work containing second- powers
century material), and by Melito of Sardis, whose *Homily on the
Passion* has lately been made available to scholars,[2] the purpose of
Christ's *Descensus* was the overthrow of Satan and the powers of
death. It is expressed by such phrases as " when He hath plundered
the angel of death " (*Asc. Is.* ix. 16 ; cf. x. 14), " and all the angels
of the firmament saw Him and they worshipped " (*ib.* xi. 23) ; by
the colloquy between Hell and Satan with his " legions of devils "
and the dramatic use of Ps. xxiv. 7-10, described in the *Gospel of
Nicodemus* (*Acts of Pilate*, v. (xxi.)-x.) [3] ; and by the words put into
the mouth of Christ by Melito (xvii. 13-17, cf. xi. 9-10) :

$$\text{ἐγώ,}$$
φησίν, ὁ Χριστός, ἐγὼ ὁ καταλύσας τὸν θάνατον καὶ θριαμβεύσας [4] τὸν ἐχθρὸν
καὶ καταπατήσας τὸν ᾅδην καὶ δή-
σας [5] τὸν ἰσχυρὸν καί . . .

In all this we have ideas very similar to those which we believe
to underlie 1 Pet. iii. 19. The allusions in the *Odes of Solomon* are
of special interest, because they are quite possibly baptismal hymns,
and they associate Christ's descent into hell and breaking of its
prison-bars with the liberation of the converted soul on earth.

(b) THE LIBERATION OF THE RIGHTEOUS DEAD

Closely allied to this is the idea, which Loofs regards as the (b) The
standard tradition of second-century teaching on the subject, that liberation
Christ liberated at the same time the souls of the patriarchs and of the
prophets of Israel. The idea was presumably unknown or unaccept- dead

---

[1] Cf. Oesterley and Box, *Apocalypse
of Abraham and Ascension of Isaiah*
(1918), following Charles.
[2] *Studies and Documents*, xii.
(1940). The Homily is edited by

Campbell Bonner.
[3] M. R. James, *The Apocryphal
N.T.*
[4] Cf. Col. ii. 15.
[5] Cf. Matt. xii. 29.

able to Hermas,[1] because he assigns this function to the Christian Apostles and teachers. But it is taught plainly by Justin, Irenaeus, and Tertullian, and possibly by Ignatius ; and it was also apparently parodied by Marcion,[2] and was known to Celsus.[3] One of its best expressions is in *Odes of Solomon*, xlii. 15 ff. [*Christus loquitur*] :

Sheol saw me and was made miserable : death cast me up and many along with me. I had gall and bitterness, and I went down with him to the utmost of his depth[4] : and the feet and the head he let go, for they were not able to endure my face[5] : and I made a congregation of living men amongst his dead men, and I spake with them by living lips : because my word shall not be void ; and those who had died ran towards me : and they cried and said, Son of God, have pity on us, and do with us according to thy kindness, and bring us out from the bonds of darkness : and open to us the door by which we shall come out to thee. For we see that our death has not touched thee. Let us also be redeemed with thee : for thou art our Redeemer. And I heard their voice ; and my name I sealed upon their heads : for they are free men and they are mine. Hallelujah.

Similar ideas are embodied in the beautiful words of comfort which the Jewish Christian who wrote 2 Esdras i., ii. was bidden to address to his people, at a date[6] probably not far different from that of the *Odes* :

And those that be dead will I raise up again from their places, and bring them out of the tombs : for I have known my name in them. . . . Remember thy children that sleep, for I shall bring them out of the secret places of the earth, and shew mercy unto them. . . . Embrace thy children until I come, and proclaim mercy unto them : for I am merciful, saith the Lord Almighty.

This liberation and restoration to life of the saints of old time by Christ's descent into hell, which is so marked a feature of the Christian literature of the second century, clearly presents close

---

[1] *Sim.* ix. xvi. 5. The place of Christ as the rock and the gate in Hermas' allegory of the tower did not leave much room for the idea that He Himself preached to the dead.

[2] According to Irenaeus, *A.H.* i. xxvii. 3, Marcion taught that the saints of O.T., since they believed in the Demiurge, refused to listen to Christ's preaching, but that only Cain and others like him did listen and were saved. Had Marcion possibly come

across the Rabbinic doctrine concerning Korah, Doeg, and Ahitophel quoted below?

[3] Orig. *c. Cels.* ii. 43.

[4] Cf. Ps. lxiii. 9, Eph. iv. 9.

[5] Cf. 1 Tim. iii. 16, ὤφθη ἀγγέλοις.

[6] Cf. Oesterley, *2 Esdras* (Westminster Comm.), Introd. p. 44, who dates these two chapters " after the middle of the second century A.D.". The verses quoted are from 2 Esdr. ii. 16, 31, 32.

doctrinal affinities with the *verba Christi* in Matt. viii. 11, Lk. xiii. 28, 29 (cf. Ign. *Phil.* ix. i) ; and Loofs aptly compares Heb. xi. 39 f. and xii. 22 f. as expressing the same idea. The kingdom of God into which the Redeemer has admitted men must embrace not only those who hear or have heard His word on earth, but also those in Israel's past who had looked forward to Messiah's advent. The extension of this by Clement of Alexandria (*Strom.* VI. vi.) to include the noblest minds of heathen antiquity is no part of the primitive idea, though it is a logical development of it for any who, like the Apologists, thought of Plato as Μωϋσῆς ἀττικίζων.

A further fact to be observed is that Christ's " preaching " in the course of His *Descensus* does not seem to be as early an idea in the second century as His " raising " or " liberating " of the saints of the Old Covenant. It is not, that is to say, in Ignatius[1] nor in Hermas, who indeed assigns this function to the Apostles and first teachers of the Gospel. But it is in Justin and Irenaeus, in the *Gospel of Peter*, and (though not very plainly) in the passages from the *Odes of Solomon* and 2 Esdras quoted above. Irenaeus, indeed, besides repeatedly citing the prophetic passage which we shall examine in a moment, says that he had heard from an elder who had it from personal companions of the Apostles and their disciples, " that the Lord descended to the parts beneath the earth preaching

The idea of Christ "preaching" to the dead is later

---

[1] I do not think that it is implied either in *Phil.* v. or in *Magn.* ix. Hermas, in *Sim.* IX, in order to represent the range of redemption and the inclusiveness of the Church, makes the Apostles and teachers of the first Christian age preach to the saints of the Old Dispensation who had predeceased them and give them " the seal of the preaching " and bring them up to life. Clement of Alexandria appeals to this passage twice in proof of his very liberal doctrine. In *Strom.* II. p. 452 [P] he writes : " And the Shepherd, speaking plainly of those who had fallen asleep, recognizes (οἶδε) certain righteous among Gentiles and Jews, not only before the appearance of Christ, but before the law, in virtue of acceptance before God—as Abel, as Noah, as any other righteous man ". In point of fact, Hermas did not allude to Gentiles, and Clement appears to be going beyond his source here. In *Strom.* VI. pp. 763 f. [P], after quoting Job xxviii. 22 to illustrate the

fact that " the Lord preached the Gospel to those in Hades ", Clement alludes to 1 Pet. iii. 19 f. (and possibly also to 1 Pet. iv. 6), and also to his own quotation from Hermas in *Strom.* II, to shew that Christ, and " the Apostles, following the Lord ", preached the Gospel to those kept in watch and guard. Here, too, he goes beyond Hermas, and indeed appears to be aware of it, since he adds : " For it was requisite in my opinion that as here, so also there, the best of the disciples should be imitators of the Master ; so that He should bring to repentance those belonging to the Hebrews, and they the Gentiles ". And this passage of the *Stromateis* is the earliest, so far as we know, in which 1 Pet. iii. 18 f. was cited as authority for this doctrine. Origen carried Clement's universalist tendencies yet one step further in *de Princ.* II. v. 3, which appeals to 1 Pet. iii. 18-21 as decisively proving that even the wicked are ultimately saved.

His advent there also and declaring remission of sins as available for those who believe in Him ", and he defines them as the " just men and prophets and patriarchs " of Israel. This points to a tradition of some standing ; but not enough reliance can be placed on its details to justify our saying that the idea of Christ " preaching " to the dead was taught in the Church earlier than A.D. 150. The most dramatic version of this idea is in the apocryphal *Gospel of Peter*,[1] where the Lord is represented as coming forth from the tomb with two others, " two of them supporting the other, and a cross following them ; and the head of the two reached to heaven, but that of Him who was led by them overpassed the heavens. And they heard a voice from the heavens, saying, Thou didst preach to them that sleep (ἐκήρυξας τοῖς κοιμωμένοις) ; and a response was heard from the cross, Yea."

(ii) *Sources of Second-Century Doctrine, in Default of Allusion to 1 Pet. iii. 18 ff.*

(ii) Sources of second-century doctrine, in default of allusion to 1 Pet. iii. 18 ff.

Such, in brief outline, are the facts with regard to the teaching of the second-century Christian literature on this subject ; and we note that there is no quotation of 1 Pet. iii. 19 nor of 1 Pet. iv. 6 to support them, and no proof that it was in the mind of any of the writers in this connexion.[2] What, then, were the sources of the belief ? We have already mentioned some of them in passing, namely Heb. xi., xii., Matt. xii. 29, viii. 11, Lk. xiii. 28, 29. Irenaeus also (*A.H.* v. xxxi. 1) quotes Matt. xii. 40 and Eph. iv. 9 to prove the *Descensus*, though without reference to any details accompanying it. Melito, again, seems undoubtedly to be drawing upon Matt. xii. 29 and Col. ii. 15 in *Homily* xvii. 13-19. Even the repeated allusions to the obscure prophecy of Jeremiah (or Isaiah) made by Irenaeus, who was perhaps following Justin, do not afford us much help ; for Justin [3] introduces it merely to illustrate Jewish mutilations of

---

[1] H. B. Swete, D.D., *The Akhmim Fragment of the Apocryphal Gospel of St. Peter*, ix. (1893). Swete gives as a probable date A.D. 165. Cf. also Harnack, *Bruchstücke des Evangeliums und der Apocalypse des Petrus*, Leipzig, 1893. Harnack emends the text, supposing that 1 Pet. iii. 19 is referred to, but Swete thinks the allusion improbable. On the other hand, he agrees—rightly, I think—with Nestle and Duhm that the two others are Moses and Elias of the Transfiguration story.

[2] It is the more important to emphasize this point in view of the surprising statements of that fine scholar, C. H. H. Wright, in his weighty essay in *Biblical Essays* (1886), p. 164, to the effect that there was no Patristic tradition on the subject of Christ's *Descensus* which was not " distinctively derived from their interpretation of 1 Pet. iii. 19 " and " entirely dependent on the expressions used by St. Peter in that single verse ".

[3] *Dial.* 72.

their own Scriptures, while Irenaeus uses it in a variety of contexts.[1]
In *A.H.* IV. xxxiii. I, moreover, he says that Jesus " was led as a
sheep to the slaughter, and by the stretching of His hands destroyed
Amalek " — a figurative expression, based on Ex. xvii. 11, which
probably refers to the overthrow of the spirit-powers of evil[2]; and
when he does quote 1 Pet. iii. 20, it is merely to illustrate the Deluge,
" through which eight persons were saved ".[3] There is nothing
here to suggest that Irenaeus identified the dead whom Christ
raised through His *Descensus* with " the spirits in prison " of 1 Pet.
iii. 19.

(a) O.T. AND RABBINIC LITERATURE

(a) O.T. and Rabbinic Literature

We have already alluded, in the note on iii. 19, to O.T. passages
which reflect a belief that the dead are prisoners in Sheol; and
Hos. xiii. 14 and Zech. ix. 12 contain the further idea that they are
to be released, though in neither passage, nor in Is. xxv. 8, xxvi. 19,
is the restoration of the dead to life ascribed to the Messiah or
associated with his work. There is, however, this curious oracle
alluded to by Justin (*Dial.* 72) and Irenaeus (*A.H.* III. xx. 9)
as found in Isaiah or Jeremiah, but not extant in our O.T., to the
effect that " the Lord God remembered His dead people of Israel
who lay in the graves, and descended to preach to them His own
salvation ".[4] The text was evidently familiar, at least in theological
circles in the second century; and it is quoted along with other
passages of Scripture as though it were equally authoritative. Did
it originally stand somewhere in Jeremiah?[5] At any rate, the differ-

---

[1] *A.H.* III. xx. 4 (to prove Christ's
divinity); IV. xxii. I (to illustrate the
comprehensiveness of salvation); IV.
xxxiii. I (without reference to any
preaching of Christ); IV. xxiii. 12
(as the reason for the Passion); V.
xxxi. I (without reference to any
preaching by Christ, and in conjunction with Matt. xii. 40 and Eph. iv. 9).

[2] So Feuardentius, quoted in
Stieren, *Irenaeus*, ii. p. 999. Cf. *Ep.
Barn.* xii. 9, with Hilgenfeld's note.

[3] *A.H.* I. xviii. 3.

[4] Justin, *Dial.* 72 (298 B, C), quotes
the words as Jeremiah's and says that
the Jews had excised them. Irenaeus
quotes them as Isaiah's in *A.H.* III.
xx. 4, but as Jeremiah's in IV. xxii. I,
and without naming an author in IV.
xxxiii. I and 12 and V. xxxi. I.
Justin's quotation runs in the Greek,

ἐμνήσθη δὲ κύριος ὁ θεὸς ἅγιος Ἰσραὴλ
τῶν νεκρῶν αὐτοῦ, τῶν κεκοιμημένων
εἰς γῆν χώματος, καὶ κατέβη πρὸς
αὐτοὺς εὐαγγελίσασθαι αὐτοῖς τὸ σω-
τήριον αὐτοῦ. Can any connexion exist between this passage and 2 Esdr.
ii. 16-32 cited above? Isaiah and
Jeremiah are mentioned together in
verse 18.

[5] Harris, *Testimonies*, i. pp. 12 f.,
thinks little of Justin's accusations
against the Jews of " excising "
prophecies that were too clearly fulfilled in Christianity. Yet there may
be something in what Justin says, for a
similar situation confronts us in Job
xxviii. 22, where we read (concerning
Wisdom) —

ἡ ἀπώλεια καὶ ὁ θάνατος εἶπαν
ἀκηκόαμεν δὲ αὐτῆς τὸ κλέος.

This and the preceding verses have

ence in the attribution of the text, to Isaiah or to Jeremiah, may be due to the fact that both Justin and Irenaeus were quoting from a book of Testimonies ; and the fact that in one of his citations Irenaeus agrees witn Justin's attribution of the text to Jeremiah makes it probable that his reference to Isaiah in *A.H.* iii. xx. 4 was a *lapsus calami*. Even if its source were a book of Testimonies, however, the text may be very early [1] ; though its ultimate source is at present unknown.

Traces of a similar belief about the Messiah also occur in a Rabbinic work, *Bereschit Rabba*,[2] but there is no certainty that this is of pre-Christian date.[3] Further, attention may be drawn to passages in Rabbinic literature which, though also in their present form post-Christian and not connected with any action of the Messiah, attest a belief that even evil-doers notorious in Hebrew history may be released from Sheol eventually : cf. Montefiore and Loewe, *A Rabbinic Anthology*, p. 587 [1623] (Doeg and Ahitophel), p. 604 [1654] (those who perished with Korah the arch-rebel), Hannah's prayer in 1 Sam. ii. 6 being cited in the latter case.

(b) " Verba Christi " : Jn. v. 19-29

(b) Verba Christi;
Jn. v.
19-29

Of far greater importance, however, in the formation of the tradition, were the words of the Lord Himself ; and there is one discourse in particular, recorded by St. John, which seems of especial relevance in this connexion, though it does not appear to have received the attention it deserves.[4] I refer to Jn. v. 19-29. Though the form of this passage may owe much to the Evangelist, the materials of which it is composed, and notably the sayings in

been a *crux* of textual criticism, and Burkitt gives reasons (*EB*, 5027, 5028) for believing that the true LXX is that given by Clem. Alex. in *Strom.* vi. p. 763 [P] : λέγει ὁ ᾅδης τῇ ἀπωλείᾳ· εἶδος μὲν αὐτοῦ οὐκ εἴδομεν φωνὴν δὲ αὐτοῦ ἀκηκόαμεν. He is concerned chiefly with the omission of Job xxviii. 21b, 22a in the Sahidic text, which would leave the 1st pers. plur. in 22b without a subject. But the case for Clement's version being correct is still further strengthened by the fact that otherwise — i.e. with the LXX as it stands — the δέ after ἀκηκόαμεν has no basis. Possibly the prophecy adduced by the Fathers may have fallen out in a similar way to the words in Job xxviii. 22. The oracle would come well, for example, between Jer. xi. 19 and 20.

[1] Cf. Harris, *op. cit.* ii. p. 2.
[2] The passage is quoted by Bigg on 1 Pet. iii. 19 from Weber, and runs : " But when they that are bound, they that are in Gehinnom, saw the light of the Messiah, they rejoiced to receive him " ; and again, " This is that which stands written : We shall rejoice and exult in Thee. When ? When the captives climb up out of hell, and Shekinah at their head."
[3] Cf. Schürer, i. i. pp. 118, 145 f.
[4] C. H. H. Wright (*Biblical Essays*, p. 150), who goes so far as to say : " It is certain that no preaching of Christ to departed spirits, whether before or after His resurrection, is alluded to in . . . the New Testament ", makes no reference to these verses of St. John.

verse 26 and verses 28, 29 have the ring of genuine utterances of Jesus[1]; and that being so, they are significant for our purpose. For they affirm the universal range of Christ's message of salvation, extending even to the dead ; they exhibit the same contrast between " life " and " judgment " as we find in 1 Pet. iv. 6 ; and they have echoes elsewhere in the New Testament.

As the passage stands, it opens with an assertion of the intimacy of the Son with the Father, which is shewn by the Son's equal, though delegated, power (i) to " quicken " ($\zeta\omega o\pi o\iota\epsilon\hat{\iota}\nu$) whom He will and to exercise judgment, and (ii) to condition the bodily resurrection of the dead. There is widespread agreement amongst expositors (e.g. Westcott, Wendt, Stevens, Bernard) that the first " judgment " and " quickening " are figurative, and have to do with the decision which the preaching of Christ forced upon men and the new life into which believers entered, while the resurrection after hearing Christ's voice, alluded to in verses 28, 29, is literal. This is not, however, to say (as e.g. von Dobschütz does [2]) that the first is mystical and the second eschatological ; for, as Hoskyns observes, both occurrences are regarded as historical, one present (verses 20-27) and the other future (verses 28, 29), and both stand within the final order of God.[3] The twice-repeated " Verily, verily " (verses 24, 25) emphasizes the urgency of the immediate decision ; and this decision is placed in the context of a more far-reaching act, or series of acts, of divine judgment which will embrace the dead no less than the living (verses 28, 29).

There is more to be said, however, than this. Is it certain that we have to deal only with a twofold division in this passage ? The majority of scholars, following St. Augustine, place the dividing line between the figurative and the literal teaching after verse 27. The assumption, however, seems too easily made. Not only is verse 25 very similar in form to verse 28 ; but the change from the present tenses consistently used in verses 21-4 to the future in verses 25 ff. is significant. Further, the references to the " hour " in verses 25 and 28 must be given full weight. " Realized eschatology ", or the doctrine that the end of all things has already arrived with the advent of the Messiah, does not mean that there is nothing further to occur ; on the contrary, the end is a highly complex series of inter-related events, which have their centre and chief significance in Jesus but have still to be unfolded in time. And in this unfolding there

Different " moments " referred to in the passage corresponding to different meanings of Christ's " hour "

---

[1] Cf. Bernard, *St. John* (I.C.C.), 1. p. clxi.

[2] *The Eschatology of the Gospels*, pp. 196 ff. He speaks of the two strands of thought as indicating distinct strata of tradition superimposed upon one another.

[3] *The Fourth Gospel*, i. pp. 298 ff.

are " moments " of special importance which lie still in the future, notably Christ's death and resurrection, the outpouring of the Spirit, and the final Judgment. It is in this context that we are to understand what Jesus says in the Fourth Gospel about the " hour ". Usually " the hour " or " my hour " has reference to His death and glorification[1] (Jn. ii. 4, vii. 30, viii. 20, xii. 23, xiii. 1, xvii. 1 ; cf. Matt. xxvi. 45) ; but in Jn. iv. 21, 23 it has reference to the establishment of the new worship and to the dispensation of the Spirit (cf. vii. 37-9), and in Jn. v. 28 to the final Judgment. In the Fourth Gospel, that is to say, the eschatological " moment " *par excellence* is in Christ's imminent sacrifice on the Cross ; and that is why it is so often insisted in this Gospel that the hour has *not* yet come. And yet there is a sense in which it *has* come, because the Messiah Himself has come and the powers of the eschatological order are already at work. This paradox of *futurum in praesenti* — of the immanent Transcendent — is expressed in a particular phrase which occurs twice (iv. 23, v. 25), " the hour cometh and now is ". In both places the " hour " which " cometh " is the hour of Christ's death and glorification and the new covenant then effectively inaugurated. In ch. iv. this hour " now is " because worship in spirit and truth is already active (iv. 23) in the company of Jesus and His disciples, but it is still " coming " because the supersession of the local churches of Jerusalem and Galilee by the Catholic Church of the new covenant has not yet taken effect (iv. 21), and cannot before Calvary.

In ch. v. the hour " now is " because the life-giving powers of the Son of God are already evident in His raisings of the dead, but it is still " coming " because He has not yet conquered death and Hades (v. 25), and in a yet more distant sense because the time for the general resurrection is not yet ripe (verses 28, 29).

Two " moments " distinguishable in our Lord's teaching here about the future

We have, then, to reckon that St. John distinguished in v. 25-9 two " moments " in Christ's predictions of the future—an imminent one, when the dead should hear Christ's voice and they that heard should live, and a more distant one when His voice should be the signal for the general resurrection of good and evil to " life " and " judgment " respectively. The authority of Christ's word or voice, which is so prominent in this passage (verses 24, 25, 28), is then represented as having effect in three different ways. It separated believers and unbelievers there and then in Palestine, and quickened those who responded (verses 21-4) : it was to be heard immediately by the dead, and those who heard it were to live ; and it was to be

[1] Cf. Hoskyns, *The Fourth Gospel*, i. pp. 196 f.

heard at the end of all things and to be the signal for the general
resurrection of all men to judgment or to life.

But, on this shewing, who are the " dead " of verse 25 ? Bernard Two views
represents the most commonly accepted opinion, namely that οἱ as to the meaning
νεκροί means " the spiritually dead ", who (unlike those referred to in of " the
verse 24) did not believe Christ's word. The use of οἱ νεκροί, how- dead " in Jn. v. 25 :
ever, in this sense, when used alone, is not easy to parallel ; for in
Eph. ii. 1, 5 the word is qualified by τοῖς παραπτώμασι. Nor can we
safely cite τῶν νεκρῶν in Eph. v. 14, for the whole sentence there is
metaphorical and taken almost certainly from a primitive baptismal
hymn. Further, the argument, which is of an *à fortiori* character,
requires at this point not a corollary or mere sequel to verse 24, but
a new fact or consideration which will underpin it. If this view is
correct, however, we have still to answer the question as to who are
" the dead " referred to. Two answers are possible : (i) In many one
ways the simplest interpretation is that Jesus was referring to those referring to Christ's
raisings of the dead which He mentioned in His reply to the disciples raisings of
of John the Baptist (Matt. xi. 2 ff.), and of which the raising of the dead ;
Lazarus was to be the most conspicuous example. These are those
" greater works " which Jesus has mentioned in verse 20.[1] In that
case the future tense in verse 25 (which contrasts with the present
in Matt. xi. 5) may be due either to the fact that *in the order of St.
John's narrative* the event is future, no instances of such miracles
occurring in this Gospel before ch. xi., or to the fact that our Lord
was claiming the fulfilment of prophecy (e.g. Is. xxvi. 19, xlii. 7).
On this view, verse 25 would not refer to the " quickening " of verses
21-4, but to a fact of a different order which illustrated it, just as
in the case of the Healing of the Paralytic in Mk. ii. 1-12 the bodily
miracle illustrated the spiritual, and certified Christ's authority.
(ii) An alternative view is that our Lord was referring to His death the other
and what should follow it, thus providing the basis for the second- to a *Descensus*
century teaching about the *Descensus*. In favour of this view it *ad*
may be urged that in the only other place where the phrase ἔρχεται *Inferos*;
ὥρα καὶ νῦν ἐστιν occurs (Jn. iv. 23) the reference is not to the
present but to the immediate future, when the break with Judaism
should have been made final and the new worship established (cf.
also Jn. vii. 39). That Jesus did contemplate entering the abode of
the dead is indicated by His promise to the penitent thief (Lk. xxiii.
43), " This day shalt thou be with me in Paradise ". Jn. v. 25, on

---

[1] Cf. W. Temple, *Readings in St.
John's Gospel*, i. p. 113. Dr. Temple's
notes on this passage are a model of
penetrating and lucid exposition ;
though St. Augustine argues strongly
against this view in Tract. xix. of his
commentary on St. John.

this interpretation, goes further than that saying ; but it is not inconsistent with it.

but these views are not mutually exclusive I have set these two views side by side as alternatives ; but that is perhaps to miss the pregnancy of this *verbum Christi*. The Evangelist, in his narrative of the raising of Lazarus, makes it plain that he regards the miracle as symbolic of the truth that Christ is " the resurrection and the life " — a Messianic truth which is also expressed in Jn. v. 26, 27. That Christ " brought life and immortality to light through the Gospel " (2 Tim. i. 10) was the settled belief of the Apostolic Church. Need we suppose that the extension of His life-giving Word to the dead was not present to His mind, as well as its extension to other generations on earth, as He saw His life-giving works of Messianic power ? May not a similar implication lie, indeed, in the words which St. Matthew records as addressed by our Lord to St. Peter (Matt. xvi. 18) : " On this rock I will build my Church ; and the gates of Hades shall not prevail against it " ? That Jesus thought of the patriarchs as living and destined to rise we know from Mk. xii. 26, 27, where He bases the fact on Ex. iii. 6, and concludes, " He is not the God of the dead, but the God of the living " ; and He gave the thought still preciser lines and a much wider range in the words He uttered after seeing the faith of the Roman centurion, " And I say unto you, That many shall come from the east and west, and shall sit down with Abraham, and Isaac, and Jacob, in the kingdom of heaven. But the children of the kingdom shall be cast out into outer darkness : there shall be weeping and gnashing of teeth " (Matt. viii. 11, 12).

I think we are justified in concluding, then, from the above evidence that our Lord did without doubt regard His message of salvation as one that would reach the dead and secure entrance for such as believed it into eternal life ; that He connected this with His miracles of healing the sick and raising the dead ; and that He regarded it as an event involving a judgment — that is to say, rejection as well as in-gathering. In Jn. v. 25 He throws this teaching into graphic pictorial form by speaking of the dead hearing the voice of the Son of God, and — if our interpretation of the " hour " be correct — by associating this with His death. It is true that it is not cited by the Fathers in this sense, and indeed is only very rarely cited at all ; but this is because it was understood before St. Augustine's time as having the same meaning as v. 28 and as referring to the General Resurrection preceding the Last Judgment : see, for instance, Hippolytus (Lagarde's edition), pp. 34 and 115, and Tertullian, *de Resurr. Christi*, xxxvii. And for that purpose there were other texts which served equally well, or better.

Jn. v. 25 is not, however, the only *logion* in this discourse which Jn. v. 26-9 concerns us here. There is also that in verses 28, 29, which bears the weight of the whole argument. This is so, even if verse 25 be regarded as no more than a corollary to verses 19-24. But, if verse 25 be interpreted as we have suggested above, the sequence of thought is as follows : The judgment implicit in the immediate decision forced upon men by Christ's teaching and its quickening effects on those who believe is of a piece with, and will at once be certified by, His raisings of the dead while He is on earth and by the judging and quickening power of His voice upon the dead after His crucifixion. But that in turn is not surprising or irrational. For His power of exercising judgment and of giving life (verses 26, 27) is one that will be ultimately decisive for the whole realm of the dead when " all that are in the graves shall hear his voice, and shall come forth ; they that have done good, unto the resurrection of life ; and they that have done evil, unto the resurrection of judgment " (verses 28, 29). There is widespread agreement amongst expositors that this saying refers to the General Resurrection and the Last Judgment, the traditional imagery of Jewish eschatology being taken over and made to serve the new truth that Christ will be the Judge of all. I believe that this view is correct, though it must be made to rest on general grounds rather than on details. The difference of phrase about the " hour " between verse 25 and verse 28 is not sufficient in itself to shew that the two verses refer to different events ; and the distinction between οἱ νεκροί in verse 25 and πάντες οἱ ἐν τοῖς μνημείοις in verse 28 is without significance in view of Is. xxvi. 19, ἀναστήσονται οἱ νεκροί, καὶ ἐγερθήσονται οἱ ἐν τοῖς μνημείοις, where the terms have the same meaning. The real reason for believing that verse 25 and verse 28 refer to different events lies partly in the requirements of the argument and partly in the character of the eschatological language used in verses 28, 29.

The importance of these verses for our present purpose lies in Bearing of their bearing on 1 Pet. iv. 6. For here too we have the distinction, this on 1 Pet. iv. 6; not between life and death (as, e.g., in St. Paul) or between life and destruction (as, e.g., in the Synoptic Gospels ; and cf. Heb. x. 39), but between life and judgment. I find it difficult not to think that St. Peter or his amanuensis had the *verbum Christi* of Jn. v. 28, 29 in mind. Moreover the preceding phrase in 1 Pet. iv. 5, τῷ ἑτοίμως ἔχοντι κρῖναι ζῶντας καὶ νεκρούς, affords a close parallel to the teaching of Jn. v. 26, 27. Further, St. Peter's interest is not in the *time* of the judgment which will secure the reversal of values and destinies, but in the fact that it is effected by the Gospel (εὐηγγε-λίσθη). For St. Peter as for St. John the deciding factor would be men's reaction to Christ's word ; and the Judge would be Christ Himself.

on Matt. Such teaching as that contained in Jn. v. 19-29, and notably
xxvii. 53; in the highly individual sayings recorded in verse 25 and verses 28, 29, was bound to arouse questions in the early Church ; and there are two passages in particular which may be noted. One is Matt. xxvii. 52, 53, where we are told how the death of Jesus was attended by the rending of the veil of the temple and by an earthquake : " and the tombs were opened ; and many bodies of the saints which slept arose, and came out of the graves after his resurrection, and went into the holy city, and appeared unto many ". Loofs (*Third Congress for Hist. Rel.* ii. p. 299) connects the passage directly with 1 Pet. iii. 19 ; but it seems to me far more probable that it was a projection — early, but not quite primitive [1] — into narrative form of a belief which derived from the *verbum Christi* recorded in Jn. v. 25.

and Again, E. C. Gibson (*The Revelation of St. John the Divine*
Rev. xx. [Churchman's Bible]), and more cautiously von Dobschütz (*op. cit.* p. 200), connect the teaching about the First Resurrection and the Second Death in Rev. xx. with Jn. v. 19-29. From the time of St. Augustine onwards the millennium referred to in xx. 4, to which the First Resurrection gives admittance, has been figuratively inter-preted [2] as an occurrence which " takes effect in the present life " (cf. Col. iii. 1, Jn. v. 24, 25). It is true that in the vision in Rev. xx. the First Resurrection is limited to the martyrs and confessors ; but from St. Paul's day onwards, when to believe in Christ meant, as 1 Peter shews, to suffer reproach, boycotting, imprisonment, and many other inconveniences, the martyrs and confessors formed the head and front of the Christian army, and we need not suppose that its rank and file were excluded. They have been raised from death and entered into life with Christ : Satan, the " strong man armed " of Mk. iii. 27, Lk. xi. 22, has been overcome by a Stronger ; the world's values have been completely reversed (cf. 1 Pet. iv. 5, 6) and the persecuted become priests and kings (cf. 1 Pet. ii. 9) ; and physical death has so far ceased to be of importance that the " First

---

[1] For example, the phrase " after his resurrection " looks as though it depended on the doctrine of Christ as " the firstfruits of them that slept " in 1 Cor. xv. 20.

[2] Cf. H. B. Swete, *The Apocalypse of St. John*, pp. 259 ff. On the error of literalist interpretation Swete's note on p. 261 should be consulted.

Death " does not need to be mentioned by the Seer.[1] And this First Resurrection or kingdom of the saints is set, as in Jn. v., against the background of the Last Judgment and the Second Death. Just as in Rev. xx. 1-6 we find mention of the First Resurrection but none of the First Death, so in xx. 7-15, conversely, we find mention of the Second Death but none of the Second Resurrection. For the new life in Christ which makes the First Death irrelevant for Christians makes the Second Resurrection equally irrelevant for them, since their life has already the quality of eternity. " He that believeth in me, though he die, yet shall he live : and whosoever liveth and believeth on me shall never die " (Jn. xi. 25, 26).

IV. Summary and Estimate of Results

We may conclude this Essay with a summary of the results reached, and an attempt to evaluate St. Peter's teaching.

Summary and estimate of results

(i) *The Interpretation of 1 Pet. iii. 18-22*

In the case of 1 Pet. iii. 18-22 the linguistic and grammatical considerations are in favour of the phrase " the spirits in prison " referring to those archetypal spirits of evil whose rebellion led to the wickedness which brought about the Flood, and whose Fall was regarded by one tradition of Jewish teaching as the *fons et origo* of human sin.[2] These considerations are reinforced by reference to the context in which the passage occurs, where the theme is the victory of the dying life exemplified in Christ and now incumbent upon Christians. It is not here the generosity of Christ's redemptive suffering and death but its triumphant issue which is the point. The Apostle's doctrine is thus in line with much Pauline teaching about Christ's conquest of the spirit-powers of evil through the Cross ; and it has specially close affinity with the credal hymn quoted in 1 Tim. iii. 16. The close connexion of this doctrine with baptism reappears frequently in the baptismal hymns and liturgies of the second, third, and fourth centuries.

(i) The interpretation of 1 Pet. iii. 18-22

[1] According to Strack-Billerbeck (Excursus in vol. iv., pt. ii.), the Rabbis from at least the first century B.C. deliberately replaced the term " Sheol " by the term " Gehinnom ", and the belief arose that the pious were not going to the underworld at all, not even to await the day of judg-ment, but were at once proceeding to heaven. This belief tallies well with the contrast between judgment and life found in 1 Pet. iv. 6 and Jn. v. 24-7.

[2] Cf. N. P. Williams, *The Ideas of the Fall and of Original Sin*, pp. 20-29, 114.

(ii) *The Interpretation of 1 Pet. iv. 6*

Linguistic reasons make it highly improbable that " the dead " of 1 Pet. iv. 6 are identical with, or included among, " the spirits in prison " of 1 Pet. iii. 19. If 1 Pet. iv. 6 were intended to recall and resume the teaching of the earlier passage, it could only be, as suggested by Loisy, in the sense that Christ " took occasion " to preach the Gospel to the dead at the time when He made proclamation to the imprisoned angels ; but there is no need to postulate even that much connexion between the two passages, since the idea contained in 1 Pet. iv. 6 needed no other warrant than the *verbum Christi* in Jn. v. 25. There are, however, weighty reasons, on grounds both of language and of context, particularly the latter, for believing that " the dead " of 1 Pet. iv. 6 are not the dead as a whole (as probably in Jn. v. 25, and certainly in Jn. v. 28, 29), but only a portion of them relevant to the writer's immediate argument, namely those Christians who had died, often in circumstances of obloquy and persecution, since receiving the Gospel.[1] Words of similar encouragement are given in a somewhat different context in 1 Thess. iv. 13-18.

(iii) *Patristic Evidence*

The Patristic evidence is in keeping with these conclusions. Though the idea of Christ preaching to the souls of the departed saints of the Old Dispensation occurs in the second half of the second century, neither of the two Petrine passages we are discussing was ever adduced in support of it. That is equally true of the other conception of the " harrowing of hell " which obtained in the second century, to the effect that our Lord descended into Hades after His crucifixion in order to triumph over the spirits of evil which had their abode there ; but this objection loses much of its weight, when we reflect that there were other passages in N.T., notably in St. Paul's Epistles (not to speak of O.T. prophecies), which lent themselves more readily to the argument. The true echo in the early centuries of St. Peter's teaching in iii. 18 ff. is to be found less in the writings of theologians than in the baptismal hymns and liturgies of the post-Apostolic Church ; and there the Petrine link between baptism and our Lord's *Descensus* is unmistakeable.

(iv) *The Witness of Catholic Liturgy and Literature*

We have seen that in the second century the idea of Christ's

[1] This point is urged with great weight by C. H. H. Wright, *Biblical Essays*, pp. 183 ff.

conquest of the powers of " death and hell " was closely allied with His liberation of the souls of the righteous whom they held in thrall ; and we may note how it was this combination of ideas rather than that of the conversion of the dead by Christ's preaching in Hades which left its mark on literature and liturgy in succeeding ages. In literature Dante and William Langland afford good examples. According to Dante, Christ's *Descensus* was into the first circle only of Hell, that Limbo where the only pain experienced was that of souls which always desired the vision of God but might not hope for it. His conception of the range of God's mercy was far narrower than Clement of Alexandria's, being limited to the patriarchs and worthies of Israel only ; but these Christ took away with Him after His *Descensus*. The event is narrated by Vergil in the 4th canto of the *Inferno*, in the passage beginning (ll. 52-4) :

> Io era nuovo in questo stato,
> quando ci vidi venire un possente
> con segno di vittoria coronato.

Langland in the closing sections of *Piers Plowman* [1] is much fuller, and in one matter goes beyond his contemporaries and appears almost as a universalist. There is the announcement by one of the friends of Christ's approach :

> Now I see where a soul · cometh hitherward sailing
> With glory and with great light   God it is, I wot well.

There is the breaking of hell's bars, and Christ's entrance, and His warning to Lucifer that his rule is doomed : the faithful are released, and Lucifer put in chains until the final Judgment. It is then that the full meaning of God's love will be revealed :

> My Righteousness and Right · shall rule all Hell,
> And give mercy to mankind · before me in Heaven.
> I were an unkind king · save I my kind help.

This looks like an intimation of universal salvation for all men, though not for the spirits of evil themselves.

The liturgical evidence [2] is very varied and widespread, ranging

Margin note: liturgy and literature

---

[1] I am much indebted for this summary to R. W. Chambers, *Man's Unconquerable Mind*, pp. 157 ff., and have also consulted Skeat's edition and Miss Hort's *Piers Plowman and Contemporary Religious Thought*.

[2] The evidence can be best studied in Cabrol and Leclercq, *Dictionnaire d'Archéologie Chrétienne et de Liturgie*, iv. pp. 682-93, in F. E. Brightman, *Liturgies Eastern and Western*, and in Karl Young, *The Drama of the Medieval Church*, i. pp. 112-77 ; and for the association of the Harrowing of Hell with the anthem known as the *Quem queritis ? ib.* p. 430. The *Depositio* was the hiding or burying of the Host or Cross (or both) in the Easter sepulchre, and the *Elevatio* its recovery in token of the Resurrection.

from the allusions in the *anaphorae* of the early liturgies and other prayers and hymns of the fourth and following centuries to the dramatic action of the Harrowing of Hell which in Germany, Italy and Switzerland, as well as in England and Ireland, formed part of the Paschal ceremonies of the *Depositio* and the *Elevatio*. The earliest allusion in an *anaphora* appears to be in the so-called " Clementine Liturgy ".[1] Here in the course of the narrative of redemption, Christ is said to have undergone the passion, " that He might loose from suffering and death those for whose sake He came, and that He might break the chains of the devil and deliver men from his wiles ".[2] This is no more than we have noted in some early baptismal rites and hymns, where the Harrowing of Hell is directed to the emancipation of *men* ; and the Eastern eucharistic rites do not seem to go beyond this. In Western rites, on the other hand, the idea of Christ's *Descensus* is the subject of rapid development ; and the purpose of the destruction of hell's bars and the overthrow of the power of the devil is that the souls of the *dead* may be released ; though it is always the righteous dead, the saints and the martyrs, who are thus set free, nor is there any suggestion of a conversion after death of the impenitent. " The Middle Ages ", says Dr. Coulton, " made even the New Testament into a fighting epic ",[3] and nowhere more so than in their treatment of this topic. A typical example is the following antiphon which occurs on a variety of occasions, and is much used in the Paschal plays which found their way into the services :

Cum rex gloriae Christus infernum debellaturus intraret, et chorus angelicus ante faciem eius portas principum tolli praeciperet, sanctorum populus, qui tenebatur in morte captivus, voce lacrimabili clamaverat : Advenisti desiderabilis, quem expectabamus in tenebris, ut educeres hac nocte vinculatos de claustris. Te nostra vocabant suspiria ; te larga requirebant tormenta ; tu factus es spes desperatis, magna consolatio in tormentis.

The influence of *The Gospel of Nicodemus* on this antiphon is evident, though it was perhaps distilled through a sermon by St. Augustine (*Sermo* clx. " De Pascha," ii.). Of the dramatic actions which were built around it we need say little, except to note how markedly they were attached to the *Elevatio* rather than the

---

[1] On the relationship of this to the " Apostolic Tradition " of St. Hippolytus cf. Gregory Dix, *The Apostolic Tradition*, p. lxxii.

[2] ἵνα πάθους λύσῃ καὶ θανάτου ἐξέλη-

ται τούτους δι' οὓς παρεγένετο καὶ ῥήξῃ τὰ δεσμὰ τοῦ διαβόλου καὶ ῥύσηται τοὺς ἀνθρώπους ἐκ τῆς ἀπάτης αὐτοῦ.

[3] *Five Centuries of Religion*, i. p. 62.

Depositio : the *Descensus*, that is to say, was thought of as the opening stage of Christ's triumph rather than as the concluding stage of His passion. If our interpretation of 1 Pet. iii. 18 f. is correct, that is also how St. Peter thought of it.

(v) *The Range of the Christian Hope in N.T.*

Many who cherish the Petrine passages as investing the article of the Apostles' Creed which speaks of our Lord's descent into hell with a peculiar tenderness and fulness of meaning will be reluctant to accept an interpretation which gives them a quite different signification. Yet we are not entitled on that ground to stretch St. Peter's statement to embrace what it did not contain, and what no Christian writer of the first two centuries (so far as our evidence goes) ever claimed that it did contain. The question was, no doubt, asked at an early date whether salvation was open to those who had never heard the Gospel, and indeed our Lord Himself forestalled it, so far as the saints of Hebrew story were concerned, in such utterances as those recorded in Mk. xii. 26, 27 and Matt. viii. 11, 12. The kingdom would not be complete until the faithful and martyrs of Israel (Heb. xi.) were gathered in.[1] The further enlargement of this hope, moreover, to include the great teachers of Greek and Roman antiquity such as Euripides and Plato and Cicero and Vergil, and the great statesmen such as Augustus, who had contributed to the *preparatio evangelica*, involved no major difficulty to minds which had been enlightened by Greek thought and had found a bridge between it and Judaism already to hand in the Wisdom literature, and saw in the Johannine doctrine of the indwelling *Logos* the theological foundation for such teaching. The question may also have been asked as to whether the benefits of Christ's redemption might be thought of as covering a still wider range, embracing not only the righteous of past ages but their impenitent sinners as well : though the evidence for this question as to a " second chance " is slender, if it exists at all, until we come to Origen, it was apparently not unknown to Rabbinism.[2] What we cannot say, however, if the conclusions hitherto reached are sound, is that to these questions the author of 1 Peter " gives the most charitable answer ".[3] It is not a question of doubting the charity of the Epistle, which indeed stands out on every page, but of whether

(v) The range of the Christian hope in N.T.

---

[1] Cf. Dodd, *The Parables of the Kingdom*, p. 55 (commenting on Matt. viii. 11) : " What has not yet happened but will happen, is that many who are not yet ' in the kingdom of God ', in

its earthly manifestation, will enjoy its ultimate fulfilment in a world beyond this ".

[2] Cf. above, p. 346 n. 2.

[3] Wand, *op. cit.* p. 112.

or not it alludes to these questions at all. And on that issue we feel bound to render a negative verdict.

Nevertheless, since these questions are still asked, we may be allowed to indicate, before passing to what St. Peter does teach, the answer which we believe the New Testament to give. It lies in germ, we suggest, in the *verba Christi* of Mk. xii., Matt. viii., Jn. v. discussed above. According to this teaching, the patriarchs, prophets, and martyrs of Israel were still living, because still in communion with the living God ; and they were waiting for the consummation of God's purpose in Christ, when they would take their places in His Kingdom. What was true of them was true also of a great multitude which no man could number, of those who left no memorial in human annals, but who lived by the same light of faith as the best of Israel's leaders. With these we must number also those outside the covenant of Israel who had responded to the Word of God in whatever form it encountered them, whether on the lips of a prophet (Matt. xii. 41) or in the wisdom of a king (Matt. xii. 42) or in the inmost promptings of a conscience which had opened itself to " the true light which lighteth every man that cometh into the world " (Jn. i. 9). Such obedience, inchoate as it was, was the beginning of repentance and would lead to salvation. And what was true then is true now ; there is no before and after in a revelation and a redemption which, while given in particular events of history, can only be fully seen *sub specie aeternitatis*. God's promise of salvation is universal to all who in this life have walked by such light as they have. That voice of Jesus which " all that are in the graves shall hear " (Jn. v. 28) will not strike upon *their* ears as something strange ; they will recognize it and welcome it ; and they will come forth to life eternal. But when we turn to those who have been wilfully blind to the light of conscience, whether they be Jew or Gentile, and " have done evil ", deliberately and without repentance, in this life, we have no clear word of hope in Holy Writ to encourage us, but rather many words of warning. What the " resurrection of judgment " means we cannot tell. There is little, indeed, in the New Testament to suggest a state of everlasting punishment, but much to indicate an ultimate destruction or dissolution of those who cannot enter into life : " conditional immortality " seems to be the doctrine most consonant with the teaching of Scripture.[1] Such a doctrine does not, perhaps,

---

[1] Cf. J. H. Leckie, *The World to Come and Final Destiny*, ch. iii. and " Review and Construction ", and R. G. Macintyre, *The Other Side of* Death, chs. xi.-xiv., for careful discussions of this doctrine, though both seem to me in error with regard to 1 Pet. iii. 18 ff. and iv. 6. A curious

rule out such a conception as Browning puts into the mouth of the Pope in *The Ring and the Book*, when he makes him speak of

> that dim, sequestered state
> Where God unmakes but to re-make the soul :

but however that may be, we cannot doubt that Scripture faces men with a very terrible alternative to its promises of salvation after death. With these promises and these warnings, the teaching of 1 Peter is fully in keeping, while it makes no significant addition to them. Belief in an intermediate state rests secure on Christ's teaching, and it is implied in 1 Pet. iv. 6 ; but for fuller elucidation of this state we are left to the inspired insight of the Church and to reverent conjecture rather than to any sure Word of God.

(vi) *The Relevance of 1 Pet. iii. 18 ff. to Modern Times*

The positive teaching of 1 Pet. iii. 18 ff., on the other hand, does not lose in deep and permanent significance because it is not concerned with the fate of the departed ; and this significance strikes home with peculiar force in an age which has seen religious persecution, war, and falsehood active on an unprecedented scale, and has felt the ravages of the powers of evil in every quarter of the world. St. Peter's statement that Christ, in the course of His passion and resurrection, made proclamation to these powers of evil — a statement which is in close accord with the teaching of St. Paul — speaks directly to our need and our condition, reminding us of the true nature of the struggle in which the Church is engaged. The form in which the doctrine is expressed is mythological, a form which none will despise who has read Plato or Milton ; indeed it is Miltonic rather than Platonic, the mythology of epic rather than of metaphysics.[1] In the Apostolic view we are considering, Christ's redemptive victory was the historical climax of an epic story which began with the Garden of Eden and closes with God's conquest of the serpent and his confederates ; and the epic called, as epic always has called since the days of Homer, for the setting and furniture of mythology : it is its proper ritual, that which makes it " solemn ". But the strangeness of

(marginal note:) (vi) The relevance of 1 Pet. iii. 18 ff. to modern times

version of the doctrine is found in Josephus, *B.J.* VI. i. 3, where the Emperor Titus, in order to fire the morale of his troops, is made to say that the souls of those who die in battle are received by the ether and placed among the stars, while those who are cowardly and afterwards die are dissolved to nothing. The doctrine of Christianity with regard to the state of the departed and its biblical foundations is well discussed in Dorner, *op. cit.* § 153, Engl. Tr. iv. pp. 401-14.

[1] Cf. C. S. Lewis, *A Preface to Paradise Lost*, pp. 12 ff. ; also the fine passage in Bridges, *The Testament of Beauty*, ii. ll. 576-639.

the form of the Apostolic teaching must not blind us to the truth of its content ; and of the existence and power of the diabolic in human life there is cogent evidence on every side. *Si monumentum requiris, circumspice.* And what St. Peter and St. Paul assert of these powers of evil, as their divine Master had asserted it before them, is that in Christ's death their end was sealed. It is true that Satan's power was not, and is not yet, broken by this defeat : the judgment on him was decreed, but not yet executed [1] : we do not yet see all things in subjection to Christ. Nor do we know the eventual issue of this decree, i.e. whether this subjection lies in the annihilation or in the reconciliation [2] of these powers of evil ; for St. Paul's teaching on the subject is ambiguous. But the note of " subordination " which St. Peter sounds here (iii. 22), as in his ethical teaching generally, points to the solution which belief in the moral ordering of the universe demands, namely that all things will be brought to a state of obedience and harmony beneath the will of God.[3]

(vii) *The Imitatio Christi*

(vii) The *imitatio Christi*

A second feature of St. Peter's teaching on our Lord's " descent into hell " which gives it a special appeal to the Church of to-day is his ethical application of it through the *imitatio Christi*. The victory which Christ won in the course of His passion and death was the victory of the dying life. From the standpoint of the doctrine of the Atonement, the doctrine of Christ's Descent into hell is the pictorial representation of the *utterness* of His victory over sin and death ; and the Swedish theologian, Dr. Aulèn, has shewn what good grounds there are for regarding this idea of victory as the central and classical element in Christian thought about the Cross. But St. Peter here is more explicit than St. Paul : the victory which Christ won was the victory of a principle of life by which the Church on earth must live. His allusion to the *Descensus* arises out of the fact of the Church's humiliation and persecution when he wrote ; and it issues in the practical injunction

---

[1] Cf. Fridrichsen, *op. cit.* p. 129.

[2] Milton ruled out any such possibility, e.g. in Satan's speech in *P.L.* iv. 94-104, especially

> For never can true reconcilement grow
> Where words of deadly hate have pierc'd so deep ;
> . . . therefore as far
> From granting he, as I from begging peace.

Cf. C. S. Lewis, *A Preface to Paradise Lost*, p. 102. Dodd, on the strength of Col. i. 20 and Eph. i. 10, believes that the reconciliation of these " *Discarnate Intelligences* " represents St. Paul's true mind on the subject. Cf. *The Epistle of Paul to the Romans*, pp. 184 f. For a curious example of the opposite view cf. the prayer of St. John in *Acta Johannis*, cxiv.

[3] Cf. J. H. Leckie, *op. cit.* p. 309.

to Christians to arm themselves with the same " counsel " (ἔννοια), the principle of the dying life, that was embodied in the Passion. The matter is discussed more fully in the Introduction.[1]

(viii) *Christian Baptism and Human Personality*

Finally, St. Peter's association of baptism with our Lord's subjection of the supernatural powers of evil is a proclamation of the worth and meaning of human personality.[2] From the very first this has been one of the cardinal principles of Christianity, as its opposition to current practices of the Graeco-Roman world such as abortion and infanticide, and its insistence on the proper treatment of slaves, made clear. To-day the depreciation of the worth of personality has other causes ; the " economic man " of the last century is giving place to the " mechanical man " of large-scale industry and the totalitarian State ; and a growing secularism throughout what once was Christendom has found itself powerless to stem the tide. To arrest this downward process, to make men once again the masters of their tools, and to restore their faith in the true nature and *wholeness* of man as made in the image of God, is one of the main tasks of Christianity to-day. Mechanical relationships or " necessity ", as Plato[3] called them, are a real fact of human life, but they are not the ultimate fact ; and of all the slanders[4] which the devil tempts man to believe few are more mischievous or more symptomatic of supernatural evil than the belief that they are. The sacrament of baptism, set in the context of Christ's overthrow of the powers of evil in His death and resurrection and ascension, is the rite by which Christianity disowns this distorted secular estimate of human personality, and asserts man's true origin, nature, and end — his true origin as the child of God, his true nature as a member of Christ, and his true end as an inheritor of the Kingdom of Heaven — and, in the very act of asserting this, proclaims also the universality of sin and the necessity of being redeemed from it.[5] One of the worst fruits of the Eucharistic

(viii) Christian baptism and human personality

---

[1] Cf. *supra*, pp. 97-101.
[2] Cf. V. A. Demant, *The Religious Prospect*, ch. ii., and p. 58, " Demonism is the effort to include Being in Becoming " ; L. Mumford, *Faith for Living*, pts. i. and iii. ; Walter Lippmann, *A Preface to Morals*.
[3] *Timaeus*, 47 E.
[4] For the devil's function as Accuser in the Bible cf. the article by Rev. R. O. P. Taylor in *The Expository*

Times, vol. liii. No. 3 (December 1941).
[5] Cf. H. W. Clark, *The Cross and Eternal Order*, p. 15, " In dealing with sin, God seeks to restore that ' wholeness ' of things, that perfect moral and spiritual structure of the universe, whereinto His relations with man enter as a most essential part, and which just at that most essential point has been broken through "

controversies which have vexed the Western Church in recent centuries has been their tendency to distract men's minds from the theology of baptism ; and it may be that we shall only recover a full sense of its significance when we have learnt more fully what the Churches in the mission field have to teach us. There, at any rate, the contrast between the Christian way of life and paganism stares the Christian as plainly in the face as it did in the Apostolic age ; and baptism, accordingly, which marks the decisive conversion from the old life to the new, is seen in all its pregnant meaning. For all who seek to restore a true and understanding faith in this sacrament we may surmise that the First Epistle of St. Peter will prove itself a source of unfailing illumination.

ESSAY II

CONTENTS

363

ESSAY II

On the Inter-relation of 1 Peter and other N.T. Epistles

Introductory

"Formgeschichte" and its Application to the Epistles

ALLUSION was made in the Introduction (II. 3) to certain sources underlying 1 Peter, and the reader was referred to this Essay for the evidence on which that view rested, since its detailed exposition would have been out of proportion in the Introduction itself. What is there written represents no more than a summary of the conclusions here reached; though it must be added that, even if these hypotheses are found to need correction, the parallels of thought and phrase which they are designed to account for constitute a significant volume of evidence, and one that is of great importance for the literary criticism of 1 Peter. An attempt is made here to set out the facts as fully and clearly as possible; and each group of them is followed by critical notes aimed at explaining both the parallels and the differences they present.

It will be well to note at the outset that our enquiry belongs to the type known as *Formgeschichte* rather than to that of the older synoptic studies; and the use of the *apparatus* of parallel columns must not be allowed to obscure the fact. *Formgeschichte* represents an attempt to understand the nature and history of the Forms in which the earliest Christian preaching and teaching were drawn up and transmitted. This attempt to give concreteness and particularity to the tradition, both oral and written, which lies behind the accepted literary sources of the Gospels, has been somewhat suspect in this country, despite the fact that St. Luke alludes in his Preface to the circulation of many such primitive accounts of the Gospel story; while in so standard a work as Bishop Westcott's *Introduction to the Study of the Gospels* the necessary place of " the oral Gospel " is fully recognized and discussed at length. Indeed, if anyone will read the first half of Chapter III of that work, he will find in it the best possible introduction to such a book as Dibelius' *From Tradi-*

tion to Gospel.[1] We note, for example, in both alike the same insistence on the missionary motive and the exigencies of preaching as the governing factor in the formation of the tradition ; the same insistence that " the Gospel was the substance and not the record of the life of Christ " ; the same view of the non-literary *genre* of document which would come from the Apostolic writers, granted that they were such men as they were. They differ, on the other hand, in their respective estimates of the operation of " mythological " tendencies in the early tradition.

While the formation of the Christian traditions was thus dictated by the missionary and propagandist interest — by the desire, that is to say, to make Christians or to edify Christians — and while the *sermon* type of tradition was therefore the most fundamental, there was none the less room for great variety of Form, owing to the various needs of different communities at different times and the various characters and tasks of those who were entrusted with teaching. Some Forms were what we should call " material for speeches ", suitable for open-air preaching ; others were intended for use in the weekly gatherings for worship, where the preacher's message could be reinforced by a familiar hymn or a reading from the prophets ; others, again, were of a paraenetic [2] character, adapted to the instruction of catechumens or the exhortation of the faithful in times of special stress or trial. The last two are of especial interest for our present purpose ; for it is reasonable to suppose that 1 Peter was meant to be read at worship in Asia Minor (and indeed it is not easy to see how otherwise any considerable number of Christians would ever have known it), and the element of ethical teaching or *paraenesis* bulks largely in its pages. Further, there is good ground for believing that collections of *verba Christi* were made at an early date, probably at Antioch, the mother-city of the Christian mission, and also that these collections were first made in the Greek tongue.[3] This, too, is of great importance for our purpose ; for we have seen how often *verba Christi* lie just below the surface of the text of this Epistle. A similar explanation

---

[1] This is the book on *Formge-schichte* which I have found most useful for my purpose in this Essay. But V. Taylor, *Formation of the Gospel Tradition*, and R. H. Lightfoot, *History and Interpretation in the Gospels*, describe the method with equal clarity. Cf. also F. H. Chase, *The Lord's Prayer in the Early Church*, pp. 8 ff., especially p. 10: " A most striking characteristic of this Epistle [St. James] is that it is built up of λόγια κυριακά. What is true of this Epistle is true in a less degree of other Apostolic Epistles."

[2] Cf. Dibelius, *op. cit.* p. xv: " Paraenetic: Hortatory, dealing with exhortations ".

[3] Dibelius, *op. cit.* pp. 240 ff.

may account for the much greater frequency with which we hear echoes of St. Matthew or Q in this Epistle than of St. Mark ; for Q and St. Matthew had the same practical interest as our author in *halakhah*, the tradition of how Christ's disciples should behave, whereas St. Mark is concerned rather with *haggada*, the tradition of what happened. Yet again, if we ask why it is that 1 Peter, despite his partiality for *verba Christi*, so often drives home a point by quoting from the Old Testament [1] when a word of the Lord would have seemed more telling, the answer is, no doubt, that the O.T. passage was already linked in Jewish tradition with the injunctions he was making, and was therefore more familiar to those Christians who had been accustomed to the synagogue. The practice was one way of applying Christ's principle that He had come " not to destroy, but to fulfil ".

The enquiry immediately before us agrees with *Formgeschichte* in the scientific assumptions with which it starts and in the analytical methods which it employs ; but it differs from it in the angle of approach. As applied to the Gospels, *Formgeschichte* begins with the finished documents and their acknowledged sources, and works downwards into the strata of underlying tradition represented by the Acts and the Epistles. Here, on the other hand, we begin on the level of these earlier strata, and are in fact driving a side-shaft into the shaft already sunk. The materials we shall be dealing with are of the same type as those which *Formgeschichte* handles, though we approach them by a different road, driving not vertically downwards but horizontally. It is surprising that so little work of this kind seems to have been done. Quite recently Bishop Carrington of Quebec has attempted to fill the gap with his illuminating monograph, *The Primitive Christian Catechism*, and still more recently Dr. A. M. Hunter's *Paul and his Predecessors* has much that is relevant to the issue. But apart from these two books, I know of no systematic attempt to explore this field since the publication of Alfred Seeberg's *Der Katechismus der Ur-Christenheit* — a work of which Dibelius speaks with great respect — in 1903.[2] What we shall be dealing with here is not the filiation of materials which ended in the Gospels as the ripe fruit of the genealogical tree, but

---

[1] Cf. 1 Pet. v. 5, quoting Prov. iii. 34, rather than, e.g., Matt. xxiii. 12, Lk. xiv. 11. Also the quotation of Lev. xx. 7 (xi. 44) in 1 Pet. i. 16, where Windisch says that a disciple of Jesus would have quoted Matt. v. 48.

[2] The distinction between " la catéchèse " and " la gnose " which Loisy makes so much of in *Les Origines du N.T.*, especially chs. viii. and ix., though superficially relevant, is based on different assumptions and developed along different lines.

rather a number of collateral relationships which present themselves to view before — or largely before — that point is reached. Moreover, these relationships bear closely upon the evidence which has been held to indicate direct literary dependence of 1 Peter upon other Epistles such as Romans, Ephesians, and James ; for they include that evidence and far more besides, and shew that we have to account for a much larger and more complicated series of data than any theories of direct dependence are sufficient in themselves to explain.

A further factor which differentiates our present enquiry from *Formgeschichte* is the part played by Silvanus in the evidence we shall be examining. The materials isolated by *Formgeschichte* are normally anonymous ; as in the mission field to-day, they were frequently put together by prophets or teachers acting in groups ; and though it is not unlikely that some of those whose names are known to us from the Acts and the Epistles took the lead in the shaping of these Forms, we cannot normally associate them with particular names. In the case of 1 Peter and the Thessalonian Epistles, however, we are on different ground, for the hand of Silvanus is common to them all, and he is a man well known to us. I had already noted the marked affinities of thought and phrase between these three documents — affinities which seem to have escaped serious attention hitherto — and had tabulated the majority of the parallels between them which will be found in the Tables that follow, before Bishop Carrington's book came into my hands. The parallels were sufficient in themselves to indicate mutual relationship and to point to the work of Silvanus as at least a contributory cause ; and the effect of Dr. Carrington's analysis was to add to that cause others of equal relevance. It was possible, for instance, that Silvanus' association with the three Epistles was twofold or threefold, in that he may have been connected in the first place with the materials which he used as well as with the finished work which bore the Apostolic names. Further, just as these materials were of different character, so he may have been connected with them in different ways — here, for example, being a joint author with others, there being the sole or at least the principal author. It was in such ways that he would have proved that " reliability " of which St. Peter speaks in v. 12.

The discussion that follows, with the accompanying Tables, will fall into the following main Parts :

I. The *first* will cover those series of parallels which indicate literary connexion between 1 and 2 Thessalonians and 1 Peter, and also in varying degrees the influence of Silvanus (Tables I, II, III). They are not exhaustive ; but the remainder will be more conveniently studied in a later Part, cf. Part III, Table XIV.

II. The *second* will cover interrelationships between a large number of the Epistles, pointing to the use of common catechetical or paraenetic materials. I propose to avail myself largely here of Dr. Carrington's *theses*, and to see how far they illuminate, or are illuminated by, other evidence which fell outside his purview. From the standpoint of the study of 1 Peter, we have to deal with two sets of parallels ; the first, that denoted by the Epistles mentioned above together with Acts xv. ; the second, that represented in Romans, Colossians, Ephesians, James, and 1 Peter.[1] We need to explain, if we can, how it is that 1 Peter appears in both lists, though otherwise they are distinct in subject and separated chronologically by about ten years ; to account for variations from the underlying pattern, where they occur ; and to see whether these variations themselves shew common features suggestive of sources independent of the pattern (Tables IV-XIII).

III. In the *third* Part we shall give special consideration to the two concluding sections of Dr. Carrington's pattern, and give reasons for supposing that one of them at least belonged to a Form of Persecution-*tōrah* which is discernible in many Epistles (Table XIV).

IV. The *fourth* Part will be devoted to a summary of the evidence, including that of Hebrews hitherto postponed, and to an attempt to estimate its bearing on the problem of the direct dependence of 1 Peter on other Epistles, or *vice versa*.

I

The Apostolic Decree, 1 and 2 Thessalonians, and 1 Peter

(1) traces of first baptismal form : influence of silvanus

Parallels traceable between Acts xv., 1 and 2 Thessalonians, and 1 Peter have a special interest for us, because, as we have seen, Silvanus was associated with them all. Dr. Carrington points out that the Law of Holiness (Lev. xvii.–xxvi., especially xvii.–xix.) laid down the rules — baptism, circumcision, and sacrifice — to be

---

[1] Hebrews also provides parallels with 1 Peter, and with 1 and 2 Thessalonians, but they will be more conveniently discussed at a later stage.

TABLE I

TRACES OF FIRST BAPTISMAL CATECHISM—B1—BASED ON A CHRISTIAN HOLINESS CODE

I Thess.	I Peter	Other N.T. Passages	O.T.
iv. 1. παρελάβετε παρ' ἡμῶν τὸ πῶς δεῖ ὑμᾶς περιπατεῖν καὶ ἀρέσκειν θεῷ.	i. 15. αὐτοὶ ἅγιοι ἐν πάσῃ ἀναστροφῇ γενήθητε . .		Lev. xix. 2. ἅγιοι ἔσεσθε, ὅτι ἐγὼ ἅγιος.
3. τοῦτο γάρ ἐστι θέλημα τοῦ θεοῦ, ὁ ἁγιασμὸς ὑμῶν, ἀπέχεσθαι ὑμᾶς ἀπὸ τῆς πορνείας.	i. 16. διότι γέγραπται, Ἅγιοι ἔσοθε, ὅτι ἐγὼ ἅγιος. ii. 11. ἀπέχεσθαι τῶν σαρκικῶν ἐπιθυμῶν	Acts xv. 29. ἀπέχεσθαι εἰδωλοθύτων καὶ αἵματος [καὶ πνικτῶν] καὶ πορνείας. Col. iii. 5-7. νεκρώσατε οὖν τὰ μέλη τὰ ἐπὶ τῆς γῆς, πορνείαν, ἀκαθαρσίαν,	Is. lii. 11. ἐξέλθατε ἐκεῖθεν, καὶ ἀκαθάρτου μὴ ἅπτεσθε, . . . ἀφορίσθητε, οἱ φέροντες τὰ σκεύη κυρίου. cf. Lev. xxii. 2.
cf. v. 22. ἀπὸ παντὸς εἴδους πονηροῦ ἀπέχεσθε.		πάθος, ἐπιθυμίαν κακήν, καὶ τὴν πλεονεξίαν, ἥτις ἐστιν εἰδωλολατρεία . .	
4. εἰδέναι ἕκαστον ὑμῶν τὸ ἑαυτοῦ σκεῦος κτᾶσθαι ἐν ἁγιασμῷ καὶ τιμῇ, cf. 2 Thess. ii. 13. ἐν ἁγιασμῷ πνεύματος.	i. 2. ἐν ἁγιασμῷ πνεύματος	ἐν οἷς καὶ ὑμεῖς περιεπατήσατέ ποτε, ὅτε ἐζῆτε ἐν τούτοις. cf. Eph. iv. 17-19, I Cor. v. 9, 10, vi. 9, 10.	
5. μὴ ἐν πάθει ἐπιθυμίας, καθάπερ καὶ τὰ ἔθνη τὰ μὴ εἰδότα τὸν θεόν·	i. 14. μὴ συνσχηματιζόμενοι ταῖς πρότερον ἐν τῇ ἀγνοίᾳ ὑμῶν ἐπιθυμίαις· ii. 11. cf. supra.	Rom. xii. 2. μὴ συνσχηματίζεσθε τῷ αἰῶνι τούτῳ. Eph. iv. 17-19. . . . ἅγνοιαν . . . ἀκαθαρσίας . . . ἐν πλεονεξίᾳ [Col. iii. 5-7].	
6. τὸ μὴ ὑπερβαίνειν καὶ πλεονεκτεῖν ἐν τῷ πράγματι τὸν ἀδελφὸν αὐτοῦ· διότι ἔκδικος κύριος περὶ πάντων τούτων, καθὼς καὶ προείπαμεν ὑμῖν καὶ διεμαρτυράμεθα.	iv. 2. εἰς τὸ μηκέτι ἀνθρώπων ἐπιθυμίας . . . βιῶσαι . . . . iii. 10-12.	I Cor. v. 9, 10 [cf. supra]. I Cor. vi. 9, 10. Eph. v. 5. τοῦτο γὰρ ἴστε γινώσκοντες, ὅτι πᾶς πόρνος ἢ ἀκάθαρτος ἢ πλεονέκτης, ὅ ἐστιν εἰδωλολάτρης, οὐκ ἔχει κληρονομίαν κτλ. Rom. xii. 19 [cf. Table VIII A].	Ps. xxxiv. 14-16. ib. 17. πρόσωπον δὲ κυρίου ἐπὶ ποιοῦντας κακά, τοῦ ἐξολεθρεῦσαι ἐκ γῆς τὸ μνημόσυνον αὐτῶν. Ps. xv. passim, esp. 4. ὁ ὀμνύων τῷ πλησίον αὐτοῦ καὶ οὐκ ἀθετῶν· 5. τὸ ἀργύριον αὐτοῦ οὐκ ἔδωκεν ἐπὶ τόκῳ, καὶ δῶρα ἐπ' ἀθῴοις οὐκ ἔλαβεν.
7. οὐ γὰρ ἐκάλεσεν ἡμᾶς ὁ θεὸς ἐπὶ ἀκαθαρσίᾳ, ἀλλ' ἐν ἁγιασμῷ.	i. 15. κατὰ τὸν καλέσαντα ὑμᾶς ἅγιον, καί, κτλ.		

8. τοιγαροῦν ὁ ἀθετῶν οὐκ ἄνθρω-πον ἀθετεῖ, ἀλλὰ τὸν θεὸν τὸν διδόντα τὸ πνεῦμα αὐτοῦ τὸ ἅγιον εἰς ὑμᾶς.	i. 13, ἐλπίσατε ἐπὶ τὴν φερομένην ὑμῖν χάριν	1 Cor. iii. 16, 17. Acts xv. 29 [D text]. φερόμενοι ἐν ἁγίῳ πνεύματι.	
9. περὶ δὲ τῆς φιλαδελφίας . . . ὑμεῖς θεοδίδακτοί ἐστε εἰς τὸ ἀγαπᾶν ἀλλήλους.	i. 22. τὰς ψυχὰς ὑμῶν ἡγνικότες . . . εἰς φιλαδελφίαν ἀνυπόκριτον ἐκ καρδίας ἀλλήλους ἀγαπήσατε . . .	Matt. xxii. 39 [v. 43 ff.] Gal. v. 14 Rom. xiii. 9, xii. 9 Jas. ii. 8 [cf. Table VIII A.]	Lev. xix. 18. ἀγαπήσεις τὸν πλη-σίον σου ὡς σεαυτόν· ἐγώ εἰμι κύριος.
11. παρακαλοῦμεν δὲ ὑμᾶς . . . φιλο-τιμεῖσθαι ἡσυχάζειν, καὶ πράσσειν τὰ ἴδια .	iv. 15. μὴ γάρ τις ὑμῶν πασχέτω . . . ὡς ἀλλοτριοεπίσκοπος·	Jas. iii. 13. δειξάτω ἐκ τῆς καλῆς ἀναστροφῆς τὰ ἔργα αὐτοῦ ἐν πραΰτητι σοφίας.	
12. ἵνα περιπατῆτε εὐσχημόνως πρὸς τοὺς ἔξω cf. 2 Thess. i. 12. ὅπως ἐνδοξασθῇ τὸ ὄνομα τοῦ κυρίου ἡμῶν Ἰησοῦ Χρι-στοῦ ἐν ὑμῖν, καὶ ὑμεῖς ἐν αὐτῷ, κατὰ τὴν χάριν τοῦ θεοῦ ἡμῶν καὶ κυρίου Ἰησοῦ Χριστοῦ.	ii. 12. τὴν ἀναστροφὴν ὑμῶν ἐν τοῖς ἔθνεσιν ἔχοντες καλήν, ἵνα, ἐν ᾧ κατα-λαλοῦσιν ὑμῶν ὡς κακοποιῶν, ἐκ τῶν καλῶν ἔργων ἐποπτεύοντες δοξάσωσι τὸν θεὸν ἐν ἡμέρᾳ ἐπισκοπῆς [idea echoed in iii. 1, 2, 16 ; and cf. iv. 14, where some MSS. add κατὰ μὲν αὐτοὺς βλασφημεῖται, κατὰ δὲ ὑμᾶς δοξά-ζεται].	Rom. xiii. 13. εὐσχημόνως περιπα-τήσωμεν . . . Col. iv. 5. ἐν σοφίᾳ περιπατεῖτε πρὸς τοὺς ἔξω. Matt. v. 16. οὕτω λαμψάτω τὸ φῶς ὑμῶν ἔμπροσθεν τῶν ἀνθρώπων, ὅπως ἴδωσιν ὑμῶν τὰ καλὰ ἔργα, καὶ δο-ξάσωσι τὸν πατέρα ὑμῶν τὸν ἐν τοῖς οὐρανοῖς.	
1 Thess. v. 15. ὁρᾶτε μή τις κακὸν ἀντὶ κακοῦ ἀποδῷ· ἀλλὰ πάντοτε τὸ ἀγαθὸν διώκετε εἰς ἀλλήλους καὶ εἰς πάντας.	iii. 9. μὴ ἀποδιδόντες κακὸν ἀντὶ κακοῦ . . . iii. 10, 11. ὁ γὰρ θέλων ζωὴν ἀγαπᾶν . . . ποιησάτω ἀγαθόν· ζητησάτω εἰ-ρήνην καὶ διωξάτω αὐτήν.	Rom. xii. 17. μηδενὶ κακὸν ἀντὶ κα-κοῦ ἀποδιδόντες·	Ps. xxxiv. 13-15.

1 Thess. iv. 1, 1 Pet. i. 15. ἀναστροφή is the Greek for *halakhah*, the Jewish word for "behaviour", and is the substantive corresponding to the verb περιπατεῖν. It is very rare in LXX, but is good Greek, e.g. Polybius, Diogenes Laertius. The "warning" and "emphatic teaching" referred to in 1 Thess. iv. 6 suggest that the ethical teaching given at Thessalonica had had an ethical colouring, as in Ps. xv. as 1 Pet. iii. 10 ff. recalls Ps. xxxiv. 1 Thess. iv. 8 shews how the ethical teaching of Ps. xv. became fused with the idea of the Church as a neo-Levitical community ; cf. 1 Cor. iii. 16, 17, vi. 19.

In 1 Thess. iv. 9 commentators take θεοδίδακτοι as "taught by conscience". But is it not an allusion to the word of God in Lev. xix. 18?

followed in the initiation of a proselyte, and that the direct initiation of Gentiles into the Christian Church was bound to assimilate itself to proselyte baptism. What the Apostolic decree did, in effect, was to maintain the first of the three Jewish ordinances, and to substitute for the other two the duty of abstention from the three major sins — idolatry, murder, and fornication — forbidden in the Holiness Code.[1] And we must remember that, while all three prohibitions would be needed amongst Gentile converts in their literal sense, they would also be interpreted in the wider meaning given them by our Lord in the Sermon on the Mount.

Commentary. — Different readers will interpret the parallels in Table I differently, but it is difficult to think that they are due simply to coincidence. Nor do they suggest that 1 Peter is dependent on 1 Thessalonians, for then the parallels would be closer. On the other hand, the substantial identity of the ideas and the extent to which they appear in near proximity in each Epistle, and in conjunction with Lev. xix. 2 and 18, is noticeable ; and these facts, when combined with variation of phrase, suggest that both are dependent on a common substratum. Such an underlying pattern would tend to stick in the mind and come to the surface in somewhat different forms in the two Epistles ; but the author would know, in both cases, that he was using ideas and words that were familiar to his readers, and already charged with emotion for them, from their previous instruction. We may note especially the following points :

(i) Certain keywords stand out. On the negative side we have ἀπέχεσθαι (Acts xv. 20, 29) ; and it is significant that the only other comparable uses of this word in N.T. are in 1 Thess. iv. 3, v. 22, written within a few months of the Apostolic decree, and in 1 Pet. ii. 11. Following Dr. Carrington's usage elsewhere, we shall speak of clauses containing this keyword as *Abstinentes* clauses. The sins to be renounced, moreover, are described as " lusts " (ἐπιθυμίαι) in 1 Thess. iv. 5 and 1 Pet. i. 14 (iv. 2) where they are said

---

[1] I think that Lake's view in *The Earlier Epistles of St. Paul* is right, and that the decree was a three-clause ethical precept. There is evidence that αἷμα can mean murder, and from that it is a short step to any act of violence. In the *Zadokite Fragment*, vi. 11, we find a triad comprising idolatry, covetousness or wealth gained by wickedness, and fornication ; and this may explain how in 1 Cor. v. we find covetousness in place of murder among the major sins to be avoided. For later Jewish ideas on the conditions on which Gentiles might be admitted, without circumcision, to the privileges of proselytes, cf. the article entitled " Noachian Precepts " in Hastings, *ERE*, vol. ix. There is something here closely akin to the " Natural Law " of Cicero, the Stoics, and Christian theology.

to spring from the heathen's ignorance of God (cf. Lev. xviii. 3) ;
and they are particularized as consisting above all in πορνεία
(1 Thess. iv. 3, 1 Cor. v. 9) or ἀκαθαρσία (1 Thess. iv. 7, Eph. iv. 19,
v. 5)—passages which are paralleled in idea in 1 Pet. ii. 11, iv. 3, 4—
and πλεονεξία (1 Thess. iv. 6, Eph. v. 5). In view of the separation
from the world involved in the Levitical idea of holiness (cf. Is. lii.
11), it is possible that the injunction not to be conformed (μὴ συσχη-
ματίζεσθαι) to the world's ways was also among the keywords of this
pattern of teaching.[1] On the positive side, we have the emphatic call
to holiness in 1 Thess. iv. 7 and 1 Pet. i. 15 ff. (the latter being hung
upon a direct quotation from Lev. xix.), and the emphasis laid in
1 Thess. iv. 9 and 1 Pet. i. 22, ii. 17, iii. 8, iv. 8 on brotherly love (cf.
Lev. xix. 18b, quoted by our Lord Matt. v. 43, xxii. 39). Likewise,
I suspect that the maxim about " not rendering evil for evil " in
1 Thess. v. 15, Rom. xii. 17, 1 Pet. iii. 9, whether or not it was, as
Lightfoot supposed, an actual *verbum Christi* which our Gospels
have omitted to record, was part of the primitive paraenetic
pattern ; for it is a fair paraphrase of Lev. xix. 18.

(ii) The idea of the importance of remembering the impression
made by Christian conduct on outsiders (πρὸς τοὺς ἔξω in 1 Thess.
iv. 12, Col. iv. 5, ἐν τοῖς ἔθνεσιν in 1 Pet. ii. 12) may well have
belonged to the primitive pattern (cf. Is. lxvi. 5) ; but the developed
idea of the glorification of God by this means (2 Thess. i. 12, 1 Pet.
i. 7, ii. 12 (iv. 14)), which is not easily paralleled elsewhere in the
Epistles, is perhaps Silvanus' own interpretation of the *verbum
Christi* in Matt. v. 16. Similarly, and with greater confidence,
I should assign to his hand the command πράσσειν τὰ ἴδια in
1 Thess. iv. 11 and its correlative warning against being an ἀλλοτριο-
επίσκοπος in 1 Pet. iv. 15.

(iii) 1 Thess. iv. 4-8 recalls Ps. xv. so often as to point to the use
of that Psalm in the preparation of the primitive Christian Holiness
Code ; and there are echoes of it in 1 Peter, which however reflects
Ps. xxxiv. much more nearly. ὁ ἀθετῶν in 1 Thess. iv. 8 is particularly significant. Commentators usually take it as governing an
implied object, " this calling ". But LS translate " *set aside,
disregard* a treaty, oath, promise, law " ; and this is exactly the
sense it has in Ps. xv. 4, which may thus have prompted the use of
the word. In LXX the word is frequently used intransitively in the
sense of " rebel " or " transgress " or " deal treacherously with ".

---

[1] Some word composed from σχῆμα
at any rate is rendered probable by the
occurrence of εὐσχημόνως in 1 Thess.
iv. 12 and Rom. xiii. 13, and by the
curious εἴδους πονηροῦ in 1 Thess.
v. 22. Cf. Dr. Daube's Note, p. 487.

May not the object to be understood here be the Law of Holiness which had been republished by the Apostolic decree, and which provided the principles on which the new Christian fellowship, with its prohibition of ἀκαθαρσία and πλεονεξία, now rested ? For it is clear that 1 Thess. iv. 8 is dealing not with conduct *in vacuo*, but with conduct appropriate to God's spiritual community. We have a glimpse of Christian ethics in process of adjustment to the priestly idea of the Church, which is fully expressed in 1 Peter. On the other hand, Psalm xxxiv., which is much used in 1 Peter and to some extent in Rom. xii. (see below, pp. 412 ff., and Table VIII A), leaves no certain trace in 1 Thessalonians, unless the warning in iv. 6 is dependent on Ps. xxxiv. 17 : a more probable source is Deut. xxxii. 35 (cf. Lev. xix. 18, Is. lix. 16 ff.)

(iv) The evidence we have been considering points to a con- ception of the Church as a " neo-Levitical " or priestly community ; and that such a conception underlies other passages in 1 Peter also will be clear in the sequel. It is particularly noticeable, for example, in ii. 1-10, which we have discussed in Add. Notes E, F, G, H (pp. 268-98), and which appears to be based on a very early Christian hymn ; and we shall observe other examples as we proceed. Meanwhile we may note that such a conception would have been congenial to what we know of St. Peter's mind from the records in Acts of his conversion ; and it would clearly have been a most valuable idea for propaganda purposes in circles where Jewish suspicions needed to be allayed. It reflected, in short, the spirit and outlook of the Apostolic decree.

Summary. — A comparison of 1 and 2 Thessalonians with 1 Peter and with certain other Epistles in the light of Acts xv. 29 points to a common catechetical pattern current in the Church, of which the keywords were ἀπέχεσθαι (*Abstinentes*) ; ἐπιθυμίαι, especially ἀκαθαρσία and πλεονεξία, which characterized the ἄγνοια of the Gentile world ; the Christian call to be holy (ἅγιος, ἁγιασμός, ἁγνίζειν) ; and the duty of ἀγάπη or φιλαδελφία as its central and indispensable expression. Abstinence from lust and avarice, and holiness embodying itself in benevolence towards fellow Christians and towards all men — these are the twin pillars of this primitive Christian formula. Its lineaments are clear enough to justify us in regarding it, with Dr. Carrington, as the nucleus of a baptismal catechism ; and this conclusion will be reinforced as we proceed. For convenience' sake I propose to denote this first baptismal Form by the symbol B[1].

So far as Silvanus is concerned, there seems no means of deciding whether he played a part in the original composition of the Form, which probably originated from the group of prophets and teachers at Antioch, or whether he used a version of it which he himself had edited and amplified. But one hypothesis or the other is rendered probable by the evidence.

(2) FURTHER CATECHETICAL MATERIAL : THE CHILDREN OF LIGHT (*FILII LUCIS*)

I pass next to a series of parallels between 1 Peter, 1 Thessalonians, and other Pauline Epistles, which present a number of somewhat complicated problems. The similarities of thought and phrase are most easily explained, I believe, by reference to an underlying pattern or patterns which the Apostolic writers have used; but the fact that some of the material appears in developed forms and in other contexts elsewhere in the Epistles makes special examination of them necessary. In particular, they raise the question whether we should assign to the first baptismal Form (B¹), or to some other primitive source, the eschatological teaching and ethics and the *motif* of darkness and light which meet us in 1 Thess. v. 1-8 and their parallels in 1 Peter and elsewhere. The evidence is set out in Table II (see pp. 376-8); and the following points may be observed :

(i) Reference is made in the first three verses to eschatological teaching already well known in the Church. This teaching appears here almost as a string of tags drawn from another source; and we shall return to the matter in connexion with Table XIV below. Here it must suffice to say that the material in itself admitted of being used in more than one way. In the context before us the eschatology is introduced not so much for its own sake as because it provides a powerful motive for conduct befitting the baptized : the ethical interest predominates and uses the eschatology for its own ends. In the context we shall consider later, on the other hand, the eschatology is introduced as part of a pattern of belief which enables the Christians to be stedfast in persecution. It is noteworthy, too, that in the parallels before us we have only to deal with 1 Thessalonians, which was probably addressed to a Gentile church; it is in 2 Thessalonians, addressed to a Jewish church, that the more full and pronounced eschatology occurs; and we may surmise that in the persecution at Thessalonica, which was fomented by the Jewish leaders, it was the Jewish Christians who were its chief victims. Moreover, the absence of echoes of the Law

Cf. Table XIV

TABLE II

FURTHER CATECHETICAL MATERIAL: THE CHILDREN OF LIGHT (*FILII LUCIS*)

1 Thess. v. 1–9	1 Peter	Acts, Cor., Rom.	Phil., Col., Eph., etc.	Verba Christi	O.T.
v. 1. περὶ δὲ τῶν χρόνων καὶ τῶν καιρῶν, ἀδελφοί, οὐ χρείαν ἔχετε ὑμῖν γράφεσθαι.	i. 11. προφῆται ... ἐρευνῶντες εἰς τίνα ἢ ποῖον καιρὸν ἐδήλου κτλ.	Acts i. 7. οὐχ ὑμῶν ἐστι γνῶναι χρόνους ἢ καιροὺς οὓς ὁ πατὴρ ἔθετο ἐν τῇ ἰδίᾳ ἐξουσίᾳ.		Mk. xiii. 32*. περὶ δὲ τῆς ἡμέρας ἐκείνης ἢ τῆς ὥρας οὐδεὶς οἶδεν ...	Amos v. 18. τί αὕτη ὑμῖν ἡ ἡμέρα τοῦ κυρίου; καὶ αὕτη ἐστὶν σκότος καὶ οὐ φῶς.
ib. 2. αὐτοὶ γὰρ ἀκριβῶς οἴδατε ὅτι ἡμέρα κυρίου ὡς κλέπτης ἐν νυκτὶ οὕτως ἔρχεται.	ii. 12. ἐν ἡμέρᾳ ἐπισκοπῆς		2 Pet. iii. 10. ἥξει δὲ ἡμέρα κυρίου ὡς κλέπτης ...	Lk. xii. 39*. τοῦτο δὲ γινώσκετε ὅτι εἰ ᾔδει ὁ οἰκοδεσπότης ποίᾳ ὥρᾳ ὁ κλέπτης ἔρχεται, ἐγρηγόρησεν ἂν, κτλ. cf. Matt. xxiv. 43*.	Ezek. xiii. 10. ... λέγοντες, Εἰρήνη, καὶ οὐκ ἦν εἰρήνη. Mal. iii. 1. καὶ ἐξέφνης ἥξει εἰς τὸν ναὸν ἑαυτοῦ κύριος ...
ib. 3. ὅταν λέγωσιν, Εἰρήνη καὶ ἀσφάλεια, τότε αἰφνίδιος αὐτοῖς ἐφίσταται ὄλεθρος, ὥσπερ ἡ ὠδὶν τῇ ἐν γαστρὶ ἐχούσῃ, καὶ οὐ μὴ ἐκφύγωσιν.			Rev. xvi. 15. Ἰδού, ἔρχομαι ὡς κλέπτης. μακάριος ὁ γρηγορῶν, κτλ.	Lk. xxi. 34*. προσέχετε δὲ ἑαυτοῖς, μήποτε ... αἰφνίδιος ἐφ᾽ ὑμᾶς ἐπιστῇ ἡ ἡμέρα ἐκείνη. Mk. xiii. 8 [Matt. xxiv. 19]. ἀρχὴ ὠδίνων ταῦτα. cf. Jn. xvi. 21 f.	Is. xiii. 6–9. ἐγγὺς γὰρ ἡμέρα κυρίου ... παραχθήσονται οἱ πρέσβεις, καὶ ὠδῖνες αὐτοὺς ἕξουσιν ὡς γυναικὸς τικτούσης ... ἰδοὺ γὰρ ἡμέρα κυρίου ἔρχεται.

* An asterisk denotes passages which were probably in Q.

v. 4. ὑμεῖς δέ, ἀδελφοί, οὐκ ἐστὲ ἐν σκότει, ἵνα ἡ ἡμέρα ὑμᾶς ὡς κλέπτης καταλάβῃ.	ii. 9. τοῦ ἐκ σκότους ὑμᾶς καλέσαντος εἰς τὸ θαυμαστὸν αὐτοῦ φῶς.	Acts xxvi. 18. τοῦ ἐπιστρέψαι ἀπὸ σκότους εἰς φῶς... Rom. xiii. 11. καὶ τοῦτο, εἰδότες τὸν καιρόν, ὅτι ὥρα ἤδη ὑμᾶς ἐξ ὕπνου ἐγερθῆναι...	Phil. ii 15. ἐν οἷς φαίνεσθε ὡς φωστῆρες ἐν κόσμῳ... Col. i. 13. ὃς ἐρρύσατο ἡμᾶς ἐκ τῆς ἐξουσίας τοῦ σκότους...	Matt. v. 14. ὑμεῖς ἐστε τὸ φῶς τοῦ κόσμου... 16. οὕτω λαμψάτω τὸ φῶς ὑμῶν κτλ.	Is. ix. 2. ὁ λαὸς ὁ πορευόμενος ἐν σκότει, ἴδετε φῶς μέγα... [cited in Matt. iv. 16].
ib. 5. πάντες γὰρ ὑμεῖς υἱοὶ φωτός ἐστε καὶ υἱοὶ ἡμέρας· οὐκ ἐσμὲν νυκτὸς οὐδὲ σκότους.	i. 14. ὡς τέκνα ὑπακοῆς.			Lk. xvi. 8. οἱ υἱοὶ τοῦ αἰῶνος τούτου φρονιμώτεροι ὑπὲρ τοὺς υἱοὺς φωτός...	
			Heb. vi. 4. τοὺς ἅπαξ φωτισθέντας, γευσαμένους τε τῆς δωρεᾶς...	Lk. xi. 35, 36. σκόπει οὖν μὴ τὸ φῶς τὸ ἐν σοὶ σκότος ἐστίν. εἰ οὖν τὸ σῶμά σου ὅλον φωτεινόν...ἔσται φωτεινὸν ὅλον κτλ.	Prov. iv. 18, 19. αἱ δὲ ὁδοὶ τῶν δικαίων ὁμοίως φωτὶ λάμπουσιν, προπορεύονται καὶ φωτίζουσιν ἕως κατορθώσῃ ἡ ἡμέρα. αἱ δὲ ὁδοὶ τῶν ἀσεβῶν σκοτειναί, οὐκ οἴδασιν πῶς προσκόπτουσιν.
	iv. 7. πάντων δὲ τὸ τέλος ἤγγικεν.	ib. 12. ἡ νὺξ προέκοψεν, ἡ δὲ ἡμέρα ἤγγικεν. ἀποθώμεθα οὖν τὰ ἔργα τοῦ σκότους, ἐνδυσώμεθα δὲ τὰ ὅπλα τοῦ φωτός.	Eph. v. 8. ἦτε γάρ ποτε σκότος, νῦν δὲ φῶς ἐν κυρίῳ· ὡς τέκνα φωτὸς περιπατεῖτε. ib. 14. διὸ λέγει, Ἔγειρε, ὁ καθεύδων, καὶ ἀνάστα ἐκ τῶν νεκρῶν καὶ ἐπιφαύσει σοι ὁ Χριστός.	Jn. viii. 12. ὁ ἀκολουθῶν ἐμοὶ οὐ μὴ περιπατήσῃ ἐν τῇ σκοτίᾳ, ἀλλ᾽ ἕξει τὸ φῶς τῆς ζωῆς. ib. xii. 36. ... πιστεύετε εἰς τὸ φῶς, ἵνα υἱοὶ φωτὸς γένησθε.	
ib. 6. ἄρα οὖν μὴ καθεύδωμεν ὡς οἱ λοιποί, ἀλλὰ γρηγορῶμεν καὶ νήφωμεν.	iv. 7. σωφρονήσατε οὖν καὶ νήψατε εἰς προσευχάς. v. 8. νήψατε, γρηγορήσατε.	Rom. xii. 12. τῇ προσευχῇ προσκαρτεροῦντες... I Cor. xvi. 13. γρηγορεῖτε, στήκετε ἐν τῇ πίστει...	Jas. v. 8. ...ἡ παρουσία τοῦ κυρίου ἤγγικε. Col. iv. 2. τῇ προσευχῇ προσκαρτερεῖτε, γρηγοροῦντες ἐν αὐτῇ ἐν εὐχαριστίᾳ. Rev. iii. 2. γίνου γρηγορῶν...	Lk. xxi. 36*. ἀγρυπνεῖτε δὲ ἐν παντὶ καιρῷ δεόμενοι ἵνα κατισχύσητε ἐκφυγεῖν ταῦτα πάντα τὰ μέλλοντα γίνεσθαι, καὶ σταθῆναι ἔμπροσθεν τοῦ υἱοῦ τοῦ ἀνθρώπου.	

TABLE II—continued

I Thess. v. 1-9	I Peter	Acts, Cor., Rom.	Phil., Col., Eph., etc.	Verba Christi	O.T.
v. 17. ἀδιαλείπτως προσεύχεσθε.	iv. 2. εἰς τὸ μηκέτι ἀνθρώπων ἐπιθυμίαις . . . βιῶσαι . . .		Col. iv. 3. προσευχόμενοι ἅμα καὶ περὶ ἡμῶν, ἵνα ὁ θεὸς ἀνοίξῃ ἡμῖν θύραν τοῦ λόγου, λαλῆσαι τὸ μυστήριον τοῦ Χριστοῦ . . .	Mk. xiii. 33*. βλέπετε, ἀγρυπνεῖτε καὶ προσεύ- χεσθε . . .	Is. lix. 17, Wisd. v. 17 f. [cf. Table V and notes]; also Is.
ib. 7. οἱ γὰρ καθεύδον- τες νυκτὸς καθεύδουσι, καὶ οἱ μεθυσκόμενοι νυ- κτὸς μεθύουσιν.	ib. 3. . . . πεπορευμέ- νους ἐν ἀσελγείαις, ἐπι- θυμίαις, οἰνοφλυγίαις, κώμοις, πότοις . . .	Rom. xiii. 13. ὡς ἐν ἡμέρᾳ εὐσχημόνως περιπατήσωμεν, μὴ κώ- μοις καὶ μέθαις, μὴ κοίταις καὶ ἀσελγείαις, μὴ ἔριδι καὶ ζήλῳ.	Eph. v. 18. καὶ μὴ μεθύ- σκεσθε οἴνῳ, ἐν ᾧ ἐστιν ἀσωτία . . . Eph. vi. 18. διὰ πάσης προσευχῆς καὶ δεήσεως, προσ- ευχόμενοι ἐν παντὶ καιρῷ ἐν πνεύματι, καὶ εἰς αὐτὸ ἀγρυπνοῦντες ἐν πάσῃ προσ- καρτερήσει καὶ δεήσει περὶ πάντων τῶν ἁγίων . . .	ib. 35-7*. γρηγορεῖτε οὖν . . . μὴ ἐλθὼν ἐξαίφνης εὕρῃ ὑμᾶς καθεύδοντας· ὃ δὲ ὑμῖν λέγω πᾶσιν λέγω, γρηγορεῖτε. Matt. xxv. 13*. Γρηγο- ρεῖτε οὖν, ὅτι οὐκ οἴδατε τὴν ἡμέραν οὐδὲ τὴν ὥραν.	xi. 5. καὶ ἔσται δικαιοσύνη ἐζωσμένος τὴν ὀσφὺν αὐτοῦ, καὶ ἀληθείᾳ εἰλημένος τὰς πλευράς.
ib. 8. ἡμεῖς δὲ ἡμέρας ὄντες νήφωμεν, ἐνδυσά- μενοι θώρακα πίστεως καὶ ἀγάπης καὶ περικε- φαλαίαν ἐλπίδα σωτη- ρίας.	i. 13. διὸ ἀναζωσά- μενοι τὰς ὀσφύας τῆς διανοίας ὑμῶν, νήφον- τες τελείως ἐλπίσατε . . . iv. 1. . . . καὶ ὑμεῖς τὴν αὐτὴν ἔννοιαν ὁπλί- σασθε . . .	ib. 14. ἀλλ' ἐνδύ- σασθε τὸν κύριον Ἰη- σοῦν Χριστόν, καὶ τῆς σαρκὸς πρόνοιαν μὴ ποιεῖσθε εἰς ἐπιθυμίας.	Col. iv. 5. ἐν σοφίᾳ περι- πατεῖτε πρὸς τοὺς ἔξω, τὸν καιρὸν ἐξαγοραζόμενοι . . . Eph. vi. 14 f. στῆτε οὖν περιζωσάμενοι τὴν ὀσφὺν ὑμῶν ἐν ἀληθείᾳ, καὶ ἐνδυ- σάμενοι τὸν θώρακα τῆς δικαιοσύνης . . . τὸν θυρεὸν τῆς πίστεως . . . τὴν περι- κεφαλαίαν τοῦ σωτηρίον . . . προσευχόμενοι . . . ἀγρυ- πνοῦντες.	Lk. xxi. 34*. προσέχετε δὲ ἑαυτοῖς, μήποτε βαρηθῶσιν ὑμῶν αἱ καρδίαι ἐν κραιπάλῃ καὶ μέθῃ καὶ μερίμναις βιω- τικαῖς. Matt. xxiv. 48-50 [cf. Lk. xii. 45]. ἐὰν δὲ εἴπῃ ὁ κακὸς δοῦλος ἐκεῖνος . . . χρονίζει μου ὁ κύριος . . . ἐσθίῃ δὲ καὶ πίνῃ μετὰ τῶν μεθυόντων, ἥξει ὁ κύριος κτλ.	
ib. 9. ὅτι οὐκ ἔθετο ἡμᾶς ὁ θεὸς εἰς ὀργήν, ἀλλ' εἰς περιποίησιν σω- τηρίας διὰ τοῦ κυρίου ἡμῶν Ἰησοῦ Χριστοῦ [cf. 2 Thess. ii. 14].	ii. 9. ὑμεῖς δὲ . . . λαὸς εἰς περιποίησιν.	Acts xx. 28. τὴν ἐκ- κλησίαν τοῦ θεοῦ, ἣν περιεποιήσατο διὰ τοῦ αἵματος τοῦ ἰδίου.	ib. i. 14. εἰς ἀπολύτρω- σιν τῆς περιποιήσεως, εἰς ἔπαινον τῆς δόξης αὐτοῦ.		

378

of Holiness in 1 Thess. v. 1-9, such as we have studied in Table I
above, is significant. For it is unlikely that a baptismal Form
based on the findings of the Apostolic Council of Acts xv. would
be confined to so strictly Jewish and Levitical a theme. Something
would be needed that would appeal to Gentile Christians too ; and
the more broadly-based teaching illustrated in Table II would
supply the need.

(ii) It is obvious that *verba Christi* underlie, and are being
interpreted in, the teaching and phraseology of these parallels,
especially in the case of 1 Thess. v. Prophetic utterances are also Is. lix. 9,
in mind, but by way of reminiscence rather than quotation, and as 10
distilled through later Jewish writings [1] and through the mind and lxii. 1
teaching of Christ. Whether the dependence on the *verba Christi* Prov. iv.
implies that these were already available in collected form is not Matt. v.
so clear. The words ἀκριβῶς οἴδατε in 1 Thess. v. 2 certainly 14
imply precise verbal instruction ; but the words of Christ referred Jn. xii. 35,
to here and elsewhere are such as could easily have been transmitted 36
orally without inaccuracy.

(iii) The sequence of thought in 1 Thess. v. is instructive. Beginning with Christ's teaching, already familiar to his readers, as
to the suddenness of the arrival of the Day of the Lord, the author Lk. xii.
proceeds (verses 4, 5) to give it a special interpretation for their 39 f.
benefit, as much as to say : " This does not apply to *you* quite as it xxiv. 43 f.
stands ; for your condition is not one of darkness, where thieves Jn. xvi. 21
operate, but of light. For you the day has already dawned."
This is to give us a glimpse of " realized eschatology " in the making.
Christians belong already to the light and the day, not the night
and the darkness. At a later date St. John was to describe conver- Jn. v. 24
sion as a passage from death to life, and to declare the proof of it 1 Jn. iii.
to consist in brotherly love ; though there too the idea of light is 1 Jn. ii. 10
closely associated with it. 1 Thessalonians, in using the metaphor
of darkness and light, followed another theme, and one no less well
authenticated by prophecy and by Christ's teaching ; and Eph. v.
8-14 shews how early this idea passed into the baptismal use and
language of the Church.[2] 1 Pet. ii. 9 tells in the same sense, for
the whole context there is baptismal ; and so does Heb. vi. 4, with
its almost technical use of φωτισθέντας. Similarly Eph. v. 8, where
St. Paul introduces the darkness-and-light metaphor, follows immediately upon a passage denouncing precisely those sins which were

---

[1] The metaphor in Jewish thought
is not metaphysical but moral: light
stands for justice or righteousness,
darkness for sin.

[2] The point is well brought out by
Bishop Wordsworth, *in loc.*

denounced in the *Abstinentes* of the first Christian baptismal code.[1]
I cannot doubt, therefore, that this theme formed part of the
Church's regular baptismal teaching at a very early date ; and its
occurrence in 1 Thessalonians ᵤuggests that it belonged to the
Form (B¹) which we have discussed above. In view of its distinctive
character, standing out clearly in 1 Thessalonians, Romans and
Ephesians, and also, though less clearly, in 1 Peter and Hebrews,
I propose to designate it by the term *Filii Lucis* — the term used of
Christians by our Lord in Lk. xvi. 8, Jn. xii. 36 (and cf. Matt. v. 14).
If we are right in regarding this idea as one very early associated
with baptism, the surmise is not unreasonable that that sacrament
played a large part in the change of doctrinal emphasis which was
involved in the introduction of what is called "realized eschatology".

1 Thess. v. 6-8   (iv) In the three verses that follow in 1 Thessalonians, the *Filii
Lucis* theme is given a more precise ethical signification. Night
is the time of sleep and of revelry, but day calls for wakefulness
and sobriety. The ethical warnings and injunctions here are clearly
based on *verba Christi*, but their context is different ; for whereas
in our Lord's teaching their motive is the approaching eschatological
crisis, in the Epistle it is the new status which Christians have as
" children of the light and of the day ".[2] The darkness-and-light
theme has intervened, that is to say, to make the eschatological
motive indirect and to give it a new meaning. For in conversion
or baptism — and the two were indistinguishable except as the
inward and outward facets of the same event — the eschatological
crisis has already in large part occurred. The behaviour inculcated
on Christians is governed not by the fear of an imminent Judgment,
but by the experience of a new spiritual order already begun. Thus,
γρηγορεῖν which in the Gospels can fairly be translated " Watch ",
as for some incalculable happening, means in 1 Thessalonians " Be
wakeful, alert " ; and νήφειν, which does not occur in the *verba
Christi* (though it might be regarded as summarizing some of His
most graphic warnings), represents a still further development of
the same ethical idea. What is enjoined is a serious and purposeful
approach to life, and the self-discipline that such an approach

---

[1] The metaphor does not occur in
the Pentateuch, nor can I discover it
in Rabbinic teaching about proselyte
baptism. But our Lord found it in
Jewish prophecy and ethical tradition,
and adapted it to His work as Rabbi.
Note its occurrence in the Benedictus
(Lk. i. 79) and the Nunc Dimittis
(Lk. ii. 32), passages where the priestly
and the prophetic are very closely
fused.

[2] A beautiful commentary on the
thought is to be found in the Com-
pline antiphon : " Save us, O Lord,
while waking, and guard us while
sleeping : that awake we may be with
Christ, and in peace may take our
rest "

requires. It is significant, moreover, that precisely the same teaching is found in 1 Peter, and is expressed in the same words, as in 1 Thessalonians. In 1 Pet. iv. 7 (but not in v. 8) the eschatological motive is immediate and direct, as in Mk. xiii. 33, 35 ; but in 1 Pet. v. 8, where the exact collocation of the words γρηγορεῖν and νήφειν occurs, the context is primarily ethical, and γρηγορεῖν has the same meaning as in our Lord's words in the Agony in Gethsemane, γρηγορεῖτε καὶ προσεύχεσθε, ἵνα μὴ εἰσέλθητε εἰς πειρασμόν. Mk. xiv. We may note, further, that in 1 Pet. iv. 7 it is self-discipline and 38, cf Lk. not wakefulness which is connected with prayer, as means to end xxii. 40 (cf. also 1 Pet. iii. 7).

(v) Christ's eschatological teaching contained very plain warnings against drunkenness and excess, which represent extreme Lk. xii. 45 examples of worldly living. In 1 Thessalonians these are echoed in xxi. 34 the allusion to drunkenness as characteristic of " night ", and thus 1 Thess. v. drawn into the ethical darkness-and-light theme which runs through 7 this passage. In 1 Pet. iv. 3 mention is made of " lusts ", amongst which drunkenness is especially singled out, as characteristic of the readers' former life, which the author has already described as a life of " darkness " (ii. 9) ; and this passage follows upon the vital baptismal teaching in 1 Pet. iii. 18–iv. 1. Both in 1 Thessalonians and 1 Peter, therefore, this particular warning is made to rest directly on ethical grounds — in the former case on the darkness-and-light *motif* and in the latter on the dying life which baptism involves for the Christian. It seems a reasonable conjecture that this explicit reference to the sin of intemperance was likewise in the primitive baptismal Form which we have denoted B[1]. Yet when we turn to Rom. xiii. 13, where the same warning is given, there is a difficulty ; for the warning occurs in a passage which is saturated in eschatology and also contains ideas that have other roots in the tradition of the early Church (cf. below, pp. 396, 456). Further discussion of this question will be found in that place. Here we may be content to note that Rom. xiii. 13, 14 are so similar in thought and phrase to 1 Thess. v. 7, 8 as to point to a common source. Nor is this view invalidated by the fact that in Rom. xiii. St. Paul has combined it with other material and given it a somewhat different significance.

I have included in this Table 1 Thess. v. 9 and its parallels, though it must be doubted whether it belonged to this source. The use of περιποίησις and its cognates is so well spread that a common substratum for it is probable ; but there were many contexts in the primitive Forms where it would have fitted equally well. Thess. v. 10 (cf. 1 Pet. ii. 21, 24), if not purely Pauline, points perhaps to a more strictly doctrinal Form than that which we have been discussing.

In the light of this evidence, I think we may confidently assign the darkness-and-light or *Filii Lucis* theme to the first baptismal Form already isolated in Table I, and regard it as marking an important stage in the " realization " of our Lord's eschatology. The duties of wakefulness, self-discipline and prayer, which had had a largely (though not solely) eschatological reference in the *verba Christi*, were early drawn into association with baptism, and probably became likewise part of the Form B¹. Of the specific warning against intemperance found in the *verba Christi*, 1 Thessalonians, Romans and 1 Peter, perhaps we cannot speak with the same confidence ; but the reasons for including it in the Form seem to me to outweigh those to the contrary. It will be seen that in assigning the above teaching to the first baptismal Form, B¹, I differ from Dr. Carrington, who connects it with the fuller Form which is discussed below, pp. 388 ff.

(3) PARALLEL SUMMARIES IN 1 PETER AND 2 THESSALONIANS

This view is still further borne out, if we make a comparison on broader lines. In 2 Thess. ii. 13-17, which follows immediately on the highly eschatological passage in ii. 3-12 — a passage we have already seen reason to assign to St. Paul personally — there is a full and compact statement of doctrine which seems to gather up a large part of the teaching of the two Epistles. There is no quite similar summary in 1 Peter, though 1 Pet. i. comes near to being such ; and it is significant that the majority of the parallels which 1 Peter offers to 2 Thess. ii. 13-17 are found in that chapter. What is most striking, however, is the strongly " Petrine " flavour of 2 Thess. ii. 13-17 ; all its distinctive ideas, and much of its distinctive vocabulary, occur in 1 Peter, and often in the same context ; one notable phrase — ἐν ἁγιασμῷ πνεύματος — is not found elsewhere in N.T. The evidence is set out in Table III (see opposite).

Commentary.—We cannot fail to observe in the Thessalonian summary the governing ideas both of 1 and 2 Thessalonians and of 1 Peter ; namely,

(1) The divine initiative of love and mercy in choosing and calling believers to their new life, which evokes the praise and thanksgiving of the Christian community ;

(2) The sanctification of their life by the Spirit, shewn in their faith and obedience to the truth ;

TABLE III

PARALLEL SUMMARIES IN 1 PETER AND 2 THESSALONIANS

2 Thess.	1 Peter
ii. 13. ἡμεῖς δὲ ὀφείλομεν εὐχαριστεῖν τῷ θεῷ πάντοτε περὶ ὑμῶν ἀδελφοὶ ἠγαπημένοι ὑπὸ κυρίου, ὅτι εἵλετο ὑμᾶς ὁ θεὸς ἀπ' ἀρχῆς	i. 3. Εὐλογητὸς ὁ θεὸς καὶ πατὴρ τοῦ κυρίου ἡμῶν Ἰησοῦ Χριστοῦ.
	i. 1, 2. ἐκλεκτοῖς . . . κατὰ πρόγνωσιν θεοῦ πατρός : cf. ii. 9.
εἰς σωτηρίαν	i. 5. εἰς σωτηρίαν : cf. i. 9.
ἐν ἁγιασμῷ πνεύματος καὶ πίστει	i. 2. ἐν ἁγιασμῷ πνεύματος.
ἀληθείας.	i. 22. ἐν τῇ ὑπακοῇ τῆς ἀληθείας.
14. εἰς ὃ ἐκάλεσεν ὑμᾶς διὰ τοῦ	i. 15. κατὰ τὸν καλέσαντα ὑμᾶς : cf. ii. 9.
εὐαγγελίου ἡμῶν,	i. 12. διὰ τῶν εὐαγγελισαμένων ὑμᾶς.
εἰς περιποίησιν δόξης τοῦ κυρίου ἡμῶν Ἰησοῦ Χριστοῦ.	ii. 9. λαὸς εἰς περιποίησιν . . .
	i. 7. εἰς ἔπαινον καὶ δόξαν καὶ τιμὴν ἐν ἀποκαλύψει Ἰησοῦ Χριστοῦ.
16. αὐτὸς δὲ ὁ κύριος ἡμῶν Ἰησοῦς Χριστός,	i. 3. ὁ θεὸς καὶ πατὴρ τοῦ κυρίου ἡμῶν Ἰησοῦ Χριστοῦ, ὁ κατὰ τὸ πολὺ . . . ἔλεος . . .
καὶ ὁ θεὸς ὁ πατὴρ ἡμῶν ὁ ἀγαπήσας ἡμᾶς	
καὶ δοὺς παράκλησιν αἰωνίαν καὶ ἐλπίδα ἀγαθὴν ἐν χάριτι,	v. 10. ὁ δὲ θεὸς πάσης χάριτος, ὁ καλέσας ὑμᾶς εἰς τὴν αἰώνιον αὐτοῦ δόξαν ἐν Χριστῷ . . . αὐτὸς καταρτίσει, στηρίξει . . .
17. παρακαλέσαι ὑμῶν τὰς καρδίας καὶ στηρίξαι ἐν παντὶ ἔργῳ καὶ λόγῳ ἀγαθῷ.	i. 13. ἐλπίσατε ἐπὶ τὴν φερομένην ὑμῖν χάριν ἐν ἀποκαλύψει Ἰησοῦ Χριστοῦ.

(3) The objective of salvation, which will mean their sharing in or possessing the " glory " accompanying Christ's appearing at the last ;

(4) The life of grace meanwhile, which is buoyed up by an infinite hope, and strengthened by God Himself.

Each of these thoughts can be paralleled elsewhere ; but the way in which they are mortised together and made to cohere, and in certain cases the language in which they are expressed, seem peculiar to these Epistles. The ideas are " in the tradition " ; but their presentation in Thessalonians and 1 Peter looks like the work of one man writing at an interval of some years, rather than of two.

And in that case we may reasonably name him as the man whom we know to have been associated with both sets of writings, namely Silvanus.

II

Further Catechetical Material : Romans, Colossians and Ephesians, 1 Peter, James (Philippians)

(i) GENERAL OBSERVATIONS : SUTURES AND OTHER FEATURES SYMPTOMATIC OF CATECHETICAL FORMS

(1) We turn now to the second group of Epistles which present marked parallels with 1 Peter, with a view to seeing whether here too interdependence upon common sources is not, at least in many cases, a more-fruitful hypothesis than direct dependence of one upon another. Dependence of 1 Peter upon Romans, and in a different degree upon Ephesians and James (though in the last two cases there is not agreement on which side the dependence lies) has been widely accepted by editors of our Epistle ; though Bigg vigorously disputes it. Moreover, it is probable enough that, if our Epistle were written from Rome by St. Peter, he would have been acquainted with Romans ; and he may also have seen the other two. The facts which have to be explained, however, are more complicated than this. We have to account for differences as well as similarities ; for differences, that is to say, precisely in those passages where it is claimed that the parallelism suggests direct dependence. Some of these differences, such as that discussed in Add. Notes E, F (pp. 268-81), turn on minute, but significant, details of language ; others, as when 1 Peter and Ephesians use similar words in quite contrary contexts (cf. 1 Pet. ii. 11 with Eph. ii. 19), or when 1 Peter and Romans discuss worship or the duty of civic obedience, lie nearer the surface. Moreover, we are not without examples of direct literary dependence in the New Testament outside the Synoptic Gospels ; but there is nothing in the relation of 1 Peter to the group of Epistles we are considering comparable to the dependence of 2 Peter on Jude (or *vice versa*), or even to the close affinities between Colossians and Ephesians. It may be questioned, indeed, whether the parallels between 1 Peter and Romans or Ephesians are nearly so sustained or so striking as those between 1 Peter and the two Thessalonian Epistles. The evidence would appear sufficiently accounted for by the broad judgment that the ideas and phrases and words which afford examples of parallelism were all alike in circulation in the primitive Christian community ; and our problem

is to see how far these parallels point to Forms of oral or written teaching which it is possible for us to isolate and in some sort identify.

In what form were the books which were in use in the Church of the first century ? What were the contents of the library of a settled local church or its presbyters, or of the travelling library of an evangelist, a prophet, or an Apostle ? We may surmise that they were of no great quantity ; but that they existed is clear from the allusions in 2 Tim. iv. 13 to " the books " and " the parchments ", in 1 Pet. ii. 6 to a written document, perhaps to " prophets' writings " in Rom. xvi. 26, and to early accounts of our Lord's ministry in St. Luke's Preface. The nature of these documents may be conjectured, moreover, from what happens in the mission field to-day ; they would have been short, and *ad hoc*, and subject to error and alteration in transcription. Their brevity results from the limited writing materials available and from the need to produce rapidly [1] ; and the first of these causes was certainly operative,[2] and probably the second also, in the first century. Then, as to-day in Africa, it is unlikely that copies of any entire Gospel were as common as copies of separate sections. They are written, moreover, to meet definite needs arising at different points in the Church's expansion ; summaries of the Christian faith, of the Lord's deeds, of His teaching, of Christian duty, of liturgical usage, and so on, are called for, and have to be provided. And in the attempts to supply what is needed discrepancies may easily creep in.

Our missionaries do a good deal of dictating to our senior lads, candidates for teachership, or Holy Orders. Our notes are lent out to others, and copied ; the copies are not always quite accurate. And if we lend our own notes to another teacher they get altered in dictation, and the resulting copy is not quite like the original in all details.[3]

There is nothing in this picture of the literary output of a modern missionary Church which we may not regard as equally true of the Church of the first century ; and it tallies with much that we know of the composition of the Synoptic Gospels. But why should we suppose that sections of narrative about our Lord's ministry and teaching were the only writings in circulation at that time ? The " parchments " referred to in 2 Tim. iv. 13 are commonly reckoned

---

[1] The position was well set out by the late Bishop Weston of Zanzibar in an article in *Theology*, vol. vii. pp. 252 ff. (November 1923).

[2] Cf. F. G. Kenyon, *Handbook to Textual Criticism of N.T.* (1912), ch. ii.

[3] Bishop Weston, *op. cit.*

to have been parts of O.T., as skins were generally used for its transcription. In Add. Note E on 1 Pet. ii. 4-10 we have given reason for believing that the "writing" alluded to there was a primitive Christian hymn, such as we know from St. Paul's Epistles were sung. And there would have been equal need of catechetical material covering the main divisions of Christian theology and ethics, if the distinctiveness of the new religion were to be preserved and the salt not to lose its savour. How congenial such a practice would have been to those who were conversant with the Jewish methods of instructing proselytes has been shewn by Bishop Carrington.[1]

It is in this context that I propose now to examine the parallels in the group of Epistles under consideration. This will involve a constructive criticism of Dr. Carrington's work already mentioned. Though I differ from some of his conclusions, his analysis of the materials is most useful; and I propose to take it as a starting-point, while endeavouring to fill in its outlines and relate it somewhat more widely to the life of the Church in the first century. Three preliminary points may be observed at the outset:

(i) Though Dr. Carrington summarizes the chief catechetical material common to 1 Peter, Colossians, Ephesians and James under four main heads or leading phrases, which occur in the same order in all four, the classification which he gives in his fifth table (pp. 42, 43) covers six principal divisions; namely the New Creation or New Birth, *Deponentes* (i.e. sections dealing with the renunciation of heathen idolatry and vice), the Worship of God, *Subiecti* (i.e. the law of humility, which embraces the strikingly subordinationist Social Code of primitive Christianity), *Vigilate* (i.e. the duty of watchfulness and prayer), and *State* (i.e. the duty of stedfastness). I believe that this sixfold division is better than the fourfold one. It enables us to assign to the instruction about the nature of baptism, and to the instruction on the worship of God, a position equivalent to that of the other four points, such as it is antecedently probable that they would have had; and it enables us to explain certain characteristics of Romans. Further, the case for the sections entitled *Vigilate* and *State* in this list does not seem to me so strong as for the other points: their eschatological colour and their suitability to times of persecution suggest that they belonged

---

[1] *Op. cit.* chs. i. and ii. Cf. A. M. Hunter, *op. cit.* p. 64: "We are driven to conclude that the substance of the Pauline paraenetic tradition is not his own creation, but something common and apostolic. . . . The only theory which will fit the facts is that Paul, in common with other apostolic writers, was drawing from a common pool, some sort of paraenetic tradition."

to a *tōrah* concerned more directly with that subject (cf. Part III below).

(ii) Attention should be drawn to a point of grammatical style which tends to bear out the view that the N.T. writers are often quoting from catechetical material, namely the use of the participle as an imperative. The usage is carefully discussed by Moulton.[1] It goes far beyond the examples of anacoluthon found in classical Greek (e.g. Herod. iii. 16. 4, Thuc. iii. 36. 2), being both more frequent and more awkward ; nor is it limited to passages charged with excitement or strong feeling, such as will often account for it in 2 Corinthians (cf. also Eph. iii. 18). On the contrary, it meets us in passages of sober and deliberate injunction, and is repeated several times in the same passage. This is notably so in Rom. xii. 9b-13, 16, 17, 18, 19a, where participial phrases are sandwiched in with imperatives and in one case an infinitive,[2] and in 1 Pet. ii. 12, 18, iii. 1, 7, 9, and perhaps iv. 8-10. Eph. v. 21, 22 should probably be included; for the ὑποτασσόμενοι in v. 21b is presumably the verb which is omitted in v. 22. One may question, indeed, whether in view of the use of ὑποτασσόμενοι in 1 Peter, Eph. v. 21b should not be separated from v. 18-20, and regarded as the beginning of a new paragraph, based on the *Subiecti* section of the primitive catechism. Eph. iv. 2, 3 and Heb. xiii. 5 are perhaps other examples. Lightfoot, commenting on Col. iii. 11, says that " the absolute participle, being (so far as regards mood) neutral in itself, takes its colour from the general complexion of the sentence ". But this broad statement does not amount to an explanation, and throws no light on the usage in 1 Peter. It is not difficult, on the other hand, to suppose that sections of the primitive catechism may have been introduced by participles, and that these gave their title to the sections concerned (as e.g. in the Canon of the Roman Mass to-day) and also led to participial constructions being used frequently in the body of the sections and in quotations from them. Much light is thrown on the matter by the evidence collected and discussed by Dr. Daube on

---

[1] *Grammar of N.T. Greek*, i. pp. 181 f., 223, 240. Moulton says that that the usage in the papyri " is not a mark of inferior education, and not very common ". Lohmeyer (*Kyrios Jesus*, pp. 8 ff., quoted by Hunter, *op. cit.* p. 48) speaks of the participial style as " a familiar feature of Semitic hymnodical prayer-speech ", and says that " only in Semitic speech can a finite verb be continued by a parti-ciple ". On this whole matter the reader is referred to the Appended Note which my friend Dr. David Daube, Fellow of Gonville and Caius College, Cambridge, has kindly pre-pared for me and generously allowed me to include in this volume.

[2] The infinitive is common for the imperative in Pseudo-Phocylides, but there is no case of the participle being so used there.

pp. 467-88 below, and I cannot do better than refer the reader to what he has written.

(iii) Examination of passages in the Epistles containing the vocative ἀδελφοί or ἀγαπητοί, with or without a verb of injunction (παρακαλῶ, ἐρωτῶ) and a resumptive particle (οὖν, δέ), is also illuminating. In many places the vocative is used simply to press home some point already mentioned (cf. Jas. ii. 1, iii. 10) or to introduce a sentence or paragraph where the direct personal relation between the writer and his readers is to be emphasized (cf. 1 Thess. v. 25, Phil. iii. 13, 17). But there are many cases where the passage thus introduced is coloured and sometimes dominated by precisely those themes which Dr. Carrington has isolated as belonging to the primitive Christian catechism. They amount to over thirty in all.

(1) Rebirth through the Word — Jas. i. 18, 21.

(2) *Deponentes* — Rom. viii. 12, 2 Cor. vii. 1, 1 Thess. iv. 1-3, 2 Thess. iii. 6, Jas. i. 19, 1 Pet. ii. 11.

(3) Worship — Rom. xii. 1.

(4) *Subiecti* — including the law of love and the Christian Social Code generally : Rom. xii. 19, 1 Cor. i. 10, xvi. 15, 2 Cor. xiii. 11, Eph. iv. 1, v. 1, 1 Thess. iv. 1-7, v. 12, 14-22, 1 Jn. ii. 7, iv. 7, Phil. iv. 8, 9.

(5) *Vigilate* — 1 Cor. xvi. 15 (παρακαλῶ δὲ ὑμᾶς, ἀδελφοί follows γρηγορεῖτε, στήκετε and precedes ὑποτάσσησθε), 2 Pet. 14, 17, 1 Thess. v. 1, 4 f., Jas. v. 7 f.

(6) *State* (especially in view of persecution) — 1 Cor. xv. 5⁵, 2 Thess. ii. 1, 15, 1 Pet. iv. 12, Jas. i. 2-4, Phil. iv. 1.

This form of address with what one may call the resumptive vocative, especially when accompanied by a phrase like παρακαλῶ ὑμᾶς, would be perfectly natural in places where the writer wished to *clinch what he had been saying by associating it with what his readers already knew* in the way of Christian faith and duty. The climax of his argument is not, like the argument itself, something new, but something familiar ; and it is to stand out afresh through being set in a new light. The cases in which they occur in places where we have already other grounds for discerning a catechetical substratum are sufficiently numerous to deserve attention.

(2) SUMMARY OF MAIN SECTIONS OF SECOND BAPTISMAL FORM

With these preliminary observations made, we can pass to examine the parallels in the Epistles named at the head of this

Part. They fall into the following groups :
  (i) The entry into the new life at baptism :
    (*a*) Its basis — the Word, truth, gospel (Table IV) ;
    (*b*) Its nature — rebirth, new creation, new manhood (Table V).
  (ii) The new life : its negative implications, or Renunciations (*Deponentes*) (Table VI).
  (iii) The new life : its faith and worship (Table VII).
  (iv) The new life : its social virtues and duties (*Subiecti*) :
    (*a*) in general (Tables VIII A and VIII B) ;
    (*b*) in particular relationships (Tables X-XIII).
  (v) Teaching called out by crisis (Table XIV) :
    (*a*) Watchfulness and prayer (*Vigilate*) ;
    (*b*) Stedfastness (*State, Resistite*).

(i) *Baptism : its Basis and Nature*

(*a*) That the Gospel is " the word of truth " is common to James, Colossians-Ephesians, and John, and implied in 1 Peter; and 1 Peter, Romans, and Colossians-Ephesians speak of it as having been " heard " or " obeyed ". In Romans it is spoken of as a τύπος διδαχῆς or " pattern of teaching " to which the converts had been " handed over ". The phrase connotes a limited course of instruction, which followed definite and settled lines. A written manual or manuals may be in St. Paul's mind. The description of the Gospel as " the truth "[1] is characteristic of all the traditions, and served to differentiate Christianity both from the Judaism which had rejected it and from the heathenism which had not known it. The importance of " hearing the word " goes back to the earliest days of our Lord's teaching ; and the emphasis laid on it as " the truth " in the Epistles suggests that the Fourth Gospel is right in attributing this also to our Lord Himself.[2] This would account for

[1] Cf. Mayor's excellent note on Jas. i. 18.

[2] The tendency of certain modern totalitarian States to prohibit the *teaching* of religion, even though they tolerate its *worship*, is thus seen to strike at the very root of Christianity. Cf. the fine passage on the power of Truth in civilizing the Teutonic races in R. W. Church, *The Gifts of Civilization*, pp. 238 f.: " Truth, as it is made the ultimate ground of religion in the New Testament; Truth, as a thing of reality and not of words; Truth, as a cause to contend for in lifelong struggle, and gladly to die for — this was the new, deep, fruitful idea implanted, at the awakening dawn of thought, in the infant civilization of the North. . . . This great idea of truth, whatever its consequences, the assumption of its attainableness, of its preciousness, comes to us, as a popular belief and axiom, from the New Testament, through the word and ministry of the Christian Church, from its first contact with the new races ; it is the

TABLE IV

BAPTISM: ITS BASIS IN THE WORD, TRUTH, GOSPEL

1 Peter	James	Romans	Colossians	Ephesians	Johannine Writings	Other Epistles
i. 14. ὡς τέκνα ὑπακοῆς ... i. 22. τὰς ψυχὰς ὑμῶν ἡγνικότες ἐν τῇ ὑπακοῇ τῆς ἀληθείας ... ἐκ καρδίας.	i. 18. βουληθεὶς ἀπεκύησεν ἡμᾶς λόγῳ ἀληθείας.	vi. 17. ὑπηκούσατε δὲ ἐκ καρδίας εἰς ὃν παρεδόθητε τύπον διδαχῆς.	i. 5. τὴν ἐλπίδα... ἣν προηκούσατε ἐν τῷ λόγῳ τῆς ἀληθείας τοῦ εὐαγγελίου τοῦ παρόντος εἰς ὑμᾶς.	i. 13. ὑμεῖς, ἀκούσαντες τὸν λόγον τῆς ἀληθείας, τὸ εὐαγγέλιον τῆς σωτηρίας ὑμῶν....	xvii. 17. ἁγίασον αὐτοὺς ἐν τῇ ἀληθείᾳ ὁ λόγος ὁ σὸς ἀλήθεια ἐστι.	1 Thess. i. 6. δεξάμενοι τὸν λόγον ... cf. conversely 2 Thess. i. 8, ii. 10-12.
23. ἀναγεγεννημέ-νοι ... ἐκ σπορᾶς ... ἀφθάρτου διὰ λόγου ζῶντος θεοῦ καὶ μένοντος. 25. τὸ ῥῆμα τὸ εὐαγγελισθὲν εἰς ὑμᾶς.	i. 21. ... δέξασθε τὸν ἔμφυτον λόγον.		6. ... καρποφορού-μενον καὶ αὐξανό-μενον iii. 16. ὁ λόγος τοῦ Χριστοῦ....			1 Thess. i. 5. τὸ εὐαγγέλιον ἡμῶν... ἐγε-νήθη εἰς ὑμᾶς... ἐν δυνάμει καὶ ἐν πνεύ-ματι ἁγίῳ καὶ πλη-ροφορίᾳ πολλῇ. ....

TABLE V

BAPTISM: ITS NATURE DESCRIBED

1 Peter	James	Romans	Colossians	Ephesians	Johannine Writings	Other Epistles
i. 3. ὁ ... ἀναγεννήσας ἡμᾶς εἰς ἐλπίδα ζῶσαν δι᾿ ἀναστάσεως Ἰησοῦ Χριστοῦ. 23. ἀναγεγεννημένοι.	i. 18. ἀπεκύησεν ἡμᾶς ..., εἰς τὸ εἶναι ἡμᾶς ἀπαρχήν τινα τῶν αὐτοῦ κτισμάτων.	vi. 4. συνετάφημεν αὐτῷ διὰ τοῦ βαπτίσματος εἰς τὸν θάνατον· ἵνα ... ὥσπερ ἠγέρθη Χριστός ... οὕτω καὶ ἡμεῖς ἐν καινότητι ζωῆς περιπατήσωμεν.	iii. 1-3. εἰ οὖν συνηγέρθητε τῷ Χριστῷ ... ἀπεθάνετε γάρ, καὶ ἡ ζωὴ ὑμῶν κέκρυπται ...	ii. 15, ἵνα τοὺς δύο κτίσῃ ἐν αὐτῷ εἰς ἕνα καινὸν ἄνθρωπον ...	iii. 5, 6. ἐὰν μή τις γεννηθῇ ἐξ ὕδατος καὶ πνεύματος, οὐ δύναται εἰσελθεῖν εἰς τὴν βασιλείαν τοῦ θεοῦ. τὸ γεγεννημένον ἐκ τῆς σαρκὸς σάρξ ἐστι, καὶ τὸ γεγεννημένον ἐκ τοῦ πνεύματος πνεῦμά ἐστι.	Gal. vi. 15. οὔτε γὰρ περιτομή τι ἐστιν οὔτε ἀκροβυστία, ἀλλὰ καινὴ κτίσις.
ii. 1, 2. ἀποθέμενοι οὖν πᾶσαν κακίαν ... ὡς ἀρτιγέννητα βρέφη.	i. 21. διὸ ἀποθέμενοι πᾶσαν ... ῥυπαρίαν κακίας ... δέξασθε τὸν ἔμφυτον λόγον.	5. εἰ γὰρ σύμφυτοι γεγόναμεν ... 6. ... ὁ παλαιὸς ἡμῶν ἄνθρωπος συνεσταυρώθη. ... 7. ὁ γὰρ ἀποθανὼν δεδικαίωται ἀπὸ τῆς ἁμαρτίας.	8-10. νυνὶ δὲ ἀπόθεσθε ... κακίαν ... ἀπεκδυσάμενοι τὸν παλαιὸν ἄνθρωπον σὺν ταῖς πράξεσιν αὐτοῦ, καὶ ἐνδυσάμενοι τὸν νέον τὸν ἀνακαινούμενον εἰς ἐπίγνωσιν κατ᾿ εἰκόνα τοῦ κτίσαντος αὐτόν.	iv. 22-4. ἀποθέσθαι ὑμᾶς κατὰ τὴν προτέραν ἀναστροφὴν τὸν παλαιὸν ἄνθρωπον τὸν φθειρόμενον κατὰ τὰς ἐπιθυμίας τῆς ἀπάτης, ἀνανεοῦσθαι δὲ τῷ πνεύματι τοῦ νοὸς ὑμῶν, καὶ ἐνδύσασθαι τὸν καινὸν ἄνθρωπον τὸν κατὰ θεὸν κτισθέντα ἐν δικαιοσύνῃ ...	cf. Mk. x. 15. ὃς ἐὰν μὴ δέξηται ... ὡς παιδίον, οὐ μὴ εἰσέλθῃ εἰς αὐτήν.	2 Cor. v. 17. εἴ τις ἐν Χριστῷ, καινὴ κτίσις ... Tit. iii. 5. κατὰ τὸ αὐτοῦ ἔλεος ἔσωσεν ἡμᾶς διὰ λουτροῦ παλιγγενεσίας καὶ ἀνακαινώσεως πνεύματος ἁγίου.
cf. ii. 9.		cf. Rom. xiii. 12, 13.	ii. 11, 12.			

its becoming " a *vox technica* of early Christianity " (Mayor).

(*b*) We observe four main types of metaphor for the change involved in becoming a Christian : (1) rebirth (1 Peter, James, John) ; (2) new creation (St. Paul, both in his earlier and his later Epistles)[1] ; (3) the contrast between the " old man " which is "put off " (Colossians-Ephesians) or " crucified and buried with Christ " (Romans) and the " new man " which is " put on " or " risen with Christ " (Romans and Colossians) ; and (4) the change from darkness to light.

As to rebirth, the metaphor is not quite identical in 1 Peter and James, as ἀποκυεῖν in Jas. i. 18 means " bear ", " bring forth " and not " beget ". It is a primitive and untechnical metaphor, used in Rabbinic theology (cf. note on 1 Pet. i. 23), and suggested by the position of Christians as (1) like new-born children, (2) the first-fruits of a harvest springing up from the sowing of the Word. These two aspects of conversion, which are traceable to the *verba Christi*, give rise respectively to the more developed ideas of re-generation and of new creation found in 1 Peter and in St. Paul respectively. The most primitive phrase in the use of this metaphor is perhaps St. Peter's ὡς ἀρτιγέννητα βρέφη.

The idea of " the old man " and " the new man " seems peculi-arly Pauline ; and he combines it with the idea of a new creation, though not in any systematic way. 1 Peter, James, and St. Paul all bring out the purposive side of the change that has taken place (εἰς ἐλπίδα ζῶσαν, 1 Pet. i. 3 ; εἰς τὸ εἶναι ἡμᾶς, Jas. i. 18 ; ἵνα, Rom. vi. 4, εἰς ἐπίγνωσιν, Col. iii. 10), shewing it to be conceived along Hebraic rather than Hellenistic and mystical lines ; and all use their several metaphors in close connexion with some part of the word ἀποθέσθαι (1 Pet. ii. 1, Jas. i. 21, Col. iii. 8, Eph. iv. 22). But the order of thought is simplest in 1 Peter and James, who made the rebirth (which is God's action) the ground of the *Deponentes*, which is man's response to it.

The metaphor of light and darkness, and the probability that it

distinct product of that great claim, for the first time made to all the world by the Gospel, and earnestly responded to by strong and simple natures — the claim of reality and truth made in the words of Him who said, ' I am the Way, the Truth, and the Life '."

[1] I am inclined to reckon Galatians with 1 and 2 Thessalonians among the earlier Epistles. I hesitate to express any opinion either as to the date or the genuineness of the Pastoral Epistles as they stand ; but the view that the greater part of 2 Timothy was written during St. Paul's imprisonment at Caesarea seems to me to merit careful consideration. Cf. F. J. Badcock, D.D., *The Pauline Epistles*, pp. 136 ff. I agree with what he says on pp. 122 f. as to the precariousness of some of the arguments based by Harrison and others on vocabulary.

formed part of the earliest catechetical teaching, have been already discussed. The facts are best explained, I suggest, by the view that the primitive catechism contained, in reference to baptism, teaching about Christians being as new-born children (teaching which had close parallels in Judaism) and being children of light, both of which points were derived from the *verba Christi* ; but that the development of the metaphors around such verbs as ἀναγεννᾶν, ἐνδύσασθαι, ἀνανεοῦσθαι, φωτίζειν was the work of individual writers.

(ii) *The New Life : its Renunciations*

The use of ἀποθέσθαι in 1 Peter, James, St. Paul (three Epistles), and Hebrews, usually with a resumptive particle (διό, οὖν, νυνὶ δέ), and its association (except in Hebrews) with κακία as a generic term, covering in particular falsehood and bad temper, are such marked features of all three traditions that Dr. Carrington is surely right in regarding them as pointing to an underlying formula. In 1 Peter and James we note that the *Deponentes* leads on to a second allusion to the Word and its saving effects ; and in all traditions alike, except Romans, it prepares the way for injunctions and teaching about worship. I conjecture that this last sequence of teaching was fundamental in the primitive Church. But the matter cannot be left to rest there ; for Romans and Colossians-Ephesians present problems of their own, and so also does 1 Thessalonians, both in what it says and in what it omits.

(*a*) 1 Thessalonians contains the *Abstinentes*[1] twice (iv. 3, v. 22), but no example of the *Deponentes* ; while on the other hand it includes (v. 7) the particular warning against intemperance which we find in 1 Peter, Romans, Ephesians (Galatians), and also the com-   1 Pet. iv. 3, Rom. xiii. 13, mand to " put on " the Christian armour (1 Thess. v. 8). I surmise   Eph. v. 18 that the absence of any *Deponentes* in 1 Thessalonians is due to the   (Gal. v. fact that the *Abstinentes* had been felt to cover the ground suffi-   20, 21) ciently at Thessalonica, and that the more vigorous *Deponentes* had not yet come into the catechism ; but that ἐνδύσασθαι was already establishing itself, under St. Paul's influence, as part of the vocabulary of baptism. We find it, for example, also in Galatians (iii. 27), which likewise has no *Deponentes* ; and we may further note that in Eph. iv. 22-4 ἀποθέσθαι is the correlative to ἐνδύσασθαι.

(*b*) In Romans the injunction about worship follows immedi-   Rom. xii. ately, and very suitably, upon the spontaneous outburst of praise in   1, 2

---

[1] I use this term for the ἀπέχεσθαι   as characteristic of a primitive Holi-
motif which Dr. Carrington regards   ness Code.

TABLE VI

THE NEW LIFE: ITS NEGATIVE IMPLICATIONS, OR RENUNCIATIONS (*DEPONENTES*)

I Peter	James	Romans	Colossians	Ephesians	Other Epistles
ii. 1, 2. <u>ἀποθέμενοι</u> οὖν πᾶσαν κακίαν καὶ πάντα <u>δόλον</u> καὶ ὑποκρίσεις καὶ φθόνους καὶ πάσας καταλαλιὰς ὡς ἀρτιγέννητα βρέφη τὸ λογικὸν ἄδολον γάλα ἐπιποθήσατε, ἵνα ἐν αὐτῷ αὐξηθῆτε εἰς σωτηρίαν....	i. 21. <u>διὸ ἀποθέμενοι</u> πᾶσαν ῥυπαρίαν καὶ περισσείαν κακίας ἐν πραΰτητι δέξασθε τὸν ἔμφυτον λόγον τὸν δυνάμενον σῶσαι τὰς ψυχὰς ὑμῶν.	xiii. 12. <u>ἀποθώμεθα</u> οὖν τὰ ἔργα τοῦ σκότους, <u>ἐνδυσώμεθα</u> δὲ τὰ ὅπλα τοῦ φωτός....	iii. 8. <u>νυνὶ δὲ ἀπόθεσθε</u> καὶ ὑμεῖς τὰ πάντα, ὀργήν, θυμόν, κακίαν, βλασφημίαν, αἰσχρολογίαν ἐκ τοῦ στόματος ὑμῶν.	iv. 25. <u>διὸ ἀποθέμενοι</u> τὸ ψεῦδος λαλεῖτε ἀλήθειαν... ib. 26. ὀργίζεσθε καὶ μὴ ἁμαρτάνετε... ib. 29. πᾶς λόγος σαπρὸς ἐκ τοῦ στόματος ὑμῶν μὴ ἐκπορευέσθω... ib. 31. πᾶσα πικρία καὶ θυμὸς καὶ ὀργὴ καὶ κραυγὴ καὶ βλασφημία ἀρθήτω ἀφ' ὑμῶν σὺν πάσῃ κακίᾳ...	I Jn. ii. 15. μὴ ἀγαπᾶτε τὸν κόσμον... Heb. xii. 1. τογγαροῦν καὶ ἡμεῖς... ὄγκον ἀποθέμενοι πάντα καὶ...
[ib. v. f. Worship.]	[ib. 27. Worship.]	ib. 14. ἀλλ' <u>ἐνδύσασθε</u> τὸν κύριον Ἰησοῦν Χριστόν, καὶ τῆς σαρκὸς πρόνοιαν μὴ ποιεῖσθε εἰς ἐπιθυμίας. [xii. 1. Worship.]	ib. 9, 10. μὴ ψεύδεσθε εἰς ἀλλήλους, <u>ἀπεκδυσάμενοι</u> τὸν παλαιὸν ἄνθρωπον σὺν ταῖς πράξεσιν αὐτοῦ, καὶ <u>ἐνδυσάμενοι</u> τὸν νέον τὸν ἀνακαινούμενον...	iv. 22. <u>ἀποθέσθαι ὑμᾶς</u>... τὸν παλαιὸν ἄνθρωπον.... [cf. v. 11.] iv. 24. καὶ <u>ἐνδύσασθαι</u> τὸν καινὸν ἄνθρωπον τὸν κατὰ θεὸν κτισθέντα ἐν δικαιοσύνῃ καὶ ὁσιότητι τῆς ἀληθείας... [cf. vi. 11, 14].	I Thess. v. 8. <u>ἐνδυσάμενοι</u> θώρακα, κτλ. Gal. iii. 27. Χριστὸν <u>ἐνεδύσασθε</u>...

<table>
<tr><td>

iv. 1. Χριστοῦ οὖν πα-
θόντος σαρκὶ καὶ ὑμεῖς
τὴν αὐτὴν ἔννοιαν ὁπλί-
σασθε. . . .

</td><td>

ib. 12. ἐνδύσασθε οὖν,
ὡς ἐκλεκτοὶ τοῦ θεοῦ,
ἅγιοι καὶ ἠγαπημένοι,
σπλάγχνα οἰκτιρμοῦ, κτλ.

[ib. 16. Worship.]

ib. iii. 5-7. νεκρώσατε
οὖν . . . τὴν πλεονε-
ξίαν, ἥτις ἐστιν εἰδωλα-
τρεία. . . .

</td><td>

ib. 32. γίνεσθε δὲ εἰς
ἀλλήλους χρηστοί, εὔ-
σπλαγχνοι, χαριζόμενοι
ἑαυτοῖς. . . .

[ib. v. 19, 20. Worship.]

ib. iv. 17-19. μηκέτι
περιπατεῖν καθὼς καὶ τὰ
ἔθνη . . . οἵτινες ἀπ-
ηλγηκότες ἑαυτοὺς παρ-
έδωκαν τῇ ἀσελγείᾳ
εἰς ἐργασίαν ἀκαθαρσίας
πάσης ἐν πλεονεξίᾳ.

</td></tr>
</table>

xi. 33-6, while the *Deponentes* is discernible in the eschatological passage at the close of ch. xiii. Here again, as in Eph. iv. 22-4, we have ἀποθέσθαι as the correlative to ἐνδύσασθαι, and it is the Christian armour (as in 1 Thessalonians) and Christ (as in Galatians) that is to be put on. The baptismal reference in Gal. iii. 27 suggests that the *Induentes* may have been an early feature of the common baptismal catechism : the metaphor of armour was, we know, a favourite one with St. Paul, though it was already fully developed in O.T. ; once established, moreover, it was natural that this metaphor should lead (as in Col. iii. 9) to the replacement of ἀποθέσθαι by the much rarer ἀπεκδύσασθαι. Further, in Romans St. Paul combines the *Deponentes* of the primitive pattern, and the metaphor of the heavenly armour, with the avoidance of specific sins and occasions of sin which belonged to the eschatological tradition. For the warning against revelry, intemperance, and sensuality is closely similar to a *verbum Christi* whish was part of His eschatological teaching (Matthew, Luke), and it appears in an eschatological context in 1 Thessalonians and Romans, and less markedly in 1 Peter. The word ἀσωτία (1 Peter, Ephesians) belongs to the same train of thought, for " profligacy " is the exact opposite of the watchfulness and sobriety (cf. the collocation of γρηγορεῖν and νήφειν in 1 Thess. v. 6, 1 Pet. v. 8) and the seriousness of thought (cf. Col. iv. 5, Eph. v. 16, τὸν καιρὸν ἐξαγοραζόμενοι) which are called for by the imminence of the End. It is difficult, therefore, to know whether we should assign it to the *Abstinentes* section of the first baptismal Form (B¹) in view of its emphasis on sins of sensuality, or to the section *Vigilate* (which I conjecture to have been part of a Persecution-document closely associated with Silvanus, cf. Part III below) in view of its eschatological context.

A similar difficulty confronts us in regard to the heavenly armour. The hypothesis that it belonged to the *Vigilate* would account for its eschatological setting in 1 Thess. v., 1 Pet. iv., and Rom. xiii. 12 ; and the allusion to " the evil day " in Eph. vi. 13 belongs to the same circle of ideas, though St. Paul has there greatly amplified and enriched it. In that event, what St. Paul does in Rom. xiii. 11-14 is to give us in concentrated form three ideas which occurred together in a pattern of Persecution-teaching — the imminence of the End, the avoidance of laxity of living, and the Christian armour ; and with these he combines the *Deponentes* which was characteristic of the baptismal catechism. St. Peter, on the other hand, transfers the metaphor of the armour to his theme of the necessity of the dying life, and adapts the warning against licentiousness to a con-

Rom. xiii. 11-14

Matt. xxiv. 49, Lk. xxi. 34

crete situation when persecution was already a fact of experience and when it was vital to separate the Christians from the heathen religions of Asia Minor, and their characteristic vices ; and he uses the eschatology to crown rather than, as in 1 Thessalonians and Romans, to introduce the argument. In any case there seems no reason, in view of the *verbum Christi* in Lk. xxi. 34 (cf. Lk. xii. 45, Matt. xxiv. 49), to suppose direct dependence between 1 Pet. iv. 2-4 and Rom. xiii. 13.

(*c*) Dr. Carrington speaks of Colossians and Ephesians as each containing a " doublet " for the *Deponentes* ; and the point merits further analysis. The issue is best studied in Colossians, which is the earlier letter. Here, in Col. iii., we find what we might more properly call a triplet for the *Deponentes* and a doublet for the *Induentes* :

Deponentes : (1) Verses 5-7, νεκρώσατε replacing ἀπόθεσθε, and introducing a catalogue of vices deriving from ἐπιθυμία, ·and marked by a strongly Jewish colour. ἀκαθαρσία, for instance, is very rare in classical Greek, but common in LXX, where nearly half the occurrences are in Leviticus (Eph. iv. 17-19) ;

(2) Verse 8, ἀπόθεσθε introducing a catalogue including κακία and with a strong emphasis on sins of speech and temper (Eph. iv. 25-31);

(3) Verse 9, ἀπεκδυσάμενοι resuming ἀπόθεσθε from the previous verse, and introducing the Pauline contrast of the old man and the new (Eph. iv. 22) ;

Induentes : (1) Verse 10, ἐνδυσάμενοι introducing the second term of the above contrast (Eph. iv. 24) ;

(2) Verses 12 f., ἐνδύσασθε introducing a summary of Catechumen Virtues (on which see below, pp. 411 f.) (Eph. iv. 32–v. 1).

We may note the following points. First, the Pauline contrast of the old man and the new can be isolated as a distinct piece of baptismal teaching, and could be taken out in each Epistle without interrupting the flow of the ethical injunctions. Secondly, the Jewish colour of the catalogue in Col. iii. 5-7, Eph. iv. 17-19 suggests that St. Paul is drawing here on the neo-Levitical pattern which we have already examined (I. 1, Table I), the original ἀπέχεσθαι being replaced in Colossians by νεκρώσατε and in Ephesians by μηκέτι ὑμᾶς περιπατεῖν. These passages derive, in fact, from the *Abstinentes* of the primitive Holiness Code. Thirdly, the true *Deponentes* of Col. iii. 8, Eph. iv. 25-31 introduces a catalogue concerned with κακία and especially sins of speech and temper ; and its correlative *Induentes* introduces in both cases Catechumen Virtues.

Further, while ἀποθέσθαι occurs in 1 Peter, James, Romans, Colossians, Ephesians, ἐνδύσασθαι does not appear in 1 Peter or James (unless it underlies ὁπλίσασθε in 1 Pet. iv. 1), but it occurs in 1 Thess. v. 8, Gal. iii. 27, Rom. xiii. 12, 14, Col. iii. 10, 12, Eph. iv. 24, vi. 11, 14, and was evidently a favourite word of St. Paul's : indeed, except for Lk. xxiv. 49, it does not occur in a metaphorical sense outside the Pauline Epistles. The object of the verb is very variously expressed : as Christ (Gal. iii. 27, Rom. xiii. 14), the new man (Col. iii. 10, Eph. iv. 24), the Christian virtues (Col. iii. 12 f.), the Christian armour (1 Thess. v. 8, Rom. xiii. 12, Eph. vi. 11, 14). The view will be advanced later that the metaphor of the Christian armour found a place in an early pattern of Persecution-teaching : the thought of the Christian life as a spiritual combat would naturally have been evoked as opposition became more widespread and pronounced. But was the root idea contained in ἐνδύσασθαι a feature of the primitive baptismal catechism also ? The question is not easily to be decided. In favour of an affirmative answer is the fact that the *Deponentes* would very quickly prompt the desire for a correlative on the positive side ; and the frequency of its occurrence in the *Odes of Solomon* and other baptismal hymns or liturgical forms indicates how well the metaphor fitted baptismal usages and ideas.[1] Still more significant is the fact that the metaphorical use of the word is frequent in LXX, e.g. Job viii. 22, Ps. xxxv. 26 (αἰσχύνην), Job xxix. 14 (δικαιοσύνην), Is. li. 9, lii. 1 (ἰσχύν . . . δόξαν) ; and cf. also *Ps. Sol.* xi. 8. On the other hand, ἐνδύσασθαι is absent from 1 Peter and James, and the first of the *Deponentes* passages mentioned above (Col. iii. 5-7) has no *Induentes* ; while it occurs with the armour metaphor in two O.T. passages, Is. lix. 17 and Wisd. v. 17-20, which undoubtedly underlie its usage in N.T., and which, being concerned with the decisive action God takes to deliver the righteous from their enemies, were eminently suited to bring strength and comfort to the Church in days of

[1] Cf. J. H. Bernard in *Texts and Studies*, vol. viii. No. 3 (1912), p. 20, and on *O.S.* vii. 10, with which cf. *O.S.* xxxiii. 10, x. 10, xiii. 2.

persecution and impending Judgment. The passages are :

Is. lix. 17	Wisd. v. 17 ff.
καὶ ἐνεδύσατο δικαιοσύνην ὡς θώρακα, καὶ περιέθετο περικεφαλαίαν σωτηρίου ἐπὶ τῆς κεφαλῆς, καὶ περιεβάλετο ἱμάτιον ἐκδικήσεως, καὶ τὸ περιβόλαιον αὐτοῦ ὡς ἀνταποδώσων ἀνταπόδοσιν ὄνειδος τοῖς ὑπεναντίοις.	λήμψεται πανοπλίαν τὸν ζῆλον αὐτοῦ, καὶ ὁπλοποιήσει τὴν κτίσιν εἰς ἄμυναν ἐχθρῶν. ἐνδύσεται θώρακα δικαιοσύνην, καὶ περιθήσεται κόρυθα κρίσιν ἀνυπόκριτον· λήμψεται ἀσπίδα ἀκαταμάχητον ὁσιότητα, ὀξυνεῖ δὲ ἀπότομον ὀργὴν εἰς ῥομφαίαν . . .

And echoing these passages in N.T. we find ἐνδύεσθαι in the places already named : θώρακα πίστεως and περικεφαλαίαν ἐλπίδα σωτηρίας in I Thess. v. 8 ; the " panoply of God ", with its θώρακα τῆς δικαιοσύνης and its περικεφαλαίαν τοῦ σωτηρίου and its shield (θυρεόν) of faith in Eph. vi. 11, 13 ff. ; and the idea of God as the divine Avenger in Rom. xii. 19, Heb. x. 30,[1] I Pet. iv. 5. We may also note possible allusions to the soldier's pack (φορτίον) in Gal. vi. 5 (cf. Lightfoot's note in loc., where three further references are given) ; to his rations (ἐφόδια) in I Clem. ii. 1 ; and to his pay (ὀψώνια) in I Cor. ix. 7, Ign. Pol. vi. 2 — a passage full of the armour metaphor. Different minds will assess the significance of this evidence differently. But I am inclined to think that ἐνδύσασθαι did find a place in the baptismal catechism, introducing the Catechumen Virtues and thus balancing the Deponentes, and that the object of the verb was δικαιοσύνην or possibly Χριστόν ; and it must be remembered that, though there is no ἐνδύσασθαι in James, I Peter gives us ἀναζωσάμενοι in i. 13, ὁπλίσασθε in iv. 1, and ἐγκομβώσασθε in v. 5. The evidence points, moreover, to the development of the armour metaphor and its application to the Christian warfare having been due to St. Paul. Much more difficult is the question whether we should assign this metaphor to the baptismal catechism (II. 2, Tables IV, V) or to the Persecution-tōrah discussed in Part III below. In favour of the former view is the association of the heavenly armour with the " light " to which the baptized are admitted through becoming Christians, in I Thess. v. 4-8 and Rom. xiii. 12 ; in favour of the latter is the eschatological

---

[1] Deut. xxxii. 35 is the primary source quoted in Rom. xii. 19 and Heb. x. 30. But the place of the thought in Is. lix. 17 may well have suggested its use.

context in which the metaphor always occurs and which seems to have marked the early teaching about persecution (cf. below, Part III, Table XIV). Perhaps the solution lies in refusing the dilemma; for we can see in 1 Thess. v. how easy the transition was from the one to the other, and we may well believe that the armour metaphor took with it into the Persecution-*tōrah* the idea of Christians belonging to the light which had been part of the baptismal catechism from the beginning.

Summary. — The facts above outlined seem best accounted for by the hypothesis that the *Abstinentes* of the primitive Holiness Code, which we have traced (Table I) in Acts xv., 1 and 2 Thessalonians, and 1 Peter, is also echoed in Col. iii. 5-7 and Eph. iv. 17-19, and perhaps v. 3-6 ; but that it was not correlated with any *Induentes*. Moreover, consideration of the catalogues alluded to in the *Abstinentes* suggests that the sins there repudiated were derived from the Levitical idea of ἀκαθαρσία. The *Deponentes* proper, on the other hand, referred to sins expressive of κακία, especially sins of speech and temper, and was balanced by a correlative *Induentes*, introducing either the simple idea of δικαιοσύνη or some such list of Catechumen Virtues as we find in Col. iii. 12 f., Eph. iv. 32–v. 1. As to the relation between the *Abstinentes* of the primitive Holiness Code (Table I) and the *Deponentes* of the baptismal catechism (Table VI) we can give only a provisional answer here. It is not satisfactory to say that they are different ways of saying the same thing ; for the first is a negative precept, a command to abstain or keep aloof, while the second enjoins an act of deliberate renunciation. It is also significant that, while ἀπέχεσθαι is fairly often used in LXX in a moral sense, ἀποτίθεσθαι is never so used. The facts point, I suggest, to distinct traditions of teaching ; the first to a period prior to or coeval with the Apostolic Decree, when manuals of instruction needed to have Jewish-Christian suspicions much in mind, and were therefore assimilated as far as possible to Levitical teaching ; while the second represents a later stage, when these suspicions were not so pressing a difficulty, and the Church was far more absorbed in the practical problem of disentangling its converts from Gentile society and its manner of life. This stage would give rise to a new version of catechetical instruction ; and we may surmise that St. Paul's missionary labours in Asia Minor and Greece quickly made the need felt.

(iii) *The New Life : its Faith and Worship*

Only brief space can be given here to consideration of the

doctrinal element in the primitive catechism, for it is not strictly
relevant to our examination of the literary parallels between 1 Peter
and other Epistles. But that there were such statements of doctrine
as distinct from practical teaching is indicated by a number of
passages in N.T. A good illustration is the summary found in
1 Thess. i. 9, 10, which embraces faith in (1) the living and true
God, (2) the Sonship of Jesus and His imminent Parusia, (3) His
resurrection, and (4) His redeeming work. The first of these
points is expressed in words in Heb. xi. 6, which may well be taken
from the primitive catechism : " he that cometh unto God (προσ-
ερχόμενον, i.e. as a proselyte of the Church) must believe that he is,
and that he is a rewarder of them that diligently seek him". There is
reason also to believe that in 1 Cor. xv. 1-4 we have a very early *credo*,
earlier than St. Paul's conversion, covering the atoning death, the
burial, the resurrection, and the appearances of Jesus [1] ; and 1 Tim.
iii. 16 is no doubt to be assigned to the same category, though we
should speak rather of a credal hymn.[2] (Cf. Kroll, *Die Christliche
Hymnodik*, and Essay I above, pp. 325-6.) Such a *credo* may
well be what St. Paul means when he writes to the Christians at
Rome (Rom. vi. 17) of "the pattern of teaching to which you have
been delivered ". The question whether this statement was oral or
written is largely otiose ; for, if originally oral, it would quickly
pass into many different manuals drawn up for missionary purposes.

Some passages in the Pastoral Epistles are also relevant. 2 Tim.
i. 13 presents a well-known crux of N.T. exegesis ; but I cannot
help thinking that the simplest explanation is also the true one, and
that the sentence should be translated, " Have (i.e. have by you) a
sketch or outline of the sound words you have heard from me, in
the study we have had together of Christian faith and conduct ".
Timothy is advised to have by him written memoranda of St. Paul's
teaching, to enable him to guard the *catholicae fidei talentum*
entrusted to him.[3] Again, in Tit. i. 9, a " bishop " is bidden to
cleave to " the word which is faithful according to the doctrine "
(κατὰ τὴν διδαχήν), a phrase which indicates a pattern or standard
of doctrine by which the reliability of the word preached may be
judged ; and this interpretation of διδαχή is borne out by the fact
that a different word, διδασκαλία, is used in the same verse (cf. also
Tit. ii. 10) for the actual teaching imparted. So understood, these

---

[1] Cf. *Essays Catholic and Critical*,
pp. 291, 292 (article by the present
writer).

[2] Cf. Loisy, *Les Origines du N.T.*
pp. 285 f. : " Le petit symbole christo-

logique qui se lit dans la Première à
Timothée (iii. 16) . . . paraît sensible-
ment plus ancien que son contexte ".

[3] See Humphries' notes (C.B.S.) on
this verse and 1 Tim. vi. 20.

passages tally with other N.T. evidence and with what we know in the mission field to-day. There is a pattern, or primitive *credo*, which underlies the regular teaching given in the Church, and is its touchstone ; and, even if not formally published like the Apostolic Decree of Acts xv., it was early committed to writing by leaders like St. Paul and his colleagues (2 Thess. ii. 15 ; iii. 6) ; and their helpers and successors in the ministry were advised to have by them notes of the teaching which the Apostles had given.

A further point worth observing is the way in which, both in 1 Peter and in Romans, the injunctions on worship are prepared for by passages on doctrine immediately preceding them.[1] The principle of Doctrine — Worship — Good Works had been enunciated long before by the celebrated Rabbi, Simon Justus, who used to say, " On three things the world is stayed ; on the *tōrah*, and on the Worship, and on the bestowal of Kindnesses "[2] ; and it is the clue to much that we find in the N.T. Epistles. In Rom. xii. 1 this is somewhat obscured by the magnificent eloquence of xi. 33-6 ; but that outburst of praise is, in fact, packed with doctrine of the profoundest significance ; and Christian worship is claimed as man's response to the abounding generosity of God towards all mankind. In 1 Peter, the doctrinal foundation is laid with the utmost deliberation. Except for the fact that Jesus is never called υἱός in this Epistle, the four points mentioned in 1 Thess. i. 9, 10 are all stated in the first chapter, and appealed to as truths well known ; Christians are guarded " through faith " in their journey through the world ; and the purpose of the resurrection of Christ is that their faith and hope might be in God. All this teaching is gathered to a practical issue in the adhesion of believers to Christ as the " living stone " ; and it is out of that relationship that Christian worship springs. It is a fruit of the Word implanted (Jas. i. 21), indwelling (Col. iii. 16), desired, and imbibed (1 Pet. ii. 2, 3).

In studying the parallel passages on Worship, we observe the following points :

(*a*) In 1 Peter, James, Colossians, and Ephesians they follow the *Deponentes*[3] and precede the Social Code comprised under the heading *Subiecti*. This relationship to the *Subiecti* is found also in Romans, though some verses dealing with Catechumen Virtues

---

[1] So, too, in Phil. ii. 10-11, following the doctrinal teaching of verses 4-9.

[2] *Pirqe Aboth*, i. 2 (with Taylor's notes).

[3] This relationship between the *Deponentes* and worship is expressed in

the place assigned to the Decalogue in the Order of Holy Communion in the Book of Common Prayer. It is quite lost when the " Summary of the Law " is substituted for it.

TABLE VII

THE NEW LIFE: ITS FAITH AND WORSHIP

I Peter	James	Romans	Colossians	Ephesians	Johannine Writings	Other Epistles
i. 17. εἰ πατέρα ἐπι-καλεῖσθε τὸν ἀπροσ-ωπολήπτως κρίνοντα ... ib. 14. μὴ συσχημα-τιζόμενοι...ἀλλά... ii. 4. πρὸς ὃν προσ-ερχόμενοι, λίθον ζῶν-τα... ὡς λίθοι ζῶντες οἰκοδομεῖσθε οἶκος πνευματικός, εἰς ἱεράτευμα ἅγιον, ἀν-ενέγκαι πνευματικὰς θυσίας εὐπροσδέκτους θεῷ διὰ Ἰησοῦ Χρι-στοῦ... ib. 9. ὅπως τὰς ἀρε-τὰς ἐξαγγείλητε τοῦ ἐκ σκότους ὑμᾶς καλέ-σαντος εἰς τὸ θαυμα-στὸν αὐτοῦ φῶς ...	i. 27. θρησκεία καθαρὰ καὶ ἀμίαν-τος παρὰ τῷ θεῷ καὶ πατρὶ αὕτη ἐσ-τίν, ἐπισκέπτεσθαι ὀρφανοὺς καὶ χήρας ἐν τῇ θλίψει αὐτῶν, ἄσπιλον ἑαυτὸν τη-ρεῖν ἀπὸ τοῦ κόσμου [cf. 1 Jn. ii. 15 and 1 Thess. v. 23].	xii. 1, 2. παρα-καλῶ οὖν ὑμᾶς, ἀδελφοί, διὰ τῶν οἰκτιρμῶν τοῦ θεοῦ, παραστῆσαι τὰ σώ-ματα ὑμῶν θυσίαν ζῶσαν, ἁγίαν, εὐ-άρεστον τῷ θεῷ, τὴν λογικὴν λα-τρείαν ὑμῶν. καὶ μὴ συσχηματίζεσθε τῷ αἰῶνι τούτῳ, ἀλλά ... εἰς τὸ δοκιμάζειν ὑμᾶς τοῦ θεοῦ τί τὸ θέλημα τοῦ θεοῦ τὸ ἀγαθὸν καὶ εὐάρε-στον καὶ τέλειον.	iii. 16, 17. ὁ λόγος τοῦ Χριστοῦ ἐνοικείτω ἐν ὑμῖν πλουσίως ἐν πάσῃ σοφίᾳ· διδά-σκοντες καὶ νουθετοῦν-τες ἑαυτοὺς ψαλμοῖς, ὕμνοις, ᾠδαῖς πνευ-ματικαῖς, ἐν χάριτι ᾄδοντες ἐν ταῖς καρ-δίαις ὑμῶν τῷ θεῷ... πάντα ἐν ὀνόματι κυ-ρίου Ἰησοῦ, εὐχαρισ-τοῦντες τῷ θεῷ πατρὶ δι᾽ αὐτοῦ.	v. 17. διὰ τοῦτο μὴ γίνεσθε ἄφρονες, ἀλλὰ συνίετε τί τὸ θέλημα τοῦ κυρίου. [cf. Rom. xii. 2.] ib. 18, 19. καὶ μὴ μεθύσκεσθε οἴνῳ... ἀλλὰ πληροῦσθε ἐν πνεύματι, λαλοῦντες ἑαυτοῖς ψαλμοῖς καὶ ὕμνοις καὶ ᾠδαῖς πνευματικαῖς, ᾄδοντες καὶ ψάλλοντες τῇ καρ-δίᾳ ὑμῶν τῷ κυρίῳ, ib. 20. εὐχαριστοῦν-τες πάντοτε ὑπὲρ πάν-των ἐν ὀνόματι τοῦ κυρίου ἡμῶν Ἰησοῦ Χριστοῦ τῷ θεῷ καὶ πατρί....	Jn. iv. 23, 24. ἔρχε-ται ὥρα καὶ νῦν ἐστιν, ὅτε οἱ ἀληθινοὶ προσ-κυνηταὶ προσκυνή-σουσι τῷ πατρὶ ἐν πνεύματι καὶ ἀλη-θείᾳ· καὶ γὰρ ὁ πατὴρ τοιούτους ζητεῖ τοὺς προσκυνοῦντας αὐτόν. πνεῦμα ὁ θεός· καὶ τοὺς προσκυνοῦντας αὐτὸν ἐν πνεύματι καὶ ἀληθείᾳ δεῖ προσ-κυνεῖν.	[Heb. xi. 6.] Heb. xiii. 15, 16. δι᾽ αὐτοῦ οὖν ἀνα-φέρωμεν θυσίαν αἰ-νέσεως διὰ παντὸς τῷ θεῷ, τοῦτ᾽ ἔστι καρπὸν χειλέων ὁμολογούντων τῷ ὀνόματι αὐτοῦ. τῆς δὲ εὐποιίας καὶ κοινωνίας μὴ ἐπι-λανθάνεσθε· τοιαύ-ταις γὰρ θυσίαις εὐαρεστεῖται ὁ θεός. cf. Phil. ii. 10, 11; and esp. 1 Cor. iii. 16 f., 2 Cor. vi. 16 f. 1 Thess. v. 16-18. πάντοτε χαί-ρετε, ἀδιαλείπτως προσεύχεσθε, ἐν παντὶ εὐχαριστεῖτε· τοῦτο γὰρ θέλημα θεοῦ ἐν Χριστῷ Ἰησοῦ εἰς ὑμᾶς... ib. 20... πάντα δοκιμάζετε....

are interpolated, and the *Deponentes*, as already mentioned, is transferred to a later place.

(*b*) The idea of thanskgiving and of glorifying God is emphasized in 1 Peter, Colossians, Ephesians, and 1 Thessalonians ; and Christian worship is offered through Christ (1 Peter, Colossians, Hebrews) and in His Name (Colossians, Ephesians, Philippians, Hebrews).

(*c*) At the same time there are differences of thought about worship. There is a Levitical background to this section of teaching in 1 Peter, Hebrews, and even Romans, which is absent in Colossians and obscured in Ephesians. In the latter, worship is conceived of in terms of hymns and psalms, which are instruments of mutual teaching and exhortation as well as acts of praise ; while the former speak of " sacrifices " which are " acceptable to God ". Behind the former lie ideas of the Church as a neo-Levitical community : the latter has behind it the customs of the synagogues of the Dispersion.

Now, we have already seen reason to believe (pp. 369 ff., *supra*) that the primitive Church used catechetical material based on the Law of Holiness in Lev. xvii.–xxvi. ; and that this was marked by teaching summarized under the heading *Abstinentes*, and by special emphasis on avoiding uncleanness and on the law of love to neighbour (Lev. xix. 18) as the highest expression of holiness. Did it also have a section on worship ? It seems to me probable. For —

(1) The first allusion to Christian worship in 1 Peter is in i. 17 (εἰ πατέρα ἐπικαλεῖσθε κτλ.), which is part of a passage steeped in Levitical ideas ; and the section ii. 1-9, which is strongly liturgical in character, arises quite simply out of this.

(2) Both in 1 Peter and in Romans the teaching on worship is closely connected with the injunction " not to be conformed " (συσχηματίζειν in 1 Pet. i. 14 and Rom. xii. 2) to the ways of the world. The word occurs only in these two places in N.T., and is well adapted to express the idea of separation involved in Jewish ideas of holiness.

(3) There are allusions in 1 Thessalonians, Romans, and Ephesians to " the will of God " which call for explanation. In 1 Thessalonians we have, " pray without ceasing, in everything give thanks, for this is the will of God towards you " (εἰς ὑμᾶς) ; in Romans the purpose of the injunction to worship and to separation from the world is "that you may prove what is the good and well-pleasing (εὐάρεστον, used immediately beforehand with θυσίαν) and perfect will of God " ; in Ephesians the injunction to worship

is prefaced by the words " understand what the will of the Lord
is ".   In none of these cases does the meaning seem to lie on the
surface, or to be easily derived from the context.   But the Law of
Holiness (Lev. xvii.–xxvi.), both in its social and its ritual and
ceremonial teaching, is punctuated by statements that its ordinances
represent the " statutes and judgments " of the Lord — an idea
which Christian catechists would certainly have preferred to express by the more general, and less legalistic, term of the " will "
of God.   The point called for emphasis, moreover, in a world
which normally sought to discover the will of heaven by recourse
to oracles : cf. the question and answer quoted by F. W. H. Myers,
Essays Classical, p. 46.   Further, we may conjecture that this
exposition of the will of God was precisely the function of the
sermon in early Christian worship : the reference to " proving "
in Romans and to " understanding " in Ephesians suggests an
exercise of the mind, on the part of the congregation no less than
of the preacher, which fits what we know of the close-reasoned
Scriptural preaching of antiquity and which was needed to balance
the more emotional parts of the service expressed in prayer and
praise.   At the same time, we must not omit the possibility that
there is also an allusion to private prayer, especially in Romans,
as an act of offering self and work to God, and of seeking His
guidance.

(4) St. Paul's language in Rom. xii. 1 is less " Levitical " than
St. Peter's in i. 17 and ii. 4-10 : if a common catechetical source
underlies both, St. Paul treats it with greater freedom than his
brother Apostle.   On the other hand, St. Paul, when contrasting
elsewhere (1 Cor. x.) Christian and Gentile worship, quotes the
Law of Holiness at a decisive point in his argument : " the things
which the Gentiles sacrifice, they sacrifice to devils, and not to God "
(1 Cor. x. 20, Lev. xvii. 7).   Throughout this whole chapter on
Christian worship St. Paul quotes the Mosaic law repeatedly ; and
we can see how effective its teaching was against precisely the kind
of pagan and idolatrous *cultus* which prevailed in the Gentile world
of the first century A.D.   Equally significant is his teaching in 1 Cor.
iii. 16 f., 2 Cor. vi. 16 f. about the Church as the " temple of God ",
where the context in each case is markedly Levitical, and in the
second case expressly directed against any compromise with
heathenism.

(5) Eph. v. 1b, 2 breathes the same atmosphere as we find in
1 Pet. i. 17–ii. 10 and Rom. xii. 1, 2, and may be assigned to a
similar basis in the tradition.   Though in the form of an ethical

injunction to imitate God and Christ, it specifies particularly Christ's sacrificial self-surrender, which embodied His love for us, as the point in which above all others we are to imitate Him. The passage thus has affinities both with 1 Peter and with Romans; with 1 Peter in its emphasis on the *imitatio Christi* (though Ephesians here thinks especially of Christ's love and 1 Peter of His humility as what the Cross embodies); and with Rom. xii. 1, 2, because Ephesians implies that Christians also, in so far as they walk in love, as Christ did, will be making " an offering and a sacrifice to God ". The context of " love ", moreover, in Eph. v. 1 as in 1 Pet. i. 17 ff., and of separation from the sin and idolatry of the surrounding world, suggests a neo-Levitical origin for this passage. The effect is to give us a doublet for the teaching about Worship in Ephesians (v. 1, 2 ; v. 19, 20).

These facts seem to me to point to the neo-Levitical *tōrah*, of which Dr. Carrington claims to find traces in certain Epistles, having contained a section on Worship. The parallels between 1 Pet. ii. 4 f. and Rom. xii. 1, 2, which have been held to indicate direct dependence of the former on the latter, are susceptible in themselves of such an explanation, for it is not improbable that St. Peter had read Romans. But when the facts are looked at *as a whole*, they seem to accord better with the view that both alike were writing on the basis of a common catechetical substratum, known to their readers as well as to themselves. At the same time, we note that the teaching on Worship in the Epistles reveals two different strains, which it will be convenient to designate as WL and WS,[1] the former signifying teaching which belongs to the neo-Levitical tradition (B[1]), and the latter that which derived directly from current synagogue custom and may be assigned to B[2]. We shall see that the same division holds good with regard to the Catechumen Virtues (CV), which we must now discuss.

(iv) *The New Life : its Social Virtues and Duties*

Dr. Carrington uses the term Catechumen Virtues to cover both the obligations of Worship and the Code of Subordination which he entitles *Subiecti*. The term itself is valuable, for it brings out the strongly ecclesiastical setting in which the ethical teaching of 1 Peter and the Pauline Epistles and Hebrews is given : the qualities demanded are thought of, not in the abstract, but as belonging to the concrete life of the Church and its members. But

---

[1] WL signifying a section on Worship governed by Levitical ideas, WS one governed by the custom of the Synagogue.

I think that a clearer analysis is obtained if the term is restricted to those general rules of conduct which, while closely associated with the rule of Worship and the Code of Subordination, occupy considerable space and have their own interesting roots. And this is especially the case if the analysis is extended to include Romans.

(a) General : Catechumen Virtues

The material is found mostly in 1 Thess. iv. v., Rom. xii., xiii.,[1] Col. iii., Eph. iv., and 1 Peter *passim.* James is difficult to bring into the picture here ; but 1 Thessalonians is of great importance. The evidence supports, I believe, Dr. Carrington's thesis that a common catechetical substratum underlies the parallels which the Epistles present. But it occurs in larger blocks than we have been handling hitherto ; and the similarities and differences of thought and form are more important than the verbal parallels, which can be discussed as they occur. The facts are set out in tabular form in Tables VIII A and VIII B (see pp. 408-11).

The following points may be observed :

1. There is a marked difference of character and form between the passages containing general teaching in 1 Thess. v. and Rom. xii., xiii. and those in Colossians-Ephesians respectively, while 1 Peter affords parallels with both. In Rom. xii. 9-19, in particular, we note the short and often antithetic clauses characteristic of Jewish paraenetic teaching, and its use of participles (and occasionally infinitives) for imperatives suggests, as we have already seen, a catechetical source ; while Rom. xiii. 8-10 is almost a conflation of two *verba Christi* which interpreted the Jewish Law. And the basis of it is Love. The phrase ἡ ἀγάπη ἀνυπόκριτος in Rom. xii. 9a is curiously solitary and abrupt, as commentators have noticed, and it would be tempting to regard it as a marginal gloss which has crept into the text, if we did not find εἰς φιλαδελφίαν ἀνυπόκριτον in close conjunction with ἀγάπη in 1 Pet. i. 22. But may it not equally well be a *heading*, i.e. " Love's sincerity ", which introduced a catechetical section in current use, and which St. Paul deliberately incorporated here with what followed it, and which St. Peter also used in his own way ? The passages in Colossians-Ephesians,[2] on the other hand, are quite otherwise constructed. Col. iii. 8-15 is a smooth, well-running passage ; and the ethical antithesis is given,

---

[1] The repeated echoes of *verba Christi* in 1 Thess. iv., v. and Rom. xii.-xiv. are well brought out by A. M. Hunter, *op. cit.* pp. 55-8.

[2] Cf. Carrington, *op. cit.* pp. 34 f.

I have no doubt that he is right in regarding Col. iii. 8-15 as the basic passage ; and his reasons for its separation into two in Ephesians seem adequate.

TABLE VIII A

CATECHUMEN VIRTUES: LOVE'S SINCERITY

I Thess.	Romans	I Peter	O. T.		Other N.T. Passages
			Psalm xxxiv.	Proverbs iii.	
iv. 1-12. See Table I	xii. 1, 2, xiii. 8-10. See Table I	i. 11 passim.			
		ii. 3, 4. εἰ ἐγεύσασθε ὅτι χρηστὸς ὁ κύριος· πρὸς ὃν προσερχόμενοι . . .	6. προσέλθατε πρὸς αὐτὸν καὶ φωτίσθητε. . . . 9. γεύσασθε καὶ ἴδετε ὅτι χρηστὸς ὁ κύριος.		
v. 12, 13. Church order based on humility and love.	xii. 3-8: Church order based on humility and modesty. 9. ἡ ἀγάπη ἀνυπόκριτος . . .	iv. 8-11. Love the basis of Church order. v. 5. Humility the basis of Church order.	12. φόβον κυρίου διδάξω ὑμᾶς.		
13. εἰρηνεύετε ἐν ἑαυτοῖς. 14. ἀντέχεσθε τῶν ἀσθενῶν, μακροθυμεῖτε πρὸς πάντας.	18. μετὰ πάντων ἀνθρώπων εἰρηνεύοντες . . . 13. ταῖς χρείαις τῶν ἁγίων κοινωνοῦντες . . . εὐλογεῖτε . . . 14 εὐλογεῖτε . . . εὐλογεῖτε . . .	iii. 8. πάντες ὁμόφρονες [cf. v. 11]. συμπαθεῖς . . . εὔσπλαγχνοι.	cf. Ps. xxxiv. 15.	3. ἐλεημοσύναι καὶ πίστεις μὴ ἐκλιπέτωσάν σε . . . 7. μὴ ἴσθι φρόνιμος παρὰ σεαυτῷ.	
15. ὁρᾶτε μή τις κακὸν ἀντὶ κακοῦ τινι ἀποδῷ· ἀλλὰ πάντοτε τὸ ἀγαθὸν διώκετε εἰς ἀλλήλους καὶ εἰς πάντας.	17. μὴ γίνεσθε φρόνιμοι παρ' ἑαυτοῖς· μηδενὶ κακὸν ἀντὶ κακοῦ ἀποδιδόντες· προνοούμενοι καλὰ ἐνώπιον πάντων ἀνθρώπων.	iii. 9. μὴ ἀποδιδόντες κακὸν ἀντὶ κακοῦ ἢ λοιδορίαν ἀντὶ λοιδορίας, τοὐναντίον δὲ εὐλογοῦντες . . .	15. ἔκκλινον ἀπὸ κακοῦ καὶ ποίησον ἀγαθόν, ζήτησον εἰρήνην καὶ δίωξον αὐτήν.	4. καὶ προνοοῦ καλὰ ἐνώπιον κυρίου καὶ ἀνθρώπων [cf. Rom. xiii. 14b].	Jas. v. 7, 8. μακροθυμήσατε οὖν, ἀδελφοί, ἕως τῆς παρουσίας τοῦ κυρίου . . . μακροθυμήσατε καὶ ὑμεῖς, στηρίξατε τὰς καρδίας ὑμῶν, ὅτι ἡ παρουσία τοῦ κυρίου ἤγγικε.

v. 16. πάντοτε χαίρετε,	12. τῇ ἐλπίδι χαίροντες, . . .	10. cf. Ps. xxxiv. 13 →	Ps. xxxiv. 13. τίς ἐστιν ἄνθρωπος ὁ θέλων ζωήν, ἀγαπῶν ἰδεῖν ἡμέρας ἀγαθάς;	
17. ἀδιαλείπτως προσεύχεσθε,	τῇ προσευχῇ προσκαρτεροῦντες	[iv. 13. . . . . χαίρετε.] iv. 7. νήψατε εἰς προσευχάς.	14. παῦσον τὴν γλῶσσάν σου ἀπὸ κακοῦ,	
18. ἐν παντὶ εὐχαριστεῖτε· τοῦτο γὰρ θέλημα θεοῦ. . . .				
19. τὸ πνεῦμα μὴ σβέννυτε . . .	11. τῷ πνεύματι ζέοντες, τῷ κυρίῳ δουλεύοντες	ii. 16. ὡς δοῦλοι θεοῦ . . .	καὶ χείλη τοῦ μὴ λαλῆσαι δόλον.	
21. . . . . τὸ καλὸν κατέχετε.	9. ἀποστυγοῦντες τὸ πονηρόν, κολλώμενοι τῷ ἀγαθῷ . .	iii. 11. . . . . ἐκκλινάτω δὲ ἀπὸ κακοῦ, καὶ ποιησάτω ἀγαθόν· ζητησάτω εἰρήνην καὶ διωξάτω αὐτήν.	Ps. xxxiv. 15. ἔκκλινον ἀπὸ κακοῦ καὶ ποίησον ἀγαθόν, ζήτησον εἰρήνην καὶ δίωξον αὐτήν.	Prov. iii. 7. φοβοῦ δὲ τὸν θεὸν καὶ ἔκκλινε ἀπὸ παντὸς κακοῦ.
22. ἀπὸ παντὸς εἴδους πονηροῦ ἀπέχεσθε.		8. φιλάδελφοι . . . . ταπεινόφρονες		
[iv. 9. περὶ δὲ τῆς φιλαδελφίας . . .]	10. τῇ φιλαδελφίᾳ εἰς ἀλλήλους φιλόστοργοι, τῇ τιμῇ ἀλλήλους προηγούμενοι			
v. 13. . . . ἡγεῖσθαι αὐτοὺς ὑπερεκπερισσοῦ ἐν ἀγάπῃ		iv. 8. πρὸ πάντων τὴν εἰς ἑαυτοὺς ἀγάπην.	19. τοὺς ταπεινοὺς τῷ πνεύματι σώσει.	

[Continued on next page

Table VIII a—continued

I Thess.	Romans	I Peter	O.T.		Other N.T. Passages
			Pentateuch	Psalms and Proverbs	
	19. μὴ ἑαυτοὺς ἐκδικοῦντες, ἀγαπητοί, ἀλλὰ δότε τόπον τῇ ὀργῇ· γέγραπται γάρ, Ἐμοὶ ἐκδίκησις, ἐγὼ ἀνταποδώσω, λέγει κύριος. 20. ἀλλὰ ἐὰν πεινᾷ ὁ ἐχθρός σου, ψώμιζε αὐτόν· ἐὰν διψᾷ, πότιζε αὐτόν· τοῦτο γὰρ ποιῶν ἄνθρακας πυρὸς σωρεύσεις ἐπὶ τὴν κεφαλὴν αὐτοῦ [citing Prov. xxv. 21, 22]. xiii. 7. ἀπόδοτε πᾶσι τὰς ὀφειλάς . . . 8-10. μηδενὶ μηδὲν ὀφείλετε, εἰ μὴ τὸ ἀγαπᾶν ἀλλήλους· ὁ γὰρ ἀγαπῶν τὸν ἕτερον νόμον πεπλήρωκε. τὸ γὰρ Οὐ μοιχεύσεις . . . ἐν τούτῳ τῷ λόγῳ ἀνακεφαλαιοῦται, ἐν τῷ Ἀγαπήσεις τὸν πλησίον σου ὡς σεαυτόν. ἡ ἀγάπη κτλ.	iii. 12. ὅτι ὀφθαλμοὶ κυρίου ἐπὶ δικαίους, καὶ ὦτα αὐτοῦ εἰς δέησιν αὐτῶν· πρόσωπον δὲ κυρίου ἐπὶ ποιοῦντας κακά. cf. iv. 14. τὸ τῆς δόξης καὶ τὸ τοῦ θεοῦ πνεῦμα ἐφ' ὑμᾶς ἀναπαύεται.	Lev. xix. 17, 18. οὐ μισήσεις τὸν ἀδελφόν σου τῇ διανοίᾳ σου. . . . καὶ οὐκ ἐκδικᾶταί σου ἡ χείρ, καὶ οὐ μηνιεῖς τοῖς υἱοῖς τοῦ λαοῦ σου, καὶ ἀγαπήσεις τὸν πλησίον σου ὡς σεαυτόν . . . Deut. xxxii. 35. ἐν ἡμέρᾳ ἐκδικήσεως ἀνταποδώσω . . . ὅτι ἐγγὺς ἡμέρα ἀπωλίας αὐτοῖς . . . 36. ὅτι κρινεῖ κύριος τὸν λαὸν αὐτοῦ . . . [Ex. xxiii. 4, 5.] Ex. xx. 13 ff, cited verbatim in Rom. xiii. 9. Lev. xix. 18. ἀγαπήσεις τὸν πλησίον σοῦ ὡς σεαυτόν.	Ps. xxxiv. 16, 17a, cited without change in I Peter iii. 12. Prov. xx. 22 [12]. μὴ εἴπῃς, Τίσομαι τὸν ἐχθρόν, ἀλλὰ ὑπόμεινον τὸν κύριον ἵνα σοι βοηθήσῃ. Prov. xxv. 21, 22 [cited without change in Rom. xii. 20]. Prov. iii. 9. τίμα τὸν κύριον ἀπὸ σῶν δικαίων πόνων, καὶ ἀπάρχου αὐτῷ ἀπὸ σῶν καρπῶν δικαιοσύνης.	Heb. x. 30. οἴδαμεν γὰρ τὸν εἰπόντα, Ἐμοὶ ἐκδίκησις, ἐγὼ ἀνταποδώσω· καὶ πάλιν, Κρινεῖ κύριος τὸν λαὸν αὐτοῦ. Eph. iv. 26. ὀργίζεσθε καὶ μὴ ἁμαρτάνετε . . . μηδὲ δίδοτε τόπον τῷ διαβόλῳ. Jas. ii. 8 . . . νόμον . . . βασιλικόν, κατὰ τὴν γραφήν, Ἀγαπήσεις τὸν πλησίον σου ὡς σεαυτόν . . . Mk. xii. 31, Matt. xix. 18, 19, xxii. 39, 40, Gal. v. 14.

TABLE VIII B

CATECHUMEN VIRTUES: ANOTHER VERSION

Colossians	Ephesians	Verba Christi	Other N.T. Parallels
iii. 12. ἐνδύσασθε οὖν, ὡς ἐκλεκτοὶ τοῦ θεοῦ, ἅγιοι καὶ ἠγαπημένοι, σπλάγχνα οἰκτιρμοῦ, χρηστότητα, ταπεινοφροσύνην, πραότητα, μακροθυμίαν· 13. ἀνεχόμενοι ἀλλήλων, καὶ χαριζό-μενοι ἑαυτοῖς, ἐάν τις πρός τινα ἔχῃ μομφήν· καθὼς καὶ ὁ κύριος ἐχαρίσατο ὑμῖν, οὕτω καὶ ὑμεῖς. 14. ἐπὶ πᾶσι δὲ τούτοις τὴν ἀγάπην, ὅ ἐστι σύνδεσμος τῆς τελειότητος. 15. καὶ ἡ εἰρήνη τοῦ Χριστοῦ βρα-βευέτω ἐν ταῖς καρδίαις ὑμῶν, εἰς ἣν καὶ ἐκλήθητε ἐν ἑνὶ σώματι· καὶ εὐχάριστοι γίνεσθε.	iv. 1. παρακαλῶ οὖν ὑμᾶς . . ἀξίως περιπατῆσαι τῆς κλήσεως ἧς ἐκλήθητε, 2. μετὰ πάσης ταπεινοφροσύνης καὶ πραότητος, μετὰ μακροθυμίας, ἀνεχόμενοι ἀλλήλων ἐν ἀγάπῃ. 32. γίνεσθε δὲ εἰς ἀλλήλους χρηστοί, εὔσπλαγχνοι, χαριζόμενοι ἑαυτοῖς, καθὼς καὶ ὁ θεὸς ἐν Χριστῷ ἐχαρίσατο ὑμῖν. v. 2. καὶ περιπατεῖτε ἐν ἀγάπῃ . . . iv. 3. σπουδάζοντες τηρεῖν τὴν ἑνότητα τοῦ πνεύματος ἐν τῷ συνδέσμῳ τῆς εἰρήνης.	σπλάγχνα οἰκτιρμοῦ: Matt. v. 7, Lk. vi. 36. ταπεινοφροσούνην: Matt. v. 3, xi. 29, xviii. 4, xxiii. 12, Lk. xxii. 24-7. πραότητα: Matt. v. 5. μακροθυμίαν: Matt. xviii. 26-9. ἀνεχόμενοι . . καθώς . . .: Mk. xi. 25, Matt. vi. 12, v. 38, 39, 43-8. σπουδάζοντες . . .: Matt. v. 6. εἰρήνης . . .: Matt. v. 9. τελειότητος: Matt. v. 48.	[Jas. v. 11.] μακροθυμήσατε . . .: Jas. v. 7, 8. εὔσπλαγχνοι: 1 Pet. iii. 9. πρὸ πάντων τὴν . . . ἀγάπην: 1 Pet. iv. 8.

not clause by clause, but by the dependence of the whole section on the contrast between the *Deponentes* and its opposite, which provide its groundwork. Further, it contains no obvious reference to O.T., but is a good summary of much of our Lord's ethical teaching, expecially in the Sermon on the Mount. I Peter presents yet another aspect. In I Pet. i. (as in I Thess. iv., v.) the emphasis of the ethical teaching is on holiness and love, and it thus has clear affinities with the Law of Holiness in Leviticus, and leads up to the *Deponentes* and the conception of the Church as a neo-Levitical community. This is followed by the *Subiecti* sections, which are interwoven with the governing idea, only faintly alluded to in Colossians (iii. 13) and Ephesians (iv. 32, v. 1, 2), of the Christian life as an *imitatio Christi* ; and the *Subiecti* sections are concluded with an avowed summary (iii. 8, 9, note the opening words τὸ δὲ τέλος) of the Catechumen Virtues, leading into a quotation of several verses of Ps. xxxiv. In Colossians and Ephesians, that is to say, the summary is attached to the *Deponentes*, in I Peter to the *Subiecti*. Further, the latter is shorter than the other; and on one specific point of teaching, the forgiveness of injuries, which Romans, I Peter, Colossians, Ephesians, and I Thessalonians all alike emphasize, I Peter presents close verbal resemblances with I Thessalonians and Romans, but none at all with Colossians-Ephesians.[1] I Pet. iii. 8, 9 looks, in fact, independent of Colossians-Ephesians ; though it might be a summary of I Thess. v. 13-22 or of Rom. xii. 9-19. And in the order of thought it is nearer to the former than to the latter, as a glance at the table shews. The verbal parallels are closest in the statement of the law of non-requital (I Pet. iii. 9 = Rom. xii. 17 = I Thess. v. 15) ; and if I Peter is the borrower here,

---

[1] The vocabulary, both in I Pet. iii. 8, 9 and in Col. iii. 12-15, is interesting. Thus, in I Pet. iii., ὁμόφρονες and εὔσπλαγχνοι are not found in LXX at all ; συμπαθεῖς is only doubtful (Job xxix. 25), apart from 4 Maccabees (three instances) ; φιλάδελφοι occurs once in 2 Maccabees, and twice in 4 Maccabees, and the noun φιλαδελφία thrice in 4 Maccabees, but not otherwise in LXX ; ταπεινόφρονες is found only once in LXX (Prov. xxix. 23). But ὁμόφρονες, συμπαθεῖς, φιλάδελφοι all occur in literary Greek, and so does εὔσπλαγχνοι in its medical sense. In Col. iii. 12 ff., σπλάγχνα οἰκτιρμοῦ, χρηστότης, πραότης, μακροθυμία all occur in LXX, though the plural

οἰκτιρμοί and not the singular is nearly always used, and μακροθυμία is rare. ἀνέχεσθαι, in the sense of "bearing patiently with ", is also found in LXX, but rarely ; though it is good classical Greek. Other LXX words which are also classical or sub-classical are χρηστότης, πραότης, and (in Menander and Strabo) μακροθυμία. On the other hand, ταπεινοφροσύνη, μομφὴν ἔχειν (" have a grievance ") and σύνδεσμος (in this sense) are not found in LXX, but occur in literary Greek. On the whole, one may say that the vocabulary of both passages is good Greek of the first century A.D., but I Peter is perhaps the more detached from the language of LXX.

dependence is more likely to be on 1 Thessalonians than on Romans, owing to Silvanus' association with 1 Peter and 1 Thessalonians.

But a more probable explanation is surely that behind all three there lies common catechetical material. For an author is more likely to summarize traditional material than a passage from a contemporary author's work, even if partly his own ; and the form of the teaching in 1 Thess. v. 13 ff. and Rom. xii. 9 ff., especially in the latter, is suggestive of a catechetical origin. Such a statement of the ethics of love might well have been prepared in the circle of prophets and teachers at Antioch, who bade God-speed to St. Paul and Silas on the second missionary journey.

2. There is striking affinity between the allusions to Leviticus xix. (with parallel passages in Deuteronomy) in 1 Peter and Rom. xii , xiii. As pointed out above (pp. 372 ff.), 1 Pet. i. is steeped in ideas found in the Law of Holiness, especially those of holiness and love ; in 1 Pet. ii. the Christian Church is portrayed as a neo-Levitical community ; and the ban on the *lex talionis*, which is expressed in similar terms in 1 Thess. v. 15, Rom. xii. 17, and 1 Pet. iii. 9, is based on Lev. xix. 17, 18, though Rom. xii. 19 (cf. Heb. x 30) amplifies it by quoting from Deut. xxxii. 35, 36. And St. Paul returns to the Law of Love in the next chapter (xiii. 8-10), when he summarizes the second table of the Decalogue, as our Lord Himself had, in the Levitical command, " Thou shalt love thy neighbour as thyself " (Lev. xix. 18). To all who thought of the primitive Church as a neo-Levitical community, this *verbum Christi* would have seemed to give all the authority they needed for developing that doctrine.

3. The influence of Prov. iii. 3-10 [1] on the language of Rom. xii. is plain from the parallels shewn in Table VIII A, and is as certain as that of Ps. xxxiv. on 1 Pet. ii. and iii. I should be inclined to see also in Rom. xiii. 6, 7 and 1 Pet. ii. 17 dependence upon Prov. iii. 9, τίμα τὸν κύριον ἀπὸ σῶν δικαίων πόνων, καὶ ἀπάρχου αὐτῷ ἀπὸ σῶν καρπῶν δικαιοσύνης (cf. also the allusions to " spiritual sacrifices " in 1 Pet. ii. 5). Further, there appear to be traces of Ps. xxxiv. in 1 Thess. v. and Rom. xii. The διώκετε of 1 Thess. v. 15 and the contrast between τὸ καλόν and εἶδος πονηρόν in 1 Thess. v. 21, 22 are very close to Ps. xxxiv. 15. That verse again may underlie Rom. xii. 9, 18 ; and the injunction to trust in God as the avenger of the innocent (Rom. xii. 19 ; and cf. the teaching on the nature of the magistrate's authority in Rom. xiii. 1-4), though it is based verbally

---

[1] How much this chapter, and indeed Proverbs generally, were used in Jewish religious teaching is well illustrated in Pereq R. Meir, §§ 7 ff. (*Sayings of the Jewish Fathers*, by C. Taylor, pp. 116 ff.).

on passages in Deuteronomy and possibly Isaiah, is closely akin to Ps. xxxiv. 16, 17. Ps. xxxiv. was so admirably adapted to the instruction of catechumens, as its use in 1 Pet. ii. 3, 4 exemplifies, that it may well have been used at a very early stage, as it stood, in the teaching of the primitive Church, or made the basis of shorter paraenetic Forms.

4. We have already observed (cf. p. 397 above) what Dr. Carrington described as a " doublet " for the *Deponentes* in Colossians and Ephesians, which further examination shewed to be more probably a case of the close interlocking of the *Abstinentes* with the *Deponentes*. Likewise, in regard to Worship, we have seen that the neo-Levitical ideas (WL) characteristic of 1 Peter, Romans, Hebrews (Ephesians) have been superseded or amplified in 1 Thessalonians, Colossians-Ephesians by teaching which appears to have quite other roots. So, similarly, with the Catechumen Virtues. The Law of Love in Rom. xiii. 8-10 is a doublet of the ἡ ἀγάπη ἀνυπόκριτος section in Rom. xii. 9-19, and is based on Lev. xix. 18 and a *verbum Christi*, while the earlier section is based on Prov. iii. and (less certainly) Ps. xxxiv. In 1 Pet. i.–ii. 12 the Catechumen Virtues are based on neo-Levitical ideas, while in iii. 8 ff. they take the form partly of a summary of the catechetical material underlying 1 Thess. v. and Rom. xii. 9-19, and partly of verses quoted from Ps. xxxiv. In Colossians-Ephesians the Catechumen Virtues are not traceable to O.T. sources,[1] either directly or indirectly, but are closely associated with the *Deponentes* and are given in a form which is probably due to St. Paul himself or his amanuensis.

Summary. — Analysis of the passages in the Epistles we are considering which contain general teaching on what Dr. Carrington calls Catechumen Virtues (CV) points to three distinct patterns of ethical teaching underlying the Epistles and current in the early Church. They are :

1. A type of *tōrah* based on the idea of the Church as a neo-Levitical community, and containing *Abstinentes*, WL, and a form of ethical teaching which we may call CVL. This pattern would have been very well adapted to Christian missionary work amongst the Jews of Palestine and those of the Dispersion who cherished especially the Levitical tradition.

2. A gnomic form of CV (which we may call CVG), modelled on and derived from Psalms, Proverbs, and other similar Jewish

---

[1] Though ἡ εἰρήνη τοῦ Χριστοῦ βραβευέτω may owe something to Zech. viii. 16; cf. Taylor, note on *Pirqe Aboth*, i. 19

literature, which appears in 1 Thess. v. 12-22, Rom. xii. 9-19, and 1 Pet. iii. 8-12. As we shall see below, it is probable that this source CVG contained teaching on Church order, with special emphasis on the duty of humility. Whether CVG circulated separately from CVL or was part of it from the first we cannot say.

3. A later version of the earlier pattern, compiled under the influence of the extension of the Church to Gentiles, and containing *Deponentes*, the idea of the Church as a " body ", a non-Levitical type of teaching on Worship (WS), and ethical teaching of which the *Subiecti* was characteristic.

St. Peter and St. Paul deal with this material in different ways. St. Peter conflates (1) and (2), if he did not find the conflation already made, and makes extensive use of the *Subiecti* from (3), but not much of the *Deponentes*. In particular, the *Subiecti* points the way to one of the great themes of his Epistle, namely the *imitatio Christi* (cf. Introd. IV. 6, pp. 90-101). St. Paul in 1 and 2 Thessalonians and 1 Corinthians shews acquaintance with many of the ideas of (1), and in Rom. xii., xiii., conflates (1) and (2), if he did not find the conflation already made. But in Colossians-Ephesians he leaves (1) and (2), and follows (3), adding to it his own metaphor of " putting off the old man " and " putting on the new ", and building his ethical teaching round this. It is these facts which lead me to the view that the " Outline of the Pattern " put forward by Dr. Carrington [1] is too simple, and that we should speak of two outlines, or of two versions of the outline, and possibly of a third source as well. And, more broadly, we may say that while (1), with or without (2), laid the main emphasis upon love, (3) laid it on humility. They stand out as the two cardinal virtues in the ethical teaching of the early Church.

(*b*) Passages on Church Order and Unity

The Epistles we have been considering contain a number of parallel passages on Church unity and order, which may be compared in detail in the appended table. The most primitive passage is that in 1 Thess. v., and it is to be observed that despite its brevity it inculcates both humility and love. St. Paul in Romans, where he is speaking of Church order, lays the emphasis on humility; while in Colossians, where he is speaking on Church unity, he lays it on love. In Ephesians, on the other hand, where he is speaking both of unity and of order, he gives equal weight to both love and humility. And St. Peter, in dealing with Church order (he does not

Table VIII c

---

[1] *op. cit.* Table VII, p. 90.

TABLE VIII c

TEACHING ON CHURCH UNITY AND ORDER

I Thess.	Romans	I Peter	Colossians	Ephesians
v. 12, 13. ἐρωτῶμεν δὲ ὑμᾶς, ἀδελφοί, εἰδέναι τοὺς κοπιῶντας ἐν ὑμῖν καὶ προϊσταμένους ὑμῶν ἐν κυρίῳ καὶ νουθετοῦντας ὑμᾶς, καὶ ἡγεῖσθαι αὐτοὺς ὑπερεκπερισσοῦ ἐν ἀγάπῃ διὰ τὸ ἔργον αὐτῶν.	**xii. 3.** λέγω γὰρ διὰ τῆς χάριτος τῆς δοθείσης μοι παντὶ τῷ ὄντι ἐν ὑμῖν, μὴ ὑπερφρονεῖν παρ' ὃ δεῖ φρονεῖν, ἀλλὰ φρονεῖν εἰς τὸ σωφρονεῖν, ἑκάστῳ ὡς ὁ θεὸς ἐμέρισε μέτρον πίστεως.	**iv. 8.** πρὸ πάντων τὴν εἰς ἑαυτοὺς ἀγάπην ἐκτενῆ ἔχοντες ...	**iii. 14, 15.** ἐπὶ πᾶσι δὲ τούτοις τὴν ἀγάπην, ὅ ἐστι σύνδεσμος τῆς τελειότητος. καὶ ἡ εἰρήνη τοῦ Χριστοῦ βραβευέτω ἐν ταῖς καρδίαις ὑμῶν, εἰς ἣν καὶ ἐκλήθητε ἐν ἑνὶ σώματι· καὶ εὐχάριστοι γίνεσθε.	**iv. 1-3.** παρακαλῶ οὖν ὑμᾶς ... ἀξίως περιπατῆσαι τῆς κλήσεως ἧς ἐκλήθητε, μετὰ πάσης ταπεινοφροσύνης καὶ πραότητος, μετὰ μακροθυμίας, ἀνεχόμενοι ἀλλήλων ἐν ἀγάπῃ, σπουδάζοντες τηρεῖν τὴν ἑνότητα τοῦ πνεύματος ἐν τῷ συνδέσμῳ τῆς εἰρήνης.
	4. καθάπερ γὰρ ἐν ἑνὶ σώματι ...	**i. 12.** διὰ τῶν εὐαγγελισαμένων ὑμᾶς.		**4.** ἓν σῶμα καὶ ...
	5. οὕτως οἱ πολλοὶ ἓν σῶμά ἐσμεν ἐν Χριστῷ ...	**iv. 10.** ἕκαστος καθὼς ἔλαβε χάρισμα, εἰς ἑαυτοὺς αὐτὸ διακονοῦντες ...		**7.** ἑνὶ δὲ ἑκάστῳ ἡμῶν ἐδόθη ἡ χάρις κατὰ τὸ μέτρον τῆς δωρεᾶς τοῦ Χριστοῦ.
	6. ἔχοντες δὲ χαρίσματα κατὰ τὴν χάριν τὴν δοθεῖσαν ἡμῖν διάφορα, εἴτε προφητείαν, κατὰ τὴν ἀναλογίαν τῆς πίστεως·	**11.** εἴ τις λαλεῖ, ὡς λόγια θεοῦ· εἴ τις διακονεῖ, ὡς ἐξ ἰσχύος ἧς χορηγεῖ ὁ θεός.		**8.** διὸ λέγει· Ἀναβὰς εἰς ὕψος ...
cf. I Tim. v. 17, οἱ καλῶς προεστῶτες πρεσβύτεροι διπλῆς τιμῆς ἀξιούσθωσαν, μάλιστα οἱ κοπιῶντες ἐν λόγῳ καὶ διδασκαλίᾳ.	**7.** εἴτε διακονίαν, ἐν τῇ διακονίᾳ· εἴτε ὁ διδάσκων, ἐν τῇ διδασκαλίᾳ·	**9.** φιλόξενοι εἰς ἀλλήλους, ἄνευ γογγυσμοῦ ...		**11.** καὶ αὐτὸς ἔδωκε τοὺς μὲν ἀποστόλους, τοὺς δὲ προφήτας, τοὺς δὲ εὐαγγελιστάς, τοὺς δὲ ποιμένας καὶ διδασκάλους,
Heb. xiii. 17, πείθεσθε τοῖς ἡγουμένοις ὑμῶν, καὶ ὑπείκετε ...	**8.** εἴτε ὁ παρακαλῶν, ἐν τῇ παρακλήσει· ὁ μεταδιδούς, ἐν ἁπλότητι· ὁ προϊστάμενος, ἐν σπουδῇ· ὁ ἐλεῶν, ἐν ἱλαρότητι.	**v. 1.** πρεσβυτέρους οὖν ... παρακαλῶ ...		**12.** πρὸς τὸν καταρτισμὸν τῶν ἁγίων, εἰς ἔργον διακονίας ...
Jas. iv. 6, 7, 10.} See be- Heb. xii. 9.} low.		**2.** ποιμάνατε ... ἐπισκοποῦντες μὴ ἀναγκαστῶς ἀλλ' ἑκουσίως κατὰ θεόν ...		
		5. πάντες δὲ ἀλλήλοις τὴν ταπεινοφροσύνην ἐγκομβώσασθε, ὅτι ὁ θεὸς ὑπερηφάνοις ἀντιτάσσεται, ταπεινοῖς δὲ δίδωσι χάριν.		

use the category of "unity" at all), is likewise synthetic, though the main emphasis is on love. St. Peter may, of course, have Romans in mind when he writes ; but this difference of approach and basis is in that case somewhat strange ; and the lines of his treatment are already laid in 1 Thess. v. The varied χαρίσματα of the Ministry presented a theological problem at an early date, and St. Paul made it the occasion for careful teaching on the unity of the Spirit in the Church and the diversity of His operations, leading up to his great hymn on the pre-eminence of charity (1 Cor. xii., xiii.). St. Peter seems to be doing the same thing on quieter lines.

There remains the further question as to why this section appears where it does in each Epistle. So far as Romans is concerned, its place is relatively to the passage we have denoted CVG the same also in 1 Thess. v. ; and it is a fair conjecture that it was part of that catechetical section from the beginning. 1 Peter, which has already in iii. 8, 9 treated that section in its own way, now transfers the teaching on Church order to a later part of the Epistle, and brings it into an eschatological context. But though our author departs here from Romans, he does not depart from 1 Thessalonians ; for the Church order passage in 1 Thessalonians follows immediately upon an eschatological passage (v. 1-11) closely akin to 1 Pet. iv. 7. The simplest explanation, perhaps, is that we have here another example of the influence of Silvanus in the drafting of the Epistle. In Colossians and in Ephesians the teaching about Church unity and order appears quite independent of that in 1 Thessalonians, Romans, and 1 Peter, though the high place given to it among the Catechumen Virtues shews how closely for the writers of N.T. the Christian ethic is bound up with Churchmanship. See Table VIII c, opposite.

We may also consider here certain striking parallels between 1 Peter, James (and Hebrews), which appear to belong to this section rather than to the *Subiecti* and which throw light on the catechetical material we have denoted CVG.

The following points may be observed :

(1) The fundamental idea is that of the theological root of humility, i.e. submission to God. In 1 Peter the reciprocal humility which Christians must shew to one another, and even the specific humility of the "younger" to the "elder" is based on this. Humility is at bottom an attitude of the soul towards God.

(2) 1 Peter and James both quote Prov. iii. 34 (with the substitution of ὁ θεός for κύριος : was this because κύριος was so largely

Proverbs	1 Peter	James	Hebrews
iii. 34. Κύριος ὑπερηφάνοις ἀντι- τάσσεται, ταπεινοῖς δὲ δίδωσι χάριν.	v. 5. ὁμοίως, νεώ- τεροι, ὑποτάγητε πρε- σβυτέροις. πάντες δὲ ἀλλήλοις τὴν ταπεινοφροσύνην ἐγκομβώσασθε· ὅτι ὁ θεὸς ὑπερηφάνοις ἀντι- τάσσεται, ταπεινοῖς δὲ δίδωσι χάριν.	iv. 5. μείζονα δὲ δίδωσι χάριν. 6. διὸ λέγει, Ὁ θεὸς ὑπερηφάνοις ἀντι- τάσσεται, ταπεινοῖς δὲ δίδωσι χάριν. 7. ὑποτάγητε οὖν τῷ θεῷ . . .	xii. 9. οὐ πολὺ μᾶλλον ὑποταγησό- μεθα τῷ πατρὶ τῶν πνευμάτων, καὶ ζή- σομεν;
	6. ταπεινώθητε οὖν ὑπὸ τὴν κραταιὰν χεῖρα τοῦ θεοῦ, ἵνα ὑμᾶς ὑψώσῃ ἐν και- ρῷ . . .	10. ταπεινώθητε ἐν- ώπιον τοῦ κυρίου, καὶ ὑψώσει ὑμᾶς.	

appropriated to Christ ?). But they approach it in different ways, St. Peter using it to give force to his injunction of humility, James to illustrate the abundance of God's grace ; though James proceeds immediately to deduce from the passage the duty of submission to God. It is unlikely that either was dependent on the other here. Furthermore, it is noticeable that the passage which both quote comes from the same chapter of Proverbs as we have seen St. Paul quoting in Rom. xii. Is it not reasonable, therefore, to suppose that this verse also formed part of the catechetical section which we have traced behind 1 Thess. v. and Rom. xii., and denoted by the term CVG ? In that case, this section was based both on Ps. xxxiv. and on Prov. iii., St. Peter using mostly the former and St. Paul the latter, but both shewing definite traces of being acquainted with those parts of the pattern which the other found most congenial. And its place in 1 Pet. v. is in favour of the view that CVG was from the first attached to a section on Church order, for that is its context there. 1 Pet. iv. 7-11 and v. 1-8 present, in fact, two lessons on Church order, the first based on love, the second on humility, and both of them against a background of eschatology made more vivid by persecution. The intervening passage, whatever its occasion, made a special address to the presbyters, and a special emphasis on humility, appropriate immediately afterwards. But the spiritual life of the Church forms the continuing interest throughout.

(c) Summary of Evidence so far considered

The evidence so far considered may now be summarized as follows :

1. The primitive Form based on the Levitical Holiness Code was drawn up at the time of the Apostolic Decree, if not earlier, for the instruction of candidates for baptism. Based on the *Abstinentes*, it laid special emphasis on the sins of uncleanness and covetousness, on the Word of God as the Truth in contrast with idolatry, and on the duty of brotherly love. It contained a section on Worship (WL), and its development of the Catechumen Virtues was strongly influenced by the Law of Holiness, contained in Leviticus and re-published by our Lord (CVL). The priestly conception of the Church so strongly marked in 1 Pet. ii. probably goes back to it likewise : all that we know of St. Peter from Acts suggests that it would have been congenial to him. The application to the baptized of the *Filii Lucis* conception and its corollaries, as we find them in 1 Thess. v., 1 Peter, and Ephesians, was also in this source. We have called this Form B¹. *Cf. Tables I and II*

2. A somewhat different Form grew up as the result of the Church's expansion in Asia Minor and elsewhere, in which the negative *Abstinentes* was amplified or superseded by the more positive *Deponentes*, with its correlative *Induentes*. In this Form Worship was conceived on freer lines familiar from the practice of the Dispersion (WS), and it contained ethical teaching based on the Jewish gnomic models, notably Psalms and Proverbs (CVG). This may have been added to CVL, or may have circulated separately in the first instance. We may call this Form B². *Cf. Tables IV-VI*

3. Teaching on Church order and unity, based on humility and love, was probably part of the catechetical teaching from the beginning, and an integral part of the Forms which contained such teaching. *Cf. Table IX*

4. St. Paul handles his materials with greater freedom than St. Peter, importing distinctive metaphors of his own, and impressing his marked personality upon the earlier Forms which he uses.

The facts are set forth in tabular form in Table IX (see p. 420).

(d) Particular Relationships : the Social Code (*SUBIECTI*)

Much attention has been devoted by scholars in recent years to the codes governing particular social relationships which meet us in several Epistles of N.T., and the comparisons they offer with similar codes current both in Jewish and in Hellenistic circles of the same

TABLE IX

SUMMARY OF EVIDENCE SO FAR CONSIDERED

1 Thess.	1 Peter	James	Romans	Colossians	Ephesians
iv. 3-12. Abstinentes. CVL.	[i. 14. Abstinentes.]		xii. 1. WL.	iii. 5-7. Abstinentes.	iv. 1-3. CV.
v. 4-8. Filii Lucis. [Vigilate.]	i. 15-23. CVL.		[xii. 2. Abstinentes.]		iv. 17-19. Abstinentes.
	i. 17. WL.				iv. 24. Induentes.
	ii. 1. Deponentes.	i. 21. Deponentes.		iii. 8, 9a. Deponentes.	iv. 25-31. Deponentes.
			xii. 3-21. CVG.	iii. 12-15. Induentes and CV.	iv. 32-v. 1. CV.
	ii. 4-10. WL.	i. 27. WL.		iii. 16, 17. WS.	v. 2. WL.
v. 19-21. WS.	ii. 9. Filii Lucis.				v. 3-6. CVL.
	[iv. 7, v. 8. Vigilate.]				v. 8-14. Filii Lucis.
v. 22. Abstinentes.	ii. 11, 12. Abstinentes.	[iv. 8. Abstinentes.]			v. 15-20. WS.
	ii. 13-iii. 7. Subiecti.	iv. 6, 7. Subiecti.	xiii. 1-7. Subiecti.	iii. 18-iv. 1. Subiecti.	v. 21-vi. 9. Subiecti.
v. 12-22. CVG.	iii. 8-12. CVG.	iii. 13-18 } CV.	xiii. 8-10. CVL.		
		v. 7-11 }	xiii. 12. Deponentes.		
v. 8. Induentes.	[iv. 1, v. 5. Induentes.]		xiii. 12-14. Filii Lucis. [Vigilate, Induentes.]	iv. 2. Filii Lucis. [Vigilate.]	

period. Despite some variations of order, the form in which the different kinds of duties are expressed, the similarity of the teaching, and the verbal parallelisms, especially the repeated use of some part of the verb ὑποτάσσεσθαι (often the *participium pendens*), point irresistibly to a common source or sources underlying the N.T. documents. This system of codes was one of the means used in the ancient world for the purposes of ethical instruction. Another was the form illustrated in the " Two Ways " of the *Didache* and the *Epistle of Barnabas*, which is traceable in Judaism to passages such as Deut. xxx. and many parts of the Psalter, and in Greek to the " antitheses " of Heraclitus, and to passages in Hesiod, Theognis, and Xenophon.[1] The third form was the " catalogue " of virtues and vices, which was much used by the Pythagoreans, and by the writers of comedy as well as by the philosophers : the most famous of these is that in Aristotle, *Eth. Nicom.* ii. vii., which governs the ethical discussion and the pursuit of the " Mean " from that point to the end of Bk. IV. They even figured on counters used in parlour games. At the same time these lists were not without criticism in the ancient world : witness Plutarch's charge against Chrysippus of creating a σμῆνος ἀρετῶν οὐ συνηθὲς οὐδὲ γνώριμον (*Vir. Mor.* 2). All these meet us in the pages of N.T., and the second and third in our Lord's own teaching. But the first, the method of the social code or code of subordination, is that which is most characteristic of the Epistles ; and it was evidently much used in the Apostolic Church.

Unfortunately no actual social codes used in education survive from antiquity ; but their germs can be surely traced both in pagan and Jewish sources. Diogenes Laertius assigns one to Pythagoras, Stobaeus to Hierocles ; and Seneca says that they had the approval of the Stoic Cleanthes.[2] To the Jews, who had the highly articulated social teaching of the Law as the bedrock of their religion, such a method of ethical teaching made a natural appeal ; and we have examples of it in Tobit iv. and xii., in *Test. XII Patr.*, in the

---

[1] For an excellent and well-documented discussion of these methods of instruction cf. K. E. Kirk, *The Vision of God*, Lecture III. Deissmann (*Light from the Ancient East* (E.T. 1911), pp. 319 ff.) gives some apt parallels to N.T. ethical teaching both from literary sources and from games. Ch. xix. of Dr. Lowther Clarke's *New Testament Problems* should also be consulted, as it contains a useful review of Weidinger's *Die Haustafeln*. For N.T. examples of the " Two Ways " method we may refer to Matt. vii. 13, 14 (*verba Christi*) and 2 Pet. ii. 2, 15, 21, and of the " catalogues " to Mk. vii. 21, 22 (*verba Christi*), Gal. v. 19-23, 1 Cor. vi. 9, 10, 1 Tim. i. 9 f., among other passages.

[2] References in Kirk, *op. cit.* p. 120, n. 8.

Story of Ahikar, and especially in Ecclesiasticus,[1] and in later times in Pseudo-Phocylides[2] and in Philo. Christianity outside Palestine was the heir of both traditions ; and in view of the vogue of these codes in the first century and earlier, we need not hestitate to assign to such a code or codes the large amount of common materials which the Epistles offer us in this *genre*. See the following Tables X-XIII.

Tables X and X A   The most convenient way of studying the parallels will be to set forth first the subjects dealt with in the different Epistles and their

Tables XI-XIII   order, and secondly the detailed treatment given to each subject with special reference to verbal similarities.

(A) The Subjects and their Order

Tables X and X A   These are set out in the adjoining Tables X and X A. The latter is a schematic version of the former, given for convenience of reference. The letters b^1, c^1, and d^1 are used on the assumption that the basic idea in these relationships is that of subordination, and they denote the reciprocal duties entailed on those to whom this subordination is due. The fact that in every case the subordinates' duties are mentioned first, and that in some cases they are without the correlative duties, implies that the approach was from the angle of subordination. The following points may be observed :

(*a*) *b*, *c*, and *d* are all balanced by their correlatives b^1, c^1, and d^1 in Colossians and Ephesians ; in 1 Peter only *e* is thus balanced. But both in 1 Peter and Romans a balance is implied in *a* in the sense that the civic authorities are said to hold their power from God (cf. Jn. xix. 11) and to hold it for a social purpose beneficial to their subjects. They are not, however, directly exhorted, as are husbands, parents, and masters of households, presumably because

---

[1] References in Kirk, *op. cit.* p. 122, n. 2.

[2] The following are the relevant passages in this curious Graeco-Jewish poem, which Schürer (II. iii. p. 315) ascribes to some period before the first century A.D. [the text is that given in Bergk, *Poetae Lyrici Graeci*, ii. pp. 450-75] :

Husbands and Wives :

στέργε τεὴν ἄλοχον· τί γὰρ ἡδύτερον
καὶ ἄρειον,
ἢ ὅταν ἀνδρὶ γυνὴ φρονέῃ φίλα γή-
ραος ἄχρις,
καὶ πόσις ᾗ ἀλόχῳ, μηδ' ἐμπέσῃ
ἄνδιχα νεῖκος (ll. 195-8).

Parents and Children :

παισὶν μὴ χαλέπαινε τεοῖς, ἀλλ' ἤπιος
εἴης (l. 207).

And in ll. 209 ff., the young are bidden αἰδεῖσθαι and γεραίρειν the aged.

Masters and Slaves :

γαστρὸς ὀφειλόμενον δασμὸν παρ-
έχειν θεράπευσιν,
δούλῳ τακτὰ νέμοις ἵνα τοι κατα-
θύμιος εἴη.
στίγματα μὴ γράψῃς, ἐπονειδίζων
θεράποντα.
δοῦλον μὴ βλάψῃς τι κακηγορέων
παρ' ἄνακτι.
λάμβανε καὶ βουλὴν παρὰ οἰκέτου εὖ
φρονέοντος.

Table X

CODE OF SUBORDINATION (*SUBIECTI*)

1 Peter	Romans	Colossians	Ephesians	1 Timothy	Titus	James (Heb.)
(*a*) ii. 13-17. Obedience to civic authority.	(*a*) xiii. 1-7. Obedience to civic authority (perhaps partly based on Prov. iii. 9).	(*e*) iii. 12. General duty of Humility.	(*e*) v. 21. Duty of reciprocal Humility.	(*a*) ii. 1-8. Prayer to be offered for all, e.g. kings and all in authority.	(*c*) ii. 4, 5. Obedience of Wives to Husbands.	(*g*) iv. 6. Duty of Humility (quoting Prov. iii. 34).
(*b*) ii. 18-25. Obedience of Slaves to Masters (based on *Imitatio Christi*).		(*c*) iii. 18. Obedience of Wives to Husbands.	(*c*) v. 22-4. Obedience of Wives to Husbands (as of the Church to Christ).	(*c*) ii. 9-15. Subordinate place of women in the Church (based on Gen. ii.): need of modest demeanour and dress (cf. 1 Pet. iii 1-6).	(*f*) ii. 6. The "younger", to be sober-minded.	(*h*) iv. 7, 10. Humility and obedience to God.
(*c*) iii. 1-6. Obedience of Wives to Husbands (based on O.T. exx., and quoting Prov. iii. 25).		(*c¹*) iii. 19. Duties of Husbands.	(*c¹*) v. 25-33. Duties of Husbands (modelled on Christ's relationship to the Church).	(*b*) vi. 1, 2. Slaves to honour their Masters.	(*b*) ii. 9, 10. Obedience of Slaves to Masters.	**cf. Heb. xii. 9.** Subjection to God as Father.
(*c¹*) iii. 7. Reciprocal duties of Husbands.		(*d¹*) iii. 20. Obedience of Children to Parents.	(*d*) vi.1-3. Obedience of Children to Parents (based on 5th Commandment).		(*a*) iii. 1. Obedience to civic authority.	Heb. xiii. 17. Subjection to Church-officers.
(*e*) iii. 8. General duty of Humility.		(*d²*) iii. 21. Fathers' duty to Children.	(*d¹*) vi. 4. Fathers' duty to Children.			
(*f*) v. 5. Obedience of "younger" to "elder".	[cf. xii. 3, 16].	(*b*) iii. 22-5. Obedience of Slaves to Masters.	(*b*) vi. 5-8. Obedience of Slaves to Masters.			
(*g*) v. 5. Duty of reciprocal Humility (quoting Prov. iii. 34).		(*b¹*) iv. 1. Duties of Masters.	(*b¹*) vi. 9. Duties of Masters			
(*h*) v. 6. Humility towards God.						

TABLE X A
ORDER OF HEADINGS

I Peter	Romans	Colossians	Ephesians	I Timothy	Titus	James
(a)	(e)	(e)	(e)	(a)	(c)	(g)
(b)	(a)	(c)	(c)	(c)	(f)	(h)
(c)		(c¹)	(c¹)	(b)	(b)	
(c¹)		(d)	(d)		(a)	
(e)		(d¹)	(d¹)			
(f)		(b)	(b)			
(g)		(b¹)	(b¹)			
(h)						

424

they were not members of the Church. It was no part of the Church's task to pose as a politically or socially revolutionary body.

(*b*) 1 Peter differs from all the other Epistles in the order of the relationships discussed. The order in Colossians-Ephesians — *c*, wives and husbands, *d*, children and parents, *b*, slaves and masters — is supported (so far as the evidence goes) by 1 Timothy which has *c* and *b* in that order, but no *d*, and by Titus which has *c* and *b* in that order, but with *f* intercalated between them, and with no *d*. 1 Peter, on the other hand, which also has no *d*, introduces *b* before *c*. It must be admitted that the order in Colossians-Ephesians, *c*, *d*, *b*, is the natural order in a code of household conduct, and we must suppose that St. Peter is here departing from his source. The reason, however, is not far to seek ; for the allusions to freedom and the service of God (ii. 16, 17) in the preceding section on civic obedience would have suggested that the position and duties of slaves should be taken next. St. Peter propounds two principal motives for the subjection and meekness which are the main theme of ii. 11–iii. 12 : one is the *imitatio Christi*, the other the converting influence of meekness on the unbelieving " superiors ". The first is illustrated in the behaviour of the Christian slave, the second in that of the Christian wife. Either would have followed quite suitably on *a* (ii. 13-17) ; but the choice was determined, I suggest, by the immediate verbal context in verse 16. The omission of *d* (duties of children) is more difficult to explain, as, if later experience is any guide, the maxim *ex ore infantium* must often have been exemplified in the primitive Church. But St. Peter was adapting the code to his own use, and may well have been content with one domestic relationship only to illustrate each principal motive. That he is using the code as a familiar peg, rather than purporting to follow it in detail, is clear from the way he breaks out into the general summary in iii. 8.

It seems to me probable, therefore, that the order of the under-lying code is more closely reflected in Colossians-Ephesians (and 1 Timothy and Titus) than in 1 Peter.

(*c*) The fact that *a*, though absent from Colossians-Ephesians, appears in 1 Timothy and Titus in conjunction with *b* and *c*, as well as in 1 Peter and Romans, makes it probable that such a section belonged to the original code.[1] The issue behind it had presented itself in our Lord's lifetime, and had been the

---

[1] The probability is, I think, reinforced by the use of πρῶτον πάντων in 1 Tim. ii. 1. This insistence on the primary importance of intercession for those in civic authority is more natural if civic duty already had a primary position in a familiar scheme of duties.

occasion of *verba Christi* of the most far-reaching kind, reinforced
in one case by a miracle (cf. Matt. xvii. 24-7, the stater in the
fish's mouth, and Mk. xii. 13-17, the tribute-money). The introduction of civic duty (τὸ πρὸς πατρίδα καθῆκον) appears to have been
a common practice in pagan codes [1] ; and a community which
desired to commend itself to society by its " well-doing " would
have been unlikely to omit such a section from its catechetical
patterns, and forego the opportunity of enlisting the support of
all who were acquainted with the high ideals of citizenship inculcated by the Stoics.[2]

(*d*) We have suggested above (p. 418) that *g* and *h* in 1 Peter
and James can be accounted for without reference to any underlying
code. *f* presents problems of its own, which will be considered
below.

(B) THE SOCIAL RELATIONSHIPS IN DETAIL

Table XI　　　1. *Civic Obedience.* — The parallel passages are set out in the
accompanying Table and the following points may be observed :

Principle
of sub-
ordination
(*a*) The dominating theme is subordination (1 Peter, Romans,
Titus), though in 1 Timothy this is replaced by intercession [3] ; and
while those in authority are variously described as ἀρχαί, ἐξουσίαι,
οἱ ἄρχοντες, the commonest word (1 Peter, Romans, 1 Timothy) is
some part of ὑπερέχειν or its noun ὑπεροχή. βασιλεύς also occurs,
in the singular or the plural, in 1 Peter and 1 Timothy, and it is
possible that this, like ὑπερέχειν and ὑποτάσσεσθαι, belonged to the
original pattern.

Nature
and
function
of the
civil
power
(β) 1 Peter and Romans are emphatic as to the divine origin
and sanction of the civil power, and as to its function of restraining
and punishing crime, though St. Paul develops both points at
much greater length than St. Peter and in characteristically Pauline
phrase. Both use ἔκδικος or ἐκδίκησις, which was perhaps in the
towards
evil
original pattern. The whole teaching marks a notable advance
on 1 Thess. iv. 6, where it is said that the Lord is the ἔκδικος
of all unfair business methods. As Christianity spread in Greece
and Asia Minor, the Church may well have had to define its
attitude more definitely towards the civil power.

and
towards
well-doing
(γ) 1 Peter and Romans also agree as to the positive function
of the civil power, in encouraging well-doing ; and such teaching
is implied in 1 Timothy ii. 2, and (more clearly) Tit. iii. 1, 8. The

[1] Lowther Clarke, *op. cit.* p. 159.
[2] Cf. Zeller, *Stoics, Epicureans and
Sceptics* (E.T. 1870), pp. 307 ff., with
the references in the notes.
[3] As in *Pirqe Aboth*, iii. 2, " Pray
for the peace of the kingdom ", etc.

TABLE XI

CIVIC OBEDIENCE

I Peter ii. 13-17	Romans xiii. 1-7	I Timothy ii. 1-3	Titus iii. 1-3, 8
13. ὑποτάγητε πάσῃ ἀνθρωπίνῃ κτίσει διὰ τὸν κύριον, εἴτε βασιλεῖ ὡς ὑπερέχοντι,	1. πᾶσα ψυχὴ ἐξουσίαις ὑπερεχούσαις ὑποτασσέσθω· οὐ γὰρ ἔστιν ἐξουσία εἰ μὴ ὑπὸ θεοῦ, αἱ δὲ οὖσαι ὑπὸ θεοῦ τεταγμέναι εἰσίν.	1. παρακαλῶ οὖν πρῶτον πάντων ποιεῖσθαι δεήσεις, προσευχάς, ἐντεύξεις, εὐχαριστίας, ὑπὲρ πάντων ἀνθρώπων·	1. ὑπομίμνησκε αὐτοὺς ἀρχαῖς ἐξουσίαις ὑποτάσσεσθαι, πειθαρχεῖν, πρὸς πᾶν ἔργον ἀγαθὸν ἑτοίμους εἶναι,
14. εἴτε ἡγεμόσιν, ὡς δι' αὐτοῦ πεμπομένοις εἰς ἐκδίκησιν κακοποιῶν ἔπαινον δὲ ἀγαθοποιῶν.	2. ὥστε ὁ ἀντιτασσόμενος τῇ ἐξουσίᾳ τῇ τοῦ θεοῦ διαταγῇ ἀνθέστηκεν· οἱ δὲ ἀνθεστηκότες ἑαυτοῖς κρίμα λήψονται.	2. ὑπὲρ βασιλέων καὶ πάντων τῶν ἐν ὑπεροχῇ ὄντων, ἵνα ἤρεμον καὶ ἡσύχιον βίον διάγωμεν ἐν πάσῃ εὐσεβείᾳ καὶ σεμνότητι.	2. μηδένα βλασφημεῖν, ἀμάχους εἶναι, ἐπιεικεῖς, πᾶσαν ἐνδεικνυμένους πραότητα πρὸς πάντας ἀνθρώπους·
15. ὅτι οὕτως ἐστὶ τὸ θέλημα τοῦ θεοῦ, ἀγαθοποιοῦντας φιμοῦν τὴν τῶν ἀφρόνων ἀνθρώπων ἀγνωσίαν·	3. οἱ γὰρ ἄρχοντες οὐκ εἰσὶ φόβος τῷ ἀγαθῷ ἔργῳ, ἀλλὰ τῷ κακῷ. θέλεις δὲ μὴ φοβεῖσθαι τὴν ἐξουσίαν; τὸ ἀγαθὸν ποίει, καὶ ἕξεις ἔπαινον ἐξ αὐτῆς·	3. τοῦτο καλὸν καὶ ἀπόδεκτον ἐνώπιον τοῦ σωτῆρος ἡμῶν θεοῦ, ὃς πάντας ἀνθρώπους θέλει σωθῆναι καὶ εἰς ἐπίγνωσιν ἀληθείας ἐλθεῖν.	3. ἦμεν γάρ ποτε καὶ ἡμεῖς ἀνόητοι, ἀπειθεῖς, πλανώμενοι, δουλεύοντες ἐπιθυμίαις καὶ ἡδοναῖς ποικίλαις, ἐν κακίᾳ καὶ φθόνῳ διάγοντες, στυγητοί, μισοῦντες ἀλλήλους.
16. ὡς ἐλεύθεροι, καὶ μὴ ὡς ἐπικάλυμμα ἔχοντες τῆς κακίας τὴν ἐλευθερίαν, ἀλλ' ὡς δοῦλοι θεοῦ.	4. θεοῦ γὰρ διάκονός ἐστι σοὶ εἰς τὸ ἀγαθόν. ἐὰν δὲ τὸ κακὸν ποιῇς, φοβοῦ· οὐ γὰρ εἰκῇ τὴν μάχαιραν φορεῖ· θεοῦ γὰρ διάκονός ἐστιν, ἔκδικος εἰς ὀργὴν τῷ τὸ κακὸν πράσσοντι.	8. . . . χωρὶς ὀργῆς καὶ διαλογισμοῦ.	
17. πάντας τιμήσατε τὴν ἀδελφότητα ἀγαπᾶτε τὸν θεὸν φοβεῖσθε τὸν βασιλέα τιμᾶτε.	5. διὸ ἀνάγκη ὑποτάσσεσθαι, οὐ μόνον διὰ τὴν ὀργήν, ἀλλὰ καὶ διὰ τὴν συνείδησιν.		
	6. διὰ τοῦτο γὰρ καὶ φόρους τελεῖτε· λειτουργοὶ γὰρ θεοῦ εἰσιν, εἰς αὐτὸ τοῦτο προσκαρτεροῦντες.		8. πιστὸς ὁ λόγος, καὶ περὶ τούτων βούλομαί σε διαβεβαιοῦσθαι, ἵνα φροντίζωσι καλῶν ἔργων προΐστασθαι οἱ πεπιστευκότες θεῷ. ταῦτά ἐστι καλὰ καὶ ὠφέλιμα τοῖς ἀνθρώποις. . . .
	7. ἀπόδοτε πᾶσι τὰς ὀφειλάς· τῷ τὸν φόρον τὸν φόρον, τῷ τὸ τέλος τὸ τέλος, τῷ τὸν φόβον τὸν φόβον, τῷ τὴν τιμὴν τὴν τιμήν.		

persistence of ἀγαθοποιεῖν, ἀγαθὸν ποιεῖν, ἀγαθὸν ἔργον, καλὰ ἔργα (1 Peter, Romans, Titus) suggests that this was in the source ; and the same may be true of ἔπαινος (1 Peter, Romans). The principle underlying the bestowal of honours and decorations by the Head of a State has thus a Christian justification.

Christian duty of loyalty

(δ) The civil power having this origin and these functions, it follows that Christians owe it an inward loyalty, and not merely an external submission ; and this is expressed by διὰ τὸν κύριον (1 Peter), διὰ τὴν συνείδησιν (Romans), ἑτοίμους εἶναι (Titus). [1 Pet. ii. 19 uses διὰ συνείδησιν θεοῦ when speaking of slaves' duties.] At the same time the difference between St. Peter's phrase and St. Paul's is instructive, the former appealing to the thought of " the Lord ", with the *verbum Christi* perhaps directly in mind, the latter writing rather as a Roman citizen in whom loyalty to the civic authority was inbred. The two together embody a high conception of the ethical obligations of citizenship.

(ε) St. Peter states clearly that one purpose of civic obedience on the part of Christians is that society may be favourably impressed by the new religion — a thought which occurs frequently in his Epistle (cf. Introd. pp. 97 f.), and derives from the *verbum Christi* in Matt. v. 14-16. Romans has nothing of this ; but 1 Tim. ii. 3 (καὶ εἰς ἐπίγνωσιν ἀληθείας ἐλθεῖν) reflects it, and so does Tit. iii. 8 (ταῦτά ἐστι καλὰ κτλ.). I suspect that it was in the source.

(ζ) All four Epistles (1 Timothy *bis*) connect the teaching of civic obedience with something *universal* in Christianity. The social duty of Christians knows no bounds: they are to "honour *all* men "[1] (1 Peter), " render to *all* their dues " (Romans), shew meekness " towards *all* men " (Titus), offer prayers " for *all* men " (1 Timothy) ; and in 1 Timothy this is grounded on the fact of the universality of the salvation offered through the Gospel. It is reasonable to think that this teaching was in the source.

(η) 1 Peter has an important verse on the nature of civic freedom and its relation to religion. This has no parallel in Romans, but its negative side is reflected in Tit. iii. 3, where κακία and δουλεύοντες offer verbal coincidences.

Conclusion. — The evidence does not seem to lend support to the view that 1 Peter is here in any way dependent upon Romans. Indeed it is easier to suppose that Romans was an expansion of

---

[1] This note of universality is a feature of the English Litany. " The word ' all ' rings through it like a bell. ' All that are in danger . . . all that travel by land or by water . . . all sick persons and young children . . . all prisoners and captives,' Nothing and no one is forgotten." (Charles Morgan, *Reflections in a Mirror*, Second Series, pp. 53 f.)

1 Peter than 1 Peter, with its crisp and concrete points, a summary of Romans. But in fact the occurrences of similar *motifs* in 1 Timothy and Titus, not least if the former is not authentic, makes any theory of direct dependence between 1 Peter and Romans unnecessary. A common source underlying all the passages is more probable ; and the workmanlike brevity of 1 Peter ii. 13-17 suggests that this version is nearest to the original.

2. *Slaves and Masters.* — The parallel passages are set out in Table XII Table XII (see p. 430), and the following points may be observed :

(*a*) The main theme is the subjection (ὑποτάσσεσθαι) of slaves to their masters. 1 Peter has οἰκέται, while the other four Epistles have δοῦλοι ; Colossians-Ephesians have τοῖς κατὰ σάρκα κυρίοις, while the other three have δεσπόταις (1 Peter) or ἰδίοις δεσπόταις (1 Timothy, Titus), and also ὑπακούειν instead of ὑποτάσσεσθαι. But these differences of vocabulary are unimportant, especially when we realize that each in its own way emphasizes the concrete and domestic nature of the relationship under discussion. The " institution of slavery " is not in any way in question : the whole interest is in the right conduct of an existing family relationship.

(β) St. Peter has in mind masters who are harsh and ill-tempered (σκολιοί), and deviates at once to the duties of slaves in such situations, and particularly to the need for meekness under injury ; and from this he passes to his great exposition of the *imitatio Christi*. The curious phrase τοῦτο γὰρ χάρις suggests that the *verba Christi* in Lk. vi. 32-4, with their repeated ποία ὑμῖν χάρις ἐστί ; were in his mind. In the other Epistles there is no suggestion that harsh masters are specially in view. Colossians-Ephesians lays stress on the idea that the Christian slave should render a willing and thorough service,[1] remembering that through it he is serving Christ the Lord; and he will be rewarded at His hands. 1 Timothy expressly contemplates the situation where the master as well as the slave is a Christian, and warns slaves against the danger of undue familiarity. Titus calls particularly for honesty and trustworthiness in the slave's calling.

(γ) Both 1 Timothy and Titus mention the favourable effect on men's attitude to Christianity which a slave's good conduct may exert ; 1 Timothy using a phrase (ἵνα μὴ τὸ ὄνομα τοῦ θεοῦ καὶ ἡ διδασκαλία βλασφημῆται) which is closely paralleled (ἵνα μὴ ὁ λόγος τοῦ θεοῦ βλασφημῆται) in Tit. ii. 5 in connexion with the duties of young married women. This sensitiveness to public opinion occurs also in 1 Peter, notably in the general passage (ii. 11, 12) which

[1] For a Rabbinic parallel cf. *Pirqe Aboth*, i. 3.

TABLE XII

SLAVES AND MASTERS

I Peter ii. 18-25	Col. iii. 22-iv. I	Eph. vi. 5-9	I Tim. vi. I, 2	Titus ii. 9, 10
18. οἱ οἰκέται, ὑποτασσόμενοι ἐν παντὶ φόβῳ τοῖς δεσπόταις, οὐ μόνον τοῖς ἀγαθοῖς καὶ ἐπιεικέσιν, ἀλλὰ καὶ τοῖς σκολιοῖς.	22. οἱ δοῦλοι, ὑπακούετε κατὰ πάντα τοῖς κατὰ σάρκα κυρίοις, μὴ ἐν ὀφθαλμοδουλείαις ὡς ἀνθρωπάρεσκοι, ἀλλ' ἐν ἁπλότητι καρδίας, φοβούμενοι τὸν κύριον.	5. οἱ δοῦλοι, ὑπακούετε τοῖς κατὰ σάρκα κυρίοις μετὰ φόβου καὶ τρόμου ἐν ἁπλότητι τῆς καρδίας ὑμῶν ὡς τῷ Χριστῷ.	1. ὅσοι εἰσὶν ὑπὸ ζυγὸν δοῦλοι τοὺς ἰδίους δεσπότας πάσης τιμῆς ἀξίους ἡγείσθωσαν, ἵνα μὴ τὸ ὄνομα τοῦ θεοῦ καὶ ἡ διδασκαλία βλασφημῆται.	9. δούλους ἰδίοις δεσπόταις ὑποτάσσεσθαι, ἐν πᾶσιν εὐαρέστους εἶναι, μὴ ἀντιλέγοντας,
19. τοῦτο γὰρ χάρις, εἰ διὰ συνείδησιν θεοῦ ὑποφέρει τις λύπας πάσχων ἀδίκως.	23. ὃ ἐὰν ποιῆτε, ἐκ ψυχῆς ἐργάζεσθε, ὡς τῷ κυρίῳ καὶ οὐκ ἀνθρώποις,	6. μὴ κατ' ὀφθαλμοδουλείαν ὡς ἀνθρωπάρεσκοι, ἀλλ' ὡς δοῦλοι τοῦ Χριστοῦ ποιοῦντες τὸ θέλημα τοῦ θεοῦ ἐκ ψυχῆς,	2. οἱ δὲ πιστοὺς ἔχοντες δεσπότας μὴ καταφρονείτωσαν, ὅτι ἀδελφοί εἰσαν· ἀλλὰ μᾶλλον δουλευέτωσαν, ὅτι πιστοί εἰσι καὶ ἀγαπητοὶ οἱ τῆς εὐεργεσίας ἀντιλαμβανόμενοι.	10. μὴ νοσφιζομένους, ἀλλὰ πᾶσαν πίστιν ἐνδεικνυμένους ἀγαθήν, ἵνα τὴν διδασκαλίαν τὴν τοῦ σωτῆρος ἡμῶν θεοῦ κοσμῶσιν ἐν πᾶσιν.
20. ποῖον γὰρ κλέος, εἰ ἁμαρτάνοντες καὶ κολαφιζόμενοι ὑπομενεῖτε; ἀλλ' εἰ ἀγαθοποιοῦντες καὶ πάσχοντες ὑπομενεῖτε, τοῦτο χάρις παρὰ θεῷ.	24. εἰδότες ὅτι ἀπὸ κυρίου ἀπολήμψεσθε τὴν ἀνταπόδοσιν τῆς κληρονομίας· τῷ κυρίῳ Χριστῷ δουλεύετε.	7. μετ' εὐνοίας δουλεύοντες ὡς τῷ κυρίῳ καὶ οὐκ ἀνθρώποις,		
21. εἰς τοῦτο γὰρ ἐκλήθητε, ὅτι καὶ Χριστὸς ἔπαθεν, κτλ.	25. ὁ γὰρ ἀδικῶν κομιεῖται ὃ ἠδίκησε καὶ οὐκ ἔστι προσωπολημψία. iv. I. οἱ κύριοι, τὸ δίκαιον καὶ τὴν ἰσότητα τοῖς δούλοις παρέχεσθε, εἰδότες ὅτι καὶ ὑμεῖς ἔχετε κύριον ἐν οὐρανῷ.	8. εἰδότες ὅτι ἕκαστος ὃ ἐὰν ποιήσῃ ἀγαθόν, τοῦτο κομιεῖται παρὰ κυρίου, εἴτε δοῦλος εἴτε ἐλεύθερος.		
21-5. Imitatio Christi.		9. καὶ οἱ κύριοι, τὰ αὐτὰ ποιεῖτε πρὸς αὐτούς, ἀνιέντες τὴν ἀπειλήν, εἰδότες ὅτι καὶ αὐτῶν καὶ ὑμῶν ὁ κύριός ἐστιν ἐν οὐρανοῖς, καὶ προσωπολημψία οὐκ ἔστι παρ' αὐτῷ.		

forms the introduction to the *Subiecti* (cf. also Introd. pp. 97 f.). This motive is so persistent in our documents that it looks as though it had a place in the primitive catechism.

(δ) Colossians-Ephesians add a verse on the reciprocal duties of masters to slaves, a fact which suggests that the Christians of the Lycus and the Mæander valleys were of a higher social status than those addressed by St. Peter.[1] (Throughout this section Ephesians is almost a reproduction of Colossians.)

(ε) St. Peter bids slaves be subject ἐν παντὶ φόβῳ, Eph. vi. 5 μετὰ φόβου καὶ τρόμου, which takes the place of φοβούμενοι τὸν κύριον in Colossians. A similar place is assigned to " fear " in St. Peter's next section (iii. 2), when he speaks of unbelieving husbands observing τὴν ἐν φόβῳ ἁγνὴν ἀναστροφήν of their wives. The corresponding section in Ephesians is introduced by the general phrase (Eph. v. 21) ὑποτασσόμενοι ἀλλήλοις ἐν φόβῳ Χριστοῦ ; and a wife is charged (v. 33) ἵνα φοβῆται τὸν ἄνδρα. These facts make it probable that φόβος was given a place in at least the preamble to the *Subiecti* section, and it would have been in place also in each of the three specific relationships where St. Peter mentions it, ii. 17, 18, iii. 2. On the meaning of the word see note on 1 Pet. i. 17.

Conclusion. — There is nothing here (apart from the case of Colossians-Ephesians) which is not more easily explained by the hypothesis of a common underlying framework of teaching than by that of direct dependence of one document upon another. While the Pastoral Epistles in this section go little beyond conduct and its motive, St. Paul in Colossians-Ephesians gives his ethical injunctions a more explicit theological background, insisting that a slave's service is service rendered to Christ, who is the true Master of all Christians. But 1 Peter goes far further than this, linking the slave's duty with the words of Christ and also with the whole example and significance of His life and death. He holds out before Christian slaves a new ambition (cf. κλέος in ii. 20), that of the highest sanctity ; and he builds this ambition into the innermost fabric of the Gospel, the passion and death of Christ. The section gives us a glimpse of how Christian ethics developed. The original command to slaves to obey their masters, which was probably pre-Christian, became a religious duty to be discharged in reverence ; St. Peter brings it to bear on the special case of slaves who serve harsh masters, interpreting in this sense the *verba Christi* ; and finally the slave's calling is magnified into a unique opportunity for

---

[1] Pseudo-Phocylides deals with the duties of masters to slaves, but not with the converse relationship.

Table XIII
WIVES AND HUSBANDS

I Pet. iii. 1-7	Col. iii. 18, 19	Eph. v. 22-33	I Tim. ii. 9-15	Titus ii. 4, 5
1. ὁμοίως, γυναῖκες, ὑποτασσόμεναι τοῖς ἰδίοις ἀνδράσιν, ἵνα, καὶ εἴ τινες ἀπειθοῦσι τῷ λόγῳ, διὰ τῆς τῶν γυναικῶν ἀναστροφῆς ἄνευ λόγου κερδηθήσονται.	18. αἱ γυναῖκες, ὑποτάσσεσθε τοῖς ἀνδράσιν, ὡς ἀνῆκεν ἐν κυρίῳ.	[21. ὑποτασσόμενοι ἀλλήλοις ἐν φόβῳ Χριστοῦ·] 22. αἱ γυναῖκες, τοῖς ἰδίοις ἀνδράσιν ὡς τῷ κυρίῳ·	[8. Βούλομαι οὖν προσεύχεσθαι τοὺς ἄνδρας ἐν παντὶ τόπῳ . . .] 9. ὡσαύτως γυναῖκας ἐν καταστολῇ κοσμίῳ μετὰ αἰδοῦς καὶ σωφροσύνης κοσμεῖν ἑαυτάς, μὴ ἐν πλέγμασιν καὶ χρυσίῳ ἢ μαργαρίταις ἢ ἱματισμῷ πολυτελεῖ,	[3. πρεσβύτιδας . . .] 4. ἵνα σωφρονίζωσι τὰς νέας φιλάνδρους εἶναι,
2. ἐποπτεύσαντες τὴν ἐν φόβῳ ἁγνὴν ἀναστροφὴν ὑμῶν.		23. ὅτι ἀνήρ ἐστι κεφαλὴ τῆς γυναικός, ὡς καὶ ὁ Χριστὸς κεφαλὴ τῆς ἐκκλησίας, αὐτὸς σωτὴρ τοῦ σώματος.	10. ἀλλ᾽ (ὃ πρέπει γυναιξὶν ἐπαγγελλομέναις θεοσέβειαν) δι᾽ ἔργων ἀγαθῶν.	5. φιλοτέκνους, σώφρονας, ἁγνάς, οἰκουργούς, ἀγαθάς, ὑποτασσομένας τοῖς ἰδίοις ἀνδράσιν, ἵνα μὴ ὁ λόγος τοῦ θεοῦ βλασφημῆται.
3. ὧν ἔστιν οὐχ ὁ ἔξωθεν ἐμπλοκῆς τριχῶν καὶ περιθέσεως χρυσίων ἢ ἐνδύσεως ἱματίων κόσμος,		24. ἀλλ᾽ ὡς ἡ ἐκκλησία ὑποτάσσεται τῷ Χριστῷ, οὕτω καὶ αἱ γυναῖκες τοῖς ἀνδράσιν ἐν παντί.	11. γυνὴ ἐν ἡσυχία μανθανέτω ἐν πάσῃ ὑποταγῇ.	
4. ἀλλ᾽ ὁ κρυπτὸς τῆς καρδίας ἄνθρωπος, ἐν τῷ ἀφθάρτῳ τοῦ πραέος καὶ ἡσυχίου πνεύματος, ὅ ἐστιν ἐνώπιον τοῦ θεοῦ πολυτελές.		25. οἱ ἄνδρες, ἀγαπᾶτε τὰς γυναῖκας, καθὼς καὶ ὁ Χριστὸς ἠγάπησε τὴν ἐκκλησίαν, κτλ.	12. διδάσκειν δὲ γυναικὶ οὐκ ἐπιτρέπω, οὐδὲ αὐθεντεῖν ἀνδρός, ἀλλ᾽ εἶναι ἐν ἡσυχία.	
5. οὕτω γάρ ποτε καὶ αἱ ἅγιαι γυναῖκες αἱ ἐλπίζουσαι εἰς θεὸν ἐκόσμουν ἑαυτάς, ὑποτασσόμεναι τοῖς ἰδίοις ἀνδράσιν·		[26-32. The unity and exclusiveness of Christian marriage symbolize the union between Christ and His Church. The point is buttressed by the *verbum Christi* in Mk. x. 7, 8, citing Gen. ii. 23.]	13. Ἀδὰμ γὰρ πρῶτος ἐπλάσθη, εἶτα Εὔα.	
			14. καὶ Ἀδὰμ οὐκ ἠπατήθη, ἡ δὲ γυνὴ ἐξαπατηθεῖσα ἐν παραβάσει γέγονε.	

6. ὡς Σάρρα ὑπήκουσε τῷ Ἀβραάμ κύριον αὐτὸν καλοῦσα, ἧς ἐγενήθητε τέκνα, ἀγαθο- ποιοῦσαι καὶ μὴ φοβούμεναι μηδεμίαν πτόησιν [cf. Prov. iii. 25]. 7. οἱ ἄνδρες, ὁμοίως, συν- οικοῦντες κατὰ γνῶσιν κτλ.	19. οἱ ἄνδρες, ἀγα- πᾶτε τὰς γυναῖκας, καὶ μὴ πικραίνεσθε πρὸς αὐτάς.	33. πλὴν καὶ ὑμεῖς οἱ καθ' ἕνα, ἕκαστος τὴν ἑαυτοῦ γυναῖκα οὕτως ἀγαπάτω ὡς ἑαυτόν, ἡ δὲ γυνὴ ἵνα φοβῆται τὸν ἄνδρα.	15. σωθήσεται δὲ διὰ τῆς τεκνο- γονίας, ἐὰν μείνωσιν ἐν πίστει καὶ ἀγάπῃ καὶ ἁγιασμῷ μετὰ σωφρο- σύνης.

the *imitatio Christi*, and what began as a rule of conduct ends as a great passage of theology.

Table
XIII

3. *Wives and Husbands.*—The parallel passages are set out in the accompanying Table XIII (see pp. 432-3), and we may note the following points :

(*a*) It seems clear that ὑποτασσόμεναι τοῖς ἰδίοις ἀνδράσιν belongs to the original source, for it appears in the *middle* of this section in Tit. ii. 5, as an obvious " tag ", not really required after the phrases in the preceding verse ; and the same holds good of the repetition of the phrase in 1 Pet. iii. 5. In Titus, moreover, as in 1 Peter, it is followed by a final clause, introduced by ἵνα, which despite great verbal differences has much the same meaning in both places. Direct dependence of one on the other is less likely than the dependence of both on a common source. Here, as in the section on slaves, we note the recurrence of ἴδιος : the writers are concerned with the concrete life of the home rather than with the " status of women ".

(*β*) There is marked similarity between 1 Pet. iii. 3 ff. and 1 Tim. ii. 9 ff. in their development of the theme, both concentrating on the need of modesty of outward demeanour, e.g. dress and ornament, in Christian wives, and of right motive and character. " Quietness " is also emphasized by both,[1] as in 1 Thess. iv. 11, and 1 Tim. ii. 2 ; and in each document the word πολυτελής occurs, though in a somewhat different context, St. Peter transferring it from the outward ornaments which are not really precious to the inner ones which are. Both Hebrew and heathen moralists were alive to the issues involved in women's dress ; and the contrast between the outer and inner ornament, which is observed by Philo,[2] is not uncommon in Greek and Latin authors.[3] The contents of this section in 1 Tim. ii., as in Tit. ii., are more ecclesiastical than in 1 Peter, and include the function of women in religious gatherings ; nor is it clear that 1 Tim. ii. has only married women in view. But both 1 Peter and 1 Timothy draw on O.T. models, the former on Sarah, and the latter on Adam and Eve, to point their morals ; and such examples or " paradigms ", as well as warnings about women's dress, may well have figured in the original catechism. And it was good Jewish teaching, based on Rabbinic lore (cf. Taylor's notes on *Pirqe Aboth*, i. 5)   A further parallel between 1 Peter and

---

[1] In 1 Timothy twice in this section, verse 11 and verse 12.

[2] *de Migr. Abr.* 97 [I. 451 M].

[3] Cf. the celebrated passage in Plautus, *Most.* I. iii. 101-21, and Eur.

Heracl. 476 f :

γυναικὶ γὰρ σιγή τε καὶ τὸ σωφρονεῖν
κάλλιστον, εἴσω δ' ἥσυχον μένειν
δόμων.

1 Timothy is latent in 1 Tim. ii. 9, ἐν καταστολῇ κοσμίῳ μετὰ αἰδοῦς καὶ σωφροσύνης κοσμεῖν ἑαυτάς, which says in less epigrammatic phrase what St. Peter means in 1 Pet. iii. 4, 5.

(γ) The view has been put forward in some quarters[1] that the Christian wives in 1 Pet. iii. are the spouses of unbelieving husbands. The Apostle's purview embraces such cases, but they are clearly not the whole number (cf. καὶ εἴ τινες ἀπειθοῦσι, iii. 1) ; and the direct address to husbands, i.e. Christian husbands, in iii. 7, suggests that they were probably not mainly in his mind.

(δ) In 1 Pet. iii. 6, μὴ φοβούμεναι μηδεμίαν πτόησιν, we have what appears to be an echo of Prov. iii. 25, καὶ οὐ φοβηθήσῃ πτόησιν ἐπελθοῦσαν. The point is noteworthy, in view of the use made of this chapter both by St. Paul in Rom. xii., and by St. Peter and St. James (cf. *supra*, p. 413 and p. 417). The inference is confirmed that this chapter was much in use in the early Church, and perhaps in the Jewish Dispersion in Asia Minor, for purposes of ethical instruction.

Conclusion.—We conclude that here, as in the preceding sections, the N.T. authors were all writing on the basis of a catechetical pattern well known to their readers, and were developing it, each in his own way. The subjection of wives to their own husbands was certainly in the pattern, and it is probable enough that the pattern also included references to the need of conciliating public opinion and to modesty in women's dress. In this case, however, it is St. Paul, not St. Peter, who develops the ethical theme into a great utterance of Christian theology, finding in the unity of man and wife and in the exclusiveness of their relationship a symbol of the unity between Christ and the Church. Though he starts from the duty of wives to be subject to their husbands, his interest does not lie there : it is simply a text for his inspired teaching on the mysterious interrelationship between God and man — a relationship fully reciprocal on either side, and deeply spiritual — which Christ has brought into being in the Church.

4. *Children and Parents: Younger and Elder: Ministers and People.* — It will be convenient to consider the remaining relationships which are treated along similar lines in the Epistles in a somewhat wider context, as the parallels are more fragmentary here and their several outlines less distinct ; and the introduction of their contexts serves in some cases as a kind of chemical to bring into view the invisible ink with which they were written.

The N.T. and the sub-apostolic literature present us with three

---

[1] Cf. Kirk, *op. cit.* p. 126.

groups of relationships, which are not always clearly distinguished:
(a) Parents and children : as in Col. iii. 20, 21, Eph. vi. 1-4, and
Did. iv. 9, οὐκ ἀρεῖς τὴν χεῖρά σου ἀπὸ τοῦ υἱοῦ σου ἢ ἀπὸ τῆς θυγατρός
σου, ἀλλὰ ἀπὸ νεότητος διδάξεις τὸν φόβον τοῦ θεοῦ.[1] Clem. Rom.
xxi. 8, τὰ τέκνα ὑμῶν τῆς ἐν Χριστῷ παιδείας μεταλαμβανέτωσαν·
μαθέτωσαν τί ταπεινοφροσύνη παρὰ θεῷ ἰσχύει κτλ. Polycarp,
ad Phil. iv. 2, τὰς γυναῖκας ὑμῶν [πορεύεσθαι] ἐν τῇ δοθείσῃ αὐταῖς
πίστει καὶ ἀγάπῃ καὶ ἁγνείᾳ, στεργούσας τοὺς ἑαυτῶν ἄνδρας . . . καὶ
τὰ τέκνα παιδεύειν τὴν παιδείαν τοῦ φόβου τοῦ θεοῦ. . . .
The background of these passages is the Christian home and
the life of the family, and they seem to derive from the domestic
code we have been considering.

(β) Older and younger members of the community : as in
1 Pet. v. 5, Tit. ii. 6, 1 Tim. v. 1. The young men or boys are
οἱ νεώτεροι or οἱ νέοι, the girls αἱ νεώτεραι or αἱ νέαι. Cf. Clem.
Rom. i. 3, . . . τιμὴν τὴν καθήκουσαν ἀπονέμοντες τοῖς παρ᾽ ὑμῖν πρε-
σβυτέροις· νέοις τε μέτρια καὶ σεμνὰ νοεῖν ἐπετρέπετε. *Ib.* xxi. 6, τοὺς
πρεσβυτέρους ἡμῶν τιμήσωμεν, τοὺς νέους παιδεύσωμεν τὴν παιδείαν τοῦ
φόβου τοῦ θεοῦ. . . .
The background is the social life of the Hellenistic towns and
cities, where the young men, described indifferently as νέοι or
νεώτεροι, were trained as a recognized group in the Gymnasia. In
some cities of Asia Minor, including probably Pergamum at one
period, this training was military or para-military ; in others it was
cultural and athletic, as in the various types of Youth Movement
now being developed in this country. [Cf. Rostovtzeff, *Social and
Economic History of the Hellenistic World*, iii. pp. 1523 ff.] The
address to νεανίσκοι in 1 Jn. ii. 13, 14 was no doubt in line with the
ethical aims emphasized in the better Gymnasia, where σωφροσύνη
was an accepted ideal. In the passages before us, from N.T. and
1 Clement, the " young men " had probably belonged lately to a
Gymnasium, and were regarded as now in training for the responsibilities attaching to citizenship of the Church. The term covers the
kind of relationships found in the Church of to-day in the Lads'
Bible Class, Scouts and Guides, and parochial club. It will be
noted that in these passages the term πρεσβύτεροι connotes age, not
office.

(γ) Ministers and their people : as in 1 Peter v. 1-4, 1 Thess. v
12, 1 Cor. xvi. 16, Heb. xiii. 7, 1 Tim. iii. 1 ff., Tit. i. 7 ff., and cf.

[1] Cf. *Ep. Barn.* xix. 5. For recent
discussions of whether *The Didache* is
dependent on *The Epistle of Barnabas*
or *vice versa* see *J.T.S.* xxxix. No. 156
(article by J. M. Creed), xl. Nos. 158
and 159 (articles by W. Telfer) and the
literature alluded to there.

Clem. Rom. i. 3, ἀπροσωπλήμπτως γὰρ πάντα ἐποιεῖτε, καὶ τοῖς νομί-
μοις τοῦ θεοῦ ἐπορεύεσθε, ὑποτασσόμενοι τοῖς ἡγουμένοις ὑμῶν. . . .
Ib. xxi. 6, τὸν κύριον Ἰησοῦν Χριστόν, οὗ τὸ αἷμα ὑπὲρ ἡμῶν ἐδόθη,
ἐντραπῶμεν· τοὺς προηγουμένους ἡμῶν αἰδεσθῶμεν. . . .

The background is that of the Church's pastoral ministry and
care. In both the passages of 1 Clement this relationship and that
between older and younger members of the community are closely
intertwined (cf. also 1 Tim. v. 1, 17, noted by Bigg), the ministers
(presbyters and bishops) being called " the leaders ", as in 1 Thessalonians and Hebrews, and the senior members οἱ πρεσβύτεροι. But
in 1 Peter the term πρεσβύτεροι is used in both senses, referring in
v. 1 to office and in v. 5 to age.[1]   Further, the duty of women to love
their husbands, to be modest in their demeanour, and to teach their
children is joined with the other two types of duty : the domestic,
social, and pastoral relationships are combined. It is not easy to
say whether the last two of these were from the beginning combined
with the first, in the sense that they were part of the social code
found in 1 Peter and Colossians-Ephesians. But the suggestion
made above (II. iv. (b)) seems to me more probable, namely that the
relationships of younger to older and of people to presbyters
belonged to teaching on Church order, which was part of the
catechetical section we have denoted CVG. Further, it is relevant
to point to a *verbum Christi* which may well have been the seed-
plot of both usages, viz. Lk. xxii. 26, ὁ μείζων ἐν ὑμῖν γινέσθω ὡς ὁ
νεώτερος, καὶ ὁ ἡγούμενος ὡς ὁ διακονῶν. The terms used here seem
of a quite non-technical kind ; but we can see ἡγούμενοι becoming
virtually an official term in N.T. (cf. Heb. xiii. 7, 17, 24, and also
1 Thess. v. 12 (προϊστάμενοι)), while διακονῶν provided the groundwork for the διάκονοι of Phil. i. 1, Col. iv. 7, Eph. vi. 21, 1 Tim. iii.
8, 12. The Lord's teaching would have embraced the relationships
both of the younger members of the community to the older, and
of the " laity " to the " clergy ".

Concluding Reflexions on the Code

One of the questions prompted by a survey of the above evidence
is whether the Code of Subordination was originally Christian or
not ; and if not, whether the Ur-Tafeln were Jewish or Gentile. We
can, I think, recognize three strata in the codes as they appear in
the Epistles. At the top there are the superstructures of theology
which St. Peter builds on to the teaching about slaves and St. Paul

---

[1] Wand's detached Note on " The Ministry in 1 Peter ", *op. cit.* pp. 126 f.,
is most valuable here.

on the passages about wives and husbands and about civic obedience. These are the products of the thought of the inspired writers
individually. Below these, and occupying the middle part of the
scene, are outstanding elements of common teaching which are
indisputably Christian. Thus, in regard to subjection to civic
authority, we have identity of teaching as to the moral function of
the State, with which is closely connected emphasis on the universal,
as distinct from the ecclesiastical, relations wherein Christians stand:
the Church, though not " of " the world, is " in " it. The allusions,
moreover, to the effect of good conduct on Gentile public opinion,
which appear in more than one document under each of the subjects
we have examined, must certainly have been in the source (even if
not in all those places), and with equal certainty were Christian.
Again, we should perhaps assign to this stratum the teaching on
quietness and on sobriety of dress which appears in 1 Peter and in
1 Timothy under the duties of wives, though a Jewish or even
Gentile origin cannot be ruled out. But when we go below this
stratum to the fundamental principles inculcated — ὑποτάσσεσθαι
τοῖς ὑπερέχουσιν (τῷ βασιλεῖ), ὑποτάσσεσθαι τοῖς ἰδίοις κυρίοις, ὑποτάσσεσθαι τοῖς ἰδίοις ἀνδράσιν, etc. — the facts are best accounted
for by the view that we are dealing with a Christian version of
a code or codes already in circulation. We note, for example,
that in Col. iii. 18-21, there is nothing specifically Christian except the formula ἐν κυρίῳ, which may easily be a Christian gloss;
while verse 21 is almost a quotation from Menander.[1] This might
seem to point to a code of a Gentile origin, as might the pride of
place given in it to the civil authority. On the other hand, the
emphasis laid on " fear ", which seems to be a basic element in the
code as we have it, is characteristically Jewish ; and so is the curious
imperatival participle which governs so many of its sections. We
have, in fact, in what appears to be the original substratum, a fusion
of Jewish and Gentile thought which may well have originated in
Hellenistic Judaism, yet is perhaps most easily explained as due
to the synthetic genius of the early Christian Mission.

A further question relates to the form of the code : was it
oral or written ? The Jews set the highest store by oral tōrah, and
some Rabbis esteemed it more highly than written tōrah. But, as
indicated above (p. 401), the question is too narrowly drawn. For
what began as oral would be unlikely to remain unwritten in a
Church pursuing an active missionary propaganda. The evidence
seems to me best accounted for by the view that between the original

---

[1] W. K. L. Clarke, *op. cit.* pp. 158, 159.

oral pattern and the versions of the code which we find in the N.T. documents lie a number of written versions of it, not verbally identical, which were in circulation for the use of teachers in different districts and groups of communities.

III. Teaching called out by Crisis : Traces of a Persecution-Form (P)

In the accompanying Table XIV (see pp. 442-9) is set forth the Table evidence pointing to a common source or sources underlying the XIV teaching on persecution found in several Epistles. The Table is divided into sections denoted by the letters from (a) to (h) ; and they are printed as one table, because it seems to me probable that they belonged originally together, though the probability varies in different cases ; and this source might well be denoted by the symbol P. The last two sections (g) and (h) correspond to those which Dr. Carrington calls *Vigilate* and *State* respectively,[1] from the keyword which gives to each its character ; and it will be convenient to follow this nomenclature. I agree with Dr. Carrington's view [2] that the remarkable parallels of thought and phrase which occur in these sections point to a common source or sources underlying the several Epistles as a more probable explanation of the facts than direct dependence of one Epistle upon another : even Ephesians here, where it amplifies Colossians, employs ideas and phrases which have parallels in other Epistles. Dr. Carrington assigns these sections, or series of parallels, which we have agreed to call *Vigilate* and *State* to the primitive Catechism (B²) chiefly on the ground that they occur at relatively the same point in a number of Epistles, including Colossians, Ephesians, 1 Peter, and James ; and this main contention is buttressed by a number of subsidiary considerations which can be discussed as they occur. But I have found Dr. Carrington's hypothesis less cogent here than elsewhere, and for the following reasons :

1. First, we may observe that Dr. Carrington's conspectus at this point does not include 1 and 2 Thessalonians or Romans ; and, when these are added to the table, the resulting situation is somewhat more complicated. For example, neither in Thessalonians nor in Romans is the *Vigilate* associated with the *Subiecti*, though its form in these Epistles presents close parallels with Ephesians and with 1 Peter. In Romans and 1 Peter, moreover, the context is

---

[1] *Op. cit.* ch. iv., and tables appended.
[2] Cf. especially *op. cit.* pp. 51-4.

strongly eschatological, and indirectly so in 1 Thessalonians.

2. Secondly, the order in which the *Vigilate* and the *State* occur in the various Epistles, relatively to one another and also to other parts of the catechetical pattern, is not, I think, as striking as Dr. Carrington's treatment of the evidence suggests. For example, in 1 Thess. v. 5-8 the *Vigilate* (which presents very close verbal affinities with 1 Peter, cf. *supra*, pp. 375 ff.), while it is bound up, as we have observed, with the idea of Christians belonging to the day and not the night, is governed by the eschatological opening of the passage in v. 1, 2. And the *State*, at least in 2 Thess. ii. 15, is still in the context of the great eschatological passage, ii. 1-12. In 1 Pet. iv. the *Vigilate* is in an eschatological setting (iv. 7), and follows a passage on behaviour in persecution, an allusion to the heavenly armour, and a special warning against intemperance and excess ; while in 1 Pet. v., though the *Vigilate* follows a quite general form of the *Subiecti*, the *State* which immediately succeeds it is governed by the idea of persecution. In Romans we notice the same features with regard to the *Vigilate* ; it is governed by the eschatological *motif* (xiii. 11), and it is associated with the heavenly armour and the same special warning against intemperance and excess as in 1 Thessalonians and 1 Peter. Even 1 Cor. xvi. 13, 14 may well be drawn from a similar store, for its association with the *Subiecti* in verse 16 seems to be due to the personal allusions in verse 15, and its place therefore accidental. In Colossians-Ephesians, on the other hand, the *Vigilate* does, it is true, follow the *Subiecti*, but not with the directness which Dr. Carrington's theory seems to require. But the context is without any eschatological suggestion, and is indeed influenced rather by the atmosphere of the flood-tide which marks these Epistles. Again in Colossians, though the *Vigilate* follows the *Subiecti* immediately, the *State* is introduced after six verses of quite other matter ; while in Ephesians it is the *State*, not the *Vigilate*, which follows the *Subiecti*, covering five verses ; the *Vigilate* coming after it in close conjunction with the heavenly armour and with prayer. The case of James is different yet again : there is no *Vigilate* at all, and the *State* (in the form *Resistite*) follows a quite general form of *Subiecti* which may have other roots than those of the social code.

3. If, then, the case for a common underlying source is very strong, but the hypothesis that this source is the catechetical pattern which we have seen reason to associate with preparation for baptism encounters formidable difficulties, it remains to be seen whether any other theory will better account for the facts. And here we must

return again in the first instance to 1 and 2 Thessalonians and
1 Peter, and to a number of parallels between them which are fully
as striking as any yet considered, and yet which belong to a different
and distinctive subject-matter. We must remember, further, that
1 and 2 Thessalonians and 1 Peter are alike in being more closely
concerned with persecution in the churches addressed than any other
Epistles of N.T. The task of formulating and imparting codes of
practical conduct was normally that of the " teacher " in the early
Church ; their application to changing circumstances and expanding horizons and opportunities was that of the " prophet ". The
glimpse of their co-operation at Antioch which we have in Acts xiii. 1
is, no doubt, characteristic of what was happening constantly and
in many places. And nowhere would the prophet's work have been
in greater demand than in infant churches exposed to persecution,
and needing exhortation ($\pi\alpha\rho\alpha\kappa\alpha\lambda\epsilon\hat{\iota}\nu$) and strengthening ($\sigma\tau\eta\rho\acute{\iota}\zeta\epsilon\iota\nu$).
Silvanus was particularly well equipped by character, experience,
and reputation for such a task ; and we are not surprised to find
that the three Epistles with which his name is associated shew much
in common in the matter of persecution.

Before setting out, however, the detailed parallels on this subject
between 1 and 2 Thessalonians and 1 Peter, we need to consider the
eschatological context in which much of the persecution teaching is
given in all three Epistles. Professor Burkitt (*Christian Beginnings*,
pp. 128-32) was so much impressed by the eschatological colour of
1 and 2 Thessalonians that he regarded them as the work not of
St. Paul, but of Silvanus. The plea is considered and rejected by
Dr. Bicknell in his edition of 1 and 2 Thessalonians in the Westminster Commentaries (pp. xxxiv ff.). But the case for Silvanus'
authorship is greatly strengthened, if we bear in mind what has
already been said as to the evidence for St. Paul's personal authorship of 2 Thess. ii. 3-12. That is far the longest and the strongest
eschatological passage in the Epistles, and St. Paul expressly claims
it as his own. Apart from that there is little — not, indeed, more than
a phrase or two — in the eschatology of 1 and 2 Thessalonians which
goes beyond that of 1 Peter ; and these differences can be easily
explained by the lapse of time. On the other hand, both in 1 and 2
Thessalonians and in 1 Peter the persecution-*motif* and the eschato
logy-*motif* are so closely intertwined that they are best handled
together ; and, when so handled, the evidence creates at least the
presumption that they were originally together. Further, the evidence of 1 Thessalonians and 1 Peter, which is supported by Acts
(Table XIV (*c*)), that the inevitability of persecution was a regular

TABLE XIV

TEACHING CALLED OUT BY·CRISIS: TRACES OF A PERSECUTION-FORM

I and 2 Thess.	I Peter	Acts and other Epistles	O.T.	Verba Christi
(a) I Thess. i. 6. ἐν θλίψει πολλῇ μετὰ χαρᾶς πνεύματος ἁγίου. 2 Thess. i. 4, 5, ὥστε ἡμᾶς αὐτοὺς ἐγκαυχᾶσθαι . . . ὑπὲρ τῆς ὑπομονῆς ὑμῶν καὶ πίστεως ἐν πᾶσι τοῖς διωγμοῖς ὑμῶν καὶ ταῖς θλίψεσιν αἷς ἀνέχεσθε, ἔνδειγμα τῆς δικαίας κρίσεως τοῦ θεοῦ, εἰς τὸ καταξιωθῆναι ὑμᾶς τῆς βασιλείας τοῦ θεοῦ, ὑπὲρ ἧς καὶ πάσχετε.	i. 6. ἐν ᾧ ἀγαλλιᾶσθε, ὀλίγον ἄρτι, εἰ δέον ἐστί, λυπηθέντες ἐν ποικίλοις πειρασμοῖς . . . ii. 20. ποῖον γὰρ κλέος, εἰ ἁμαρτάνοντες καὶ κολαφιζόμενοι ὑπομενεῖτε; ἀλλ' εἰ ἀγαθοποιοῦντες καὶ πάσχοντες ὑπομενεῖτε, τοῦτο χάρις παρὰ θεῷ. iii. 14. εἰ καὶ πάσχοιτε διὰ δικαιοσύνην, μακάριοι. iv. 13. καθὸ κοινωνεῖτε τοῖς τοῦ Χριστοῦ παθήμασιν, χαίρετε . . .	(a) Acts v. 41. οἱ μὲν οὖν ἐπορεύοντο χαίροντες . . . ὅτι κατηξιώθησαν ὑπὲρ τοῦ ὀνόματος ἀτιμασθῆναι. 2 Cor. viii. 2. ἐν πολλῇ δοκιμῇ θλίψεως ἡ περισσεία τῆς χαρᾶς αὐτῶν . . . ἐπερίσσευσεν . . . Jas. i. 2. πᾶσαν χαρὰν ἡγήσασθε . . . ὅταν πειρασμοῖς περιπέσητε ποικίλοις. Rom. v. 3,4. καυχώμεθα ἐν ταῖς θλίψεσιν, εἰδότες ὅτι ἡ θλῖψις ὑπομονὴν κατεργάζεται, ἡ δὲ ὑπομονὴ δοκιμήν, ἡ δὲ δοκιμὴ ἐλπίδα. Phil. i. 29, ὑμῖν ἐχαρίσθη τὸ ὑπὲρ Χριστοῦ οὐ μόνον τὸ εἰς αὐτὸν πιστεύειν, ἀλλὰ καὶ τὸ ὑπὲρ αὐτοῦ πάσχειν. Heb. x. 34. τὴν ἁρπαγὴν τῶν ὑπαρχόντων ὑμῶν μετὰ χαρᾶς προσεδέξασθε, γινώσκοντες ἔχειν ἑαυτοὺς κρείττονα ὕπαρξιν καὶ μένουσαν.		Matt. v. 10-12. μακάριοι οἱ δεδιωγμένοι ἕνεκεν δικαιοσύνης· ὅτι αὐτῶν ἐστιν ἡ βασιλεία τῶν οὐρανῶν. μακάριοί ἐστε ὅταν ὀνειδίσωσιν ὑμᾶς καὶ διώξωσι, καὶ εἴπωσι πᾶν πονηρὸν καθ' ὑμῶν ψευδόμενοι, ἕνεκεν ἐμοῦ [Lk. vi. 22. ὅταν μισήσωσιν ὑμᾶς οἱ ἄ[νθρωποι], καὶ ὅταν ἀφορίσωσιν ὑμᾶς, καὶ ὀνειδίσωσιν, καὶ ἐκβάλωσι τὸ ὄνομα ὑμῶν ὡς πονηρόν, ἕνεκα τοῦ υἱοῦ τοῦ ἀνθρώπου]. χαίρετε καὶ ἀγαλλιᾶσθε [Lk. σκιρτήσατε] ὅτι ὁ μισθὸς ὑμῶν πολὺς ἐν τοῖς οὐρανοῖς· οὕτω γὰρ ἐδίωξαν τοὺς προφήτας τοὺς πρὸ ὑμῶν. Lk. xx. 35. οἱ δὲ καταξιωθέντες τοῦ αἰῶνος ἐκείνου. Lk. vi. 32 f. εἰ ἀγαπᾶτε τοὺς ἀγαπῶντας ὑμᾶς, ποία ὑμῖν χάρις ἐστί; . . . καὶ ἐὰν ἀγαθοποιῆτε τοὺς ἀγαθοποιοῦντας ὑμᾶς, ποία ὑμῖν χάρις ἐστί; . . . Lk. xxii. 28, ὑμεῖς δέ ἐστε οἱ διαμεμενηκότες μετ' ἐμοῦ ἐν τοῖς πειρασμοῖς μου.

(b) 1 Thess. ii. 4. ἀλλὰ καθὼς δεδοκιμάσμεθα ὑπὸ τοῦ θεοῦ πιστευθῆναι τὸ εὐαγγέλιον, οὕτω λαλοῦμεν, οὐκ ὡς ἀνθρώποις ἀρέσκοντες, ἀλλὰ θεῷ τῷ δοκιμάζοντι τὰς καρδίας ἡμῶν. 2 Thess. i. 7. . . . ἐν τῇ ἀποκαλύψει τοῦ κυρίου Ἰησοῦ . . .	i. 7. ἵνα τὸ δοκίμιον ὑμῶν τῆς πίστεως, πολυτιμότερον χρυσίου τοῦ ἀπολλυμένου διὰ πυρὸς δὲ δοκιμαζομένου εὑρεθῇ εἰς ἔπαινον καὶ τιμὴν ἐν ἀποκαλύψει Ἰησοῦ Χριστοῦ. v. 4. καὶ φανερωθέντος τοῦ ἀρχιποίμενος κομιεῖσθε τὸν ἀμαράντινον τῆς δόξης στέφανον.	Jas. i. 3. γινώσκοντες ὅτι τὸ δοκίμιον ὑμῶν τῆς πίστεως κατεργάζεται ὑπομονήν. 1 Cor. iii. 13. καὶ ἑκάστου τὸ ἔργον ὁποῖόν ἐστι, τὸ πῦρ αὐτὸ δοκιμάσει. Jas. i. 12. μακάριος ἀνὴρ ὃς ὑπομένει πειρασμόν· ὅτι δόκιμος γενόμενος λήμψεται τὸν στέφανον τῆς ζωῆς, ὃν ἐπηγγείλατο τοῖς ἀγαπῶσιν αὐτόν. Rom. v. 3 [cf. supra].	Prov. xvii. 3. ὥσπερ δοκιμάζεται ἐν καμίνῳ ἄργυρος καὶ χρυσός, οὕτως ἐκλεκταὶ καρδίαι παρὰ κυρίῳ. Prov. xxvii. 21. δοκίμιον ἀργύρῳ καὶ χρυσῷ πύρωσις. cf. Ecclus. ii. 1 (περασμόν), 4, 5 (ἐν πυρὶ δοκιμάζεται χρυσός . . . ταπεινώσεως), Wisd. iii. 4-6, 2 Esdr. xvi. 73, Mal. iii. 3. Ecclus. i. 11. φόβος κυρίου δόξα καὶ καύχημα καὶ εὐφροσύνη καὶ στέφανος ἀγαλλιάματος.	Mk. xiii. 13*. καὶ ἔσεσθε μισούμενοι ὑπὸ πάντων διὰ τὸ ὄνομά μου· ὁ δὲ ὑπομείνας εἰς τέλος, οὗτος σωθήσεται. [cf. Matt. x. 22.] Matt. xix. 28. ὑμεῖς οἱ ἀκολουθήσαντές μοι, ἐν τῇ παλιγγενεσίᾳ ὅταν καθίσῃ ὁ υἱὸς τοῦ ἀνθρώπου ἐπὶ θρόνου δόξης αὐτοῦ, καθήσεσθε καὶ ὑμεῖς, κτλ. . . . Matt. v. 12*. ὁ μισθὸς ὑμῶν πολὺς ἐν τοῖς οὐρανοῖς·
(c) 1 Thess. iii. 2-5. ἐπέμψαμεν Τιμόθεον . . . εἰς τὸ στηρίξαι ὑμᾶς καὶ παρακαλέσαι ὑπὲρ τῆς πίστεως ὑμῶν. [cf. ib. 13. εἰς τὸ στηρίξαι ὑμῶν τὰς καρδίας ἀμέμπτους ἐν ἁγιωσύνῃ . . .] τὸ μηδένα σαίνεσθαι ἐν ταῖς θλίψεσι ταύταις· αὐτοὶ γὰρ οἴδατε ὅτι εἰς τοῦτο κείμεθα. καὶ γὰρ ὅτε πρὸς ὑμᾶς ἦμεν, προελέγομεν ὑμῖν ὅτι μέλλομεν θλίβεσθαι . . . διὰ τοῦτο ἔπεμψα εἰς τὸ γνῶναι . . . μή πως ἐπείρασεν ὑμᾶς ὁ πειράζων . . .	iv. 12. μὴ ξενίζεσθε τῇ ἐν ὑμῖν πυρώσει πρὸς πειρασμὸν ὑμῖν γινομένῃ, ὡς ξένου ὑμῖν συμβαίνοντος· ii. 21. . . . εἰς τοῦτο γὰρ ἐκλήθητε . . . iii. 14, 15. τὸν δὲ φόβον αὐτῶν μὴ φοβηθῆτε, μηδὲ ταραχθῆτε, κύριον δὲ τὸν Χριστὸν ἁγιάσατε ἐν ταῖς καρδίαις ὑμῶν.	Acts xiv. 22. ἐπιστηρίζοντες τὰς ψυχὰς τῶν μαθητῶν, παρακαλοῦντες ἐμμένειν τῇ πίστει, καὶ ὅτι διὰ πολλῶν θλίψεων δεῖ ἡμᾶς εἰσελθεῖν εἰς τὴν βασιλείαν τοῦ θεοῦ. Phil. i. 28. . . . μὴ πτυρόμενοι ἐν μηδενὶ ὑπὸ τῶν ἀντικειμένων . . .	Prov. xxvii. 21 [cf. supra]. Is. viii. 12, 13. τὸν δὲ φόβον αὐτοῦ οὐ μὴ φοβηθῆτε οὐδὲ μὴ ταραχθῆτε· κύριον αὐτὸν ἁγιάσατε, καὶ αὐτὸς ἔσται σου φόβος.	Matt. x. 25. ἀρκετὸν τῷ μαθητῇ ἵνα γένηται ὡς ὁ διδάσκαλος αὐτοῦ, καὶ ὁ δοῦλος ὡς ὁ κύριος αὐτοῦ. Mk. xiii. 7. μὴ θροεῖσθε· δεῖ γενέσθαι· ἀλλ' οὔπω τὸ τέλος. ib. xiii. 11. ὅταν ἄγωσιν ὑμᾶς παραδιδόντες, μὴ προμεριμνᾶτε τί λαλήσητε . . . Matt. x. 28 [Lk. xii. 4, 5]. καὶ μὴ φοβηθῆτε ἀπὸ τῶν ἀποκτεννόντων τὸ σῶμα, τὴν δὲ ψυχὴν μὴ δυναμένων ἀποκτεῖναι. φοβήθητε δὲ μᾶλλον τὸν δυνάμενον καὶ ψυχὴν καὶ σῶμα ἀπολέσαι ἐν γεέννῃ.

* An asterisk denotes passages which were probably in Q.

TABLE XIV—continued

I and 2 Thess.	I Peter	Acts and other Epistles	O.T.	Verba Christi
(d) I Thess. ii. 14. τὰ αὐτὰ ἐπάθετε καὶ ὑμεῖς ὑπὸ τῶν ἰδίων συμφυλετῶν, καθὼς καὶ αὐτοὶ ὑπὸ τῶν Ἰουδαίων.	v. 9. εἰδότες τὰ αὐτὰ τῶν παθημάτων τῇ ἐν κόσμῳ ὑμῶν ἀδελφότητι ἐπιτελεῖσθαι.	Heb. x. 32, 33. πολλὴν ἄθλησιν ὑπεμείνατε παθημάτων, τοῦτο μὲν ὀνειδισμοῖς τε καὶ θλίψεσι θεατριζόμενοι, τοῦτο δὲ κοινωνοὶ τῶν οὕτως ἀναστρεφομένων γενηθέντες.		Mk. xiii. 32*, 33. περὶ δὲ τῆς ἡμέρας ἐκείνης ἢ τῆς ὥρας οὐδεὶς οἶδεν, οὐδὲ οἱ ἄγγελοι ἐν οὐρανῷ οὐδὲ ὁ υἱός, εἰ μὴ ὁ πατήρ. βλέπετε, ἀγρυπνεῖτε, οὐκ οἴδατε γὰρ πότε ὁ καιρός·
(e) I Thess. v. I. περὶ δὲ τῶν χρόνων καὶ τῶν καιρῶν, ἀδελφοί, οὐ χρείαν ἔχετε ὑμῖν γράφεσθαι.	i. 10, 11. προφῆται ... ἐρευνῶντες εἰς τίνα ἢ ποῖον καιρὸν ἐδήλου τὸ ἐν αὐτοῖς πνεῦμα Χριστοῦ, προμαρτυρόμενον τὰ εἰς Χριστὸν παθήματα καὶ τὰς μετὰ ταῦτα δόξας.	Acts i. 7. οὐχ ὑμῶν ἐστι γνῶναι χρόνους ἢ καιροὺς οὓς ὁ πατὴρ ἔθετο ἐν τῇ ἰδίᾳ ἐξουσίᾳ.	Is. xiii. 6-9. ἐγγὺς γὰρ ἡμέρα κυρίου ... ταραχθήσονται οἱ πρέσβεις, καὶ ὠδῖνες αὐτοὺς ἕξουσιν ὡς γυναικὸς τικτούσης ... ἰδοὺ γὰρ ἡμέρα κυρίου ἔρχεται ...	ib. 35. γρηγορεῖτε οὖν, οὐκ οἴδατε γὰρ πότε ὁ κύριος τῆς οἰκίας ἔρχεται.
ib. 2. αὐτοὶ γὰρ ἀκριβῶς οἴδατε ὅτι ἡμέρα κυρίου ὡς κλέπτης ἐν νυκτὶ οὕτως ἔρχεται·	Jas. v. 8. στηρίξατε τὰς καρδίας ὑμῶν, ὅτι ἡ παρουσία τοῦ κυρίου ἤγγικε.		Lk. xiii. 39*, 40*. τοῦτο δὲ γινώσκετε ὅτι εἰ ᾔδει ὁ οἰκοδεσπότης ποίᾳ ὥρᾳ ὁ κλέπτης ἔρχεται, ἐγρηγόρησεν ἂν, κτλ. ...καὶ ὑμεῖς γίνεσθε ἕτοιμοι, ὅτι ᾗ ὥρᾳ οὐ δοκεῖτε ὁ υἱὸς τοῦ ἀνθρώπου ἔρχεται.
ib. 2. ἐν ἡμέρᾳ ἐπισκοπῆς. iv. 7. πάντων δὲ τὸ τέλος ἤγγικε·	2 Pet. iii. 10. ἥξει δὲ ἡμέρα κυρίου ὡς κλέπτης ...			
		[Rev. xvi. 15. Ἰδού, ἔρχομαι ὡς κλέπτης. μακάριος ὁ γρηγορῶν, κτλ.]	ib. 11. καὶ ἐντελοῦμαι τῇ οἰκουμένῃ ὅλῃ κακά, καὶ τοῖς ἀσεβέσιν τὰς ἁμαρτίας αὐτῶν· καὶ ἀπολῶ ὕβριν ἀνόμων, καὶ ὕβριν ὑπερηφάνων ταπεινώσω.	cf. Matt. xxiv. 43, 44.
ib. 3. ὅταν λέγωσιν, Εἰρήνη καὶ ἀσφάλεια, τότε αἰφνίδιος αὐτοῖς ἐφίσταται ὄλεθρος, ὥσπερ ἡ ὠδὶν τῇ ἐν γαστρὶ ἐχούσῃ, καὶ οὐ μὴ ἐκφύγωσιν.	iv. 3, 17, 18 [cf. infra].	Rom. xiii. 11. καὶ τοῦτο, εἰδότες τὸν καιρόν, ὅτι ὥρα ἤδη ὑμᾶς ἐξ ὕπνου ἐγερθῆναι· νῦν γὰρ ἐγγύτερον ἡμῶν ἡ σωτηρία ἢ ὅτε ἐπιστεύσαμεν.	Ezek. xiii. 10. ... λέγοντες, Εἰρήνη, καὶ οὐκ ἦν εἰρήνη.	Lk. xxi. 34*. προσέχετε δὲ ἑαυτοῖς, μήποτε... αἰφνίδιος ἐφ' ὑμᾶς ἐπιστῇ ἡ ἡμέρα ἐκείνη.
		I Cor. vii. 29. ὁ καιρὸς συνεσταλμένος ...	Mal. iii. 1. καὶ ἐξέφνης ἥξει εἰς τὸν ναὸν ἑαυτοῦ κύριος. ...	Mk. xiii. 8 [Matt. xxiv. 8]. ἀρχὴ ὠδίνων ταῦτα.
				cf. Jn. xvi. 21.

(ƒ) Thess.		Phil./Rom./Heb.	Prov./Deut./Is.	Matt./Lk.
(ƒ) Thess. i. 4 . . . τῆς ὑπομονῆς ὑμῶν καὶ πίστεως ἐν πᾶσι τοῖς διωγμοῖς ὑμῶν	iv. 17. ὅτι ὁ καιρὸς τοῦ ἄρξασθαι τὸ κρίμα ἀπὸ τοῦ οἴκου τοῦ θεοῦ· εἰ δὲ πρῶτον ἀφ᾽ ἡμῶν, τί τὸ τέλος τῶν ἀπειθούντων τῷ τοῦ θεοῦ εὐαγγελίῳ [cf. ii. 8].	Phil. i. 27, 28. ὅτι στήκετε ἐν ἑνὶ πνεύματι . . . ἥτις ἐστὶν αὐτοῖς ἔνδειξις ἀπωλείας, ὑμῶν δὲ σωτηρίας, καὶ τοῦτο ἀπὸ θεοῦ·	Prov. xi. 31. εἰ ὁ μὲν δίκαιος μόλις σώζεται, ὁ ἀσεβὴς καὶ ἁμαρτωλὸς ποῦ φανεῖται;	Matt. x. 32*, 33* [Lk. xii. 8*, 9*]. πᾶς οὖν ὅστις ὁμολογήσει ἐν ἐμοὶ ἔμπροσθεν τῶν ἀνθρώπων, ὁμολογήσω κἀγὼ ἐν αὐτῷ ἔμπροσθεν τοῦ πατρός μου. . . . ὅστις δ᾽ ἂν ἀρνήσηταί με ἔμπροσθεν τῶν ἀνθρώπων, ἀρνήσομαι αὐτὸν κἀγὼ . . . .
ib. 5. ἔνδειγμα τῆς δικαίας κρίσεως τοῦ θεοῦ, εἰς τὸ καταξιωθῆναι ὑμᾶς τῆς βασιλείας τοῦ θεοῦ, ὑπὲρ ἧς καὶ πάσχετε.			Deut. vii. 10 [cf. Ex. xx. 5, 6]. . . . καὶ ἀποδιδοὺς τοῖς μισοῦσιν κατὰ πρόσωπον ἐξολεθρεῦσαι αὐτούς.	
ib. 6. εἴπερ δίκαιον παρὰ θεῷ ἀνταποδοῦναι τοῖς θλίβουσιν ὑμᾶς θλῖψιν,	ib. 18. καὶ Εἰ ὁ δίκαιος μόλις σώζεται, ὁ ἀσεβὴς καὶ ἁμαρτωλὸς ποῦ φανεῖται;	Rom. ii. 5-11. . . . ἐν ἡμέρᾳ ὀργῆς καὶ ἀποκαλύψεως δικαιοκρισίας τοῦ θεοῦ, ὃς ἀποδώσει . . . τοῖς μὲν . . . δόξαν καὶ τιμὴν καὶ ἀφθαρσίαν ζητοῦσι, ζωὴν αἰώνιον τοῖς δέ . . . ἀπειθοῦσι τῇ ἀληθείᾳ ὀργὴ καὶ θυμός . . .	ib. xxxii. 35 f. ἐν ἡμέρᾳ ἐκδικήσεως ἀνταποδώσω . . . ὅτι ἐγγὺς ἡμέρα ἀπωλίας αὐτοῖς . . . ὅτι κρινεῖ κύριος τὸν λαὸν αὐτοῦ . . .	
ib. 7. καὶ ὑμῖν τοῖς θλιβομένοις ἄνεσιν μεθ᾽ ἡμῶν, ἐν τῇ ἀποκαλύψει τοῦ κυρίου Ἰησοῦ ἀπ᾽ οὐρανοῦ μετ᾽ ἀγγέλων δυνάμεως αὐτοῦ ἐν πυρὶ φλογός,	iv. 13. ἵνα ἐν τῇ ἀποκαλύψει τῆς δόξης αὐτοῦ χαρῆτε	Heb. x. 30. οἴδαμεν γὰρ τὸν εἰπόντα, Ἐμοὶ ἐκδίκησις, ἐγὼ ἀνταποδώσω· καὶ πάλιν, Κρινεῖ κύριος τὸν λαὸν αὐτοῦ.	Prov. xx. 22 [12]. μὴ εἴπῃς, Τίσομαι τὸν ἐχθρόν· ἀλλὰ ὑπόμεινον τὸν κύριον, ἵνα σου βοηθήσῃ.	Lk. xviii. 7. ὁ δὲ θεὸς οὐ μὴ ποιήσῃ τὴν ἐκδίκησιν τῶν ἐκλεκτῶν αὐτοῦ τῶν βοώντων αὐτῷ ἡμέρας καὶ νυκτός, καὶ μακροθυμεῖ ἐπ᾽ αὐτοῖς;
ib. 8. διδόντος ἐκδίκησιν τοῖς μὴ εἰδόσι θεὸν καὶ τοῖς μὴ ὑπακούουσιν τῷ εὐαγγελίῳ τοῦ κυρίου ἡμῶν Ἰησοῦ.	iv. 5. οἳ ἀποδώσουσι λόγον τῷ ἑτοίμως ἔχοντι κρῖναι ζῶντας καὶ νεκρούς.		Is. lxvi. 4-6. ὅτι ἐκάλεσα αὐτοὺς καὶ οὐχ ὑπήκουσάν μου	
ib. 9. οἵτινες δίκην τίσουσιν . . .				

TABLE XIV—continued

1 and 2 Thess.	1 Peter	Acts and other Epistles	O.T.	Verba Christi
2 Thess. i. 10. ὅταν ἔλθῃ ἐνδοξασθῆναι ἐν τοῖς ἁγίοις αὐτοῦ καὶ θαυμασθῆναι ἐν πᾶσι τοῖς πιστεύσασιν.... ἐν τῇ ἡμέρᾳ ἐκείνῃ.	i. 7. εἰς ἔπαινον καὶ δόξαν καὶ τιμὴν ἐν ἀποκαλύψει Ἰησοῦ Χριστοῦ. ii. 9. ὅπως τὰς ἀρετὰς ἐξαγγείλητε τοῦ, κτλ. . . .	I Cor. i. 7, 8. . . . ἀπεκδεχομένους τὴν ἀποκάλυψιν τοῦ κυρίου ἡμῶν Ἰησοῦ Χριστοῦ, ὃς καὶ βεβαιώσει ὑμᾶς ἕως τέλους ἀνεγκλήτους ἐν τῇ ἡμέρᾳ τοῦ κυρίου . . .	Is. lix. 18. ὡς ἀνταποδώσων ἀνταπόδοσιν ὄνειδος τοῖς ὑπεναντίοις. ib. lxvi. 4. καὶ τὰς ἁμαρτίας ἀνταποδώσω αὐτοῖς . . .	Mk. xiii. 27. καὶ τότε ἀποστελεῖ τοὺς ἀγγέλους, καὶ ἐπισυνάξει τοὺς ἐκλεκτοὺς αὐτοῦ. . . . ib. viii. 38. ὅταν ἔλθῃ ἐν τῇ δόξῃ τοῦ πατρὸς αὐτοῦ μετὰ τῶν ἀγγέλων τῶν ἁγίων.
(g) I Thess. v. 4-11. 4. ὑμεῖς δέ, ἀδελφοί, οὐκ ἐστὲ ἐν σκότει, ἵνα ἡ ἡμέρα ὑμᾶς ὡς κλέπτης καταλάβῃ. ib. 5. πάντες γὰρ ὑμεῖς υἱοὶ φωτός ἐστε καὶ υἱοὶ ἡμέρας· οὐκ ἐσμὲν νυκτὸς οὐδὲ σκότους. ib. 6. ἄρα οὖν μὴ καθεύδωμεν ὡς οἱ λοιποί, ἀλλὰ γρηγορῶμεν καὶ νήφωμεν.	iv. 7. σωφρονήσατε οὖν καὶ νήψατε εἰς προσευχάς. . . . v. 8. νήψατε, γρηγορήσατε.	Rom. xiii. 13. . . . μὴ κώμοις καὶ μέθαις, μὴ κοίταις καὶ ἀσελγείαις . . . Col. iv. 2. τῇ προσευχῇ προσκαρτερεῖτε [cf. Rom. xii. 12], γρηγοροῦντες ἐν αὐτῇ ἐν εὐχαριστίᾳ, ib. 3. προσευχόμενοι ἅμα καὶ περὶ ἡμῶν ἵνα κτλ.	Ps. lxxxix. 8. ὁ θεὸς ἐνδοξαζόμενος ἐν βουλῇ ἁγίων.	Lk. xxi. 34.* προσέχετε δὲ ἑαυτοῖς, μήποτε βαρηθῶσιν ὑμῶν αἱ καρδίαι ἐν κραιπάλῃ καὶ μέθῃ καὶ μερίμναις βιωτικαῖς [cf. Matt. xxiv. 49*, Lk. xii. 45*].

ib. 7. οἱ γὰρ καθεύδοντες νυκτὸς καθεύδουσιν, καὶ οἱ μεθυσκόμενοι νυκτὸς μεθύ-ουσιν.	iv. 3. . . . ἀσελγείας, οἰνο-φλυγίας, κώμοις, πότοις . . .	Eph. vi. 14 ff. στῆτε οὖν περιζωσάμενοι τὴν ὀσφὺν ὑμῶν ἐν ἀληθείᾳ, καὶ ἐν-δυσάμενοι τὸν θώρακα τῆς δικαιοσύνης . . . τὸν θυρεὸν τῆς πίστεως . . . τὴν περι-κεφαλαίαν τοῦ σωτηρίου . . . διὰ πάσης προσευχῆς καὶ δεήσεως προσευχόμενοι . . . καὶ εἰς αὐτὸ ἀγρυπ-νοῦντες.	Is. lix. 17, Wisd. v. 17 ff. [cf. Table V and notes]; also Is. xi. 4.	ib. 36*. ἀγρυπνεῖτε . . . δεόμενοι ἵνα κατισχύσητε . . . σταθῆναι ἔμπροσθεν . . .
ib. 17. ἀδιαλείπτως προσ-εύχεσθε.	i. 13. διὸ ἀναζωσάμενοι τὰς ὀσφύας τῆς διανοίας ὑμῶν, νήφοντες τελείως ἐλ-πίσατε . . .	Rom. xiii. 14. ἀλλ᾽ ἐν-δύσασθε τὸν κύριον Ἰησοῦν Χριστόν.		Lk. xii. 35*. ἔστωσαν ὑμῶν αἱ ὀσφύες περιεζωσμέναι, καὶ οἱ λύχνοι καιό-μενοι . . .
ib. 8. ἡμεῖς δὲ ἡμέρας ὄντες νήφωμεν, ἐνδυσάμενοι θώ-ρακα πίστεως καὶ ἀγάπης καὶ περικεφαλαίαν ἐλπίδα σω-τηρίας.	i. 21. ὥστε τὴν πίστιν ὑμῶν καὶ ἐλπίδα εἶναι εἰς θεόν.	Acts xx. 28. τὴν ἐκ-κλησίαν τοῦ θεοῦ, ἣν περι-εποιήσατο διὰ τοῦ αἵματος τοῦ ἰδίου.		Mk. xiii. 33*. βλέπετε, ἀγρυπνεῖτε καὶ προσεύχεσθε. . . .
ib. 9. ὅτι οὐκ ἔθετο ἡμᾶς ὁ θεὸς εἰς ὀργήν, ἀλλ᾽ εἰς περιποίησιν σωτηρίας διὰ τοῦ κυρίου ἡμῶν Ἰησοῦ Χριστοῦ [cf. 2 ii. 14].	ii. 8. οἳ προσκόπτουσι τῷ λόγῳ ἀπειθοῦντες, εἰς ὃ καὶ ἐτέθησαν.	Eph. i. 14. . . . εἰς ἀπο-λύτρωσιν τῆς περιποιή-σεως, εἰς ἔπαινον τῆς δόξης αὐτοῦ.		ib. 35-7*. γρηγορεῖτε οὖν . . . μὴ ἐλθὼν ἐξαίφνης εὕρῃ ὑμᾶς καθεύδοντας. ὃ δὲ ὑμῖν λέγω πᾶσιν λέγω, γρηγορεῖτε.
ib. 10. τοῦ ἀποθανόντος ὑπὲρ ἡμῶν, ἵνα εἴτε γρηγο-ρῶμεν εἴτε καθεύδωμεν ἅμα σὺν αὐτῷ ζήσωμεν.	ib. 9. ὑμεῖς δὲ . . . λαὸς εἰς περιποίησιν . . .			Matt. xxv. 13*. γρηγορεῖτε οὖν, ὅτι οὐκ οἴδατε τὴν ἡμέραν οὐδὲ τὴν ὥραν.
ib. 11. διὸ παρακαλεῖτε ἀλλήλους, καὶ οἰκοδομεῖτε εἰς τὸν ἕνα, καθὼς καὶ ποιεῖτε.	ii. 21. ὅτι καὶ Χριστὸς ἔπα-θεν (v.l. ἀπέθανεν) ὑπὲρ ὑμῶν . . .			
	ii. 24. ἵνα ταῖς ἁμαρτίαις ἀπογενόμενοι τῇ δικαιοσύνῃ ζήσωμεν [cf. iv. 6].			
	ii. 4, 5. πρὸς ὃν προσερχό-μενοι . . . καὶ αὐτοὶ ὡς λίθοι ζῶντες οἰκοδομεῖσθε οἶκος πνευματικός . . .			

TABLE XIV — continued

I and 2 Thess.	I Peter	Acts and other Epistles	O.T.	Verba Christi
(h) I Thess. iii. 8. νῦν ζῶμεν, ἐὰν ὑμεῖς στήκητε ἐν κυρίῳ.	v. 8, 9. ὁ ἀντίδικος ὑμῶν διάβολος . . . ᾧ ἀντίστητε στερεοὶ τῇ πίστει, εἰδότες κτλ.	I Cor. xvi. 13. γρηγορεῖτε, στήκετε ἐν τῇ πίστει, ἀνδρίζεσθε, κραταιοῦσθε. Phil. iv. I. οὕτω στήκετε ἐν κυρίῳ, ἀγαπητοί. Col. iv. 12. . . . ἵνα σταθῆτε τέλειοι καὶ πεπληροφορημένοι ἐν παντὶ θελήματι τοῦ θεοῦ. Eph. vi. 11. ἐνδύσασθε τὴν πανοπλίαν τοῦ θεοῦ, πρὸς τὸ δύνασθαι ὑμᾶς στῆναι πρὸς τὰς μεθοδείας τοῦ διαβόλου [cf. iv. 27].		Lk. xxi. 36*. ἀγρυπνεῖτε δὲ ἐν παντὶ καιρῷ δεόμενοι ἵνα κατισχύσητε ἐκφυγεῖν ταῦτα πάντα τὰ μέλλοντα γίνεσθαι, καὶ σταθῆναι ἔμπροσθεν τοῦ υἱοῦ τοῦ ἀνθρώπου. Mk. xiii. 13*. ὁ δὲ ὑπομείνας εἰς τέλος οὗτος σωθήσεται. Cf. Matt. vii. 24-7.
2 Thess. ii. 15. ἄρα οὖν, ἀδελφοί, στήκετε, καὶ κρατεῖτε τὰς παραδόσεις . . .	10. ὁ δὲ θεὸς πάσης χάριτος . . . ὀλίγον παθόντας αὐτὸς καταρτίσει, στηρίξει, σθενώσει (v.l. optative) . . .	13. . . . ἵνα δυνηθῆτε ἀντιστῆναι ἐν τῇ ἡμέρᾳ τῇ πονηρᾷ, καὶ ἅπαντα κατεργασάμενοι στῆναι. 14. στῆτε οὖν περιζωσάμενοι τὴν ὀσφὺν . . . καὶ ἐνδυσάμενοι κτλ.		
ib. ii. 17. αὐτὸς δὲ ὁ κύριος ἡμῶν . . . παρακαλέσαι ὑμῶν τὰς καρδίας καὶ στηρίξαι ἐν παντὶ ἔργῳ καὶ λόγῳ ἀγαθῷ.	12. . . . ἀληθῆ χάριν τοῦ θεοῦ· εἰς ἣν στῆτε.	Jas. iv. 7. ὑποτάγητε οὖν τῷ θεῷ, ἀντίστητε δὲ τῷ διαβόλῳ, καὶ φεύξεται ἀφ᾽ ὑμῶν. I Cor. xv. I, τὸ εὐαγγέλιον . . . ἐν ᾧ καὶ ἑστήκατε.		

ib. iii. 3. πιστὸς δέ ἐστιν ὁ κύριος, ὃς στηρίξει ὑμᾶς καὶ φυλάξει ἀπὸ τοῦ πονηροῦ [cf. I Thess. v. 24].	Rom. v. 2. . . . τὴν χάριν ταύτην ἐν ᾗ ἑστήκαμεν . . .	cf. *Test. Naphth.* viii. 4. ἐὰν ἐργάζεσθε τὸ καλὸν . . . ὁ διάβολος φεύξεται ἀφ' ὑμῶν: and Hermas, *Mand.* xii. 5. 2.	Matt. x. 30*, 31*. ὑμῶν δὲ καὶ αἱ τρίχες τῆς κεφαλῆς πᾶσαι ἠριθμημέναι εἰσίν. μὴ οὖν φοβεῖσθε κτλ.
iv. 19. οἱ πάσχοντες κατὰ τὸ θέλημα τοῦ θεοῦ πιστῷ κτίστῃ παρατιθέσθωσαν τὰς ψυχὰς ἐν ἀγαθοποιΐᾳ.	I Cor. i. 8, 9. . . . ἀνεγκλήτους ἐν τῇ ἡμέρᾳ τοῦ κυρίου . . . πιστὸς ὁ θεὸς δι' οὗ ἐκλήθητε κτλ.		Matt. vi. 13*. καὶ μὴ εἰσενέγκῃς ἡμᾶς εἰς πειρασμόν, ἀλλὰ ῥῦσαι ἡμᾶς ἀπὸ τοῦ πονηροῦ.
	Heb. x. 23. κατέχωμεν τὴν ὁμολογίαν τῆς ἐλπίδος ἀκλινῆ, πιστὸς γὰρ ὁ ἐπαγγειλάμενος.		

part of the Apostolic teaching from the beginning, renders it probable that a pattern of such teaching would have been prepared and made available at an early date. I believe that this pattern is discernible in these epistles as well as in St. James and elsewhere, and that it accounts for much that is common to them : it rested, moreover, upon undoubted *verba Christi*. The original drafting of this pattern was perhaps a corporate rather than an individual matter ; but the extent of the parallels between 1 and 2 Thessalonians and 1 Peter seems to me to indicate either that Silvanus was one of those who took part in this work or that he had his own version of it from which he was accustomed to teach.

Table
XIV

Commentary. — The evidence assembled in Table XIV indicates a large measure of common ground here, both in thought and in language, which may be summarized as follows :

(*a*)

(1) The thought of rejoicing in suffering for the faith is specifically Christian and goes back to our Lord's own teaching ; and it is found in several Epistles, though the grounds often differ.[1] Thessalonians and 1 Peter agree in offering certain reasons for fortitude in persecution which are not found, or occur in different contexts, in

(*d*)

other letters ; namely, the facts that (i) the sufferings of those addressed have been experienced also in other parts of the Church,

(*c*)

(ii) there is nothing in them to cause surprise or shock, for they are

(*h*) (*f*)

part of the Christian vocation, (iii) they can count on God to guard them spiritually and strengthen them, and to vindicate their cause. Unlike the idols from which they have turned, He is living and true, and has shewn His power by Christ's resurrection.

(*e*) (*f*)

(2) The experience of persecution is closely related to the expectation of Christ's revelation in glory, and rests also on *verba Christi*. That " day " will come suddenly, and will be a day of judgment and redress, when the unbelieving persecutors will be punished for their crimes ; the outbreak of persecution and the stedfastness of Christians in face of it are a kind of foretaste of God's visitation — an anticipation of the glory in which they will share at Christ's appearing, and a significant pointing to the final punishment of the wicked.

It is noticeable that much of this teaching is concentrated into " blocks " in 2 Thess. i. 4-12 and 1 Peter iv. 14-19. It may well represent an agreed formula lying behind Thessalonians and 1 Peter, used by Silvanus on each occasion.

(*b*) (*c*) (*e*)
(*f*) (*g*)

(3) The references in the table to the " eschatological discourse " recorded in Mk. xiii., Matt. xxiv., Lk. xxi., and to similar passages

---

[1] 2 Cor. viii. 2 affords interesting confirmation here of 1 Thess. i. 6.

in the Sermon on the Mount, in Matt. x. and in Lk. xii., shew how closely the primitive teaching stuck to the *verba Christi*, and particularly to the *verba Christi* as they stood in Q.

(4) Verbal similarities must not be pressed, for often they are due to the fact that the words used are such as would most naturally come to a writer's pen ; though if ξενίζεσθαι is the right reading in 1 Thess. iii. 3,[1] the word is rare enough to arrest attention. But there are certain keywords, and certain combinations of words, which are in a different category. Notable keywords, for example, are μακάριος, ἀγαλλιᾶσθαι, θλῖψις (Mark, Matthew), πειρασμός (Luke) in section (*a*), which all go back to *verba Christi* ; δοκιμάζειν and its correlatives in section (*b*), which derives from the LXX, and which is frequently associated both there and in N.T. with πῦρ ; πιστός as applied to God in section (*h*) ; κρίσις (κρῖμα) and ἐκδίκησις in section (*f*), the latter having the authority of a Lucan *verbum Christi* as well as LXX, and the sufferings and stedfastness of Christians being its ἔνδειξις or ἔνδειγμα ; and a number of words for the End in section (*e*), some of which, such as ἡμέρα, ὥρα, and the metaphor of the κλέπτης ἐν νυκτί, were characteristic of *verba Christi*. Among significant combinations of words we observe (οἱ)

---

[1] Milligan cites *Od.* x. 217, Aesch. *Choeph.* 194 (σαίνομαι δ' ὑπ' ἐλπίδος) for the meaning " allured ", " drawn aside " ; but this is to strain the meaning. Hesychius says the word is equivalent to κινεῖσθαι, but gives no authority. Lachmann felt the difficulty and read μηδὲν ἀσαίνεσθαι, a word not given in LS or MM. Two MSS. (F, G) read σιένεσθαι, i.e. σιαίνεσθαι, for which LS cite a scholiast and Hesychius for the meaning " be disquieted ". Alford says that σαίνεσθαι is a *vox media*, with the idea of agitating or disquieting, whether painfully or pleasurably depending on the context. He cites Soph. *Ant.* 1214, παιδός με σαίνει φθόγγος, Eur. *Rhes.* 55, σαίνει μ' ἔννυχος φρυκτωρία, to which add Eur. *Hippol.* 862 f., τύποι . . . προσσαίνουσί μέ (Theseus recognizing the seal on the tablets left by his dead wife) ; and Jebb points out that in *Antigone* and *Hippolytus* the word connotes " a recognition attended by pain ". Yet none of these passages suits the context in 1 Thess. iii. 3. Greater probability attaches to A. D. Knox's suggestion, in *J.T.S.* vol.

xxv. No. 99 (April 1924), pp. 290 f., that the original word corrupted into what he calls " this monstrosity " was παθαίνεσθαι, a word found in Dio Cass. li. 12, Menand. *Epitr.* 587, and elsewhere, and meaning here "descend to womanly appeals," " break down ". There is something histrionic, however, in the connotation of the word which seems foreign to the context in 1 Thess. iii. 3. I suggest that St. Paul wrote τὸ μὴ ξενίζεσθαι ἐν. . . . For the confusion of αι and ε cf. Moulton, *Grammar*, ii. p. 69, " ε and αι were as completely identical as ι and ει in the uncial period " ; and " when in 1 Tim. vi. 20 and 2 Tim. ii. 16 some δ-text authorities (FG and a few cursives) read καινοφωνίας for κενοφωνίας, we recognize it as a legitimate interpretation of what when read aloud is an ambiguous word ". Cf. the variant ἀγαλλιᾶσθαι in 1 Pet. i. 6. It is to be noted that F and G are the MSS. that give us here σιένεσθαι. The consonantal changes are such as might easily arise if a scribe were copying from dictation.

χρόνοι καὶ (οἱ) καιροί which occurs in 1 Thessalonians and in Acts, in the latter place as a *verbum Christi*, while in the former it is introduced as a subject-heading well known to the readers. νήφειν, again, occurs twice in 1 Thessalonians and thrice in 1 Peter, and only once more in the whole N.T. ; while the combination of γρηγο-ρεῖν and νήφειν occurs nowhere else but in 1 Thess. v. 6 and 1 Pet. v. 8.

What conclusions may be drawn from these facts ? They seem to me to be inconsistent either with mere coincidence or with direct literary dependence of 1 Peter on 1 and 2 Thessalonians: the parallels are too numerous for the former hypothesis, and too widely scattered for the latter. On the other hand, the facts are what we should expect if both sets of writings rest upon a common basis of oral or written admonition compiled in view of persecution, particularly if they were both penned by the same hand and represent specimens of Silvanus' regular teaching. And a similar plea for relationship to a common source can be put in to account for the parallels between 1 Peter and James. The similarity both in idea and word between 1 Pet. i. 6, 7 and Jas. i. 2, 3 is more easily explained by a common source than by borrowing of one from the other ; and the same is true of the parallels between 1 Pet. iv. 7 and Jas. v. 8 (the immin-ence of the End) and 1 Pet. v. 4 and Jas. i. 12 (the crown), though here the presence of the ideas in the tradition generally might suffice to account for them. Further, if such a common source is to be inferred, the evidence points to its being directed towards the needs of the Church in times of persecution ; and since the readers of 1 and 2 Thessalonians, 1 Peter, and James were all enduring per-secution, such a source would have been a good foundation on which their authors could build.

(5) In (g) there is a striking correspondence between 1 Thess. v. 4-8 and Rom. xiii. 11-14, which can hardly be accidental ; and we have given reasons above (pp. 375-82, and Table II) for believing that the darkness-and-light *motif* found here belonged to the earliest baptismal Form, which we have designated B¹. That Christians belonged not to the darkness, the time for sleep and drunkenness, but to the light, the time when men are alert and wakeful, was evidently a settled part of Christian teaching, which is touched here, in both Epistles alike, with the peculiar urgency that comes from the imminence of the End ; and the order of thought is too closely parallel, despite the fact that in Rom. xiii. it has other strands interwoven into it, to be attributed to chance. The main ideas occur also in 1 Peter, though often in isolation. The conclusion

seems irresistible that the underlying Form was firmly established Cf. Table
when Romans was written. I Thessalonians is very much simpler II
and less complicated, and is clearly earlier. Whether the Form was
earlier than I Thessalonians or was what we should call an " off-
print " from it cannot easily be determined; though in I (2) above
(pp. 375-82) I have adopted the former view. In either case the
compilers of the Persecution-Form used such parts of it, or of the
eschatological *verba Christi* underlying it, as they needed for their
purpose.

(6) This view is borne out by a more detailed examination of
the parts of (*g*) which contain the *Vigilate*. It will be seen from
Table XIV that the command to be awake and sober (γρηγορεῖν,
ἀγρυπνεῖν, ἐξ ὕπνου ἐγερθῆναι, νήφειν, σωφρονεῖν) is associated
(i) with *prayer* in I Peter, Colossians, and Ephesians, and less
directly in I Thessalonians and Romans, (ii) with *donning the
heavenly armour* in I Thessalonians, I Peter, Romans, and
Ephesians.[1] In I Peter and Romans, moreover, and by implica-
tion in I Thessalonians, the injunction is connected with a special
warning against intemperance and excess, dealing particularly
with drink and revelry — a warning which recalls the *verba Christi*
recorded by St. Luke (xxi. 34) in his version of the Eschatological
Discourse. Furthermore, in I Thessalonians, I Peter, Romans,
the *Vigilate* is governed by eschatological teaching which is in
close accord with that Discourse, both substantially and verbally.
In Colossians-Ephesians this is not so : persecution is not in the
Apostle's mind, and the eschatology has been broadened out to
describe the whole moral and spiritual crisis in which Christians
stand. But in Thessalonians, I Peter, and James the fact and
menace of persecution underlie the Epistles ; in I Thessalonians,
I Peter, and Romans the thought of imminent crisis is to the fore ;
and in our Lord's eschatological Discourse on the Mount of Olives
both are found together and are expressed in terms which are
reproduced in the text of the Epistles.

(7) Many of the above arguments apply also to the *State* (*h*).
The *motifs* we have been tracing — watch, pray, be sober, be strong,
etc. — are interwoven round the main stem of eschatological belief

---

[1] Dr. Carrington (*op. cit.* p. 51) lays
some stress on the association of the
command to watch with the preaching
of the word. But the case seems to me
rather thin. In Acts xx. 31, 32, for
example, the association seems purely
verbal and fortuitous ; in I Pet. iv. 11
the λόγια have to do with the injunction
to unity rather than to vigilance ; and
in Colossians and Ephesians the
Apostle's preaching of the word is
bound up not with wakefulness but
with prayer.

like tendrils of ivy round the bole of a tree, and they are as difficult as such tendrils to disentangle. And the *State* appears to be among them. Its place, for instance, in 1 Cor. xvi. 13 and in Eph. vi. 11 ff., as well as in 1 Pet. v. 12 and in the form *Resistite* in 1 Pet. v. 9, Jas. iv. 7, and Eph. vi. 13, is most significant. At the same time, it differs from the *Vigilate* in having no obvious root in the *verba Christi*, and this fact imposes a certain hesitation in assigning it to the same primitive Form.

(8) The hypothesis which seems to me to account best for the facts is that the *Vigilate* certainly, and possibly also the *State*, are derived from a Persecution-*tōrah*, or Form of teaching drawn up with persecution in view. The need of such a Form or Forms of teaching would have quickly made itself felt when persecution arose ; and it is not improbable that Matt. x. 24-41 represents a " Persecution Discourse " compiled from the *verba Christi* either by the Evangelist himself or by some earlier writer.[1] Moreover, persecution was an experience which inevitably raised questions as to the proximity of the divine Judgment and Deliverance, of which it was regarded as one of the premonitory signs ; and the two issues are closely associated in the great Eschatological Discourse which occupies Mk. xiii., Lk. xxi., and Matt. xxiv. Some scholars are inclined to attribute much of this Discourse to the prophets of the early Church rather than to our Lord Himself ; but even so we are left with a series of sayings which were presumably in Q, and which are therefore probably authentic *verba Christi*. It is significant that it is precisely these sayings which are most prominently reproduced in the parallels we have examined. The importance of this fact is obvious : it means that they belong to the period before the eschatological traditions had received the accretions and special emphases which are traceable in the final Synoptic versions, and especially in the Matthaean version, of our Lord's teaching. And likewise the more prominent eschatological passages of St. Paul's Epistles, e.g. 2 Thess. ii., are conspicuous by their absence from the series of parallels.

SCHEME OF THE PERSECUTION-FORM

We may now summarize the results of our criticism and analysis in positive form, setting it out in relation to the main

---

[1] W. C. Allen in *Oxford Studies in the Synoptic Problem*, pp. 299 f. The relevant critical questions can be well studied there and in Dr. Streeter's *The Four Gospels*, especially the Appendix. It is to be noted that in *Oxford Studies* Dr. Streeter assigned Mk. xiii. to a date later than A.D. 70, but in his later books asserted his belief that it must be earlier than that year.

sections of Persecution-teaching which we have already traced in
the earliest N.T. writings, 1 and 2 Thessalonians, and following the
lettering of these sections given in Table XIV.

1 and 2 Thess.

(*a*) Persecution a ground of rejoicing — Q, 1 Peter, 2 Corin- 1 i. 6
thians, Romans, Acts, James (Hebrews), and

(*b*) a testing of character — 1 Peter, James, 1 Corinthians.   1 ii. 4

(*c*) It had been foretold — Q, Mk. xiii., Acts, 1 Peter (iv. 12), 1 iii. 4
and therefore there was no cause for surprise or alarm — Q, 1 iii. 2-4
Mark, Acts, 1 Peter, and

(*d*) It is the common experience of Christians — 1 Peter 1 ii. 14
(Hebrews).

(*e*) You ask, When ? Its advent is near, and will be sudden — 1 v. 1-3
Q, 1 Peter, James, 1 Corinthians.

(*f*) Persecution indicates that divine Judgment and deliverance 2 i. 5-10
are at hand — Q, Acts, 1 Peter, Hebrews : so believers
must steel themselves to endure — Luke, 1 Peter, James,
Revelation : having the promise of eternal reward — Q,
Romans, 1 Corinthians, 1 Peter, James, Revelation : at 2 i. 10
the Lord's appearing — Q, 1 Peter, James, 1 Corinthians.

(*g*) Therefore, be vigilant, wakeful, and sober — Q, Mark, 1 v. 4, 8
Luke (xxi. 34 f.), 1 Peter, Romans, Colossians-Ephesians :
and gird your loins — Q, 1 Peter (i. 13), Ephesians
(vi. 14): and pray — Q (Luke), Mark (Romans), Colos- 1 v. 17
sians-Ephesians, James : Put on the heavenly armour — 1 v. 8
1 Peter (iv. 1), Romans, Ephesians : and

(*h*) Stand firm against the powers of evil — Mark (xiii. 13), 1 iii. 13,
1 Peter, James (iv. 7, v. 8), Colossians, Ephesians, Hebrews, 2 ii. 17,
Revelation; knowing that God is faithful (1 Peter, 1 ii. 3
Corinthians, Hebrews, Q).   1 v. 24
2 iii. 3

It will be observed at once that such a form of teaching is
both coherent in itself, and also lies close, verbally as well as in
substance, to some of the most certainly authentic *verba Christi*. It
enables us to account, moreover, for a large number of parallels, in
words and phrases, between several N.T. Epistles belonging to
different streams of tradition. In particular, the following points
may be observed :

(*a*) The doctrine that persecution indicates the proximity of the
divine Judgment and Deliverance, though its clearest statement is
in verses of the Eschatological Discourse which may not be authentic, is so plainly implied in *verba Christi* which are vouched for
by Q that it can be regarded as going back to our Lord Himself.

(*b*) The command to be vigilant is found by itself in verses of that Discourse which Streeter assigns to Q ; and its association with the command to pray was undoubtedly in Q. The context of this prayer is differently given by different writers. In Lk. xxi. 36 [1] it is for grace to escape from the impending calamities, and to " stand before the Son of Man ". In Mk. xiv. 38 (in Gethsemane) it is that the disciples may not " enter into temptation ". In 1 Thessalonians, 1 Peter, and Romans the context is not stated, though in 1 Thessalonians and Colossians it is associated with thanksgiving. In Colossians and Ephesians prayer is to be offered for the Apostle, that the Word may have free course through his preaching, and in Ephesians this is expanded into prayer which is perpetual, all-absorbing, and embracing the whole body of believers.

(*c*) We have already seen in connexion with Table II that the combination of wakefulness (γρηγορεῖν) with soberness (νήφειν) is especially noticeable in 1 Thessalonians and 1 Peter. The word νήφειν is not found in the Gospels ; but that does not mean that the teaching it conveys does not go back to our Lord. We have already drawn attention (*supra*, p. 396) to the existence in 1 Thessalonians, 1 Peter, and Romans of a special warning concerned with abstention from drunkenness and revelry. For this there is Dominical authority in more than one well-attested saying of our Lord, cf. Lk. xii. 45 (Q), xxi. 34 (Q), and Matt. xxiv. 49 (Q) ; and I suggest that the νήφειν of Thessalonians and 1 Peter is a brief form of the same injunction. Another synonym for this form of warning may be found in the command to " gird up the loins " which occurs in 1 Pet. i. 13 (ἀναζωσάμενοι τὰς ὀσφύας τῆς διανοίας ὑμῶν), Eph. vi. 14 (στῆτε οὖν περιζωσάμενοι τὴν ὀσφὺν ὑμῶν ἐν ἀληθείᾳ), and Lk. xii. 35 (ἔστωσαν ὑμῶν αἱ ὀσφύες περιεζωσμέναι κτλ.). The idea, as Dr. Creed observes,[2] is of being ready for any activity. It is, moreover, a Messianic trait, cf. Is. xi. 4. I suspect that this combination of γρηγορεῖν and νήφειν was drawn into this Persecution-Form either from the baptismal Form we have called B[1] or from a still earlier Form of which the compilers both of B[1] and of P made use.

(*d*) The idea of the heavenly armour, which reaches its fully developed form in St. Paul's great picture of the Christian warrior (Eph. vi. 10 ff.), cannot be assigned to this context with the same

---

[1] For the reference of Lk. xxi. 34-6 to Q see Sir John Hawkins in *Oxford Studies*, p. 135 n. and J. M. Creed, *St. Luke's Gospel, in loc.*
[2] *Op. cit. in loc.*

confidence ; though its place in 1 Thess. v. 8 points in that direction. The relevant facts are :

(i) The picture of the armour of *Deus Vindex* in Is. lix. 17, 18, where God takes action Himself against the apostate Jews, and arms Himself accordingly.

(ii) A fuller picture given in Wisd. v. 17-23, where God rewards the righteous with eternal life (verses 15, 16) and punishes the ungodly and the persecutors (cf. verses 1, 2) by arming Himself against them and bringing in as allies on His side the whole created world (τὴν κτίσιν, v. 17 ; ὁ κόσμος, v. 20). The description of the armour is based on Is. lix. 17, 18.

(iii) The idea of God arising in Judgment against the ungodly and persecutors which occurs in 2 Thess. i. 6, 8, 1 Pet. iv. 5, 17, 18, Rom. xii. 19, Heb. x. 26-31, but without any reference to His arming Himself. In Rom. xii. 19 and 1 Pet. iv. 19 the inference is drawn that, because God will thus act, Christians should entrust their vindication to Him and not take it into their own hands.

(iv) In 1 Thess. v. 8, 1 Pet. iv. 1, Rom. xiii. 12, Eph. vi. 10 ff., Christians are exhorted to arm themselves against the power or powers of evil ; and the language used is drawn from that applied to God's armour in Is. lix. and Wisd. v. In 1 Thessalonians, Romans, and 1 Peter the context is eschatological, but not so directly in Ephesians ; and in 1 Peter a peculiar turn is given to the image by the statement that the armour to be put on is " the same mind " as that of Christ in His Passion and subsequent Resurrection and Harrowing of Hell, i.e. meekness to the uttermost, which results in the victory of His redemptive work.

These facts seem best explained by reference to the idea of the conflict of Christ and His kingdom and Church against the kingdom of Satan and his attendant spirits which is given striking expression in His teaching,[1] and was a cardinal feature of His Ministry. The Lord's own conflict underlies the story of the Temptation, the eschatological *verbum Christi* in Jn. xii. 31, and especially the Q-Mark group of sayings in Mk. iii. 23 ff., Lk. xi. 17 ff., Matt. xii. 25 ff. about the " strong one " being overcome and bound by a stronger than he, who takes away his armour (πανοπλίαν, Lk. xi. 22). And this conflict between the two kingdoms was, like persecution (of which, indeed, it was the obverse), a sign that the final End and Deliverance were at hand (Lk. xi. 20). A similar idea occurs in Col. i. 13, and ii. 15 ; and the inevitable participation of Christians in

---

[1] Cf. Lightfoot's note on Col. ii. 15, and article by Anton Fridrichsen in *Theology*, xxii. pp. 122 ff. ; and above, Essay I on 1 Pet. iii. 18 ff.

the spiritual conflict is implied in the Petrine passage, Matt. xvi. 18, and in 1 Pet. iii. 17–iv. 6 and made fully explicit in Eph. vi. 12 (and cf. Rom. viii. 37-9). We can see, moreover, why the stress on the eschatological association varies. As in the case of the doctrine of the Holy Spirit, which also had originally an eschatological reference (cf. Acts ii. etc.), the conflict itself was a fact of experience conditioning the whole of Christian life ; and its practical upshot in the necessity of adequate spiritual equipment and stedfastness in defence and attack was of no less importance than its doctrinal implications with regard to the imminence of the End.

Finally, we may observe the consistency of the idea of the heavenly armour which St. Peter puts forward in the one allusion he makes to it with the whole conception of Christ's work and office set before us in his Epistle. For his idea he does not go to Is. lix. or Wisd. v., as St. Paul does, but to the prophecy of the Suffering Servant which underlies his soteriology and ethics in chapters ii. and iii. For that prophecy closes with a passage which at once recalls our Lord's teaching about " the strong one " and " the stronger ". " Therefore shall I divide him a portion with the great, and he shall divide the spoil with the strong (LXX, τῶν ἰσχυρῶν μεριεῖ σκῦλα) ; because he hath poured out his soul unto death : and he was numbered with the transgressors ; and he bare the sin of many, and made intercession for the transgressors " (Is. liii. 12). That is the idea which underlies the idea of the armour in 1 Pet. iv. 1 ; and we may surely refer it to the Apostle himself.

The command to " stand " or to " resist " — two forms of the same injunction — fits well into this context, especially in view of the references to the devil which (as Dr. Carrington rightly observes) yield such distinctive parallels in 1 Pet. v. 8, Eph. vi. 11 (cf. iv. 27), Jas. iv. 7, Heb. ii. 14. And we shall surely connect with these the passages where στηρίζειν occurs in, e.g., 1 Thess. iii. 13, 2 Thess. ii. 17, iii. 3, 1 Pet. v. 10 ; for the root of στηρίζειν and of στῆν .ι is the same. The Christian's firm standing is the result of God's grace in stablishing him. If the *State*, moreover, belongs to the context of the heavenly conflict, we have a reason why its order relatively to the *Vigilate* varies in different Epistles.

IV. General Summary

We must now attempt to sum up the conclusions to which our enquiry has led us. The parallels between 1 Peter and other N.T. Epistles have long been familiar to scholars, and have provided much of the supposed evidence for the alleged Paulinism of our Epistle. The investigation of the relevant facts has involved a wide induction and has taken us far beyond the confines of the immediate problem which it was our primary purpose to elucidate ; but if the theories we have advanced are found to explain other facts and difficulties as well as those they were originally designed to account for, that event must be set to their credit. Incidentally, the conclusions reached are not all of the same degree of probability. That common catechetical and liturgical sources underlie most of the Epistles of N.T. seems to me proven beyond a doubt ; but the isolation and differentiation of the sources, and the attribution of particular pieces of teaching to this or to that source, are a more difficult and a more dubious matter. The task is still further complicated, moreover, by the lack of any established technique for the synoptic study of the Epistles, similar to that which prevails for the Gospels ; and, even if it did exist, we should have to recognize that in many cases it would need to be supplemented and corrected by methods more usually found in the work of the *Formgeschichte* school. Nevertheless it has seemed worth while to make the attempt, not least since the work of Dr. Carrington had opened the ground. Even where our conclusions are questioned, the facts set out in this Essay and its accompanying tables will demand explanation along historico-literary lines ; and one may hope also that many who are not interested in this critical problem as such may nevertheless find the tabulation of the facts helpful for the practical purposes of teaching and preaching.

FORMS UNDERLYING THE EPISTLES

1. Comparison of 1 and 2 Thessalonians with 1 Peter reveals a number of parallels in thought and phrase which have hitherto received little attention. The fact that Silvanus appears as a joint author in both cases is significant in this connexion, and may be held to account for many of the resemblances. *Silvanus*

Table III

2. The resemblances, however, seem to point beyond the influence of an individual mind to a pattern or patterns of catechetical teaching familiar both to him and to his readers. In particular, we can discern behind 1 and 2 Thessalonians and 1 Peter the traces of what Dr. Carrington has called " A Christian Holiness Code " (B¹). Its marks are the emphasis on " abstaining " (ἀπέχεσθαι) from sensual lusts and uncleanness ; and the positive consecration (ἁγιάζειν, καθαρίζειν) which it inculcates is specially expressed in the exercise of charity. The idea of the baptized as *First baptismal Form (B¹)*

Table I

having passed out of darkness and being already the Children of
Light was probably also in this Form. In this pattern of teaching
the Christian Church was thought of as a neo-Levitical community,
at once sacerdotal and sacrificial ; and it included teaching on worship (WL) conceived on these lines. Its ethical teaching enumerated
virtues based on the principle of Charity, and so well suited to the
instruction of catechumens that they may fairly be called Catechumen Virtues (CVL). The whole pattern probably provided the
first outline of a baptismal catechism, and seems to have had
specially in mind the elementary needs of Gentile Christians, and
the fears of Jewish Christians, as these were made clear at the
Council of Jerusalem. The occurrence of its *motifs* in the Epistles
of A.D. 60 and later shews that it was never discarded, though it was
combined with something broader.

3. The rudimentary pattern of teaching which was summarized
in, or derived from, the Apostolic Decree — for either course may have
occurred — was amplified by a baptismal catechism (B²) which was
conceived on more positive and imaginative lines. It began with the
idea of " the Truth " or " the word of truth " as the divine foundation of baptism, and described the change involved in baptism in a
variety of metaphors. The *Abstinentes* of the earlier pattern was
superseded or reinforced by the *Deponentes*, which referred especialy
to the repudiation of κακία in all its forms, including sins of speech
and of temper ; and the *Deponentes* was followed by an *Induentes*
introducing another version of Catechumen Virtues which we have
called CVG, based largely on Ps. xxxiv. and Prov. iii. B² seems
also to have included a section on Worship (WS) which derived from
the customs of the synagogues ; and there was a section on Church
order and unity which is reflected in different ways in Romans,
1 Peter, and James, and was perhaps part of CVG. The ethical
teaching of B² turns upon the triad, truthfulness, humility, and love.
The idea of humility was worked out in detail in a social code
(*Subiecti*), of which the keynote was subordination, and thus applied
to civic duty and to domestic life.

The date of the pattern we have designated as B² appears to lie
between A.D. 50 and 55. In favour of the earlier date is the fact that
much of 1 Thess. v. seems based upon the section designated CVG
which also underlies Rom. xii. and probably 1 Pet. iii. 8-12. In
favour of the later date is the absence from 1 and 2 Thessalonians
of two of the keywords of B², *Deponentes* and *Subiecti*. The solution depends on the view taken of the genesis and history of CVG.
If it was originally independent of both B¹ and B², and circulated

Marginal notes (left column):

Table II

Table VII

Table
VIII A

Second
baptismal
Form (B²)

Table IV

Table V

Table VI

Table
VIII A

Table VII

Table
VIII C

Tables X-
XIII

among teachers as a separate fragment of catechetical material, it might well have been known in that form to the authors of 1 Thessalonians and have been incorporated only later, perhaps under their influence, in the baptismal pattern B². Or indeed it may have remained always detached, and been used independently by St. Peter and St. Paul. Its close affinities with Ps. xxxiv. and Prov. iii. gave it a unity of its own, and its brevity would be no argument against its continued separate existence ; though the baptismal context in which Ps. xxxiv. 8 is quoted in 1 Pet. ii. 3 shews how suitable it was for baptismal purposes. In any case, the section was such as we may well suppose that the circle of prophets and teachers at Antioch would have rejoiced to compile.

4. Other resemblances between 1 and 2 Thessalonians, 1 Peter, Romans, and James point to an underlying source (P) compiled with persecution in view, based largely on *verba Christi* and possibly prepared, at least in part, by Silvanus. This source contained injunctions to wakefulness (*Vigilate*) and stedfastness (*State*), the former being perhaps derived from the earliest baptismal catechism. The metaphor of the heavenly armour, even though originally it may have been in the baptismal catechism, probably belonged here in its developed form ; and the source had a markedly eschatological character, persecution being premonitory of the End when God or Christ should be manifested as *vindex*.

A Persecution Form (P) Table XIV

BEARING OF EVIDENCE ON THE SUPPOSED DEPENDENCE OF 1 PETER ON OTHER EPISTLES

So much common ground having been shewn to underlie the Epistles of St. Paul, 1 Peter, and St. James, it remains to be seen what remnant of Petrine parallels, supposed to prove the dependence of 1 Peter on St. Paul or on James, still stands now. The parallels are well set out in Bigg's Commentary, in B. Weiss's *Manual of Introduction*, and A. Meyer's *Das Rätsel des Jacobsbriefs* [1] (for St. James), and in Moffatt's *Introduction* (quoting from E. C. Selwyn's *St. Luke the Prophet*, for Ephesians) ; and readers who refer to these lists will observe how much of the evidence has already been covered.

Romans. — The six parallels with 1 Peter in Rom. xii., xiii. are traceable to the use, in both, of the sources we have designated B¹, CVG, and B². The similarities and differences between Rom. ix. 33 and 1 Pet. ii. 6, 7 have been traced in Add. Note E to a primitive hymn used by both authors ; and the same explanation may account

---

[1] I have to thank Dr. Lowther Clarke for references to this book.

for the allusion to Christ as " on the right hand of God " in Rom. viii. 34, 1 Pet. iii. 22 — a doctrine found on the lips of St. Stephen in Acts vii. 56. For Rom. iv. 24 = 1 Pet. i. 21, Rom. vi. 7 = 1 Pet. iv. 1, Rom. vi. 11 = 1 Pet. ii. 24, Rom. viii. 18 = 1 Pet. v. 1, nothing need be added to Bigg's observations, except that in 1 Pet. v. 1 there is probably a personal reference to St. Peter's own experience at the Transfiguration. There is no reason, therefore, to suppose direct dependence of 1 Peter on Romans, though echoes of its language need not be ruled out.

Ephesians. — Of the thirteen parallels given in Moffatt (*Introduction*, pp. 382, 383) seven are accounted for by common derivation from B², especially the *Subiecti* section. The form of the opening address and benediction in Eph. i. 1-3 = 1 Pet. i. 1-3 (cf. 2 Cor. i. 1-3), and the phrase πρὸ καταβολῆς κόσμου in Eph. i. 4 = 1 Pet. i. 20, represent common forms of expression. Eph. ii. 18 = 1 Pet. ii. 4, Eph. i. 14 = 1 Pet. ii. 9, Eph. i. 20 f. = 1 Pet. iii. 22, all derive from liturgical sources pointed out above in the Notes and the relevant Additional Notes, and in Essay I, pp. 325 f. On the resemblance between Eph. iii. 5 f. and 1 Pet. i. 10 f. see Add. Note D, pp. 262 f. : if, as we have suggested, the " prophets " in 1 Pet. i. 10 are Christian prophets, the parallel is a true one, and arises naturally out of the historical situation. To these parallels noted by Moffatt we might add Eph. iii. 10 = 1 Pet. i. 12, iii. 22, where the credal hymn quoted in 1 Tim. iii. 16 would amply account for such resemblance as exists. Hort's dictum [1] that " the connexion (between 1 Peter and Ephesians) though very close does not lie in the surface ", though Bigg disallows it, is justified, we believe, in the light of the above facts.

Titus. — Bigg thinks that the parallels of thought between 1 Peter and Titus are significant enough to suggest at least that St. Paul was now " approximating to the Petrine view ". It would be safer, perhaps, to speak of the common tradition expressed in the Petrine view. The λουτρὸν παλιγγενεσίας of iii. 5 is traceable to B², Tit. ii. 12 to the *Abstinentes* of B¹, Tit. iii. 1-3, 8, ii. 9, 10, 4, 5 to the *Subiecti*. The use of λυτροῦσθαι in ii. 14, as in 1 Pet. i. 18, rests upon the *verbum Christi* in Mk. x. 45, Matt. xx. 28, and occurs in the catechetical Ps. xxxiv. 23 ; and λαὸς περιούσιος in ii. 14 recalls the hymn quoted in 1 Pet. ii. 9.

James. — The individuality of this Epistle, and the uncertainty as to its date, make the parallels between it and 1 Peter more difficult

---

[1] *The First Epistle of St. Peter, i.–ii. 17*, p. 5. But a somewhat different judgment is given in *The Romans and the Ephesians*, p. 169.

to account for. The source we have called P accounts sufficiently for i. 2, 3 = 1 Pet. i. 6, 7, and for the injunction of stedfastness in v. 8 = 1 Pet. iv. 7, v. 10; the allusions to honest "walking" in iii. 13 = 1 Pet. ii. 12, and to lusts making war in iv. 1 = 1 Pet. ii. 11, may derive from B¹ and current modes of expression ; the crown of i. 12 = 1 Pet. v. 4 may have been in P, but occurs also in 1 Cor. ix. 25, 2 Tim. iv. 8, and eight times in Revelation,¹ and has a Rabbinic origin. The allusion to worship in Jas. i. 27 is of the WL type, but is verbally too far from anything in 1 Peter to require explanation.

The parallels between Jas. iv. 7, 10 and 1 Pet. v. 5, 6 are discussed on pp. 417-18 above, and the baptismal teaching in Jas. i. 18, 21 on pp. 392-3. The only difficulty is in regard to the use of O.T. in James. Jas. iv. 6 = 1 Pet. v. 5 is a quotation from Prov. iii. 34, a chapter underlying CVG, where the different approach of the two writers is stongly marked. This is likewise the case in Jas. i. 11 = 1 Pet. i. 24, where the former paraphrases, while the latter quotes, Is. xl. 6 f. ; the idea itself was a commonplace. The possible use of Prov. x. 12 in Jas. v. 20 = 1 Pet. iv. 8 is discussed in the note on the latter passage, and it is suggested that a proverb or *verbum Christi* current in the Church is a more probable source. If direct dependence exists, then 1 Peter is much more likely to be original than James : B. Weiss' arguments (*Manual*, ii. p. 106 n.) seem to me far more cogent than those of A. Meyer on the opposite side.

Hebrews. — We have noted in the Tables accompanying this Essay only incidental references to Hebrews, but the affinities between the two Epistles are striking. They are of three kinds. (i) Bigg gives a list of words and phrases peculiar to the two Epistles, some of which may be more than fortuitous. Thus γεύεσθαι in vi. 4, 5 may in view of its context be derived, as in 1 Pet. ii. 3, from Ps. xxxiv., which was used for catechetical purposes in the early Church ; and a similar cause may underlie the collocation of εὐλογίαν with κληρονομεῖν in Heb. xii. 17 and in 1 Pet. iii. 9, where it serves to introduce a quotation from Ps. xxxiv. The injunction to " pursue peace " (εἰρήνην διώκετε) in Heb. xii. 14 has also, as in 1 Pet. iii. 11, the same source. The idea of the Church as the οἶκος of God presided over by Christ as High Priest (Heb. iii., x. 21) is similar to the neo-Levitical conception underlying 1 Pet. ii. The classical word κομίζεσθαι occurs in Heb. x. 36, xi. 39 and in 1 Pet. i. 9, v. 4 in contexts so similar as to strike the attention and to suggest that it may have been amost a *vox technica* in the early Church.

---

¹ Cf. Carrington, *op. cit.* p. 56 n.

(ii) Other words and phrases appear to reflect similarities of doctrinal development or of historical circumstances behind the two Epistles. " The word of God is living " of Heb. iv. 12 recalls 1 Pet. i. 23, on which see the exegetical Note *in loc.* Jesus is the Shepherd (ποιμήν) in Heb. xiii. 20 as in 1 Pet. ii. 25 (cf. ἀρχιποίμην in 1 Pet. v. 9) — a conception which goes back to such *verba Christi* as Mk. vi. 34, xiv. 27, and Jn. x. 2, 11 ff. In Heb. i. 2 as in 1 Pet. i. 20 the revelation of God in Christ has occurred " at the end of " the times or days, and is regarded as an eschatological event. There is a particularly close affinity in the doctrine of the Atonement, as we find it in Heb. ix. and 1 Pet. ii., iii., and in the terms used in connexion with it. Christ was ἄμωμος (Heb. ix. 14 and 1 Pet. i. 19) ; He suffered for sins ἅπαξ (Heb. ix. 28, 1 Pet. iii. 18) ; He bore (ἀνήνεγκεν) our sins (Heb. ix. 28, 1 Pet. ii. 24) ; His blood was " blood of sprinkling " (Heb. xii. 24, 1 Pet. i. 2). Though the ideas in 1 Peter seem simpler and more primitive than those in Hebrews, they are essentially the same ideas. Even the characteristic Petrine idea of the *imitatio Christi* has an echo in Heb. xii. 1, 2, where Christ is set before us as our example in His endurance of the cross, an endurance which culminated in triumph (cf. 1 Pet. iii. 22). And these close resemblances of doctrine are matched by resemblances in the underlying situation in each case. Both Epistles were written in the context of persecution. Heb. xiii. 13 (cf. also xi. 26) contemplates Christianity involving reproach (ὄνειδος) no less than 1 Pet. iv. 14, and the lesson is given in both cases (Heb. x. 29-31, 37 f., 1 Pet. iv. 17-19) that God will take the Church's cause into His own hand and vindicate His own. In such circumstances Christians could scarcely be other than " strangers and pilgrims (παρεπίδημοι) on the earth ", like the patriarchs of long ago (Heb. xi. 13, 1 Pet. i. 1, ii. 11).

These parallels are of a very striking character. Von Soden's view, cited by Bigg, that they are sufficiently accounted for by " the supposition that the authors were contemporaries and breathed the same spiritual atmosphere", is rendered still more concrete if the sources we have endeavoured to lay bare behind 1 Peter and the Pauline Epistles were also familiar to the author of Hebrews.

(iii) There is, however, a third group of affinities which we must consider, though they are more difficult to indicate in detail. But I cannot get away from the impression of a relationship between Heb. xiii. and 1 Peter which goes beyond what common sources or common doctrinal tradition or even common circumstances will explain. There seem to be the same problems of Church life, and the same attitude to them, behind both — the same need of hospitality, of sympathy, of active well-doing, of inner cohesion, and subjection towards the Church's leaders ; the same sense of reproach and of being without a settled earthly home ; the same necessity to imitate Jesus in His suffering ; the same hope of an inheritance awaiting believers at the last. And the great chapter of Hebrews reaches its climax in words redolent of 1 Peter, and of 1 Peter when most near to 1 and 2 Thessalonians :

Heb. xiii. 20, 21	1 Pet. and 1 and 2 Thess.
ὁ δὲ θεὸς τῆς εἰρήνης.	1 Thess. v. 23. ὁ θεὸς τῆς εἰρήνης.
ὁ ἀναγαγὼν ἐκ νεκρῶν.	1 Thess. i. 10. ὃν ἤγειρεν ἐκ τῶν νεκρῶν (cf. Acts ii. 24, 32).
	1 Pet. i. 21. τὸν ἐγείραντα αὐτὸν ἐκ νεκρῶν.
	1 Pet. ii. 25. ἦτε γὰρ ὡς πρόβατα . . .
τὸν ποιμένα τῶν προβάτων τὸν μέγαν.	ἐπὶ τὸν ποιμένα καὶ ἐπίσκοπον τῶν ψυχῶν ὑμῶν.
	1 Pet. v. 4. φανερωθέντος τοῦ ἀρχιποίμενος.
ἐν αἵματι διαθήκης αἰωνίου.	1 Pet. i. 2. ῥαντισμὸν αἵματος Ἰησοῦ Χριστοῦ.
τὸν κύριον ἡμῶν Ἰησοῦν,	1 Pet. i. 19. τιμίῳ αἵματι ὡς ἀμνοῦ ἀμώμου καὶ ἀσπίλου Χριστοῦ.
	2 Thess. ii. 17. στηρίξαι ἐν παντὶ ἔργῳ καὶ λόγῳ ἀγαθῷ.
	1 Pet. v. 10. ὁ δὲ θεὸς πάσης χάριτος . . . καταρτίσει, στηρίξει, σθενώσει.
καταρτίσαι ὑμᾶς ἐν παντὶ ἀγαθῷ.	1 Pet. iv. 19. παρατιθέσθωσαν τὰς ψυχὰς αὐτῶν ἐν ἀγαθοποιίᾳ.
εἰς τὸ ποιῆσαι τὸ θέλημα αὐτοῦ.	1 Pet. iv. 2. θελήματι θεοῦ . . . βιῶσαι.
ποιῶν ἐν ἡμῖν τὸ εὐάρεστον ἐνώπιον αὐτοῦ.	1 Thess. iv. 3. τοῦτο γάρ ἐστι θέλημα τοῦ θεοῦ, ὁ ἁγιασμὸς ὑμῶν.
	1 Thess. v. 18. τοῦτο γὰρ θέλημα θεοῦ ἐν Χριστῷ Ἰησοῦ εἰς ὑμᾶς.
ᾧ ἡ δόξα εἰς τοὺς αἰῶνας τῶν αἰώνων. ἀμήν.	1 Pet. iv. 11. ᾧ ἐστιν ἡ δόξα καὶ τὸ κράτος εἰς τοὺς αἰῶνας τῶν αἰώνων. ἀμήν.

The author of Hebrews may have read 1 Peter and been haunted — as who would not be ? — by its language. But is it not equally possible that among " those from Italy " (Heb. xiii. 24) who were beside him as he wrote there was one who had been the close associate of St. Paul in writing to Thessalonica and of St. Peter in his First Epistle ? The hypothesis would do much to explain the intimate links (to use Bigg's adjective) which seem to bind Hebrews and 1 Peter together.

APPENDED NOTE

PARTICIPLE AND IMPERATIVE IN 1 PETER

BY DR. DAVID DAUBE

IN 1 Peter and other epistles the participle occasionally stands for the imperative. It is proposed first to discuss the current explanation of this, which is unsatisfactory; then to suggest a different explanation; and finally to go through the passages concerned one by one and test the theory advanced.

I

There is agreement that it would be wrong to dispose of the difficulty by assuming an anacoluthon, regarding a convenient imperative such as ἐστέ as implied, or the like. To do so would be making the texts suit our notions of grammar instead of deducing our grammar from the texts. Another reason why the usage cannot be due to carelessness will be mentioned below.[1] We have to put up with the fact that, in certain passages of the New Testament, the participle has a value different from what it has in classical Greek. We want to know how this comes about, and it seems universally held that J. H. Moulton has supplied the correct answer. According to him,[2] it is clear from the papyri that the use of the participle for the imperative was a genuine Hellenistic development.

Let us examine his evidence. He gives seven references, which, however, may be reduced to three or even two cases. First, there is the formula ἑαυτῶν δὲ ἐπιμελόμενοι: G 35, ParP 63, G 30, PathP 1, TbP 12, etc. Secondly, the participle, he says, is used for the imperative in TbP 59, where a genitive absolute is followed by ἐν οἷς . . . ἐπιτάσσοντές μοι. Thirdly, he adduces FP 112, ἐπέχον Ζωίλωι καὶ εἶνα . . . μὴ δυσωπήσῃς, asserting that ἐπέχον represents ἐπέχων.

To begin with the formula ἐπιμελόμενοι, it is true that, in G 35, we are almost forced to treat it as an imperative. This letter ends (ll. 7 ff.): ἑαυτῶν δὲ ἐπιμελόμενοι ἵν' ὑγιαίνητε. ἔσμεν ἐν Πτολεμαΐδι. ἔρρωσθε. The natural translation is . "Take care of yourselves that you should be fit. We are in Ptolemais. Keep well." But in all other letters where the formula occurs it can easily be connected, as a proper, classical participle, with ἔρρωσθε. The letter to be found in ParP 63, col. 1, ends thus (ll. 18 f.): ἐπιμελόμενος δὲ καὶ σαυτοῦ ἵν' ὑγιαίνῃς. ἔρρωσο. It is perfectly possible to translate: "Taking care of yourself that you should be fit, keep well". Similarly, the conclusion of the letter G 30 runs (ll. 9 ff.): ἐπιμελό[μενο]ι δὲ καὶ ἑαυτῶν ἵν' ὑγιαίνητε. ἔρρωσθε. PathP 1 reads (ll. 11 f.): καὶ ἑαυτῶν δ' ἐπιμελόμενοι ἵν' ὑγιαίνητε. ἔρρωσθε. The first of the two drafts preserved in TbP 12 concludes (ll. 12 f.): τὰ ἄλλα σαυτοῦ ἐπιμελόμενος ἵν' ὑγιαίνῃς. ἔρρω[σ]ο.

These texts afford little support to Moulton's thesis. (Others might be adduced, but in all of them the participle may be construed in the classical

[1] See pp. 470 f.
[2] *A Grammar of New Testament Greek*, i. pp. 180 ff. and 232 ff. His view is accepted, for example, by A. T. Robertson, *A Grammar of the Greek New Testament*, pp. 945 f.

manner.)[1] The only one with anything remarkable about the participle at all is the first, G 35.[2] But, bearing in mind the evidence as a whole, we shall hardly claim that G 35 argues a genuine Hellenistic use of the participle for the imperative. The truth is that it was usual to finish a letter with some friendly phrase like " Take care of yourself ". We come across the actual imperative, ἐπιμέλου[3] ; combinations like χαιριεῖ σαυτοῦ ἐπιμελόμενος[4] ; and combinations like ἐπιμελόμενος σαυτοῦ ἔρρωσο — namely, in all the texts cited above except G 35. And even in explaining G 35 it is from this combination that we have to start. Probably the writer was just careless. It is not only in the papyri that when a man comes to the stereotyped conclusion of a letter, his style and grammar are apt to grow laxer. The English " With kindest regards from " may conceivably be defended (" This letter comes with . . ."). But in ParP 63, col. 12, a copy of a letter may be found with part of the conclusion missing, the copyist having left off in the middle of a word because he got bored by the formula (ll. 99 ff.) : τῆς δὲ τοῦ σώματος ἐπιμελή[ας προ]νωούμενος ὅπως ὑγιαίνοντά σ⟨ε ἀσπασώμεθα or the like, ἔρρωσο⟩.[5] The writer of G 35 probably intended to conclude in the normal fashion, put ἑαυτῶν δὲ ἐπιμελόμενοι ἵν' ὑγιαίνητε, and then, instead of immediately going on to ἔρρωσθε, was careless enough to insert ἐσμεν ἐν Πτολεμαΐδι. However, even if it were true that ἐπιμελόμενοι, at the close of a letter, could be used as a real imperative, no sweeping conclusions ought to be drawn. A formula for ending letters is a very special case. Even if the ἐπιμελόμενοι used in finishing letters should at some date have become so detached from its governing verb that it assumed the character of a real imperative (an evolution for which there is no evidence), this would not entitle us to infer that, in Hellenistic speech, the participle might quite generally stand for the imperative.

Moulton's second case is TbP 59. But it is the same, in essence, as the first and just as weak. For once again the participle appears towards the end of a letter and can be construed classically, by connecting it with ἔρρωσθε. Here is the passage (ll. 8 ff.) : ἐν οἷς ἐὰν προσδέησθέ μου ἐπιτάσσοντές μοι προθυμότερον διὰ τὸ ἄνωθεν φοβεῖσθαι καὶ σέβεσθαι τὸ ἱερόν. ἔρρωσθε. This may be rendered thus : " In which, if you need me, commanding my services (since of old I revere and worship the temple), keep well ". There is no need to make ἐπιτάσσοντές an imperative : it goes with ἔρρωσθε, as a proper participle. The letter in question is very brief : we should call it a note, and the telegraphic style (ἐν οἷς . . . ἐπιτάσσοντές μοι . . . ἔρρωσθε) seems quite natural. In English letters, the subject of the concluding phrase is the writer himself. Hence we find clauses like " Looking forward to seeing you, Yours ". There is no reason, in interpreting letters where the subject of the concluding phrase is the addressee, to boggle at clauses like ἑαυτῶν ἐπιμελόμενοι — or ἐπιτάσσοντές μοι — ἔρρωσθε.

FP 112 (ll. 8 ff.) remains, but it is even less convincing than the other texts[6] : τῶν ὤγμ[ον] τῆς 'Απίαδος ἕως σήμερον οὐ ἐθέρ[ι]σας ἀλλ' ἠμέληκας αὐτοῦ καὶ μέχρι τούτου τὼ ἥμυσυ αὐτοῦ ἐθέρισας, ἐπέχον τῷ δακτυλιστῇ Ζωίλωι

---

[1] See, for instance, TbP 19 (ll. 14 ff.), ἐπιμελόμενος δὲ καὶ σαυτοῦ [ἵν' ὑ]γιαίνῃς ἔρρωσο ; or TbP 20 (ll. 10 f.), καὶ σαυτοῦ ἐπιμελόμενος ἵν' ὑγιαίνῃς ἔρρωσο.
[2] It is only G 35 and TbP 59 (to be discussed below) which are quoted for the view here combated by Robertson.

[3] ParP 32, TbP 55.
[4] TbP 12.
[5] See Wilcken, *Urkunden der Ptolemäerzeit*, i. pp. 629 ff.
[6] Robertson, though accepting Moulton's thesis, does not quote it ; see above, n. 2.

καὶ εἶνα αὐτὸν μὴ δυσωπήσῃς. ἀθέρισ⟨τον⟩ αὐτὸν ἕως σήμερον ἄφικας, διὼ μέμ-
φομαί σαι μεγάλως. The rendering of the editors runs [1] : " Up to to-day you
have not harvested the field at Apias, but have neglected it, and so far have
only harvested the half. Give heed to the measurer (?) Zoilus ; don't look
askance at him. Up to to-day you have left it unharvested, wherefore I
blame you greatly." Moulton declares that ἐπέχον represents ἐπέχων and
has the value of an imperative. But Gemellus, the author of this letter,
was a man whose spelling and grammar were " peculiarly atrocious ", according to the editors. ἐπέχον, therefore, might be meant as some aorist imperative ; or, if it represents ἐπέχων, Gemellus may have connected it, as
a proper participle, with ἐθέρισας even though speaking of an action to be
performed by the addressee in the future. (Gemellus was fond of carousing
with his friends ; he may have written this when he had not recovered from
one of his bouts.) However, a rendering slightly different from that of the
editors would seem not only to exclude any imperative meaning but also to
make better sense in the context. ἐπέχον may be taken to signify " according to ", " to judge by the report of ". This would give : " Up to to-day
you have not harvested the field . . ., according to the measurer Zoilus, and
don't look askance at him (sc. for letting me know). Up to to-day you have
left it unharvested, wherefore I blame you greatly." We need only assume
that Gemellus put an accusative absolute on the model of παρέχον, ἐξόν
and the like. (Admittedly, this form is rarer in the papyri than in earlier
Greek, but it does still exist.) Or if ἐπέχον represents ἐπέχων, he may have
used an unattached participle, possibly connecting it in mind with " I blame
you greatly " ; or even more simply, he used the participle instead of the
indicative, a usage of which Moulton himself gives convincing examples.[2]
In any case, on this interpretation, the argument of the letter becomes
coherent : while, if we follow the editors, the sentence " Give heed to the
measurer Zoilus, don't look askance at him " is an abrupt and obscure inter-
jection. Moreover, the meaning here preferred would be consistent with
what we should expect from Gemellus, who was " a shrewd man of business,
somewhat wilful and exacting, but of a kind and generous disposition ".
Needless to add, should δακτυλιστής mean " musician ", as Preisigke thinks
possible,[3] no conceivable translation of ἐπέχον would make the sentence
really intelligible.

This is all Moulton's evidence from the papyri, and it does not shew that
the participle was a substitute for the imperative in Hellenistic language.
(Still less does it shew that this use is " not a mark of inferior education ".
Moulton emphasizes that TbP 59 is a letter from an important official. This
is true, and one might even add ParP 63, col. 1. But the participle in the
former agrees with ἔρρωσο, that in the latter with ἔρρωσθε.) Two texts
only are remarkable at all, G 35 and FP 112. In G 35, ἑαυτῶν ἐπιμελόμενοι
is separated from ἔρρωσθε by a statement of the place, ἔσμεν ἐν Πτολεμαΐδι :
the writer was careless about the concluding formula of his letter. In FP
112, we find the word ἐπέχον in a difficult sentence, in a letter by a man
who, as regards spelling and grammar, was a law to himself. There is,

[1] See Grenfell, Hunt and Hogarth, *Fayum Towns and their Papyri*, pp. 261 ff.
[2] See *l.c.* p. 223. Actually, one of the cases adduced by Moulton, TbP 14 (ll. 50 f.), is remarkably like the one under notice : γράψας ὅπως εἰδῇς καὶ σὺ ἀναγωνίατος ἴσθει, " I write

this for your information, and do not have any anxiety ".
[3] Liddell and Scott accept the meaning " measurer " without reservation, but Preisigke gives the choice between this and " musician ".

however, a further consideration. Even if the evidence from the papyri were valid in itself, it would yet be inapplicable to the cases from the New Testament that it is sought to explain, for three reasons. In the first place, among those cases we find some where not only participles but also adjectives are used in an imperative sense: ἀποστυγοῦντες τὸ πονηρόν . . . φιλόστοργοι and the like.¹ Obviously, an explanation, to be satisfactory, must account for both. But in none of the papyri relied on by Moulton is there any trace of an imperative meaning of an adjective. Curiously, it is precisely in the passages with adjectives in an imperative sense that Moulton would detect the rationale of the usage. It is these, he thinks, which shew that the usage originated in an anacoluthon, the omission of the ἐστέ. Gradually, what was at first an anacoluthon became a proper grammatical form. But if this were right, we should expect the usage mainly in connexion with adjectives, not participles. In point of fact, as has been stated, not one of Moulton's papyri contains an adjective in an imperative sense. And as for the New Testament, while there are passages where participles unaccompanied by adjectives are used as imperatives (οἱ οἰκέται ὑποτασσόμενοι . . . τοῖς δεσπόταις),² there are none where adjectives independent of participles are so used : adjectives are used as imperatives only where they follow participles, as in the text quoted (ἀποστυγοῦντες . . . φιλόστοργοι). In the second place, when we say that in Hellenistic speech the participle could stand for the imperative, we are using convenient but dangerously vague terms of grammar. For one imperative or participle is not like another. As will be shewn, wherever a participle has an imperative sense in the New Testament, it expresses not a command addressed to a specific person on a specific occasion, but a rule. It is always of the type ἀποστυγοῦντες τὸ πονηρόν : this is a rule, namely, that good Christians should abhor the evil. It is never of the type, say, " Go and fetch me a glass of water ". (Lk. xxiv. 47 f. would be an exception if it were correct to regard ἀρξάμενοι as opening a new sentence and translate it by " begin ". So would be three verses from 2 Corinthians if the participles had to be treated as imperatives. But these interpretations are not convincing.) ³ Moulton's examples, however, even if they were valid in themselves, would none of them have the character of a rule : ἐπιμελόμενοι, " keep well ", ἐπιτάσσοντές μοι, " command my services ", ἐπέχον Ζωίλωι, " give heed to Zoilus ". True, as a result of the nature of the sources, in the New Testament rules may well be more frequent and specific commands less frequent than in the papyri, which consist largely of private correspondence. Any particular form, therefore, we may expect to be more common in rules in the New Testament and in specific commands in the papyri. But there do occur many specific commands in the New Testament and many rules in, for instance, official circulars preserved in the papyri; and the fact remains that even if we accepted Moulton's evidence as such, it would give us not a single parallel for the participles of the New Testament, which express rules. In the third place, Moulton tries to prove that the use of the participle for the imperative was a genuine Hellenistic development. But if this were the case, why, then, should the usage be confined to one specific kind of context in the New Testament ? Ought we not to find it anywhere ? Yet in the New Testament it occurs

---

¹ Rom. xii. 9 f. For other examples see below, pp. 483 f.
² 1 Pet. ii. 18. For other examples see below, pp. 480 ff.
³ See below, pp. 481 f.

solely in the *Haustafeln* and similar rules ; solely in rules concerning the social behaviour of Christians within their new community and within their families. This clearly speaks, on the one hand, against its being due to mere carelessness (for carelessness would not be so rationally restricted — there must be something more serious behind it) ; but, on the other hand, also against its being a recognized, grammatical form of the Hellenistic age.

The upshot seems to be that Moulton, in this case, has " innovated too fast " [1] and overrated the testimony of the papyri, a mistake committed by many and in many provinces since his day. (Papyrology has done less for Roman Law, for example, than one would think, to go by the huge output of literature.) It is not maintained that the way in which the participle is employed in some passages of the New Testament cannot conceivably be Greek. Any day fresh papyri may come to light vindicating Moulton's theory (though it is likely, in view of some of the difficulties pointed out, that it would have to be considerably modified). But, if such papyri exist, they have yet to be discovered.

II

In the meantime, it may be permissible to try and submit a different solution. It is suggested that the participles in question may be due to Hebrew or (though less probably) Aramaic influence.

The Hebrew participle often corresponds to our present tense. Of the first river going out from Eden, the Bible says הוא הסבב, [2] " that is it which compasseth the whole land " ; literally, " that is the one compassing ".[3] The third river " is it which goeth toward the east ", הוא ההלך ; lit., " it is the one going ".[4] Again, God says to Cain,[5] דמי אחיך צעקים, " the voice of thy brother's blood crieth unto me ". A more literal translation would be, " the voice of the blood crying ". Frequently, it is our future tense to which the Hebrew participle seems nearest in meaning. When Jacob hesitates to let Benjamin go to Egypt with his brothers, they tell him, ואם אינך משלח, " but if thou wilt not send him, we will not go down " ; lit., " but if thou not sending him ".[6]

In particular, the Hebrew participle denotes a repeated or habitual event or action, where we should mostly put either the present or the future. The Ecclesiast says that דור הלך, " one generation passeth away, and another generation cometh ".[7] We might translate, " one generation will pass away. . . ." Literally, however, it means " one generation passing away . . ." Or take הולך וסובב הרוח, " the wind goeth and turneth about " ; lit., " the wind going and turning about ".[8] Or הכסיל חבק, " the fool foldeth his hands together, and eateth his own flesh " ; it would be equally good to say, " the fool will fold. . . ." Once again, literally translated, this would be " the fool folding . . ." [9]

A habitual action that is desirable may be called customary, an action that custom requires us to perform. Accordingly, in many languages, that form of the verb which expresses a habitual action can also express one that ought to be performed. In other words, to describe a custom may be very much the same as to convey the proper line of conduct. An English states-

---

[1] This was his own fear : see his Preface, p. x.
[2] Hebrew quotations will be reduced to the minimum necessary for the reader to be able to follow the argument.

[2] Gen. ii. 11. Comp. ii. 13, of the second river, with the same form.
[4] Gen. ii. 14.
[5] Gen. iv. 10.
[6] Gen. xliii. 5.
[7] Eccles. i. 4.
[8] Eccles. i. 6.
[9] Eccles. iv. 5.

man may say, " During a war, people fight and do not think of personal profit ", and mean by it, " During a war, people ought to fight. . . ." The phrase " it is not done " normally means " it ought not to be done ". At any rate, in Tannaitic Hebrew, though not yet in Biblical, the participle, equivalent to our present or future tense, is common in rules of conduct and even in actual religious precepts. In fact, it is by far the most frequent form of the laws of *Mishnah, Tosefta* and *Baraita*.

The following examples are chosen at random. *Mishnah Berakoth* ii. 4 says : האומנין קוראין בראש האילן, " Craftsmen may recite (the *Shema*) on the top of a tree " [1] ; lit., " craftsmen reciting ". *M. Moed Katan* iii. 8 f. runs : נשים במועד מענות, " Women may sing lamentations during the Feast but they may not clap their hands. . . . On the first days of months they may sing lamentations and clap their hands, but they may not wail ; after the corpse has been buried, they may neither sing lamentations nor clap their hands " ; lit., " women singing lamentations but not clapping their hands . . . singing lamentations and clapping their hands, but not wailing ; neither singing lamentations nor clapping their hands ". In *M. Yadaim* iv. 3 we are told that עמון ומואב מעשרין, " They voted and decided that Ammon and Moab should give Poorman's Tithe. . . R. Eliezer wept and said, Be not anxious by reason of your voting, for I have received a tradition from Rabban Johanan ben Zakkai, who heard it from his teacher, and his teacher from his teacher, as a *Halakah* given to Moses at Sinai, that Ammon and Moab should give Poorman's Tithe " ; lit., " Ammon and Moab giving ". *M. Berakoth* vi. 6 reads : כל אחד ואחד מברך, " If men sit apart to eat, each should say the Benediction for himself ; if they recline together, one should say the Benediction for all " ; lit., " each saying for himself . . . one saying for all ". *M. Peah* ii. 6 says : אם עשאן גורן אחת נותן פאה אחת, " Nahum the Scrivener said, I have received a tradition from R. Measha, who received it from his father, who received it from the Pairs (*i.e.* the President and Father of the Court), who received it from the Prophets as a *Halakah* given to Moses from Sinai, that if a man sows in two kinds of wheat and makes them up into one threshing-floor, he need grant but one Peah, but if two threshing-floors, he must grant two Peahs " ; lit., " granting but one . . . granting two ". *M. Bikkurim* i. 4 says : הגר מביא, " The proselyte may bring (the First-fruits) but he may not make (the Avowal of Deuteronomy xxvi. 5 ff.) " ; lit., " the proselyte bringing but not making". To take a *Baraita, Babylonian Berakoth* 19a contains this passage : הן יושבין, " Our teachers have taught, Those who occupy themselves with the burial ceremony, they have to sit down and read (the *Shema*) but he (the mourner) sits down and is silent ; they have to stand up and pray but he has to stand up and confess the righteousness of the judgment that has come upon him " ; lit., " they sitting down and reading but he sitting down and keeping silence ; they standing up and praying but he standing up and confessing ".

In all the rules adduced so far, the addressees are specified : the craftsmen in *M. Berakoth* ii. 4, the women in *Moed Katan* iii. 8 f., Ammon and Moab in *Yadaim* iv. 3, the person saying the Benediction in *Berakoth* vi. 6, the person sowing wheat in *Peah* ii. 6, the proselyte in *Bikkurim* i. 4, and those taking part in a burial ceremony in *Bar. Bab. Berakoth* 19a. The plural of the participle appears in the first three instances (the feminine in

[1] For most passages from the *Mishnah*, Professor Danby's translation is used.

the second), the singular in the next three, the plural and the singular
in the last. The participle expresses a permission (e.g. *M. Berakoth* ii. 4),
a positive injunction (e.g. *M. Peah* ii. 6) or a negative injunction (e.g.
M. Moed Katan iii. 8 f.). At least two of the rules belong to an ancient
stratum of tradition, *M. Peah* ii. 6 and *M. Yadaim* iv. 3. It may be noted,
however, that the use of participles in formulating rules has survived in
Hebrew up to this day. In the abridged *Shulhan Aruk* by S. Ganzfried,
a late nineteenth-century work to be found in the library of even the poorest
practising Jew, paragraph cxxxiii. 21 opens thus : מזכירין נשמות ביום הכפורים
" One should commemorate the dead on the Day of Atonement " ; lit.,
" commemorating ".

This last example is one where the addressee of the rule is not specified.
The rule is formulated as of a universal nature, no subject such as " those
praying " or even " the people " or " they " or " a person " is named, the
mere participle, plural or singular, expresses the teaching. We find a great
many such cases in Tannaitic literature. *M. Berakoth* i. 5 says : מזכירין יציאת
מצרים בלילות, " One has to rehearse the going forth from Egypt (say the
third section of the *Shema*) also at night " ; lit., " rehearsing ". In *M.*
Shabbath i. 6 we are told : אין נותנין אונין, " The School of Shammai say,
One must not put bundles of flax in an oven (on Friday) unless they can
steam off the same day, and the School of Hillel permit it " ; lit., " not
putting ". *M. Taanith* iv. 6 says : משנכנס אב ממעטין בשמחה, " When Ab
comes in, one has to diminish gladness " ; lit., " diminishing ". The
singular may be found, for instance, in *M. Berakoth* vi. 1 : כיצד מברכין על
פירות האילן אומר בורא פרי העץ, " What Benediction should one say ? Over the
fruit of trees one should say, (Blessed art thou) who createst the fruit of
trees ". The question employs the participle plural (" what Benediction
saying ? "), the answer the participle singular (" saying "). Very naturally,
the singular is used chiefly where the person performing the rule would act
singly ; the plural is used in this case and in that where several would
act collectively.

The role of the participle here described becomes very clear from the fact
that a rule with a participle not infrequently appears next to one with a better
recognized imperative form, such as the imperfect or a phrase like " it is
necessary to ". Sometimes the change in form corresponds to a change in
meaning or rather nuance. For example, *M. Shabbath* i. 3 lays down :
החזן רואה אבל לא יקרא, " Rightly they have said, The schoolmaster may
look where the children read (on Friday, towards nightfall) but he himself
may not read (lest, forgetful of the commencement of the Sabbath, he should
tilt the lamp for a brighter light) ". Here we find a participle at the beginning (" the schoolmaster looking "), but an imperfect at the end (" himself shall not read ") ; and while the former expresses a permission, the
latter expresses a negative injunction. In a large number of cases, however,
a change in form indicates no change in meaning whatever. Let us take
M. Hagigah ii. 1 ff. : אין דורשין בעריות בשלשה כל המסתכל בארבעה דברים ראוי לו כאלו
לא בא לעולם יוסי בן יועזר אומר שלא לסמוך בית שמי אומרים סביאין ואין סומכין, " One
may not expound the forbidden degrees (Lev. xviii. and xx.) before three
persons, nor the story of the Creation before two. Whoever gives his mind
to four things, it were better for him if he had not come into the world —
what is above ? what is beneath ? . . . Jose b. Joezer says, One may not
lay (one's hands on the animal to be offered on a Festival-day), Joseph b.

Johanan says, One may lay. The School of Shammai say, One may bring Peace-offerings but one may not lay (one's hands on them on a Festival-day), and the School of Hillel say, One may bring and lay." There is here a great variety : first a participle for a negative injunction (" not expounding degrees "), secondly a threat for a negative injunction (" he who ponders four things it were better for him had he not been born "), thirdly an infinitive for a negative injunction (" not to lay one's hands "), fourthly an infinitive for a permission or positive injunction (" to lay "), fifthly a participle for a permission or positive injunction (" bringing Peace-offerings "), sixthly a participle for a negative injunction (" not laying ") and seventhly two participles for permissions or positive injunctions (" laying and bringing "). All these come one immediately after the other, and changes occur even where the subject discussed remains the same. In fact, the rules under notice refer to two subjects only ; yet we find participle and threat in the section concerning dangerous problems, forbidden degrees and the above and the beneath, and we find infinitives and participles in the section concerning offerings on the Festival-day. (Certainly, the presence of different forms in one section is often due to the latter's being derived from different sources. But for one thing, it would be wrong to deny that the same original author might use different forms in the course of the same discussion ; and for another thing, it is sufficient for the purpose of this article to shew that a small section of a Tannaitic code, homogeneous or going back to several sources, could contain a fair number of imperative forms.) An example from the abridged *Shulhan Aruk* is cxciv. 7 : מעצימין עיניו של מת ומי שיש לו בנים יעשה זאת בנו, " One must close the eyes of the dead, and if he has sons his son must do it ". Manifestly, the two rules are on one level, except that the first is general, the second special. But a participle is used for the first (" closing "), the imperfect for the second (" shall do it "). As a medieval writer with an excellent Tannaitic style, Maimonides is of interest. *Hilkoth Deoth* iii. 2 runs : צריך האדם שיכון לבו ויהיה שבחו וקומו . . . מי שהיה בשרו חם לא יאכל ושותה מי העולשין, " Man must direct his heart to know God, and his lying down and rising be with a view to this end. . . . He whose constitution is hot should eat no meat and should drink no wine, and should drink chicory water though it is bitter ".[1] The forms employed are a phrase stating the need for a certain course (" it is necessary for man that he direct "), a positive imperfect (" his lying down shall be "), negative imperfects (" he shall not eat, drink ") and a participle (" drinking chicory water "). *Hilkoth Tefillah* iv. 2 may also be cited : רוחץ ידיו ואחר כך יתפלל מקנח ידיו ומתפלל, " (When the time of prayer arrives) one has to wash one's hands and after that one may pray ; if one finds oneself abroad and has no water, one may wipe one's hands on a stone and pray ". A participle (" washing "), an imperfect (" he shall pray ") and two participles (" wiping and praying ") follow one another.

However, if the participle thus has the value of an imperfect-imperative, an infinitive-imperative or the like in countless texts, it is important to note that there are definite limits to its imperative use. It cannot stand for the imperative everywhere, and the reason is that something of its function as denoting a custom always remains. This means, first, that it is never used in a command addressed to a specific person on a specific occasion ; never

---

[1] The French, in preparing coffee, follow this advice. Curiously, they seem to like it.

used for an imperative of the type "Go and fetch me a glass of water".[1]
It is used exclusively in rules, cases like *M. Moed Katan* iii. 8, נשים במועד
מענות, "Women singing lamentations during the Feast but not clapping
their hands". This is a rule, namely, that women may go only to certain
prescribed lengths in mourning the dead during a Feast. Secondly, a
participle cannot be indiscriminately employed even for every kind of rule.
We never find it in an absolute, unquestioned and unquestionable law. It
would not, for example, be possible to say, אין רוצחין, "not killing"; just
as, in English, it would not do to state the prohibition of murder in the
present indicative, "one does not kill". There must be some qualification,
however slight, if the participle is to be the appropriate form. A pacifist
might teach that "a good man does not kill his fellow-being", or in Hebrew,
אין חסיד רוצח את חברו. But here, there are several points to make the rule
less absolute: the rule is disputed, specifies its basis (each man is the other's
fellow), appeals to the conscience of the addressee (a good man — surely you
want to be one), and so on. *M. Sanhedrin* viii. 7 lays down that you may
kill a man in order to prevent him from committing certain crimes, but you
may not in the case of certain others. ואלו הן שמצילין אותן בנפשן הרודף אחר
הזכר אבל הרודף אחר הבהמה אין מצילין, "These one may deliver (from transgression) at the cost of their lives: him that pursues after his fellow to
slay him, or after a male (to have unnatural intercourse). But one may
not deliver him that pursues after a beast (to have intercourse) or him
that profanes the Sabbath." The participle occurs in both parts of the text
("delivering, not delivering") even though in the second we have before
us a prohibition of killing. But, clearly, even the second part is an injunction qualified, not absolute. The cases where killing is prohibited are
opposed to those where it is permissible, and we are given not the fundamental prohibition of murder but a prohibition of killing in certain circumstances. To quote a text from Maimonides, *Yesode Hatorah* v. 7 says:
ומנין שאפילו במקום סכנת נפשות אין עוברין, "And whence do we know that these
three prohibitions (idolatry, unnatural intercourse, murder) one must not
transgress even in danger of life?" Once again, there is the participle
("not transgressing"), in a rule directed against, among other things,
idolatry. Once again, however, the rule is qualified. We are not simply
told not to commit any of the three cardinal sins; and indeed, it would not
be Hebrew to formulate an absolute law like this with the participle, אין עוברין
על עבודת כוכבים, just as no English catechism would say, "One does not
commit idolatry". We are told not to commit those sins even in a certain
situation, namely, when we could save ourselves by committing them. Moreover, we are told so indirectly: the author poses the question what is the
scriptural proof of this rule. Here the participle is suitable, just as in English
it would be correct to ask, "Where does Scripture say or imply that one
does not commit idolatry even in order to save one's life?" In brief, the
participle is in its place in all admonitions to a proper conduct and even the

---

[1] There are some uses, very rare, which look
like exceptions but probably are not. For
example, a command may be expressed as a
statement of fact, in which case a participle
seems possible. Compare, in English, a
sentence like "You will take this route and he
the other". Again, complications arise where
a command occurs in a subordinate clause ("I
decree that . . ."). It would lead too far afield
to go into all these possibilities. Suffice it to
say that the participle plural with no specified
subject at any rate never makes even an apparent exception. אין כופין אותו להוציא (*M.
Ketuboth* vii. 9) means always "Given certain
facts, one may not compel him (lit., not com-
pelling him) to put away (his wife)"; never
"Do not compel him at this particular moment"
or "They must not compel him just now".

vast majority of fixed and exact precepts ; but not where a precept is an unqualified, hard, fundamental " must " or " must not ", having absolutely nothing to do with custom. A third result of this persistence of the function of the participle as denoting custom is a slightly impersonal touch, which becomes noticeable when we compare its use with that of the imperfect, the phrase " it is necessary to " or the imperative proper. When a father exhorts his sons, he would not employ the participle but one of the " warmer " forms — unless, indeed, he were relying on a code. The imperative participle seems restricted to codes and quotations from or allusions to codes. In the many Talmudic stories where a man receives advice from a Rabbi outside the professional discussion of the law and with no reference to a previously formulated teaching, the participle seldom, if ever, occurs. This point will come up again below.[1] There exist other consequences, besides the three discussed, of this fact that the participle never quite loses its original character. For example, slight differences in application may be observed between the imperative participle without אֵין (" not ") and that with אֵין, differences probably to be explained as such a consequence. But there is no need here for further examination.

It is suggested that the imperative participles of the New Testament may be translations of the Tannaitic ones. This theory would seem at least to avoid the objections that can be raised against Moulton's. First, whereas the participles adduced from the papyri are not really independent but can all be reduced to the classical, attached participle, the Tannaitic participles here analysed are unattached, like those under notice from the New Testament. Secondly, whereas the participles from the papyri occur in the concluding part of letters, a case *sui generis*, the Tannaitic participles are very frequent in *Mishnah*, *Tosefta* and *Baraita*. Thirdly, while the papyri cannot explain the imperative adjectives of the New Testament, this theory can. Hebrew is poor in, and rather averse to, adjectives ; Greek is not. Consequently, when Hebrew rules are done into Greek, it will often be easiest to render an adverbial phrase by an adjective. *M. Berakoth* v. 1 lays down that אֵין עוֹמְדִין אֶלָּא מִתּוֹךְ כּוֹבֶד רֹאשׁ, " One should stand up (lit., standing up) to pray only in sober mood ". At greater length, *Bar. Bab. Berakoth* 31a says, אֵין עוֹמְדִין לֹא מִתּוֹךְ עַצְבוּת וְלֹא מִתּוֹךְ עַצְלוּת, " Our Rabbis have taught, One should not stand up (lit., standing up) to pray from the midst of sorrow, idleness, jocularity, frivolous conversation, levity or idle chatter, but from joy of the commandment ". In Greek, one would probably replace some of these phrases by adjectives ; which might result in " Standing up to pray, sober, joyful in the commandment ". Maimonides, *Hilkoth Talmud Torah* v. 5, tells us : וְאָסוּר לְתַלְמִיד לִקְרוֹת לְרַבּוֹ וְלֹא יִתֵּן שָׁלוֹם אֶלָּא שׁוֹחֶה בְּיִרְאָה וְכָבוֹד, " And it is forbidden to a disciple to call his master by his name and he must not greet his master in the way one greets one's fellow, but he must bow before him and say to him (lit., but bowing and saying) in fear and respect, Peace be with you, Rabbi ".[2] In this case also, " in fear and respect " might become adjectives in Greek, so that we get something like, " A disciple bowing and saying to his master, Peace be with you, reverential and respectful ". Even the Hebrew imperative participle itself would perhaps now and then be represented by an adjective in translation. *M. Berakoth* ix. 4 reads : וְנוֹתֵן הוֹרָאָה . . . שָׁנִים מִתְפַּלֵּל, " He that enters a

---

[1] See pp. 484 ff.
[2] Observe the change in imperative forms :

"it is forbidden to", " he must not " (imperfect), " bowing and saying " (participles).

town should pray (lit., praying) twice, Ben Azzai says, Four times . . . and he should offer thanks (lit., and offering thanks) for what is past and he should make supplication (lit., and making) for what is to come ". This, in translation, might appear as " He that enters a town praying, thankful for what is past ". Or take *Bar. Bab. Gittin* 61a : מפרנסים עניי נכרים ומבקרין חולי נכרים, " Our Rabbis have taught, One has to maintain the poor non-Jews with the poor Israelites and one has to visit the sick non-Jews and one has to bury the dead non-Jews (lit., maintaining and visiting and burying) ". With a little more emphasis on motives, this might become, " Helping the poor non-Jews, friendly to their sick, careful about their dead". The point is that this translation theory accounts not only for the presence of the imperative adjectives in the New Testament, but also for the fact, already mentioned, that they never stand by themselves but always go with imperative participles, while the latter can stand by themselves. The Hebrew text here postulated as the original would contain one or more injunctions in the form of participles. If, in translating, some adverbial phrase or even one of several participles were turned into an adjective, the dominant participle would none the less remain for the adjective to lean upon. On the other hand, imperative participles without imperative adjectives are obviously to be expected : it is exactly what we get in the Hebrew. The fourth objection against Moulton's thesis is that, even if the participles from the papyri did represent imperatives, they would yet be " specific " imperatives ; but the participles of the New Testament are confined to rules, general directions. There is no difficulty of this sort about the theory here advocated. The imperative participles of Tannaitic literature are used in precisely the same way as those of the New Testament, in rules only. Fifthly and lastly, if we proceed from Moulton's assumption of a genuine Hellenistic development, it is hard to see why the imperative participles of the New Testament should be limited to one subject, social conduct — just as hard, in fact, as if we ascribed them to carelessness. On the basis of the theory submitted in this article, the problem is easily solved : we have only to suppose that some writers of epistles, in dealing with that subject, drew on Hebrew codes. Some more will be said about this point later.[1]

The following argument may perhaps support the suggestion here advanced. It is maintained that the imperative participles of the New Testament reflect those common in Tannaitic rules. If this is correct, we may expect to find that to a good many teachings laid down or referred to in the New Testament, whatever the form employed, parallels exist in Tannaitic writings with the imperative participle. This is indeed the case. Here is a haphazard collection from *Mishnah, Tosefta, Mekiltha, Baraita* and Maimonides. *M. Shekalim* iii. 2 says : בשלש קופות תורמין אין התורם נכנס לפי שאם צריך לצאת ידי הבריות, " In three baskets one has to take up (lit., taking up) *Terumah* out of the Shekel-chamber. He that takes up *Terumah* may not go in (lit., not going in) either in a sleeved cloak or with shoes, lest if he becomes rich men should say that he became rich from the *Terumah* ; for it is necessary for a man to satisfy mankind even as it is to satisfy God . . . and again Scripture says (Prov. iii. 4), So shalt thou find favour in the sight of God and man." [2] With this, Rom. xii. 17 may be compared, one

---

[1] See pp. 484 ff.
[2] Observe the different imperative forms, " taking up " (participle plural, with no specific subject named), " he that takes up not going in " (participle singular with the subject named), " it is necessary to satisfy ".

of the New Testament cases of an imperative participle, " Provide (προνοού-
μενοι) things honest in the sight of all men ". *M. Baba Metzia* ii. 11 says,
מניח את של רבו, " If his father and teacher each bore a burden, he must
first relieve his teacher and afterwards he must relieve his father (lit., first
relieving and afterwards relieving) ; if they were each taken captive, he must
first ransom his teacher and afterwards he must ransom his father (lit., ransoming) ". Somewhat similar in spirit is Matt. x. 37 : " He that loveth
father or mother more than me is not worthy of me ". In *M. Temurah* vi. 5
we are told : כל הקרשים אין פורים אותם, " All holy (animal-offerings) that
have been rendered *terefah* (and therefore unfit to be offered) one may not
redeem (lit., not redeeming) since one may not redeem (lit., not redeeming)
the holy (offerings) in order to feed the dogs with them ". The waste of
spiritual goods is considered in *Bar. Bab. Hagigah* 13a : אין מוסרין, " And
R. Ammi said, One should not deliver (lit., not delivering) the words of the
Law to a Samaritan (Gentile ?) ". These texts are related with Matt. vii. 6 :
" Give not that which is holy unto the dogs ". *M. Tohoroth* iv. 5 reads :
על ששה ספיקות שורפין, " Because of six suspicions (of uncleanness) one must
burn (lit., burning) the Heave-offering, because of . . . what is perhaps
earth from the land of the Gentiles ". One may compare Matt. x. 14 f.,
" And whosoever shall not receive you, when ye depart out of that house or
city, shake off the dust of your feet ". To go on to the *Tosefta*, we are
warned in *T. Demai* iii. 6, 9 that הוא . . . לא ישחמש חבר במשתאו של עם הארץ
נאמן לוקחין היצנו, " An Associate (*Haber*) may not wait at the feast of a
Vulgar (*Am-Haaretz*), unless all has been tithed under his hands. . . . If
he (the *Am-Haaretz* husband) is trustworthy but his wife is not, one may
buy (lit., buying) produce from him, but one may not be his guest (lit., but
not being his guest) ".[1] From the New Testament may be quoted Jn. vii. 49,
" But this people who knoweth not the law are cursed ", and 1 Cor. v. 11,
" But now I have written unto you not to keep company, if any man that is
called a brother be a fornicator or covetous . . . with such an one not to
eat ". Or take *T. Shabbath* xv. 11, 15 : מפקחין על ספק נפשות, " One may
make arrangements (lit., making arrangements) for the saving of human life
on the Sabbath. One may prepare warm water (lit., preparing) for a sick
man, be it to let him drink, be it to cure him ; and one must not say (lit.,
and not saying), Wait, perhaps he will remain alive (without assistance) ".
Matt. xii. 10, 12 deals with this subject : " Is it lawful to heal on the sabbath
days ? . . . Wherefore it is lawful to do well on the sabbath days." *Mekiltha
Exodus* xxii. 25 says, מכאן אמרו מסשכנין . . . שאחה מחויר זה כסות יום, " This
(Exodus xxii. 25) speaks of the day garment that thou must restore it
(lit., thou restoring) to him (the debtor) for the whole day. Of the night
garment, whence do we know that thou must restore it too (lit., thou restoring) to him for the whole night ? Scripture says (Deut. xxiv. 13), Thou
shalt deliver him the pledge again when the sun goeth down. On this basis
they (the Sages) said, One has to take as pledge (lit., taking) the day garment
for the night and the night garment for the day, and one has to return (lit.,
returning) the former for the day and the latter for the night ".[2] Teachings

---

[1] Observe the changes in form : " may not
wait " (imperfect), " buying but not being
guest " (participles).
[2] It should be noted that the first part of this
text, as it is an immediate interpretation of the
Biblical commandment which uses the direct
address (" thou shalt deliver "), also uses the
direct address, " thou restoring ", and person
participle. In the second part, where a previously formulated rule is quoted (" they said "),
we find the impersonal participle plural as in
most rules cited in this article, " taking and restoring ". Below (pp. 485 f.) some remarks will
be made on the influence of Biblical forms.

of this kind are alluded to in Matt. v. 40, " And if any man will sue thee at the law and take away thy coat, let him have thy cloke also ", and xviii. 33, " Shouldest not thou also have compassion on thy fellowservant ? ". *Bar. Bab. Berakoth* 16b reads : אין קוראין אבות אלא לשלשה, " Our Rabbis have taught, One calls (lit., calling) fathers only the three (Abraham, Isaac, Jacob), and one calls (lit., and calling) mothers only the four (their wives) ". Matt. xxiii. 9 says : " And call no man your father upon the earth : for one is your Father, which is in heaven ". In *Bab. Yoma* 87a we are told : כל המקנים את חברו צריך לפייסו אל יבקש יותר . . . ואם מת סביא עשרה, " R. Isaac said, He who annoys his fellow, even if it be only with words, it is necessary for him to reconcile him ; and R. Jose b. Hanina said, Whoever apologizes need not apologize more often than three times . . . and if the wronged man is dead, he should bring (lit., bringing) ten persons and should place them (lit., and placing them) at his grave and should say (lit., and saying), I have sinned ".[1] We may compare Matt. v. 24 f., " First be reconciled to thy brother. . . . Agree with thine adversary quickly . . . lest at any time he deliver thee to the judge " (quite possibly a metaphorical warning, with the point that one should reconcile the wronged man before he dies), and xviii. 21 f., " How oft shall I forgive him ? . . . Until seventy times seven." Finally, two examples from Maimonides. *Hilkoth Deoth* v. 7 runs : תלמיד חכם לא יהא צועק ולא ינביה . . . ומקדים שלום רואה שדבריו מועילים אומר ואם לאו שותק כיצר לא ירצה את חבירו בשעת כעסו, " A scholar should not be shouting and should not raise his voice . . . and should forestall (lit., and forestalling) every man in greeting and should judge (lit., and judging) every man with a bias in his favour, he should speak (lit., speaking) in praise of his fellow, he should love (lit., loving).peace, if he sees that his words are appreciated he should talk (lit., talking), but if not he should keep silent (lit., but keeping silent) — how for example ? he should not seek forgiveness from his fellow while he is in his first rage ".[2] This reminds one of Rom. xii. 9 f., another passage with imperative participles : " Cleave (κολλώμενοι) to that which is good, be kindly affectioned (φιλόστοργοι) one to another with brotherly love, prefer (προηγούμενοι) one another in honour ". *Hilkoth Teshubah* vii. 2, 3, 8 says : לעולם יראה אדם עצמו ולא יאמר . אל תאמר אלא כשם . שצריך אדם לשוב מאלו . . . בעלי תשובה דרכן להיות שפלים אם חרפו הכסילים אל ירגישו אלא שומעין ושמחים וחטא גמור הוא לאמור זכור, " A man ought ever to regard himself as if he were about to die, and he must not say, When I am older I shall repent. . . . Do not say that repentance applies only to sins that involve a deed ; but just as it is necessary for a man to repent these, so it is to consider his evil thoughts. . . . The ways of the penitent are to be particularly humble and meek ; if the fools vilify them, they should take no notice but should listen and rejoice (lit., but listening and rejoicing) ; and it is an absolute sin to say to a penitent, Remember thy deeds." [3] Allied with

---

[1] There are various forms, " it is necessary for him to reconcile ", " he need not apologize " (imperfect), " bringing and placing and saying " (participles).
[2] Again, there is variety : " he should not be shouting " (imperfect of " to be " with participle), " and he should not raise " (imperfect), " and forestalling and judging, speaking, loving, talking but keeping silence " (participles), " he should not seek forgiveness " (imperfect). The source of the rule that one should be the first to greet is *M. Aboth* iv. 15 : הוי מקדים, " R. Mattithia said, Be forestalling in greeting every

man ". Here we find not the imperative participle as in Maimonides, but the imperative of " to be " with a participle. The reason will be explained later (see p. 484), in the course of some general observation on the forms of *Mishnah Aboth*.
[3] Note the various imperative expressions : " a man ought to regard " (imperfect), " he must not say " (imperfect), " do not say " (imperfect, 2nd person, direct address), " it is necessary for man to repent, examine ", " the ways of the penitent are to be this or that ", " they should take no notice " (imperfect),

this in spirit is Matt. v. 11 f., " Blessed are ye when men shall revile you. . . . Rejoice, and be exceeding glad ", and Rom. xii. 14, " Bless them which persecute you ". From all this it will be seen that there was probably no scarcity of Hebrew rules with imperative participles by which an early Christian writer might let himself be influenced.

Before proceeding to the relevant texts from the New Testament, it may be remarked that the participle in rules is to be met with not only in Hebrew but also in Aramaic. Very naturally, however, it is far less frequent in the Aramaic part of the Talmud than the Tannaitic. The later Rabbis largely confined themselves to interpreting the earlier ones and did not lay down so many fresh rules ; and when they quoted their predecessors, they rarely made the Hebrew into Aramaic. A few brief examples from the Aramaic part may suffice. *Bab. Berakoth* 52a says, מאי לאו דמברך עילויה ושתי ליה, " Surely this means that one should say the blessing (lit., saying) over it (the wine) and should drink it (lit., and drinking) ? ". In *Bab. Shabbath* 153b it is decreed, דזריק ליה, " He should throw it down (lit., throwing) with the back of his hand (the burden which he carried home after he was surprised by the commencement of the Sabbath) ". In *Bab. Pesahim* 104a the question is raised : מחתם מאי חתים, " What should one say in conclusion of the blessing (lit., what saying) ? ". *Bab. Hagigah* 7a says : כל היכא דאתא כולי עלמא לא פליגי דעייל ומחזי ומפיק, " If he has come and has nothing (to offer, despite Ex. xxiii. 15, And none shall appear empty), it is undisputed by all that he should go in (into the temple) and appear (before God) and go out again (lit., going in and appearing and going out again) ". It is conceivable that the New Testament participles derive from Aramaic speech. But Hebrew origin is much more likely in this case. Religious codes at that period were normally written in Hebrew. It has been long realized by students of the New Testament that " Semitisms which are in common use belong mostly to the technical language of religion ".[1] In the passages from the epistles here under discussion, the Semitism belongs to the technical language of religious codes — which was Hebrew.

III

In Rom. xii. 9-19 " adjectives and participles, positive and negative, are interrupted by imperatives in verses 14, 16, 19 and infinitives in verse 15 ".[2] Actually, a series of what, in Greek, are badly elliptical clauses begins before this. They reach from εἴτε προφητείαν in verse 6 down to ἀνυπόκριτος in verse 9 ; and though they are perhaps not surprising in Paul, it is worth noting that they would all be easily translatable into the language of Hebrew codes, when their elliptical character might disappear. As is well known, nominal sentences without copula are commoner in Semitic languages than Indo-European. Tannaitic rules, in particular, are often formulated in this way. The form of an injunction like ὁ μεταδιδοὺς ἐν ἁπλότητι is rather reminiscent of that of a similar warning by R. Judah the Prince, in *Bab. Moed Katan* 16a f. On Solomon's Song vii. 2, " The joints of thy thighs are like jewels ", he based the teaching that a scholar should not instruct his disciples publicly, for the sake of glory. For מה ירך בסתר אף דברי תורה בסתר,

---

" but listening, rejoicing " (participles), " it is a sin to say ". The exclamation " Remember thy deeds " in this context is a " specific " admonition, not a rule. The form employed is the imperative ; the participle would be impossible.

[1] See Moulton, *l.c.* p. 18, quoting Thumb, quoting Deissmann.

[2] See Moulton, p. 180.

" As the thighs are hidden, so the words of the Law should be hidden " : lit., " As the thighs in secret, so the words of the Law in secret ". R. Hiyya referred the same verse to secret almsgiving and loving deeds, a subject that Paul mentions in verse 9, once more in a somewhat un-Greek sentence, ἡ ἀγάπη ἀνυπόκριτος. The imperative participles commence in verse 9. We find two in verse 9, an imperative adjective and an imperative participle in verse 10, one adjective and two participles in verse 11, three participles in verse 12, two in verse 13, two imperatives proper in verse 14, two imperative infinitives in verse 15, three participles and one imperative in verse 16, two participles in verse 17, a participle in verse 18, and a participle and an imperative in verse 19. The injunctions have regard to the proper social conduct within the new community. The participles are in the plural, and no subject is specified. There is a variety of imperative forms, participles, imperatives, infinitives. All this, we have seen, is typical of Hebrew codes. Regulations as to social behaviour are sufficiently near the customary to admit of the participle. It is indeed possible that, in Paul's source, the addressees were named (" The members of the new community abhorring the evil ", not simply " Abhorring the evil "). But enough examples of general rules with no specified subject have been adduced under II to shew that Paul's directions might come straight from the Hebrew. Again, it is possible that the rules with an imperative proper or an infinitive, which interrupt the participles, were not in the original code. But this also it is not necessary to assume. In many of the instances given above different imperative expressions follow one another with no corresponding difference in meaning.

Rom. xiii. 11 may be another case in point. It also comes in the course of an explanation of the new duties, and a rule that the initiated must understand the time is quite conceivable in a code. It seems better, however, to regard εἰδότες not as of imperative force but as the complement of the preceding injunctions : " And this (observe), knowing the time ".[1]

The three texts from 2 Corinthians which Moulton brings are of a very different nature. viii. 24 does not belong here. If ἐνδεικνύμενοι is the correct reading — which is doubtful in view of the ἐνδείξασθε of א, A, B and C — it is best explained as loosely connected with the εἰς ὑμᾶς of verse 22. Similarly, ix. 11 goes with verse 8, from which it is separated merely by scriptural proof, verses 9 and 10. The δοξάζοντες of verse 13 is a complement, though carelessly attached, of διὰ πολλῶν εὐχαριστιῶν in verse 12. Its rendering as an imperative would be artificial : Paul does not ask the Corinthians to glorify God, but says that the saints will do so on account of the subjection of the Corinthians. In any case, the use of the participle in these three passages evidently is most unlike that in Rom. xii. 9 ff.

The participles of Eph. iv. 2 f. may be considered either as going with the " you " of verse 1, or as imperative participles, deriving from a code such as underlies Rom. xii. 9 ff. A comparison of the contents with Rom. xii. 9 ff., as also with Col. iii. 12 ff., makes the latter alternative more probable.

In Col. iii. 16 f. again the participles may be laxly connected with ἐν ὑμῖν in the first part of verse 16. But again it appears more likely that we have before us imperative participles from a code enumerating rules of conduct within the new community. If so, it is true that the ὑμῶν at the

---

[1] See Moulton, p. 182.

end of verse 16, or maybe the entire clause beginning with ἐν ταῖς and ending with θεῷ, would have to be considered as inserted by the writer of the epistle. It is to be noted that the πάντα ἐν ὀνόματι, which in Greek sounds wrong without an imperative supplied, is good style in a Hebrew law. *Mekiltha Exodus* xxi. 2 says, עבד עברי עובד ביום רבי יוסי אומר הכל לפי אומנותו, " A Hebrew slave is to work (lit., working) only during the day. R. Jose says, All (is to be arranged) according to his trade." The principle הכל לשם שמים, " All in the name (for the sake) of heaven ", would be perfectly possible in a Hebrew code.

Outside Peter and Paul, Heb. xiii. 5 is a case of an imperative participle. This also occurs in an enumeration of rules of conduct. The three rules immediately preceding (from τίμιος in verse 4 to τρόπος in verse 5) are formulated, like some Pauline injunctions discussed above, as nominal sentences without copula.

Lk. xxiv. 47 f. Moulton " inclines to add with great hesitation ".[1] Actually, ἀρξάμενοι does not stand for an imperative but signifies " the preachers beginning at Jerusalem ". It is put with a laxity surprising in Luke. But there is a close parallel in Acts x. 37, where an imperative is out of the question. So we have to admit that Luke here gives the word almost the meaning of an adverb.[2]

When we now examine 1 Peter, the first passage to be mentioned is i. 14. It is a doubtful case since the participle can be read as agreeing with ἐλπίσατε in verse 13. On the other hand, it may well go back to a Hebrew rule, " They (the members of the new community) must not fashion themselves ", אין מודמים.[3] If so, the phrase ἐν τῇ ἀγνοίᾳ ὑμῶν, spoken directly to the recipients of the epistle, must be ascribed to the writer. The Hebraism τέκνα ὑπακοῆς may be noted : it reminds one of expressions like בן דעה, " a son of understanding ".[4] There is a parallel injunction in Rom. xii. 2. On this something will be said later.[5] ii. 12 is also doubtful. Probably ἔχοντες is attached to ἀγαπητοί, παρακαλῶ . . . ἀπέχεσθαι. It may, however, be due to a Hebrew rule, something like הולכים (מהלכים) חמים. If so, the ὑμῶν would be inserted by the writer of the epistle.

ii. 18, it is suggested, reflects a Hebrew rule. The participle cannot be construed in the classical manner, and it obviously has the force of an imperative. On the basis of the translation theory, we have to assume a Hebrew rule, formulated by means of the participle plural, the persons concerned, the servants, being specified ; it might be העברים נכנעים (מחכנעים) תחת ידי אדניהם, " The servants subjecting themselves to their masters ". The injunction forms part of a series of rules of conduct within the new community and family, like the similar Eph. vi. 5 and Col. iii. 22. In verses 19 ff. it is probably the author of the epistle who speaks again, though the switching over to the direct address as such is not conclusive : we have seen many examples of it in Hebrew collections of laws, and besides, verse 17, which may well come from the same code as 18, employs imperatives proper. A small point seems to corroborate the theory here advanced. The verse in question opens with οἱ οἰκέται, the definite article being used. On the translation theory, since " the servants " must be a nominative, this is in order : " The servants subjecting themselves ". But what are we to say if

---

[1] See *op. cit.* p. 182.
[2] See Creed, *The Gospel according to St. Luke*, p. 301.
[3] Comp. below, p. 487, on the Hebrew.
[4] E.g. *Bab. Baba Metzia* 8a.
[5] See p. 487.

we render the two words as a vocative ? True, in pieces translated from Hebrew, the nominative with article is frequent in the New Testament instead of the vocative (representing the determined Semitic vocative). But if verse 18 is spoken personally by the writer and not taken from a code, there is no reason to regard it as a translation and the definite article in the vocative remains unaccounted for. Blass-Debrunner would probably explain it as they do αἱ γυναῖκες, οἱ ἄνδρες, τὰ τέκνα of Col. iii. 18 ff.[1] They say, rightly, that where a vocative is accompanied by any additions (like ὑμεῖς οἱ Φαρισαῖοι), the nominative can replace it even in pieces not translated from Hebrew ; and they go on to claim that, in Col. iii. 18 ff., such additions are, though not expressed, yet implied : (ὑμεῖς μὲν) αἱ γυναῖκες . . . (ὑμεῖς δὲ) οἱ ἄνδρες. This, however, is begging the question ; and before accepting it, one would want independent evidence that the vocative may give place to the nominative, in Greek, not only if there are additions but also if additions could be thought of. In the absence of evidence to this effect, it is at least equally probable that in Col. iii. 18 ff. — another enumeration of rules of behaviour in the Christian family — we have Hebrew vocatives, from Hebrew rules, and that in 1 Pet. ii. 18 we have a nominative as outlined above.

The case of iii. 1, with another Hebrew participle, is very similar. There are parallel rules in Eph. v. 22 and Col. iii. 18. The original might have been הנשים נכנעות (מתכניעה) החת ידי בעליהן וכן, " Likewise the wives subjecting themselves to their husbands " ; or perhaps וכן הנשים נכנעות אשה לפני בעלה, " The wives subjecting themselves each to her husband ", which would immediately explain the τοῖς ἰδίοις (though there are satisfactory alternative explanations[2]). Modern editions omit the article before γυναῖκες, and it may well be that the Hebrew law also had not got it. There exists, however, good authority in the apparatus for αἱ γυναῖκες. It looks as if this *lectio difficilior* were the better reading, and some scribe dropped the article when it was no longer understood why the direct address used in ii. 25 and iii. 2 should be interrupted by verse 1. In verse 2, in all probability, the author of the epistle himself is speaking : he addresses the recipients directly (ὑμῶν), enlarging on the usefulness of the rule. The directions are resumed in verse 3.

The next instance, iii. 7-9, is again very much the same. There are two imperative participles in verse 7, five imperative adjectives in 8, and two participles in 9, the first of these in a negative injunction. The subject of participles and adjectives is named : οἱ ἄνδρες (resumed by πάντες), with the article again. The adjectives most likely correspond to phrases like " of one mind " or to participles in the Hebrew. The variety of imperative forms is common in Hebrew codes. The injunctions concern behaviour in the family and community. Parallels are to be found in Rom. xii. 14-19, Eph. v. 25 and Col. iii. 19. The Hebrew would run approximately thus : וכן יושבים עמהם האנשים ברעת נוחנים כבור . . . פן תכלאנה (תהעקרנה) תפלתיכם וסוף דבר כלם לב לב אחד חוסלים איש על רעהו . . אין משלמים רעה חחת רעה . . . כי לואת נקראתם, " Likewise, the husbands dwelling with them according to knowledge, giving honour . . . that your prayers be not hindered ; finally, all of one mind, sympathizing one with the other . . . not rendering evil for evil . . since thereunto ye are called ". At least ὑμῶν, but more probably

[1] See *Grammatik des neutestamentlichen Griechisch*, 5th ed., p. 89.
[2] See Moulton, *l.c.* pp. 87 ff.

the whole clause εἰς τὸ μὴ ἐγκόπτεσθαι τὰς προσευχὰς ὑμῶν at the end of verse 7, and also the end of verse 9, from ὅτι εἰς τοῦτο, are due to the writer himself. Quotations from a code (verses 7a, 8-9a) and comments on them (verses 7b, 9b) seem to alternate.

Lastly, there is iv. 7-10, with two imperatives proper in 7, a participle in 8, an adjective in 9 and a participle in 10. It is possible to connect participles and adjective with νήψατε in verse 7 ; but, in view of the passages discussed above, one is inclined to interpret them as of imperative value, deriving from a Hebrew code. If this is correct, we have here before us the participle plural without any specified subject used for a general rule ; though there is no certainty that the original code did not name the persons admonished, " The members of the community having charity ". Rom. xii. 3 ff. and Heb. xiii. 2 may be mentioned as containing similar exhortations. The Hebrew might have been : אוהבים איש את אחיו מאַרחים איש את . . . היו צנועים, מאַרחים) רעהו עוזרים איש לרעהו) participle which, in Greek, becomes adjective).

Here this article might be concluded. Its object has been to shew that underlying that strange use of the participle in Romans, Ephesians, Colossians, Hebrews, and 1 Peter may be the participle of Hebrew rules, of *Mishna*, *Tosefta* and so on ; the participle expressing a duty, positive or negative, with the person or class concerned sometimes named, and sometimes omitted, and other imperative forms employed in the same context, as on the same level. It may be permissible, however, to finish by touching on one or two questions that arise in connexion with this theory. One is : What sort of code or codes did the writers of the epistles draw upon ? It was mentioned above [1] that all the rules in question bear upon the social duties within the new family and community ; and that, indeed, this homogeneity of the rules with imperative participles is one of the serious arguments against a genuine Hellenistic usage, and in favour of a Hebrew origin — even in the case of 1 Peter, otherwise not very Jewish. But what kind of code are we to think of ?

The first possibility that suggests itself is the tractate *Mishnah Aboth*, a body of directions as to the right mode of living, the attitude to be adopted in the family and community, specially important qualities, and so forth. Yet when we look through *Aboth*, a surprising feature emerges : there is not a single imperative participle. While the participle is by far the most frequent form in the rules of all other Mishnic tractates, here we come across imperatives proper of verbs, or the imperative of " to be " with participle, or imperfects (" A man should ever do this or that "), but not a single imperative participle. This fact becomes even more striking when we consider that rules which elsewhere shew the participle are here formulated in a different way. The principle to be the first to greet has a participle in Maimonides, *Hilkoth Deoth* v. 7, תלמיד חכם מקדים שלום, " A scholar forestalling every man in greeting ", and in Rom. xii. 10, τῇ τιμῇ προηγούμενοι, but the imperative proper of " to be " with participle· in *Aboth* iv. 15, הוי מקדים, " R. Mattithia b. Heresh said, Be forestalling in greeting ". There are indeed cases that approach the imperative participle, such as v. 7, שבעה דברים בגלם ושבעה בחכם בחכם אינו מדבר, " There are seven marks of a clod and seven of a wise man. A wise man not speaking before one that is greater . . ." [2] But if we try to translate this as " A wise man should not speak ", the conclusion of the saying will prove us wrong : וחלופיהן בגלם, " and the

---

opposites of these are the marks of a clod ". Clearly, it is impossible to
construe the opposites as " The clod should speak before one that is
greater ". In other words, the participles are not of an imperative
character, though they may be on the way, but descriptive. What is the
cause of this singular feature of *Aboth* ? In the first place, as pointed out
above,[1] the participle, equivalent to the English " One does (not) this or
that ", is suitable for codes but not for personal, intimate advice. For the
latter, " warmer " forms are preferred, the direct address with the imperative
proper in positive injunctions and the imperfect in negative, or such warnings as " Ever should a man act thus " with the imperfect ; the participle
has a flavour of the impersonal, customary, that makes it unfit for spontaneous advice. When Bar Kappara sold mottos for coppers,[2] he gave
people words like עד דכפנת אכול, " While thou art hungry, eat ; while thy
kettle is hot, pour it out".[3] It would not have done to cite real laws, עד דכפנו
אוכלים, " While one is hungry, one ought to eat (eating) ". *Mishnah
Aboth* tells us what the great Rabbis had to hand on to their audience as
the essence of study and experience. In contradistinction to the rest of the
Mishnah, it is a " historical " sketch designed to shew how there leads an
intimate, uninterrupted tradition from mount Sinai to the Tannaites (" Moses
received the Law from Sinai and committed it to Joshua . . .", *Aboth* i. 1)
and how these again instructed the people. The maxims of the Rabbis are
given as their ultimate teachings uttered to their very own disciples. This
is not a codification of rules, but a collection of sayings : hence the absence
of the usual form of impersonal precepts with the participle. There is, however, a second reason (closely connected with the first) : the traditional forms
of Wisdom Literature. In the Wisdom Literature of the Old Testament,
Proverbs, Ecclesiastes, the instructions are often given by a wise old man to
an imaginary youth ; the latter may be addressed as " my son " — whether
the author has in mind two persons actually father and son or a comparable
spiritual relationship does not matter. Here, very naturally, the direct
address is employed. Indeed, the Tannaitic use of the participle examined
in this article does not exist in Biblical language at all. There can be no
doubt that the old forms had an enormous influence on later Wisdom. (Needless to say, the forms are many of them universal, and it would be worth
investigating them from a comparative point of view. Here it is sufficient
to pursue the Jewish development.) Whenever " my son " was to be
directed on the right path, this influence would make itself felt. We can
trace it in, for example, the book of Sirach (בני כבד אביך, " My son, in word
and deed honour thy father "),[4] the words of Tobit to his son when he
prepares to die (παιδίον, ἀγάπα τοὺς ἀδελφούς σου),[5] the reminders given by
the Rabbis to their sons in the *Gemara* (אמר להו רבא לבניה אל תחתכו, " Raba
said to his sons, When you cut meat, do not cut it on the hand "),[6] and the
principles of good governorship communicated by Don Quixote to Sancho,
about to take up office (*Primeramente, oh hijo, has de temer à Dios*).[7] The
same influence is present in *Aboth*, which in some respects does belong to
Wisdom Literature. There is confirmation of this view. In all Biblical
Wisdom Literature, if the person to be instructed is not directly addressed,
sentences like " The wise man does this — the fool does that " are frequent.
In Sirach, wise saws of this kind occur : " Three things my soul desireth

. . . Nine I call happy."[1] The same structures are to be met with in *Aboth*, particularly in chapter v., which consists of anonymous, less personal maxims.[2]

It follows that when we think of the codes underlying those injunctions from the epistles as resembling *Aboth*, we are only half right. The contents may have been similar, but while *Aboth* is a collection of sayings, the codes must have been codes, a real system of social duties in which imperative participles had their place. Are there any analogies ? For one thing, there are the non-canonical tractates (*i.e.* tractates not properly belonging to the Talmud) dealing with special occasions and relationships, such as *Kallah*, on marriage, or *Semahoth*, on mourning (the title, " Joys ", being a euphemism). For another thing, there are those dealing with moral conduct in general, *Derek Eres Rabba* and *Derek Eres Zuta*. The latter seems of particular relevance. For it is intended as the guide of a superior group, the תלמידי חכמים, the Scholars. It is a work of this kind, a guide for the elect, that we may suspect behind the epistles here discussed. *D. E. Zuta* opens thus : דרכן של תלמידי חכמים עניו ושפל רוח, " The ways of the Scholars are, Meek and humble in spirit, industrious, filled (with virtue ?), oppressed, beloved by every man, humble to the members of his household, fearing sin and judging man by his deeds and saying, All that is of this world I have no desire for it, sitting and studying and making dusty his garment at the feet of the Scholars and no man can find any bad thing in him ". These ideals are not unlike those proclaimed in the epistles. There are two points, how-ever, that give one pause. First, the imperative participle is rare in *Derek Eres Zuta* and *Rabba*. True, it occurs. *Zuta* 19b (the section beginning with " R. Simeon ") says : הוא היה אומר אין מעמידין מהם, " He (R. Jose) said, The barber and the tanner and the bath-attendant one does not make any of them (lit., not making) head of the congregation ". Here we have the participle plural, with no subject named, used in a negative injunction. *Rabba* 18a (beginning of a section) says : הגדול שולח יד תחילה, " When two sat down at one table, the elder should take first and the younger after-wards (taking) ". Here, the participle singular is employed, the subject is specified, and the injunction is positive. Again, *Rabba* 19b (beginning of a section) tells us : הנכנס אין . . . . הנכנס אומר יהי רצון וקודם שיכנס כיצד יעשה חולץ, מתעמל ולא ירוק אדם בבית המרחץ, " He that goes in to have a bath should say (saying), May it be thy will that thou leadest me in in peace, and before he goes in how should he do ? He should take off (taking off) his shoes. . . . He that goes in to have a bath should not practise gymnastics (not practising) and should not gargle (and not gargling), and a man should not spit in the bath-house." There is a variety of imperative expressions following one another : a participle (saying), an imperfect (how should he do ?), a participle (taking off), two participles in negative injunctions (not practising nor gar-gling) and an imperfect in a negative injunction (he should not spit). Still, it remains the case that the imperative participle in the two tractates is rare. The reason is that large portions were put together in much the same way as, if not on the model of, *Mishnah Aboth*. (The influence of *Aboth* was great. In *Aboth deRabbi Nathan* there seems to be not one imperative participle : the work was fashioned entirely on *Mishnah Aboth*.) Thus even *Derek Eres Zuta* and *Rabba* do not quite possess the character of codes ;

[1] xxv. 1, 7.

[2] See v. 7, already quoted, " There are seven marks of a clod and seven of a wise man ".

they stand somewhere between collections of sayings and proper codifications of social duties. The second point to be considered is that the two tractates are of unknown date. It is indeed probable that they are Tannaitic, and the material certainly is. But this is all that one can say.

Perhaps the matter may be clinched by adding a further work, parts of which are very old, *Mishnah Demai*. This contains the rules to be observed by a scrupulous person in regard to produce of which, as it comes from or goes to a less scrupulous one, the proper tithes may possibly not be given. The rules originated in the community of the *Haberim*, the Associates, the antagonists of the *Ame-Haaretz*, the Vulgar. This community goes back to the second temple, and so no doubt do portions of *Demai*. Strack-Billerbeck hold, with good reasons, that the first half of *M. Demai* ii. 3 formed part of the original constitution of the sect.[1] המקבל עליו להיות חבר אינו מוכר לעם הארץ, " He that undertakes to be an Associate may not sell to an *Am-Haaretz* (produce) wet or dry, and may not buy from him (produce) wet, and may not be the guest of an *Am-Haaretz* and may not receive him as a guest in his own raiment". The main objects of these rules, it will be noticed, are to preserve the Associate from having anything to do with things not adequately tithed and from the uncleanness assumed in a Vulgar. It is clear that, though primarily concerned with " levitical " questions, they have an immediate bearing on social conduct. Separation from the Vulgar is the gist of them. (An early synonym of " Associate " is פרוש, " Separated ".[2]) The rules, as they stand in the *Mishnah*, all shew the imperative participle : " He that undertakes to be an Associate not selling, and not buying, and not being the guest, and not receiving as guest ". Here, then, is an ancient, real codification — not a mere collection of sayings — stating the duties of a community of the elect. When we combine *Demai*, *Aboth* and *Derek Eres*, we may be able to form some idea of what the codes behind Romans and so on looked like. It should be borne in mind that, if those codes said nothing of ritual obligations and barriers (in this respect more like the gentler *Aboth* and *Derek Eres* than *Demai*), the idea of chosenness, not being and acting like the others, must none the less have played a prominent part in them. When we find μὴ συσχηματίζεσθε τῷ αἰῶνι τούτῳ in Rom. xii. 2, just where the series of instructions opens, and μὴ συσχηματιζόμενοι ταῖς πρότερον ἐν τῇ ἀγνοίᾳ ὑμῶν ἐπιθυμίαις in 1 Pet. i. 14, in a similar position[3] ; and when we consider that the verb occurs nowhere else in Biblical Greek,[4] it does appear possible that the warning comes from an introductory paragraph of a code. Not to do after the doings of the sinners is a slogan ever recurring in the Old Testament and throughout Jewish catechisms ; to be like the sinners is the worst that can be said of a man or group at any time. Deut. xxxii. 32, " For their vine is of the vine of Sodom ", is paraphrased by the Jerusalemite Targum thus : עובדיהון מרמיין לעובדי עמא דסרום, " Their deeds are to be likened to the deeds of the people of Sodom ". A form of רמה may well underlie συσχηματίζομαι.

Some further problems may be mentioned only to be dismissed.[5] Did

[1] See *Kommentar zum Neuen Testament aus Talmud und Midrasch*, ii. pp. 506 f.
[2] *M. Hagigah* ii. 7, *T. Shabbath* i. 15.
[3] See on these texts above, p. 482.
[4] See G. W. Blenkin, *The First Epistle General of Peter*, p. lx.
[5] Carrington's *The Primitive Christian Catechism* became available to the author too
late to be discussed. A comparison of the *Haustafeln* as appearing in several epistles leads Carrington to conclude that they go back to one source which is prior to the epistles. This part of his argument clearly supports, and is supported by, the results of the present article.

the authors of epistles quote from the Hebrew or from translations made before by someone else ? Has the translation theory any bearing on questions of date and authorship ? And of the relation between different epistles ? As for this latter point, it is important to note that 1 Peter occasionally has the imperative participle where Paul has not (1 Pet. iii. 1 against Eph. v. 22 and Col. iii. 18 ; 1 Pet. ii. 18 against Eph. vi. 5 and Col. iii. 22). This puzzle may be solved in many ways. Slightly differing codes may have been drawn upon by different writers ; or Paul may have made, or used, a better translation than others. The most plausible answer is that these variations prove extremely little. We have seen that imperative participles are freely paired off with other imperative expressions in the same code ; also that Paul has the participle in Rom. xii. 10, like Maimonides, *Hilkoth Deoth* v. 7, but unlike *M. Aboth* iv. 15. The number of factors that may make for this form or that is so large, and chance so prominent among them, that few inferences can be drawn from isolated cases. One suspicion, however, that emerges is that 1 Peter, in the rules concerned, hardly borrowed direct from Paul's epistles in their present form. Why, on any theory, should 1 Peter, with its good Greek, have put imperative participles for Paul's clearer imperatives proper ? On the similarity between Rom. xiii. 1-7 and 1 Pet. ii. 12-17, Blenkin remarks [1] : " But in one passage we have, what must be regarded as conclusive evidence (of borrowing), the same ideas in the same order ". Is it conclusive ? What if both authors used the same source, an early Christian code of behaviour within the new community ? If this is assumed, one of the arguments against the authenticity of 1 Peter, its so-called Pauline character, loses much of its force.[2]

---

[1] See *l.c.* p. lxviii.
[2] The author is indebted to Professor F. S. Marsh for much valuable advice. The latter is not responsible, however, for any flaws in the reasoning.

INDEXES

I. QUOTATIONS FROM THE BIBLE AND JEWISH LITERATURE

A. OLD TESTAMENT

489

B. New Testament

C. APOCRYPHA, PSEUDEPIGRAPHA, AND HELLENISTIC JEWISH WRITINGS

D. RABBINIC

II. CLASSICAL

A. Greek

499

B. Latin

III. PATRISTIC

IV. GREEK WORDS

V. PROPER NAMES

VI. SUBJECT INDEX

Abstinentes, 372-4, 393, 396 f., 404, 414, 419, 453, 455, 457 f., 460, 462

Angels, 138 f. Fallen Angels, 198 f., 200 f., 205, 328. See also under Spirits

Apostle, The term, 117

Armour, The Christian, 209, 396-400, 456-8, 461

Asia Minor, Peoples of and Conditions in, 44-52, 173, 211

Atonement, The, 90-100, 464. See also under Christ, Sacrifice

Authority, 3 f., 27 f., 102, 117

Authorship, 7 ff., 31 ff., 242, 461-6

Baptism, Christian sacrament of, Regarded by St. Peter as the seal of conversion, 34, 82, 110; and of admission to the Church, 181 f., 327, and a sign of its universality, 327. Connexion of, in early centuries, with Christ's baptism, 335, descent into hell, 202-08, 335, 354, and resurrection, 147, 206 f. Typified by the Flood, 5, 41, 204-06, 327 f. Reflexion of this in baptismal rites, 333-6. N.T. teaching on, in primitive baptismal Forms, 19, 369-375, 375-82, 386, 388-439, 459-61. Remarks on St. Peter's teaching on, 361 f.

" Because ", in 1 Peter, 64 f.

Benediction, Jewish and Christian forms of, 69 f., 121 f.

Calling, 65 f.

Catechism, Scottish, 340

Catechism, The Primitive Christian, 18

Catechumen Virtues, 19, 188, 190, 397-400, 402, 406-15, 419, 460

Charity, 109, 139, 150; its "covering" power, 217 f.; relation to humility, 220

Children (in figurative sense), 140 f., 185

Christ (see also *imitatio Christi*), St. Peter's doctrine of, 122, 248-50. His Incarnation, 152, 193, 231. His Transfiguration, 31, 228 f. The passion and death of, 30, 62, 120 f., 195, 197, 228; its relation to the sacraments, 285; its atoning efficacy, 67 f., 90-7, 120 f., 179. His " descent into hell ", 197 ff., 319-22; and " preaching " there, 200, 322-4; His domination over supernatural beings, 207 f., 320-2; mediaeval doctrine of, 354-7. Resurrection of,

28 f., 69 f., 76 f., 97, 121-4, 147, 162; Ascension of, 146, 198, 200, 206 ff., 320-3; Second coming of (see Parusia). Represented as the " Stone ", 158 f., 164, 309 f.; the Cornerstone, 83, 163, 289; and stone of stumbling, 164; the " Suffering Servant " of Is. liii., 30, 35, 94, 179 ff.; the Scapegoat, 94 f.; the (Chief) Shepherd, 31, 84, 182, 231 f., 464; our High-Priest, 290 f.; the Judge of all, 213 f., 337 f.; the Subject of the Gospel, 214, 316, 337. Consecration of, 192 f. Adherence of man to, 157; stages in men's apprehension of, 131. Meekness of, 91-6, 98, 195. Example of, 92 ff., 179, *Christus patiens*, *Christus victor*, 195, 318, 334; " in Christ ", 83, 194 f., 240, 245; " unto Christ ", 136, 263 f. Spirit of, 135 f., 249 f. Name of, 34, 222 (see Persecution). Glory given to, through the Resurrection, 147; and in Christian doxologies, 220. Revelation of, 111, 113, 251

Church, The, Word not found in 1 Peter, 81. St. Peter's doctrine of, 81-4, 107, 109 ff., 153, 160, 165, 243 f., 327; as a neo-Levitical community, 374, 404 ff., 412-14, 459 f. Conceived as God's " house " or temple, 159 f., 289 ff., 463; a palace, 165 f.: a holy priesthood, 160, 166, 291-4: a chosen people, 166 f., 168 f.; a brotherhood, 239; the Hope of the World, 241. Divine foundation of, 82 f.; priestly and sacrificial, 83 f.; its subordination to God, 84 f. Relation of, to civil power, 87-9. Unity and order in the, 415-18, 419. Mixed character of churches in Asia Minor, 44

Civic Duties, St. Peter's teaching on, 5, 59 f., 87-9, 103, 171-4, 422-9. Comparison with St. Paul, 86, 171 f., 426

Clergy, 231

Code, Jewish and Gentile use of ethical codes, 101, 421 f., 471-80. The primitive Christian code or codes in N.T., 19, 101-09, 422-39, 481-8

Community, 168

Conscience, 176 f.

Consecration, Prayer of, 161

Conversion, 306-09

Covenant, Jewish Covenant-sacrifice fulfilled in the Cross, 68, 120 f. The Noachic Covenant, 329 f.

514

THE END

Thornapple Commentaries

Baker Book House, Box 6287, Grand Rapids, Michigan 49506